The World of the Oratorio

KURT PAHLEN
with the collaboration of
Dr. Werner Pfister
Rosemarie König

The World of the Oratorio

Oratorio, Mass, Requiem, Te Deum,
Stabat Mater and Large Cantatas

Translated by
Judith Schaefer

Additional material for the English language edition by
Thurston Dox, Ph.D.

Reinhard G. Pauly, General Editor

Scolar Press

German edition © 1985 as *Oratorien der Welt* by
SV international/Schweizer Verlagshaus AG, Zurich

Translation and Dox additions © 1990 by Amadeus Press
(an imprint of Timber Press, Inc.)
All rights reserved

Printed in Hong Kong

First published in the United Kingdom in 1990 by

Scolar Press
Gower Publishing Company Limited
Gower House
Croft Road
Aldershot
Hampshire GU11 3HR

British Library Cataloguing in Publication Data
Pahlen, Kurt 1907–
    The world of the oratorio: oratorio, mass, requiem, Te
    Deum, Stabat mater and large cantatas.
    1. Oratorios
    I. Title II. Pfister, Werner III. Konig, Rosemarie IV.
    Pauly, Reinhard G.
    782.23

ISBN 0-85967-866-0

Contents

Preface

A list of all operas ever performed reveals the unbelievable fact that there are 58,000 in existence. However, a count has never been taken of the oratorios that have been sung somewhere or other. We would not be wrong if we estimated the total to be slightly less than that for opera. This is clearly the place to explain that this book can, as a consequence, deal with but a very, very small selection from a very, very broad field. I freely admit that the most difficult part of writing this book was the selection of the material to be presented. The decision could have been made to include only those works that are part of today's musical life, but such a choice would have risked becoming outdated at least in some measure in a few years, because many of the oratorios performed today will be forgotten, and the continual search by musicians for lost treasures might rediscover works that have long been lost. The most important thing to keep in mind is that frequency of performance, or even popularity and renown are extremely unjust criteria. How many valuable works have disappeared from our memories! I believe it is worthwhile to resurrect works that have been forgotten unjustly and to draw attention to their lost beauties. But who would dare maintain that the choice represented in this book was the only fair one? I, for one, would not.

In my earlier books *Operas of the World* and *Symphonies of the World*, the titles indicated fairly clearly and precisely what the reader could expect to find inside. This is less true of this volume. Half of the works presented here are not even oratorios in the strict sense of the word. The reader might feel deceived if he fails to find familiar works closely related to the oratorio. But then think of all the related forms there are: the Mass, for example, and therefore, also, the Requiem. If these two are included, then the group must be expanded to include the *Stabat Mater* and the *Te Deum*, Vespers and Litanies, and even Magnificats and other forms from the Catholic liturgy. Many works similar to opera may also spill over into this category. Other questions arise: Should cantatas be included? Song cycles with continuous text and orchestral accompaniment? The gentle reader can see how the circle of those works which, in keeping with slightly different criteria, should be included, grows ever wider.

Is there any definition at all, then, for the content of our book? The important thing is that in the works presented here, the vocal and instrumental components should mesh. The vocal parts are primarily choral, and the instrumental parts played by some kind of orchestra. But we shall also speak of works in which the orchestra is replaced by the organ, and even touch here and there on unaccompanied vocal, usually choral, music. Is it, perhaps, the narrative aspect of all these oratorios and related works that results in inclusion? Even here, there are exceptions. Is the distribution of the story action among different voices the deciding factor? This criterion, too, although often invoked, is not one hundred percent valid. Quite superficially, we might say that the term oratorio includes only works of a certain minimum length; a cantata lasting only a few minutes would, therefore, not belong here. Although there is something to be said for this consideration, it, too, is not totally acceptable. In the area of music theater there are such things as mini-operas (composed by Darius Milhaud and called by him *Opéra Minutes*). Theoretically, then, could there not also be mini-oratorios?

Now that I have probably confused my readers completely, rather than laying their doubts to rest, I would like to attempt the simplest possible definition. This book is about musical works that combine various vocal elements (solo and chorus) with instrumental accompaniment (primarily organ and orchestra), impart their message without using scenery, require none of the trappings of theater, may be of either a secular or sacred nature, and possess a certain level of intellectual and musical development.

This book is intended for the music lover who either actively or passively is concerned with the types of music just described. There are countless enthusiasts who belong to choral societies that undertake works involving more than the simple singing of songs; and the even more numerous public that is particularly partial to these great compositions, heard all over the world—whether Mozart's, Verdi's, or Dvorak's *Requiem*, Beethoven's *Missa Solemnis*, Haydn's *Creation*, Bach's *St. Matthew Passion*, Handel's *Messiah*, Bruckner's *Te Deum*, Brahms's *German Requiem*, or one of the hundreds of other works that this book tries to bring closer to the interested reader. In addition I have included many others known only to the most informed specialists. I also hope that my book—and this was and remains my dearest wish—wins new friends for music. I hope this with all my heart, because in these inhuman times, music is one of the most powerful weapons in the struggle to create a new kind of humanism.

Kurt Pahlen

Historical and Other Observations on the Oratorio

Oratorio is opera without theater—without sets, without costumes, without stage business; but in fact including action. The oratorio does not impart its "subject matter," whatever it may be, in such a way that it can be seen but rather tells it. The form can be lyrical, epic, or dramatic. An opera is made up of three components: text, music, and staging; the oratorio limits itself to the first two. Whether these limitations—and we will come to see that they do not have to be considered as such—came about through the internal logic of the form or were forced upon the form by social pressure is debatable. The fact is that from the very beginning, oratorio had a different function than opera. But it is true that at certain periods the fundamental separation between these two music forms was so loosely construed that intermediate forms developed, in Handel's time as well as in our own. Many works discussed in these pages represent such intermediate forms. This fact is underscored by this book's illustrations: if the oratorio were limited to the concert framework and no effort was ever made to make a visual impression, there could be no photographs showing modern theatrical versions of oratorios.

The oratorio makes great demands on the listener's imagination. Whereas opera goers see the entire work unfold graphically before their very eyes, the audience of an oratorio is called upon to recreate the story being told in their imagination. Although many people may find this demand difficult and are scarcely able to meet it, those with little more than an ordinary gift of mental creativity will find the oratorio a source of the most wonderful riches, for the imagination knows no limits; a wondrous realm beckons, an amazing realm opens out to them.

Oratorio and opera have their roots deep in the Middle Ages. Their forbears were the mystery and passion plays and portrayals of the legends of the saints. In these plays, in addition to the more or less historical figures, there were symbolic ones such as Death, Beauty, Good Works, Faith, Mammon, Pride, Jealousy, and Curiosity. This personification of abstract concepts made the plays easier to understand for the common people who gathered in city squares and market places and, most often, at the portals of churches to see them. From the outset, there was a connection between such theatrical plays or pageants and the church's effort to inculcate morality into daily life. But there were also other, more popular offerings, embellished with street ditties and carnival songs, which often had to keep their distance from the precincts of the church. Opera and oratorio drank from both springs, the sacred and the secular.

The birthplace of both was Italy. In Florence, in the highly cultured circles of the "Camerata Fiorentina," particularly at the palazzo of Count Bardi, there arose a theatrical genre at first called *dramma per musica, melodramma,* or *favola in musica,* decades before it assumed the name "opera." The oratorio took its name from the Latin word for oratory or prayer room, of which there were many in the Rome of that time. Oratories were usually additions made to churches in which spiritual plays and representations of the passion were put on: *Laude* were sung here as well; religious folk songs in praise of the Virgin Mary and the saints. These were sung in Italian, whereas in the church proper songs and prayers were only in Latin. In one such oratory, that of the Roman church of Santa Maria of Vallicella, the art form of the same name is supposed to have originated. Here worked the man to whom we ascribe a founding, probably decisive role in the history of the oratorio.

San Filippo Neri was born on July 21, 1515, in Florence. As a youth he journeyed to Rome, where in 1548 he founded the "Brotherhood of the Holy Trinity," later known as the "Congregation of the Oratorians." Filippo became a passionate preacher, and also ministered to the many unfortunates who were drawn to him. In 1551, he was ordained a priest. One of the more distinctive features of his activity was his greater emphasis on the use of music; in his oratory, the singing of spiritual songs became an important, inspirational activity. He acquired the valuable coopera-

9

tion of the papal choir master Giovanni Animuccia, who died, however, in 1571. He was later succeeded by the late master of polyphony, the great Palestrina, who as a consequence also entered the history of the development of the oratorio. In 1583, Neri moved to the oratory of Santa Maria in Vallicella, which in turn came to play a decisive role in the new art form. Filippo died on May 26, 1595, at the age of 80, and was canonized in 1622.

Seen from this point of view, it could seem coincidental that opera and oratorio arose at virtually the same time, but there is an important, purely musical reason. The end of the 16th century marked the decline of polyphony, and with the 17th century, melody supported by harmony, also called homophony or monody, came into prominence. During the Baroque period, this form was characterized by the development of the *figured bass*. This development made possible the longer, accompanied vocal solo which forms the basis for both opera and oratorio. At the outset, there was scarcely any difference between the two forms; only gradually did opera tend to move toward the stage, toward a theatrical representation of the narrative. The oratorio, by contrast, maintained the connection with sacred themes, and positive efforts were made to insure that the narrative unfolded through words and music alone. Its most important subject matter was found in the Bible—Biblical stories and the accounts of the gospels, retold in a dramatic musical form. In order to bring the contents within the grasp of as wide a public as possible, a narrator was used to describe the action; this role was generally called *testo* by the Italians ("speaker," "commentator," "reader of the scriptures," and in a wider sense, also "witness"). He reads—in recitative—the Biblical text, after which he gives the various characters in the drama their cues to come in: to the soloists, if the matter to be sung was a dramatic declaration or reflection upon the meaning of what was happening, or an observation; and to the chorus, if the feelings of the masses or moral sentiments were to be expressed.

The first oratorio written is a matter of some uncertainty, though the work most frequently mentioned is the *Rappresentazione di anima e di corpo* by Emilio Cavalieri, which appeared in 1602. It was not yet called "oratorio" but was titled a *rappresentazione per l'oratorio*—a work to be given in the prayer hall.

In the 17th century, there were two kinds of oratorio: the more learned *oratorio latino*, in which Biblical texts were sung in Latin; and the *oratorio volgare*, which used freely chosen poetic texts in the Italian vernacular. The form clearly derived from the *Laude*, which Filippo Neri had first arranged to be sung at San Girolamo della Carità, and later at Santa Maria in Vallicella. Their development can be traced in 10 anthologies that appeared between 1563 and 1600. We can observe how the plots grew appreciably more dramatic. There appeared in Ferrara in 1598 *Dialog between Christ and the Samaritan*, as well as *The Prodigal Son*; the musical forms used in madrigals, which had dominated in the 16th century, were slowly left behind in favor of songs representing dialogue between individual voices. Opera became more and more worldly, ever more suited to theater and entertainment; the oratorio, although giving up nothing in plot (only sung, not represented visually), drama, and suspense, became more serious and dignified. One of the most significant 17th-century composers of oratorio was Giacomo Carissimi (1605–1674). He cultivated the Latin oratorio, which he usually called *historia sacra*, with dramatic action, in a style similar to the motet. Directly or indirectly, he became the teacher of many composers, including the Italians Alessandro Scarlatti, Marco Antonio Cesti, and Marco Antonio Bononcini, the Frenchman Marc Antoine Charpentier, and the Germans Johann Kaspar Kerll, Johan Philipp Krieger, and others. The oratorio had by this time spread throughout Europe.

Bologna and Modena soon became significant Italian centers for the cultivation of the oratorio, second only to Rome. Vienna became especially important, for not only was Emperor Leopold I an accomplished composer, but his court maintained the poets Apostolo Zeno and Pietro Metastasio, who collaborated to produce librettos that decisively influenced the genre. Their texts were set to music hundreds of times, and were still being used in Mozart's day, the Classic period in music. In the manner of opera, they emphasize the aria at the expense of the *testo*, the "narrator," a tendency noticeable as early as 1700.

With the appearance of Handel, the oratorio flourished anew. He composed his first—the *Resurrezione*, or resurrection—in 1708, during his Italian "apprenticeship," and became, with *Esther*, composed in 1732, the creator of the English oratorio. He reached the summit of his achievement in this genre in 1742 with the *Messiah*. The musical scene in Vienna was dominated by Antonio Caldara, Antonio Lotti, and Johann Joseph Fux writing oratorios in Italian and Latin.

Meanwhile, a new type of oratorio was developing in Protestant Germany. Among his countless works, Bach's Passions stand out, carrying on the style of the three significant Baroque masters Schütz, Schein, and Scheidt. Bach's oratorios are still acknowledged as masterpieces of the form. Hamburg, Frankfurt am Main—cities both closely tied to the name Telemann—Lübeck, and

Magdeburg all played a role in the development of the Protestant oratorio.

Haydn created a new form around 1800 with his precedent-setting *The Creation* and *The Seasons*; although deeply influenced by Handel in London, Haydn's preferences ran to a much more popular genre. During the first half of the 19th century the oratorio flourished, especially in German-speaking countries. Powerful intimations of the approaching Romantic era are to be found in Mozart's *Requiem*, left unfinished as he lay on his death bed. Mendelssohn, with *St. Paul* and *Elijah*, attained new heights in the genre.

Since then, the oratorio has assumed so many forms that it can now be employed for virtually any intellectual content or social purpose. It can be either sacred or secular, can take its subject matter not only from the Bible or the lives of the saints, but can also depict historical figures; it can contain dramatic, epic, or lyrical styles, can be pensive and meditative, can convey weighty thoughts, can be accusatory, controversial, can report completely factually or be given over to pure feeling. It can, from a purely technical standpoint, accept large forms or small; give a prominent role to the orchestra or leave it out entirely; focus on the chorus or reduce its importance to only a filler role, or even ignore it completely. The 20th century also multiplied its uses in other ways. Many famous composers steered toward intermediate forms, for which a concert rendition is by no means out of the question—Stravinsky's *Oedipus Rex*, Honegger's *St. Joan at the Stake*—but for which some theatrical amplification seems to have been intended. The oratorio clearly can by no means be thought of as a purely historical form, as an art form of the past. It is pregnant with so many possibilities that it will never grow old, but must perforce maintain its vitality. The future of opera has been called into question hundreds of times, that of the oratorio, never. Furthermore, in the course of its history the oratorio has been called on to assist its sister, even to save it from the threat of disappearance. As long as people are deeply affected by music, the oratorio will live on as one of the most complete art forms, for the good and sufficient reason that it appeals to that inexhaustible human quality—the imagination.

THE COMPOSERS AND THEIR WORKS

Samuel Hans Adler   1928–

Sam Adler studied composition with Paul Hindemith, Randall Thompson and Walter Piston. Currently Professor of Composition and Department Chairman at Eastman, he has earned distinguished recognition as an educator and composer. Serial techniques, blended with tonal harmonic procedures, form a distinctive style feature in later works. Adler has published over 200 compositions.

His Jewish heritage provided the inspiration for several choral works: *The Vision of Isaiah* (cantata, 1962); *Behold Your God* (cantata, 1966); *The Binding* (oratorio, 1967), and *From Out of Bondage* (cantata, 1968). *The Binding* stands out among these works. It focuses on the central teaching in Judaism—unswerving obedience, and steadfast faith in God.

The Binding

Original Language: English
Text: Based on *Genesis* Chapter 22, and upon traditional teachings of the Midrash and Aggadah compiled by Hugo Ch. Adler. English adaptation by Albert Friedlander.
Date of Writing: 1967
First Performance: May 4, 1967 in Dallas, Texas.
Form: An oratorio in three parts.
Cast: Roles for Abraham, Isaac, Satan and the Narrator are sung by soloists, but God's voice speaks only through the chorus. Soloists and chorus also carry reflective and didactic texts.
Scoring: Five soloists, mixed chorus and orchestra.
Discussion of the Work: After a short choral statement "Look to Abraham your father," and an orchestral interlude, the story begins. God summons Abraham and orders him to sacrifice his son. Abraham only questions: "Which of the two [sons] do you demand from me?" The following words flow from the chorus as this scene reaches a climax (Example 1). Abraham and Isaac begin their journey to the place of sacrifice.

Example 1

Part Two dramatizes this journey. Satan confronts the travellers and attempts to undermine Abraham's resolve. Their dialogue, except for a few bars of chorus, forms the musical framework for this movement (Example 2). In contrast, Part Three uses no soloists in character roles: They join the chorus in commentary and reflection. At the denouement, the chorus couples *Sprechstimme*

Example 2

with energetic rhythms in a dramatic passage (Example 3). The reflective aria which follows uses a twelve-tone melody against a tonal background, forming a bridge to the closing events (Example 4). The opening text returns; the oratorio ends.

Example 3

Example 4

A reviewer described the work as ". . . a document of literary merit and theological integrity, speaking in a contemporary musical language which communicates instantly."

—*Thurston Dox*

Dominick Argento   1927–

The Pulitzer Prize in music was awarded to Dominick Argento in 1975. An innate skill in writing for the voice is his special gift as a composer, enabling him to produce over 15 successful works for the stage, a wealth of solo songs and song cycles, and several large compositions for chorus. Argento's formal training did not begin until he was 16. After his interests turned to composing, he studied with Nabokov, Weisgall, Cowell, Hovhaness, Hanson and Rogers before completing a doctorate at Eastman in 1957. Like many 20th-century composers, he writes in an openly eclectic style. He acknowledges the voice as the source of his personal power: "The voice is our representation of humanity."

Three successful choral works of moderate length are *The Revelation of St. John the Divine* (1966), *Easter Cantata* (1970) and *Peter Quince at the Clavier* (1979). Argento's outstanding achievement among his choral works is the full-length oratorio *Jonah and the Whale*.

Jonah and the Whale

Original Language: English
Text: Compiled from medieval writings on Jonah (translated by the composer), scripture and folk songs.

Date of Writing: 1973
First Performance: March 9, 1974, at Plymouth Congregational Church in Minneapolis.
Form: Two major divisions and 11 titled subsections, each moving to the next without a pause. Total performance time: one hour.
Cast: Jonah (tenor soloist), the Voice of God (bass soloist), Narrator, incidental baritone and soprano solos.
Scoring: Three trombones, percussion, harp, piano, organ, soloists, mixed chorus.
Discussion of the Work: In keeping with the story's didactic spirit, teachings such as "face woe with fortitude and joy will follow" and "patience is a princely thing" form the text for a chorale which opens section one, "The Lesson." The choral writing is purely syllabic. Using the exact chorus rhythms, the narrator enters over the closing cadence, "God's charge came to him [Jonah], roaring in his ear." These words form a bridge to section two, "The Charge to Jonah." In an angry, declamatory recitative style, God instructs Jonah to carry His message of displeasure to the Ninevites. God "shakes the heavens"—a rapidly repeated 16th-note figure—as He orders Jonah to "Go!"

Stunned by God's uncompromising demands, Jonah ponders: "If I speak of such tidings, they will seize me at once, put me in prison, set me in shackles and scratch out my eyes." This jocular aria in six-eight meter, formed in chains of arched phrases, characterizes Jonah as a diffident, unwilling prophet. He quickly decides to escape to Tarshish and, with an air of nonchalance, goes off to find passage, as the narrator explains (Example 1). [Musical examples Copyright 1976 by Boosey and Hawkes, Inc. Reprinted by permission.]

Example 1

In section three, "His Flight," Jonah and the sailors (the SATB chorus) sing a lusty whaling song, "The Greenland Fishery," while the narrator reports on the voyage. Naively joyous at having outwitted God, Jonah becomes one of the sailors and takes musical leadership in the song. As the story of the "whale that got away" fades to pianissimo unison, the narrator reminds us of God's continuing involvement in Jonah's life. The three trombones announce God's voice with a solemn fanfare, and section four, "The Storm at Sea," follows. God commands the East wind to blow (Example 2). Throughout this entire section, the chorus sings only textless vowels, imitating the wind. Together with the raging rhythms of the instrumental ensemble, the fury of the storm steadily increases. The narrator's description heightens the effect until the waves of music reach their peak and threaten to sink the ship. At the narrator's words "They resigned all hope and each prayed to the god who could comfort him best," the chorus calls out to a myriad of gods in frenzied choric speech. The sailors decide Jonah is to blame for their misfortune. They sing textless,

Example 2

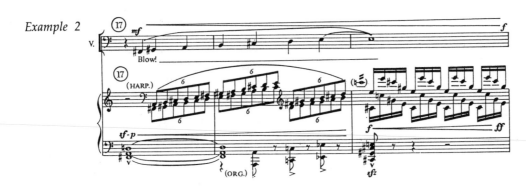

swinging phrases that increase in height and volume as the narrator describes how the sailors "took him by top and by toe, and into the tumultuous sea he was thrown." The storm subsides. Choral phrases decrease in energy and compass until the final calm is mirrored in long, sustained cadence notes.

Section five, "In the Belly of the Whale," is the shortest. At the outset, rapid, upward instrumental lines and a graceful cantabile melody accompany the narrator as he describes the whale "beaten up from the abyss" and floating by the boat. Staccato, broken fourths picture the whale as he swims toward Jonah "to swallow him up," in a rush of thirty-second notes. Narration and instruments place Jonah "seated in his stomach, safe and secure" to ponder this lesson. The chorus becomes Jonah's inner voice and quotes two phrases from the opening chorale, telling him to "face woe with fortitude." Jonah prays. His prayer becomes the text of section six, evolving into a three-part musical form. In part one, Jonah's petition "Out of the belly of hell cried I" is intoned while the chorus repeats a Latin psalm in unison: "De profundis clamavi ad te" (Out of the depths I cry to Thee). This choral melody then becomes the subject of a brief fugue for chorus alone, continuing the Latin text of the chorale and forming a middle section. When Jonah re-enters to continue his prayer of repentance, the chorus shifts to a free syllabic style and concludes the psalm, forming a structural recapitulation. As Part One ends, the narrator announces:

Then our Father firmly commanded the fish to spit up the sinner on some dry shore.

Part Two begins when the repentant Jonah agrees to go to Nineveh. Steady, determined chords accompany Jonah as he approaches Nineveh. He unleashes his indictment of the city and all its inhabitants, using a melodic line that projects vigorous determination (Example 3).

Example 3

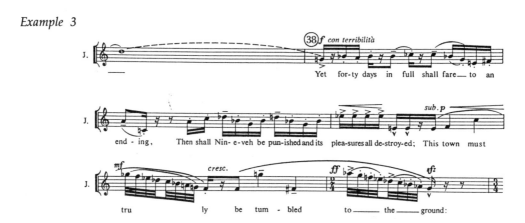

He delivers this complete message four times without stopping. The King is aroused and calls for his people to fast and pray for mercy. In the role of the people, the chorus begins a polyphonic "Kyrie Eleison" (Lord, Have Mercy) which increases steadily in its activity and volume, gradually equalling Jonah's searing call for repentance. Finally, chorus and brass overpower the voice of Jonah, silencing the prophet, symbolizing that God has heard the Ninevites. A soprano soloist guides the chorus in an exquisite "Christe Eleison," and according to liturgical custom the opening Kyrie returns. After the final choral cadence of this section, the narrator reports:

And God through his goodness forgave them, for in spite of his vow, the Lord withheld his vengeance.

Jonah is angered: "He waxed like a whirlwind towards our Lord." These words from the narrator begin section eight. Jonah unleashes his rancor in a long aria, bitterly begging God to take his life, "Since it seems to me sweeter to die at once than to play the prophet and be found a fool." God scolds Jonah: "Haughty man, have I harmed you here?" The narrator ends this section, picturing the sulking, "grumbling" prophet leaving the city to find shelter and rest.

Section nine develops into the most elegant choral movement of the work. The chorus describes the "beautiful woodbine" which blossomed over the sleeping Jonah, giving him comfort, pleasure and protection from the sun (Example 4). As the vine withers and dies the section ends. Jonah again falls upon God's injustice: "Why me?" The question is asked six times, with increasingly impassioned rhythmic emphasis. The melody rises step by step, as Jonah stretches his arms to heaven, crying out: "Why must your mischief always fall on me?"

Example 4

Three timpani form a muffled minor chord to summon the Voice of God at the outset of section ten, "God's Rebuke." This entire movement is essentially a recitative and aria for the Voice of God. He upbraids Jonah:

> Should you become so choleric, all because of a woodbine? Such a sulky servant, and for something so slight? And you would find fault with me, when Nineveh I set free.

At length, in much the same manner as He dealt with Job, God reveals to Jonah the protective comfort which His omnipotence assures: "I myself made them all, out of primal matter; I have watched over them from the start, as I shall watch unto the end of the world." God continues to explain how His mercy goes out to all in His creation and, close to the end of this section, the chorus surrounds the Voice of God with a simple diatonic setting of the hymn "Praise to the Lord, the Almighty, the King of Creation."

God directs His final words to Jonah, in vocal lines of majesty and mercy, forming a bridge to the last section, "The Lesson Restated."

> Be not so angry, my good Jonah, for he who is so choleric that he rips his own clothes must then sullenly suffer to sew them together himself.

The chorus returns to the music and text of the opening chorale, "Face woe with fortitude." Then, in quiet, flowing harmonies, continues the hymn "Praise to the Lord". As the instruments generate propelling rhythmic activity a momentous climax is reached on the cadence of the final phrase (Example 5). Three resounding echoes of the first "Amen" die away in decreasing dynamic levels until the last melts into a one-line reprise of the hymn. As the closing "Amen" stretches out from the reprise to an almost inaudible triple piano, the voice of Jonah rises above the chorus in delicate and confident tones: "Salvation is of the Lord."

Example 5

> I myself made them all, out of primal matter;
> I have watched over them from the start, as I shall watch unto the end of the world.

—Thurston Dox

Emanuele d'Astorga   1680–1757

Emanuele d'Astorga is a forgotten name today—a lifetime of work has almost all been lost. Only a single composition is still played occasionally, and for its sake a few lines are dedicated here to its creator, Baron Rincón. Though of Spanish ancestry, for generations his family had possessed property in southern Italy—Astorga and other villages—where the composer-to-be was born in 1680. Out of his hectic life, which took him to all the leading cities of Europe—Palermo, Genoa, Mantua, Venice, Vienna, London, Lisbon, and Madrid—the period that particularly interests us is the autumn of 1707 and the first few months of 1708, when he appears to have been in Naples and Rome. Here he composed his *Stabat Mater*, which at the time was often mentioned in the same breath with that of his contemporary Pergolesi, and which has survived him all these years.

For neither of the two works have we been able to ascertain the form in which they were originally performed. The vocal parts could have been intended for either soloists or chorus and were most likely interchangeable. Whereas Pergolesi's work was written for high voices exclusively—probably for a children's choir, although today usually given to a female chorus—Astorga's *Stabat Mater* was written for mixed voices. The instrumental accompaniment was almost surely performed by strings. After the four-part, probably choral, setting of the first movement ("Stabat Mater") comes an elaborate imitative trio (soprano, tenor, bass): "O quam tristis." A double duet follows, probably sung by soloists, first between alto and soprano and then between tenor and bass, never moving to four-part texture ("Quis est homo" and "Pro peccatis"). The "Eia Mater" that follows seems to have been conceived as a choral fugue. Then the soprano sings an emotional Baroque aria, "Sancta Mater."

Richness in forms marks this work, whereas in Pergolesi's work, arias alternate with duets, excluding the use of larger ensembles. D'Astorga obviously loved diversity of structure and sound. "Fac me tecum" is a duet between alto and tenor, followed by the chorus singing "Virgo virginum." The bass soloist sings the aria "Fac me plagis," and the work ends with a beautiful, variegated "Christe" sung by the full chorus.

Jacob Avshalomov   1919–

Jacob Avshalomov spent the first three decades of his life in China. His mother was American, his father the noted Russian composer, Aaron Avshalomov. Music remained essentially an avocation for Jacob until 1937, when he reached a decision to become a composer. In that year he visited the United States and remained to become a citizen. Studies with Ernst Toch, Bernard Rogers and Aaron Copland brought success as a composer and led to a position on the music faculty of Columbia University. In 1954 he was appointed conductor of the well-established Portland Youth Philharmonic—a position he has held to the present.

Five large works for chorus and instruments distinguish his catalog: *How Long, O Lord* (1948), *Tom O'Bedlam* (1953), *Inscriptions at the City of Brass* (1956), *Praises from the Four Corners of the Earth* (1964), and *City Upon a Hill* (1964). The composer considers *Inscriptions at the City of Brass* his *magnum opus*; in his words, ". . . the most ambitious work I have ever produced." A new translation of *The Book of the Thousand Nights and One Night* by E. Powys Mathers inspired Avshalomov to select this particular tale and set it as a narrative oratorio.

Inscriptions at the City of Brass

Original Language: English
Date of Writing: 1956
First Performance: March 12, 1957 in New York, with Hugh Ross as conductor. Dedicated to Ernst Toch.
Form: The story unfolds in three large divisions and nine subdivisions.

> Prelude
> I.   A. The Entrance
>   Interlude
>   B. The Hawk-eyed Kings

II.   Kush ben Shaded ben Ad,
      Surnamed the Great
      Interlude
III. A. The Stranger
      B. A Short Passing to Another Place
      C. The Web of the World
      D. The Fair Things You Do

Performance time: 23 minutes.

Scoring: The scoring is unusual; an orchestra of winds, brass and four percussionists, but no string section. Prepared piano, guitar, two banjos, four contrabasses and harp are added. There is a female narrator and mixed chorus.

Discussion of the Work: Shahrazad's discoveries while searching for the City of Brass are described by the narrator. In each city he visits, inscriptions are found on the city walls. They carry a common theme: Mankind's quest for wealth and power is vanity. The chorus sings the words of each inscription.

General characteristics of Avshalomov's style are clear throughout this work. Melodies are lyrical and overflowing with expressive beauty. All instruments are considered potential melody bearers, producing continuous melodic movement. Text declamation adheres very closely to correct natural accents, and important words are stressed by placement on the downbeat. A two-voice choral texture is common, the full chorus arranged in octave pairing.

New texts are often introduced in the space following an orchestral release, facilitating comprehension. The harmonic style employs relatively moderate dissonances and tonality is maintained with or without major/minor modes.

An oriental flavor pervades this music, clearly and deliberately influenced by the composer's early years in China and by his father's works. Avshalomov is lucid on this point, reminding us, "Music is stilted if it does not reflect one's environment." The ornamental figure in the winds which precedes the opening narration, for example, immediately evokes strong feelings of the mysterious and remote (Example 1).

Example 1

Such figures reappear in exotic patterns throughout the work. The masterful combination of transparent orchestral colorings—appropriate to mood and text—brilliantly illuminates the various scenes and helps to maintain the oriental hue.

Word painting adds moments of imagination and expressive interest to the music. The words "they were dispersed" are set to abruptly divergent lines in contrary motion; a rapid eight-measure chromatic passage illustrates a "hot wind." The simple word "far" is extended for eight bars. Text painting characterizes a passage which entangles the words "web of the world" in a net of intricate counterpoint (Example 2). The closing text—"for tomorrow the earth will claim you, but the fair things you do shall blow like flowers on the red and fiery day"—ignites the orchestra to a glowing display of color and dynamic intensity.

Jacob Avshalomov combined technical and coloristic resources to create music that is tenaciously faithful to the drama. Each detail of action, each turn of events on this strange and wondrous journey comes to life. The dramatic power of this unusual orchestral ensemble, sup-

Example 2

porting the provocative texts, often approaches the operatic, an impression confirmed by the composer's own words:

> The choral work I have done takes the place of operatic settings in my output. I have a closer feeling for the non-staged works of dramatic literature than the staged. In a way, it's a kind of opera. The fact is, where other people would have turned things into operatic setting, I have turned to the choral literature—the cantata and the oratorio. I have never ventured into opera because I prefer to deal with exalted and humanistic texts directly with this combined medium, without the distractions and conventional silliness of plot, costume and lighting.

—Thurston Dox

Johann Sebastian Bach 1685–1750

Johann Sebastian Bach was born in Eisenach, in Thuringia, on March 21, 1685, to a musical family, the likes of which we will probably never see again. From the death in 1626 of the great-grandfather, Hans Bach, each new generation brought forth new musicians, who played a considerable role in Thuringia as organists, cantors, and choral directors. Johann Sebastian was certainly the most important member of the family; without a shadow of doubt, we think of him today as one of the greatest musical geniuses of all times and peoples, a man who encompassed the entire Baroque tradition and foretold the future development of music as well. Of his 20 children, born to him in the course of two happy marriages, four became famous musicians: Wilhelm Friedemann (the "Halle Bach"), Carl Philipp Emanuel (the "Berlin" or "Hamburg Bach"), Johann Christoph Friedrich (the "Bückeburg Bach"), and Johann Christian (the "Milan" or "London Bach"). Only with them, after five creative generations, did the Bach family run out of musicians.

After the early death of his parents, Johann Sebastian moved to the nearby town of Ohrdruf, where he was educated by a brother. When 15 years old, he moved to Lüneburg to attend the cloister school, where he met French musicians from the nearby town of Celle, and from where he traveled to Hamburg to hear Johann Adam Reinken, already well along in years, play the organ. In 1703, he became a violinist in the palace orchestra at Weimar. He was drawn to the organ, and obtained posts as organist in Arnstadt and later in Mühlhausen, both of which offered very limited musical opportunities. In 1708 he returned to Weimar, where, in 1714, he became concertmaster of the ducal orchestra. He left this post in 1717 to move to Anhalt-Köthen, where he assumed the duties of Kapellmeister at the court. In 1722 he applied for a more prestigious post in Hamburg, which was ultimately given to the much more famous Telemann. Instead he became, in 1723, Kuhnau's successor in Leipzig, as cantor at the church of St. Thomas, also having responsibility for the music performed in other churches in the city. Here, until his death on July 28, 1750, he performed his duties faithfully and diligently, esteemed by the local congregations and admired by many musicians, but far from having won renown in the rest of Europe.

His workaday life flowed smoothly and uneventfully, at least on the surface. In 1736, having written parts of the *B Minor Mass*, he received the title "Composer to the Court of Poland and Saxony," and experienced the external high point of his life in May, 1747, when his son, then working in Berlin, arranged a visit for him to Potsdam, to meet King Frederick the Great of Prussia, a very talented musician.

Bach composed in all musical genres except opera, which for many reasons did not interest him. The five works falling within the scope of this book are all sacred: two are Passions (the *St.*

John and *St. Matthew Passions*); the *Mass in B Minor;* and two works usually called the *Easter Oratorio* and the *Christmas Oratorio.* They were all composed between 1722 and 1739, with possible later additions to the *B Minor Mass,* according to recent findings. As with most of Bach's works, these oratorios were not widely known during his lifetime. Generations went by—exactly a century in the case of the *B Minor Mass*—before these works, true masterpieces of the genre, entered the consciousness of the wider musical world.

St. John Passion

Original Title: Passio secundum Johannem
Original Language: German
Text: From the Gospel according to St. John (Chapters 18 and 19); in addition, excerpts from Barthold Heinrich Brockes's poem "Der für die Sünde der Welt gemarterte und sterbende Jesus" (1715) ("Jesus Martyred and Dying for the Sins of the World").
Date of Writing: Anhalt-Kothen, 1722–23; revised in 1725, around 1730, and again around 1739.
First Performance: April 7, 1724 (Good Friday) in the church of St. Nicholas in Leipzig.
Form: In two parts; includes a total of 40 musical numbers (68 according to the old numbering).
Parts: Evangelist (tenor), Jesus (bass), Pilate (bass), Peter (bass), four solo voices (soprano, alto, tenor, bass), and a four-part mixed chorus. *Orchestra:* Two flutes, two oboes, oboe d'amore, two oboes da caccia, two violas d'amore, viola da gamba, strings, continuo with cello, possibly bassoon, contrabass, and organ or harpsichord.
Contents: Using the words of the Holy Scriptures, the work tells the story of Jesus' capture in the Garden of Gethsemane, a "garden above the river Kidron," frequented by him and his disciples; of his interrogation by Annas, a brother-in-law of the High Priest Caiphas; of being handed over to Caiphas and then to the Roman governor Pilate, who was convinced that Jesus had committed no crime; of the insistence of the Jews that Jesus be condemned to death because he had purportedly called himself their "King"; of his crucifixion and death; of the removal from the cross by Joseph of Arimathaea and the hasty, stealthy burial, due to the approaching Sabbath, which they dared not break with activities of this sort. The narrative is interrupted again and again with insertions sung by the chorus (dramatic, lyrical, [i.e., non-scriptural], contemplative pieces; chorales) and the soloists (arias).
History of the Work: The *St. John Passion* seems to have been the first work of its kind composed by Bach. An earlier *St. Luke Passion,* presented under his name, has since turned out to be fairly certainly spurious. Bach, exceptionally receptive to other musicians' compositions, probably performed this rather weak work and for that purpose copied it out, even adding his customary "J.J.," Jesu juva (with the help of Jesus). However, the view that there were, in addition to the *St. John* and the *St. Matthew* Passions, two other Bach works in this genre stubbornly persists, but they are thought to have been irrevocably lost.

When Bach was certain that he had indeed obtained the position in Leipzig and would soon begin his work there, he began, while still in Köthen, to compose the *St. John Passion.* Because he could not find a suitable libretto there, he wrote one himself, using the text of the Gospel according to St. John and interjecting parts of the Passion verses written years before by the poet and town councillor of Hamburg, Barthold Heinrich Brockes. Brockes's words had already been set to music by several composers, all of whom had worked at least for a time in Hamburg: Reinhard Keiser (1712), Handel and Telemann (1716), and Mattheson (1716).

Why Bach chose to compose a Passion upon assuming his new office is not easily explained. Johann Kuhnau (1660–1722), Bach's predecessor as cantor at the church of St. Thomas in Leipzig, had, after much soul searching, finally brought himself to accept this "modern" art form related to opera. Toward the end of his service he finally embraced it by composing one of his own. Bach probably did not complete the *St. John Passion* until after he had moved to Leipzig; he had made two journeys there at the beginning of 1723 in order to present himself and his works before taking up his duties officially. When the work was first performed was for some years not clear. Earlier Bach scholars, among them Wolfgang Schmieder, refer to the year 1723, giving the exact date as March 26, Good Friday. This date has since proved invalid: The *St. John Passion* was performed for the first time at the Good Friday Vespers on April 7, 1724, at the church of St. Nicholas in Leipzig.

A work treating the theme of Christ's suffering and death was entirely appropriate for the Good Friday services. Five years later Bach also introduced his *St. Matthew Passion* on Good Friday. The *St. John Passion,* repeatedly and fairly thoroughly revised by Bach, was performed twice or perhaps three times more during his lifetime. The first was in 1725, as it is sung today, with the altered opening chorus; the next, probably before 1730. In the meantime, he seems to have composed two other Passions, now lost, using texts written by the young Leipzig postmaster and later tax collector Christian Friedrich Henrici, who used the pen name Picander. Bach's admiration for him is hard for us to understand.

We know nothing of how the *St. John Passion* was received at its first performance. It was not performed in concert, but as part of the Good Friday liturgy in the sanctuary of the church, thus precluding a written critical account; such accounts have come down to us under other circumstances, albeit seldom. The few performances given during the remaining quarter century of Bach's life seem to have left no deep impression upon the devout.

The *St. Matthew Passion* is generally better loved and esteemed than Bach's setting of the Gospel according to St. John. But contrary opinions have been voiced, the most important, perhaps, that of Robert Schumann. Albert Schweitzer's experience is noteworthy in this connection. In his great biography of Bach, he tells of performances of the *St. John Passion* for which he prepared the chorus and played the organ. During the first rehearsals he found the work difficult, but by the time it was ready for performance, he had taken the work to heart and preferred it to all others of its kind.

Performance Practice: Today's listeners (and performers) should always bear in mind that Bach worked under conditions fundamentally different from those to which we are accustomed. His usual choruses included at the most 20 voices, and his orchestra numbered about the same, or sometimes, even fewer. On special occasions, perhaps on great holidays, the forces increased to 50 or at the very most, 60. Today, we often hear Bach's Passions, as well as his *B Minor Mass*, sung by choruses of imposing size and vocal strength, which naturally leads to a corresponding strengthening of the accompanying orchestra. The orchestras of his time included two violins for each oboe or flute; in an augmented orchestra, this relationship may reach 6:1 or an even more distorted ratio. The question of the doubling of the winds is pressing, but one that is difficult to answer because many of the passages for wind instruments were intended by Bach as expressive solos and when doubled, lose their individuality of expression and phrasing. Many other questions come to mind. Did Bach have massive choirs in mind—as might be assumed from the dramatic choruses? He must have been aware that at the same time he, in Leipzig, was compelled to perform works using such small forces, Handel, in London, could count on masses of singers and players, and that even his friend Telemann found more generous support in Hamburg. Did Bach write his "great" works for the performance possibilities at his disposal, or did he have in mind those that might be available to his successors?

In our epoch, with its new understanding of Baroque music, we must give serious consideration to problems like this, whereas in the 19th century it was customary to perform all music, even that of earlier times—if it was played at all—according to the tastes of the time. With increasing frequency Bach's Passions are presented not as mass spectaculars—which certainly possess their own attraction and can be powerfully effective—but in an effort to approximate performance conditions of his time: a small orchestra (using historical instruments, when possible) and a chamber chorus of about 25 voices.

With respect to solo parts, it should be noted that Bach had to rely for the most part on experienced members of the chorus. In view of the often extreme difficulty of these roles, we find this truly astonishing. People then must have been less demanding than we, who live in the "Age of Perfection." Neither Bach nor Beethoven would probably be able to believe their ears if they were able to hear contemporary performances of their works. It is therefore all the more astonishing that such consummate masterpieces could be produced in those centuries.

Discussion of the Work: The opening chorus, "Herr, unser Herrscher, dessen Ruhm in allen Landen herrlich ist!" (which Bach added only after the first performance of the work, as a replacement for a more tranquil chorus in E-flat major) is one of the most distinctive and impressive sections. It begins after an orchestral introduction, which establishes the key of G minor, the key which may be said to be the principal one of the work. After three mighty calls of "Herr! Herr! Herr!" and the lively development of each in running sixteenth-note passages, each repeated with increasing intensity, Bach begins a magnificent fugato. The massive theme runs from the basses upwards through all four voices of the chorus, the last (soprano) entering a fourth higher (Example 1). After the introductory chorus, the Narrator begins his account, accompanied, as was customary, by a basso continuo, played on either harpsichord or organ, which may be augmented in a lower register by a cello or gamba, if available.

Example 1

The longer recitative (taken from chapter 18 of the *Gospel of St. John*) remains in a somber minor key and describes the place where Jesus, walking with his disciples, was overheard and confronted by Judas and his henchmen. Not until Jesus counters them with the question "Wen sucht ihr?" (Whom do you seek?) does the tonal structure suddenly lighten to a D major chord. While not wishing to ascribe to Bach and the Baroque period too great a tendency toward tone painting, the point of this unexpected modulation surely must be to immediately characterize Jesus as a shining, godly figure. Without a pause, the chorus bursts in, again in G minor, singing "Jesum von Nazareth" four times. Another short recitative by the Evangelist, with Jesus' questions interspersed, follows, and again the chorus cries out in G minor. And then, in a deeply expressive declamation, Jesus speaks; he surrenders without resistance, asking only for his disciples' freedom. Bach uses this occasion to insert a chorale based on the melody of the Lutheran hymn "Herzliebster Jesu, was hast du verbrochen?" (Dear Jesus, what wrong have you done?), which, simply harmonized in a traditional way, is sung with the words "O grosse Lieb' ohn' alle Masse" (O great and endless love). Here we have a fine example of one of the most basic characteristics of Bach's Passions: his wish to bring art and folk music together. The chorale is also in G minor, but in the final chord brightens to G major. Another recitative, and then, surprisingly soon, another chorale, "Dein Will' gescheh" (Thy will be done).

The narration by the Evangelist, describing how Jesus was captured, bound, and led before Annas and Caiphas, comes next, followed by the first aria: the alto sings "Von den Stricken meiner Sünden" (From the shackles of my sin). The chorales and arias in Bach's Passions are seldom directly related to the dramatic action; they are contemplative in nature (earlier commentators called them "philosophical"). Their introspective quality was intended to reflect the moods, thoughts, and feelings aroused in the listeners at a given moment in the drama. Sometimes they do indeed refer to the action, but immediately move away from it to give themselves up to lyrical reflection.

After the alto aria, the Evangelist sings a single sentence: "Simon Petrus aber folgete Jesu nach, und ein and'rer Jünger" (Simon Peter followed Jesus and another disciple). This gives the solo soprano the occasion to expand upon the words with: "Ich folge dir gleichfalls mit freudigen Schritten" (I, too, follow Thee with joyous steps). The relationship may seem strained, because although "folgen" makes sense, the words "freudige Schritte" do not fit at all, for at this moment Peter's heart must have been grieved and anxious. Then comes another chorale, "Wer hat dich so geschlagen" (Who has beaten you so?), sung to the well-known chorale tune "O Welt, ich muss dich lassen." In the episode in which Peter, warming himself in the chilly night, is assailed by the crowd singing "Bist du nicht seiner Jünger einer?" (Are you not one of his disciples?), the chorus, having just sung a lyrical lament, suddenly is transformed, becoming once more the basic dramatic element of the work. The next recitative, in which Peter denies his relationship to Jesus but then recalls His prophecy and "bitterlich weinete" (wept bitterly), is significantly expanded. Bach gives the Evangelist, who is telling the story, an especially expressive melodic passage, which contrasts with the recitatives he has sung heretofore (Example 2). What follows, in the same key (F-sharp minor) in which these remarkable six adagio measures of the Evangelist close, is a tenor aria (which leads musicologists to the conclusion that Bach used the same singer for both the solo tenor role and the Evangelist): "Ach, mein Sinn, wo willst du endlich hin?" (O my soul, what lies ahead for you?). Once more, with these very first words, the relationship to Peter's confusion and shame is established, and once more, the aria goes on to assume a separate identity, one scarcely connected to the plot. The first part of the passion closes with another chorale, the fourth ("Petrus, der nicht denkt zurück"—Peter, without conscience), based on the melody "Jesu Kreuz, Leiden und Pein." The text here clearly refers back to the action: from Peter's weeping it goes on to a call to Jesus," . . . blicke mich auch an, wenn ich nicht will büssen; wenn ich Böses hab' getan, rühre mein Gewissen" (. . . see me, when I do not repent; when I have done evil, awaken my conscience).

Example 2

The second part begins with a chorale, this time using a melody Bach composed himself: "Christus, der uns selig macht" (See the Lord of life and light). The action begins with the handing over of Jesus to the Romans and their governor, Pilate. An angry crowd demonstrates, demanding nothing less than the death of the prisoner. The dialogue between Jesus and Pilate is treated as a long recitative, interrupted only once by a chorale. To the melody of the original "Herzliebster Jesu, was hast du verbrochen," the words "Ach, grosser König, gross zu allen Zeiten" (Ah, mighty King, forever great) are sung. This melody occurs here for the second time; it formed the first chorale of the first section. Here Bach has not only transposed it a whole tone higher but scored it entirely differently, which was important, not only for dramatic reasons, but for a purely musical one as well— his fondness for writing variations finds expression here. The story takes a dramatic turn after the Evangelist's long recitative with the brief, violent outcry by the chorus of Jews, who demand that Pilate release the murderer Barrabas instead of Jesus, as Pilate had recommended. The Evangelist, as though caught up in the crowd's excitement, now sings an equally tempestuous, almost operalike recitative, stirred from his usual objectivity to the most dramatic kind of singing (Example 3).

Example 3

Next come two splendid pieces of music: a bass arioso and a tenor aria, the latter surely one of the most ravishing Bach ever wrote. Its accompaniment, a mixture of the sounds of the viola d'amore and the cello, give the delicately conceived orchestral accompaniment an unearthly, almost mystical cast. In contrast, the mocking chorus of soldiers is all too earthly, as they dress him in a purple mantle and place a crown of thorns upon his head: "Sei grüsset, lieber Judenkönig!" (Greetings, dear King of the Jews). The chorus, with its "Kreuzige!" (Crucify him!), reaches a new high; this one outcry surges wildly through the vocal parts, which are rhythmically sharp at variance. In the next chorus, the Jews demand from the still hesitant Pilate the execution of Jesus, who has broken their strict law by declaring himself the Son of God. At this most dramatic point, a new chorale breaks in: "Durch dein Gefängnis, Gottes Sohn" (Through your capture, Son of God), sung to the melody of "Mach's mit mir, Gott, nach deiner Güt'," but the people's tumultuous outcry continues as, with mounting excitement, they continue to assail Pilate. A bass aria brings no respite, because Bach interrupts the mostly coloraturalike melody of the soloist with excited interjections from the soprano, alto, and tenor voices of the chorus, which in great agitation cry out the single word "Wohin?" (Where?). The realism of this scene is gripping. In the next chorus, the High Priests address Pilate, demanding that he not place the words "Der Juden König" (King of the Jews) on Jesus' cross, but rather that Jesus, himself, *claimed* to be their king. But Pilate refuses. A chorale interrupts the action: to the melody of "Valet will ich dir geben" the chorus sings the words "In meines Herzens Grunde" (Deep in my heart). In the next chorus, the Roman soldiers cast lots for Jesus' tunic. The mother of Jesus appears in the following recitative, and is told she may take one of Jesus' favorite disciples as her son. A chorale emphasizes the gentle mood, using once more the melody "Jesu Kreuz, Leiden und Pein," this time with the text "Er nahm alles wohl in Acht" (He has thought of everything), which here departs from the usual pattern and refers directly to the immediately preceding action. The harmonization and even the melody itself are different from the first appearance of this chorale. Then the alto sings a sublime aria ("Es ist vollbracht"—The end has come), accompanied by the viola da gamba. The first part is quite solemn, while the second is heroic ("Der Held aus Juda siegt mit Macht"—The hero from Judah is victorious) and precedes the finale in which "Es ist vollbracht" is repeated twice, accompanied once more by the stately, expressive melody of the viola da gamba. A bass aria with chorus sings of Jesus' death, representing a new climax. The chorale "Jesu Kreuz, Leiden und Pein" appears again, this time with the words "Jesu, der du warest tot" (Jesus, who once was dead) and is interwoven with the expressive melody sung by the soloist.

Now the Evangelist describes the events following Jesus' death: The curtain in the temple is ripped asunder, an earthquake causes the rocks to burst, and many graves break open. Here Bach uses musical imagery, but limits himself to either the harpsichord or the organ to describe with a rapid downward passage how the curtain is torn, and with a dense tremolo, the quaking of the earth. In the tenor solo arioso that follows, we hear an echo of this musical imagery in the orchestra, while the text, too, repeats the events. The connecting soprano aria fits the situation exactly: "Zerfliesse mein Herze" (Overflow, my heart), with the repeated, painful assertion, "Dein Jesus ist tot!" (Your Jesus is dead!).

However, the work does not end here. The Evangelist, in a somewhat stiff manner, goes on to recount the subsequent events of Christ's Passion. Another chorale follows: "O hilf, Christe" (O help us, Christ) to the melody "Christus, der uns selig macht," and another long recitative, the final one. Now comes the lovely, peaceful chorus "Ruht wohl, ihr heiligen Gebeine" (May your holy body rest in peace). With the chorale "Ach Herr, lass dein lieb' Engelein" (Ah, Lord, send your dear angels), the *St. John Passion* comes to an end.

The St. Matthew Passion

Original Title: Passio D. N. J. C. secundum Matthaeum
Original Language: German
Text: From the Gospel of St. Matthew (Chapters 26 and 27); in addition, texts by Christian Friedrich Henrici (Picander) from his "Ernst-Schertzhaffte und Satyrische Gedichte," Part 2 (1729).
Date of Writing: Leipzig, 1728/29; revisions 1736, 1739, 1745.
First Performance: March 15, 1729 (Good Friday) in the church of St. Thomas in Leipzig.
Form: In two parts, including a total of 68 musical numbers (78 according to the old system).
Characters: Evangelist (tenor), Jesus (bass), Judas (bass), Peter (bass), Pilate (bass), Pontifex I/II (basses), Maids I/II (soprano and mezzosoprano), Witnesses I/II (alto and tenor), Pilate's Wife (soprano), four solo voices (soprano, alto, tenor, bass), two four-part mixed choruses, boys' chorus.
Orchestra: Two recorders, two flutes, two oboes, two oboes d'amore, two oboes da caccia, viola da gamba, strings, continuo with cello, bassoon, contrabass, organ, and harpsichord.
Contents: This work, like the *St. John Passion*, recounts the story of the capture and crucifixion of Christ, using the words of the Holy Scriptures, interrupted again and again by the poetic interjections of the chorus—dramatic, lyrical, contemplative pieces. The action, however, here begins earlier than in the *St. John Passion* and there are more scenes, so the emotional variety is correspondingly greater. Because of the magnitude of this work, which contains no fewer than 68 musical numbers and requires almost five hours to perform, it is a unique depiction of the suffering and death of Christ.
History of the Work: At the time of the death on November 19, 1728, of Bach's former employer, the Duke of Anhalt-Köthen, the cantor of the St. Thomas church and the poet Picander, a young Leipzig postal clerk, were probably already planning a Passion based on the Gospel of St. Matthew. When the possibility arose that Bach would be asked to compose music for the memorial services—which would, as was customary, take place two or three months after the death—he discussed with his librettist the possibility of changing the texts of certain parts of the Passion they were already working on and combining them to form a *Trauermusik* (music of mourning). The resulting composition consists of seven arias, an aria with chorus, and a concluding chorus, all identical to pieces in the *St. Matthew Passion*. The great introductory chorus of the Passion seems to have made its first appearance as part of the *Trauermusik*.

This was not the first collaboration between the cantor of St. Thomas and the young poet. In 1725, Picander wrote a Passion text in which he used some ideas of the Hamburg poet Brockes, who was responsible for the non-Biblical texts of the *St. John Passion*. Was it, then, Picander's text that Bach had set to music? There are indications that this is the case, for just six years later Picander wrote—certainly for Bach again—the text for a *St. Mark Passion*. But the 1725 Passion—based on a nontraditional Gospel or perhaps on a text entirely of Picander's writing—as well as the *St. Mark Passion* of 1731, have disappeared.

Scholars have also maintained that some of the pieces in the *St. Mark Passion* also derived from the *Trauermusik* already mentioned (for which, moreover, some Bach experts give a different origin than I do, and thus a different year of composition). Because it never occurred to Bach to write a history of his compositions, much about his life and works remains in dispute or simply unknown. One such disputed matter is the allegorical figure of the "Tochter Zion" (Daughter of Zion), the source of which is probably Brockes's poem, who leads a chorus of the faithful souls, but who does not figure in the final cast of the *St. Matthew Passion*. In the final version her part has been divided among various other roles, but there are allusions to her throughout the text.

At the time of its composition, Bach was at the height of his creative powers. He provided the score of the *St. Matthew Passion* with such a treasure of truly Baroque ideas and such musical mastery that it is hard to take it all in; it is simply overpowering.

Unfortunately, we cannot know how he conceived of the performance of this huge work. Did he think a performance five hours long was possible? It is always a problem for today's audiences. The best solution is to divide the performance into two parts corresponding to Bach's own division. It has often been suggested that the first part be performed on Holy Thursday and the second on Good Friday, the days during which the tragic events depicted were played out. On the day of its first performance, Good Friday, 1729, Bach had placed both parts, the entire work, on the program of his afternoon services. No one knows whether the hours-long church service wore the faithful out or whether they were simply incapable of following this magnificent, in many ways unusual, music. That evening, Bach probably gathered up the score and took it home with him. It is very doubtful that the *St. Matthew Passion* was performed again during the lifetime of its creator. It slept the sleep of Sleeping Beauty for an entire century before the 21-year-old Felix Mendelssohn, perhaps acting on a hint from his former teacher, Karl Friedrich Zelter, discovered the forgotten score in a Berlin library and performed it on March 11, 1829, with the Singakademie. The success was so enormous that the performance had to be repeated 10 days later, on March 21. Since that time, the *St. Matthew Passion* has been considered one of the greatest of musical masterpieces.

Performance Practice: Much of what has already been said about the *St. John Passion* is true of this work. But from the point of view of sound, the *St. Matthew Passion* is more richly conceived, and the power of the double chorus is employed. The question of the interpretation of old music, including the matter of faithfulness to the original, naturally arises. We know from memoranda to the town council of the modest forces with which Bach had to make do during his tenure at Leipzig. Should we try to imitate these limitations, or should we allow the score to lure us into producing a mighty extravaganza of sound? Should we try to imitate the sound of his orchestra, for which we would need many instruments no longer in general use, or should we not worry about all that and just use the modern instruments we have? The question is not a superficial one, touching as it does on a most difficult, central problem, of which the layman knows little and with which, happily, he does not have to concern himself. There is furthermore the matter of pitch, which was considerably lower than that of today's instruments, and the consequences of which are quite dramatic. The key of C major in which Bach wrote in order to achieve a very particular effect sounds like our B major, perhaps even a little lower. If he were to hear a modern performance of one of his C major works, he—master of absolute pitch that he was—would be astonished and perhaps not exactly delighted with the C-sharp major that he hears. But if in interpreting old music we reduce the forces to what used to be, the result would be chaos. The consequences of these factors is that every performance we give, even the best, must be a compromise.

But it would be totally wrong to assume that performances of Bach's music then were much less expressive than what we are used to today. With simpler means he achieved amazing effects. Karl Schumann clarifies this somewhat when he says:

> The introductory chorus unfolds on three levels: the first chorus as the knowing congregation, the lamenting Daughter of Zion ("Kommt, ihr Töchter, helft mir klagen"—Come, daughters, join the lamentation); the second chorus as ignorant heathens who ask what is going on ("Wen? Wie? Was? Wohin?"—Who? How? What? Where?); the boys' chorus with the Passion chorale that begins in a strident G major ("O Lamm Gottes"—O lamb of God), a melody that first appeared in 1542 in an old German song collection. . . .

This means that Bach did not use the double chorus just to achieve a certain sound effect, as was done during the Golden Age of Italian Renaissance polyphony in the church of St. Mark in Venice. A second organ loft was built in St. Mark so that on each there was room for both an instrumental and a vocal group. Bach rather used it because for this drama he needed to sharply delineate characters without recourse to a stage. Should the two choruses called for in the *St. Matthew Passion* be placed next to each other or as far apart as possible? Should performances given in a church be different from those given in a concert hall? These are important questions that cannot be answered with certainty. The treatment of Jesus' recitatives in the *St. Matthew Passion* is fundamentally different from that in the *St. John*. In the former, they are no longer accompanied by harpsichord or organ but are supported and given a special dignity and solemnity by a string quartet, increasing their expressiveness. Perhaps it is just this quality—allowing the performers more leeway in interpretation than is possible in works closer to us in time—that is so bound up with any good performance of the *St. Matthew Passion* and similar Baroque works.

Discussion of the Work: Even the orchestral introduction in E minor is a significant piece; it is dominated by two themes, which are treated in double counterpoint. This means that each can be either the upper or the lower voice, either the melody or the accompaniment. Then the chorus enters, immediately demonstrating what Karl Schumann explained in words, that this piece is a dramatic element of the first rank. The voices of the first chorus begin, calling upon the entire world to lament and weep with them, after which the second chorus enters. One must imagine the action: It is as if, in an old city, a mass of people streamed in confusion from every street and alley toward the square, from which they have heard a call. They besiege the gathered assembly with astonished questions: Whom? How? What are you weeping about? The frightened curiosity, the insistence on learning the cause of the weeping and lamenting become more and more intense, until the second chorus also comes in in a continuous, four-part texture. But even the eight-part texture he has thus achieved is not enough for Bach. Hermann Kretzschmar has an absolutely beautiful explanation for this passage: "Just like Raffael, in his Sistine Madonna, he has the massed faces of angels looking down from the vault of heaven upon the scene of this holy burial. As the Daughter of Zion calls to the souls of the faithful: 'Seht ihn als wie ein Lamm' (Look, He is like a lamb), a boys' chorus sings in unison the old Passion chorale 'O Gottes Lamm unschuldig' (Oh innocent lamb of God).... In its grave simplicity it stands above the artfully constructed vocal fugue like a radiant emanation from the other world..." Here, in addition to the stereophonic effect of the first two choruses, which may, or perhaps even should, stand apart from each other, Bach achieves a third dimension. If the effect were not too theatrical for an oratorio, one might suggest that, as in the Grail scenes in *Parsifal*, the boys' chorus not be seen but that their voices ring down from above. The use of children's voices is only traditional, not a prescription; but it is completely justified by the nature of children's voices—they are pure, or, in the basic meaning of the word, innocent; furthermore, they stand out effortlessly from the eight-part adult chorus with a special kind of beauty, particularly because Bach wrote the part for the best ranges of children's voices, certainly no accident. He noted in the score only the remark "soprano in ripieno," meaning roughly "additional voices." This mighty section, closing brightly in E major, is, as an introduction, in a way set apart from the main body of the work. Here too a very modern explanation is possible: The conclusion is presaged at the beginning, the story being told as in the film device of flashback.

The first part now begins, made up of three large scenic blocks: Jesus and his disciples up to and including the Last Supper, Jesus in Gethsemane, and his arrest. The first scene opens with a recitative: Jesus speaks to his disciples and his speech immediately is set off from that of the Evangelist, whose objective account is sung virtually without accompaniment. The words of Jesus are not only underscored by a softly played string quartet, but are melodic as well. His prophecy of his crucifixion leads to the first chorale, which appears again and again with different texts throughout the work. The chorus seems to take these terrible words deeply to heart and, despairing, asks: "Herzliebster Jesu, was hast du verbrochen?" The chorale character is very clear here: contemplation, inwardness, sometimes quiet examination of conscience, the world of thought and reflection. Again the chorales recount nothing of the story, but are, rather, statements of the believer's experience. The Evangelist then tells of the assembly of the High Priests and Scribes of the Jews, who discuss how they can be rid of Jesus. In a brief, excited double chorus, they conclude that, to avoid creating an uproar and resistance among the people, nothing should take place during the approaching Passover holiday. The episode in the house of Simon the leper follows, where a woman anoints Jesus with a costly perfume, thereby upsetting the Disciples. Jesus defends her, and Bach then inserts the magnificent alto aria "Buss und Reu" (Repentance and Remorse), the song of a repentant sinner who wants to consecrate her tears to Jesus. The anguished chromaticism and harmonization of the first four measures is very moving (Example 1).

The Evangelist reports Judas' decision to betray Jesus for 30 pieces of silver. A soprano aria follows ("Blute nur, du liebes Herz"—Bleed, thou loving heart), another one of those lyrical insertions that form such an important part of Bach's Passions. They occupy slightly less than half of the 5 hours but are musically characterized by a special inwardness and most affecting beauty. Even when, at first glance, they seem to distance themselves from the action of the drama, they continually emphasize the mood of the moment. The action proceeds: The Disciples, thinking of the "Fest der süssen Brod'" (Festival of the Unleavened Bread)—the Jewish holiday at Eastertime, called Pessach or Passover, when unleavened bread called matzoh is served—ask where they can celebrate it with their Master in a dignified way: "Wo, wo, wo willst du, dass wir dir bereiten das Osterlamm zu essen?" (Where, where, where do you want us to prepare the Passover feast?). Here the Disciples present a picture of unanimity, musically speaking. Upon Jesus' prophecy that one of them will betray him, the mood changes: in horrified voices, in chaos and confusion, they sing "Herr, bin ich's?" (Master, am I the one?). Before Jesus can answer, the introductory chorale interrupts the action with "Ich bin's, ich sollte büssen..." (I am the one, I must atone...). The charge may be leveled that the language and poetry of the texts used in Bach's Passions are old-fashioned, but this chorale is a masterstroke. The frightened questions of the Disciples about the impending betrayal linger in the hearts of the congregation: Is it not I who have sinned? Is it not I who should repent, so that he will be pardoned? We do not know whether this psychologically telling device should be attributed to Bach or to Picander. The mood of the following scene, which depicts the Lord's Supper, becomes increasingly urgent. Jesus' words—first "Nehmet, esset, das ist mein Leib" (Take and eat, this is my body) and, after a brief interruption by the Evangelist, "Trinket alle daraus.." (Everyone, drink this...)—are a moving arioso (Example 2).

Then, in an aria preceded by a recitative, the solo soprano expresses the ambiguous feeling of the pious, again a very fine psychological touch: their pain at the thought of Christ's death and their consolation in his legacy ("Ich will dir mein Herze schenken"—I make you a gift of my heart).

Example 1

Example 2

The action now moves to Gethsemane; the scenes of Jesus' suffering are intensely and movingly portrayed. The first chorale appears twice and may be taken almost as a sort of *Leitmotif,* though not in the Wagnerian sense. It permeates the work in ever changing keys and new settings of the three voices that underlie the simple, beautiful melody, always with a different text. As "Erkenne mich, mein Hüter" (Recognize me, my protector) it is in the key of E major and, a little later, as "Ich will hier bei dir stehen" (I want to stay by you), in E-flat major. The question naturally arises whether such changes in key have a psychological meaning; should the second version sound "darker" than the first? In Bach's day, when the tuning of instruments was at least a half tone lower than is customary today, did E major sound "brighter" than E-flat major, and was C minor a typical key for mourning? The debate can go on and on. I mention the problem only because it is a technical issue which arises at this point, but it is a controversy into which I do not want enter here.

The chorale sung twice is very soothing, but the inner anguish remains. It leads to Jesus' call to his disciples to keep watch with him ("Meine Seele ist betrübt"—My soul is full of sorrow), a call that grows out of the recitative in which this time even the words of the Evangelist give the impression of an odd stirring of sympathy. The piece that follows is one of the most artful and affecting of the entire work. The solo tenor begins as though with a recitative ("O Schmerz! Hier zittert das gequälte Herz"—O pain! Here trembles a tormented heart) but is interrupted by the chorus singing, to the melody of the chorale "Herzliebster Jesu, was hast du verbrochen" (the first chorale of the work) the words "Was ist die Ursach' aller solcher Plagen?" (What has caused all this suffering?) This alternation between soloist and chorus leads to a great aria ("Ich will bei meinem Jesu wachen"—I want to watch with my Jesus), once more with choral accompaniment ("So schlafen unsre Sünden ein"—So do our sins go to sleep). After a short recitative, Bach inserts a longer scene (recitative and aria) sung by the solo bass ("Der Heiland fällt vor seinem Vater nieder"—The Savior throws himself at the feet of his Father). In the following recitative, Jesus once more, more urgently, calls upon God to allow the cup to pass him by, but when this is not to be, "trinke ich ihn denn, so geschehe dein Wille"—but if I drink it, Thy will be done). The words are taken up in the next chorale: "Was mein Gott will, das g'scheh' allzeit" (Let God's will be done).

The last section of the first part now begins: with varied shaping, but with one mighty, uninterrupted, dramatic breath pulsing through it, story and music press on to judgment. The Evangelist tells of the sleeping Disciples, whom Jesus chides sadly because at this decisive moment they must sleep; of the crowd of armed bailiffs led to the place by the traitor Judas, and of the arrest of Jesus. A duet sung by two solo female voices is interrupted several times by the chorus calling to the bailiffs "Lasset ihn, haltet, bindet nicht!" (Leave him alone, stop, do not bind him!). This duet is not a lyrical reflection: it observes the events with the greatest inner sympathy, portrayed by excited passages and leaps of major intervals: "So ist mein Jesus nun gefangen, Mond und Licht ist vor Schmerzen untergegangen... Sie führen ihn, er ist gebunden..." (Now my Jesus has been taken, moon and light have gone down in anguish... they are taking him away, he has been bound...). Now, in one of the most magnificent moments of all, the eight-part double chorus bursts forth violently: "Sind Blitze, sind Donner in Wolken verschwunden..." (Have thunder and lightning disappeared in the clouds?). A mighty storm seems to sweep the earth, but really takes place only in the imagination of those who sense the weightiness of the moment; in reality, not the tiniest cloud has passed before the moon. Is it a premonition of the events that will soon take place, when Jesus dies? Once more, we can only admire the modernity of the work. If we choose, we can see here not only 19th-century Realism but also many dramatic effects used in the last half of the 20th century. Jesus calls upon his disciples to refrain from using force ("denn wer das Schwert nimmt, der soll durch's Schwert umkommen"—he who takes up the sword shall die by it), after which they flee. The first section concludes with a fantasia on the chorale "O Mensch, bewein' dein' Sünde gross" (O Man, weep for your sins). If shortly before, Bach was closer to opera or to the Italian opera-oratorio than he was probably aware, this chorale fantasia definitely reestablishes his distance from those forms. With quiet but by no means untroubled contemplation, the first part of the *St. Matthew Passion* comes to an end.

The drama that must inevitably take place in the second part is not announced at its opening. It begins with an alto aria with chorus. The Daughter of Zion is looking for Jesus, her friend. Her expressive lament is joined by the four-part chorus singing a fugue: " Wo ist dein Freund hingegangen, o du Schönste unter den Weibern?" (Where has your friend gone, O you loveliest of women?), thus personifying this symbolic figure for the first time. The light, floating melody has sometimes been likened to a madrigal, while the treatment of the chorus, too, is reminiscent of this delightful form of Renaissance music. The piece ends as it began, the music sung by the alto tying back to that sung at the beginning. The action proceeds: The Evangelist describes how Jesus is taken before the High Priest, Caiphas, and how he, with all his councillors, tries unsuccessfully to find evidence unfavorable to Jesus. Once more a chorale refers directly to this scene: "Mir hat die Welt trüglich gericht't" (The world has judged me falsely). Finally, two witnesses are located who, singing closely in a duet, as if they wanted to support each other in their lie, give false testimony. Jesus meets these accusations with silence. Now we hear a great aria for the solo tenor: the preceding recitative begins with "Mein Jesu schweigt zu falschen Lügen stille" (My Jesus is silent in the face of false lies), and the aria, with "Geduld, Geduld, wenn mich falsche Zungen stechen" (Patience, patience, when false tongues jab me). In the following recitative, Caiphas asks Jesus if he is really Christ, the Son of God. Jesus' answer rises in an arioso, to a rapidly swelling orchestral accompaniment. The High Priest's answer is harsh, accompanied only by brief instrumental insertions. Now the eight-part chorus bursts forth, condemning Jesus: "Er ist des Todes schuldig!" (He deserves to die!). After a few words from the Evangelist, who describes how Jesus is flogged, the chorus, as one, rages on: "Weissage uns, Christe, wer ist's, der dich schlug?" (Prophesy now, Christ, who has beaten you?). A chorale interrupts the drama: "Wer hat dich so geschlagen?" (Who has beaten you so?) sings the chorus, lamenting now in the artless manner of simple people. Then Peter denies his master, just as Jesus had foretold: Twice the maids accused him of keeping company with Jesus, but the third time, the chorus sings the accusation "Wahrlich, du bist auch einer von denen..." (Truly, you are also one of them...). And then Peter declares "Ich kenne des Menschen nicht!" (I do not know this man!). Then the rooster crows—the Evangelist tells this—and Peter remembers Christ's prophecy. "Und weinete bitterlich" (And weeps bitterly) is sung in an unusual anguished melodic phrase in the highest register. A long aria for the solo alto ("Erbarme dich, mein Gott!"—God have mercy!) seems to express Peter's sobs (Example 3).

A chorale follows, also referring to the episode with Peter: "Bin ich gleich von dir gewichen..." (Although I turned away from you...). Then the action turns to Judas, who is ready to return the 30 pieces of silver he received for betraying Jesus to the councillors. But the priests refuse him with cold words: "Was geht das uns an?" (What has that to do with us?). After taking the money to the temple, Judas hangs himself. The priests do take the money back; a duet sung by two of them, called by Bach "Pontifex primus" and "Pontifex secundus," offers the explanation: "Es taugt nicht, dass wir sie in den Gotteskasten legen, denn es ist Blutgeld" (It is not fitting that we put the money into the treasury, for it is blood money). The bass aria, which begins immediately, refers to this episode: "Gebt mir meinen Jesum wieder!" (Give my Jesus back to me!). The next dramatic element focuses on the interrogation of Jesus. The Evangelist narrates, and Pilate, the Roman governor questions Jesus, who has been handed over to him by the Jews. But in the long recitative, Jesus sings only three notes: "Du sagest's" (You are the one who says it). He says nothing about the false accusations, leading the Governor to wonder ("dass sich auch der Landpfleger sehr verwunderte"). In the following chorale, it is explained to him that Jesus has long committed himself to a higher power (Example 4).

Example 3

Example 4

The drama rushes on to its climax. When Pilate asks the people which of the guilty ones should be released to them, as was the custom on a feast day, the people, in an eight-part fortissimo outburst, cry "Barrabam!" Barrabas was a convicted murderer whom Pilate would rather have crucified than Jesus, who he knew was innocent. Pilate's wife had told him shortly before that she, too, had been told this, in a dream. But the people, in their hatred, stand fast: "Lass ihn kreuzigen!" (Let him be crucified!), they demand (referring to Jesus); the mood is emphasized by a brief, tumultuous choral piece. Shrill intervals (among them the so-called tritone, called *Diabolus in musica* in the Middle Ages—the Devil in music) give the sound a sharp edge. Before Pilate commands the crucifixion of Christ to proceed, Bach delays the inevitable with the chorale "Wie wunderlich ist doch diese Strafe!" (How strange this punishment is!), and the soprano aria, answering Pilate's question "Was hat er denn übels getan?" (What evil has he done?) with "Er hat uns allen wohl getan . . ." (He has done good for all) and "Aus Liebe will mein Heiland sterben . . ." (My savior dies for love of us). But it is to no avail. The voices of the people have become more angry: even more shrill—a whole tone higher—they demand once more "Lass ihn kreuzigen!" Pilate declares he is "unschuldig an dem Blut dieses Gerechten" (innocent of the blood of this blameless man), and the people take responsibility for the deed in a mighty chorus—again, as often before, both choruses sing together—singing "Sein Blut komme über uns und unsere Kinder!" (His blood be upon us and our children!). The Evangelist reports soberly that Barrabas was set free while Jesus was bound and led to his crucifixion. The action seems to digress once more with the interjection here of a great solo scene for the alto, composed of an arioso-like recitative 'Erbarm' es Gott!" (God have mercy!), in the sharply rhythmical orchestral accompaniment of which some commentators claim to hear the sound of the whip on Jesus' body, and the aria "Können Tränen meiner Wangen" (If the tears on my cheeks). The Evangelist enters again to tell how Jesus, wearing his crown of thorns and purple mantle, is mocked by the soldiers who ridicule him in an eight-part chorus: "Gegrüsset seist du, Judenkönig!" (Greetings, King of the Jews!). Then they beat him, upon which the chorale "O Haupt voll Blut und Wunden" (O Sacred Head, now wounded) begins, a chorale that with various texts is the *Leitmotiv* of the entire work (Example 4). The bass soloist, in a very long scene composed of accompanied recitative and aria, meditates deeply upon guilt and expiation ("Komm, süsses Kreuz"—Come, sweet cross), while the listener perhaps imagines he is accompanying Jesus along the way to Golgotha, the place where the crucifixion is to take place.

The Evangelist reports on the crucifixion, on the inscription they place above his head—the wording of which (I. N. R. I., Iesus Nazarenus, Rex Iudaeorum—Jesus of Nazareth, King of the Jews) provokes a new outburst of hatred: the eight-part double chorus sings "Der du den Tempel Gottes zerbrichst" (You who destroy the temple). The High Priests gather and mock him: "Andern hat er geholfen, und kann sich selber nicht helfen..."—He has helped others but cannot help himself). The alto soloist—here once more cast as the Daughter of Zion—now sings one of the most affecting pieces in the entire work: "Ach Golgotha, unsel'ges Golgotha!" (Golgotha, unholy Golgotha), recitative and aria, full of harsh harmonies, unused since the Middle Ages, which must have startled Bach's listeners. Here, too, we can point to a most realistic kind of art, a rare kind of musical realism. The chorus interjects into this aria four times, at irregular and completely unexpected intervals, the question—quickly and harshly—"Wo?" (Where?). It seems to accompany the phrase "... in Jesu Armen sucht Erlösung..." (In Jesus' arms we seek salvation); is this meant to portray mockery, or does it, rather, express longing?

The hour of Jesus' death approaches. We hear his last words and their incorrect interpretation by those standing nearby: He calls out to the Prophet Elijah. Then his final cry is heard, followed by a gentle chorale, again the *Leitmotiv*, this time with the text "Wenn ich einmal soll scheiden..." (When I must leave at last). The next recitative is very dramatic; it reports how, at the hour of Jesus' death, the curtain in the temple was torn in two: swift instrumental runs are used to create this image. It tells of earthquakes that have broken open many graves—a dense tremolo in the orchestra reinforces the image. The Evangelist tells how Joseph of Arimathea received permission from Pilate to take Jesus' body down from the cross. Bach takes this opportunity to give the solo bass another extended recitative and aria: "Am Abend, da es kühle war..." (In the evening, when it was cool...). The drama ends with the visit of the High Priests and Elders to Pilate, to tell him of their misgivings; in an eight-part chorus they reveal to him that Jesus had prophesied his own resurrection after three days, and tell him that in order to avoid a new "Betrug, ärger als der erste" (Fraud, one more troublesome than the first one), the grave should be sealed and guards posted before it, a wish which Pilate grants. A choral recitative with short solos sung by all four solo voices bids Jesus farewell and, in a manner of speaking, brings the drama to an end. The great, eight-part final chorus is only a soft, introspective farewell, a final laying-to-rest: "Wir setzen uns mit Tränen nieder..." (We sit here weeping...).

The Mass in B Minor

Original Title: Missa/Symbolum Nicenum/Sanctus/Osanna, Benedictus, Angus Dei et Dona nobis pacem
Original Language: Latin
Text: The five parts of the Ordinarium Missae, with the wording used in the Lutheran liturgy.
Date of Writing: All four parts were composed in Leipzig: 1. *Missa* (= Kyrie and Gloria) 1733, 2. *Symbolum Nicenum* (= Credo) 1732, 3. *Sanctus* 1736, and 4. *Osanna, Benedictus, Agnus Dei,* and *Dona nobis pacem* 1738/39. According to the most recent research (Georg von Dadelsen) the Sanctus was composed as early as 1724, and parts 2 and 4 not until 1748.

On July 27, 1733, Bach sent the first part of the *B Minor Mass*, the *Missa*, together with a letter requesting the title of Court Composer of Saxony, to the Saxon Prince Friedrich August II, who was also King August III of Poland. About 1748 he combined the four separate parts into one complete Mass. The title, *Hohe Messe in h-moll* (High Mass in B Minor) appeared for the first time when his collected works were printed in Bonn by the publisher Simrock, in 1845.
First Performance: The first part of the *B Minor Mass* was first performed on either April 21 or July 27, 1733. The entire work was never performed during Bach's lifetime, the first complete performance being given on February 12, 1835, by the Berlin Singakademie.
Form: In four parts:
    1. *Missa* (= Kyrie and Gloria; 12 musical numbers)
    2. *Symbolum Nicenum* (= Credo; 9 musical numbers)
    3. *Sanctus*
    4. *Hosanna*, etc. (5 musical numbers)
Scoring: Five solo voices (sopranos I/II, alto, tenor, bass), four- to eight-part mixed chorus, two flutes, three oboes, two oboes d'amore, two bassoons, corno da caccia, tympani, strings, continuo with cello, bassoon, contrabass, and organ.
History of the Work: Bach wrote the *Kyrie* and *Gloria* of this Mass probably less out of his own need for material to perform (as was customary during the Baroque period and on into the following

Classic period) than for the purpose of gaining the title of Court Composer by dedicating it to his Catholic Sovereign. He sent the two parts and a humble letter on July 27, 1733, to Dresden. More than three years later, in November of 1736, he received the title. The religious balance in Saxony was precarious. The people were Protestant, but the Prince, in support of his claim to the Kingdom of Poland, had converted to Catholicism in 1697. Tensions between the two confessions arose repeatedly: August's wife, Christine Eberhardine, remained aloof from all religious ceremonies, the church authorities in Leipzig attempted to suppress the use of Latin, and no official religious funeral ceremony was held upon the death of the Prince. Although Bach had grown up as a strict Protestant, he doubtless thought and felt in a more ecumenical way, for which the *B Minor Mass* stands as testimony. We can only surmise as to why no performance of the entire work was mounted during his lifetime. Nor do we know why Bach's son Wilhelm Friedemann—who, having been recommended by his father and having passed a trial performance with flying colors, became organist in Dresden in 1733—did not at least make the effort to perform the two sections already composed. Further, another son, Carl Philipp Emanuel Bach, made no effort to introduce the work at any of his influential posts. Whether their unwillingness is attributable to a rebellion against their father (whose abilities they admired but viewed as "old hat," in contrast to their own "progressive work"), or whether out of protest against this "Catholic" work, or even, more simply, whether these portions of the Mass were not then considered a complete musical entity, we do not know. It seems significant in this respect that Bach, in his efforts to garner the title he sought, did not present the additions to the *Kyrie* and *Gloria* he had already sent, which he had finished in the meantime, but rather other, shorter Masses which, moreover, were not new compositions but mere combinations of parts of cantatas composed earlier.

That there is an original manuscript in Bach's hand is incontestable. This in itself, however, would not guarantee authenticity, as the *St. Luke Passion* illustrates. But because in the latter work many weak passages are evident, leading to the conclusion that perhaps Bach copied someone else's work in order to perform it, the *B Minor Mass* is clearly a masterpiece whose grandeur of conception and completeness of execution leave no doubt as to its authenticity. It must certainly strike the listener as even more amazing, then, that this Mass remained unpublished for more than a century. Indeed, the Zurich publisher Hans Georg Nägeli, best remembered for his far from friendly relationship with Beethoven, inaugurated a subscription in 1818 to fund the publishing of the Mass, but published only the first part, the *Kyrie* and *Gloria*, referred to as the *Missa*, in 1836. Not until 1845 did the publisher Simrock in Bonn publish the entire work. It was included in the *Complete Works* published by the Bach-Gesellschaft in 1855.

Performance Practice: It is most important to remember that Bach often made no fundamental distinction between the choral and solo voices; therefore, capable choral voices can perform the solo parts. This is a basic difference between opera and oratorio: each important role in opera requires a specific performer, while in most oratorios, including Bach's, the same singer can sing for several roles.

On the whole, the *B Minor Mass* mainly raises basic questions of interpretation. Albert Schweitzer finds in this work a joining of Protestant subjectivity with Catholic objectivity, a mixture that the director can realize in various proportions without violating the spirit of the work. The interpretation chosen will affect orchestral sound and the timbre of the singers, as well as expression, which may run the gamut from great restraint to an almost Romantic exuberance.

Discussion of the Work: The work begins slowly and solemnly with a complete B minor chord sung by the five-part chorus. Then the orchestra, in a long introduction, presents the solemn theme, from which the chorus will soon develop its great fugue. From the very outset, the movement sounds "like the cry for help from a people sorely tried" (H. Kretzschmar), as in the Introitus of the *St. Matthew Passion* and also in Handel's oratorio *Israel in Egypt*. The fugue theme of the "Kyrie eleison" (Example 1) is—at a very slow tempo!—fully two-and-a-half measures long, an indication of the great dimensions Bach conceived of for this piece and for the work as a whole. The theme is introduced by the tenor; the alto answers at the fifth, in keeping with traditional rules. But already the form of this *comes* surpasses that of the original *dux* considerably. The first soprano enters, again as *dux*, and after two-and-a-half measures, the second soprano as *comes*.

Example 1

Six bars of a four-part development follow before the fifth and last voice enters—the bass, who, conforming to tradition, once more repeats the form of the *dux*. Here the fugue reaches its first climax and the end of the first part. At this point Bach gives the orchestra an expressive sostenuto episode, followed by the second part of the fugue. This time, the voices enter in a different order: the bass begins and the tenor follows as *comes* (therefore, at the fifth). The third voice is the alto—in an unusually low register difficult to sing, which the director may choose to support with tenor voices; the fourth, the first soprano, and, again after a long contrapuntal passage, the fifth and last, the second soprano.

The development that follows creates a mounting intensity, rich in modulations, of the highest artistry—a more magnificent or more difficult passage is hardly to be found in the music of that time. The text of the entire, mighty piece consists of only two words: the call to God, in Greek, "Kyrie eleison" (Lord, have mercy upon us). The first part of the Catholic Mass bears this title, as does the Protestant liturgy. The second piece is a duet between two sopranos: "Christe eleison" (again, only two words); it is lyrical, elegiac, full of feeling. Moving passages for violin leave their mark on the prelude, interlude, and postlude. No. 3 is a second "Kyrie," completely different from the first. The contrast lies in the use of only a few weighty notes, which, in spite of the now lively tempo, impart a restful character, as well as a harmonically interesting melodic step (G to E-sharp) that sounds oriental and which Bach works out with extensive chromaticism (Example 2). This second "Kyrie" also employs a choral fugue, although in only four parts because the two sopranos sing in unison. The sequence of keys for the three parts that make up the "Kyrie" is: B minor (in the first fugue), D major (in the "Christe eleison"), and F-sharp minor (in the second fugue), which ends, as is so often the case with Bach's use of the minor, in the major. No. 4, the "Gloria," is one of Bach's most jubilant compositions. In the brightest D major, with vigorous strings reinforced by trumpets, it reflects a joyful people paying thankful homage to God. The chorus is once more in five parts, the first two entries (alto and tenor) follow each other in canon; then all the voices come in, fortissimo; the pattern is repeated in the second attack: first and second soprano in canon, then the five-part chorus. Bach moves ever closer to his favorite polyphonic form, the fugue, which he, better than any other composer, had mastered in all its permutations. The jubilation gives way to a more contemplative, peaceful section, sung to the words "et in terra pax" (and peace on earth). This plea comes first as an entreaty in several parts; then—after a short orchestral interlude—this melody is used as the theme of a new fugue, which, because of its numerous coloratura passages, should be sung by a small vocal ensemble. In addition, because of its introspective mood, one of an inner longing for peace, a chamber chorus formed from the nucleus of the large chorus is most appropriate. The next aria (No. 5) is to be sung by a darker female voice—the second soprano, accompanied by a solo violin and small orchestra: "Laudamus te" (We praise thee). With a wavelike melodic pattern, in long note values, after the preceding uninterrupted motion in both instruments and solo voice, No. 6, the hymn of thanks "Gratias agimus tibi" (We give thanks unto thee), begins. It again is a choral fugue in which the entrances succeed each other at short intervals, from low to high. It is for four voices, since the two sopranos again sing in unison (Example 3).

Example 2

Example 3

A solo flute introduces the following duet (No. 7), sung by the first solo soprano and the solo tenor, with a cheerful melody. There are repeated canonlike passages without, however, a strict canon being formed. Nevertheless, in this close meshing of the voices we have the sense of the merging of God the Father and God the Son: the first voice (tenor) begins with "Domine Deus," and is immediately followed by the second (soprano) singing "Domine Fili unigenite." The long duet leads into a four-part chorus (No. 8, "Qui tollis peccata mundi"—thou who bearest the sins of the world) and should merge with it because the chorus is really the inevitable continuation of the appeal begun with the duet. The alto, tenor, soprano, and bass enter in turn with the lovely melody, canonlike or in a fugato in keys that freely change (Example 4).

Example 4

"Qui sedes ad dexteram Patris" (He who sits at the right hand of the Father) (No. 9), is an aria for the solo alto, with an expressive accompaniment by the oboe d'amore. A horn (hunting horn, if possible, of the type used in Bach's time) and two bassoons accompany the solo bass in the aria (No. 10) "Quoniam tu solus sanctus" (Only thou art holy). The five-part choral number that follows (No. 11, "Cum sancto spiritu"—With the Holy Spirit) is one of the most glorious inspirations of the Mass. What Bach, in his genius and absolute mastery creates here, in a dense and extended display of power, is beyond the power of words to describe. The form constantly changes, following no traditional pattern. The beginning may be called a double fugue, to which a fifth, "free" voice is added contrapuntally. From about the middle on, a solemn fugue with a long theme seems to emerge, ascending with mighty chords ever higher, until the end. No. 12, "Credo in unum Deum" (I believe in one God), makes the heart of every musician beat faster: it is one of the great moments in music. Bach makes use of a Gregorian melody to construct a towering piece of music (Example 5). The age-old tune, from the very oldest Catholic liturgy, attains new grandeur through a five-part fugue and majestic ascending and descending organ passages.

Example 5

The sovereign way in which Bach manipulates the form (the theme enters on the notes e,a,a,e,a) and finally crowns it with a grand stretto is especially notable; it not only looks remarkable on paper, as is often the case in passages reflecting great technical skill, but is a living reality. Once more, as in the "Kyrie," Bach is not content with a single "Credo;" he adds another, part homophonic, one (No. 13). No. 14 is a duet between the solo first soprano and the solo alto: "Et in unum Dominum," another expression of belief in the Father and the Son. The explanation of the mystery of the union of God and his Son Jesus gains credibility through Bach's close joining of the two voices, which follow each other almost canonlike at intervals of only a quarter-note. The completely introspective beginning of No. 15, ("Et incarnatus est"—And the word is made flesh), reflects Bach's deep piety. Once more the five parts of the chorus enter canonlike or in fugue, not storming dramatically but gathering together, at the slowest of tempos, in prayer. The next piece, No. 16, "Crucifixus" (He was crucified), is as mystical as the preceding piece. Before its brief, staggered, fuguelike choral entrances with the word "crucifixus," there is a remarkable orchestral introduction in which the organ figures prominently: a chromatic passage for the bass, descending in slow, somber movement (Example 6).

The Resurrection follows the Crucifixion; it is the subject of No. 17 ("Et resurrexit"—And he rose from the dead). Once more, as in the *Gloria*, the five-part chorus sings jubilantly, but in a

Example 6

slightly more measured way, perhaps because the victory was so dearly won. The form Bach uses here has no technical name, but is the one that he, at least in this Mass, so obviously prefers: a solemn, forceful opening, with all voices singing together. Twice they call out the reason for their joy ("Et resurrexit, resurrexit!"). Then the orchestra clearly establishes the musical character, after which the voices begin a great fugato. The first exclamation serves as the theme, which is now continued in joyful coloraturas, more elaborate with each entry. Bach places heavy demands on the voices—the first sopranos must sing a high B, and the basses in several places as high as E and as low as F-sharp, so the two orchestral interludes offer a welcome and necessary resting place. A rather long bass passage is better sung by the soloist than by the basses of the chorus (although Bach does not positively indicate this), so that the five-part entry of "cuius regni non erit finis" (whose reign has no end) has an even greater effect.

Without a doubt, No. 18 ("Et in spiritum sanctum"—And in the Holy Spirit)) belongs to the solo bass. And in this piece—incomprehensible to some—is the confession of belief "in unam sanctam catholicam et apostolicam ecclesiam" (in one, holy, Catholic, apostolic church). Bach, raised in the Lutheran faith and serving in a Protestant church, musically states his belief in one "Catholic, i.e., universal, Church," and not in a fleeting, musically subordinate passage but repeatedly and conspicuously. Was it difficult for him, as it was for Beethoven, who believed in a natural pantheism rather than in any churchly sect? Would he rather have left it out, as Schubert was to do in all of his Masses, just a century later? Apparently Bach had no such problem, a matter which calls for reflection. Indeed, earlier in this same work he had revealed his reverence for Gregorian Chant—the most Catholic of all musical expressions—and does it again in No. 19

Example 7

"Confiteor" (I believe). From the middle of the latter on, almost hidden as a canon between the bass and the alto (while the other three voices weave a melodious counterpoint), is the old Gregorian melody that has been associated with these words for a thousand years. How well the Protestant cantor must have known the old Catholic Gregorian Chants! This extended piece is quite remarkable for other reasons as well: it presents intimations of a double fugue; it suddenly decreases its tempo, hardly a fast one but sprightly nevertheless, suddenly to an adagio with an almost longing quality; and then proceeds, practically in the Italian style, to a very lively stretto, powerfully intensified as the piece draws to an end. No. 20 the "Sanctus," expands to a six-part chorus. It is an indescribably festive piece of music, full of majesty and grandeur, stunning the listener with the triumphal brilliance of voices and orchestra (Example 7).

Now, after almost nothing but mighty chords, the music moves on to a sprightly fugato: "Pleni sunt coeli" (The heavens are full). The people are ecstatic at the unspeakable brilliance breaking from the clouds. Those who are acquainted only superficially with Bach would not believe him capable of such spirited music. The "Hosanna" (No. 21) follows without pause, a happy, joyous piece for two four-part choruses. It is in three-eight time, a meter Bach uses surprisingly often in the *B Minor Mass* to express exultation. The monumental double-chorus effect allows for the sonorous interplay of thoroughly melodic, greatly varied counterpoint. The tenor aria "Benedictus" (No. 22) follows; a contemplative piece accompanied by a solo violin or transverse flute; then the chorus is heard again, rejoicing, singing its Hosanna. After this bright exultation there is once more a reflective, solemn piece in minor: the "Agnus Dei" (Lamb of God, No. 23), sung by the solo alto. Its key of G minor, far removed from B minor, makes a marked contrast to the succession of keys we have heard thus far. Did Bach hear in this key the painful resignation that the key of G minor would soon come to represent in the works of composers who followed him—especially Mozart, who wrote not only his penultimate, and probably his most melancholy, symphony in that key, but also the profoundly sad aria for Pamina in the second act of *Die Zauberflöte*? With "Dona nobis pacem" (Give us peace), No. 24, this monumental work comes to an end. Once more the chorus, reduced to four parts, solemnly intones the plea for peace. It is a very free fugue, whose ascending entries consist of a very short theme: bass, tenor, alto, soprano. The fact that Bach also took this piece, like others in this work, from an earlier composition—Cantata No. 29, "Wir danken dir"—and that it is almost identical, tone for tone, with the chorus No. 6, "Gratias agimus tibi," in no way diminishes its beauty. There could be no more expressive setting for those final words emanating from the depths of the human heart—"Gib uns Frieden!" (Give us peace).

The Christmas Oratorio

Original Title: Weihnachts-Oratorium
Original Language: German
Text: From the *Gospel of St. Luke*, Chapter 2, Verse 1 and Verses 3–21; from the *Gospel of St. Matthew*, Chapter 2, Verses 1–12; and in addition, texts from church hymns and madrigalesque works, which possibly were written by Christian Friedrich Henrici (Picander).
Date of Writing: Leipzig, 1734
First Performance: On the Christmas and New Year holidays of December 24, 1734 to January 6, 1735, in the churches of St. Thomas and St. Nicolas in Leipzig.
Form: Six individual parts in cantata form, which Bach combined to form a single work, and called "Oratorium"; a total of 64 musical numbers.

　　1st. Part: Feria 1 Nativitatis Christi (the first day of Christmas)
　　2nd. Part: Feria 2 Nativitatis Christi (the second day of Christmas)
　　3rd. Part: Feria 3 Nativitatis Christi (the third day of Christmas)
　　4th. Part: Festo Circumcisionis Christi (the day of Christ's Circumcision)
　　5th. Part: Dominica post Festum Circumcisionis Christi (the Sunday after New Year) 6.
　　6th. Part: Festo Epiphanias (Twelfth Night)

Cast: Evangelist (tenor), Angel (soprano), Herod (bass), four solo voices (soprano, alto, tenor, bass), four-part mixed chorus.
Orchestra: Two flutes, two oboes, two oboes d'amore, two oboes da caccia, two corni da caccia, three trumpets, timpani, strings, continuo with cello, bassoon, contrabass, and organ.
History of the Work: The Leipzig postmaster and later tax collector Christian Friedrich Henrici, who wrote under the name Picander, probably contacted Bach in 1724, a year after the latter had moved to Leipzig, and arranged to provide a number of librettos to the cantor of St. Thomas. Probably the most significant of these is the *St. Matthew Passion*. It seems that in 1734, Bach asked Picander to

help him with a large Christmas composition; whether he had in mind an oratorio like those he had already composed (the *St. John* and *St. Matthew* Passions, and probably the two that have disappeared, as well), or rather had planned from the beginning to compose a loose series of several cantatas for the separate holidays of the joyful Christian holiday season, we do not know. Picander arranged the poem in six sections, assigning each to one holiday: 1. the first day of Christmas; 2. the second day of Christmas; 3. the third day of Christmas; 4. New Year's Day; 5. the Sunday after New Year's Day; 6. the day of the Epiphany.

From the outset, Bach must have referred to the entire work as the *Christmas Oratorio*, which raises an interesting question: Did Bach think that a succession of cantatas, or similar vocal works such as, perhaps, motets or madrigals could be integrated into an oratorio? Such a plan was not consistent with later concepts and definitions, but as we see here, entirely possible. We should keep clearly in mind that in earlier times such distinctions were not taken as seriously as they are today. It is pointless to argue the matter here, for Bach knew what he was doing. The fact is that to the best of our knowledge, Bach never performed his *Christmas Oratorio* as a whole, but rather divided among the holidays indicated: It continues to be performed in this way since Bach himself established the tradition. After Bach's death the work was forgotten. Not until after the *St. Matthew Passion* was rediscovered (1829) was the *Christmas Oratorio* performed—first in 1857 by the Berlin Singakademie, under the direction of Eduard Grell.

Discussion of the Work: The first part begins with the radiant opening chorus "Jauchzet, frohlocket!" (Rejoice, exult!), whose timpani passages and fanfarelike wind motifs suggest worldly brilliance. The fact is that this piece was taken from a *Dramma per musica* (not an opera, in our sense of the term) that Bach had composed in honor of the Queen of Saxony, Christine Eberhardine, in which the text sung was "Tönet, ihr Pauken, erschallet, Trompeten!" (Sound, drums, ring out, trumpets!). The chorus begins in unison, not separating into the usual four parts until the third entry. Then the Evangelist reads from *St. Luke*, Chapter 2: "Es begab sich aber zu der Zeit, dass ein Gebot von dem Kaiser Augusto ausging..." (And it came to pass in those days, that there went out a decree from Caesar Augustus...). A recitative and aria sung by the solo alto takes up the thread and announces the birth of Christ: "Bereite dich, Zion!" (Prepare yourself, Zion!). Then we hear the chorale that surely was Bach's favorite, for he had already used it several times in the *St. Matthew Passion* (see Example 4 of that section). In the latter it was sung to the words "Befiehl du deine Wege" (Commend thy ways) and "O Haupt voll Blut und Wunden" (O sacred head, now wounded) and here, to "Wie soll ich dich empfangen?" (How shall I receive thee?) in the rather dark key of A minor, that in the *St. Matthew Passion* signified the gloom of mourning at the time of Jesus' death. Does its use here indicate that the one just born is destined to suffer a martyr's death? No. 7 combines chorale and recitative in a very unusual way: after every phrase of the chorale melody, sung by the soprano, the solo bass interrupts with a short recitative. The bass then sings the aria "Grosser Herr, o starker König" (O great Lord and mighty King), a proud and sumptuous piece telling how little it matters to the Lord of the World that he was born in a wretched crib. The end of first part is formed by a traditional chorale that is still often sung as the Christmas carol "Vom Himmel hoch da komm' ich her," but here to the words "Ach, mein herzliebes Jesulein!" (Ah, my dear Jesus!) accompanied by the full orchestra, with brilliant trumpet passages heard between each of the four phrases of the chorale.

The second part opens with an orchestral "sinfonia." The rocking 12/8 rhythm, the bright G major key, the lovely sound of the flutes and the various oboes all contribute to the impression that Bach wanted to create a kind of "pastorale" here, as angels and shepherds hurry over the fields to the newborn Christ child. After a chorale ("Brich an, o schönes Morgenlicht!"—Shine on, o beautiful morning star!), the voice of an angel (solo soprano) confirms in a recitative the Savior's birth; a bass recitative and a very difficult tenor aria ("Frohe Hirten eilt..."—Happy shepherds, hurry...) follow. The Christmas chorale "Vom Himmel hoch" is now heard again with the words "Schaut hin! Dort liegt im finstern Stall..." (Look, there in a gloomy stable...). The solo bass, accompanied by four oboes, calls upon the shepherds to witness the miracle, and the solo alto sings a tender lullaby, ornamented by passages on the oboe d'amore: "Schlafe, mein Liebster, geniesse der Ruh..." (Sleep, dear one, enjoy your rest...). No. 21 is an artfully constructed hymn of the heavenly host ("Ehre sei Gott in der Höhe!"—Glory to God in the highest!). The solo bass joins in in a brief recitative: "So recht, ihr Engel, jauchzt und singet" (Rejoice and sing, angels), whereupon the chorus once more sings the Christmas carol, this time with the words "Wir singen dir in deinem Heer..." (We sing to you).

The third part opens forcefully, again with a choral fugue: "Herrscher des Himmels, erhöre das Lallen..." (Ruler of Heaven, hear the murmuring), and in a second section, separated only by a brief interjection by the Evangelist, tells the shepherds to follow the angels' advice: "Lasset uns gehen gen Bethlehem!" (Let us go to Bethlehem!). A bass recitative looks ahead, prophesying Jesus' future deeds. Chorale No. 28 follows, to the well-known melody of "Gelobet seist du, Jesu Christ" but with the words "Dies hat er alles uns getan!" (He did all this for us!). In quiet contemplation the soprano and bass sing the duet "Herr, dein Mitleid" (Lord, your pity), to the sonorous, expressive melodic accompaniment of the oboes d'amore. The Evangelist reports the arrival of the shepherds who find everything to be as it was foretold by the angels. Mary, the mother of the Child, sings (solo alto) a most moving aria, "Schliesse, mein Herze, dies selige Wunder" (Enfold this wonder, my heart), accompanied by the sweet sound of a solo violin. Two choruses, separated by short measures sung by the Evangelist, follow: "Ich will dich mit Fleiss bewahren" (I will guard you diligently) and "Seid froh dieweil!" (Meanwhile, rejoice!); then, to bring the third part to a close, Bach repeats his opening chorus "Herrscher des Himmels," thus creating an impressive finale.

The fourth part, intended for New Year's Day, is the most worldly of all. It tells of Jesus' childhood and begins with a striking, homophonic (and therefore more simple) opening chorus ("Fallt mit Danken"—Fall down in thanks) and a heartfelt duet between the solo soprano and the solo bass. The bass then continues alone in a recitative. The aria No. 39 is quite unusual, dealing with the naming of Jesus. It contains an echo to the soprano voice—a second soprano who calls out several times "Ja" und "Nein," repeating the words of the first soprano, which may represent the voice of the child Jesus. This aria, which deeply affects the listener, especially if the echo comes from a point the audience cannot see, has often been thought to be odd and stylistically out of place. In fact, the piece derives from the secular, dramatic, almost theatrical cantata Bach wrote entitled "Die Wahl des Herkules," (The choice of Hercules), in which Hercules questions the oracle, and the oracle replies. Then comes another duet between soprano and bass, still dealing with the naming of Jesus: "Wohlan, dein Name soll allein..." (So be it. Only your name...). An extended tenor aria ("Ich will nur dir zu Ehren leben!"—I shall live only to honor you) leads to the final chorale, "Jesus, richte mein Beginnen" (Jesus, show me my beginning), in which once again the individual phrases are separated by richly orchestrated interludes.

The fifth part begins with a great chorus, "Ehre sei dir, Gott, gesungen!" (God, let your praises be sung!). Double fugal entries lend grandeur to the piece. The Evangelist recounts from the Gospel of St. Matthew, Chapter 2, the arrival of the wisemen from the East. They seek Jesus ("Wo, wo, wo ist der neugeborene König der Juden?"—Where, where, where is the newborn King of the Jews?), to which the solo alto answers in recitative, "Sucht ihn in meiner Brust!" (Look for him in my heart!). When the wisemen continue their questioning ("Wir haben seinen Stern gesehen!"—We have seen his star!), she answers again, "Wohl euch, die ihr dies Licht gesehen habt!" (Blessed be you who have seen this light!). A chorale ("Dein Glanz all' Finsternis verzehrt"—Your brilliance dispels all gloom) and the bass aria "Erleucht' auch meine finstre Sinnen..." (Illuminate my darkened soul) interrupt the narrative, which continues with a short recitative (No. 48) and two more ariosolike recitatives (Nos. 49 and 50). Then we come to a trio sung by the solo soprano, solo alto, and solo tenor in which, to the prophecy already cited—"Aus dir [Bethlehem] soll kommen der Herzog, der über mein Volk Israel ein Herr sei!" (For out of you shall come a prince to rule over my people Israel)—is added "Ach, wann wird die Zeit erscheinen...?" (Ah, when will the time come...?). This unusual ensemble is quite dramatic, heightened by an excited orchestral accompaniment. With the chorale "Zwar ist solche Herzensstube" (The heart's humble dwelling) (No. 53), the fifth part comes to a close, quietly, but with deep assurance.

The sixth part begins with an unusually forceful chorus: "Herr, wenn die stolzen Feinde schnauben..." (Lord, when proud enemies threaten us...). It is constructed partly as a four-part fugue; its content is the hope, indeed the certainty, of victory over all enemies, of stubborn faith overcoming all dark powers. The Evangelist, elaborating upon this theme, tells of King Herod, who is a dangerous enemy; he pretends to seek the Child in order to worship him, but a soprano recitative immediately discovers his dark purpose. The great soprano aria "Nur ein Wink von seinen Händen..." (Only a wave of his hand...) expresses the same sentiment. The Evangelist continues the narrative with the visit and gifts from the Kings from the East, which introduces the chorale "Ich steh' an deiner Krippen hier" (I stand here by your crib). After further extended reports from the evangelist and observations by the solo tenor, the latter sings the great aria, "Nun mögt ihr stolzen Feinde..." (Now may the proud enemy...). It is in two parts accompanied by the expressive playing of the oboes d'amore. Next the four soloists begin a fugal but melodic recitative, which leads to the contemplative final chorus, again based on the often used chorale "Befiehl du deine Wege," this time using the words "Nun seid ihr wohl gerochen..." (Now you have been avenged...). The *Christmas Oratorio* ends with quiet certainty: "Tod, Teufel, Sünd' und Hölle sind ganz und gar geschwächt, bei Gott hat seine Stelle das menschliche Geschlecht" (Death, Devil, Sin, and Hell are doomed, mankind now has its place near God). The full radiance of the orchestra is heard in a victorious D major, Bach's most joyful key.

Magnificat

Original Title: Magnificat
Original Language: Latin
Text: From the *Gospel of St. Luke,* Chapter 1, Verses 46–55
Date of Writing: First version in E-flat major, 1723; revised in 1732 to form the second version in D major, the only one extant today.
First Performance: In the church of St. Thomas in Leipzig, Christmas Vespers, 1723.
Form: Composed of 12 musical numbers.
Cast: Five solo voices (two sopranos, alto, tenor, bass), five-part mixed chorus, two flutes, two oboes, three trumpets, timpani, strings, continuo with cello, contrabass, bassoon, and organ.
History of the Work: When Bach took up his duties as cantor in the church of St. Thomas in Leipzig (which also included liturgical duties at the church of St. Nicholas) in 1723, demands upon him for compositions increased enormously. Every Sunday he had to prepare two new motets for the main service and another work for Sunday afternoon Vespers. In addition, he had to write a *Magnificat* and a *Sanctus* for each Christmas season. This heavy compositional burden explains why Bach "also composed seemingly Catholic church music, such as several Sanctus and Magnificat settings, in addition to Latin and German motets." (A. E. Cherbuliez, in his biography of Bach).

Of these, surely the *Magnificat* composed for Christmas of 1723 is the foremost. One version of this composition, a solo cantata, has been lost, as have Bach's Latin motets. We have two very different versions of the Magnificat as a choral work, however. The first, from 1723, is in E-flat major and contains typical Christmas interpolations: the chorales "Vom Himmel hoch, da komm ich her" and "Freut euch und jubiliert," as well as the Latin song "Virga Jesse floruit." These additions to the Biblical text are lacking in the second version, which was probably composed in the spring of 1732. In this version, the entire work has been transposed to the key of D major. Even the parts that remain show evidence of having been altered. Whereas the first version was without doubt written in the course of his duties, the second was probably composed only out of the joy of creation and in the certain knowledge that he had here created a work that incorporated his highest accomplishments in this form. It is entirely possible, even probable, that he had composed other settings of the *Magnificat,* but this is the only one to come down to us.

Discussion of the Work: The hymn of praise, *Magnificat* is a traditional part of the cult of Mary. It is based upon Mary's words when she learns from the angel that she will give birth to the Savior of the World. The work begins resplendently, the three trumpets heralding with festive D major chords the extended, lively orchestral prelude, from which the five-part chorus bursts out in highly embellished phrases: "Magnificat anima mea Dominum" (My soul doth magnify the Lord). The aria for second soprano, "Et exultavit spiritus meus in Deo salutari meo" (And my spirit rejoices in God, my savior), also in D major, follows without a pause in three-eight time, used by Bach to signify great joy (Example 1). Slowly and solemnly, filled with great emotion, the B minor soprano aria "Quia respexit humilitatem ancillae suae" (For he has regarded his lowly handmaiden) follows. The music becomes lively again and, once more in a joyous D major, Mary exults "Ecce, ecce, ecce . . . enim ex hoc beatam . . ." (Behold, from now on I will be called blessed). With the last words of this verse, Bach has the five-part chorus enter again, repeating the majestic words ". . . omnes generationes" (. . . all generations).

Example 1

Example 2

The A major bass aria that follows, "Quia fecit mihi magna..." (The Mighty One has done great things with me, holy is His name), is more reflective. Then comes a lovely E minor duet for alto and tenor, rocking, almost rustic in its naive joy: "Et misericordia a progenie in progenies timentibus eum" (And His mercy extends from generation to generation, for those who fear Him). The voices sing at intervals of a sixth, while the orchestration is reduced to the sound of the flutes and strings.

After the E minor piano conclusion, there is a very energetic choral piece which begins in G major: "Fecit potentiam in brachio suo" (He can do mighty deeds with His arm). While four of the voices build a solid framework of firm chords, a fifth moves in highly embellished coloraturas: first the tenor, then the alto, then the second soprano, the bass, and finally, the first soprano, this main melody being handled like a fugue. A contrapuntal and, at the same time, harmonic stroke of genius finally rises with dramatic intensity: "Dispersit superbos mente cordis sui" (He scatters the proud in heart). But it is as if after a few agitated measures Bach thought better of it, and reduces the fortissimo of his chords, closing the section quietly. (The custom of then returning in the final chord once more to fortissimo is debatable. Bach seldom wrote expression marks in his scores.)

Now we hear a tenor aria: "Deposuit potentes de sede et exaltavit humiles" (He throws the mighty from their thrones and raises the lowly). The F-sharp minor signifies inner agitation, contrasting with the following, lighter alto aria, in which the key of E major sounds charming and tender: "Esurientes implevit bonis et divites dimisit inanes" (He feeds the hungry and lets the rich go away empty). We are repeatedly astounded not only by Bach's rhythmic variety but that of other composers of the time as well (Example 2). Now three solo voices (two sopranos and the alto) join in a peaceful but exceedingly expressive D minor movement: "Suscepit Israel puerum suum, recordatus misericordiae suae" (He has received His servant Israel, mindful of His mercy). We might call this beginning an artful canon: the second voice is the mirror image of the first, and the third again follows the first (Example 3). Two choral pieces end the work: the thoroughly fugal "Sicut locutus est ad patres nostros, Abraham et semini eius in saecula" (As he promised our

Example 3

fathers, Abraham and his descendants for ever and ever), and the mighty "Gloria Patri, Filio et Spiritui sancto" (Glory to the Father, the Son, and the Holy Ghost). Here, dense, sonorous interjections confront fugal entries ascending and descending through all five parts.

Finally, with varied references to the introductory chorus, the work comes to a thundering conclusion: "Sicut erat in principio, et nunc et semper et in saecula saeculorum, amen" (As it was in the beginning, is now, and ever shall be, Amen), in the key of D major moving majestically in three-quarter meter, masterfully shaped to a compelling oneness—a religious service and an affirmation of life, a devotion and an exultation.

Easter Oratorio

In 1725, his third year in Leipzig, Bach composed for the birthday festivities of Duke Christian of Saxony-Weissenfels on February 23rd, a pastoral cantata using the works "Entflieht, verschwindet, entweicht, ihr Sorgen!" (Flee, disappear, go away, O Cares). A few weeks later he changed the text to "Kommt, eilet und laufet" (Hurry, come running), and thus was born the Easter cantata, performed for the first time on April 1, 1725. Ten years later Bach composed a new version of this cantata and called it *Oster Oratorium* (Easter Oratorio). The name "Oratorio" is entirely justified not only because of its considerable scope, which combines in 11 musical numbers the forces of soloists, choruses, and orchestra, but also because the style is reminiscent of earlier Italian oratorios. In addition, this work differs from all of Bach's other compositions for the church in that it is based on a story told not just by an Evangelist, but sung by several different characters. Upon the request of the two Marys, the Disciples follow them to Jesus' grave to find it empty; the angel who had announced the Resurrection had spoken the truth. Bach's original score contains three trumpets, two oboes, timpani, strings, and continuo with harpsichord or organ and bassoon.

Carl Philipp Emanuel Bach   1714–1788

Johann Sebastian Bach, the great cantor of St. Thomas, had 20 children from two marriages—11 sons and nine daughters. Only 10 lived past early childhood. Four of the sons, an unusually large number, were musical geniuses. But what is even more astonishing is that they were so unlike each other, both as human beings and as musicians. Carl Philipp Emanuel was the second eldest of them. He became one of the leading German musicians of his time, unlike his brother Wilhelm Friedemann, a sort of Bohemian who led an adventuresome life and was thought of by many as something of a vagabond. The pre-Classical *galant* or *sensitive* (empfindsam) style found in Carl Philipp Emanuel its most interesting representative. He first studied law in Leipzig and Frankfurt/Oder, but then became chamber musician to the Prussian king Frederick II, whose court was served by many brilliant musicians, including the master flutist Johann Joachim Quantz, the Graun brothers (see the section on Karl Heinrich) and the Benda brothers. It was at his instigation that his father visited the court at Potsdam in 1747. He inherited many of Johann Sebastian's manuscripts upon his death, but was unfortunately anything but careful with this estate, which should have been of value to him for two reasons: filial piety and artistic esteem. He sold the copper plates laboriously engraved by his father who had risked his eyesight to do so, and co-opted many of his father's themes and melodies in his own work. He also allowed his stepmother, his father's dear companion, to live in need.

For 30 years Carl Philipp Emanuel lived in Berlin and upon Telemann's death, in 1767, became his successor in Hamburg. Here he directed a great many concerts, cultivated the music of Handel and Haydn, and was very busy with composition. He composed an extraordinary number of works: hundreds of pieces for keyboard instruments, 22 Passions, and 2 oratorios; cantatas, odes, songs, and so on. While much of his instrumental work is still extant, and his textbook *Versuch über die wahre Art, das Klavier zu spielen* (Essay on the True Art of Playing Keyboard Instruments, 1753–62) is still considered a basic text, his vocal music is not widely known. This is true not only of the more than 250 spiritual and secular songs, odes, and psalms, but also of the great choral works. In the course of the new interest in early music, some have at last been recorded.

One that deserves mention is the *Magnificat a 4 Voci*, composed in 1749, first performed in Berlin in 1787, an especially lively work, full of diverse forms and moods and lasting three-quarters of an hour. Its key of D major and the rich orchestration (three trumpets, two flutes, two oboes, two horns, timpani, strings, continuo with organ) are reminiscent of Johann Sebastian's D major *Magnificat*.

Two oratorios also must be mentioned: *Auferstehung und Himmelfahrt Jesu* (1787) (The Resurrection and Ascent of Jesus) and *Die Israeliten in der Wüste* (The Israelites in the Wilderness), first performed on December 14, 1769, in Hamburg. With their epic-idyllic style, galant melodies, and emotional treatment of words, they can in no way be compared with Handel's monumental Baroque oratorios. But Carl Philipp Emanuel's lyrical, contemplative music forms a logical transition from Handel's Baroque musical language to the *empfindsam* Classic oratorios of Joseph Haydn.

Ludwig van Beethoven   1770–1827

Beethoven was born in Bonn, probably on December 16, 1770. He was baptized the next day, for which there is a record, whereas there is none of his birth. He grew up in Bonn and was musically precocious, leading his father, who was only a mediocre singer in the Hofkapelle, to toy with the idea of making a "second Mozart" of his son. When he was "six years old," Ludwig made his first appearance as a pianist. Though he was really already eight, his father wished him to appear younger. A good music teacher, Christian Gottlob Neefe, saved him from an early career as a virtuoso and understood how to steer him toward higher goals, both ethical and technical. We do not know for certain whether Beethoven traveled to Vienna in 1787, spent three weeks there, and performed for Mozart, as some stories have it. He did travel south, that much is known, but had to return quickly due to the fatal illness of his beloved mother. In any case, we know that shortly thereafter, he really did make the trip. A friend, the Austrian Count Waldstein, presented Beethoven to Haydn, who was passing through. Haydn's favorable opinion, together with some funds which had been collected by friends in Bonn and valuable letters of introduction, enabled Beethoven to go to Vienna toward the end of 1792. The music-loving aristocracy of the city on the Danube opened its doors to him almost at once. There, as Waldstein wrote in Beethoven's travel diary, he would receive "the spirit of Mozart from the hands of Haydn." Beethoven briefly became Haydn's pupil, after which he also studied under Salieri and Albrechtsberger. The first years in Vienna were eminently successful; portraits of him from that time show an elegant man-about-town. But fate had something else in mind for him. In 1796 he suffered an ear inflammation that would not heal and the physicians of the time were not able to save his hearing, a musician's most valuable sense. Beethoven began to withdraw. His inward journey was acutely painful: his *Heiligenstädter Testament*, written during the autumn of 1802, shows him at the brink of suicide. But his calling was stronger. A quarter of a century of creative life still lay before him.

Composition was for him—unlike Haydn, Mozart, and Schubert, his immediate contemporaries—a struggle, the full difficulty of which can only be appreciated by those who share a similar problem. A glance at his sketchbooks, drafts, and manuscripts reveals the self-torture and sometimes self-destructiveness of a battle whose only bright moments came with successful, well received performances. On the one hand we have Mozart, who could write a sonata or a quartet movement in a few hours, a symphony in a few days, and an opera in a few weeks; and on the other we have Beethoven, who required months, often years to compose the same kinds of works. Were they really doing the same thing? How easily Schubert's Masses flowed from his pen, and what effort Beethoven had to expend to put the final version of his *Missa Solemnis* on paper! Every composition became a monument to a hard-won victory after a ferocious battle. The nine symphonies, the 32 piano sonatas, the five piano concertos, the violin concerto, the triple concerto, the 16 string quartets are all more comprehensive than those of his predecessors, denser in content, more complex technically, but their relatively small number—surpassed by a wide margin by each of the three contemporaries mentioned—is largely attributable to the fact that they arose out of a completely different creative process, and that their creator was, in character and temperament, a completely different kind of man.

Several of Beethoven's works must be included in a book on oratorios: the oratorio *Christus am Ölberg* (1803), the "little" *Mass in C Major* (1807), the *Fantasia* for piano, chorus, and orchestra (1808) (the so-called choral Fantasia), the cantata *Der glorreiche Augenblick* (1814), and the *Missa Solemnis* (1823) are the most important. But two youthful cantatas written in 1790 must not be overlooked—one composed on the death of Emperor Joseph II and the other on the coronation of his successor, Leopold II—nor the cantata *Meeresstille und glückliche Fahrt* (1815). Beethoven's fame spread far and wide during his lifetime.

Music lovers throughout Europe recognized his greatness and anxiously awaited each of his new works. But the greater his fame, the more he withdrew personally from public life. Long wrapped in a cloak of loneliness and deep suffering, he died on the afternoon of March 26, 1827. His funeral on the 29th was a great and notable demonstration of veneration for the master.

Christ on the Mount of Olives

Text by Franz Xaver Huber. Earlier biographers place its composition in 1801–02, but more recent research by Dieter Rexroth assigns it to the spring of 1803. The first performance took place at one of Beethoven's "Academies" in Vienna on April 5, 1803; it seems to have been performed several times more in the same year. The high opus number (85) has nothing to do with the date of composition, but with the later date of publication (1811), as was then customary.

The work calls for three solo voices: Christ (tenor), a seraph (soprano), and Peter (bass), as well as a four-part chorus further subdivided into the chorus of angels, the chorus of soldiers, and the chorus of Disciples. The story is taken from the Passion: from the point when Jesus prays on the Mount of Olives to his arrest in Gethsemane. Little remains today of the great affection felt for this work during Beethoven's lifetime and the several subsequent decades. This decline in esteem is probably attributable to the text rather than the music, although Beethoven did not count it among his best compositions. He used the late Classical orchestra of his time—two flutes, two clarinets, two bassoons, two horns (E-flat), a tenor and a bass trombone, timpani, and strings—but oboes and trumpets are noticeably absent.

The work begins in somber dignity with a fanfarelike, ascending E-flat minor triad. A lengthy orchestral introduction bearing unmistakable traits of tone painting leads to Jesus' first recitative: he calls upon his Father in heaven asking for strength and consolation in the hour of suffering he feels approaching. His aria "Meine Seele ist erschüttert von den Qualen, die mir dräun..." (My soul trembles before the torment that awaits me...) follows, which critics have often charged with being too "human."

Certainly the Christ of this work is different from the lofty figure of Bach's Passions, one who is above all worldliness, but the 70 years that separate the two compositions brought a new era of "heightened sensibility," of humanizing the godly, leading to Romanticism, a tendency also noticeable in the verses by the completely unknown Franz X. Huber. Beethoven clearly stood on the threshold of this new sensitivity, which led to a vision of a more "modern" direction in art. About 1800 it was he who led the way from Classicism to Romanticism.

An example is found in the passage of tone painting after Jesus' aria announcing the arrival of the seraphim sent from heaven: a swelling roll on the timpani and the passage work in the violins seem like giant wings floating earthward. In spite of its many limitations, the work shows touches of genius throughout.

Among them is the angels' chorus that from time to time accompanies the voice of the seraph as he sings his highest notes. The following scene is also very affecting: Jesus asks the seraph if his Father will spare him the agony of the fearful death prophesied. The angel answers with the words of Jehovah, bathed in a sense of mysticism created by a solemn chorale in the winds: "Eh' nicht erfüllet ist das heilige Geheimnis der Versöhnung, so lange bleibt das menschliche Geschlecht verworfen und beraubt des ew'gen Lebens" (The holy mystery of reconciliation cannot be fulfilled as long as mankind remains depraved and deprived of eternal life). Thus is confirmed the crushing burden of his task. The mood changes, as, to a march, the soldiers return: "Wir haben ihn gesehen nach diesem Berge gehen... sein wartet das Gericht!" (We have seen him going toward this mountain... the court awaits him!) The collision of the Disciples with the arriving soldiers is a thoroughly dramatic scene in which we hear, not surprisingly, sounds that remind us of *Fidelio*. A trio by the soloists is as varied as an opera scene: Jesus warns Peter reaching for his sword, not to use force. The drama ends with Jesus' capture, and the angels' chorus sings the conciliatory finale.

Fantasia for Piano, Chorus, and Orchestra

The Choral Fantasia, Op. 80, is for many reasons a curious piece, but also remarkable, even lovely. Should we call it a piano concerto, as its form might suggest? Why then does it have a chorus? But then is Beethoven's Ninth not a symphony because a chorus with solo voices joins the orchestra in the last movement? Is it, then, a very freely constructed cantata? Many of his works exhibit very free structures, for Beethoven experimented endlessly with musical form, using nothing from tradition without first adapting it to his own ends.

The idea of crowning an instrumental work with a chorus seems to have occurred to Beethoven early on. He first gives expression to the idea in the Choral Fantasia and returns to it again in the Ninth Symphony. These two works, different as they are, share certain common traits: Beethoven made the same observation when, on March 10, 1824, he offered the Leipzig music publisher H. A. Probst his last symphony, with the words,"... It is like my piano fantasia with chorus, but of much greater dimension..." Both works share a great, songlike melody which has something hymnlike about it: the famous "Freude, schöner Götterfunken" from the Ninth

Symphony, sung today the world over, and the similar-sounding but not as well known "Schmeichelnd hold und lieblich klingen unseres Lebens Harmonien" from the Choral Fantasia. Another shared trait is that these themes are first heard in the orchestra before being taken up by the voices. It also appears that both themes had been turning in the composer's head long before he put them on paper. Sometime in the 1790s Beethoven wrote in his notebook "Let us sing the song of the immortal Schiller!" which surely was an early reference to the chorus of the Ninth, composed almost 30 years later. The long melody of the Choral Fantasy first appeared in a song composed in the 90s, "Gegenliebe" (Requited Love) (1796), based on a text by Gottfried August Bürger.

This theme appears in the Choral Fantasy with a completely different text, so the first question that arises is who wrote it. Beethoven, as was customary at that time, failed to provide the author's name, and the circumstances surrounding this composition shed no light on the matter. Karl Czerny, for a short time Beethoven's pupil, said it was the poet Christoph Kuffner. Kuffner purportedly was given only a few days by the composer as the choral parts were already finished. Subsequent research has thrown doubt on this account, and in fact, it seems unlikely that it is true. We can only say that the author of the text is unknown.

The Fantasy for Piano, Chorus, and Orchestra, Op. 80, is one of the few works Beethoven was able to complete in a short period of time and without interruption. There was, however, one major omission: In the original manuscript the long, very important piano introduction that gives the work the name *fantasia* was missing. It seems that Beethoven did not have time to finish it before the first performance, but since he was playing the piano, he supplied the introduction as a free improvisation. The final version of this section, the one used today, was apparently not written down in the master's notebook until 1809, a year after the work had been performed. The performance took place during the course of a memorable, probably unique concert given on December 22, 1808.

For this concert Beethoven had invited his supporters and admirers to an "Academy" at the Theater an der Wien, which lasted four to five hours. It included the first performances of his Symphonies No. 5 in C Minor, Op. 67 and No. 6 in F Major, Op. 68, the *Pastoral*; and the Piano Concerto No. 4 in G Major, Op. 58; the extended concert aria *Ah, perfido!*; and a few "hymns" (from the *Mass in C Major*, which, as a sacred work, could not be performed in its entirety in a secular hall, nor under its proper name). This would have been more than enough, but in keeping with a pleasant custom of the time, the artist who gave the concert provided an extended free improvisation at the keyboard. All of this, which probably would have taken about 200 minutes, did not seem to him sufficient, so Beethoven decided to realize his plan for a piano fantasia with chorus which he began composing a few weeks before the "Academy" was to take place, thinking that it would be an especially effective finale. We have already noted that he wrote it at an unaccustomed speed, possibly starting at the beginning of December, 1808. Unfortunately, we know far too little about any rehearsals of those days, let alone Beethoven's. It seems that a few, good Viennese musicians stood by him. They helped with the coaching and rehearsing for this gigantic program, which presented difficulties we, today, can only vaguely appreciate. The parts were written out by hand, probably resulting in mistakes and inaccuracies, the corrections of which made some parts difficult to read. The musicians were not part of an integrated ensemble accustomed through long hours of work to performing as a unit. In addition to these difficulties, and probably the most important, was Beethoven's manner of conducting, about which more than one of his contemporaries have left us very critical observations (for example, Louis Spohr, the famous violinist and composer, and one of the earliest conductors in the modern sense).

In addition to the virtuoso piano solo, the Choral Fantasia uses a typical late Classical/early Romantic orchestra: two each of flutes, oboes, clarinets, bassoons, horns, and trumpets, a pair of timpani, as well as the usual five-part augmented string section, in which the cellos and double basses parallel each other. In addition a four-part mixed chorus (soprano, alto, tenor, bass) with some solo passages, which were likely sung by members of the chorus, was required.

The work begins with the long piano improvisation, which Beethoven wrote down only after the first performance had already been given. This section, best compared to a very free cadenza in a piano concerto, is full of surprising harmonic effects and must be played in the most virtuosic manner. In the manuscript, at the end of the composition, there is a curious sentence written by Beethoven in Italian: "Qui si da un segno all'orchestra o al direttore di musica" (Give a signal here to either the orchestra or the director). The sentence must be a remnant from either the first performance or the one that followed it, before the first part was committed to paper, for it means that at the end of his improvisation, the pianist should provide a cue for the entry of the orchestra. The orchestra begins pianissimo, with the cellos and contrabasses playing their lowest notes; an interplay between this theme and the now very melodic piano follows. A hesitation: horns call, the oboes answer like a distant echo. Then the main theme appears in the piano, accompanied softly by the horns.

What follows can be called a cumulative variation movement, which moves through various tempos, rhythms, and meters. A repetition of the echo passage between the horns and the oboes leads finally to the entry of the solo voices and then of the chorus: "Schmeichelnd hold und lieblich..." (Fondly and sweetly flattering...). The joyful, almost triumphant movement swells to its finale as the three groups (voices, orchestra, piano), now in ensemble, join in a hymn to art.

Mass in C Major

Original Title: Missa in C, Op. 86
Original Language: Latin
Text: The five parts of the Ordinarium Missae
Date of Writing: Begun possibly in 1806, completed in 1807.
First Performance: September 13, 1807, in Eisenstadt (Burgenland, Austria).
Form: The five parts of the Ordinarium Missae are combined into three hymns: Hymnus I (= Kyrie and Gloria); Hymnus II (= Credo); Hymnus III (= Sanctus, Benedictus, and Agnus Dei). This unusual nomenclature is related to the first performance in Vienna (see the History of the Work).
Vocal Scoring: Four solo voices (soprano, alto, tenor, bass), four-part mixed chorus.
Orchestra: Two flutes, two oboes, two clarinets, two bassoons, two horns, two trumpets, timpani, strings, and organ.
History of the Work: Prince Nicholas II von Esterhazy commissioned Beethoven to write a Mass to celebrate the name day of his wife. Nicholas had acceded to the title at the time when Joseph Haydn, after 30 years of service in Eisenstadt and at the Esterhazy summer palace in the Hungarian Puszta, retired and returned to Vienna. Haydn had remained on good terms with Beethoven, who often visited Eisenstadt.

It was through Haydn that Beethoven became acquainted with the Prince, who then became his student for a time. Now, in the first decade of the new century, as Beethoven's works were heard with increasing frequency, Esterhazy requested him to compose the Mass. Beethoven was at that time in one of his most creative periods. In 1806 he composed the Fourth Piano Concerto (in G major), the Violin Concerto, the Fourth Symphony, and three string quartets; and in 1807, the *Coriolanus* Overture, the Fifth and Sixth Symphonies, the Choral Fantasy, and a good deal of chamber music.

Beethoven traveled to Eisenstadt for the first performance of his Mass, reporting in a letter that it was "warmly received." However, an anecdote circulating at the time contended that the Prince was displeased, and was supposed to have said: "*Now* what have you done, my dear Beethoven?" This seems very unlikely since Esterhazy must surely have known that Beethoven's work would differ markedly from the Mass he had commissioned simultaneously from Haydn (his last). Even more unlikely is another rumor that "the people standing around, among whom was Hummel, had laughed." Johann Nepomuk Hummel (1778–1837), Haydn's successor at Eisenstadt, was a brilliant musician who surely must have recognized the composition's value.

One source reports that Beethoven departed from Eisenstadt offended. The fact is that one of his great "Academies" was to be presented at Eisenstadt; however, it did not work out. The "Academy" was presented in Vienna on December 22, 1808; it is no exaggeration to say that it was one of the greatest concerts in history. (For its program see the discussion of Beethoven's Choral Fantasy.)
Discussion of the Work: Beethoven begins the work with the chorus: the basses intone the keynote C, and not until the next measure do the upper voices and the orchestra enter with the lovely main theme (Example 1).

Soon, an unusual feature of this work becomes evident: the quick alternation between chorus and solo voices, which imparts a restless, typically Romantic quality. With a mighty outburst in the chorus and orchestra, the Kyrie leads without a break into the Gloria. The solo alto returns to a lyrical mood with the "Qui tollis peccata mundi," sung against a "floating," syncopated, F minor background. Then come the words "Quoniam tu solus" in a radiant C major; a mighty choral fugue on the words "Cum sancto spiritu" closes the movement. In the second part, the Credo, which begins softly, perhaps the most impressive moment is the "Et incarnatus est" (Example 2).

Once more a choral fugue, "Et vitam venturi," this time with some solo passages, forms the finale. The brief orchestral prelude to the third part (Sanctus) is a fine example of the melodic heights to which Beethoven could rise (Example 3). Because this movement also flows without interruption, the individual parts are very closely related: the Benedictus (marked by the interplay between the soloists and the chorus) and the Agnus Dei, with its concluding "Dona nobis pacem," which leads back to the beginning, to the tender melody (No. 1) of the Kyrie, moving in the same harmonious thirds.

Example 1

Example 2

Example 3

Der glorreiche Augenblick (The glorious moment)

Much has been written of Beethoven's political views. Two events have usually been singled out. The first is the angry obliteration of the dedication to Napoleon on the title page of his Symphony No. 3 in E-flat major, Op. 55. Shortly before the work was made public, he erased the dedication, deeply disillusioned by Bonaparte's coronation. Exactly 10 years later, he composed several works celebrating Napoleon's downfall, the end (supposedly) of the wars fought in his name, and the convening of the Congress of Vienna. One was the musical battle painting *Wellingtons Sieg oder die Schlacht bei Vittoria* (Wellington's Victory or the Battle of Vittoria), which called for an outsized orchestra with a mighty percussion section to describe realistically the tumult of battle, and which included the national anthems of the victors. The cantata *Der glorreiche Augenblick*, Op. 136, also appeared at this time. The work is included here less for artistic reasons than for the light it sheds on an interesting, if hardly "glorious," moment in the master's life. Throughout his lifetime Beethoven passionately supported human rights. His sympathies were with the French Revolution, which proclaimed them, and with Napoleon, whom he saw as the highest expression of these values. It was Napoleon as emperor and more importantly, Napoleon as conqueror, who led his troops through Europe in support of personal aggrandizement and unlimited power, not human rights, whom Beethoven rejected. Together with all the continent Beethoven breathed a sigh of relief when the tyrant was struck down. He joined in the general exultation when the news of Napoleon's defeat was announced and leaders of Europe converged on Vienna to establish a new order. He little knew that the promised new beginning would result in a backward turn of the wheel of European politics, a return to the times of unfettered absolutism, that the old injustices would appear again—that the handful of progressives of the day would be rendered impotent at the hands of those reactionaries whom Beethoven had always hated. He was carried along by the delirious, exultant crowds, especially since these crowds began to honor him in a way he had never before experienced. Neither before nor after was he to be as famous and popular as at that moment. That this adulation was due to the success of works that did not really deserve it should have given him pause for thought; but that may be too much to ask. He undoubtedly believed this widespread approval was directed to him personally and to the music he had composed.

The Viennese municipal authorities commissioned him to compose a festive cantata to celebrate the Congress, for which Aloys Weissenbach, a Viennese doctor, supplied the text. The cantata might still be performed occasionally were it not for Weissenbach's text, which has made the work impossible. (In 1836, Ludwig Rellstab, a Berlin poet widely read at the time, undertook to replace the text with a hymn to music. And in our century, the conductor Hermann Scherchen tried to turn it into a paean to peace. But both efforts were unsuccessful.) Weissenbach used the popular phrase "glorreiche Augenblick," originally coined to describe the meeting of the three victorious monarchs on the battle field at Leipzig, and extended it to include the Congress of Vienna.

The work was performed for the first time on Tuesday, November 29, 1814, "in the large Royal and Imperial Ballroom," as the posters read (the ballroom or concert hall of the Vienna Hofburg). The evening began with the Seventh Symphony, only recently performed for the first time, followed by the cantata and then by "a great, resounding instrumental composition written to celebrate Wellington's victory in the battle of Vittoria." The setting was magnificent; accounts written at the time tell of an audience numbering 5,000 among whom were many of Europe's most distinguished figures who had flocked to Vienna. Among them was the Prussian king, Frederick William III, to whom Beethoven dedicated his Ninth Symphony some 10 years later. The concert was repeated a few days later but attracted only half as many, and a third performance was cancelled. Yet everyone seemed to recognize the rather odd man in the streets of Vienna, remarking, "There goes Beethoven... the musician who wrote the Battle Symphony and the cantata to the Emperors."

The cantata *Der glorreiche Augenblick*, in six parts, sings the praises of the victorious monarchs, who are elevated to luminous, godlike figures. In the second section, the four-part chorus gives way to soloists who sing the roles of *Genius* and *Leader of the People*. Vienna is honored, once under its German name and then as the Latin Vindobona, "kronengeschmückte, götterbeglückte, herrscherbewirtende Bürgerin" (a citizeness, wearing a diadem, favored by the gods, gracious hostess to rulers); the exultant chorus sings "to the queen of cities." At this point Vienna, the solo soprano, greets each of the lords in dithyrambic verse, in an aria accompanied by the chorus: "And all the lords stretch out their hands to grasp the right hand of our Emperor, to weave an eternal ring...." Reconciliation, peace among nations, the "glorreiche Augenblick." In the fourth part, an "oracle" sings: "The eye sees the sunrises and sunsets, the stars and the people go their ways.

Behold it, above that coming and going of the crowned heads! This eye is the Last Judgment . . ." In the fifth part the four soloists (Vienna, the Oracle, the Genius, the Leader of the People) join together to sing "For ever, for ever will the olive branch be green, fashioned by those who now build the edifice, wound around the pillars of Europe."

The work comes to a close with a hymnlike chorus of rejoicing, ending in a stretto in which separate choruses of children, women, and men each give their blessing before coming together with the mighty orchestra in a C major exultation: two each of flutes, oboes, clarinets, bassoons; four horns, two trumpets, three trombones, timpani, a large string section with occasional violin and cello solos. As has been said—a classic instance of talent for hire. But, did Beethoven not feel that he, of all people, should never have composed such a work? Our only consolation is that his greatness is such that this piece need not be held against him.

Missa solemnis

Original Title: Missa solemnis in D major, Op. 123
Text: The five parts of the Ordinarium Missae
Language: Latin
Date of Writing: The concept of the Mass goes back to 1814; the first sketches date from 1818; the work was actually composed between 1819 and 1822.
First Performance: April 6, 1824, in St. Petersburg (Leningrad), Russia.
Form: In five parts—Kyrie, Gloria, Credo, Sanctus, Agnus Dei
Scoring: Four solo voices (soprano, alto, tenor, bass), four-part mixed chorus, two each flutes, oboes, clarinets, and bassoons; contrabassoon, four horns, two trumpets, three trombones, timpani, strings, organ ad libitum.
History of the Work: In 1807, Beethoven had composed the *Mass in C major,* but in the years that followed wrote no sacred music. On June 4, 1819, Archduke Rudolf of Austria, the Emperor's brother, was named Archbishop of Olmütz, in the then crownland of Morovia. The solemn enthronement was to take place on March 20, 1820.

Rudolf had not only been a student of Beethoven from the age of 15, but as time passed had become his most faithful and supportive friend. Thus when Jerome Bonaparte, in 1808, offered Beethoven the post of Hofkapellmeister in Kassel, Rudolf was one of the highly placed Viennese who saw to it that the Master had the funds to remain in Vienna and would be completely free to compose.

Beethoven dedicated more important works to Rudolf than to any other human being: the two piano concertos Nos. 4 and 5; three great sonatas, including *Les Adieux,* which referred to the departure on and return from a journey his friend made; the *Hammerklavier* Sonata; his last, the Sonata in C minor, Op. 111; the Great Fugue for string quartet, Op. 133; and what was probably his greatest gift, the *Missa solemnis.*

When Beethoven began to work on this Mass is not totally clear. It was formerly assumed that it coincided with Rudolf's appointment, but Beethoven's "assistant" Anton Schindler—a rather unreliable man and a proven forger—sets the beginning of the composition back several months. Was the rumor of Rudolf's appointment enough to cause such a great plan to mature in Beethoven's head? It is somewhat unlikely, especially since his religious inclinations had never been very strong.

This point has been of burning interest in the Beethoven literature. Beethoven did believe in God, but not in any dogma. In a conversation notebook from 1820 we read, written in his own hand: "The moral law within us and the starry heaven above! Kant!!!" There are other indications as well that Beethoven maintained no church affiliation and that his views were closer to a sort of eastern pantheism. That despite this evidence, the *Missa solemnis,* a statement of Christian faith, became one of his most important compositions is probably attributable to a gesture of friendship for the Archduke and Archbishop. But a careful listening to this mass reveals that its sources lie in another kind of belief than that which informed the works of Bach, Bruckner, and César Franck. Here no peaceful piety reigns, no quiet devotion to God's inscrutable power, but rather a wrestling with the meaning of life, a struggle to find peace in confronting the "Last Things." Work on the *Missa solemnis* dragged on and on; a performance at the installation ceremonies in Cologne was out of the question. For a while he worked simultaneously on this composition and the Ninth Symphony.

Beethoven seems to have done some preparation before taking up such a massive religious work. He obtained an exact translation of the text of the Mass into German, he studied the works of Palestrina, and occupied himself with Gregorian chant. It seems that the composition excited him greatly. Visitors during that summer of 1819 reported the indescribable chaos they found in his rooms, and a neglect of his person even more extreme than usual. Subsequent research has revealed that the miseries attendant to the unremitting hiring and firing of servants; the unusually frequent quarrels with copyists; and the unnerving struggle with his sister-in-law over the guardianship of his nephew, with its disputes and litigation, greatly distracted him.

Understandably, the almost total disruption of his daily life, coupled with the inflation triggered by the Napoleonic wars which greatly reduced the value of his pension, led to financial embarrassment. So, shortly before the *Missa solemnis* was finished in 1823, the idea came to him of paying off the debts he had acquired—not always honorably—by selling subscriptions to this work. He offered the work "in manuscript"—in actuality done by a copyist—to several European courts as well as to a select few, prominent people, among them Cherubini and Goethe, for 50 ducats. The earnings from this dubious subscription plan finally amounted to 1600 gulden. He sold the actual manuscript to the Mainz publisher Schott for 1000 gulden, after having already signed a contract with Simrock in Bonn and C. F. Peters in Leipzig and having received large advances for it from both of them.

The *Missa solemnis* must have been finished early in 1823. A Russian nobleman, Prince Nikolaus von Galitzin, who found his way into Beethoven's biography as commissioner and dedicatee of some of the master's quartets, had the work performed for the first time at a benefit in St. Petersburg, the capitol of czarist Russia, on March 26, 1824. The score, published soon after, bore the dedication, in Latin, to Archduke Rudolf: "summa cum veneratione" (with deepest reverence). On May 7th, a month and a half after the premiere in St. Petersburg, three parts of the *Missa solemnis* were performed in Vienna—the Kyrie, the Credo, and the Agnus Dei—designated, for this occasion, as "Three Great Hymns." At the same concert the Ninth Symphony was first performed. A complete performance of the Mass was not possible on this occasion, not because of lack of time (considerations of length seemed meaningless), but because the performance of sacred works in secular settings such as concert halls was forbidden.

Thenceforth the course of the *Missa solemnis*, which Beethoven often called his most important and best work, is difficult to follow. Hermann Kretzschmar, even at that late date (1916) much closer to the events than we are, gives the dates of subsequent performances as follows: In Warnsdorf/Lausitz, Bohemia in 1830; at a private concert in London in 1832, directed by Beethoven's friend and student Ignaz Moscheles; and at a music festival in the Rhineland in 1844. Does this mean, unbelievable as it may seem in light of Beethoven's fame, that this is the only one of his major works which he never heard? Strictly speaking it can be said that he was never present at a performance of the *Missa solemnis*, because for at least 15 years he had actually not heard a single note of anything he had written...

Discussion of the Work: Beethoven's "Festival Mass" or "Solemn Mass"—for this is what Missa solemnis means, in contrast to a Missa brevis, the "short" mass for liturgical use—included the usual parts of the Ordinarium Missae (Kyrie, Gloria, Credo, Sanctus, Agnus Dei). But it possesses a number of unusual characteristics that set it apart from all other works of this genre. None of the Haydn or Mozart Masses that preceded it is as personal as this one. A comparison with Schubert's Masses, composed at about the same time, is hardly conceivable. It is as if Beethoven prays in another language, using a different vocabulary, yet everything is exactly as prescribed. Possibly Beethoven conceived of God differently than the other masters mentioned, as revealed in the way he distributed musical emphasis, in his choice of climactic moments, perhaps also in the very proportions of the work and in the stressing of certain concepts.

Beethoven repeatedly made exceptional demands on the voices, in terms of range as well as length of breath (this practice usually compels the choral director to resort to certain "tricks," so that notes to be held particularly long, especially in the soprano, do not lose their force). Beethoven's critics have often voiced the opinion that he did not understand voices well or that he had lost contact with the voice due to his deafness. They point particularly to the *Missa Solemnis* and the Ninth Symphony as examples of this shortcoming. But such problematic passages also occur in the opera *Fidelio*, composed 15 to 20 years earlier, so the reason must be sought elsewhere. We might recall Beethoven's remark to the violinist Schuppanzigh, when this good friend found fault with a difficult passage in a string quartet: "Do you really believe I think about your miserable violin when inspiration strikes me?" Beethoven—very much unlike Mozart—threw all other considerations aside when he was in the throes of creating a way to express an idea. And he was right: supreme effort coupled with great technical skill can master even the most difficult passages in his works.

After a short, devotional introduction—Beethoven wrote the now famous words "From the heart, may it go to the heart" above it—the chorus enters sonorously, majestically, with the call

"Kyrie," the word used in both classical and modern Greek for "Lord." At the end of each of the three calls, a solo voice enters (tenor, then soprano, then alto) during the last note of the chorus, an echo floating in the air after the chorus has broken off. The solo alto completes the call with "Kyrie eleison," from which the chorus now fashions a melodic movement. The "Christe eleison," following without a pause, is presented by the quartet of solo voices in double fugal entries and is an especially artful section, which, after fading away, leads to a return of the mighty choral "Kyrie" with its echo effects by the solo voices. The "Gloria" is almost stormy when compared to its solemn character in most other compositions. Not until "et in terra pax" does the storm abate, only to gather strength again in the "laudamus te," where it forms a bridge to a joyful fugue in the "glorificamus te." Then, in a wonderfully contrasting passage, the solo tenor sings the gentle and lyrical "Gratias tibi;" the alto, the soprano, and the bass join in, until the chorus, softly, almost imperceptibly, takes over the lead. It maintains the lead in the once more lively "Domine," which describes God's might in an almost tone-painterly way.

The "Qui tollis" begins with wind solos, tenderly and lovingly, with great expression but more delicate intonation on the part of the four soloists; they melt into the chorus almost imperceptibly, which then, in a great outburst, sings "qui sedes ad dexteram patris;" for a moment it is as if the heavens had opened. This section comes to an end slowly and with deep devotion, as the chorus, almost in a murmur, begs for mercy ("miserere nobis").

With a transitional roll in the timpani and fortissimo entrance of the full orchestra, the "Quoniam" begins, mounts powerfully ("maestoso," Beethoven demands), and with "in gloria dei patris" develops a mighty fugue, which sustains its excitement through harsh, rhythmic beats. It comes to a climax on the exultant, repeated "Amen," before the voices of the chorus once more rejoice in God's majesty ("Gloria") in a presto stretto. The Credo begins with a solid, thoroughly resolute theme, which is then developed fugally (Example 1). The confession of belief in God, the Almighty Father, stands like a fortress, sacrosanct, unconquerable. We hear the same theme, also presented fugato but spun out with much variation, in the avowal of belief in Jesus; it rises to a new climax with the final assurance that he descended from heaven ("descendit de coelis"). Then, with bewildering abruptness, the mood changes to one of deep mysticism. With an adagio like a ray of light from heaven, the orchestra modulates to the key of D minor. The solo tenor sings the tender "Et incarnatus," floating mysteriously over the quartet of soloists, highlighted by a wonderfully expressive flute solo, while the clarinets and bassoon weave an almost inaudible carpet of sound.

Example 1

With "Et homo factus est" (D major) we return to earth. The "Crucifixus," again in D minor, is almost dramatic, with the victorious certainty of the resurrection and the kingdom without end. Then once more, in the transition to the next article of faith ("Credo in spiritum sanctum"), there is a pronounced modulation, underscored by the entire orchestra (D major, G minor, D minor as the six-four chord, and B-flat major). In this part of the creed, the theme of the Credo (No. 1) appears again, this time as the main motive in the lower voices, until in the next part it courses once more through three voices (bass, soprano, and alto). But the fourth, the tenor, recites the contents of this article, "in unam sanctam catholicam et apostolicam Ecclesiam," while the rest of the voices sing out the word "Credo" powerfully and repeatedly.

This moment forces us to stop and reflect: All the other articles of the Credo are presented repeatedly with varying degrees of emphasis, all clearly audible; only this one, which addresses the church, is almost inaudible. Does this have anything to do with Beethoven's belief in God not extending to the church?

Schubert deleted the article in the confession of faith, "the holy catholic and apostolic church," the "only one offering salvation," entirely. He probably did not believe in it, so preferred not to express an untruth, even in music. Moreover, he did not write his Masses for a friend who was an Archbishop, as Beethoven did.

Is this setting of the Mass a compromise between Beethoven's personal beliefs and his deep friendship with Archduke and Archbishop Rudolf? It can scarcely be assumed that these odd passages crept into the work unintentionally and unwittingly. Immediately following this passage Beethoven avows his belief most convincingly in baptism, the forgiveness of sin, the resurrection of the dead, and eternal life, and makes out of the latter, followed by countless "amen"s, an over-powering, contrapuntal eight-part hymn supported by radiant orchestration.

Above the "Sanctus," which follows, Beethoven once again wrote "with devotion"; it forms a unit with the "Benedictus." After a solemn beginning by the quartet of soloists, joined by a transparent texture in the orchestra, a new fugue begins (Example 2) with "Pleni sunt coeli." The solo soprano begins with the broad, fanfarelike theme, brightened further by the jubilant violins. The second entry (the solo tenor) does not follow the rules, but simply turns the D major chord around; the third entry (the solo alto) imitates the first, this time in G major, and the fourth (the bass) turns this one around, just as in the case of the tenor and the soprano. Then comes a whirling "Osanna," also fugato, which can hardly contain itself for joy. It breaks away from this climax and moves immediately to a contemplative orchestral passage, which leads to the Benedictus. Here we meet one of Beethoven's most magnificent inspirations. The music, no less stirring than the "Et incarnatus," mounts from the depths of the soul; two flutes accompany a solo violin that seems to float in the clouds.

Example 2

Almost inaudibly, reciting the text, the basses enter with the murmured "Benedictus qui venit in nomine Domini," and then suddenly leave the field to the instruments: the solo violin (Example 3) alternating with two clarinets. Not until after a long, melodious interlude do we hear the voices again: first the alto and the bass in a duet, then the soprano, and last, the tenor, in a dignified tempo, each voice melodic, usually beginning with the basic motive (Example 4). The relationship of this motive to the one in the preceding violin solo is unmistakable; its ethereal sound marks the whole passage, which could be compared with the slow second movement of a Romantic violin concerto.

The last movement, the "Agnus Dei," contains a quite unusual turn of phrase. It begins with an expressive bass solo, answered by the male voices of the chorus. After a few bars the solo alto and solo tenor enter, and finally the soprano, and together they develop an extended melody. The mood of restraint is maintained as the chorus enters, expressing with the colorful solo voices the burden of sin, of repentance and remorse. According to Beethoven's notes on the score, he wanted the "Dona nobis pacem" to express "a plea for inner and outer peace." It is no melancholy pleading, but rather a cheerful vision conjured up by the choruses and soloists. But suddenly, with one of those abrupt harmonic changes so beloved by Beethoven the dramatist, who often used them to startle us, the picture of peace seems to change to a scene of war. Trumpets blare the call to battle, dense tremolos in the strings underscore the now anxious pleading of alto and tenor, the drums beat out a harsh march rhythm, and the chorus calls out in terror "miserere nobis." The solo soprano cries out, the ghostly vision fades, returning to a gentle mood. Then just before the conclusion, Beethoven the symphonist comes imperiously to the fore: an imposing fugue builds in the orchestra before the work and its many moods come to an end.

Example 3

Example 4

William Bergsma 1921–

The success of his ballet *Paul Bunyan* (1937) prompted the young William Bergsma to study with Howard Hanson at Eastman, opening the way to a brilliant career as music administrator, teacher and composer. *Confrontation from the Book of Job* (1962) is Bergsma's major choral work. Selected scriptural passages carry the essence of the story—Job's despairing protest and God's loving response.

Confrontation from the Book of Job

Original Language: English
Text: The biblical Book of Job
Date of Writing: 1962
First Performance: December 1, 1963 at the Plymouth Congregational Church, Des Moines, Iowa, with chorus and orchestra under Mr. Dexter's direction. On October 17, 1965 it was telecast by the same group over the Columbia Broadcasting System on their religious program, "Lamp Unto My Feet."
Form: Two parts
Cast: The chorus sings the entire dialogue; there are no soloists.
Scoring: Instrumental scoring is for winds, brass, piano and percussion.
Discussion of the Work: Job's opening outcry condemns God (Example 1). [Musical examples copyright 1966 by Galaxy Music Corporation. International Copyright Secured.] His protest soon weakens into pleas for justification, and the chorus whispers his first petition (Example 2). "Spicy" dissonance is normal throughout this work, but occasionally there are extremes. The following cluster accumulates as Part One ends, underscoring the moment of Job's ultimate despair (Example 3).

Example 1

Example 2

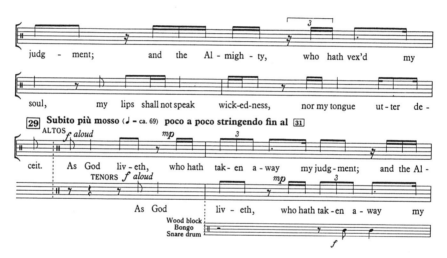

Example 3

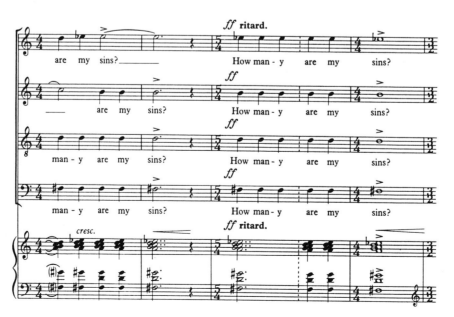

Tympani and percussion open Part Two with an instrumental whirlwind, to announce God's first response: "Who is it that darkeneth counsel by words without knowledge?" Passages of strong, buoyant music follow, overcoming the dark, ignorant mood in Part One (Example 4). The phrases laugh, at times taunting Job with whimsical word pictures (Examples 5 and 6). God's summation brings the answer to Job's quest: "Everything that is under the whole heaven *is mine.*" The final two words occupy 21 bars. This encounter with the Almighty rekindles Job's childlike faith, and the oratorio closes with music of symbolic simplicity.

Example 4

Example 5

Example 6

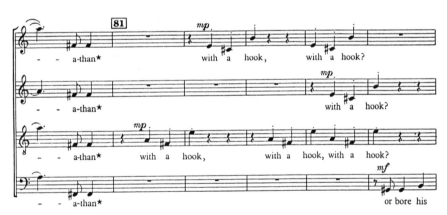

Confrontation radiates intense dramatic energy. To amplify this, the organizers of its premiere (December 1, 1963, Des Moines) presented a staged adaptation, with lighting, costumes, dancers and action, using actors to portray God and Job. The reviewer for *The Des Moines Register*, Ogden Dwight, took exception to this treatment of the work.

> As conceived for its premiere here, the choral depiction of this storied conflict, which Bergsma's score quite ably dramatizes by itself, has for some reason been illustrated by narration, dance, pantomime, costumery and stage makeup. In concert performance this is open to serious question.
>
> Bergsma composed his oratorio to be heard, and when the eye directs the mind, intense concentration is required to understand and appreciate. Confusion ensues—at least for some listeners.
>
> Disregarding this (by looking away, say, or closing one's eyes), the new oratorio becomes an emphatic, dynamic narrative of Job's despair, agitation and self realization—at the climax—of Divine might and redemption.
>
> —*Thurston Dox*

Hector Berlioz   1803–1869

Berlioz, a revolutionary Romantic of uncommon genius, wrote a number of oratorios, both sacred and secular. Among his most important works: a *Messe solennelle* (1824), a *Grande Messe des Morts* or *Requiem* (1837), the *Damnation de Faust* (1846), a Te Deum (1850), and the sacred trilogy *L'Enfance du Christ* (1854)—compositions scattered throughout the creative period of his life.

He was born on December 11, 1803, in Côte-Saint-André in the Department of Isère in France, changed his studies from medicine to music and in 1830 won the Prix de Rome of the Paris Conservatory; in the same year he created a masterpiece, the *Symphonie Fantastique*. His life was full of paradox: although he successfully championed new musical principles such as "reminiscence themes," tone-painting, program music based on extramusical motifs, and revolutionary forms of instrumentation, his native country hardly took note of him, whereas he was celebrated through-out most of Europe—Germany, Hungary, Russia. He led a wretched existence as librarian at the Paris Conservatory. He was an eccentric, his private life awash with absurdities. He died in Paris on March 8, 1869. Only then did much of the world begin to comprehend his greatness; his influence on countless of his contemporaries, the foresight of his predictions made as critic for the promi-nent "Journal des Débats"; the magnificence of his visions in sound, which anticipated Wagner, Scriabin, and Mahler; and his use of "stereo," even "quadraphonic" effects (as in the *Requiem*, with its groups of wind instruments installed in the four corners of the hall). All of these were innova-tions whose time would not really come until the 20th century.

Requiem

Original Title: Requiem. Grande Messe des Morts, Op. 5
Text: Mass for the Dead (Missa pro defunctis) of the Catholic liturgy.
Language: Latin
Date of Writing: Commissioned by the French government in 1837 to be given at a memorial ser-vice for the victims of the July Revolution of 1830.
First Performance: On December 5, 1837, in the Cathedral of St. Louis des Invalides, for the entomb-ment of General Damrémont, who fell in North Africa. The conductor was François Antoine Habeneck.
Form: The work is in 10 parts: 1. Requiem and Kyrie; 2. Dies Irae; 3. Quid sum miser; 4. Rex tremendae; 5. Quaerens me; 6. Lacrimosa; 7. Offertorium; 8. Hostias; 9. Sanctus; 10. Agnus Dei.
Scoring: Mixed chorus, frequently divided into as many as seven parts; solo tenor; four flutes, two oboes, two English horns, four clarinets, 12 horns, eight bassoons, six trumpets, four cornets, eight trombones, four tubas, eight pairs of timpani, bass drum, large numbers of strings. (In some move-ments, the brasses are divided into four groups, each with a separate percussion section. Doubling and larger scoring are possible.)
History of the Work: Berlioz described the origin of his *Requiem* in detail in his memoirs, which we will quote here, leaving out a few personal attacks made by this *enfant terrible* of French music, who was always ready to do battle with anyone.

> In 1836, M. de Gasparin was Minister of the Interior. . . . Hoping to restore French reli-gious music, which had long been ignored, to its former glory, he provided that 3,000 francs be granted annually from the funds of the Department of Fine Arts to a French composer designated by the Minister for the composition of a large scale Mass or oratorio. Moreover, the work was to be performed at government expense. "I am going to begin with Berlioz," he said; "he is to compose a Requiem Mass; I am sure he can do it well." When I learned of this . . . I made an appointment with the Minister, who con-firmed the correctness of the rumor I had heard. "I shall soon be leaving the Ministry," he added; "this will be my musical testament". . . . Nevertheless, days went by, and the commission (which had to be issued by the Ministry of Fine Arts) had not come. There, a Monsieur X., the director, did not at all approve of the minister's project for religious music, and even less of his choice of me to carry it out. He knew, moreover, that M. de Gasparin would retire in a few days. By delaying issuance of the decree . . . he could easily defeat the project. . . . But on the day before M. Gasparin was to leave the Minis-try, he ordered Monsieur X. to deliver the commission to me immediately. . . . As soon as I had received it, I set to work. The text of the *Requiem* was prey I had long coveted, and now that I had it, I threw myself upon it with a sort of fury. The turbulence of my

thoughts threatened to split my head.... Because I could not write things down as fast as they came to mind, I developed a system of shorthand which was very helpful, especially for the Lacrymosa.... Consequently, I was able to compose the work very quickly and made only a few changes long after it was finished.... The terms of the decree stipulated that my *Requiem* would be performed at the government's expense on the day commemorating the victims of the revolution of 1830. When July came, the month in which the ceremony was held, I had the parts for chorus and orchestra copied and began rehearsals. But almost immediately I received a letter from the office of the Minister telling me that the memorial service was to be held without music and instructed me to suspend all my preparations.... For five months I tried unsuccessfully to collect money to pay the debts I had incurred (with vocalists and copyists).... I was beginning to lose patience when one day, as I was leaving the office of Monsieur X. after having had an argument with him on the subject, the cannon of Les Invalides announced that Constantine (in Algeria) had fallen. Two hours later I was asked to rush back to the ministry.... General Damrémont had died in the assault, and there was to be a solemn service in the church of the Invalides for him and the French soldiers who had died during the siege.... Scarcely had Cherubini received the news that my *Requiem* was to be performed soon at a very grand, official ceremony, when he fell ill with a fever. It had long been the custom to use one of his funeral Masses for such affairs. He saw it as an attack on his rights, his dignity.

Berlioz then tells how friends of Cherubini tried to stir up trouble in the press, but finally settled for the awarding of a high honor to the illustrious old master, now 77 years old.

Berlioz's work was to be performed as scheduled, but in its performance Berlioz suffered another setback. He had counted on conducting the work himself but was unable to overcome the objections of the long-time choral director, Habeneck. In Berlioz's detailed description of the performance, Habeneck (who had earned a reputation as a conductor of Beethoven's music) is blamed for having nearly caused disaster through an act of carelessness that seems absolutely grotesque today: at the most difficult moment of the whole work, he supposedly pulled out his snuff box and took a pinch! Berlioz, who was standing next to him, "to watch over the percussion," jumped to the podium and rescued the performance, as he describes in detail, not forgetting to add: "Could it be possible that this man, in concert with Monsieur X., who hates me, and Cherubini's friends, dared conceive and very nearly carry out such a piece of skullduggery? I cannot bear to think of it... but do not doubt it. God forgive me if I have wronged him."

Quotes from two letters are illuminating: one was sent on April 17, 1837, to his sister Adèle:

I hope to be finished in two months. It took great effort to master this material. In the early days this poetry of death so intoxicated and excited me that I could hardly think straight. My head was seething and I had dizzy spells. Now some order has come to this volcanic eruption, the stream of lava has dug a bed for itself, and with God's help everything will go well. It will be a truly great work! Undoubtedly I will be charged with striving for novelty, because I am trying to express *truth*, from which, in my opinion, both Mozart and Cherubini frequently deviated. I am writing terrifying combinations of sounds, which have never been tried before....

And 30 years later, on January 11, 1867, he wrote to a friend: "If everything I had ever written was to be burned, except for a single work, I would plead for my Mass for the Dead."

The effect of the *Requiem* must have been stunning. Berlioz himself recalled in his memoirs:

The memorial service attracted all of Paris: the Paris of the opera, of the Théâtre des Italiens, the crowd that attends openings at the race track, of the balls at M. Dupin's, and the high society around Mr. de Rothschild.... The impression was overpowering.... The curé of the Invalides wept at the altar; after the ceremony was over, he embraced me tearfully.... The terror at the moment of the "Last Judgment," produced by the five orchestras and timpani accompanying the "Tuba mirum," was indescribable... It was really both frightening and grandiose.

Discussion of the Work: The first movement begins with a motive in soft, slow crescendo, ascending step by step. The basses of the chorus enter with a muted "Requiem aeternam." The tenors counter it with a chromatically descending motive, separated by eloquent pauses between the syllables, like sobs that interrupt the flow of tears; this is repeated in the other parts. The tenors, divided into two parts, sing a tender, melodic motive with the words "Dona eis...." The movement then arrives at its full strength and momentum, and the voices enter fortissimo with a fugue on "Requiem aeternam. . . ." Now we hear the main motive, its call ringing out in relays, interrupted by the mystical sounds of "et lux perpetua. . . ." The finale of this section is of overpowering beauty, the basses murmuring like a choir of monks chanting in some dim chapel, the countermelody descending chromatically, pleading: finally a crescendo, an outcry, and then a quiet "rest in peace."

The next section, the "Dies irae," is marked by somber magnificence. This is the movement that stimulated so many composers to enlist the ultimate in musical resources, and understandably so—but no one approached Berlioz, not even Verdi, 30 years later. Indeed, this part of the Mass was somehow especially meaningful to Berlioz, for seven years earlier he had put a magnificent Dies irae into a purely instrumental work, the fifth movement of his *Symphonie Fantastique*.

The terror and dismay of Judgment Day are depicted as the terrifying end of the human race is described. It begins rather quietly with a long melody in the lower strings, with the whispered words "Dies irae" in the female voices, breathless, faltering, filled with fear. Fear mounts relentlessly in an inexorable crescendo in both voices and orchestra, until the first climax is reached. In order to fully experience this moment it is necessary to hear a well considered performance: from the four corners of the church or concert hall the four wind orchestras begin to blare forth, as if the heavens are calling out the end of the world. An abyss of death and decay seems to open. To a fortissimo chord of stunning power, a long, mighty roll is played on all 16 timpani, and the boom of the bass drum tears open the gates of hell.

The basses of the chorus—and almost 200 are needed to make themselves heard above this din—begin the "Tuba mirum." Then a short pause, as the horror of death is felt: "Mors stupebit." Once more the threat "Judicanti responsura," with thunderbolts which subside and sound again. Berlioz's imagination in sound is inexhaustible; even today, aspiring composers and choral directors study the effects he created. How quietly, how eternally wretched, is mankind mirrored in the third section, "Quid sum miser," and yet how sincere is its pleading! There is a single melodic line in the tenors, a single one in the lowest strings, and a prayerful melody in the English horns to the soft counterpoint of the bassoons.

Horror reappears in the "Rex tremendae" (No. 4); the fearful Majesty, whose glance no mortal can bear, stands before us. The voices grow more urgent: "Salve me, fons pietatis" they sing in terrible fear. But there is yet no consolation. What is there to cling to when the earth is quaking and collapsing? Then the storm passes, followed by a long, oppressive pause; is it over? Have we been condemned or saved? A whisper—"Libera me," Lord, save me! It swells, and once again, from all sides, we hear the fearful trombones. The judgment rages on, and with its last bit of strength, the movement comes to an end; softly, softly, it disappears: "Salva me, fons pietatis," Save me, O source of all pity, . . . Save me, God, only You can save me.

Berlioz formed the "Quaerens me" (No. 5) as a purely choral movement; all the instruments are still and the effect is most impressive. In the following "Lacrymosa" (No. 6) the tenors sing a sweeping, almost Italianate melody, which remains monophonic even as the female voices and, finally, the basses enter. Tension steadily increases in the melancholy basic melody in A minor: as the groups of winds enter once more, the movement again becomes dramatic, and a new climax is reached. It ends in triumph, in a shining A major, sung in unison like a hymn—in contradiction of the text, actually. The "Offertorium" (No. 7) begins even more quietly in D minor and proceeds through many changing moods. We seem to feel the same enormous excitement Berlioz experienced while composing the work. He, whose volcanic temperament never experienced periods of calm, must have been in a state of continuous exaltation as he composed the *Requiem*, but this is not the place to try to examine whether this ecstasy was religious or artistic. The "Hostias" (No. 8) is written for male chorus with various short orchestral interjections. Here, too, is another unusual sound effect: most of the interjections are of a single chord played by three flutes supported by four trombones, which begin softly, swell, and then return to piano. The following "Sanctus" (No. 9) is in the key of D-flat major, dignified, yet warm. After a short melody in the violins, four solo violins and a flute enter; they play the slow, solemn motive previously played by all the violins, now stated by the solo tenor. It is a tender movement, wreathed in magical sounds, which then, with the "Osanna in excelsis," moves on to a brilliant fugue. Each section of the chorus is supported by a string ensemble: tenors and second violins make the first entrance, basses and contrabasses follow after eight measures, and eight measures after that, the second tenors with the cellos. Then the beginning with its iridescent sounds returns ("Sanctus"), once more delineated by the soloists. The second part of the fugue follows, again with "Osanna in excelsis," and this time it is carried through to completion.

Now the conflict is over, all battles have been fought, and the "Agnus Dei" begins softly, with long chords. Earlier passages are cited, as though recalling past sorrows, but also past consolation.

Once more the musical structure becomes lively and the chorus gains in strength and expression. Finally, the "distant orchestras" come into play once more, bringing reconciliation to the work, one of the most imposing of Western music. Whether it should be ranged among the most soulful manifestations of religious art is a question we cannot answer. But the nature of true faith is beyond arguing.

The Damnation of Faust

Original Title: La Damnation de Faust. Légende dramatique, Op. 24.
Original Language: French; the chorus of students, Latin.
Text: By Hector Berlioz, with the help of Almire Gandonnière. Based upon the medieval legend of Dr. Faustus, and very freely based on Goethe's *Faust.*
Date of Writing: Mostly during his second concert tour through Austria, Hungary, Bohemia, and Silesia in 1845.
First Performance: December 6, 1846, in Paris (concert version) February 18, 1893, in Monte Carlo (stage version).
Form: Oratorio in four parts with an epilogue; a total of 20 scenes.
Cast: Faust, an aging philosopher (tenor); Mephistopheles (bass); Margareta (soprano); Brander, a student (bass). Choruses of male and female citizens, students, soldiers, tavern guests, gnomes and sylphs, male and female peasants, the damned, and the spirits of heaven and hell.
Orchestra: Three flutes (with piccolo), three oboes (with English horn), two clarinets, four bassoons, four horns, two trumpets, three trombones, timpani, strings.
History of the Work: Toward the end of 1842, Berlioz for the first time freed himself from his agonizingly cramped Parisian existence and undertook a concert tour to Brussels and several German cities, where he found, to his indescribable joy, that his music was understood. The returning traveler found Paris a little more sympathetic: he conducted four concerts of his own works in 1845. He then decided to embark upon another concert tour, for he was not lacking invitations. This journey, which he undertook at the end of October, 1845, took him to Vienna, Prague, and Budapest, cities that made indelible impressions on him. It was during the course of this trip that *The Damnation of Faust* came into being. He describes the process vividly in his memoirs:

> During this voyage I began to compose my *Faust* legend, which I had been thinking about for a long time. As soon as I had decided to begin it, I also decided to write almost all of the libretto myself.... While rolling along in the old German post chaise, I tried to write the verses that would go with my music. I began with Faust's invocation to nature, trying neither to translate nor even to imitate Goethe's masterpiece, but to use as inspiration the musical substance it contained. Once started, I wrote the verses I needed as the musical ideas came to me, and I composed the score with an ease I had only rarely experienced with my other works. I wrote when and where I could—in carriages, in trains, aboard the steamer, and even in the cities, in spite of my various other obligations in connection with the concerts I was giving. Thus, in an inn in Passau, on the border of Bavaria, I wrote the introduction "Le vieil hiver a fait place au printemps" (Old winter gave way to spring). In Vienna I wrote the scene set on the banks of the Elbe, and Mephistopheles's aria "Voici des roses, de cette nuit écloses..." (Here are roses that bloomed last night) and the ballet of the sylphs. I have noted elsewhere when and how, in one night, also in Vienna, I composed the march on the Hungarian Rakoczy theme.* The extraordinary effect that it produced in Pest** persuaded me to insert it in my *Faust* score, taking the liberty of placing my hero in Hungary as the story begins, and having him watch troops of the Hungarian army cross the plain where he wanders, sunk in reverie. One German critic found it very strange that I had Faust traveling in such a place. I do not see why I should not do it, and I would not have hesitated for one moment to put him anywhere at all, if it would benefit my score. I did not feel compelled to follow Goethe's plan, and a character such as Faust could make the most eccentric kinds of journeys without offending verisimilitude. Other German critics took up this line of criticism again later, attacking me more violently because of the way I

*Prince Franz II von Rakoczy, a legendary Hungarian freedom fighter at the beginning of the 18th century.

**Then the capital of Hungary; later joined with Buda to form the city of Budapest.

modified the text and plan of Goethe's *Faust* to suit my libretto ... I was stupid enough to answer them in the foreword to *The Damnation of Faust*. I have often asked myself why these same critics did not reproach me for the libretto for my symphony *Romeo and Juliet*, which hardly resembles the immortal tragedy at all! It is probably because Shakespeare was not German. Patriotism! Fetishism! Cretinism! While strolling one evening in Pest I wrote the choral refrain for the peasants' dance in the light of a shop window. In Prague, I got up in the middle of the night to write down a song, trembling lest I forget it; it was the chorus of angels for Marguerite's apotheosis: "Remonte au ciel, âme naive" (Rise to heaven, pure soul).

In Breslau I wrote the words and music for the Latin song of the students "Iam nox stellata velamina pandit ..." After my return to France ...* I composed the great trio "Ange adoré dont la céleste image" (Adored angel, whose heavenly image). The rest was written in Paris, but always on the spur of the moment—at home, in a cafe, in the Tuilerie gardens, and even on the Boulevard du Temple....

When the work was finished, Berlioz explored ways to have it performed. He remembered how, in spite of high costs, he had made a small profit with *Romeo and Juliet*, but this time things did not turn out as well. The premiere he organized for December 6, 1846, was a failure:

I performed *Faust* twice to a half-empty hall. The fashionable Parisian public, the one that attends concerts, the one that is supposedly fond of music, remained quietly at home, caring as little for my new score as if I had been the meanest pupil at the Conservatory.... Nothing in my artistic career wounded me so deeply as this unexpected indifference.... I was ruined; I owed a great deal of money I did not have.

Very shortly thereafter, the work was performed in concert from, as it had been at the premiere in St. Petersburg, Moscow, and Berlin, but never again in Paris until after his death. *Discussion of the Work:* The musical foundation of the work is the *Eight Scenes from Goethe's Faust*, which Berlioz had already set to music in 1828; based on the poetic translation of Goethe's *Faust* (Part I) by Gérard de Nerval**. Among the many differences between Berlioz's work and Goethe's, perhaps the most significant is the fact that Goethe has his aging and then rejuvenated philosopher, after many adventures, redeemed and taken to heaven, whereas Berlioz damns him, as the title says, to hell, a much more interesting place than heaven to the French composer. He had always felt an affinity for the "demonic and satanic" (Werner Oehlmann); the unearthly orchestral colors in his music, never before tried, were ideal for ghosts and spirits. The piece begins with Faust contemplating nature; the aria changes to more philosophical observations but retains its bucolic background. It leads to the chorus of peasants, whose bright, happy melody interrupts the scholar at his studies. But this charming scene gives way to warlike sounds: to the proud strains of a splendid military march, troops march off to war (Example 1). It is the national anthem of Hungary, the *Rakoczy* March, which Berlioz orchestrated for a concert in Budapest and now inserted into this dramatic legend for its stirring effect, thereby providing a Hungarian setting, which had never before been used for the Faust legend.

In the second part the scene shifts to northern Germany; Faust pores over his books and recognizes the futility of his existence. Here Berlioz follows Goethe closely. Faust seizes a beaker of poison and is about to drink it when suddenly, instead of dramatic music, we hear a distant chorus singing pious Easter music. Faust recalls his childhood and, deeply moved, adds his voice to the lovely chorus of the devout. Suddenly Mephistopheles, announced by a rapid sequence of chromatic chords, stands before him (Example 2). His first words, in recitative accompanied by a dynamically varied tremolo in the strings, are cutting and ironic. (A comment is important here: Berlioz wrote the role of Mephistopheles not only for bass, but also wrote a variation for baritone, with considerable differences in the melodic line).

The next scene takes place in "Auerbach's cellar" in Leipzig, where songs sung by a male chorus set the tone. If sung in a straightforward manner, the songs lose the intended effect: they must be sung as a parody, expressing the repugnance Faust feels for these drunken gamblers and habitues of common tastes. Brander's song is also intended as a parody, for it is no elegant couplet but rather a coarse, plodding chanson, very effective in its way. Its refrain is bellowed or howled by

---

*Berlioz spent a few weeks on an estate near Rouen.

**1808–55; "literary child prodigy, eccentric, dabbler in the occult, globetrotter, adventurer, drug addict, suicide" (Sigrid Metken).

the chorus. But the disgusting, macabre scene is not yet over. The rage such people aroused in Berlioz is almost tangible. The "rat" Brander sings about deserves an "honorable" burial. The drunken crowd, now barely up to it, sings a four-part fugue with a single word as the text: "Amen." Here we have several parodies at once: of Baroque music (of which Leipzig had been an important center) but now mocked by the hollow, textbook fugue; and perhaps also of Berlioz himself, who often worked fugues into his great religious works. He was always inclined to take an ironic, often almost self-deprecating view of himself.

The character of the music changes as Mephistopheles enters into the proceedings. His "Song of the Flea," clever and witty, far surpasses the songs usual in this tavern. But Faust is weary of this scene. Is this all the visitor from hell can offer him? He longs for youth, but not for that of these dull-witted carousers.

The third act takes place in a lovely meadow on the banks of the Elbe, a veritable garden of love.

The third act takes place in a lovely meadow on the banks of the Elbe, a veritable garden of love. It brings to mind Wagner's almost contemporary creation of the kingdom of love of the goddess Venus in *Tannhäuser:* the shimmering orchestral brilliance, the sensual mood, the distant chorus. Mephistopheles lulls Faust to sleep with a melodious aria, and an image of the lovely Margareta appears to him in his dreams. The scene closes with a dance of the sylphs, one of the composer's most elfinlike inspirations, full of ethereal magic, perhaps the most often performed part of the entire work (Example 3). Then we find ourselves in the city, with its sounds of soldiers marching by, students singing a song in Latin, and finally, a chorus of citizens. The whole, colorful scene comes to life in the mind's eye of the listener. It might seem that a concert performance cannot convey the vividness of such a scene as clearly as one that is staged, but in this work, the opposite is true; nowhere does Berlioz's music seem so dramatic, so able to create pictures in the mind, as here. The same holds true for the scene that follows: Faust sings an expressive aria on entering Margareta's house. The odd, chromatic shift (No. 2) announces, like a *Leitmotif*, the arrival of Mephistopheles, who gives Faust some final advice before allowing him to join Margareta. The maiden enters in all her loveliness, sunk in thought, singing the song of "The King of Thule." Berlioz calls it simply "A Gothic song," supported by archaic orchestral sounds and melodic turns. The low tessitura of this song indicates that Berlioz originally had a mezzo-soprano in mind for the role.

Margareta falls asleep, and Mephistopheles conjures up dancing spirits and will-o'-the-wisps, which Margareta sees in her dreams. As she awakens she sees Faust, and they sing an intimate love duet—in no way different from a scene in an opera. The hour of love passes too swiftly; Mephistopheles interrupts it as the idyll has been discovered, and mocking, scolding neighbors are on their way. A theatrical finale: the lovers' duet disappears dreamily while the coarse voices of cruel daily life combine with that of Mephistopheles, now certain of victory, in one magnificent,

Example 1

Example 2

oppressive tonal image. The next scene shows Margareta pondering her experience. With mounting passion the maiden sings a song of longing ("D'amour, l'ardente flamme"—The ardent flame of love), which approximates Goethe's text, and then the lament, often set to music, "Meine Ruh ist hin, mein Herz ist schwer" (My peace is gone, my heart is heavy) in which Berlioz departs occasionally from Goethe's verses. Margareta sits alone, full of longing, set apart from the soldiers and students singing merry songs outside her window. With a deep sigh and the melody heard as the scene opened (Example 4), played by the English horn, the scene closes.

The title of the next scene is "Invocation to Night," opening with a long monologue by Faust, interrupted by Mephistopheles who lurks nearby. Finally Faust, gripped by feelings of guilt for Margareta's unhappy plight, asks that time stand still to atone for his actions. That is exactly what Mephistopheles has been waiting for—it is the sign of his victory. Now Faust's soul belongs to him. Their journey to hell begins; Berlioz, master of sound, has the orchestra and chorus of spirits rage in a way heard at that time only in Wagner's *The Flying Dutchman*. During the frenzied ride to the underworld they pass through the stages of Faust's life, but the forms have grown vague; they plunge on into the deepest abyss, into the dark realm of Mephistopheles with its raging devils. A narrator (or male chorus), without orchestral accompaniment, introduces the final transfiguration. As a chorus of seraphs sings, heaven opens and Margareta ascends to eternal blessedness.

Te Deum

Original Title: Te Deum, Op. 22
Original Language: Latin
Text: Ambrosian hymn of praise "Te Deum laudamus" from the 4th century.
Date of Writing: 1848–49
First Performance: April 30, 1855, in the church of St. Eustache, Paris.
Form: In six parts: 1. Te Deum (hymn); 2. Tibi omnes (hymn); 3. Dignare (prayer); 4. Christe, rex gloriae (hymn); 5. Te ergo quaesumus (prayer); 6. Judex crederis (hymn and prayer).

In the original version the Te Deum included two additional movements: a "Prelude" (after No. 2) and as a finale, a "Marche pour la présentation des drapeaux" (March for the Presentation of the Flags). Neither movement, written for victory celebrations and other military ceremonies, is performed today because they are not considered an integral part of the work.
Scoring: Solo tenor, two mixed choirs (three-part, in the French manner: sopranos, tenors, and basses), unison children's chorus; four each flutes, oboes, clarinets, bassoons, horns, trumpets, and cornets; six trombones, two tubas, a powerful percussion section (timpani, bass and side drums), cymbals, strings, organ.
Performance Practice: The composer wrote in the score:

The orchestra and the choirs must be placed at the farthest end of the church facing the great organ. If the conductor has no metronome to keep exact time with the organist, there must be a "time beater"* on the organ platform who can see the conductor's movements and imitate them, communicating them directly to the organist; otherwise the organist's tempos will continually lag. The children's choirs, as large as possible, must be isolated from the two other choirs, on a raised platform not far from the orchestra. There must be two or three choral directors to direct the choirs and transmit the conductor's tempos to them. The third, the children's choir, can be dispensed with if necessary, although it contributes considerably to the effect. If the work is to be performed in a large concert hall or in a theater lacking an organ, a harmonium may be used instead.

History of the Work: The last 20 years of Berlioz's life are compressed into a single chapter of his memoirs: the later addenda deal largely with an encounter with a woman with whom he had been in love in his youth. Little is said about the *Te Deum*. As a consequence the events surrounding it must be reconstructed from other sources.

At the end of October 1848, Berlioz conducted a concert at Versailles, but received little encouragement from the new court of Prince Louis Napoleon—later President and Emperor Napoleon III. On April 15, 1849, for the first time since 1833, the Conservatory put one of Berlioz's works on its concert program: two parts from *The Damnation of Faust*. Ignored by officialdom and the city's music establishment Berlioz felt increasingly isolated in Paris. In response, he founded in 1850 his own "Société Philharmonique," which, with a membership of two hundred vocalists and instrumentalists, commenced operations on February 19, 1850. Spurred on by the prospects of such an ensemble, he began to compose a great religious work—the opera seemed totally closed to him—in the style of his mighty *Requiem*, which was slowly gaining favor. In April he was appointed to the position of curator of the Conservatory library, a very lowly position in Parisian musical circles. Despite his own musical organization, performance of the *Te Deum*, which was probably finished by the end of 1850, proved impossible.

He composed *L'Enfance du Christ*, which was performed for the first time on December 10, 1854, but no opportunity to perform the *Te Deum* had yet arisen. At last a handful of friends got together and arranged to give this difficult work a hearing. Thanks to their efforts, the premiere was held in the church of St. Eustache on April 30, 1855. Nearly 1,000 performers were mustered, of which 600 were children, making a mighty chorus indeed. The performance made a deep impression, just as had the *Requiem*, but additional performances were few and far between.

Russia took to the work early on; there, the young Mily Balakirev, founder and leader of the "Group of Five" and pioneer of a national school of music, performed the *Te Deum* several times. It became a kind of article of faith for the young Russian school who saw in Berlioz one of the great masters of all time. Berlioz dedicated the work to Prince Albert, husband of the English queen Victoria; he donated the autograph to the imperial library in St. Petersburg. On the subscription list for the printing were the names of the English royal couple, the Czar and his mother, the King of Belgium, five German kings, the Emperor of Austria (who sent a diamond ring), but only a single French minister. Seldom has the saying that prophets are not honored in their own countries been so painfully apt as in the case of Berlioz.

Discussion of the Work: In a letter to his friend Liszt in Weimar, Berlioz told of the first performance of the *Te Deum*, describing it as a "scene out of the apocalypse." "This gigantic fresco, this jutting pyramid of eternal praise can be understood in no other way" (Hans Kühner). The inspiration for the composer's conception was purportedly the solemn moment when Napoleon I, still consul of the French Republic, returned home triumphantly from the Italian campaign and entered the cathedral of Notre Dame. Perhaps it was this vision that marked the work with a greatness even his enemies could not deny.

The first part, entitled "Hymn," begins with an interchange between mighty chords in the winds supported by timpani and the full organ. The choirs then embark on a double fugue, with increasingly dense textures, accompanied by an increasingly sonorous orchestral accompaniment. The second piece is also called "Hymn," beginning with a long, lyrical organ introduction; the sopranos enter singing "Tibi omnes angeli" to the accompaniment of the winds in a high register, creating a truly heavenly, angelic vision. This movement, too, mounts gradually and organically above the call of "Sanctus" to a tutti with "Pleni sunt coeli," which reaches a climax drowned out by

---

*Berlioz writes "batteur de mesure" which implies a lesser function than "conductor."

thundering drums and clanging cymbals. Softly, the organ takes up the broken threads once more; the tenors in both choirs continue the "Sanctus, sanctus," while the music mounts again to a climax, breaking off once more with drum strokes and cymbals. Again Berlioz begins with the soft sound of the organ to build an extended, tension-filled passage of mounting intensity, which culminates for the third time in the monumental, "apocalyptic" stroke. Finally there is a wonderful, quiet concluding phrase in the orchestra, reduced to a sigh in the organ's final passage.

The third movement begins calmly with two expressive organ measures, which, interrupted by pizzicati in the strings, form an eight-bar melody. At the same time the sopranos of the choir begin to sing tenderly, in a whisper; the basses interject their "Domine" as the sopranos and tenors add intensity with a melodious, free canon. By piling up voices and orchestral forces Berlioz creates another of those mounting intensities characteristic of this work. Is this why some say it is theatrical? But the climax does not endure and is much less dramatic than in the following "Tibi omnes."

The next movement, the fourth, rises again in a hymn; the third had been subtitled "Prayer." Christ in all his glory is presented by Berlioz in another colossal outburst of sound. It gives way in a somewhat slower transitional passage ("Ad liberandum") to lyrical tones sung by soloists from the choir. A new, lengthy upswing begins as tempo I returns, leading to the ardent outcry "Christe, rex! Rex gloriae" with which the movement ends.

Another prayer follows: "Te ergo quaesumus," No. 5. This is the only solo movement in the work. A tenor intones a tender melody which the violins have already sung to him as if from the clouds. The only accompaniment is the restrained women's choir. From G minor Berlioz modulates to G major, from gloomy pleading to radiant hope ("Speravimus in te"). The solo voices become more lively, full of exultation, higher, after which the choir sings (in eight parts, ppp) a soft, whispered conclusion.

"Hymn and Prayer" is the title given the sixth part ("Judex crederis"). It begins with solemn organ sounds; the choral entrances are majestic. With "Salvum fac populum tuum" there is a change: the voices become pleading, but the movement moves on through many moods before returning to the grandeur of the beginning. Then, in an ecstasy of religious feeling, it goes on through a number of climaxes to its conclusion in a blaze of trumpets.

The Childhood of Christ

Original Title: L'Enfance du Christ. Trilogie sacrée, Op. 25
Original Language: French
Text: Hector Berlioz
Form: Oratorio (sacred trilogy), in three parts
      1. "Le Songe d'Hérode" (Herod's Dream), six scenes
      2. "La Fuite en Egypte" (The Flight into Egypt), one scene
      3. "L'Arivée à Sais" (The Arrival at Sais), two scenes
Date of Writing: Begun in 1850 with "La Fuite en Egypte"; continued in 1853 with "L'Arivée à Sais"; completed in 1854 with "Le Songe d'Hérode".
First Performance: "La Fuite en Egypte" was first performed in Paris on November 12, 1850, as an "Oratorio by Pierre Ducré." The entire work was heard for the first time, under Berlioz's name, on December 10, 1854, also in Paris.
Cast: Narrator (tenor), Mary (soprano), Joseph (baritone), Herod (baritone), Polydor (bass), a Roman centurion (tenor), a patriarch (bass); four-part mixed chorus.
Orchestra: two flutes, two oboes, English horn, two each clarinets, bassoons, horns, and trumpets; three trombones, timpani, strings.
History of the Work: In 1767, Jean-Jacques Rousseau noted in his famous *Dictionnaire de Musique* that there were no French oratorios. As a matter of fact, it seems that Berlioz's teacher, Jean-François Lesueur (1760–1837) was the one who introduced this genre to his country with his composition *La mort d'Adam,* among others.* This work must have had a profound effect on Berlioz, because

---

*There are some earlier French oratorios, such as those by M. A. Charpentier, 1634–1704. Ed.

even though his operatic talent is questioned by some, his supreme mastery of dramatic concert works requiring no recourse to the stage (*Requiem, Te Deum, La Damnation de Faust, L'Enfance du Christ*) is not.

The last named is truly a "sacred oratorio," in the style then popular in Germany. Berlioz emphasizes this relation by the use of a Narrator, a successor to the old Italian *Testo* and to the Evangelists in the Passions. Apparently Berlioz had carried the idea for such a work in his head for some years—a work in which he could create a variety of moods to express an increasingly perceptible mystical preoccupation.

He began the composition with a chorus of shepherds, which in turn was to become the first song of the second section. He combined archaic harmonies with an extremely simple choral texture. Perhaps it was this achievement which gave him the odd idea to perform the scene in Paris, in 1850, long before the other parts had been composed, claiming it was a 17th-century piece by an unknown composer named Pierre Ducré which he had discovered. Why did he do this? Was it to take revenge against the Parisian audiences who had so often disappointed him? Was it a trap set for the music critics of the press who, in spite of the old saying that crows do not scratch each other's eyes out, usually treated him very badly? Or was it simply an effort to discover the effect such music would have? The deception passed unnoticed; it was nothing to be proud of for public, press, or composer. Audiences were generally indifferent; Ducré was not much of a discovery. Berlioz described the episode in his memoirs, half jokingly, half in anger.

On the other hand the real premiere, which took place more than four years later, was one of the most warmly received of Berlioz's Paris performances.

Discussion of the Work: The oratorio begins with a short "announcement" by the Narrator in a recitative accompanied by the orchestra. Then the drama begins and, guided by Berlioz's scenic directions, it almost seems as if we were attending a theatrical production. "Street in Jerusalem, Roman soldiers on their nightly rounds." There is a long, soft horn call in the distance over low pizzicati in the strings, making us think of a patrol marching nearer. The leader of the troop meets an old comrade who he thought was in Rome, but who now serves King Herod, for the King's fear grows daily and he requires the constant presence of his men. The soldiers continue their nightly patrol, and we hear their footsteps receding in the distance.

The second scene takes place in Herod's palace, where the king wanders distracted: he has dreamed of the child again, the one who will lead to his fall and his death. These confused and baleful thoughts are expressed in one of the great arias of the work. He commands the elders and soothsayers of the Jewish people to assemble, recounts his fearful dream, and demands their assistance. The cabbalistic processions and invocations are accompanied by a quite uncanny music: Berlioz is in his element with anything having to do with the mystical and the extrasensory. The mysterious music is written in seven-four time, a meter almost never used at the time and whose unevenness reflects the ghostly mood of disquiet and disarray. Mysteriously, in the lowest bass register, the wisemen whisper to the king the meaning of his dream and offer their advice: Because he is threatened by an infant, all the newborn babies of the Israelites must be killed. Raging wildly, Herod agrees, and in a four-part male chorus the soothsayers emphasize the soundness of his cruel decision.

The scene changes to Bethlehem. Mary sings a lullaby by her child's cradle. Joseph joins in to form a lovely duet full of natural poetry and happy feelings. A chorus of angels (women's and children's voices) calls to them, accompanied by the soft sounds of the organ, revealing to them the deadly danger overhanging their child, and advising them to flee secretly to Egypt. With a bright, hopeful "Osanna!," the chorus of angels brings the first part to an end.

There is a long orchestral prelude to the second part, "The Flight into Egypt," after which we hear the shepherds' chorus referred to earlier, bidding a fond farewell to the holy family. There is an aura of bucolic peace surrounding the events. A tender orchestral introduction accompanies the fleeing family as they prepare for their first night's rest. The Narrator describes the road taken and the beautiful spot chosen, carpeted by soft, green grass full of flowers, which "the Lord created for them in the midst of the desert." As they prepare to sleep, a distant chorus of angels sings "Hallelujah".

At the beginning of the third part, the "Arrival in Sais," the Narrator describes the events of the journey: After three days in the desert, the faithful donkey died; Joseph often fell; only Mary walked on in peace and tranquility, carrying her golden-haired child in her arms. Finally she, too, weakened, and it was only with the most desperate effort that they reached Sais, a city of the Roman Empire "full of cruel and haughty people." The completely exhausted couple went from house to house in the huge city but were everywhere harshly turned away as beggars. Mary and Joseph take turns asking for shelter, the last time, summoning the last bit of strength, at a wretched hut. They are taken in and the patriarch, an Ismaelite, welcomes them heartily. He and the others who live in the house gather with their children and in a choral fugue come to the aid of the pitiful refugees.

The mood is now one of love and hope. The guests rest and are looked after. The young Ismaelites sing a trio with two flutes and a harp, which turns into an enchanting, floating, dancelike piece. A joyful conclusion by the whole ensemble—Mary, Joseph, the patriarch, chorus, and orchestra—brings the drama to a close. But the work is not over; in an epilogue the Narrator hints at the fate that awaits the child. Ten years after being saved by heathens, Jesus returned to his native land with his parents to meet his destiny. The chorus piously reflects on the human soul which, with the help of the miracle of Jesus, will enter into eternal heavenly grace. With a multipartite whispered "Amen" the work comes to an end.

Leonard Bernstein 1918–

After Gershwin, Bernstein is the most American of all American musicians. A conductor of the first rank; an enthralling interpreter of music for children (at his exciting matinee concerts in New York) and students (at Harvard University); and a thoroughly intelligent musician (his books deal with real and important musical problems in a way that is understandable and pleasantly undidactic). Above all he is a composer who has something new and revolutionary to say; he does not experiment with sound—he is completely indifferent to theories but rather has blazed a new direction in music.

He has set high goals for his music. He is concerned with the deepest questions facing mankind today, questions of belief and love, brotherhood and peace. With the musical *West Side Story* he created a new kind of music theater, writing brilliant music for a drama of the underworld as it is played out every day and became a bitter commonplace in modern cities. But a new hope arises out of this tragedy. Bernstein believes in mankind and has expressed this faith nowhere as clearly as in his *Mass*. He calls this Mass a "theater piece," but the action is only hinted at; rather, it grows out of the words, sound, and imagination: it has been written to make itself felt without images, so that its full effect can be comprehended by radio or on records.

Prior to 1971 neither an opera house nor a concert hall worthy of the name existed in Washington, D.C. President Eisenhower set plans for such a structure in motion. Before its completion, President Kennedy was assassinated. His widow suggested that the new hall be named the "John F. Kennedy Center for the Performing Arts" and that it be inaugurated with a work by an American composer. Bernstein received the commission for which he wrote the *Mass*, performed there for the first time on September 8, 1971. Performances in Philadelphia followed, and in New York the Metropolitan Opera played it continuously from June 28 to July 22, 1972. In 1973, an outstanding student production originating at Yale University toured Europe.

Soon, despite the difficulties presented by its American slang, the text was translated into several other languages. It was sung in Swedish in Malmö. On February 16, 1981, the first production in German was given at the Vienna State Opera. The translation was done by Marcel Prawy, who wrote the following program notes:

> One after the other, several voices begin the Kyrie. They are not together. Is it that their hearts are not close? A young man with a guitar, that magical instrument of youth, interrupts the chaos to praise God with a simple song. He is presented with liturgical garments by the others and begins to teach the word of God as a celebrant. A church choir sings the Mass. The young people are clearly believers, but during the course of the Mass we learn of their thoughts, questions, reservations, and cynicism. Despite these difficulties the celebrant manages to keep these diverse groups together in their faith, for a time. But then he loses the trust of the young people because he cannot help them in their search for faith. A transformation, a Transubstantiation, starts to develop. With "Dona nobis pacem" he feels that he is not equal to the task. Now all the people turn against him, and he, too, is tormented by doubt. He collapses, madly smashing the holy vessels, and ripping his vestments to shreds. This dramatic episode is followed by a long, meditative pause. The celebrant is transformed back into a young man once more, one among many, as at the beginning. With the closing chorale, all discover themselves as pilgrims seeking their way to God.

Bernstein used the text of the Latin Mass (with its Greek insertions) for the church choir. The Sanctus is in Latin and Hebrew. The text sung by the youths is in English, largely written by Bernstein with help from Stephen Schwartz. In the sequence "The Word of the Lord," Paul's second letter to Timothy, his first to the Corinthians, and the first letter of John are quoted; in addition, letters from an American conscientious objector to his parents and from his wife after her first visit to him in prison are also quoted. Here Bernstein is probably referring to his encounter with the Jesuit priest Daniel Berrigan who was jailed for destroying draft records in 1968. The composer mixes all the musical forms current at the time: symphonic and choral music in the actual Mass, and rock, jazz and indeed dances for the group of young people. In addition the Southern folksong "Simple Song," blues and deliberately alien sounds of various kinds are used. In one place Beethoven's Ninth Symphony is quoted ("Ihr stürzt nieder, Millionen? Ahnest du den Schöpfer, Welt?"—Are you crashing down, all you millions? Do you know your creator, World?) It is a thoroughly colorful mosaic intended to mirror our times. An ideal performance would result if the performers did not play a role but rather played themselves, identifying completely with their roles.

Bernstein's message is that every human being is a part of God; there is no higher meaning in life. This Mass is the plea of a believer, whose burning hope is for the salvation of the world.

Boris Blacher   1903–1975

Boris Blacher, a German composer of Baltic ancestry, born in China, is perhaps not one of greatest composers of his time but rather one who greatly inspired others. His music, always intelligent and technically interesting, sprang not from feeling but rather from a cool intellect. He lived in Berlin, where in 1938 he was a professor at the Hochschule für Musik and in 1953 became its director, succeeding Werner Egk. His compositions were performed remarkably often during his lifetime, but few have been presented since his death. Nevertheless, a number of his works deserve lasting consideration; some of them fall within the gambit of this book. One is the Cantata *Träume vom Tod und vom Leben*, which he composed in 1955 to a text by the Alsatian painter, sculptor, and writer Hans Arp (whose fantastic visions also inspired other contemporary musicians, including Wladimir Vogel).

The oratorio *Der Grossinquisitor* is one of his major works. This figure, for whom the world can find no civilized name, whose features are not those of a human being, but who is yet the representative of the summit of worldly and ecclesiastical power in the waning days of the Middle Ages, plays an interesting role in music. Perhaps the most unforgettable is found in Verdi's opera *Don Carlos*, where, in an almost ghostly scene, the inquisitor puts the mightiest emperor in the world in his place. Luigi Dallapiccola, too, created a frightening inquisitorial role in *Il Prigionero*. In his oratorio, Blacher uses the character created by Dostoyevsky. This Grand Inquisitor, whose inhumanity exceeds belief, has his bailiffs arrest Jesus, who has returned to earth and, as during his first sojourn on earth, goes about healing the sick, raising the dead, and preaching love and peace among men. He is condemned to death because his appearance conflicts with established religious belief. Blacher created a terrible and magnificent role for this figure, whose dramatic and vocal opportunities remain attractive to many top-ranking baritones. The chorus, which incorporates all the other roles, including the "People" and the "Narrator," plays opposite him.

More than 10 years later, Blacher composed his *Requiem* (1959, Op. 58, for solo soprano and baritone, mixed chorus with as many as eight parts, and orchestra), which clearly shows his musical development. The music of this work is less traditional, based upon mathematical relationships and as "objective" as a laboratory report. Yet this music produces extreme tension and evokes emotions capable of touching the spirit of 20th-century man.

Howard Leake Boatwright   1918–

After an early career as a concert violinist, Howard Boatwright turned to composition. Following study with Hindemith, he received an appointment to the faculty at Yale and went on to become Dean of the School of Music at Syracuse University. His compositions include over 30 works for chorus.

The Passion According to Saint Matthew (1962) ranks high among Boatwright's large choral compositions.

The Passion According to Saint Matthew

Original Language: English
Text: From the Gospel of Matthew
Date of Writing: 1962
First Performance: April 28, 1962, at St. Thomas Episcopal Church, New Haven, Connecticut.
Form: Cast in the traditional baroque mold, this work uses an Evangelist to narrate in simple recitative and designated characters to enact the story. The chorus sings 11 well-placed, reflective hymns and numerous short passages in which it acts as the multitude or the High Priests. There are no large, reflective choruses.
Discussion of the Work: Two verses of the hymn "Go to Dark Gethsemane" by the chorus begin the oratorio in a dark, contemplative mood. The Evangelist (tenor) narrates the account of Christ's arraignment before Pilate in a combination of unaccompanied chant and accompanied recitative to which the chorus responds with the chorale "Ah, Holy Jesus, how hast Thou offended." Judas betrays Christ, confessing his guilt in a brief six-measure arioso, and the crowd responds with a polyphonic chorus of the same length (Example 1). [Musical examples Copyright 1967 by E. C. Schirmer Music Company, Boston. Used by permission.] Again the chorus reflects on the meaning of this event with the chorale "Who was the Guilty?" A pattern of narration and dramatic action, followed by a reflective hymn, is established at this point as the basic formal plan for the work.

Example 1

Disposition of the betrayal money is the subject of the next episode; the chorus responds with two verses of "For Sins of Heedless Word and Deed." Pilate's trial of Jesus is set entirely in recitative. The Evangelist narrates and prepares for entrances of the dramatic characters, here and in all episodic sections. A joyous hymn, "All praise to Thee," is an atypical response to this scene, as Pilate calls for Barabbas or Christ to be crucified, but it serves to deepen the spirituality of this work by reflecting on the religious significance of the moment rather than the event itself. After this hymn, Pilate calls again upon the crowd. It demands Barabbas and cries out for the death of Jesus (Example 2). At the end of this episode, the Evangelist reports, "he delivered him to be crucified."

Example 2

Here the chorus sings the beautiful polyphonic motet "Alone thou Goest Forth, O Lord," a departure from the homophonic chorale settings. Its gentle, plaintive lines express the suffering and rejection of the condemned Savior (Example 3). Jesus is mocked—"led away to be crucified"—and, again, the choral response transcends the mere role of reflection, offering a majestic hymn of praise: "The Royal Banners Forward Go." The true import of this tragic event is envisioned in the line "the cross shines forth in mystic glow."

Example 3

The Evangelist narrates the crucifixion scene in a syllabic recitative style, using a melisma only to express an outpouring of grief and anguish in the final moment (Example 4).

Example 4

As in many famous Passion settings, the sublime strains of the passion chorale, "O Sacred Head, Sore Wounded" are heard at this particular point. Immediately, onlookers mock Jesus in the most extended choral section of the work, with angry, derisive imitative passages and declamatory chords.

> Thou that destroyest the temple in three days, save Thyself. He saved others, Himself he cannot save. (Example 5)

Using a setting based on the medieval melody *Guidetti*, the choir sings Isaac Watts' immortal Passion hymn, "When I Survey the Wondrous Cross." The evangelist describes the scene as Jesus calls from the cross "My God, My God, why hast Thou forsaken Me," and dies. The hymn "Jesus, all Thy labor vast" is woven into a liquid polyphonic setting in response to Christ's sacrifice on the cross.

> May Thy life and death supply
> Grace to live and grace to die.

Example 5

Example 6

Events following the crucifixion are condensed by the Evangelist into a small musical space of some 20 measures. A sublime choral passage follows, enclosing the Centurion's telling words within the warm, hushed polyphonic frame (Example 6). Contrary to tradition, Boatwright's setting of the Passion concludes triumphantly, with the hymn "Sing My Tongue, the Glorious Battle." This work is suitable for both concert performance and worship.

—Thurston Dox

Johannes Brahms   1833–1897

Johannes Brahms was born May 7, 1833, in one of Hamburg's most modest neighborhoods, son of a minor musician and his wife, who was 17 years his senior. After his first piano lessons, given by his father, he came under the wing of the capable Eduard Marxsen, who recognized his unusual gifts and who strenuously and successfully resisted turning his protege, scarcely more than a child, over to an impresario who had planned an American piano concert tour for the youth.

When barely 20, he journeyed as accompanist to a Hungarian violinist through northern Germany. In the course of these travels he visited the prominent violinist Joseph Joachim in Hannover, and in Düsseldorf, on September 30, 1853, knocked at the door of the revered Robert Schumann. After Mendelssohn's death, Schumann was considered the foremost of the German Romanticists, second only to Liszt. Scarcely had the young man unfolded his few manuscripts, which he carried in his knapsack, than Schumann called out excitedly to his wife, the famous pianist Clara Wieck, "Here is some music for you; you've never heard anything like it!" He invited Brahms to stay with them, almost as another son, the eldest in a family of growing children. Schumann published in the October issue of his music journal an article singing the praises of the young musician, whom he presented as a genius, the fulfillment of all goals and dreams of the Romantics. Such an accolade was completely unheard of and could have (thanks to the heavy responsibility imputed) broken a weaker character. But Brahms went steadfastly on his busy, quiet way.

He was soon called upon to make a decision. In February 1854, Schumann attempted suicide by throwing himself into the icy waters of the Rhine, and spent the next two years in a mental institution at Endenich, near Bonn, drowsing away the last two years of his life. An unacknowledged bond had begun to develop between Brahms and his "stepmother" Clara, one that grew deeper as time went by. They traveled to Switzerland together and returned having made the decision to deny their love, but to remain friends. Brahms lived alone—but it was more than just that. His loneliness went deep into his heart; he was as lonely as Beethoven, with whom he had much in common, had been. From 1857–1859 he was court pianist and choral director in Detmold, then returned to his native city for two years, where he directed a female chorus; all of which was artistically unsatisfying. In 1862 he set out for Vienna where, after leaving for two short intervals, he settled down, making it his home. Here, too, he cultivated close contacts with various choruses; human voices enthralled him, and although he never composed an opera, he wrote a great many important and beautiful vocal works: almost 200 songs and the *Deutsches Requiem*, one of the world's greatest choral works.

Brahms's predilection for clarity and order contrasted with the ever hazier forms and colors of dying Romanticism. No matter how rapturous and dreamy his music, he was a "neo-Classicist" for whom form was of fundamental importance. He undertook extensive tours as a pianist, often playing his own works, and early on tried his hand at conducting. But his performance on the podium was far from virtuosic—the style favored during his lifetime. He was devoted to nature and to Classical civilization; he traveled to Italy eight times and spent his summers in the beautiful rural areas of Germany, Austria, and Switzerland. His works, sold and performed throughout Europe, brought him more income than his modest way of living required. This small man with the very long, full beard and solitary ways became a legendary but highly honored figure in Vienna. Almost every year which passed saw a new work from his pen. He was a sought-after guest at music festivals. His life flowed along, outwardly calm and regularly creative, a musical city at its center, an uninterrupted climb to fame, a circle of good friends. He never spoke of loneliness; but he aged surprisingly quickly. A young singer visiting him at his idyllic summer home in Thun when he was 55 years old, remarked that he would have seemed like a very old man were it not for his lovely, youthful, blue eyes. When he returned from Clara Schumann's funeral in Frankfurt, he was marked for death, which came to him in Vienna on April 3, 1897.

Ein deutsches Requiem (A German Requiem)

Original Title: Ein deutsches Requiem, Op. 45
Original Language: German
Text: Passages from the Holy Scriptures
Date of Writing: The first thoughts of a work like this probably came to him at the time of Schumann's death; first draft, 1861; he took up the composition again in 1866 and completed it in the first half of 1868.

First Performance: The first three movements on December 1, 1867 in Vienna; the first four and the last two movements on April 10, 1868, in Bremen; the complete, seven-movement work on February 18, 1869, in the Leipzig Gewandhaus.

Form: In seven parts:

1. Selig sind, die da Leid tragen (Blessed are they who mourn); chorus.
2. Denn alles Fleisch (Because all flesh . . .); chorus
3. Herr, lehre doch mich (Lord, teach me); baritone and chorus
4. Wie lieblich sind deine Wohnungen (How lovely are thy dwelling places); chorus.
5. Ihr habt nun Traurigkeit (Now you are full of sadness); soprano and chorus.
6. Denn wir haben hier (We have here); baritone and chorus
7. Selig sind die Toten (Blessed are the dead); chorus

Cast: Two solo voices (soprano, baritone); four-part mixed chorus; two flutes, one piccolo, two each oboes, clarinets, bassoons; one contrabassoon, four horns, two trumpets, three trombones, one bass tuba, three timpani, two harps, strings, organ ad libitum.

History of the Work: Probably no other composer in the history of music began thinking about a Requiem as early in life as Brahms. Not even Mozart, who was just over 35 when he received the anonymous commission to compose a Requiem, which, as we know, he was unable to finish. Ulrich Dibelius maintains that the "normal" time for composing a Requiem is "after the midlife crisis," and goes on to give supporting evidence: "Saint-Saens (age 42), Fauré (43), or Dvorak (49), if not even older, as in the case of Cherubini (56), Verdi (61), or Cavalli (ca. 70)." Berlioz was the closest to Brahms in age—he composed his Requiem when he was 34. But there were for the Frenchman other contributing factors, many of them external, whereas Brahms' motivation came from within, arising out of his melancholy disposition.

Dibelius is correct when he maintains that the horrible death of Schumann, the rejection of his application for a position in his native city of Hamburg, and the death of his mother all contributed "with mounting intensity to the emotional prerequisites" necessary for such a work. To this list must be added his painful experience with Clara, which must have caused a "deep confusion of emotions" (Stefan Zweig) in the soul of this young man—so inclined to loneliness, yet so longing to escape it—which led even to thoughts of death. Soon after Brahms had settled in their city, the Viennese, who so delighted in mockery, began circulating a witticism by the concert master of the Philharmonic, Joseph Hellmesberger, their favorite joker, who said that when Brahms was in a particularly good mood he would set to music the words, "The grave is my joy." There was a deep truth behind this remark, as the one who made it up and those who spread it probably suspected.

With the composition of the *German Requiem,* Brahms freed himself from the unbearable pressure of those trying events and painful feelings. His work was not a Mass for the Dead in the Catholic sense—there is no description of Judgment Day, no struggle between the powers of heaven and hell. Brahms, a Protestant, wrote a work of mourning and consolation for the living, for those left behind. He felt as Bach did that death had no sting but was like an older brother, a great peacemaker who opened his arms with love to receive the tired and heavy laden to lead them home to eternal rest. Thus the *German Requiem* is not a liturgical work but a freely formed, artistic confrontation with the problem of death as must be faced by all mankind.

Brahms believed in God but was not "pious" in the churchly sense. He loved the Bible and read it constantly. It was probably around 1861 that he collected the first verses for his work. The first three movements, "Selig sind, die da Leid tragen," "Denn alles Fleisch, es ist wie Gras," and "Herr, lehre doch mich," composed in 1866, were first performed at a concert of the Vienna "Gesellschaft der Musikfreunde" (Society of Friends of Music), directed by Johann Herbeck. This institution was founded in 1812—Beethoven had participated—and had come to play a central role in Vienna's musical life.

The public was not particularly enthusiastic about the new work; after the first performance, some in the audience whistled. Nevertheless, Brahms continued to work on it and shortly thereafter received an invitation to conduct it himself on Good Friday, April 10, 1868, in the Bremen cathedral. For this performance he added three new movements: "Wie lieblich sind deine Wohnungen," "Denn wir haben hier keine bleibende Statt," and "Selig sind die Toten." The performance was given in the course of a concert tour in northern Germany requiring frequent trips from Hamburg to conduct rehearsals in Bremen. Close friends came from various parts of Germany for the premiere: the Joachims from Hannover: the publisher Rieter, who first published the *German Requiem,* from Winterthur: and, at the last minute, Clara Schumann from Baden-Baden. Brahms brought his father from Hamburg. They experienced and noted the overpowering effect it had on the thousands who were in the audience.

But deep inside, the composer felt the work was not finished. Perhaps it was the visit he paid the next day to his mother's grave in Hamburg that led him to proceed with another, already planned section. With "Ihr habt nun Traurigkeit," sung by a solo soprano, he introduced a brighter sound. Then the whole, seven-part work—the new addition was put in fifth place—was performed for the first time in its entirety on February 18, 1869, in the Leipzig Gewandhaus under the direction of Karl Reinecke. The work was not received with universal approval, but 20 performances in Germany and Switzerland in that same year are incontestable proof that the work had gained acceptance. German Romanticism had been presented its greatest oratorio, a work that can take its place beside those of the older masters, a companion piece to Mozart's unfinished Latin Requiem, a work that today is an essential part of the repertoire of all great choral societies and of international concert life.

Discussion of the Work: A feeling of gentle consolation hovers over the beginning of the work, a quiet transfiguration. Out of the lowest register—a repeated, soft heartbeat in the contrabasses on the note F—a motive (Example 1) rises slowly through the cellos, the second, and the first violas to the higher registers, until the chorus enters (Example 2), emphasizing the peaceful mood with the words ". . . denn sie sollen getröstet werden . . ." (for they shall be comforted). These words from the Sermon on the Mount (*St. Matthew,* 5:4) enfold the human heart in a calm certitude that may be seen as the underlying theme of the *Requiem.* It is a deeply serious work, shadowed with wistfulness, but not informed by pain. "Die mit Tränen säen, werden mit Freuden ernten" (They that sow in tears shall reap in joy) brings movement to the voices, after which the beginning returns: the long, calm throbbing in the lowest registers, the motive No. 1, which enters here in imitation, but remains calm ("Sie gehen hin und weinen"—They go away to weep) until there is a new upswing with "Und kommen mit Freuden" (And come with rejoicing) (*Psalm* 126, 5–6), which leads to the distant key of D-flat major. In this key a reprise begins: the chorus enters pianissimo with "Selig sind, die da Leid tragen." There is much thematic work carried out in short motives, but with no real melody formed. A brief climax ("Sie sollen getröstet werden"—They shall be comforted); then, with the sounds of the harp, the music fades away.

Example 1

Example 2

The second movement is like a funeral march, although it is written in three-four time; the altos, tenors, and basses sound somber and pale as they enter in unison in the lowest registers with "Denn alles Fleisch, es ist wie Gras" (For all flesh is as grass) (*I. Peter*, 1, 24–25) (Example 3); the sopranos join in at the next entry. The music sounds archaic, like a funeral procession in a medieval city. Sometimes intensity mounts, as in "So seid nun geduldig" (Therefore be patient) (*James* 5:7) and "Aber des Herrn Wort" (But the word of the Lord), which leads to a lively canonlike passage "Die Erlösten des Herrn" (Those the Lord has delivered) (*Isaiah* 35:10). Step by step, the funereal mood is transformed into one of joy. The baritone soloist opens the third movement: "Herr, lehre doch mich, dass ein Ende mit mir haben muss..." (Teach me, Lord, that my life must end) (*Psalms* 39, 4–7). The chorus takes up the words in a deeply reverent chorale (Example 4). The voices alternate as in a responsive reading.

Example 4

Then a cry breaks through the tranquility (Example 5) and forms a recurring *Leitmotif* on the theme of the futility of man and his works. The baritone meditates upon this theme as it is taken up by the chorus. The chorus reaches a climax in an imposing fugue with a long theme: "Der Gerechten Seelen sind in Gottes Hand" (The souls of the just are in God's hand) (*Wisdom* 3:1) (Example 6).

The fourth movement paints the text in tones: "Wie lieblich sind deine Wohnungen, Herr Zebaoth!" (How lovely are thy dwellings; *Psalm* 84: 1–2, 4). It is one of those sunlit but pensive moods that so enchants us in many of Brahms's songs.

In the fifth movement, "Ihr habt nun Traurigkeit" (Ye now have sadness; *John* 16:22), a solo soprano joins the chorus, lending a bright note of gladness. The main motive in G major (Example

7), which returns later to the words "Ich will euch wiedersehen und euer Herz soll sich freuen" (I will see you again and your heart will rejoice) is a happy one. The intimate, quiet lines of the chorus "Ich will euch trösten, wie einen seine Mutter tröstet..." (I will console you as a mother would) (*Isaiah* 66:13) are a wonder to hear.

After this idyllic moment, the drama of the sixth movement seems even more intense. It sets a vision of Judgment Day before us, the time of the "last call." Here, the bitter winds of the "Dies irae" of the Catholic Mass of the Dead blow through, but the battle, described in great excitement, ends in triumph: "Tod, wo ist dein Stachel? Hölle, wo ist dein Sieg?" (Death, where is thy sting? Hell, where is thy victory?) (*I. Corinthians* 15: 51–55).

Example 5

Example 6

Example 7

And at the word "Sieg" (Victory) Brahms modulates to C major with a brilliance and radiance achieved heretofore only by Haydn on the word "Licht" (Light) in the *Creation* (Example 8). Then a concluding fugue begins, strong and splendid: "Herr, du bist würdig..." (Lord, thou art worthy...) (*Revelations* 4:11), which ends with an overpowering apotheosis on "Preis und Ehre und Kraft" (Glory and honor and power.)

Example 8

The last movement is a refrain—Brahms wrote "solemnly" above it: "Selig sind die Toten, die in dem Herrn sterben..." (Blessed are the dead who die in the Lord) (*Revelations* 14:13). A long melody for the sopranos of the chorus is answered by the basses at the fifth, but Brahms does not continue this fuguelike beginning, moving on to a compact choral movement that repeatedly presents imitative elements. As the finale approaches, the music of the first movement reappears in the chorus (Example 2): "Selig sind. . . ." The work ends tranquilly in the same F major with which it opened.

Schicksalslied/Triumphlied/Nänie

Even in his youth, Brahms had a lively feeling for vocal music. In Hamburg, and later in Vienna, he directed choruses for which he often composed. The great number of vocal compositions testify to this fondness; hundreds of songs and arrangements of folk songs for solo voices and for chorus, as well as duets, quartets, and motets. His choral works arise out of this same preoccupation: the *Schicksalslied*, Op. 54; the *Triumphlied*, Op. 55; *Nänie*, Op. 82; the cantata *Rinaldo*, Op. 50; the magnificent *Alto Rhapsody*, Op. 53; and the *Gesang der Parzen*, Op. 89. His greatest choral work, the *German Requiem*, was discussed previously. It is interesting to note that three consecutive opus numbers have been assigned to works of this genre: Op. 53 (*Alto Rhapsody*), Op. 54 (*Schicksalslied*), and Op. 55 (*Triumphlied*), which were composed in three consecutive years, 1869, 1870, and 1871. We can really include the *German Requiem* in this grouping since Brahms composed the last remaining movement in 1868, and the whole work, now seven movements long, was first performed in 1869. It should also be noted that all these choral works were composed many years before the first symphony, which he did not take up until the summer of 1876.

The text for Brahms's *Schicksalslied*, Op. 54, is based on "Hyperions Schicksalslied" from Friedrich Hölderlin's novel *Hyperion*.

> Ihr wandelt droben im Licht
> Auf weichem Boden, selige Genien!
> Glänzende Götterlüfte
> Rühren Euch leicht,
> Wie die Finger der Künstlerin
> Heilige Saiten.
> Schicksallos, wie der schlafende
> Säugling, atmen die Himmlischen;
> Keusch bewahrt
> In bescheidener Knospe
> Blühet ewig
> Ihnen der Geist,
> Und die seligen Augen
> Blicken in stiller
> Ewiger Klarheit.
> Doch uns ist gegeben
> Auf keiner Stätte zu ruhn;

Es schwinden, es fallen
Die leidenden Menschen
Blindlings von einer
Stunde zur andern,
Wie Wasser von Klippe
Zu Klippe geworfen,
Jahr lang ins Ungewisse hinab.

(You walk above in light, blessed spirits, on forgiving ground. Sparkling, divine breezes caress you gently, like the fingers of a harpist on sacred strings. No fate awaits the holy ones; they breathe like sleeping babies; chastely guarded in shy buds. Their spirit blooms forever, and their blissful eyes witness only clarity, quiet and eternity. But it is our lot to know no resting place; we, suffering mankind, with failing strength fall headlong, from one hour to the next, like water thrown from crag to crag, down through the years we fall into uncertainty).

Brahms wrote this work for four-part mixed chorus and orchestra in May, 1871, during a stay in Lichtental in Baden. It was first performed on October 18, 1871, in Karlsruhe, under the direction of the composer.

The musical form of the *Schicksalslied* stems from Hölderlin's poem, which is clearly divided into two images: the idyllic lives of the gods and the tragic uncertainty of human existence. Brahms expresses both with an almost tone-painterly quality. He compensated for the brevity of the second part by repeating many phrases, thus making the music more dramatic, greatly supported by the orchestra. Brahms gave a great deal of thought to the conclusion. In order to round off the work (as would have been done in the Classic era, ever his model) he first planned to follow the terrible pessimism of Hölderlin's conclusion with a repetition of the first part of the poem, which would result in the old A-B-A form. A draft exists clearly showing this intention. It seems that his good friend Hermann Levi (who at the time still was Hofkapellmeister in Karlsuhe, shortly before he was called to Munich, and then, in 1882, to Bayreuth to conduct the first performance of Wagner's *Parsifal*), who was thoroughly familiar with Brahms's work, discussed this problem of form with him and advised against a complete repetition of the first part. So Brahms repeated only its gentle, thoroughly melodic music for the conclusion, leaving out the chorus and text. Therefore, after repeating several times "ins Ungewisse hinab," (into uncertainty) the work ends with a wonderful transfiguration in an orchestral postlude, which brings back the lovely mood of the opening in all its sweetness. In October, 1871, Brahms wrote to the choral director of the cathedral in Bremen, Karl Martin Reinthaler, ". . . the chorus is silent in the last adagio. It is a stupid mistake or what you will, but there is nothing to be done about it. I had even gone so far as to write something for the chorus, but it did not work. It may be an experiment that fails, but to tack something on at the end would not have made sense." After the first performance, the astonished Brahms remarked, "It made quite an impression in Karlsruhe."

The origin of the *Triumphlied* is quite different, as is the work itself. It is suspect from many points of view, if not from a purely musical one. The triumph honored here is Germany's victory over France in the war of 1870–71 and the founding of the German Empire under Emperor Wilhelm I, to whom Brahms dedicated the work. In view of the general patriotic enthusiasm of the time, and Brahms's esteem for Bismarck, the "iron chancellor," this is understandable.

Wagner's inclusion of this cantata in his malicious critique of Brahms (who, without having had much to do with it, had been elevated to a sort of "Anti-Pope" to Wagner's "Pope" by a strong faction in Vienna) is of no import here. "Compose, compose, even if you haven't got an idea in your head! Why do we say 'compose'—meaning 'to put together'—when the element of invention is also necessary? But the more boring you are, the more the pretense shows; that, at least, is amusing! There are famous composers whom one might meet at concert-masquerades today costumed as a ballad singer,* tomorrow wearing Handel's Hallelujah wig,** some other time gotten up as a Jewish czardas player,*** and yet again in the guise of a solid symphonist..." wrote Wagner in the *Bayreuther Blätter*, 1879, very clearly referring to Brahms.

Rather, *Triumphlied* is suspect because words from the Holy Scriptures have been used with reference to political events of the day, and even more so since many of the Biblical passages must be very loosely interpreted in order to have meaning in the profane sense intended here. Other

---

*Reference to Brahms's *Liebeslieder Waltzer*

**Reference to Brahms's *Triumphlied*

***Reference to Brahms's *Hungarian Dances*.

texts should have been found or written. The *Triumphlied* for solo baritone, eight-part double chorus, orchestra and organ ad libitum, bears the opus number 55. Brahms began the composition in October 1870. When Wilhelm I was crowned emperor in 1871, Brahms dedicated the now finished *Triumphlied* to him: "To Your Imperial and Royal Majesty from Your Most Humble Servant Johannes Brahms." The work is in four parts and contains some magnificent music, especially in the rich choral writing. The orchestration clearly demonstrates Brahms' musical maturity—the sound is dense yet transparent, and its color has become unmistakable.

Like many other composers, Brahms had long struggled with the problem of finding texts suitable for setting to music. He wrote to his good friend Elizabeth von Herzogenberg these very revealing lines: "Try to see if you can't find some texts for me! Only the young can accept those fabricated to order; later one becomes spoiled by too much good reading. The Bible is not sufficiently pagan for me; I have just bought a copy of the Koran, but can't find anything there, either..."

He fell back again on Schiller when, deeply affected by the death in Venice in 1880 of his great friend, the painter Anselm Feuerbach, he composed a lament dedicated to the artist's mother ("Dedicated to Frau Hofrat Henriette Feuerbach"). The great German poet had included a lament in the mythological *Nänie*, which inspired Brahms to write a song of the same name for four-part mixed chorus and orchestra. Whether this text is, on the whole, well suited for music is open to question; apart from its strict meter, whose rigidity would seem to constrict the music from the beginning, the poem abounds with Greek expressions and concepts, a knowledge of which only a few very well educated listeners possess. Probably two lines particularly attracted Brahms and started his imagination working:

> Siehe, da weinen die Götter, es weinen die Göttinnen alle,
> Dass das Schöne vergeht, dass das Vollkommene stirbt...

> (See how the gods are weeping; all goddesses are weeping, because beauty fades and perfection dies...)

As in *Ein deutsches Requiem*, the pervasive mood of *Nänie* is one of sadness rather than of despair; of consolation rather than hopelessness. The piece moves from a bright D major into the powerful, but at the same time gentle and soothing F-sharp major, as the goddess Thetis rises from the river to mourn her fallen son, Achilles, with whom beauty and perfection had died. Brahms repeats these words until, with the last two lines

> Auch ein Klaglied zu sein im Mund der Geliebten ist herrlich,
> Denn das Gemeine geht klanglos zum Orkus hinab.

> (It is also glorious to be a lament on the tongue of the beloved, because all that is vile goes soundless down to Orcus.)

he returns to D major and concludes the work with the word "Herrlich," coursing over and over through all the voices, forgiving and full of love.

Nänie was composed in the summer of 1881 in Pressbaum, near Vienna, and was performed for the first time in Zurich on December 6, 1881. This was a historic moment for the Swiss city, as Hans Erismann writes:

> The Concert Society had announced an extra concert featuring works by Brahms, with the assistance of the composer himself. This concert included *Nänie*, Op. 82, for chorus and orchestra, its premiere; and Brahms played the Second Piano Concerto in B-flat Major, Op. 83, from the manuscript, for only the second time (it had been performed for the first time in Budapest on November 9). He also conducted the *Academic Festival Overture*, Op. 80, as a novelty, and closed with the Second Symphony in D Major, Op. 73.

Brahms, a "modern" composer at that time, did not reach the hearts and minds of his listeners with all of his works. Erismann quotes the review that appeared a few days later in the *Neue Zürcher Zeitung*:

> ... The choral piece *Nänie* is made of different stuff. "Even beauty must die," but where it lives, as here, in its purest, most noble form, it will outlive generations. The tones lie against the glorious words of the poet like a soft, billowing garment; it is infused with the most noble simplicity and warm, humanly beautiful sensitivity. May this work, performed here for the first time, uplift and quicken the hearts of thousands as it goes its way through the world.

Alto Rhapsody

Original Title: Rhapsodie für Altstimme, Männerchor und Orchester, Op. 53 (Rhapsody for alto, male chorus, and orchestra)

Original Language: German

Text: From the poem "Harzreise im Winter" (Journey through the Harz Mountains in Winter) by J. W. von Goethe.

Date of Writing: In the second half of 1869.

First Performance: "Dress rehearsal" in late autumn of 1869 in Karlsruhe; official premiere in Jena, March 3, 1870.

Cast: Solo alto, four-part male chorus (tenor I and II, bass I and II); two flutes, two oboes, two clarinets, two bassoons, two horns, strings.

History of the Work: Brahms's remark that this "rather intimate music" should not be printed or performed (an idea he soon gave up) lends weight to the supposition that this composition has something to do with another disappointment in love experienced by the composer, by then a famous man. It is not much consolation that once again he was his own enemy, this time due to his excessive shyness. It seems that Brahms, 15 years after his love for Clara Schumann, which resulted in a close lifelong friendship, harbored more than just friendly feelings for her daughter Julie—without ever saying a word about it to her. When, in July, 1868, the young woman, then 25 years old, became engaged to an Italian count, Clara noticed that "Johannes has changed completely, he seldom comes to visit and speaks in monosyllables, even to Julie, to whom he used to be so kind."

He began, at the same time, to set the Goethe text to music, a text that probably reflected his own bitterness and disappointment. He called the work, the *Alto Rhapsody*, a "wedding song for the countess Schumann," but added "With rage do I write this—with fury!" The work came from his soul, perhaps in the sense that Ibsen meant when he said that to write poetry was to put oneself on trial. The work was completed in a few short months. He tried it out in Karlsruhe, as he liked to do when a work had something new about it. When it was given its official premiere in Jena, on March 3, 1870, the choral society of the Academy there produced and performed it; the world-famous alto Pauline Viardot-Garcia* sang the solo.

Discussion of the Work: The orchestral prelude is painted in melancholy colors. The melody, sighing in pain, enters in the lowest instruments (bassoons, cellos, and contrabasses, in unison); then there is a chromatically descending tremolo in counterpoint to the violins and violas. We hear repeated accents depicting deep agitation, until the strings enter with a gentler, comforting passage that descends like heavenly consolation to a magnificent counterpoint in the cellos, and which drops three octaves, becoming softer and softer before it dies away.

Then the voice enters with a kind of recitative: "Aber abseits wer ist's? Ins Gebüsch verliert sich sein Pfad . . ." (But who is that off to the side? His steps disappear in the underbrush). It is the odd, winter encounter with the stranger in the Harz Mountains. Now the orchestra repeats as accompaniment what had been displayed symphonically in the prelude. A long, extremely soft note in the contrabasses fills a ghostly pause between the soloist's words "Die Öde verschlingt ihn" (The wilderness swallows him up). The tempo, slow until now, increases, developing into the three-part song "Ach, wer heilet die Schmerzen des, dem Balsam zu Gift ward? Der sich Menschenhass aus der Fülle der Liebe trank?" (Ah, who will heal the pain of him for whom balsam has become as poison? Of him who has drunk the hatred of mankind out of the cup of love?). A long, melancholy melody unfolds—pure Brahms; but it, too, contains those exceptionally wide intervals—from one to one-and-a-half octaves—characteristic of this work, probably symbols of emotional disintegration and boundless suffering.

The third part of the work opens with the male chorus in the oppressive C minor, a symbol of grief and pain since Beethoven and Mozart. But it brightens to C major with "Ist auf Deinem Psalter, Vater der Liebe, ein Ton seinem Ohr vernehmlich, so erquicke sein Herz!" (If he can hear the sound of your psaltery, father of love, then will his heart once more come to life). Here and there beams of light break through the dark clouds until finally the last rays of the sun shine on an evening landscape. Did Brahms paint the picture of his own soul in sound?

---

*Pauline Viardot was one of the two famous daughters of the great Spanish singer Manuel Garcia. Her sister, Maria Malibran (1808–1836) died at the age of 28 in a riding accident. Pauline (1821–1910) was a star at the Paris opera, revered as the greatest Orpheus (Gluck). She lived for years in Baden-Baden, where she came to know Brahms and turned her attention to song.

Gesang der Parzen (Song of the Fates)

Original Title: Gesang der Parzen, Op. 89
Original Language: German
Text: From *Iphigenie auf Tauris* by Johann Wolfgang von Goethe.
Date of Writing: In Bad Ischl, Austria, in the summer of 1882.
First Performance: December 10, 1882, in Basel, conducted by the composer.
Cast: Six-part mixed chorus (soprano, alto I and II, tenor, bass I and II); two flutes (with piccolo), two oboes, two clarinets, two bassoons, contrabassoon, four horns, two trumpets, three trombones, tuba, timpani, and strings.
History of the Work: Brahms was very well read and took texts for his songs from a great variety of poets, but his two principal sources were the Bible (for *Ein deutsches Requiem*), and Goethe (for the *Alto Rhapsody,* the *Gesang der Parzen,* and the cantata *Rinaldo,* Op. 50, for solo tenor, male chorus, and orchestra). As he grew older, however, his interest in antiquity grew. He used Schiller's classic setting for the lament *Nänie,* honoring his friend Anselm Feuerbach. Some time later he attended at the Vienna Burgtheater, the best of the German theaters producing Classical drama, a performance of *Iphigenie auf Tauris* with the great tragedienne Charlotte Wolters in the title role. Thereupon he composed a monologue based on this work, whose author he did not name in the manuscript, for some strange reason, and thus completed his triptich of "classical" choral works, which he had begun with the *Schicksalslied,* Op. 54 (based on poetry by Hölderlin) and Schiller's *Nänie.* The *Gesang der Parzen* stands oddly alone in that summer of 1882 in Ischl; all the other works produced during that happy time were cheerful and sunny: the String Quintet. Op. 88 (which has been called the "Springtime Quintet"); the Piano Trio in C major, Op. 87, and others. Those who really understand Brahms, however, are not surprised at this "relapse" into earlier dejection for he had always been a melancholy sort, one who observed life gravely and only seldom shared in its joys. But Brahms was not nearly as independent as he would have people believe. He often sought the opinion of sympathetic friends who understood music before placing it before the public. Thus after completing *Gesang der Parzen,* he sent it to Theodor Billroth, the famous physician, avid music lover, and closest of friends.

> You do not know how important and dear to me your approval is and how thankful I am for it. One knows what one is trying to do, and how badly one wants to do it right. One should also really know how well one has done, but needs to hear it from others in order to believe all favorable comment. This is the way it is with me this time; only now does this piece please and satisfy me.

Discussion of the Work: An orchestral introduction in D minor, deeply agitated in spite of the tempo prescribed (maestoso), leads to the more peaceful, rhythmic entrance of the chorus, which takes up the first orchestral theme in variation. At first, the male and female choruses sing antiphonally "Es fürchte die Götter das Menschengeschlecht! Sie halten die Herrschaft in ewigen Händen und können sie brauchen, wie's ihnen gefällt" (It is mankind's lot to fear the gods! They hold all power in their eternal hands and use it as they please). Then the orchestral theme sounds again, with great fervor, and leads to the combined forces of the mighty chorus, now in six parts.

Now Brahms describes with tone painting and uncanny realism the collision of men as they are plunged into "the blackest depths" and "wait there in vain, in bondage, in the gloom," while the gods "live lives of eternal feasting at golden tables. They stride from mountain to mountain. . . ." After dramatic descriptive passages, the opening returns: "Es fürchte die Götter das Menschengeschlecht. . . ." But the work does not end in despondency and despair in the face of human powerlessness. The concluding passage begins softly, legato, which—also in a musical reprise—although mulling over dark thoughts, seeks a conclusion of reconciliation, however modest—it has always been so, even in the time of our ancestors. The Fates, goddesses of antiquity, bring their song to an end in a muffled whisper, pianissimo: So was it, so is it, so will it always be.

Cesar Bresgen   1913–

Cesar Bresgen is one of the most spirited musicians of our time. He has not dealt with theory despite a lifelong interest in introducing young people to music; his knowledge and his works flow from experience. He views the artist as "a representative of society" (as Oskar Kokoschka said, and

Bresgen likes to quote) and feels that the task of creative people, especially in times of turmoil, is the most serious of social missions. He chooses his themes accordingly; they are related to their time, yet are timeless. More than anything else, Bresgen is a composer of vocal works who selects his literary subjects with unusual sensitivity and appreciation for their true meaning. He has set to music texts from St. Augustine and medieval poets, from Michelangelo, Eichendorff, Hans Carossa, Josef Weinheber, Georg Trakl, H. C. Artmann, and the former president of Senegal and Nobel Prize winner, Leopold S. Senghor (who wrote in French). He does not simply add music to words but deepens the meaning of the text; his music opens pathways of thought that have only been hinted at and drenches the images with shining, intimate color, always relating the word closely to the image. It is no accident that he is very gifted with language, music's sister-art. The works of this Austrian, born October 16, 1913 in Florence, make an impressive catalogue. Many of his songs have become popular, a claim few composers of his generation can make. A number of his most important works fall within the scope of this book.

During the war he wrote the oratorio *Der Strom* based on a text by Hans Baumann, for four solo voices, mixed chorus, and large orchestra. After its premiere in Vienna in May, 1944, the work was lost in the general destruction at the end of the war. In 1951, he composed the ludus tragicus *Der Wolkensteiner*, which is discussed separately. In 1955 came the mystery play *Der ewige Arzt*; in 1959, the *Christkindl-Kumedi*, a sacred play based on old, anonymous Bavarian texts, for vocal soloists, a speaker, youth chorus, and small orchestra. At Easter, 1966, the *Salzburger Passion*, for five solo voices, speaker, dancers, mixed chorus, youth chorus, and large orchestra, was given its premiere at the Festspielhaus in Salzburg; it was revised and abridged in 1982, resulting in a more oratoriolike work, the *Loferer Passion*. It, too, was performed successfully and recorded for television. *Surrexit Dominus* is the title of the resurrection oratorio he wrote in 1970 (for three solo voices, mixed chorus, brass, percussion, and organ), which was performed first in 1974 in Erl in the Tyrol. In 1972, Bresgen published a work he had begun in 1945, *Requiem für Anton von Webern* (who was shot in 1945 by an American soldier when he broke curfew, in Mittersill, Austria). In 1973, the oratorio *De Tempore* was performed for the first time in Salzburg; it will be discussed separately.

Four Masses appeared in rapid succession: the *Kleine deutsche Orgelmesse* (1969); the *Missa secunda*, also in German, for mixed chorus and organ (1970); the *Grossgmainer Kindermesse* for children's chorus, glockenspiel, and organ (1971); and the *Totenmesse*, German, based on a text by H. Oosterhuis, for mixed chorus and organ (1972). In 1984, Bresgen's important *Spiel vom Menschen* had its premiere. In 1985 the oratorio *Invocazione*, for soprano, male voices, percussion, and organ, was performed at the New Music Days in Würzburg, accompanied by the projection of 55 "sun pictures" made by P. K. Hoenisch of Haifa. Also in 1985 he composed the chamber oratorio *Lumen* (The Blind Man), based on a text by Jacques Lusseyrand, which had its premiere in the sumptuous church at Wies in Bavaria, as well as the children's cantata *Die Stadthüpfer*, for the week of children's music at the Carinthian Summer in Villach, Ossiach, Austria.

Der Wolkensteiner, called "Do frayg amors" (Of Cold Love) in an earlier version and subtitled "Visiones amantis" (roughly: Visions of Love), is a ludus tragicus—a "tragic play," something between an opera and an oratorio and performed both ways with great success: in the unstaged form in Salzburg in 1952, at the Festival of the International Society for New Music, IGNM, and staged at the Tiroler Landestheater in Innsbruck in 1971.

It is based on the story of the fateful love of the last of the Minnesänger, Oswald von Wolkenstein (who died in 1445 in his castle in the south Tyrol, an adventurer and a tough, old soldier, but a greater poet) for Melusine, an enigmatic, fairylike creature. He fell under her spell, and when he wanted to leave her, found he could no longer do so. The operatic literature is full of works based on similar subjects, but Bresgen's interpretation differs from those of Lortzing, Dvorak, Respighi, Henze, and Reimann, to name a few. He finds an archaic, medieval tone and yet is contemporary; he is not a Romantic, yet arouses the deepest feelings. He uses the form of the "report," which puts him in the company of such contemporaries as Stravinsky (Oedipus Rex), Frank Martin (Le vin herbé), and Werner Egk (Columbus), among others.

De Tempore holds more closely to the concert form of oratorio. The work is composed of three sections: I. Von der Unruhe der Menschen (On the Restlessness of Men). II. Von der Ordnung der Zeit (On the Orderliness of Time). III. Gottes Zeit ist die allerbeste Zeit (Das Ende der Zeiten) (God's Time is the Best Time—The End of Time). The text is taken from the *Confessions* of St. Augustine, with many insertions from Michelangelo, Angelus Silesius, Paracelsus, Alexis Carrel, from the books of *Jeremiah, Ecclesiastes, Revelations* and the *Psalms*, all of which serve to emphasize and deepen the meaning. Taken all together, they give the impression of great, spiritual unity, which also becomes a musical unity. The first performance was held in the Kollegienkirche in Salzburg on August 28, 1974.

Das Spiel vom Menschen is based on a text by Wolfgang Greisenegger and combines mystery play and church opera. Its language is timeless, as is Bresgen's lovely, often deeply affecting music. It does not "historicize" and yet forms a mighty bridge between the age of Gregorian music and today. The human condition is explored in scenes ranging from Adam and Eve through Cain's fratricide to the miraculous saving of the young men from the fiery furnace. Man's fall is vividly portrayed in such a way that it relates easily to today's world; it is a frightfully contemporary work. Bresgen uses several soloists, as in an opera, and an instrumental chamber ensemble. The premiere at the Carinthian Summer of 1982 made such a strong impression that it was performed again the following year.

Benjamin Britten   1913–1976

Britten was not only England's most prominent musician of the 20th century and probably the most performed opera composer of his generation, but one of the most multifaceted musicians of our time; a man inspired and possessed of great technical abilities. He successfully composed works for the stage, chamber music, orchestral music, songs, and in other genres as well. His works for the stage and the symphony orchestra have earned him an important place in music. He warrants a place of honor in this volume with his magnificent Mass for the Dead, the *War Requiem*, and the church operas *Curlew River*, *The Burning Fiery Furnace*, and *The Prodigal Son*, all of which can be performed in concert. I must also call attention to several works that resemble the cantata: *A Boy Was Born* (1933), *Te Deum* (1936), *Ballad of Heroes* (1939), *A Ceremony of Carols* (1942), *Rejoice in the Lamb* (1943), *Saint Nicolas* (1948), *Spring Symphony* (1949), *A Wedding Anthem* (1949), *Cantata academica* (1959), *Missa brevis* (1959), *Cantata misericordium* (1963), and *Voices for Today* (1965), among others.

Britten was a "child of the sea," of the English North Sea coast, which played a critical role in his life and works. He was born in that region, in Lowestoft, Suffolk, on November 22, 1913, and after spending the years of World War II in the United States, settled down in Aldeburgh, where he later founded an important music festival. He died there on December 4, 1976.

War Requiem

Original Title: War Requiem, Op. 66
Original Languages: Latin and English
Text: Mass for the Dead (Missa pro defunctis) of the Catholic liturgy; interspersed with poems by Wilfred Owen.
Date of Writing: 1961; the score gives the completion date as December 20, 1961.
First Performance: May 30, 1962, in the rebuilt Coventry cathedral.
Form: In six parts: 1. Requiem; 2. Dies irae; 3. Offertorium; 4. Sanctus; 5. Agnus Dei; 6. Libera me.
Cast: Three solo voices (soprano, tenor, baritone), mixed chorus (up to eight parts), two-part children's chorus; two orchestras: the large one accompanies the Latin Requiem text and consists of three flutes (one piccolo), two oboes, English horn, three clarinets with bass clarinet, two bassoons, contrabassoon, six horns, four trumpets, three trombones, tuba, piano, organ (or harmonium), 14 percussion instruments, strings. The chamber orchestra accompanies the texts by Wilfred Owen: flute and piccolo, oboe, English horn, clarinet, bassoon, horn, various percussion instruments, harp, strings; the children's chorus is always accompanied by the organ (or harmonium).
History of the Work: On November 15, 1940, the cathedral of the English city of Coventry, in the county of Warwick, one of the most beautiful edifices in Great Britain, was destroyed in a German air raid. Although during the course of the war there were many other bombings with more horrible results, this one is of special significance because it was one of the first instances of terror and devastation falling from the air on an unarmed city of no strategic significance, its sole purpose being to sow panic among civilians and thus bring the opponent to his knees. This meaning became clear when the verb "coventrisieren" (to Coventry-ize) became a strategic term in the vocabulary of National Socialism and was used when threatening similar attacks. The rebuilding of the magnificent religious monument required more than 16 years.

For the formal consecration, ceremonies were planned that were to emphasize international reconciliation. Benjamin Britten, England's leading musician, was commissioned to write a work expressing the mood of the time, almost an obsession, which called for the stigmatization of war and the vow to never again allow the inhumanity and cruelty that had led to such unspeakable disaster.

It was more than a just a nice gesture that on May 30, 1962, the two main male roles of the *War Requiem* were entrusted to two singers who 20 years before had been on opposite sides of a murderous war: Peter Pears (tenor) on the English, and Dietrich Fischer-Dieskau (baritone) on the German side. Both sang the deeply moving verses of Wilfred Owen with burning conviction. (Owen was a British officer who had been killed at the age of 25 in World War I; his poems are one sustained, despairing outcry of accusation, not against an enemy but against the incomprehensible cruelty of war itself.) This was more than just the premiere of an important work of art; it was an unforgettable moment of celebration of brotherhood among peoples. The quality of the performance was worthy of the occasion: in addition to the two male soloists, the soprano Heather Harper also sang, as did the specially-formed Coventry Festival Chorus and the boys' chorus from Stratford. The Birmingham Symphony Orchestra, directed by Meredith Davies, and the Melos Chamber Ensemble, conducted by the composer, played.

Discussion of the Work: What was new about the *War Requiem* derives its unique significance from the juxtaposition of the eternally valid words of the Mass with the burning actuality of the words of a contemporary poet. The incomprehensible awe of Judgment Day stood side by side with the horrors recently experienced by mankind; the mind comprehends the one no better than the other. The propriety of this juxtaposition has become an issue among theologians. But the question has become virtually meaningless in view of the fact that here the words of the liturgy, sung in the context of agonizing experience, acquired new life.

The voices begin as in a funeral march, almost reciting their words; the instruments play mutedly in their deeper registers, and a lonely death knell sounds. Slowly, the interval C/F-sharp crystallizes; the bell strikes it, the chorus sings it; the sound is eerie, weird, just as it sounded to people in the Middle Ages, who called this interval, the tritone, *diabolus in musica* (the devil in music). And today, following 400 years of use, its effect has not been diminished. With "et lux perpetua" the psalmodizing on the same tone takes on a denser motion but even here moves within the hollow-sounding C/F-sharp interval. Then the boys' chorus enters, accompanied by the organ and high, sustained notes in the violins (in the C/F-sharp interval) singing homophonically, with alternating parts, its "Te decet hymnus," until the voices, too, reach the C/F-sharp interval. At this point the choruses enter, again almost reciting their words—the sound is ghostly, as if they were emerging from a grave.

The bells of the death knell toll again, softly and far away, as the harp and the low strings of the chamber orchestra prepare agitatedly for the first solo tenor entrance: "What passing bells for these who die as cattle? / Only the monstrous anger of the guns. / Only the stuttering rifles' rapid rattle / Can patter out their hasty orisons." Suddenly we are in the midst of war, and the singer passionately cries out his accusation, resignation and despair. The two tones C and F-sharp of the bell sound as the music breaks off abruptly. Then the chorus enters, in triple piano, with "Kyrie eleison," the eerie tritone predominating until the song and the death knell fade away in the distance as if finally set free—in an eight-part, F major chord that leaves an indelible impression on the soul of the listener. No greater contrast can be imagined than that between the "Requiem aeternam" just heard and the "Dies irae" that follows. Trombones, trumpets, and horns issue the call to battle very softly, as if from a distance, and suddenly there is a rushing, out of breath, as the world disintegrates in fear. The chorus stammers, words come out singly, with great effort; the very rapid seven-four meter is syncopated, like the panting of men fleeing in terror. Again the call in the brasses, heralding the imminent calamitous scene, approaching slowly but irrevocably, and again the sudden rush of men frightened to death. Then it is there: war, or hell, or the Day of Judgment. The air is torn with blaring sounds of rage. Into this frenzy, still with the irregular, choppy, horrified stammering, the chorus, now in eight parts, cries its "Tuba mirum" (The trumpets will sound even into the graves).

The score is full of magnificent details that send chills down the listener's spine. Death is everywhere, awful, inescapable—"Mors stupebit. . . ." A roll on the timpani, supported by a long, low sound by the piano, leads to the chamber orchestra; a horn calls out softly, like an echo of the storm of death that has just passed; the trumpet motive, which before had descended in agitation, sounds again, this time ascending in the woodwinds like a call to heaven. And the baritone enters singing "Bugles sang, sadd'ning the evening air / And bugles answered, sorrowful to hear." Then again the large orchestra, this time accompanying a solo soprano; the liturgical text is "Liber scriptus" (And a book will be opened; every bad deed committed on earth is faithfully recorded in it). The timpani enter and beat a relentless, uninterrupted, inescapable rhythm; and the chorus, reduced for the sake of clarity, sings a fugue, different from Baroque fugues only in the much more complicated entrances, which follow each other mostly at intervals of a second, and in an extremely intensified realism of expression. The words are "Quid sum miser . . . ?" (What shall I, a poor wretch, say?) The soprano continues with "Rex tremendae majestatis" (King of awful majesty), and now the melody is an inversion, the mirror image of the first—clearly seen in the score (Examples 1, 2). The choral entry that follows—"Salva me, fons pietatis" (Save me, font of mercy)—is also an inversion, mirroring the one that preceded it, which is not a little trick in imitation of the artistry of past centuries but rather a conviction based on an understanding of subtle text relations and on formidable technical skill. Up to this point the timpani have kept up their penetrating, relentless beat which now fades away. The chamber orchestra begins an odd piece, heavily, almost awkwardly, with a forced cheerfulness; the tenor and bass soloists sing a duet describing a ghostly companionship with death: "Out there, we've walked quite friendly up to Death; / Sat down and eaten with him, cool and bland." It is a scene set to a march rhythm, gay yet horrible. We almost breathe a sigh of relief when the orchestra enters with a more gentle mood and the chorus, accompanied by the bassoons, embarks upon one of the most melodious pieces of the work: "Recordare Jesu" (Remember, O Jesus) (Example 3). Britten constructs the movement powerfully; tension mounts as the sound goes higher and higher, the liturgical text becomes more oppressive, with elaborations of great intensity and expression. Another baritone solo is embedded in it: "Be slowly lifted up, thou long black arm / Great gun towering toward Heaven, about to curse." There is something solemn about these words, which break off with rapid trumpet signals that finally seem to plunge into an abyss. Then the chorus returns in a shudder of fear and despair, singing "Dies irae, dies illa" (Day of wrath), but the stammer has become a cry. They subside into sobs as the solo soprano adds "Lacrimosa . . ." (Day of tears), once more in seven-four time, a meter that for Western man does not feel like a steady rhythm but is slightly unearthly, especially if reinforced by the instrumentation. It merges with an almost whispered tenor solo: "Move him, move him into the sun / Gently its touch awoke him once, / At home. . . ." This poetic insertion, backed by a very soft tremolo in the strings and similar effects in the winds, lasts only a minute; then the chorus repeats its "Lachrimosa," but the tenor interrupts: "Think how it wakes the seeds, / Woke, once, the clays of a cold star. . . ." This episode is over in a flash, and the movement proceeds with the chorus and soloist singing alternately, the soloist asking again and again for the meaning of it all, and then finally blurting out in despair "O what made fatuous sunbeams toil to break earth's sleep at all?" But the chorus does not seem to feel it has been addressed; in the same hovering, somewhat other-worldly rhythm it completes the words "Pie Jesu Domine . . ." (Gentle Jesus, Lord . . .).

The boys' chorus introduces the third part, the "Offertory," accompanied by the organ. Its two parts psalmodize in alternation. Then the large chorus enters in a lively movement and describes accurately and specifically the image of Saint Michael, the flag bearer of the heavenly host, who is to lead men "into the holy light," "which you promised to Abraham and his children." Following tradition, Britten sets the words "Quam olim Abrahae" as a fugue with a very distinct theme. It goes without saying that since it is composed by a 20th-century composer, it does not follow the rules precisely; some of the entrances are in inversion, in mirror image, but the basic concept is carried out, as in fugues by Bach or Handel.

The two male soloists intone a long, substantial passage that finally becomes a true duet. They tell the story of Abraham, and of how he sacrificed his son, Isaac. Their words become accusatory, and the meaning is extended to include the sacrificing of half of Europe: "So Abraham rose and clave the wood. . . ." The boys' chorus interrupts the agitated singing with a lovely melody: "Hostias et preces tibi . . ." (To you, O Lord, we bring gifts and prayers).

It is this juxtaposition and overlapping of thanksgiving and accusation that is so unsettling. It fades away to the soft strains of the organ, and then the chorus and large orchestra again take up the fugue "Quam olim Abrahae," this time developing it in the softest tones possible, almost like a distant memory, as though God's promise to Abraham were today no longer valid.

The solo soprano opens the next section, the "Sanctus," in the midst of an orgy of percussion—vibraphone, glockenspiel, cymbals,* and bells—which increases in tempo and dynamics. She calls out three times "Holy, holy, holy"; the last time in a long, melismatic melody that contains all 12 tones of the chromatic scale (Example 4). This structure led some commentators to believe that at some point in his creative life Britten had become a follower of Schönberg's twelve-tone system (actually no longer relevant in 1962). This contention is insupportable because several pitches are repeated in this phrase, which runs counter to the principles of the dodecaphonic system. Several similar melodies in the *War Requiem* (and other Britten compositions) are not based on any "theory"; his music is never constructed but rather spontaneously conceived.

Example 4

Then the chorus enters reciting the text on a fixed pitch: "Pleni sunt coeli" (Heaven and earth are filled with thy majesty). This passage, in eight parts with staggered entrances, creates a strange effect in the listener: it sounds both very ancient and extremely modern. In the "Osanna in excelsis" that follows, chorus and orchestra break out with a rejoicing that lasts until subdued in the "Benedictus." At that point they accompany the solo soprano in great, shining arcs of melody. Once more the chorus exults: "Osanna!" Suddenly the joyful sound breaks off; to the most meager accompaniment of the chamber orchestra the baritone sings "After the blast of lightning from the East, / The flourish of loud clouds, the Chariot Throne; / After the drums of Time have rolled and ceased, / And by the bronze west long retreat is blown, / Shall life renew these bodies?" Fearful questions are uttered and remain unanswered. The "Sanctus", quite contrary to all other settings of this Mass text, ends in painful stillness. The "Agnus Dei" which follows does not begin with the liturgical text, but with a tenor solo singing Owen's words "One ever hangs where shelled roads part. . . ." Britten again chooses a "hovering" rhythm—here five sixteenth notes per measure—using it to express inner unrest. Very quietly, the chorus sets its "Agnus Dei qui tollis peccata mundi, dona eis requiem" (Lamb of God, who takes away the sins of the world, give them rest) against the deeply melancholy melody of the tenor; both the large and the chamber orchestras are playing here.

The last section, the "Libera me," begins with a very calm march, barely hinted at in the percussion, which mounts gradually, leading to a great outburst. The plea for redemption moves very quietly through all parts of the chorus, becoming more expressive as it comes to "Quando coeli movendi sunt et terra" (When the heavens and the earth shake, when You come to judge the world in fire). The solo soprano has the sequence "Tremens factus" (I stand there in fear and trembling), sung to the agitated pizzicato of the strings and the staccato of the piano, without pedal. The chorus joins in delicately, in a low register, and together they surge to a new climax (a high C for the soprano), following which a new, marchlike section begins. Chorus and soloists now call out to be saved, canonlike although at various pitches: "Libera me." With the outburst "Dies illa, dies irae" the music literally explodes, and calms down only later.

The tenor, as always with the chamber orchestra, begins a passage of free recitative: "It seemed that out of battle I escaped / Down some profound dull tunnel. . . ." Stationary chords in the strings spread an atmosphere of detachment from the world. The baritone answers the tenor. In a long, affecting melody sung to an extremely varied and spare orchestral accompaniment with solo passages by various instruments, the dead soldiers take each other by the hand; the din and the hatred subside and disappear: "Let us sleep now. . . ." The sound of the organ comes as from an infinite distance, and the boys' chorus sings a deeply moving lullaby (Example 5). "In paradisum

---

*Britten calls for "antique cymbals," which, however, are seldom used; they are small, thick metal disks that produce a very hard, shrill sound.

deductant te angeli; in tuo adventu suscipiant te martyres..." (Angels will lead you to paradise; martyrs will receive you there and take you to the holy city, Jerusalem). Once again we hear the two male solo voices as they sing "Let us sleep now..."; the boys' chorus and mixed chorus join in a hymn, varied, solemn, otherworldly. The last word is sung by the chorus, which gently modulates to a pure F major ("Requiescant in pace..."), resolving the dissonance of the tritone *Leitmotif* (C/F-sharp) forever.

Example 5

The Church Operas

The church opera is a very old, early form of oratorio, related to mystery plays and similar offerings of medieval sacred theater. The 20th century has pioneered the revival of all kinds of older artistic expressions, with a view less to enlarging our knowledge of museum pieces than to trying to create vital new forms. Britten's church operas are among the most successful of these new creations.

The first, *Curlew River*, was inspired by a trip Britten made to Japan, and more particularly by the Japanese No theater. This almost mythological kind of play, concise in message, its action barely hinted at, spare in gesture and word, seems an unlikely form for Western imitation. On his return he carried on long conversations with the poet William Plomer, who had spent his youth in Japan, about his experiences there. Finally the idea came to him that the closest Western form was that of the old church operas. *Curlew River* was the first attempt made in this direction. It was first heard at Britten's Aldeburgh Festival in 1964; called a "parable of the church," given in a sacred performance space from which the genre had vanished long ago.

Britten's other two church operas, more frequently performed than *Curlew River*, were also strongly influenced by the No theater but are based on the Bible: the *Burning Fiery Furnace*, also performed for the first time at Aldeburgh, in 1966, and the *Prodigal Son*, produced two years later, in 1968.

Burning Fiery Furnace is based on the Old Testament book of *Daniel*. The Babylonian king Nebuchadnezzar (the same one the young Verdi chose for the title role in his opera *Nabucco*) had three Jewish youths (Shadrach, Meshach, and Abednego) who had refused to worship a golden image, thrown into a blazing oven. But the fire did not consume them; bystanders listened in horror as the youths sang their hopeful songs, and when the king looked into the glowing oven, he thought he saw four figures. Half crazed with fear, he had them plucked from the fire and asked who the fourth person whom he had seen was. They were quite amazed because they had not known that a fourth had shared their fate; then they remembered that the prophet Daniel had promised to help them in time of need. Nebuchadnezzar recognized the power of the true God and from then on declared himself to be His follower.

Peter Gradenwitz has added some interesting information on this subject:

Since the 11th century dramatic representations of biblical episodes, legends from the lives of the saints, and miracles worked by holy men have been given in churches, with text and music. The parable of the saving of the three innocent boys from the fiery furnace by an angel sent by God seems to be the oldest of these musical dramas. The library of the monastery of St. Catherine on Mt. Sinai, the archives of the monastery on Mt. Athos, and the National Library in Athens all contain manuscripts recording the melodies of a Byzantine liturgical drama based on this same story, all dating from the 11th century. They even bear the author's name—Kasenos Koronas, who was perhaps either the composer, or the one who adapted the melodies. The existence of the manuscripts was forgotten until our century, though the play itself remained a living tradition for centuries in the Byzantine church where it was performed over and over. The legend is also depicted on the doors of the cathedral in the city of Pskov in northern Russia. Sergei Eisenstein worked scenes from a traditional production into his film *Ivan the Terrible....*

Plomer and Britten follow the old drama closely; the poet fleshes it out with only a few additions, taken either from the book of *Daniel* or written by himself. Britten uses a small orchestra, consisting of flute, horn, viola, contrabass, trombone, harp, organ, and percussion. The singing roles are Nebuchadnezzar (tenor); his court astrologer, who also sings the abbot of the monastery (baritone); a herald, who is also the leader of the courtiers (baritone); the three Jewish youths (tenor, baritone, and bass); two boys' voices; and a small male chorus, composed of only of three tenors, two baritones, and two basses.

Before the play begins, all the performers—singers and instrumentalists—enter the church in procession singing the Gregorian hymn "Salus aeterna indeficiens mundi vita;" with which they leave the church, again in procession, when the play is over. This device is used to bring home the sense that the performance is a parable: "See, now, this is our story of how God's miraculous power saved three boys from the flames. . . ."

The Prodigal Son is also based on a Biblical story, this time from the New Testament, the story having been arranged as the libretto. It seems that this theme occurred to Britten while he was looking at Rembrandt's famous painting.

William Plomer again wrote the text (as he did for Britten's coronation opera *Gloriana*), drawing principally on the Gospels of *St. Matthew* and *St. Luke*. Nevertheless, there are differences: in the Bible, the younger son willingly goes to a foreign land to seek a better life; "he seems more of an emigrant than a frustrated "dropout" interested only in life's pleasures. He only goes wrong when in another land" (Max Ulrich Balsiger).

In Plomer and Britten's version, it is a tempter who tears the son from the bosom of his family and leads him into reckless and extravagant behavior by placing seductive pleasures before him. Repeated disappointments in the foreign land follow, and eventually the loss of everything: penniless and full of remorse he returns home where he asks to work for his father as a servant. His father, however, greets him with open arms, gives him his own best garment, and orders a feast prepared. The older son, who has worked faithfully for which he has received neither praise nor pay complains of this behavior. But the father's actions conform to the words of Jesus, long subject to various interpretations: Heaven is more pleased with a repentant sinner than with 99 just souls.

It is interesting to note that the English title of the parable and church opera carries a different connotation than it does in many other languages, including German. In English, "prodigal" means "extravagant," making the story one of the reckless son, whereas the German title means "lost." So the father refers to him as lost when he explains to the older son: "Your brother was dead and is now alive again. He was lost and has now been found." The French, Spanish, Italians, and others speaking a Romance language also refer to the "extravagant" son. Debussy wrote a work on the subject: *L'Enfant prodigue;* the correct title for which should probably be "The parable of the son who was lost and found again."

The premiere of this third church opera by Plomer and Britten took place in 1968, again in the church in Orford, a village near Aldeburgh, during the music festival that has come to be an annual event in Benjamin Britten's home town. Not only because they are fairly easy to perform, but also because of their profound meaning and affecting music, these church operas, which can be considered oratorios, have been widely performed throughout the world.

David (Dave) Brubeck 1920–

David Brubeck was brought up in a rural environment, and his talent for music was nurtured within the rich cultural life at home. The opportunity for study with Darius Milhaud was, in Brubeck's words: "The single most important influence in my musical life." Later, experimentation with various jazz styles helped synthesize his own and elevated him to leadership in the world of progressive jazz. Tours by the Dave Brubeck Quartet made jazz history.

In the late 1960s Brubeck turned his full attention to writing sacred choral works. *The Light in the Wilderness* (1968) came first. Other works, *The Gates of Justice* (1969), *Truth is Fallen* (1971), *La Fiesta de la Posada* (1975), *Beloved Son* (1978) and *Festival Mass to Hope* (1980) followed. During the decades when American jazz was gaining wider acceptance in the church, these works united jazz with traditional sacred music forms.

The Light in the Wilderness

Original Language: English
First Performance: January 1968 at the University of North Carolina.
Form: Two large divisions contain 18 numbers, with eight optional opportunities for jazz-style keyboard improvisation. Qualities of progressive jazz are ever present. Polyharmony, quartal structures, superchords, mixed meter and syncopation are the norm.
Scoring: Chorus, organ, and baritone, with optional string bass and percussion (or full orchestra).
Discussion of the Work: In the opening number, "The Temptations," the chorus moves in hollow, text-less sounds like "the wind on the desert" (score notation) to evoke an atmosphere appropriate for the encounter of Jesus with the devil. In flowing lines, warm and rhythmical, the chorus becomes "the voice from heaven," repeating the words "This is my beloved Son in whom I am well pleased." An energetic rhythm pattern is used which will recur many times in the work as a unifying motive (Example 1). [Musical examples Copyright 1968 St. Francis Music Co. and Malcolm Music, Ltd. All Rights Reserved. Sole Selling Agent: Shawnee Press, Inc.; Delaware Water Gap, PA 18327. Used with permission.] Clearly, this motive has only musical significance, as it is used even in this movement for the devil's words "If Thou be the Son of God, cast Thyself down." The baritone soloist fills the role of Jesus throughout the work, in a manner typified in this movement (Example 2).

Example 1

Example 2

Section IIa is for chorus alone and is a narrative reflection on the 40 days of temptation. Chorale-like homophonic phrases, at times alternating between the male and female choruses, stress the loneliness Jesus experiences in the wilderness. A brief organ interlude follows to provide a reflective moment and a bridge to a baritone solo, "Repent, Follow Me." This aria begins the series of sections in which Jesus "preaches the gospel," using familiar biblical verses. "The Sermon on the Mount" (Section IV) follows without pause. One by one, the Beatitudes, sung by the chorus alone, flow in connected phrases. The melodic and rhythmic texture of each is distinctly suited to the words (Example 3). Frequent use of a descending eighth-note line, on the other hand, creates a structural balance and provides a sense of unity throughout this extensive choral movement. To frame this section, the text and music of "Repent, Follow Me" return at the opening of Section V, which is extended beyond the original statement and develops into patterns of choral echoes to the call of Jesus (baritone): "Follow me, repent, for the Kingdom of Heaven is at hand." Solo and choral phrases are very short and texture changes frequent. The smooth, carefree rhythms of an earlier jazz style provide a lighthearted, jovial picture of the spirited multitude—complete with high-hat cymbal and a "big band" feel. Jesus calls the 12 disciples. Choral soloists identify each by name. With the words "I will make you fishers of men" the chorus repeats "forgive, forgive" and fades into pianissimo at the closing cadence. One of the unique features of this work is used at this point. On cue, a small instrumental ensemble begins to improvise in progressive jazz style until the full ensemble returns, also on cue. These improvisatory moments are optional at several places throughout the work and may be performed by a solo pianist or an ensemble. This element of jazz performance, so much a part of the composer's renowned style, is a significant innovation for this form of sacred music.

Example 3

Section VI, titled "The Great Commandment," uses a double chorus; the first responds in a typical fashion to the voice of Jesus; the second repeats a four-bar choral pattern (32 repetitions) based on the "rhythmic motive" in Section I (see Example 1). Both choirs sing this ostinato at the outset (Example 4). Section VII, *Love Your Enemies,* is closely related in spiritual tone to the previous movement. It generally follows the common solo-chorus pattern and is the most extensive and complex of all the choral numbers—the oratorio's centerpiece. Frequent changes of meter and texture—more than in any other chorus—produce vivid word pictures and concise expressive moments.

Example 4

As the oft-quoted passages on Christian love from *Matthew* 5 and *Luke* 6 build in fervor, "Love your enemies—Do good to those that hate you—Do not judge and you shall not be judged—Give and it is given to you," the meters change with increasing urgency. Eleven measures before the final cadence a unique summary section in two-four meter begins. The voice of Jesus soars above the chorus, recapitulating the textual theme, "Love your enemies, Do good to those who hate you," and the chorus adds support, using a variety of texts. In each measure the meter increases by one unit of pulse: two-four, three-four, four-four and so on, until the final twelve-four measure. Metrical emphasis loses its significance in this overpowering statement, however, as more frequent breath marks lead to a declamatory emphasis on each individual word (Example 5).

Example 5

Part II—shorter by half than Part I—begins at this point. Its seven sections contain two baritone solos, three for chorus and baritone, and two for chorus alone. Again, familiar passages of scripture—known to many by their first lines—bring further messages of spiritual import, but speak more of Christ's death and ascension than did the first part.

"What Does it Profit a Man"
"Where is God?"
"We Seek Him"
"Peace I Leave with you"
"Let Not Your Heart Be Troubled"
"Yet a Little While"

The organization of musical material and distribution of text between solo and chorus does not radically depart from earlier patterns, except in one unusual choral movement, "We Seek Him" Section IXa. Here, the chorus is given a five-measure succession of chords in four parts to repeat over and over, while the pianist improvises above this ostinato. Upon cue from the pianist the improvisation moves without pause into the next section.

The final section of the oratorio is a triumphant chorus, "Praise Ye the Lord," the text taken from Psalm 148:1–13. All sections of the chorus sing consistently in the extremes of their ranges, and the sonority glows with radiant brilliance. "His glory is above the earth and heaven," the chorus proclaims at the closing phrase (Example 6).

Example 6

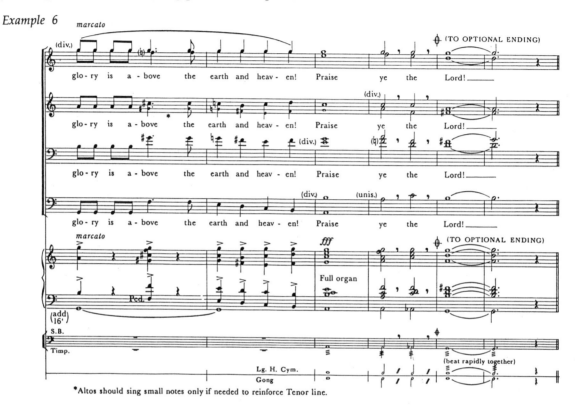

*Altos should sing small notes only if needed to reinforce Tenor line.

The *Light in the Wilderness* had its choral premiere in January, 1968 at the University of North Carolina at Chapel Hill. In February of that year a symphonic premiere was given by the Cincinnati Symphony and Miami University Singers. The *Christian Science Monitor* captured the significant impact of these performances.

> Brubeck's personal appearance will signal the advent of a revolutionary musical form: live jazz improvisation as a continuing embellishment to a fully-realized sacred work which involves both choral and symphonic elements.
>
> Jan. 12, 1968

> Mr. Brubeck notes that the oratorio started out to be a simple sacred service, and it can be performed without the orchestra or the piano improviser, depending on the group's resources. He emphasizes that any future improviser need not follow the Brubeck jazz idiom, but should feel free to play in any manner appropriate to the musical ideas in the score.... Mr. Brubeck's view of the Judeo-Christian tradition, like his use of music to express it, is inclusive rather than exclusive. And its warmth and sincerity cannot be doubted, any more than the courage of an established talent giving up a sure thing to try something big and new.
>
> March 4, 1968
>
> —*Thurston Dox*

Anton Bruckner   1824–1896

The very composer from whom the world could most reasonably have expected a great oratorio never composed one. Sacred music occupied a preeminent place in Anton Bruckner's life. Although his symphonies are longer and may have involved more intense work, the number of his religious compositions is incomparably greater. Bruckner repeatedly turned to the composition of Masses; he completed a total of five, and there are more or less detailed sketches of others. He experimented three times with a Requiem, but completed only the D minor work of 1848–49. In addition, he wrote a Magnificat (1852), a Te Deum (1881–84) and settings of various Psalms, among them the 150th Psalm, written in 1892. He also composed motets and many small sacred works for a cappella chorus.

Scarcely any other major master was so devout a believer as Bruckner; no other felt so at home in the Catholic Church. Even his symphonies are mighty hymns of glory and praise, intended for the ears of heaven as much as for his earthly audience. The last bears a dedication probably not found on any other work of art: "To the good Lord."

To form a true picture of Bruckner—something more than that of an awkward peasant flung into a great metropolis; more than a shy, idealistic, childlike and naive but kindhearted man, one must imagine him at the great organ of the splendid Baroque abbey of St. Florian, presiding serenely and unconstrained over a gigantic ocean of sound, master of limitless tonal resources which he heaped up into a towering brilliant offering of praise to the One on high. But this masterful, somewhat divided persona never wrote an oratorio, never a Passion in which he might have described with all the mastery at his disposal his feeling for the Savior he so loved. This is a matter worth thinking about. Perhaps it was only his time, the second half of the 19th century—an era none too fond of the oratorio. Yet Liszt, dissimilar from Bruckner in every other way save in his later mysticism, loved the form. Verdi and Dvorak each composed a Requiem large enough in scope to fill an evening, and Brahms, whom Bruckner so often met on the streets of Vienna, poured his most intimate feelings into a religious composition of the grandest style—*Ein deutsches Requiem*. Bruckner probably knew little of his Belgian colleague in Paris, César Franck, except that he, too, was counted one of the greatest organists of his time. But he who feels he must create a work that springs from his innermost being will do so, even though it goes against the current of his time. Was Bruckner not driven to it? His superb Masses are no "substitute" for another genre, nor are they intended to be. They are magnificent works for religious services. In them, Bruckner speaks directly to his God, without having to concern himself about public reaction, as he would have had to in a concert hall or theater. Bruckner's masses are liturgy first and only secondarily works of art.

Anton Bruckner was born on September 4, 1824, in the small town of Ansfelden in Upper Austria, amid green fields and forests, a somewhat remote part of the world. Between 1837 and 1840 he was a member of the boys' choir at St. Florian, near Linz. That towering abbey church of wonderful proportions became his true home, his refuge in the difficult times of his life. And difficult times he had: his path was trying; recognition came slowly; he suffered confrontations with virtually every aspect of life. He could not easily make his way in the city because he could never learn to play the game, and never shared the hollow pleasures of city life. In its turn, the city showed little understanding for his concerns. After having held a series of minor teaching positions in outlying villages, he became cathedral organist in Linz, from 1856 to 1868. From there he travelled once a week to Vienna to continue his education with Simon Sechter, the teacher to whom Schubert had turned during his final illness. In 1868, Bruckner received professional recognition in the capital and imperial city of Austria, being appointed a lecturer at the conservatory and the university, where, for a time, Gustav Mahler and Hugo Wolf were his students. He soon became acquainted with Richard Wagner's work and then with the man himself, falling under the spell of both. His regard for Wagner made his life in Vienna even more difficult because the "official" artistic position was one of opposition to the master of Bayreuth. Nevertheless Bruckner received further recognition: an honorary doctorate from the University of Vienna (1891), the Order of Franz Joseph (1886), and increasing public attention. Audiences began to understand that his work could not be measured by the usual standards, that it represented a confession of faith in the spiritual, godly elements of human life. One of his most affectionate biographers, Ernst Decsey, called him "God's musician," which is perhaps the best way to describe him.

Bruckner died in Vienna on October 11, 1896, while working on his ninth symphony. He only had time to recommend that in place of the unfinished finale, his Te Deum should be played, which still is often done. He was not buried in Vienna, where he was certainly entitled to a place in its cemetery honoring great musicians, but laid to eternal rest beneath the great organ of St.

Florian's, amid green fields and forests, far from the world but close to God.

The Masses

As a young man, Bruckner worked as a teacher's assistant: from 1841–1843 in Windhaag near Freistadt, and from 1843–1845 in Kronstorf, near Steyr—both tiny villages in Upper Austria. The composer in him was already stirring. He later said that one of "the greatest mysteries" had been "the memory of the setting out of the Eucharist representing the Last Supper, on the night of Holy Thursday." Inspired by this experience, Bruckner composed a four-part *Choralmesse für den Gründonnerstag* (the "Kronstorf Mass") during his last year at Kronstorf; his first work of any size. At the beginning of the score, he wrote the letters OAMDG (Omnia ad majorem Dei gloriam—all for the greater glory of God). This inscription is reminiscent of Bach, who headed many of his manuscripts with the letters "JJ" (Jesu juva—with Jesus' help) and ended them with "SDG" (Solo Dei gloria—Glory only to God). Bruckner's Mass is written for a cappella chorus; an organ accompaniment is provided only in the Gloria.

In 1848, Bruckner was appointed to the post of temporary abbey organist at St. Florian's. In the very first year of his service there he set to work composing his D minor Requiem for solo voices, four-part mixed chorus, orchestra, and organ. He noted the date of completion in the first draft as March 11, 1849; almost half a century later, in 1892, he revised this Mass for the Dead and presented it in a new and improved version.

Here we have the first instance of the serious problem of Bruckner's versions. Most of Bruckner's compositions, even some of his great symphonies, exist in several, sometimes quite different versions. Again and again he felt compelled to revise and correct earlier works, which he considered to be "unfinished." He often did quite a thorough job, pasting whole pages of corrections over pages already in the score, or striking out entire pages, thereby changing not only the form of the work but also, not infrequently, its inner meaning.

Among Bruckner's most important sacred choral works are the three numbered Masses composed in his later years. The Mass No. 1 in D minor for four solo voices, four-part mixed chorus, orchestra, and organ was composed in 1864, while Bruckner was still organist at the cathedral in Linz. He had just completed a symphony in D minor to which the composer himself later assigned the number "zero" in the series of his symphonies. Sketches for the Mass were made at the beginning of the year, and its completion took up the months of July through September, as can be seen from the dates Bruckner gave for the completion of the individual sections: the Kyrie was finished on July 4, the Credo on September 6, the Benedictus on September 29. The surprising element in it is the daring harmonic language. Max Auer, a leading biographer of Bruckner, ascribes this to the "one who awakened his ego"—Richard Wagner; although at that time, the only work by Wagner Bruckner knew was *Tannhäuser*. The often thoroughly harsh, incisive chromaticism sometimes reminds us of *Tristan und Isolde* (Example 1). This Mass No. 1 was performed for the first time, under Bruckner's direction, on November 20, 1864, in the Linz cathedral. He revised the work in 1876 and again in 1881 and 1882.

Example 1

The Mass No. 2 in E minor was also composed during the years in Linz. A greater role is assigned to the chorus, this time in eight parts, but the instrumentation is reduced: only winds are used and without organ accompaniment. Bruckner gives the completion date as November 25, 1866; he revised it in 1876, 1882, 1885, and 1896.

The work begins a cappella with an artful fugue. The second soprano follows the second alto at an interval of four quarter notes, at the fifth, after which the first alto and the first soprano enter at shorter intervals at the third and the sixth, all the harmonies being built on the E pedal point of the second alto (Example 2). The theme of the canon Bruckner uses in the eight-part Sanctus is taken from a Missa brevis composed by Palestrina, probably because Bruckner wished to show his reverence for this greatest of masters of Catholic church music. This is the only occasion on which Bruckner borrowed a theme. The E minor Mass was not performed until after the Mass No. 3 in F minor was finished; its premiere was held in the cathedral square in Linz on September 29, 1869.

Example 2

The year 1868 was one of the most decisive in Bruckner's life: His first symphony in D minor was given its premiere on May 9 in Linz. As greatly as he and Brahms differed in almost every respect, they had one thing in common—both were attracted to the symphony late in life. On July 6, Bruckner was appointed lecturer in harmony, counterpoint, and organ at the Vienna Conservatory, and on September 9 received the additional appointment of interim court organist. A new life lay before him. He had become quite unhappy in Linz and looked upon the call to Vienna with relief, but had no way of knowing that the origins of his depressions lay within himself, and that the city had many bitter experiences in store for him. Shortly thereafter he fell severely ill, spending several months of 1867 in a clinic for nervous disorders. He initially was forbidden all "intellectual" work, but how could he survive without composing? The doctors soon recognized that creative activity did their patient good, and with this work his condition began to improve rapidly. He composed the Kyrie of a new mass while hospitalized.

The Emperor's chief controller had approached Bruckner wanting a new Mass, and so he began the Mass No. 3 in F minor, the "Great." After its Kyrie had been completed in the sanatorium on March 2, 1867, Bruckner revised it in September and continued to work on it until October 10. The Gloria, too, was composed during this illness—from March 2 to May 6, 1867. On December 30 of that year, Bruckner wrote to his great friend and active supporter Johann Herbeck, one of the leading figures in Vienna's musical life, "Soon the Credo of my new Mass will be finished. The Kyrie and Gloria are sketched out. I am really pulling myself together . . ." He evidently considered the two parts composed in the sanatorium to be only "sketches," and did, in fact, work on them further. The final version of the Kyrie was completed on February 16, 1868, and that of the Gloria on August 11, 1868—at St. Florian's. The Credo was completed on February 15, the Benedictus, roughed out on Christmas Eve 1867, was completed on August 27, 1868. The Sanctus was composed between August 18 and 22, 1868, and the Agnus Dei between August 29th and September 9th.

Some time passed, however, before this magnificent, deeply introspective and movingly devout work was first performed. "If I were not truly religious, how could I have composed the Credo of my F minor Mass?" was his only reply when someone in that metropolis, Vienna, questioned his faith, sometimes described as naive or exaggerated. He was partial to this Mass for a special reason: he felt that it had saved his life, for was it not this Mass which had snatched him back from the brink of madness? How ill he must have been, and in what despair, for him, a true believer in Christ, to have contemplated suicide.

The F minor Mass is one of the most beautiful testimonies in liturgical art, one of the most brilliant achievements in church music. On June 16, 1872, this, the last of Bruckner's Masses, was performed for the first time in the church of St. Augustine in Vienna. By then Bruckner had long been known to the initiated as a great master. As an organist, he had realized triumphant successes in Nancy, Paris, and London; greater than any of his contemporaries. But in Vienna, the resistance of the critics—with Hanslick, the enemy of the Wagnerites, in the lead—had not been overcome, and would not be as long as both men lived.

Te Deum

Original Title: Te Deum
Original Language: Latin
Text: Ambrosian hymn of praise "Te Deum laudamus" from the 4th century.
Date of Writing: A first, fragmentary version was sketched in May, 1881; the work received its final form in 1884.

First Performance: In Vienna, conducted by Bruckner, on May 2, 1885, with two pianos substituting for the orchestra. It was first performed in its final form on January 10, 1886, also in Vienna.
Form: In five sections: 1. Te deum laudamus; 2. Te ergo quaesumus; 3. Aeterna fac; 4. Salvum fac populum tuum; 5. In te domine speravi.
Scoring: Four solo voices (soprano, alto, tenor, bass); four-part mixed chorus; two each of flutes, oboes, clarinets, bassoons; four horns, three trumpets, three trombones, bass tuba, timpani, strings, and organ ad libitum.
History of the Work: After the work was finally finished (it had taken several years), Joseph Hellmesberger, Hofkapellmeister in Vienna, who had ordered or at least suggested it, thought it was "too long" and asked the composer to shorten it. But Bruckner—who had had similar unreasonable requests from well-meaning friends in connection with his symphonies, requests that had not turned out well—was firm. Therefore Hellmesberger refused to perform the *Te Deum* at any of his important concerts. The Wagner Society came to the rescue. The work met with immediate success and was performed many times in the next few years in many cities. Gustav Mahler, once a pupil of Bruckner's and whose star was now rising, conducted it in Hamburg. (Mahler was appointed director of the Vienna Hofoper after Bruckner's death.) On April 16, 1892, the day after the concert, Mahler wrote to his teacher, "The performers and the entire audience were deeply moved by the powerful structure and truly sublime concept. When it was over, I experienced what to me is the greatest triumph a work can have: the audience sat there in silence, motionless, and only after the conductor and the performers had left their places did a storm of applause burst out."

At about the same time, the *Te Deum,* probably the first of Bruckner's works to be played in North America, was performed in Cincinnati, conducted by Theodor Thomas. There were 800 singers and an orchestra of 120 musicians in a hall holding 7,000 people; the work was received with a storm of approval.
Discussion of the Work: After two solemnly radiant introductory measures in C major, played by the entire orchestra, the chorus begins majestically, in unison, with "Te Deum laudamus" (Example 1).

Example 1

The soloists sing a delicately contrasting "Tibi omnes Angeli" in G major. The chorus enters again, softly, with the "Sanctus," going from F minor to A minor and then back to C major, and finally to the overpowering opening theme (No. 1), this time with "Te gloriosus...." Bruckner the symphonist demonstrates here his ability to write developments with changing moods, stirring climaxes, and surprising modulations. The "Te ergo" has a pleading character, sung only by the soloists, that is to say, by the solo tenor, since only at the end of the lovely melody do the other solo voices join in. Then the "Aeterna fac" is heard, powerful, with trumpets and full choral setting; toward the end it increases in tension as the tenor calls out "Gloria" and the very high, hymnlike harmonies of an exultant song of praise are heard. Once more, with the "Salvum fac," the soloists bring a tender, peaceful mood, which is taken up by the chorus. Then the opening theme (No. 1) bursts forth mightily, and we hear once more the spacious orchestral background in a bright C major ("Per singulos dies"), before the soloists enter again with a new, introspective song, "In te Domine speravi." At this point there is a truly breathtaking gathering of forces culminating in an apotheosis in C major, which, with its daring modulations, places enormous demands for strength and purity of intonation upon the chorus. After an extended, uninterrupted ascent of long notes, the sopranos of the chorus must maintain their luminosity on a high C—it is as if all heaven opened up and a host of angels were singing a hymn to eternity: "In aeternum, aeternum...."

Just before Bruckner's death, which occurred before he could complete his Ninth Symphony, he voiced the hope that the mighty work would not be performed without a conclusion and suggested, surely thinking of the vocal finale of Beethoven's Ninth as a precedent, that his *Te Deum* be so used, which is now commonly done. He had especially loved this work and thought it one of his best. It has been reliably reported that once when the conversation turned to the subject of death, he said, "When the good Lord finally calls me and asks 'What have you done with the talent I gave you?' I'll hand Him the score for my Te Deum, and He will judge me mercifully."

How well the Ninth Symphony and the *Te Deum* fit together musically is a matter of opinion, but they are spiritually related: the Ninth is dedicated to "The good Lord." When Bruckner had finished the *Te Deum* and showed it to Hellmesberger, the latter suggested that the composer dedicate it to the Emperor. Bruckner only shook his head and said, "Unfortunately, I cannot do that; it already belongs to a higher power... to the good Lord...."

The 150th Psalm

On June 29, 1892, Bruckner completed his last sacred choral work, the *150th Psalm*, which was first performed on November 15, 1892, in Vienna. Bruckner had been invited to compose a cantata or a hymn for a meeting of musicians to be held in conjunction with a great musical and theatrical exhibit that had been planned for Vienna. He decided on the Psalm, one that praised God and was close to his heart. He used a solo soprano, a four-part (in some places subdivided into 10 parts) mixed chorus, and a symphony orchestra.

It would not be wide of the mark to regard this composition as a "miniature" Te Deum. There is once again the brilliance of C major in which the work begins, with the oft-repeated cry of "Hallelujah!" Then the contrasting part, "Alles, was Odem hat, lobe den Herrn!" (All who have breath, praise the Lord!) is restrained, and forms the peaceful, contemplative center section of this much more concise composition. With a renewed "Hallelujah," the return to C major, and the hymnlike chorus, it seems that the climax has arrived, but it is not enough for Bruckner. In a suddenly slower tempo he continues with an imposing fugue; "Alles, was Odem hat..." sing the basses, making a passage of an impact and force like few others (Example 1). The tenors take over from the basses, then come the altos and, finally, the sopranos. This magnificently structured masterpiece of counterpoint is relatively short, in keeping with the length of the whole work, but maintains an enormous tension. With an ingenious use of octave leaps which form the core of the theme, Bruckner manages to create sounds that are ever more massive. With a thundering chord the opening tempo appears again, an apotheosis begins, reminding us once more of the *Te Deum* (albeit much abridged), and the sopranos rise to high C, bringing the work to an exultant close.

Example 1   Langsam

Al — les, was   O – dem hat,   lo — be den Herrn.

Willy Burkhard   1900–1955

The work of Willy Burkhard, the most important Swiss composer of our century, includes cantatas both sacred and profane, as well as a number of more extensive pieces that may be classified as oratorios and, indeed, deserve the greatest attention as such. Burkhard, born near Biel, held a teaching position at the Zürich Conservatory from 1942 until his death. He developed his own, completely individualistic style, a blend of linear, old polyphony, incisive as a woodcut, with visionary, mystical sounds of great insistence. Of his cantatas for solo voices with various kinds of accompaniment we must mention the following: *Herbst* (after Christian Morgenstern) for soprano and piano trio: *Die Versuchung Jesu* for alto or bass and organ; *Das ewige Brausen* (after Knut Hamsun) for bass and chamber orchestra; *Magnificat* for soprano with organ; *Christi Leidensverkündigung* for tenor, chamber chorus, and organ; *Und als der Tag der Pfingsten erfüllet war* for low voice, unison chorus ad libitum, and organ; and the *Psalmenkantate* for soprano, mixed chorus, and chamber orchestra. Among other choral works the following stand out: *Till Ulenspiegel* (after the Strassburg folk tale) for male chorus and orchestra; *Spruchkantate* (after Joseph von Eichendorff) for male chorus and string orchestra; *Genug ist nicht genug* (after Conrad Ferdinand Meyer) for mixed chorus, string orchestra, two trumpets, and timpani; a Mass for soprano, bass, mixed chorus, and small orchestra; as well as several pieces for chorus alone.

His *Te Deum*, Op. 33, composed in 1931, is curiously scored for two-part mixed chorus with trumpet, trombone, timpani, and organ. It opens with a two-voice fugue, the male voices entering together on the sustained pedal point D, and the female voices answering at the fifth, on A. There is a third entry for the trumpet on E, also at the fifth. A whole-tone scale is used; modal harmonies provide an archaic quality. Then, without any break, the music moves into "modern" harmonies with harsh dissonances, but the voice leading of each group remains logical and relatively simple. Melismas in the voices alternate with the same in the organ ("Sanctus"), until with the "Pleni sunt coeli" the chorus once more has a fugal entry. The male voices begin with an ascending B minor chord and the female voices answer with a G-sharp minor triad, leaving B as the common tone of both key areas. Nevertheless, the work is to be understood as contrapuntal rather than harmonic. The organ part is especially richly conceived. With "In te, Domine" the opening theme, slightly varied, returns, but now the female voices enter not at the fifth, but at the second. With a mighty build-up and ascending runs in octaves in the chorus the work comes to a most effective conclusion.

Das Gesicht Jesajas, Op. 41, composed in 1935, has the dimensions of a great oratorio. The orchestration is symphonic: two concert flutes (alternating with piccolos), two oboes (one of which doubles on the English horn), two clarinets, two bassoons, two horns, two trumpets, two trombones, tuba, large percussion section (with large and small drums, cymbals, triangle, tamtam, castanets, xylophone, and glockenspiel), organ, and augmented strings. There are also three solo voices (soprano, tenor, bass) and a four-part, mixed chorus. The Biblical text (from the book of *Isaiah*) is treated in a contemporary and extremely varied way; as in Baroque oratorios, the choruses are exceedingly dramatic or meditatively chorale-like. The orchestra, too, plays in varied, often surprising ways, in long and expressive instrumental solos as well as in passages with symphonic effects. It is a truly great oratorio, composed in an era when few others have appeared.

Das Jahr, Opus 62, based on a text by the Swiss lyric poet Hermann Hiltbrunner (1892–1961), is also an oratorio that would fill an entire evening. The orchestra used is like that in the work just described, but reinforced with a bass clarinet and a contrabassoon. There are also three soloists, but instead of a tenor, an alto. The text includes, between an introduction and conclusion, four images of the seasons, giving the musician ample scope to treat this theme, so beloved from medieval times. Burkhard, with his often sumptuous sonorities, took full advantage of the opportunity. The tonal language is austere. Quartal harmonies and passages of atonality make this work difficult to perform, especially for amateur choruses; but there are things in it quite worth studying. Here a very gifted man struggles for expression without courting easy popularity.

Dietrich Buxtehude 1637–1707

The most gifted musicians of the subsequent generation—Bach, Handel, Telemann—made pilgrimages to Lübeck, where from 1668 until his death, Dietrich Buxtehude, one of the most formidable masters of the organ and of Protestant church music of his time, gave heavily attended evening recitals in St. Mary's church. Buxtehude was probably born in 1637 in Oldesloe, Holstein; although it was long thought that he had been born in Helsingör, Denmark, or Helsingborg, Sweden, recent research points to the north German birthplace. Buxtehude was not only one of the leading organists of the German Baroque; his compositions were widely known as well. He was especially devoted to the cantata, which he usually called "Konzert," whereas Heinrich Schütz defined the form more narrowly as "geistliches Konzert" (sacred concert). In recent decades, with renewed interest in Baroque music, many works by Buxtehude have been discovered; although we can assume that some are still slumbering in archives, for example, in the library of the university at Uppsala in Sweden, which began to collect his works very early. Buxtehude died in Lübeck on May 9, 1707, a famous and highly respected man.

His major work is probably *Das Jüngste Gericht* (The Last Judgment). It is composed of five cantatas based on the theme of Judgment Day. Though there is no continuity of action it may still be considered an oratorio because it is a cohesive composition. For more than 200 years it was thought to be lost, but was rediscovered in 1924. It bears the curious yet informative subtitle "Das allerschröcklichste und allererfreulichste, nämlich Ende der Zeit und Anfang der Ewigkeit, gesprächsweise in fünf Vorstellungen auf Opern-Art mit vielen Arien und Ritornellen in einer musikalischen Harmonia gezeiget" (The most horrible and the most joyful event—the end of time and the beginning of eternity—presented in dialogue, operalike, with many arias and ritornellos with harmonious music). "Operalike" refers to musical dialogue and dramatic scenes, even when performed in concert and not on a stage. We are here reminded of the close relationship between the "sister arts," opera and oratorio. (Actually only a century had gone by since the two genres had originated).

Das Jüngste Gericht was not intended to be performed in a single evening, but rather to be heard between the last Sunday after Trinity and the fourth Sunday of Advent. It is for this reason that the images are so forceful yet have scarcely any connection with each other. Choruses and arias are unevenly distributed. Individual human vices—particularly avarice, lust, and pride—are represented struggling with the virtues. In spite of the seriousness of the theme there is no lack of coarse, popular humor, for example, "Ich kann nicht mehr, ganz voll und toll bin ich gesoffen, o weh, o Kopf, o Herz, ich vergeh!" (I'm done for, I'm thoroughly drunk, o woe is me, o head, o heart, I'm dying). The judgment does not occur until the fifth cantata; five trombones call the living and the dead, whereupon the evil sink together to eternal damnation. Only the "good" are saved: "Ich will zu euch kommen und euch zu mir nehmen, dass ihr seid, wo ich bin" (I will come to you and take you to me, so that you will be where I am). There is a conciliatory ending which reminds in many ways of the medieval dances of death.

A few of Buxtehude's many cantatas are selected at random for mention here. *Jesu, meine Freude* (Jesus, my joy) uses the same text that Bach used a few decades later, as did countless other Baroque composers. A three-part overture leads into the first chorus, set in three parts throughout the work; the female voices probably sing in unison. Three solo voices, two sopranos and bass, each have an aria. The chorus participates in the action a total of three times; the last piece is a repetition of the first with a different text ("Weicht, ihr Trauergeister, denn mein Freudenmeister Jesus tritt herein"—Begone, funereal spirits; Jesus, master of my joy, is coming).

Even simpler is, for example, *Befiehl dem Engel, dass er komm'* (Command the angel to come), a cantata for four-part chorus with strings and the obligatory Baroque harpsichord continuo. The cantata *Das neugebor'ne Kindelein* (The newborn child) uses the same resources and was clearly intended for Christmas Eve. *Fürwahr er trug unsere Krankheit* (Indeed, he bore our sickness), a Passion cantata, is more ambitious and has soloists along with the chorus. *Erstanden ist der heilig Christ* (The holy Christ has arisen) sings of the Resurrection. Of greater importance is the cantata *Wo soll ich fliehen hin?* (Whither shall I flee?). It is not only one of the most artistic but perhaps one of the most meaningful works of the German high Baroque.

Giacomo Carissimi   1605–1674

Carissimi, born in April, 1605, in Marino, then in the Church State, and baptized on April 18, was one of the most important fathers of the oratorio and of the newer form, the cantata. Even though many of his works have been lost—most of them when the Jesuits were driven out of Rome (he had taught at their German-Hungarian school there), the remaining 16 oratorios in Latin, as well as cantatas, spiritual "concerts," Masses, Psalms, and so on, are quite sufficient to place him among the greatest of the Italian masters (as he was also recognized in his own time) and to establish the fact that he had a direct influence on Handel. A few works allow us to see him as one of the founders of the oratorio: *Abraham et Isaac, Baltazar, Diluvium universale, Ezechia, Jephte, Job, Jonas, Judicium Salomonis, Lucifer, Martyres,* and *Esther.* It was Carissimi who intentionally divided the solo numbers into two parts—the recitative and a closed form, the aria. His harmonies, with figured bass, were richer than those of his predecessors and his writing for the chorus more expressive. The Catalan musicologist Carreras has tried to prove that Carissimi owed important stylistic details to the Spaniard Tomas Luis de Victoria, who lived most of his life in Rome and was a close friend of Palestrina. Thanks to his outstanding students, among whom were the Germans Kerll and Krieger; the Italians Alessandro Scarlatti, Cesti, and Bononcini; and the Frenchman Marc-Antoine Charpentier, Carissimi's influence lived on well into the future.

Emilio de'Cavalieri   1550?–1602

Because we have no exact or complete records—never written, or if so, not preserved or not yet found—the life and works of so important a figure for this book as the Roman Emilio de' (or dei, or del) Cavalieri (or Cavaliere) remain largely a mystery. He seems to have come from a family with a great interest in the arts; his father was a friend of Michelangelo. From 1578–84 he is supposed to have put on musical programs in the oratorio, i.e., prayer hall, of the Holy Crucifix in San Marcello, which led to the new forms of church opera, oratorio, etc.—called *Rappresentazione* in Italian. In an enlightening preface to his best-known work he discusses the staging or partial staging of these compositions. Whether he was also active in Rome as a composer, or only as an organizer, is unclear. It is striking, however, that he is never referred to as *Maestro*, the obligatory title even then given any practicing musician. It is certain that he went to Florence in 1588. Starting in September of that year, he was "Director of Fine Arts" at the court of the art-loving Medici. Whether he was called there from Rome or went on his own in order to be close to the new musical directions that were attracting attention throughout Italy, we do not know.

It was around this time that the *Camerata Fiorentina*, that unusual and famous circle of artists, scholars, and patrons of the arts, began to form in the Tuscan capital. Their conversations, experiments, and musical evenings (held in the house of Count Bardi and in the Pitti Palace) were the source not only of the art form known as opera, but more importantly, of the *Stile rappresentativo*, that partly declamatory partly sung, recitativelike, arioso style that soon drove out the old polyphony and led to a new musical era. Cavalieri was successful not only in putting on the sumptuous festivities for the marriage of Ferdinand de Medici and Christine of Lothringen in 1589, but also at least helped to compose the music for the festivities. A number of other works he composed to texts by Laura Guidiccioni Lucchesini (*Aminta*, after Tasso, 1590; *Il satiro*, 1590; *La disperazione di Fileno*, 1594; *Dialogo di Giunone e Minerva*, 1600) have not survived. On the other hand, we do have, from 1600, perhaps his most important work: *La rappresentazione di anima e di corpo* (The Play of the Soul and the Body), which Cavalieri wrote in and for Rome, to which he must have returned at the end of the century.

Here, too, great artistic innovations were taking place: the decisive steps in the development of oratorio, making it possible for us to say, perhaps a little too simply, that opera arose in Florence and oratorio in Rome—simultaneously and from the same impetus. Moreover, we are fairly certain that Emilio de'Cavalieri stood by the cradle of both forms. In the course of performances of his *Rappresentazione* in Rome, he was recalled to Florence to participate in the lavish ceremonies scheduled for the wedding of Maria de'Medici and Henry IV of France. A few months later we find him once more in his native city, where he became increasingly ill and slowly went blind. He died in Rome on March 11, 1602.

The *Rappresentazione di anima e di corpo* was first performed in Rome, in February of 1600, in the oratorio Santa Maria della Vallicella of Saint Filippo Neri. Today the work is considered to be the venerable first oratorio, but could also correctly be called a church opera as it was performed at least partially staged, with costumes and movement. The work was published soon after. Cavalieri wrote an interesting preface in which a performance of that time almost comes to life before our eyes. It also shows how little notions of "Gesamtkunstwerk" have changed from that distant time, through Richard Wagner, right down to today. He wrote, "He who would like to perform the following work on the stage and wants to follow the suggestions of Emilio de'Cavalieri, should take into consideration that this new kind of music may evoke varied effects, such as pity, exultation, lament, laughter, and so on. It seems essential, then, that everything that goes with it should be carried out as perfectly as possible." He goes on to discuss the singers and their art, their diction, the plausibility of their gestures "not only of the hands, but accompanied by a corresponding way of walking." He speaks of the instruments, which should be well played and should be in such numbers as suit the size of the hall. The hall should not seat more than 1,000 people, and the audience should "sit comfortably" so as to provide "great quiet and attention." Cavalieri warns against larger halls, in which the words would not be heard clearly so that singers would have to force their voices, causing a loss of expressivity, thereby making the music boring. Then follow some precise "recipes" for good plays of this kind: There should be variety in the musical numbers; the poetic text should consist of not more than 600 lines; the action should be easy to follow; and so on. He follows with specific advice about oratorios which I quote: "The chorus should be onstage, sometimes seated, sometimes standing, endeavoring to show a sympathetic interest in all that goes on there." Then there is more on scenic and theatrical effects: "Some members of the chorus must change their places from time to time and join in the action. And when it is their turn to sing they should stand so that they can make gestures, then return to their original place."

Down through the centuries, the *Rappresentazione di anima e di corpo* seems never to have completely disappeared from the awareness of musicians and cultivated lay people. A major revival took place at the Salzburg Festival in 1968, when a new production under the musical direction of the festival's president, Bernhard Paumgartner, and the stage direction of Herbert Graf was given. This production remained in their repertory for years, a great counterpart to *Everyman* and a symbolic yet readily understood play on the themes of vice and virtue, damnation and salvation.

The "action," if it can so be called, is concerned with mankind's endeavor to reach Heaven—to sit at the side of God. The four elements are: *Corpo* (body), *Anima* (soul), *Intelletto* (intellect, understanding, powers of reasoning), and *Consiglio*, which we might think of as "good advice" or "reason." Traps are set out for man in the course of his earthly life to divert him from the path to God. These include *Il piacere* (pleasure) with various companions, called in many similar works by names such as avarice, gluttony, lust, gambling, search for power, and so on, but which in this play are left unspecified. The action is played out in the context of *Il mondo* (the world) and *La vita mondana* (earthly life and strife). In addition to this earthly scene, we are presented another world, where the *Angelo custode* (the guardian angel possessed by each person), the *Anime beate* (the souls of the dead, of the blessed), and finally, the *Angeli nel cielo* (the angels in heaven), bent on defeating the powers of evil and the *Anime dannate nell'inferno* (the souls of the damned condemned to Hell), save men of good will and faith.

In this sense, the *Rappresentazione* is a sacred play, whose roots were hundreds of years old when it was composed. Such mystery plays, sacred theater and related dramatizations, can be traced back through the Middle Ages to the early years of Christianity. But this tradition did not become fully articulated as musical drama—of the sort to which much of this book is devoted—until the Renaissance. At this time all the elements including vocal soloists, choruses, instruments, a narrator (where such a figure is required to make things clear), and continuous music were finally integrated. Cavalieri's enduring play is based on an ancient *Lauda*, an Italian song of praise, probably from the 13th century. The librettist was Agostini Manni, who deserves the highest praise for a work that moves even today's audiences.

There is, of course, the possibility that in the future, thanks to the reawakened interest in Baroque and Renaissance music, other works by Cavalieri, or more or less authentic arrangements of fragments, will come to light.

It should be noted here that in 1550, Gianfranco Maselli published the *Lamentazione di Geremia* (The Lamentations of Jeremiah), a work probably intended for performance by soloists and chorus during Holy Week. It came from the church of St. Nicholas in Pisa, where we know that not only Giulio Caccini (singer and composer), but also the famous female vocalist Vittoria Archilei, who often is mentioned in documents relating to Cavalieri, were active. Whether she (and other women) performed in church as well as in early operas is a matter of dispute. For the most part we assume that the high voices of the chorus and solos were sung by boys or castratos. These questions play an important role in adapting such works for today's purposes, but increasingly the prevailing point of view is that old music should be "beautiful," performed in a way that moves us today, rather than being merely historically accurate. Taste, which should be the only yardstick, has changed.

With the exception of its Italian title, the text of *Lamentazione* is in Latin, although each strophe is introduced with the sung letter of the Hebrew alphabet: aleph, beth, ghimel, vau, zain, heth. . . . We do not know if the work was sung a capella or, and this is more likely, with at least organ accompaniment. The inclusion of other instruments was purely a practical matter in those days: if any were available, they took part.

Francesco Cavalli 1602–1676

It is a truism that composers in the first generations of homophonic, monodic music cultivated the new genres of opera and oratorio regularly and often simultaneously. An obvious example was Cavalli, who was born on February 14, 1602, in Crema, a little town in the Italian province of Cremona, and died in Venice on January 14, 1676, after a very successful career as a composer. Of his 42 stage works (among them the operas *L'Ormindo* and *La Callisto*, which remain in the repertory today) *Serse* was selected to celebrate the peace treaty of the Pyrenees between France and Spain in 1660, while his *Ercole amante* was Louis XIV's wedding opera, in 1662. A Requiem was performed at Cavalli's funeral; he had composed it himself only a short time before—a lovely, eight-part composition. Among his sacred compositions, the Masses and Psalms, the *Messa concertata* for solos, chorus, and orchestra (1656) stand out; the cantata *Se la giù negl'abissi* has been reissued in our century and is often sung.

George Whitefield Chadwick 1854–1931

At the age of 22, without a complete high school education, Chadwick received a one-year appointment as Professor of Music at Olivet College in Michigan. Further organ study in Boston with Dudley Buck and Eugene Thayer, in addition to other private study at the New England

Conservatory, established his reputation as a promising young musician. Success as a composer came quickly. Study in Leipzig, Dresden and Munich (1877–1880) was crowned by prize-winning European premieres. Following his return to Boston, Chadwick led a prominent life as composer, conductor, organist and educator. In 1892 he was appointed to the faculty of the New England Conservatory and five years later became its Director. He remained in that position for 34 years.

Chadwick is one of America's great composers, with over 375 compositions to his credit. One-third of these are for chorus, including 21 large works with orchestra. The choral work which stands out above all others is the lyric drama *Judith* (1901).

Judith

Original Language: English
Date of Writing: 1901
First Performance: September 26, 1901, at the Worcester Festival in Massachusetts.
Form: Judith is in three acts, divided into 14 scenes. The similarities of the first and third acts—with their large choruses in hymn, fugue and anthem style—provide formal balance and account for the oratorio-like character. Act Two uses marches, dance rhythms, extended arias, and shorter choruses which relate directly to the dramatic action. It is thoroughly operatic.
Cast: Five major characters in the drama have extended roles: Judith, mezzo-soprano; Holofernes, baritone; Achior, tenor; Ozias, bass; and the Sentinel, tenor. The chorus acts as the Israelites, captive Hebrews, soldiers and camp followers. Though its position in the drama is often relegated to static commentary, the chorus is never without character identity.
Scoring: Soloists, chorus and full orchestra.
History of the Work: Apparently Chadwick intended the work to be viewed as an opera. Its numerous and detailed stage directions would indicate this. Each of the four complete performances to date, however, has been in concert form, as an oratorio. Producers seem unwilling to face the difficulties and risks involved in staging the long, static choral sections, even though many dramatic scenes seem to call for effective staging. In 1902, a writer for the Boston *Transcript* summarized this view:

> The libretto suffers severely from being neither opera nor oratorio, and the music, of necessity follows the text. The great climax of the second act, the long duet between Holofernes and Judith, the music of the camp followers and the soldiers and the dancing girls, also the ballet music, will never be effective without staging and dramatic action. As an opera, on the other hand, it would be sent to disaster by the numerous long choruses in operatic style.

Frederick Burton, composer and music critic for *The New York Times,* was even more pointed in his review of the premiere:

> *Judith* is unmistakably a kind of opera. That is, it belongs on the stage and can never be expressed in all its force until the music and text are supported and enhanced by action and spectacle.

Chadwick's choice of the designation "lyric drama" is an acknowledgment of this ambiguity.
Discussion of the Work: The story is essentially about Judith, the widowed Israelite beauty. Judith saves her people from certain defeat at the hands of the Assyrians by gaining entrance to the enemy camp, enticing their leader, Holofernes, into a drunken sleep and then beheading him with his own sword. Act I opens as the Israelites, Ozias, their leader, and Judith despair over the threat of the invading Assyrians in the massive chorus "Proud Ashur's Host." The motive introduced here in the soprano (Example 1) is one of many *Leitmotifs* (e.g. Judith, Judith's vision, protection of Jehovah, Holofernes, death knell) to appear throughout the work; they reflect Chadwick's interest in the Wagnerian style. Ozias counsels the people that their obedience to Jehovah will insure his aid and bring ultimate victory. In the next scene, Judith prays that God will show her how to save the people from destruction.

Example 1

Assyrian soldiers enter in scene three and remind the Hebrews that the siege will doom them and they will soon be without water—a situation akin to the story in Mendelssohn's oratorio *Elijah*. The Hebrews then lose confidence in God, curse Ozias and cry out in desperation for relief from the drought.

The final scene of Act I is in two dramatic sections. First, Judith sings a lengthy monologue. She chides the people for their lack of faith by explaining a vision in which God has unfolded his plan for her to subdue Holofernes. In the second section—a long choral finale to the act—the Israelites repent and pray that Judith will have divine protection on her sacred mission. This chorus contains a sublime passage in Chadwick's "anthem style"—one of the few unaccompanied sections in the work (Example 2).

Example 2

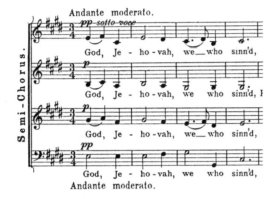

Example 3

Act II is pure opera. In the opening scene victorious Assyrian soldiers parade their Hebrew prisoners. Jeering camp followers throw barbed taunts at the beleaguered captives as they lament their fate (Example 3). In a savage aria, Holofernes shows his character as a brutal tyrant and then condemns one of his own commanders to death as a traitor for betraying fear of Israel's God. Intense dramatic moments such as this one, which need full staging to be convincing, characterize this act. The centerpiece of the work is the fourth scene, as Judith approaches the Assyrian camp. Hebrew captives lament her presence in an expressive a cappella passage of 32 measures (Example 4):

> The palm tree of mighty Judah
> Why comes she alone to the camp of the foe?
> Why did she leave the walls of the city?
> Trusted she here to find human pity?
> Never will sun rise to light thee hither,
> Ever in shame thy beauty shall wither,
> Judith, our fairest,
> Judith the pure.

Example 4

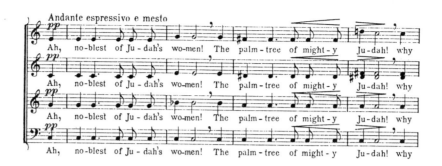

Example 5

Judith's beauty overcomes Holofernes. He bids her to his victory feast and proclaims she will be treated as a princess. Under this guise Judith gains entrance to the tent of Holofernes. In the long duet which follows, Chadwick's sensuous music effectively underscores the drama of this moment. Holofernes entices Judith with offers of gifts, wealth and station. She coyly resists responding. Then, seizing the opportunity, she asks for his jeweled sword. He hastily grants her request without suspicion, "Be all my power thine, thou hast it now. Then kiss me, come, thou dost delay too long!" With the weapon in hand, Judith feigns interest in his advances, encouraging him to continue drinking—"Drink, mighty chief, the bowl of wine"—until he falls into a drunken sleep. For 130 measures the music sustains Judith's fervent resolve to obey God's charge to her: "Thy fair arm shall slay." At the climax of her aria, a descending scale and sforzando chord picture the sword as it falls on Holofernes. Judith, unobserved, leaves the tent with the head of Holofernes concealed under her mantle. The curtain falls as the Sentinel dutifully intones "All's well."

The final act is relatively brief. Judith returns in triumph to Bethulia, displays the head of Holofernes and recounts the story. Released from the fear of imminent defeat and again confident in Jehovah's power to save, an inspired Israelite army rallies to victory. The craftsmanship and musical grandeur of the choral finale equals that of any major work (Example 5).

In composing *Judith*, Chadwick was undoubtedly influenced by Saint-Saëns' *Samson and Delilah*. He had conducted *Samson* as an oratorio in Boston and saw the story of Judith as comparable in moral tone and therefore acceptable to Victorian Boston. Chadwick had absorbed Wagnerian operatic fashions, but not to excess. Harmonically and melodically, the style is his own. Romantic chordal relationships are more blunt, more rough-hewn than Wagner's, and the flow of counterpoint is less chromatic. Yet the music is dramatically proper, direct, and powerfully expressive.

Judith was revived in 1977 and given a complete concert performance at Dartmouth College under the direction of Steven Ledbetter. It stands as a major work by a major American composer.

—*Thurston Dox*

Marc-Antoine Charpentier 1634?–1704

By a stroke of luck—shortly after Charpentier's death a nephew sold his musical estate (28 thick volumes entitled *Mélanges autographes*) to the royal library in Paris, which later formed the core of the French National Library—the works of this extremely important Baroque composer have been preserved. For many generations they lay practically unnoticed; Charpentier's name appeared only in encyclopedias, and his secular and sacred works were seldom performed. Only in the 20th century, when the great rediscovery of distant centuries began, when the demand for music of all kinds increased hugely and could not be met by contemporary production, did jewels of the past, especially from the Baroque, begin to appear. Not the least of these were works by this master, highly respected and famous in his own day, details of whose life remain unclear to this day. He should not be confused with the much later composer of the same name, Gustave Charpentier, who in 1900 composed the highly successful opera *Louise*.

Charpentier came from Paris; the year given for his birth, 1634, has been often disputed and a later date suggested. It is certain that as a youth he went to Rome, probably to follow family tradition and become a painter. Once there, he fell under the influence of the great Giacomo Carissimi who, as noted in the preface to this book was one of the fathers of the oratorio, and turned to music. It seems that toward the end of the 1650s he returned to Paris, where he entered the service of the Duchess of Guise whose palace orchestra he directed. He also wrote the music for some of Molière's plays, including *Le malade imaginaire* (1673), performed at Versailles, as well as for plays by Corneille and other leading French dramatists. In the 1680s he entered the service of the Jesuits, becoming "master of music" in their church and school at Clermont. In 1698 he reached the peak of his career when he was appointed musical director at Sainte Chapelle.

Only a very few of his extremely numerous compositions were printed in his lifetime. H.Wiley Hitchcock, the New York editor of a series of scores from the Baroque era, enumerates the most important of these: secular cantatas, arias, choruses, and incidental music for more than 25 plays. In addition, there is much sacred music, including more than 100 motets, 30 hymns, 32 antiphons, psalms, 10 Magnificats, 12 Masses, litanies, and Christmas songs ("Noels"). Probably most important are his 34 Latin oratorios which he called "Historiae." They are scored for soloists, one or two choruses, and one or more narrators. Many of them could, in my judgment, be performed today with great success. We also have the manuscript of a small textbook of composition, *Règles de Composition*, probably written for his long-time student, the Dauphin of France. Charpentier, viewed as one of the leading musicians of his country and of his time, died on February 24, 1704, at his residence in Paris.

From the enormous body of his works we have chosen two for discussion in this book. Like most Baroque compositions, Charpentier's contain few performance indications; often there is no more than a melodic line and a figured bass, to which is sometimes added information on the instruments to be used. There are neither tempo nor expression marks. Interpretation was left largely to the discretion of the performer, which for contemporary performances necessitates the preparation of "practical editions" that often differ greatly from each other. Let us briefly discuss Charpentier's *Te Deum*. It is a festive, thoroughly melodic piece, performed with five vocal soloists, a four-part mixed chorus, and a small instrumental ensemble typical of the Baroque era. Many of the instruments used then (oboe d'amore, various gambas, and others) are not in general use today; we can try to find them in museums or in private collections and put them into working order again; or we can undertake to "modernize" the works without sacrificing their original sense, so that they have the same effect on today's audience that they had on the Baroque audience. This has been done with a piece from Charpentier's *Te Deum*, which has become one of the most popular melodies of our time, for international television uses it as the introductory theme for its Eurovision broadcasts, resulting in its reaching a vast audience. No one can deny that this is a great, brilliant melody, combining the pomp of the most magnificent royal court of its time with the easy catchiness of a hymn (Example 1) (quoted from the edition by Walter Kolneder, Vienna, 1957).

Example 1

The oratorio *Judicium Salomonis* is broader in scope, and seems to be one of his later Historiae. It calls for two characters called "Historicus" (narrator), the solo voice of God (bass), Solomon (tenor), the true and the false mothers (soprano and alto), and a four-part chorus. It tells the Biblical story of how Solomon, the wisest king of his time, with the help of divine inspiration, decided the quarrel between two women, each of whom claimed to be the mother of the same child. Solomon initially delivered a sham verdict: the child claimed by the two women was to be cut in two so that each could have her share. The real mother instantly relinquished her half to spare her child, at which point Solomon, having discovered the genuine mother, awarded the child to her.

Luigi Cherubini 1760–1842

Cherubini's name was a byword among the musicians of his generation. A well known letter by Beethoven tells how much he valued and loved Cherubini and with what excitement he awaited each new work—an honor no other composer can boast of. Adolphe Adam, his respected French contemporary, referring to Cherubini's sacred music, called him the "Palestrina of the 19th century" and added that the C minor Requiem was "without equal in the world." Even Brahms, decades later, expressed high regard for the long dead composer. Born in Florence, trained by the greatest masters in Bologna and Milan, Cherubini began a career in opera. After a successful sojourn in London he settled down in Paris, where his operas (among them *Médée* and *Les deux journées*) assured him of a high position. Except for a few short concert trips he did not leave the city on the Seine from 1786 until his death in 1842, even though bitterness as well as fame had been his lot there. Napoleon was not favorably disposed toward him, and during his rule Cherubini remained in obscurity. While out of favor he dedicated himself to the less noticeable genre of church music. In 1811 he wrote the greatest of his Masses, in D minor, one of the most inspired of all religious compositions. With Napoleon's fall and a changed political climate, Cherubini's rehabilitation began. In 1816 he became professor at the conservatory, and in 1824 its director, a post he held until just before his death. Also in 1816, King Louis XVIII requested him to compose a Requiem for the service planned to commemorate the death of Louis XVI, executed during the Revolution. Exactly 20 years later he composed a second Mass for the Dead—for his own death, one might say. Cherubini died at the age of 82 in Paris, famous and heaped with honors, although his thoroughly Classic style that had come straight from Haydn was by then a little out of date.

Requiem in C minor

Wishing to present a memorial service for the Bourbon king Louis XVI, who, together with his wife, the Habsburg princess Marie Antoinette, had been executed during the French Revolution, Louis XVIII commissioned a Requiem from Cherubini in 1816. Cherubini wrote a work calling for four-part mixed chorus (without solo voices) and the usual "classic" orchestra: two each of oboes, clarinets, bassoons, horns, trumpets; three trombones, timpani, gong or tamtam, and strings. Wanting a darkly colored sound he omitted flutes entirely and left the violins out of the introductory pieces—the Introitus, Kyrie, and Graduale.

The first theme rises out of the depths; cellos and bassoons singing a gloomy song of mourning. After three attempts it almost painfully reaches the tonality of C minor (Example 1), and the chorus enters in somber colors. In this register, the voices sound little more than pale, disengaged, not of this world. It is long before they climb to higher registers. Motive No. 1 sounds again and again, like a "Memento mori." The violas, pianissimo, introduce the Gradual, again in minor, after the Kyrie closes with an unexpected brightening in C major. Softly, with restraint, and with a single, fleeting climax, only the low strings accompany the song of mourning "Requiem aeternam dona eis." As in many Requiems, the third section, the "Dies irae", portrays the horror of Judgment Day and therefore employs the most strident orchestral coloring. The brasses open the movement blaring a sustained pitch of G in unison. Then the gong sounds; its reverberating fortissimo is accentuated in that except for the timpani, no other percussion instrument is heard, and that it is struck only this once. The strings enter, and then the chorus, both with a ghostly softness, the voices again in that low, pallid register precluding any sensuousness. Then comes a pronounced upswing in the music, continuing through the "Tuba mirum." The brasses now call forth in all their might and the timpani enter loudly for the first time. It all breaks off eerily: "Mors stupebit..."—death is once more at hand. Face to face with its majesty, the male voices plead "Salva, salva me...," the strings subside in mournful sobs, and the tenors join in the weeping with a long solo: "Quaerens me...." The female voices answer softly, the basses intone a broad solo ("Ingemisco") and the female voices again answer. The mood becomes dramatic: with the words "Confutatis maledictis," the music mounts to new climaxes, which then break off, and the pleading voices return: "Voca me cum benedictis." Then the tempo slows, and the "Lacrimosa" begins like a great song of prayer, continuing with short, painful accents as if shaken by suppressed sobs until with its "Amen," it dies away.

Example 1

Larghetto sostenuto

Another important piece is No. 4, the Offertorium "Domine Jesu Christe." It contains many alternating moods and the magnificent finale "Quam olim Abrahae." Here Cherubini has constructed a fugue worthy of Bach. Technically it is a triple fugue because the main subject, introduced in the basses ("Quam olim..."), is accompanied by a second subject ("et semini" in the tenors) and a third (also "et semini" in the altos). The first answer of the fugal subject (as *comes*) follows in the sopranos with slightly altered intervals; the basses take over the second subject and the tenors, the third (Example 2). The tempo increases as the fugue enters a stretto, where only the main subject occurs (Example 3), and concludes with a concentrated choral passage. The delicate "Hostias" follows, a clear contrast to the contrapuntal edifices and linear voice leading that had gone before; here, Cherubini shows himself as one of the most skilled harmonists of his time. The powerful and majestic "Sanctus" leads to the most tender "Pie Jesu." In the final movement, the "Agnus Dei," the Lamb of God is called upon three times, and three times the call subsides with a gentle "dona eis requiem." The work comes to rest with an otherworldly brilliance ("et lux perpetua"), the voices flowing very quietly into the last harmony, C major, a breath of peace and light.

Example 2

Example 3

The *C minor Requiem* was first performed on January 21, 1816, in the crypt of St. Denis. It gained immediate acceptance, so much so that it was played at Beethoven's funeral.

When the Archbishop of Paris let it be known that he was reluctant to have the work performed at the funeral of the renowned composer Boieldieu, because he objected to female voices in church choirs, Cherubini decided to compose a second Requiem for male chorus alone. Thus the *Requiem in D minor* was created.

Requiem in D minor

Cherubini composed his *D minor Requiem* between 1834 and 1836; it was first performed on March 25, 1838 by the Concert Society of Paris. There is no doubt but that the composer really wrote it for his own funeral, and it was, in fact, played on that occasion four years later. To preclude the possibility of an argument over the participation of women in the Catholic liturgy—a source of considerable friction then and still a problem in orthodox congregations—Cherubini used a three-part male chorus (in the old form: two tenors and bass), at times subdivided. The orchestra is slightly larger than that in the *C minor Requiem:* it calls for four horns instead of two, as well as two flutes, the second of which plays the piccolo part.

The structure is similar to that of the earlier work, and many of the same ideas are used, including the pianissimo beginning with its subdued tone color—without flutes, oboes, violins, and violas. No. 2 is a Gradual; after a four-bar somber introduction it leads into an a cappella chorus. Then there is a dramatic "Dies irae." The "Pie Jesu" is structured like the Gradual (No. 2): only short phrases performed by a few instruments support the mostly a cappella male chorus, forcing it to reveal its best tonal quality in this passage. In general, it can be said that the *D minor Requiem* is more austere than its earlier counterpart, its rhythms harsher and its lyrical passages less sweet—but it provides a magnificent experience for those especially fond of the sound of a male chorus.

Paul Creston (originally Giuseppe Guttoveggio) 1906–1985

During his early years, Creston's first love was the keyboard and he aspired to become a concert pianist. Study with a theater musician eventually led to a position as organist for a silent movie house. At age 14 he stopped formal lessons and became his own teacher in piano, violin, and composition. After 1932 composing became his consuming interest. His first work to command attention, *Threnody* (1938), was premiered by the Pittsburgh Orchestra under Fritz Reiner, but it was Symphony No. 1 (1940) which brought international acclaim. Paul Creston received numerous awards and honors, held several college positions and wrote extensively about rhythm in Western music. The latter effort resulted in a ten-volume series, *Rythmicon*, which brought special attention to the deficiencies he found in traditional rhythmic practice. In his own words, composition was a "spiritual practice." The vitality of his rhythmically innovative and harmonically aggressive style characterizes his music; it brought him recognition as one of America's leading composers.

The fact that Creston produced many more instrumental than vocal works—perhaps 80% of his output—by no means indicates lack of interest in or capacity for expressive strength in vocal writing. His large works for chorus include *Missa Solemnis* (1949), *Isaiah's Prophecy* (1962) and *Missa cum Jubilo* (1968). Of these, *Isaiah's Prophecy*, for soloists, orchestra and chorus alone is designated an oratorio.

Isaiah's Prophecy

Original Language: English
Text: The Book of Isaiah
Date of Writing: 1962
First Performance: December 12, 1962, at the University of Florida at Tampa.
Form: There are no large divisions, merely a succession of 16 titled numbers.
Cast: Six soloists: The Prophet (baritone), Mary (mezzo-soprano), The Evangelist (tenor), Caspar (tenor), Melchior (baritone), and Balthazar (bass).
Discussion of the Work: The opening chorus invites all nations to hear the Christmas story (Example 1). [Copyright 1963 Franco Colombo, Inc. c/o CPP/Belwin, Inc., Hialeah, FL 33014. International Copyright secured. Made in U.S.A. All rights reserved. Used by permission.] In simple recitative the tenor sings a beloved prophetic passage from the book of Isaiah, "and there shall come forth out of the stem of Jesse....," foretelling the Messiah's coming. To complement these words, the chorus adds an Advent hymn, "O Come, O Come Emmanuel" (verses 1 and 3, Service Book and Hymnal, LCA) in a new strophic setting by the composer. The second verse "O Come Thou Rod of Jesse" particularly reinforces the recitative.

Example 1

Now the Annunciation story is told by the Evangelist through scripture taken from Luke's gospel; "And the Angel Gabriel was sent from God." After a brief recitative, the Evangelist continues the story as spoken narration over an expressive orchestral interlude. Mary responds, as in scripture, with the complete Magnificat (My soul doth magnify the Lord), set as an aria in warm, graceful lines over a flowing accompaniment. The final phrase reaches its climactic notes as the result of a gradual increase in pitch over several measures.

Narration resumes. The Evangelist sings a gentle accompanied recitative to the well-known nativity account found in Luke (And it came to pass in those days). The prophecy is fulfilled and the shepherds wait for God's revelation to them. This scene is narrated by the chorus through the hymn "While Shepherds Watched their Flocks by Night." All six verses are used but have been grouped in consecutive pairs to form three verses for a new strophic setting. A gently moving 6/8 meter preserves the pastoral mood.

An orchestral interlude titled "Pastoral Night" follows, depicting the awesome mystery in impressionistic colors and chordal patterns. Strains of the Gregorian introit "Puer natus est nobis" become a melodic companion for the parallel harmonies (Example 2). Suddenly, the Evangelist, unaccompanied, interrupts this serene mood to announce "a multitude of the heavenly host praising God." The orchestra's brief, incisive introduction opens the heavens and the full chorus bursts into song—the song of the Angels (Example 3). Three exuberant passages in fugetta style follow; then the opening exultation returns, and the words "on earth peace, good will toward men" call for an abrupt change to a mood of motionless, quiet calm. In one of these sections Creston displays his creative command of counterpoint. The subject appears in parallel thirds. Each voice dutifully imitates in thirds until a shimmering eight-voice texture results, the voices maintaining the thirds as strictly as possible in the underlying contrapuntal lines.

The male chorus now changes its role to represent the inquiring shepherds. A balance of homophony and animated counterpoint allow the four voices to picture the conversation of the shepherds in their excited approach to the manger scene.

The Evangelist's report, "And they came with haste and found Mary and Joseph, and the babe lying in a manger," sets the scene at the manger, calling for a lullaby to the Holy Child. A soprano solo carries the text of "Sleep, Holy Babe," cushioned by the humming chorus. Again, the verses follow an original strophic setting, helping to provide variety and contrast in the succession of numbers.

One scene remains to complete the miraculous dramatic narrative—the arrival of the Three Magi. A brief passage from the Gospel of Matthew announces their arrival at the manger.

The scene of Adoration is enacted by the Wise Men, using five verses from the Ephiphany carol, "We Three Kings of Orient Are." Verse one is sung by the Magi as a trio and the chorus responds with the refrain. For the next three verses, each individual sings the verse appropriate to the special gift he bears; gold, frankincense and myrrh. The choral refrain is not sung after verse four, however, and the chorus concludes the carol with verse five. As with the previous hymns, the composer has created new music for old, familar words.

The last line of the carol "Alleluia, alleluia, earth to heaven replies" flows without interruption into the closing choral "Alleluia." A single thematic idea binds the movement's phrases together (Example 4). At the same time it supplies a constant source of rhythmic energy, giving buoyancy and thrust to the mounting succession of alleluias. Polymelodic sections sustain long melismatic lines, alternating with crisp, homophonic phrases until the summation is reached and "all alleluias" unite in praise of the Christ Child.

Example 4

—*Thurston Dox*

Johann Nepomuk David 1895–1977

Three very different German composers were born in 1895: Paul Hindemith, Carl Orff, and Johann Nepomuk David. Their paths led in completely different directions, not surprising in those disjointed times, but each found his own, unmistakable style. Nevertheless they have one trait in common: a clear predilection for the old—the pre-Classic or even the medieval. Hindemith was the first, with his opera *Mathis der Maler*; Orff reflected the orgiastic joy of living at the dawn of Western civilization, and David turned quietly inward, to himself and to God.

David was born on November 30, 1895, in Eferding, Upper Austria, and in some ways took after his countryman Bruckner: the organ was also life-sustaining for him, and the chorus an important means of expression. He was an exponent of polyphony of Bach's stamp, a master of counterpoint, in which he discovered ever new, modern possibilities. He required no revolution, no new doctrines or systems in order to compose music that was completely valid for the 20th century; even though it was solidly rooted in traditions hundreds of years old, its spirit is remarkably contemporary. He was not interested in gaining recognition, but composed and taught—mostly in Stuttgart. When asked which was his best work, he answered modestly, "the one I will write tomorrow."

Several of his works belong in this book, among them the oratorio *Ezzo-Lied*, a setting of the old German poem by the Bamberg canon Ezzo. Dating from the 11th century, it is a sort of Christian chronicle of the world, in which the story of creation is tied in with Christ's redemption. David set this work twice; the first version was lost during World War II (but later recovered), so he composed another in 1957, which bears the opus number 51. It combines the most diverse stylistic elements; old forms such as the fugue and the passacaglia are found side by side with jazzlike sounds.

Other works that should be noted here are the *Evangelienmotetten*; the *Deutsche Messe*, Op. 42, composed in 1956; the *Missa choralis de angelis*, Op. 43, which uses Gregorian themes; as well as the *Requiem Chorale*, Op. 48, also composed in 1956. The latter consists of eight sections: Requiem, Tractus ("Absolve Domini"), Sequence ("Dies irae"), Offertorium ("Domine Jesu Christe"), Sanctus, Agnus Dei, Lux aeterna, and Libera me. Twenty-two years after its composition and four years after David's death, his *Pollio* was given its first performance on February 11, 1982, in Vienna. It is an unusual work for solo bass, mixed chorus, and instruments (one each flute, oboe, clarinet, bassoon; two horns, harp, timpani, percussion [three performers], and strings). The great Latin poet Virgil composed his lovely eclogues around the year 40 B.C. These pastoral poems, which sing the praises of Sicily, are dedicated to the consul Arsinius Pollio. The fourth eclogue, which forms the text for this work, has given rise to various interpretations, among them the assumption that Virgil, in projecting a Golden Age related to the anticipated birth of a child, had foretold the birth of Jesus, as Constantine the Great suggested in a speech A.D. 325. David composed the work while on sabbatical in 1960, at the Villa Massimo in Rome.

In his obituary for David, Rudolf Klein wrote the following remarkable lines for the *Österreichische Musikzeitschrift* 1978:1: "His music ennobles to the highest degree that spirit of humanity that seeks a balance between order and freedom and creates a model for it in art.... What is new in David's music is more than just the quality of the works—it is an essential contribution to the evolution of style in our century, in an area that acknowledges the fundamental demand for a conciliatory, effective language...." His time will come, must come, when calmer times have separated the wheat from the chaff of a chaotic era.

Frederick Delius   1862–1934

England's reemergence toward the end of the 19th century as one of the leading centers of musical creativity, following roughly 200 years of virtual silence, is related to four important names: Edward Elgar, Frederick Delius, Ralph Vaughan Williams, and Gustav Holst. With his *Dream of Gerontius*, Elgar created the best known English oratorio of the time. Delius's *A Mass of Life*, less known to his contemporaries, probably due largely to the completely different conditions under which the two composers lived, is no less esteemed by those who love choral music. Holst, too, created a work for chorus and orchestra, the *Ode to Death*, after Walt Whitman; it was composed in 1919 as a Requiem for his friends who had fallen in World War I. Since the days of Handel the oratorio has played such an integral part in England's musical life that we can speak of England as its second home, after its origin in Italy.

Delius shares with Handel another connection, despite the differences in their mode of life, characters, and fate: that of their origin and emigration from the land of their nativity. Handel was a German, educated in Italy and famous in the south. He lived in England for more than 40 years, until his death, and was, in fact, an Englishman; he composed in that language (except for his Italian works) and was laid to rest in the Poets' Corner of Westminster Abbey. Delius came from a German family of possibly Dutch origin that had moved to England. He was born on January 29, 1862, in Bradford, Yorkshire, and spent part of his youth working in the orange groves of Florida. He later studied at the Leipzig conservatory, settled in Paris in 1888, but moved in 1899 to the tiny village of Grez-sur-Loing (Dep. Seine et Marne) to satisfy his need for a more natural landscape. After years of serious illness, he died there on June 10, 1934, crippled and blind. (1934 was a tragic year for English music—Elgar and Holst died in that year as well.) In spite of the fact that its creator was so out of touch with real life (he left Grez only to spend time in the even more isolated fjord country of Norway), the music of Delius is part and parcel of the intellectual/spiritual atmosphere of his time. It is as closely tied to Debussy's overrefined Impressionism as to the fragile, nostalgic *Art nouveau*. It has about it a thoroughly subdued, "phantasmal twilight," (Hans Hollander) emanating from nature and dissolving into it again, and often seems lost in dreams. Delius's finest creations are in the genres of opera and the symphonic poem.

For so introspective a man as Delius, poetry in all its forms was especially meaningful. Three famous poets particularly inspired him: Gottfried Keller, Jens Peter Jacobsen, and Friedrich Nietzsche. Fritz Cassirer compiled the text for Delius' *A Mass of Life* from Nietzsche's *Also sprach Zarathustra*, whose basic perspective is not the abstract philosophy of Professor Nietzsche, the philosopher/poet who went insane and died young, but the life-affirming Dionysus cult of the art-inspired Nietzsche. *A Mass of Life*, composed for four solo voices, eight-part double chorus, and large orchestra (three flutes with picolo, three oboes, English horn, bass oboe, three clarinets, bass clarinet, three bassoons, contrabassoon, six horns, four trumpets, three tenor trombones, bass tuba, two harps, percussion, and strings) was composed in 1905, the same year as Richard Strauss's opera *Salome*, Debussy's symphonic poem *La mer*, and Mahler's Seventh Symphony. It is significant that Mahler and Strauss, like Delius, referred to Nietzsche: Strauss in the tone poem *Also sprach Zarathustra* and Mahler in the songs of his Third Symphony, where some of the same verses are set as in Delius's *Mass of Life:*

> O Mensch! Gib acht! Was spricht die tiefe Mitternacht? Ich schlief! Aus tiefem Traum bin ich erwacht! Die Welt ist tief! Und tiefer als der Tag gedacht! Tief ist ihr Weh! Lust tiefer noch als Herzeleid! Weh spricht: Vergeh! Doch alle Lust will Ewigkeit, will tiefe, tiefe Ewigkeit!

> (Take heed, Oh man! What does midnight have to say? I was asleep. I was awakened

from a deep dream. The world is deep, deeper than the day had thought. Its woe is deep, but its joy is deeper than heartache. Woe speaks: Begone! But all joys want an eternity, a deep and everlasting eternity!)

But by 1905, Delius was no longer just a herald of joy; perhaps he had never really been one. The most beautiful passages in his oratorio, or probably in all of his music, are the wistful, ineffable moments of deep melancholy, which are often best conveyed in sound—that Fin-de-siècle mood that is so pervasive in the art of the time, and so prophetic. This mood bridged national cultures and brought Delius close to a poet whom he hardly could have known—Ady Endre, the superb Hungarian poet who wrote (roughly translated), "I am related to death; I love the love that suffers, I kiss most tenderly the one who departs." The songs of the living in *A Mass of Life* are for this reason more original and introspective than the somewhat sumptuous double chorus of the opening: "O du mein Wille! Du Wende aller Not!" (Oh, thou, my will, turning point of all necessity). The second section of the Mass also begins with a sort of hymn: "Herauf! Nun herauf, du grosser Mittag!" (Arise! Arise now, high noon!) Patently this Mass is not intended for a particular church or liturgy. Delius would indeed not have been able to write such a work, for he was a convinced atheist who opposed all established churches, dogmas, and confessions of faith. This became especially clear when people interpreted his *Requiem*, dedicated to those who had died in World War I, in this way. Thomas Beecham, the noted English conductor who discovered Delius and promoted his music, has left us this description: "The meaning of his earthly existence lay in the turning of his gaze always inward to the depths of the soul, bringing to light the best that he found there and translating it into the language of music, without worrying much if his work would be applauded or even noticed." As Delius himself said, from the very bottom of his soul (and this from a man who had had his share of happiness—love, inexhaustible experiences in the natural world, and even almost unwanted success): "There is only one true happiness on this earth—the happiness of creativity."

Robert Nathaniel Dett 1882–1943

An extraordinary talent for keyboard improvisation drew Dett to an early musical career. His accomplishments at the Hampton Institute in Virginia (1913–1931) distinguished him as an educator, choral conductor and composer. In 1932—at 50 years of age—he completed a Master's degree in composition at the Eastman School of Music.

Dett was at home writing in impressionistic and jazz-related idioms, though earlier styles were easily under his command. A major choral work, *The Ordering of Moses*, claims distinction as the first oratorio written by a black composer.

The Ordering of Moses

Original Language: English
Text: Based on scripture and folklore.
Date of Writing: 1937
First Performance: May 7, 1937, at the Cincinnati May Music Festival.
Form: Though the music is through-composed, the text arrangement clearly delineates three sections: Israel's oppression under Pharaoh, God's "ordering of Moses," and Israel's deliverance. Only essential Biblical detail is provided.
Cast: Five character roles are designated for soloists; the chorus represents "the Children of Israel."
Scoring: Chorus and orchestra
Discussion of the Work: Nathaniel Dett was an innovator in his use of black American melodies as themes. In this work, quotes from the beloved spiritual *When Israel Was in Egypt's Land* figure prominently. A remembrance motive drawn from the melody begins the overture (Example 1). [Musical examples copyright 1937 (renewed 1964) J. Fisher & Bros. c/o CPP/Belwin, Inc., Hileah, FL 33014. International Copyright secured. Made in U.S.A. All rights reserved. Used by permission.] Several short passages then picture Israel in bondage, and a large choral section carries the promise of deliverance, culminating in "let my people go" (Example 2). Instruments depict Moses in deliberation. A spiritual, "When Moses Smote the Water," fixes Israel poised at the Red Sea. "The March" begins. Determined rhythmic movement in the orchestra energizes the freely flowing vocal lines

(Example 3). A programmatic orchestral section in galloping 6/8 meter—titled "The Egyptians Pursue"—interrupts this march. Waves of whole-tone harmony submerge the pursuers. The remembrance motive reappears, recalling Israel's struggle, as the triumphant choral finale begins.

Black American music commonly has drawn a parallel between this Biblical drama and black slavery. Dett's oratorio establishes a musical monument to this relationship. After the first performance critics for *The Cincinnati Enquirer* wrote in the most favorable terms.

Musically speaking, this Biblical folk scene of Dett might be loosely described as a sort of extended development of the spiritual, "Go Down, Moses," interrupted by declamatory and rhapsodic passages for soloists and some orchestral interludes.... The composer has treated the material with naivete appropriate to the outlook of his drama.... His choral fugue "Go Down, Moses" can hold its own with some of the best of them.

Dwight Bicknell's comments preserve the spirit of the audience reaction.

> The fourth concert of the May Festival series last night was marked by one of the most rousing ovations ever witnessed in the staid auditorium of the Music Hall—an ovation to the composer of "The Ordering of Moses," Dr. R. Nathaniel Dett, whose oratorio received its world premiere before a wildly enthusiastic audience.
>
> Dr. Dett's composition is said to be the most important contribution to music yet made by a member of the Negro race, and judging from the reaction of the festival audience, that statement may be classed as an understatement.
>
> —*Thurston Dox*

Antonio Diabelli 1781–1858

We tend to associate the name Diabelli only with the names of two more notable people: Beethoven, who wrote variations on a theme Diabelli had composed (*Diabelli-Variationen*, Op. 120), and Schubert whose works Diabelli published. But this Viennese musician and music publisher, born on September 6, 1781, in Mattsee, near Salzburg, was a widely honored composer in his day. A large number of works flowed from his pen, primarily exercises for piano which enjoyed great popularity for many years. His operas and other large-scale works have mostly been forgotten, probably forever. But one of his Masses, the *Pastoralmesse* in F major, Op. 147, has reappeared in our time, and is a thoroughly attractive, engaging, harmonious work.

Gaetano Donizetti 1797–1848

We often think of Rossini, Bellini, and Donizetti together as the "three stars of bel canto opera," as well as the last practitioners of this genre. Rossini, at the peak of his fame, chose to retire from all further work in the theater after the wildly successful premiere of his opera *Guillaume Tell*, although he was only 37 years old. Bellini's star rose like a meteor; in constant competition with his friend Donizetti, he experienced triumph after triumph, until fate put an end to his life when he was 34 years old. That left Donizetti the only one active in the international musical arena, but in his 40s he plunged into the night of madness and was taken from Paris, where all three "belcantists" had lived for a time, to his home town, Bergamo. His illness worsened, and he died on April 8, 1848. He was one of the most important creators of opera, and our own era has seen the enthusiastically received revival of a number of his works for the stage. Compared to these, his sacred works appear somewhat pale.

It should be noted that Donizetti wrote a large number of religious compositions: two practically forgotten oratorios (*Oratorio Sacro* and *Le siete chiese*); more than a hundred small pieces of church music (such as Ave Maria, Gloria, Kyrie, Miserere, Te Deum); and a quantity of both secular and sacred cantatas. He also composed Masses and Masses for the Dead; one of the latter is included here because it is occasionally performed and also because its origin is a beautiful gesture of friendship for Bellini, who had just died.

Requiem

Original Title: Messa di Requiem, scritta espressamente pei funerali del Maestro Cav. Vincenzo Bellini ed alla sua memoria dedicata
Original Language: Latin
Text: Mass for the Dead (Missa pro defunctis) of the Catholic liturgy.
Date of Writing: End of 1835; remained unfinished.
First Performance: In the basilica Santa Maria Maggiore in Bergamo, on April 28, 1870.
Form: That of the Mass for the Dead, but only the following sections were finished: Introitus, Kyrie, Requiem, Dies irae, Tuba mirum, Judex ergo, Rex tremendae, Ingemisco, Preces meae, Confutatis, Oro supplex, Lacrimosa, Domine, Lux aeterna, Libera me.
Scored for: Four solo voices (soprano, alto, tenor, bass), four-part mixed chorus, and orchestra.

History of the Work: After Rossini had decided to give up composing operas (1829), the two sharpest contestants in Italian opera, but true and devoted friends, were Gaetano Donizetti and Vincenzo Bellini. Bellini's early death on September 23, 1835, shook Donizetti deeply and led him to compose several works: a *Lamento per la morte di V. Bellini* to verses by *Andrea* Maffei; a *Sinfonia per orchestra sopra motivi di Bellini;* and most notably the *Messa di Requiem.* It remained unfinished, was not performed until 22 years after Donizetti's death, and has since been somewhat overshadowed by other Masses for the Dead.

Discussion of the Work: The main key, D minor, is established during the solemn introduction. The voices of the chorus enter in imitation of each other, first the basses, then the tenors, the altos, and finally, the sopranos, each voice persisting on a single pitch as in a litany, until their respective half cadences. The simplicity of Donizetti's melodic style is evident here, but it expresses well the deeply religious feeling of the "Requiem". The solo quartet enters with "Te decet hymnus" in F major, finally modulating to A major, and then back to D minor for the start of the "Kyrie." Here begins a rather free-form fugue with much chromaticism. Then the Requiem section is repeated in a condensed form ending in a stretto. The "Dies irae" is striking: the syncopation of the choral entries reminds us of Verdi's overwhelming *Messa di Requiem,* more than 30 years in the future, where this nuance is expanded to become an unforgettable experience. Was it a coincidence? Probably, because it is most unlikely that Verdi knew of the work of his predecessor. The priority given male voices over female is most striking, but because the work is incomplete, explanations are futile; it is entirely possible that Donizetti would have reestablished the balance in the missing sections. Or was he thinking of boy sopranos and altos, certainly less suitable for the solos than professional male singers? We know that Donizetti's Bavarian-born teacher, Simon Mayr, who became a famous musician in Italy, had a hand-written copy of Mozart's *Requiem* which he held up to his students as a masterpiece of the highest, most unattainable quality. Whoever listens to Donizetti's Requiem attentively will discover the composer's deep respect for Mozart and for his *Requiem* in particular, inculcated by his teacher.

Maurice Duruflé   1902–1986

Maurice Duruflé was born on January 11, 1902, in Louvriers on the Eure, in the department of Eure et Loire, and lived chiefly in Paris. He had already made a name for himself with his famous improvisations on the organ before he turned to the composition of various, primarily sacred, compositions. With his Requiem, composed in 1947, he produced an undisputed masterpiece. Inspired somewhat by Gregorian chant, this piece shows a classic sense of order and clarity but is nevertheless completely contemporary. As a child, Duruflé attended the famous cathedral school for vocal music, St. Evode, in Rouen. He studied at the Paris conservatory from 1920 to 1928, and later taught organ there, an instrument he continued to play in the best tradition of French organists.

Antonin Dvorak   1841–1904

Loved by his people, highly esteemed by the major musicians of his time, successful yet modest, an artist with close popular ties but also possessed of a technical mastery of the first order: that was the quintessential Bohemian musician, Antonin Dvorak. He inherited from his predecessor Smetana his preoccupation with Czech national music and carried out his intentions with great success in all musical genres. Among these are the sacred and secular choral works with orchestra, five of which fall within the scope of this book. They were composed primarily during the composer's early and middle years prior to his journey to America and world-wide fame.

Dvorak was born on September 8, 1841, an innkeeper's son, in the village of Nelahozeves on the Moldau. When he was 16 years old he went to Prague, where he earned his living playing the violin and the viola. In 1873 he won a scholarship for composition, and he was on his way. When Oxford University bestowed an honorary doctorate upon him, England welcomed him with open arms. In 1892, the National Conservatory in New York called him to be its director. The three-year stay in the United States broadened his intellectual as well as musical horizons; he became acquainted with the musical language of the Indians and the Blacks, and taught the rising generation of composers in this land so unburdened by tradition. Upon his return, he became the director of the Prague conservatory but devoted most of his time to composition. He died in Prague on May 1, 1904.

Requiem

Original Title: Requiem. Missa pro defunctis, Op. 89
Original Language: Latin
Text: Mass for the Dead (Missa pro defunctis) from the Catholic liturgy.
Date of Writing: From February until the end of October, 1890.
First Performance: October 9, 1891, in Birmingham, England, conducted by the composer.
Form: In six parts:
    1. Introitus and Kyrie
    2. Gradual
    3. Sequentia: Dies irae (subdivided into six musical numbers)
    4. Offertorium (subdivided into two musical numbers)
    5. Sanctus and Benedictus (with Pie Jesu)
    6. Agnus Dei and Communio: Lux aeterna
Scoring: Four solo voices (soprano, alto, tenor, bass), variously subdivided mixed chorus; two flutes (one piccolo), two oboes, English horn, two clarinets, bass clarinet, two bassoons, contrabassoon, four horns, four trombones, three trumpets, tuba, timpani, strings.
History of the Work: In 1887, the committee for the music festival in the English city of Birmingham proposed to Dvorak that he compose a work for this occasion and suggested the text "Dream of Gerontius" (which would be fashioned into an impressive oratorio 15 years later by the noted English composer, Edward Elgar). Dvorak accepted the offer but could not warm to the subject; instead he promised a composition of his own choice. When he began to work, the form of the Requiem was of particular interest to him, and the result is one of his most beautiful, most mature and affecting works. His close relationship to England had been formed over the course of several visits he had made to that country, during which time several important works had been conceived. When he returned in 1891, he conducted the premiere of his Requiem in Birmingham. Posterity remembers that great choral work as one of his most impressive achievements.
Discussion of the Work: The first motive, played by the violins in the most delicate pianissimo, suggests a Gregorian chant melody. The pitch F (the dominant of the key of B-flat minor) is embellished by neighboring half-tones. In the second phrase the melody expands a bit but keeps to the minor third F/A-flat in the same melancholy, funereal mood (Example 1). The voices enter, again emphasizing this gloom. Only slowly does the first section free itself from the prevailing somber mood and reaches its first climax with "Te decet hymnus, Deus, in Sion." The composer inserts many solo passages into the choral parts. The second section, the Gradual, is set for the solo soprano, who repeats the opening phrase at a higher pitch and then, accompanied by the female voices of the chorus, increases its range and ends in a great cantilena. The "Dies irae" gets its dramatic movement and sharp accents from the orchestra, while the chorale-like, unison choral melody has a medieval flavor (Example 2).

The introduction to the "Tuba mirum" is one of the most beautiful parts of this Requiem. There are no trumpets or trombones blaring forth the call to Judgment Day, as is typical. Softly, uneasily, with all the melancholy of the first motive (No. 1), the horrors awaiting mankind are only suggested. This motive, which we can think of as the main idea of the entire work, is heard three times, each time a half-tone higher and each time closing on an augmented chord—a "chord of longing"

(Example 3). Now the melody passes to the solo alto. After a brief outburst in the chorus, the horror of death courses through all the voices, recited on the same note ("Mors stupebit") and descends to the deepest registers in the bass. The tenor begins a solo, "Liber scriptus." The repetition of the angular Dies irae motive with the sforzato chords in the orchestra brings the mighty structure of this movement to a close. "Recordare, Jesu" is sung by the quartet of soloists. Dvorak, otherwise so independent, holds to tradition by providing a fugue for the "Quam olim Abrahae," though we notice in certain passages that their composer is no Baroque master but a thoroughgoing Romantic, in the few magnificent moments he was able to wring from a theme that is not especially expressive.

Example 3

This makes the "Sanctus" all the more affecting, and the light-filled "Benedictus" is overpoweringly beautiful, as is the "Pie Jesu," in which three solo voices (soprano, alto, and tenor) sing against a five-part chorus. The beginning of the "Agnus Dei" cites once more the "main motive" (No. 1), which rises in a great arc until the entry of all the vocal forces—four solo voices and four-part chorus. Then the theme recurs; the sound recedes as the section comes to a close.

Stabat mater

On September 21, 1875, Dvorak's young daughter Josefa died. In his anguish he began to compose, on February 19, 1876, his *Stabat mater*, Op. 58. The text comes from a poetic sequence probably written by the Franciscan monk Jacopone da Todi around 1300 for the Feast of the Seven Sorrows of the Blessed Virgin Mary. Dvorak finished his sketch on May 7, 1876, but never completed the work due to pressures from commissions and other tasks. It took another tragedy to bring him back to it: two more of his children died. He completed the *Stabat mater* on November 13, 1877, but it was three years before it was first heard—in Prague, on December 23, 1880, performed by the soloists, choruses, and orchestra of the Czech Interim Theater (the forerunner of the splendid National Theater, founded by Smetana), conducted by Adolf Cech.

This work, probably the first Czech oratorio, quickly found widespread acceptance. On April 2, 1882, Leos Janacek conducted it in Brünn, and at the beginning of September, 1884, the composer took it with him on one of his trips to England. He had been invited on this occasion to participate in a music festival planned to celebrate the 800th anniversary of the cathedral in Worcester. He conducted the work there on the morning of September 11, 1884; the evening of the same day he appeared before a very large audience to conduct his Sixth Symphony in D major, Op. 60. The next morning he reported happily to his dear wife Anna, at home, "Yesterday was another glorious day. The *Stabat mater* made a tremendous impression in a huge, magnificent church (4,000 people). It was the greatest day of the entire festival, as everyone here says. As we were leaving the church, everyone looked at me and wanted to shake my hand."

A very prominent English conductor of the time, Joseph Barnby, presented the work in London's Royal Albert Hall, where it was a complete triumph; Dvorak had been "discovered" in England, something he joyfully acknowledged: "I am convinced that a new and happier time is beginning for me here in England; I think and hope it will be beneficial for our Czech art. The English are a good people, devoted to music, and it is also known that they remain faithful to those who have pleased them. God grant that this also applies to me."

In few of his great works is Dvorak so close to popular tradition, so true to his people, as in the *Stabat mater*. He has assembled a number of melodies of varying quality but always sincere, often naive, which appeal to the simplest heart, sometimes for solos, sometimes for ensembles. There is one passage ("Ut sibi complaceam") that sounds like a Bohemian dance, but slower and more reflective, "an idea that has many parallels and much precedent in the Baroque" (Alec Robertson).

It is not so far-fetched to refer to the Baroque tradition in connection with this work, in spite of the century and a half that separates them. In England, Dvorak witnessed the marvelous way in which Handel's music was kept alive, and it is understandable that his non-intellectual, music-loving soul absorbed something of it. Otakar Sourek, the Czech musicologist, calls Dvorak's *Stabat mater* one of the "richest in musical values and therefore deepest in feeling and purity of style of any setting of this sequence" and "a simple and upright, extremely realistic, comprehensive image of human feelings, from the depths of heart-breaking anguish to the heights of plaintive and compassionate prayer."

The 149th Psalm

Dvorak composed his 149th Psalm in March, 1879, for the famous Czech chorus "Hlahol," which, along with the gymnastic team "Sokol," was one of the places where the Czech heritage was cultivated before the founding of the country in 1918. The composer had already worked with this group six years previously, when, on March 9, 1873, they had performed his hymn *Die Erben des Weissen Berges* (The Legacy of the White Mountain) to a storm of applause. It was a political tale by Vitezlav Halek dealing with the oppression of the Czech people. This time Dvorak had chosen a Psalm, but it, too, alluded to a similar theme, although there was nothing in the music to draw attention to it. It is a happy, jubilant work, with a sonorous, full symphony orchestra and four-part mixed chorus without soloists. Of course, "Hlahol" sang the Psalm in the Czech language, but it is performed today in many languages whenever a festive work is needed. "Sing a new song unto the Lord, your joyful Hallelujah shall ring out to honor Him! Sing His praises aloud, sing a new song in honor of Him!"

Mass in D major

In 1886, a leading patron of music, Josef Hlavka, president of the Czech Franz Josef Academy in Prague, commissioned a religious work from Dvorak to be performed at the consecration of a chapel on his estate. The result was the *Mass in D major*, which bears the composer's opus number 86 (these numbers are not always a reliable indication of chronology). Although it is by no means one of the more important of Dvorak's works, it contains a number of lovely melodies which continue to evoke devout feelings in today's listeners and to bring joy to performers. Even with a prescribed form like the Mass, Dvorak's music never became routine; his very personal approach colored all his creations. Almost every other composer would set the Credo in a strong, confident mood, free of doubt. Dvorak uses a reflective, lyrical melody for his, sung by four solo altos in unison to a simple orchestral background (Example 1). The miracle of the Incarnation ("Et homo factus est") is sung by the chorus in mysterious, somewhat other-worldly tones. All the more frightening are the four chiseled syllables that then burst forth from chorus and orchestra: "Cru-ci-fix-us," which, repeated, become a motive of anguish and suffering.

Example 1

Die heilige Ludmilla

When, at the beginning of September, 1885, Dvorak returned from his triumphal journey to England, he took a few days off to rest in the village of Vysoka, near Pribram. From there he wrote to the poet Jarolsav Vrchlicky in Prague on the subject of an oratorio that both of them had been planning:

> I read your 'St. Ludmilla' [in Czech *Svata Ludmila*] to some of my friends in Birmingham, and they were highly pleased. We should shorten it a bit in some places and expand it in others. The work should last about two-and-a-half hours. We'll talk more about it when I go to Prague, which should be soon, and I will look you up as soon as I get there. I am hard at work on it, and immerse myself in it more and more; I can only

admire the great beauty you have built into the work. I hope my part goes as well! If it does, I am convinced our efforts will be crowned with the greatest success.

The poetically admirable text retells a medieval Bohemian legend. Ludmilla, the bride of Duke Boriwoj I, is celebrating, together with other noblemen, priests, and common people, the erection of a pillar in honor of the old Slavic weather goddess, Baba. The Hermit Ivan joins the crowd and begins to preach Christianity. As though divinely inspired, Ludmilla is converted and follows the venerable sage to his hermitage to receive the teachings of Christ. The Duke while hunting shoots a doe, thinking he has mortally wounded it. He sees to his astonishment that the bleeding animal has, with its last strength, dragged itself to a hermit who lives in the middle of the forest, at whose feet Ludmilla is kneeling, and that the holy man gives the animal new life. Full of joy he, too, embraces the new faith and leads his people to do the same. Ludmilla is later killed by opponents of Christianity (around A.D. 920) and subsequently beatified. Shortly thereafter she was made the patron saint of Bohemia. (She is also the grandmother of St. Wenceslas.)

Vrchlicky's poem as set to music by Dvorak is a legend in oratorio form, arranged in three parts or acts, and occasionally staged. In the first act we see the heathen festival at the court of Castle Melnik and the appearance of the apostle Ivan. The second act takes place deep in the forest and recounts Ludmilla's final enlightenment, her meeting with the Duke and his conversion. In the third scene, the reunited noble pair and their people are baptized.

Dvorak created an imposing historical tableau with solo voices, choruses, and large orchestra. There are a number of short, melodic phrases that we could well call "leitmotifs," since they are used in a way that closely resembles the way Richard Wagner used them. A clear example is the way the motives for paganism and for the cross confront each other.

Dvorak, like his librettist, is far from presenting the pagan feast of the goddess Baba as a dark and despicable ceremony; it is instead a lovely celebration of spring, with folkloristic and historical touches, even though the composer did not intend to conjure up the Middle Ages musically.

Dvorak dedicated the score to the Zerotin musical society of Olmütz (Olomouc). The first performance of *St. Ludmila* took place on October 15, 1886, in Leeds, conducted by the composer. It was the jewel in the crown of his fifth English journey, which he had made this time with his wife. On October 18th, he reported to his friend Antonin Rus in Pisek:

> Finally everything is over; my triumph was magnificent, and I hasten to give you the details. *St. Ludmila* made a tremendous impression on everyone and was the high point of the festival, as all the London newspapers agreed.... I have never heard such a chorus and such an orchestra in England; they were literally fabulous! Words cannot describe it. I was so heartily and sincerely acclaimed by the audience, the chorus, and the orchestra, that I could hardly keep to my feet. During the performance almost all the numbers were wildly applauded, and at the end of the first part they broke out in such a storm of joy that I was deeply moved.... There were 350 singers in the chorus and 120 of the best musicians in the orchestra.

The performance in Leeds was done in English; since then *St. Ludmila* has been translated into many languages and performed in many lands, but it is seldom heard today.

Te Deum

In 1892, Dvorak signed a three-year contract as the director of a leading school of music in New York. A patroness of the arts, Mrs. J. Thurber, founder of the National Conservatory, flooded the composer with correspondence concerning every conceivable detail. Among other things, she asked him to compose something for the 400th anniversary of Columbus's discovery of America in 1492. Dvorak thought there was not enough time to compose a work to a text that was not yet finished, so he suggested in its place a Te Deum which he immediately began to write and which was performed in New York in October, 1892. It was Dvorak's last sacred work and bears the opus number 103. It is a significant work for two soloists (soprano and bass), four-part mixed chorus, and large symphony orchestra (with doubled woodwinds, four horns, two trumpets, three trombones, tuba, timpani, bass drum, cymbals, and triangle). Its division into four parts is reminiscent of a symphony, and even the tempo marks are similar: the first part ("Te Deum laudamus") is labeled allegro moderato, maestoso; the second ("Tu, Rex gloriae"), lento maestoso; the third ("Aeterna fac"), vivace, which corresponds to the scherzo in a symphony; and the fourth ("Dignare, Domine") begins slowly, gathers force as it moves into a hymn, and ends with an exultant "Hallelujah." The main theme of the first movement turned up again almost note for note in his violin sonata Op. 100 (Example 1).

Example 1

Te De – um lau – da – mus, te Do – mi – num con – fi – te – mur.

Cecil Effinger 1914–

Cecil Effinger's career developed in his home state of Colorado, where he has held distinguished positions as conductor of the Colorado Springs Symphony, first oboist with the Denver Symphony Orchestra, Assistant Professor of Music at Colorado College, and Professor of Music at the University of Colorado at Boulder (1948–1984).

After study with Bernard Wagenaar in 1937, he produced his first successful composition, *Piece for Ochestra*. During military service as band director and composition instructor in World War II, his first work, *Prelude and Fugue for Organ* (1942) appeared in print. His published catalog contains over 100 commissioned works for orchestra, small ensembles, chorus, and the stage, with over 15 large-scale choral works to his credit.

An oratorio, *The Invisible Fire* (1957), remains one of his most highly regarded compositions; widely performed and judged by some critics to be among the finest sacred oratorios in the 20th century.

The Invisible Fire

Original Language: English
Text: The text by John F. Driver is a compilation drawing on documents of the Wesley family: sermons of John Wesley; hymns of Charles Wesley; the journals of both, and passages of scripture. The story of John Wesley's struggle to achieve a dynamic Christian faith gives form and purpose to the work. Although the libretto is allusory, with little that passes for direct dialogue, surging movement towards a dramatic climax is achieved through careful ordering of the textual material. This sense of story and an overall didactic purpose supply the necessary ingredients for a powerful dramatic oratorio.
Date of Writing: 1957
First Performance: Commissioned by the National Methodist Student Movement and the Department of Worship and the Arts of the National Council of Churches, the first performance appropriately took place at the national Methodist Student Conference in Lawrence, Kansas, December 31, 1957, and marked the 250th anniversary of Charles Wesley's birth.
Form: Five parts; performance time is one hour.
Scoring: Full orchestra, chorus and four soloists: The Singer (soprano); Susanna Wesley (contralto); John Wesley (tenor), and The Moravian (baritone).
Discussion of the Work: Part One opens with a choral hymn of praise, "Christ Whose Glory Fills the Skies." The closing hymn, "Come Holy Ghost, All Quickening Fire," calls for the presence of the "invisible fire"—the Holy Spirit. Framed by these two brief unison choruses, The Singer raises questions about philosophy's role in the search for God and offers the hope of "a fire the sage philosopher knew not, burning invisibly, slow to consume." The Singer's role combines a narrator function with that of the chorus in Greek tragedy; setting the scene, speaking indirectly to a character or commenting in a detached manner on the progress of the drama (Example 1). [Musical

Example 1

It is a flame _ mys - te - ri-ous-ly lit,

(Flute)

Ped. 8' only

After this "invocation," Part Two focuses directly on John Wesley and his search for the consummate Christian life. Susanna Wesley, his mother—spiritual beacon of his life—begins with a straightforward directive: "God is altogether inaccessible, there is none can find Him, but by Jesus Christ." Wesley responds that he has "walked a straight and narrow way," as he was reared to do. He prays that God will see his good works.

> Lord, hear my cry! Doing so much, and
> living so good a life, I shall be a good Christian!

In a powerful section, the chorus speaks directly to Wesley in strong phrases: "You began, Holy Man, perfect law to fulfill. Purify, clear as sky, every part of your will." This chorus leads into the hymn by Charles Wesley "Long Have I Seemed to Serve Thee, Lord" (verses 1,5,6,7), and the audience is invited to join with the chorus, as it is again later, to close the section. Wesley's spiritual state of mind comes vividly to the fore in the last verse of this hymn:

> Where am I now, or what my hope?
> What can my weakness do?
> Jesus, to Thee my soul look up;
> 'Tis Thou must make it new.

Wesley's celebrated "Aldersgate experience" of rebirth and belief in salvation through faith alone, captures full attention in Part Three. The Moravian becomes involved in Wesley's spiritual struggle, symbolizing the inspiring association Wesley had with members of the Moravian sect. The Moravian also represents a particular individual in this scene, Peter Bohler, an exiled Moravian zealot who exerted a powerful influence on Wesley immediately prior to Aldersgate. The chorus characterizes Wesley's laborious striving with the lines "The hero moves with calm to every task which duty poses for his proven strength." Wesley responds in kind, but is driven to despondency: "The fiend is present with me and makes me captive to the law of sin. I fall, and rise, and fall again." The Moravian queries Wesley at this point, asking "What is the end of all your serving?" and is joined by the chorus in a litany, recounting Wesley's good works; his fasting, prayer, charity and preaching in foreign lands (a reference to the Georgia missionary expedition) (Example 2).

Example 2

The Moravian presses the crucial point with the very words Wesley actually heard as he entered the Aldersgate meeting place: "All who rely on the works of the law are under a curse; they die. But the righteous by faith shall live." Wesley felt his "heart strangely warmed" and cried out: "Lord, I believe!" Almost immediately, he adds the words "help Thou my unbelief." With faith professed he confesses it is "with dullness and coldness." "God is altogether inaccessible," he reasons, and the chorus echoes his emptiness:

> Hear in the sky our echoing cry,
> We would long to die.

Part Four is unusual in oratorio composition as it constitutes a dramatic "flashback." The Voice of God, sung in unison by the chorus men, thunders through the underpinnings of Wesley's wavering faith:

> Servant of my Holy law,
> Abandon thy dismay!
> Unknown to thee through all thy life
> I made thee a way.

The chorus and Susanna then join to recount the incident in which Wesley, as a child, was miraculously rescued "in the dead of night" when his home was ravaged by fire (Example 3). God speaks again: "I sent thee out into the sea to overflood the soul." The chorus plunges into a description of the terrifying storm which befell Wesley's ship on his voyage to America, then divides into male and female choruses to represent the Moravian men, women and children on the ship. The women and children pray for help while the men sing "On this my steadfast soul relies; Father, Thy mercy never dies," set to the ancient chorale tune "Aus tiefer Not" (From deepest need).

Example 3

Example 4

Wesley calls out "Lord, I am afraid to die," admitting fear of death, while those around him appear confident in God's power. In direct dialogue with the Moravian, Wesley is again pressed to expose a lack of faith in his calling as "a child of God." Finally God's plan unfolds before Wesley "when all thy works were vain, I sent thee, unwilling, to a chosen place" (Aldersgate). Using the second and third verses of Charles Wesley's hymn "Jesus Mine All Victorious Love," Wesley prays "O that in me the sacred fire might now begin to glow" and with exuberant zeal sings (Example 4). Here, at this climactic moment, the congregation is again invited to join the chorus, singing verses 1,2,5 and 6 of Charles Wesley's hymn "Author of Faith, Eternal Word." The last stanza expresses the fulfillment of Wesley's spiritual quest:

> Faith lends its realizing light
> The clouds disperse, the shadows fly;
> The Invisible appears in sight,
> And God is seen by mortal eye.

Part Five functions as an epilogue and is the shortest. The Singer begins " 'Twere new indeed to see a bard all afire" and, together with the chorus, vividly depicts a world ignited with the blazing fire of the Holy Spirit—alluding to Wesley's subsequent ministry and founding of the Methodist Church. The chorus sings the concluding paean, "And lo! We fall before His feet and silence heightens heaven."

Cecil Effinger has written a wealth of accessible choral music for American audiences. The cantatas *The St. Luke Christmas Story* (1953), *Paul of Tarsus* (1968), and *Cantata for Easter*, along with the oratorio *This We Believe* (1974) are well known and frequently performed. His harmonic language is clear and unencumbered. Though he readily identifies with accepted 20th-century practices to whatever extent his expressive purpose requires this, he is an avowed opponent of serial techniques.

In October 1959, a reviewer for *The American Organist* wrote about *The Invisible Fire:*

> Effinger's setting is modern in the finest sense: music of true distinction, free of any cerebral striving for mere effects, spiritually at one with the text, spontaneous, communicative, making the word come alive.

> *—Thurston Dox*

Edward Elgar   1857–1934

A greatly revered English composer, much performed there as well as in the United States, Elgar is much less known in central Europe and in the Latin countries—in fact, is hardly a familiar name there at all. At the most, his brilliant *Enigma Variations* for orchestra and less often, the violin and cello concertos are performed. Probably most frequently heard—though not often in a concert hall—are some of his *Pomp and Circumstance* marches, dazzling parade pieces, both literally and figuratively. After almost 150 years of mediocrity, England found itself, at the turn of the century, in the position of being one of the leading nations in music; Elgar and Holst, as well as Delius and Vaughan Williams, less well known at the time, had much to do with this "Renaissance." They followed in the footsteps of the great virginalists of the 16th century, Purcell in the 17th century, and Handel in the 18th century, and restored the composition of music to a place of prominence in the life of this always musical nation.

Edward Elgar, later knighted, was born on June 2, 1857, in Broadheath, Worcester; he grew up far from centers of music and never really had a formal education in music. He matured as one of those "original" composers, glowingly defended by some, roundly criticized by others. He probably gained recognition later in life than any other musical master, and indeed found his own style later than most. In 1889 he moved to London, but it was fully 10 years later before he had compositions to show and had gained some measure of success. From that time forward his influence justly spread.

In 1893 Elgar began to write those works that lead to his inclusion in this book. In that year he composed the cantata *The Black Knight* and in 1896 the oratorio *Lux Christi* (*Light of Life*). In the same year his cantata *King Olaf* was performed for the first time at the North Staffordshire festival in Hanley. In 1898 came the cantata *Caractacus* and two works for the diamond jubilee of Queen Victoria, which earned him the title of "Court Composer" but contributed little in the way of recognition by the public. This situation changed suddenly in the next two years with the appearance of his song cycle *Sea Drift*, his orchestral work *Enigma Variations*, and finally the oratorio *The Dream of Gerontius*. Elgar wrote two other oratorios (*The Apostles*, 1903, and *The Kingdom*, 1906) as well as the cantata *The Music Makers* (1912), but never again found as wide an audience as that for *The Dream of Gerontius*. He wrote a number of large and small choral works, both sacred and secular. The main body of his work was orchestral, although he also composed chamber music, piano music, and songs (as a matter of curiosity it should be mentioned that among other things, he wrote *Scenes from Upper Bavaria*, based on texts of Bavarian folk songs). Elgar died, a "national" figure, in Worcester on February 23, 1934. In the same year, Holst and Delius followed him in death; within the space of a few months England had lost three of its most important contemporary composers.

The Dream of Gerontius

Original Title: The Dream of Gerontius, Op. 38
Original Language: English
Text: by Cardinal Henry Newman
First Performance: October 3, 1900, at the Birmingham Festival, conducted by Hans Richter.
Cast: Angel (mezzosoprano), Gerontius and His Soul (tenor), priests and the Angel of Death (bass), four- to eight-part double chorus (demons, angels, souls, friends).
History of the Work: On one of his trips to England, the Czech master Antonin Dvorak met in Birmingham with Bishop Henry Newman, who showed him a sketch for an oratorio, *The Dream of Gerontius*. Dvorak, easily excited when it came to plans for music, agreed to set it to music, but never managed to fulfill his promise. The text was then given to Elgar, who had meanwhile been discovered by the famous Hungarian conductor of German ancestry, Hans Richter. Richter had conducted the premiere of Richard Wagner's *Ring des Nibelungen* in 1876 at the festival theater in Bayreuth, had been the director of the music festival in Birmingham since 1885; and, since 1897, directed the Manchester Symphony Orchestra, usually called the Hallé Orchestra, after its founder. He conducted the premiere of *Enigma Variations*, which opened the way for Elgar, and placed *The Dream of Gerontius* on the program of the Birmingham festival in 1900, where it was a smashing success. Richter also had it translated into German so that he could perform it in Düsseldorf in 1902. It soon conquered the cities of the world and was so often performed in England that it became almost a popular work, appearing frequently on the programs of large choruses wherever they performed, including the Three Choirs Festival in Gloucester, Worcester, and Hereford; at the festivals in Leeds, Norwich and Sheffield; and finally at the one best known today, at Edinburgh.
Discussion of the Work: The Dream of Gerontius is an oratorio without a real plot. It describes the "Death and Transfiguration"—to use the title of a tone poem by Richard Strauss—of an aging man whose life is drawing to a close. (The use of the name Gerontius to describe such men should be explained. In ancient Greece, the wise old men who stood at the king's side to give him advice were called Gerontes, from which the word gerontology also derives.) In the first part of the work we witness the hour of his death and in the second the entrance of his soul into eternity. Elgar used the most varied styles to depict these events. Short ariosi, developed from recitatives, and long arias, depict the state of the dying man's soul as he feels his hour approach. A small chorus of friends gathered at his deathbed sings a "Kyrie eleison," and the entire chorus prays for the deliverance of his soul. The small chorus enumerates God's deeds of deliverance, almost like a Gregorian litany; they are recited and end with an ancient cadence and an "Amen": "Noah from the water, by an ark . . . Job from all his suffering and bitter sadness . . . Moses from slavery and the foreign land . . . David from Goliath and the anger of Saul . . ." With a dying phrase—to the almost leitmotivic strains in the orchestra, which, already in the prelude, seemed to express reconciliation in death—Gerontius breathes his last (Example 1), as the priests and the choruses bring the first part to a close.

In the second part, the soul of the dead man tells of its feelings since it has left its earthly frame behind: "I went to sleep; and now I am refreshed. A strange refreshment; for I feel in me an inexplicable lightness, and a sense of freedom." His soul is led before God, and along the way to the longed-for goal hears the cries of demons struggling with angels for the souls of the dead, and the songs of the angels in heaven who will save them. It is accompanied by an imperceptible procession of the heavenly host, whose song leaves the sounds of earth farther and farther behind. The path to God leads the soul through Purgatory, past new and-ever changing, dreamlike images, through a brighter and brighter transfiguration, into brilliance and majesty. It is late romantic music, which from today's vantage point seems to derive from Wagner's opera *Parsifal*, or from Liszt's oratorio *Christus*, and in which we hear sounds of great beauty. It is a deeply introspective work, one that admonishes us to contemplation, and for at least two hours should make us forget earthly materialism.

Example 1

Manuel de Falla 1876–1946

Manuel Maria de Falla y Matheu was born on November 23, 1876 in the Andalusian city of Cadiz. He studied for three years with Felipe Pedrell and then went to Paris where he remained from 1907 to 1914. He developed close friendships with Debussy, Dukas, Ravel, and Stravinsky. When World War I broke out he returned to his native land, where he conducted various orchestras and composed. Some of his more important works were written for the stage: *La vida breve* (The Short Life, 1905); the ballet *El amor brujo* (Love the Magician, 1915); *El sombrero de tres picos* (The Three-cornered Hat, 1919); and the curious piece *El retablo del Maese Pedro* (Master Pedro's Puppet Show, 1922), based on an episode from Don Quixote, with parts for both singers and marionettes. In 1939 Falla emigrated to Alta Gracia, Cordoba, in the mountains of Argentina, where he died on September 14, 1946. He had been unable to complete *Atlantida*, on which he had been working for several decades. This, his greatest work, did not receive its premiere until 16 years after his death.

Atlantida (Atlantis)

Original Title: La Atlántida
Original Language: Spanish and Catalan
Text: After Jacinto Verdaguer, by M. de Falla
Date of Writing: De Falla began this work in 1928, but it remained unfinished.
Cast: The Narrator (baritone), a youth (boy's voice), Pirene (alto), Hercules (silent role), a giant (baritone), the Leader of Atlantis (tenor), Christopher Columbus (silent role), Queen Isabel of Spain (soprano), the Pleiades, the Archangel, a female courtier, and others.
First Performance: On November 24, 1961, the most important fragments were performed in concert in Barcelona; the staged version was first produced on June 18, 1962, at La Scala in Milan, and was sung in Italian. (Falla's score is based on both the original Catalan poem and a Spanish translation, so that both languages can be considered original for the work.) The first performance in German took place only a few weeks later, in the newly opened West Berlin opera house.
Description of the Work: It is extremely difficult to summarize the multiplicity of events dealt with in this "cantata for the stage." It is really an enormous saga of gods and heroes, a kind of Edda. Falla transferred the action to his native land, thus resurrecting the sunken continent of Atlantis in Spain, so to speak. As a consequence Spain inherits the old, long-vanished Atlantian culture, the spirit of which Spain then diffuses throughout the world. In order to bring some measure of unity to the many events, Falla opens the work on an island in the Atlantic Ocean, where an old man—a true "ghost of the sea" as Verdaguer calls him—recounts fantastic tales to a shipwrecked youth. The youth, named Christopher Columbus, is enraptured by these tales of the future which one day, when he is grown, will be realized. The ancient one tells of the burning of the Pyrenees; the rescue and death of Queen Pirene; of the founding of the city of Barcelona; Hercules' battle with a three-headed monster (which quite logically Falla has sung in three parts); the magic gardens of the Hesperides, where the Pleiades play; the wanton and blasphemous inhabitants of Atlantis; the Archangel's announcement of the death of the sinful island; and of its disappearance beneath the sea. The work concludes with Queen Isabella's vision of new islands, of Columbus' planned voyage, his setting forth, and his triumph.

This is a work of epic proportions; it reminds one of Wagner's monumental tetralogy, despite the dissimilarity of the music. The choruses carry the burden of the exposition: the solo roles are very limited, many only in pantomime. It is unquestionably an important piece of music. Many see in it the story of life while others are put off, for it lacks the spontaneity of inspiration that characterizes Falla's earlier works. Although many parts of the score were completed by Ernesto Halffter, the unity of the whole has been largely maintained. Some of its highlights, such as Isabella's dream, will stand the test of time, even if the entire work does not.

Gabriel Fauré 1845–1924

Many music lovers may recognize Fauré's name but would be hard put to name even a handful of the most important works of this French master. Since the same observation can be made for Dukas, d'Indy, Messager, Saint-Saëns, Messiaen, and even César Franck, we must assume a real lack of knowledge of French 19th-century repertory.

Fauré composed a wide range of works, from opera to delicate miniatures for piano or voice. His inclusion here is attributable to his religious choral works, including a *Messe basse* for female voices and organ, three *Tantum ergo* settings, and an outstanding masterpiece, deserving of a place of honor in the international repertory of sacred music: his *Requiem*. It would not be wrong to place it with those of Mozart, Cherubini, Berlioz, Verdi, Brahms, and Dvorak.

Fauré was born on May 13, 1845 in Pamiers, in the department of Ariège in southern France. He studied at the School of Religious and Classical Music in Paris, which was to have a decisive influence on his career. He became organist in Rennes and later in various churches in Paris, succeeding Saint-Saëns at the Church of the Madeleine in 1877. In 1896, when Massenet retired from his teaching position at the Conservatory, Fauré was appointed to fill the vacancy. He served as its director from 1905 on. His last years were troubled by a hearing disorder that occasionally left him deaf. He died on November 4, 1924 in Paris but had lived long enough to see some of his students—notably Maurice Ravel and Nadia Boulanger—become famous.

Requiem

Original Title: Requiem, Op. 48
Original Language: Latin
Text: Mass for the Dead of the Catholic liturgy (Missa pro defunctis).
Date of Writing: 1887–88
First Performance: First version: on January 16, 1888, in the Church of the Madeleine (Paris), conducted by the composer. Second version: on January 28, 1892, at a concert in Paris.
Form: The first version is in five parts, the second, in seven (the additions are from the Office for the Dead). Neither version includes the *Dies irae.*
Scoring: Two solo voices (soprano and baritone), four- to seven-part mixed chorus; the instrumentation is different in each version. In the first one there are no woodwinds or violins. It is possible that Fauré had not intended that there be any in the second version either, and only included them to satisfy the publisher who issued the *Requiem* in 1900. The added woodwinds only double parts already in the score, while violins are called for in only a few places, and in those cases play in unison. The violas and cellos, however, are divided even in the first version, which probably corresponds with the musical sounds Fauré wanted to achieve. The final instrumentation printed in the score (sometimes also called the third version) is: two flutes, two clarinets, two bassoons, four horns, two trumpets, three trombones, timpani, two harps, organ, and strings.
History of the Work: It is possible that the composition of the *Requiem* extended over many years, and that when the "Libera me" section was written, probably as early as 1877, the overall plan had not yet been worked out. Fauré's father died in 1885 and his mother on December 31, 1887. It was likely that one of these deaths prompted him to compose a Requiem. In any case, the manuscript of the "Agnus Dei" bears the date of January 6, 1888, and that of the "Sanctus," January 9. The *Requiem* was first performed in its original, five-movement form (Introitus and Kyrie, Offertorium, Sanctus, Pie Jesu, Agnus Dei) in the Church of the Madeleine where Fauré was organist and choral director. The orchestra was composed of a solo violin, heard only in the Sanctus, low strings, timpani, a harp in the Kyrie, and the organ, which played almost uninterruptedly. The composer must have had in mind that the work would most commonly be performed without orchestra, accompanied only by the organ. The next performance, now expanded to seven parts with added brasses,* took place two years later, on January 28, 1892, in a concert presented by the Société Nationale in the church of St. Gervais, in Paris. In both performances the soprano solo was sung not by a woman but by a boy. Boys sang the soprano and alto parts of the chorus. In 1900, the work was performed at the World's Fair. For this occasion the composer provided the instrumentation that is commonly used today, added at the request of the publisher who wanted to issue it to take advantage of Fauré's growing fame.

*According to research done by Roger Fiske and Paul Inwood.

Discussion of the Work: Here, by way of a preface, are a few remarks made by Nadia Boulanger, one of Fauré's foremost students, published in the *Revue musicale* in 1922:

> The church has the power to judge us, to condemn us, which the Master did not want to express in his work. Further, he did not want to content himself with merely restating the dogmatic aspect of the text musically. It would be better to say that he understood religion in the gentler terms of the Gospel of St. John, in the spirit of St. Francis more than in that of St. Bernard. . . . His music seeks to mediate between Heaven and man, in a peaceable way, calmly and inwardly, sometimes serious and sad but never threatening or dramatic.

In fact, Fauré eliminated all passages of the Mass of the Dead that speak of fear, horror, punishment, and tears, of the menacing call of the last trumpet, and of the day of wrath. He was probably the only composer to do so in all the history of Requiem settings. It is more difficult to explain other textual exclusions. However, Fauré really did not intend this to be a liturgical composition, even though he was a church choral director, but rather a work of art reflecting his innermost thoughts. This is not to say that there are no lively moments in this score; there is excitement, even drama, to be found in the "Libera me." There the words "Dies illa, dies irae, calamitatis et miseriae" are heard at least for a moment and set to suitable music, but the text moves on immediately to the words "requiem aeternam." Fauré added the seldom-set "In Paradisum" in a calm mood, transfigured, heavenly, as only few composers have been able to do.

Wolfgang Fortner   1907–1987

Wolfgang Fortner was born on October 12, 1907 in Leipzig and has long been in the forefront of German musical life. As a young man he conducted a chamber orchestra and made arrangements of early music; later he was cofounder of the Kranich-Darmstadt Summer Courses for New Music; professor at the Hochschule in Detmold, then in Freiburg/Breisgau; and also president of the German section of the International Society for New Music, to name only some of his activities. His many compositions have invariably attracted the attention and esteem of musicians, but never the spontaneous applause of music lovers. He was a staunch supporter of the twelve-tone system but was always open to other 20th-century currents. The following compositions have earned him a place in this book: *Grenzen der Menschheit* (after Goethe, for baritone, five-part mixed chorus and orchestra, 1931); *Nuptiae Catulli* (for tenor, chamber chorus and chamber orchestra, 1937); *Herr, bleibe bei uns* (vespers for solo voice in the middle register, mixed chorus, organ, and instruments, 1944); *An die Nachgeborenen* (after Bertolt Brecht, for speaker, tenor, mixed chorus and orchestra); and *Chant de naissance* (after St. John Perse, for solos, chorus, orchestra, 1959). In addition, he wrote a *Deutsche Liedmesse* for a cappella chorus (1934) and numerous works for solo voice and instruments or orchestra.

The *Pfingstgeschichte* was commissioned by the Lutheran church of the Rhineland. It uses the words of the Gospel of St. Luke and is scored for tenor solo, six-part mixed chorus, organ, and chamber orchestra. The composer calls for the following instruments: oboe, English horn, bassoon, trumpet, xylophone, vibraphone, bass and side drums, wood block, several cymbals, maracas, gong, four bells (D-flat, F, A-flat, C), organ, and strings (sometimes soloistic). The work is extremely difficult; the intervals to be sung by the chorus are almost without exception consciously "unmelodic." In passages where confusion is to be expressed, the phrases of the text are often interrupted again and again, sometimes after each syllable, and continued by other voices. Only time will tell whether such an intense expenditure of effort is justified by its artistic value.

César Franck   1822–1890

Few great masters remained in such obscurity during their lifetimes as César Franck; few harvested such meager, arduously acquired returns as this shy, quiet "Musician of God" (this epithet, coined for Bruckner, is also fitting for Franck.) He was born on December 10, 1822, in Liège, Belgium, but is often thought of as French because he lived and worked in Paris most of his life. His work in the service of a French school of organ playing, which has trained a number of leading church musicians, cannot be overestimated. However, his importance as a composer of sacred works continues to be undervalued and, indeed, little known.

When he was 13 years old, his father took him to Paris for the first time; he did brilliantly at the conservatory and won many honors. Then it seems he was compelled to return home; he did not finally settle in Paris until he was 21 years old. He first sought to support his parental family by giving private music lessons but shortly thereafter was appointed as organist at the church of St. Jean-St. François. He later moved to St. Clotilde, and finally, in 1872, became a teacher of organ at the Conservatory. In the same year a careless, poorly prepared performance of his oratorio *Rédemption* was given in Paris, which did nothing to help the composer. Little notice was taken of his works, which included many sacred pieces: the Biblical cantata *Ruth* (1846), a *Messe solennelle* (1858), three motets (1858), the short oratorio *The Tower of Babel* (1865), three offertories (1871), and short, individual pieces, among them the *Panis angelicus* which was later widely sung. While at the Conservatory he worked steadily on his greatest composition, the oratorio *Les béatitudes*. Only late in life did a ray of sunshine fall into Franck's life, when the noted violinist Eugene Ysaye took Franck's violin sonata with him on a world tour, causing a sensation. But it was too late. One evening, as Franck was hurrying to the home of a student, he was run over by a horse-drawn omnibus. He died on November 9, 1890. To the very end, he earned his living by teaching, which—second only to the organ, which he played with all his soul—was his true calling. At his funeral, "official" Paris and its cultural leaders were conspicuous by their absence.

Les béatitudes

Original Title: Les béatitudes
Original Language: French
Text: From the fifth chapter of the Gospel of St. Matthew (the Sermon on the Mount); additional texts by Mme. Colomb.
Date of Writing: 1872 to 1879, in Paris
First Performance: On February 20, 1879, in César Franck's residence on the Boulevard St. Michel. The unfinished orchestral part was performed on the piano; the first performance of the final version took place on June 15, 1891, in Paris.
Scoring: Eight solo voices (soprano, mezzosoprano, alto, two tenors, baritone, and two basses), four-part mixed chorus, and orchestra.
History of the Work: Quietly, as usual, Franck went about setting this text, one very close to his heart. Some sources say he began it as early as 1869, while according to others it was in 1872 or 1873. Opinions as to when it was completed also differ. Kretzschmar maintains the first part was ready in 1870, before war broke out between France and Germany. Franck is said to have composed during the entire siege of Paris, but it is possible that he interrupted work on *Les béatitudes* to take up the *Rédemption*, which he finished in a single sustained effort over a short period of time. In 1879 the composition was so nearly completed that Franck wanted to try it out with a few friends and musicians. He therefore invited a handful of guests to his home, rehearsed the choruses with his students and replaced the unfinished orchestral part with a piano version. The few accounts we have concur in the judgment that it was an unsuccessful, even miserable, evening. Many of the "important" figures had sent their regrets or simply failed to attend. Furthermore, many of the guests left without a word during the course of the admittedly long evening. Only a few of his friends held out until the end—two, according to one report, which should probably not be taken literally. Even this limited effort to bring his work to the public proved futile. The few notices in the press attracted hardly any attention, which they really should have done because they contradicted each other. One paper reported, "This composition is not only one of the longest since Beethoven, but seems to surpass everything written since his death." (René de Récy); another, "It may be that César Franck has seen the Good Lord in some of his works, but he did not even give us a glimpse of Him! He celebrated the eight 'Beatitudes' without giving us a single moment of happiness. . . . What misery!" (Camille Bellaigue).

In 1887, friends and students got together to plan a great concert aimed at giving a chance to some of Franck's major works in a manner worthy of them. This concert proved an even greater failure because the public was invited. The orchestra proved poorly prepared and lackluster, in spite of the fact that the concert's first part was conducted by a noted conductor, Jules Etienne Pasdeloup. Franck conducted the second half, which included selections from the opera *Hulda* and the third and eighth song from *Les béatitudes*. Only a few steadfast, faithful friends applauded. Following the concert the composer tried to console them in his quiet, kind-hearted way: "You expect too much, dear children. . . . I was completely satisfied."

He never heard *Les béatitudes* in its entirety. It did not receive a proper performance until it was given in Dijon, on June 15, 16, and 18, 1891, after his death. It was heard in Paris for the first time on March 12, 1893. Thereafter it was performed more widely.

Discussion of the Work: Franck divided the work into a prologue and eight sections, each of which treated one of the blessings:

1. "Blessed are the poor in spirit. . . ."
2. "Blessed are the meek. . . ."
3. "Blessed are they that mourn. . . ."
4. "Blessed are they that hunger and thirst for righteousness. . . ."
5. "Blessed are the merciful. . . ."
6. "Blessed are the pure in heart. . . ."
7. "Blessed are the peace makers. . . ."
8. "Blessed are they that are persecuted for righteousness' sake. . . ."

The distribution of the voices varies considerably throughout these sections, but except for the fourth, in which there are only two solos for male voices, each section contains music for the chorus in various configurations. The text of the Sermon on the Mount would not have been long enough for an oratorio that would fill an evening, so Franck enlisted the help of a poetess named Madame Colomb, who attempted to make the words of Jesus more graphic.

In a tenor solo, the prologue describes the mean and difficult times of a distant, unspecified era—it is, of course, just prior to the birth of Christ. The oppressed people long for freedom and seek a sign from Heaven. Then the first section begins with a song in praise of wealth and sensuous delights, followed by the opposing voice of Christ singing the praises of human moderation. A heavenly chorus answers the earthly one with the same broad cantilena that Jesus has just sung. In the second section, a quintet of soloists dramatically describes human loneliness, to which the chorus replies in consolation with an almost folklike, traditional melody. The voice of Christ is heard again, and the second blessing rings out.

It is debatable whether the additional texts add any deeper meaning; many seem disconnected, and most are quite commonplace. More than once, Franck's music must compensate for their triteness; in this it is almost completely successful. There are gripping, even deeply moving passages in this work, which convince the listener of the strength of Franck's faith and create wonderful images in sound.

The third section presents us with a realistic scene: A widow, an orphan, and a mother who has lost her child, represented by three female voices, lament their fate, while the tenor sings the role of a husband who has lost his loved ones: "O toi que j'aimais, adieu pour toujours!" (O, beloved, farewell for ever!) becomes the center of a deeply felt ensemble. Then comes a chorus of slaves longing for their lost freedom; philosophers answer. The text is all very hazy, until once more we hear the voice of Jesus: "Blessed are they that weep, for they shall be comforted." and a chorus of "heavenly voices" develops these words into a great ensemble.

The shorter fourth section includes an almost operalike tenor aria with very forceful orchestral accompaniment. Only with Jesus' words does peace return: "Blessed are the hearts that call for righteousness." The work reaches its emotional climax in the fifth section. The masses cry out for revenge, for punishment of the unjust; earthly voices and heavenly choirs engage in a long struggle. Then the voice of Christ is heard again: "Revenge is mine alone!" The sixth section comforts people of goodwill and pure heart, whom neither the powers of evil nor of death can harm.

The seventh section opens with the voice of Satan, accompanied by a chorus of tyrants; a mighty chorus of the people oppose them, but this thought is not elaborated. Finally the godly voice displaces Satan: "Blessed are the peacemakers" (once again, as several times in almost every section, the syncopated, ascending sequence of notes is heard, a sort of "*Leitmotif* of the godly" [Example 1]). The Devil appears again in the eighth section; three times the chorus of the Just opposes him. But Satan does not admit defeat until he hears the lament of the "Mater dolorosa." Jesus and the heavenly choirs, singing Hosannas, bring the work to a close.

Example 1

Charles Gounod   1818–1893

Few of today's countless devotees of the successful operas *Faust, Romeo et Juliette, Mireille,* and others know that Charles Gounod had once planned to enter the priesthood and compose sacred music. He was born on June 17, 1818. In 1839 he won, with his cantata *Fernand,* the coveted Prix de Rome of the Paris Conservatory. His three-year stay in the Eternal City introduced him to the music of Palestrina, for which his admiration steadily grew. Throughout his life, a good part of his artistic effort was devoted to the composition of Masses. They range from a three-voice orchestral Mass, first sung in the French church in Rome in 1841; to the Requiem, first performed in Vienna in 1842; to various Masses composed for the "Orphéon" male chorus which he directed for many years, and to the works of his old age, the *Messe solennelle Ste. Cécile, Messe angeli custodes,* and *Messe à Jeanne d'Arc.* His abundant life's work also includes other compositions for the church: *Les sept paroles de N.S. Jesus-Christ,* an Ave verum, a Te Deum, and a Stabat mater. Several oratorios flowed from his pen as well: *Tobias, Redemption* (with an English text), and *Mors et vita.* Gounod did not give up his plan to enter the priesthood until after his return from Rome, followed by studies in theology and other classes at a Paris seminary.

Influenced deeply by the works of Berlioz and Schumann, he became increasingly involved in secular music and discovered his special talent for music theater, a genre in which he ultimately achieved world fame. But it would be a mistake to ignore his contributions to the Mass and the oratorio. He was always particularly attracted by choral music, an interest that repeatedly led him back to the church and the concert hall. He died on October 17, 1893 in Paris, a highly respected and much honored composer.

The *St. Cecilia* Mass is considered the most beautiful of Gounod's many sacred compositions. It was composed in 1855, after the composer had withdrawn from the hectic life in Paris to spend some time in Avranches in Normandy. His opera *Sappho* had satisfied neither him nor the public, raising again the question he had thought settled once and for all: to what kind of music—stage or church—should he devote himself. Further, the many years spent in writing for choruses led him to see new possibilities in this genre. The Mass in Honor of St. Cecilia reflects this deepened understanding and profoundly-held religious beliefs as well as his unusual gift for expressive melody. Thereafter, beginning with his next opera, *Faust,* he put this gift to use largely in the service of the theater. However, in later years his mystical inclinations returned with overwhelming force, finding expression in an outpouring of sacred works that paralleled his final estrangement from the world.

Karl Heinrich Graun   1701–1759

Under the patronage of the Prussian king Frederick II, a kind of "Berlin School" formed at his court. It included the Benda brothers from Bohemia, Bach's son Carl Philipp Emanuel, and first and foremost, the Graun brothers, of whom the most important was Karl Heinrich. The latter was born on May 7, 1701, in Wahrenbrück in Saxony, and attended the famous Dresden Kreuzschule, noted for its music training. Upon graduation he became a singer and later, Kapellmeister in Braunschweig until Frederick, who was then crown prince of Prussia, appointed him future director of a magnificent opera house the prince was planning to build in Berlin. This new theater, designed by the famous architect Geog Wenzeslaus von Knobelsdorff, was completed in 1742 and opened with a work of Graun's. With his 17 operas, numerous songs, arias, and other works, he became one of the most famous composers of his time. His concert works, Passion cantatas, and oratorios were equally well received. One of them, *Der Tod Jesu* (The Death of Jesus) long remained popular, not only in Berlin, where it was performed every Easter for a century and a half, but in other cities as well. It was, for all intents and purposes, to be considered *the* Passion setting and was only displaced 80 years later, when Bach's *St. Matthew Passion* was rediscovered. Other Graun works that deserve mention in this book are the funeral music for Duke Wilhelm of Braunschweig (1731) and Friedrich Wilhelm of Prussia (1740), as well as a Te Deum to celebrate the battle of Prague in 1756.

Der Tod Jesu is a Passion cantata composed in 1755 and performed for the first time in Berlin on March 26 of the same year. It was the last of the five works in this genre that Graun composed after 1730. The text was by Karl Wilhelm Ramler. There is little sense in arguing about texts written in those days; they fulfilled their purpose, which was essentially to form a scaffolding upon which the music could be built and should be considered from this point of view. Moreover, C. P. E. Bach and Telemann also used Ramler's texts, which were much appreciated in their day. If we remember that *Der Tod Jesu* was composed only five years after Bach's death—and before Handel's—the stylistic similarities are not surprising.

Among the 17 musical numbers in Graun's work, there are no fewer than seven Protestant chorales. The work begins with the famous one used by Bach several times in his *St. Matthew Passion*, "O Haupt voll Blut und Wunden." Ramler's text for the same music was "Du, dessen Augen flossen / sobald sie Zion sah'n / zur Freveltat entschlossen / sich seinem Falle nah'n / wo ist das Tal, die Höhle / die, Jesu, dich verbirgt? / Verfolger seiner Seele / habt ihr ihn schon erwürgt?" (You, who wept when you saw Zion bent on sacrilege, close to collapse; where is the valley, the cave that hides you, Jesus? Persecutors of his soul, have you already strangled him?) The characters are not clearly drawn, so it is often not easy to separate what has been experienced from what is being told. But the work contains melodies of unusual beauty, even in the recitatives. It goes without saying that since it is a Baroque work there is no lack of fugues. There is one as early as in the second piece, others in Nos. 10 and 14, all of considerable merit. The parts for the soprano and bass soloists are richly endowed, those for the high voice so extravagantly that it is better to divide them between a soprano and a tenor. In one of the duets for two high voices Graun expressly called for "Soprano I" and "Soprano II", but it is better to use a mezzo in place of the second soprano. The work is moderately difficult for chorus and orchestra, with rewarding solo parts—all in all, well worth performing today.

Francisco Guerrero   1528–1599

Francisco Guerrero, child of a musician's family in Seville, was one of the most outstanding masters of the 16th century, and one of the last masters of the age of polyphony. His many sacred compositions in all genres deserve much greater attention. With his St. Matthew and St. John Passions, which appeared in 1585, he is one of the first great masters of this genre. It seems that in his own time, Europe held him in high esteem. His works were printed in the leading musical countries of the day—France, Italy, and Flanders—and often performed there. He lived and worked in Spain, was director of church music in Jaén, Malaga, and finally, in the cathedral of Seville. He once made a pilgrimage to the Holy Land, visiting the most important cities in Italy along the way. He died in his native city of Seville on November 8, 1599.

Joseph Haas   1879–1960

Joseph Haas, born on March 19, 1879, in Maihingen near Nördlingen in Bavaria, is one of the great figures in 20th-century oratorio. The folk oratorio is viewed as his creation, and his contribution to the German folk song Mass is of the greatest significance. There is something deeply affecting in the simplicity of his melodic inspiration; his style is immediately accessible, and his high musical intentions far exceed much of what his era heard and created. He was intensely active in music. For a quarter of a century he headed the department of church music at the Munich Academy of Music; he guided the Donaueschingen Music Festival in the early 20s, and he led the fight for musicians' professional rights. Of his many sacred and secular works for chorus and orchestra the most important are noted here.

Die heilige Elisabeth (1931) is scored for speaker; unison male, unison children's and four-part mixed choruses, and soprano solo. The orchestra has ad libitum instrumentation, which is helpful for amateur musicians, as are the songs and hymns dispersed throughout. These songs and hymns may, indeed should be sung by the audience as well. *Christnacht* (1932) was composed to words by W. Dauffenbach and is subtitled "Ein deutsches Weihnachts-Liederspiel" (A German Christmas Song-play). In it he has adapted melodies from Upper Bavaria and the Tyrol for solo voices, chorus (possibly a children's chorus), and small orchestra. *Das Lebensbuch Gottes* (1934) is one of the loveliest heartfelt works of the time. Haas called it "an oratorio based on the words of Angelus Silesius for soprano and alto solos, women's chorus, mixed choruses, both unison and in parts (or only women's voices), with small orchestra (or piano, or organ)." *Lied von der Mutter* (The mother's song) (1939), based on a text by Willi Lindner, is for soprano and baritone solos; choruses for mixed, children's, female, and male voices; and orchestra which plays mostly interludes. *Das Jahr im Lied* (the year in song) (1952) is an oratorio using folk songs from the 15th to the 18th centuries, with a connecting text by Ludwig Andersen. It calls for solo quartet, mixed chorus, and orchestra. *Die Seligen* (1957), subtitled "Variations on the Sermon on the Mount," uses, in a composite text by Ludwig Schuster and poems by Angelus Silesius, soprano and baritone solos; male, female, children's, and mixed choruses; and orchestra. Among Haas's numerous Masses, the following stand out: *Deutsche Singmesse, Speyerer Domfestmesse, Christ-König-Messe* (for the 800th anniversary of the cathedral in Limburg), and *Deutsche Weihnachtsmesse*. He also composed a German Vespers, a canonic motet, and a Te Deum, whose authentic folk quality deserves special notice. Haas died on March 30, 1960 in Munich.

George Frideric Handel 1685–1759

Madame de Staël very perceptively remarked that Michelangelo was the "Bible's painter." Handel must then be called its composer. The number of his oratorios based on Biblical subjects runs to over 30, even though he did not begin composing in this genre until he had suffered great disappointment in the field of opera and withdrew from it, after having composed about 50 operas. If we add to this the vast number of orchestral, organ, and harpsichord works, as well as sacred and secular vocal works, we arrive at a life total that can scarcely be comprehended; it is of a magnitude imposing in every respect which can only be called amazing.

Handel was born in Germany (in Halle an der Saale, probably on February 23, 1685), attained youthful mastery in Italy, and matured to his highest powers in England. The life of this Titan presents a colorful, kaleidoscopic view of an exciting age whose musical life he did much to shape.

When he was four years old, and it was already clear that he loved music and had an ear for it, Handel encountered his father's firm objections. He somehow surmounted them as he did the many other obstacles which marked his life. At 17, he became assistant organist in his native city, but the next year moved to Hamburg, then the most progressive music center in Germany. Handel became a violinist in the opera house orchestra and presented his first opera, *Almira*, there when he was only 20. Within a year, Hamburg, too, had grown too small for him. Opera flourished in Italy, so in 1706 Handel journeyed to Florence. It was in Florence that the famous double contest with Domenico Scarlatti, who was just his age, took place. The Italian won on the harpsichord, the German (whom the Florentines called "il Sassone," the Saxon) on the organ. For five years he worked in various Italian cities and composed some successful operas as well as cantatas and instrumental music. Then he was ready to take on a greater role in Germany where, in 1710, the Prince of Hanover appointed him Hofkapellmeister. But London, the brilliant city of music, beckoned, all the more so since the death of Henry Purcell had left it without a leader. After a six-month stay in England (1710–11) Handel returned to Hanover, but in the fall of 1712 again asked permission to depart for London. Then began so dizzying a rise in popular success that the 27-year-old composer no longer considered returning to Germany. He was sought after in the highest circles, received a stipend from the queen, directed and composed opera, and soon became a leading figure in London's musical life. In 1718, he composed his first oratoriolike work, the English masque *Acis and Galatea*. As the years passed, Handel experienced both triumph and defeat; he became severely ill and recovered; he earned and lost quantities of money. Everything about this physically enormous man was larger than life, colossal, sensational—in fact, the direct opposite of his contemporary, Johann Sebastian Bach, who followed his profession in a modest way in small musical centers in Germany. Following Handel's biography year by year, we note that opera gradually retreated into the background while the oratorio became increasingly important. The old Baroque opera, with its pompous gods and heroes, its sumptuous costumes that thwarted any kind of realistic movement, its language that had long since become artificial and mannered, and its mythological themes—no longer of much interest—had become not only unpopular but a subject of satire (*The Beggar's Opera*, 1728) and was facing financial collapse.

In such circumstances, the advantages of the oratorio form come to the fore: the concentration on literature and music, which offer the opportunity to treat symbolic themes—abstract concepts that affect everyone such as time, death, the devil, wealth, beauty, and love—and to see them with the inner eye, giving imagination full rein. For a century opera and oratorio had been sisters complementing each other, the advantages of the one never surpassing those of the other. Now they became rivals, each trying to prove its superiority. This development is clear in Handel's works, which speak for the entire era. As Baroque opera declined, oratorio ascended. Social factors played a significant role in this change. Baroque opera is unthinkable in anything but Italian, and in a few instances, in French; in England, as in Germany, only a very small upper class understood both languages. But the vernacular was preferred in the oratorio, which expanded the circle of admirers enormously. Furthermore, opera is the very exclusive domain of the professional musician; amateurs can hardly mount a performance. Amateur choruses on the other hand have typically provided the musical foundations for the great oratorio performances; an especially welcome turn of events that has generally had a salutary effect on "popular culture" and made music available to other strata of society. The participation of such massed choruses has come to be the foundation of a new kind of musical life that is not likely to pass from middle-class culture. Not only Haydn, who visited England at the end of the "Handelian century," but other observers as well have been impressed by the extraordinarily wide-ranging effect of music on the island. Probably no other artist contributed as much to this outcome as Handel, whose oratorios during that early, decisive period were a rich and valuable element in this development. Handel's works in English cover almost half a century, beginning with the *Utrecht Te Deum* and ending only with his death in 1759. They can be divided between liturgical works and oratorios, but are treated here chronologically. The former extend over a period of 30 years, from the *Utrecht* (1713) to the *Dettingen* (1743) *Te Deum*, and the oratorios from *Acis and Galatea* (1718) to *Jephtha* (1751). Handel bade farewell to the world with a magnificent performance of his *Messiah* on March 30, 1759, in Covent Garden, still a theater today. It was his final triumph over pain and blindness. He died on April 14, 1759, and was buried in Westminster Abbey among England's greatest lights, the greatest composer of his age.

Utrecht Te Deum and Jubilate

At the beginning of 1713, it seemed that the end of the War of Spanish Succession was in sight. It was certain that a peace treaty was not far off, which would particularly benefit Austria and England. Handel prepared for it by composing a Te Deum. He finished the work on January 14, 1713 but when the treaty was signed on April 13, in the Dutch city of Utrecht, Handel added a *Jubilate* (Psalm 100). Victory and peace celebrations in London were set for July 7, in St. Paul's Cathedral. Handel's *Utrecht Te Deum and Jubilate*, his first sacred work and his first composition in the English language, was the centerpiece of the solemn ceremony.

Although oratorios, operas, and instrumental music make up the bulk of Handel's work, his contribution to music for the service should not be underestimated. This group includes numerous anthems (motet- or cantatalike songs to Biblical texts used by the Anglican church), as well as five Te Deums: the *Utrecht Te Deum* of 1713; another in D major, supposedly composed the following year; a third, in B-flat major (1719); a fourth, in A major (1727?); and finally the crowning work, the *Dettingen Te Deum* of 1743.

The *Utrecht Te Deum* calls for the typical late Baroque ensemble: flute, two oboes, two trumpets, strings, and a group of instruments designated as "continuo," in which bassoons, cellos, and contrabasses supplied the musical foundation, in addition to the organ. Added to the mighty chorus were five solo voices (soprano, mezzo soprano, two tenors, bass). As usual in Baroque music, there were fugues and double fugues, fugatos and imitative sequences. The orchestral part contained solos, especially for oboe and violin, which were accompanied either by the organ or a harpsichord. In the Baroque manner, Handel had written out a basso continuo part—a figured bass—so that a musician could realize the harmonies in a more or less artistic way. The work is composed of individual sections but forms an indivisible whole: it can be thought of as a mosaic of highly expressive sound images.

Acis and Galatea

Handel had explored the oratorio form as early as 1708, in Rome; he composed *La Resurrezione* as well as the cantata *Il trionfo del tempo e del disinganno*, which he revised much later, in London. In 1708, after his youthful sojourn in Rome, he visited Naples, where he composed the serenata *Aci, Galatea e Polifemo*. When he had established a foothold in England, he decided to revise some of the things written in Italy to make them suitable for London audiences; among the first of these was this serenata, which he reworked as an English masque, a form that implied a scenic or partially scenic performance. This form, so beloved in 17th-century England, was one of the early types of opera and was usually based on allegorical or mythological matter.

In 1717, Handel accepted the invitation of a notable patron of the arts, the Earl of Carnarvon, who was elevated to Duke of Chandos in 1719 and lived in Cannons castle. As musical director for this immeasurably wealthy aristocrat Handel had plenty of time to compose. While there he created his *Chandos* Anthems, wrote the theatrical oratorio *Esther*, the first group of harpsichord suites, and the reworked version of *Acis and Galatea*, now in English, the title shortened by dropping Polyphemus that had been included in the Italian version of 1708.

The English text was supplied by John Gay, with help from Alexander Pope and John Hughes. Gay was a well-known London poet who became a regular contributor of "Ballad Operas," a folk-like type of opera employing ballads or songs. The most famous of these was the *Beggar's Opera*, the parody of opera that was to be the ruin of Handel's Italian opera company in 1728. All of London ran to see it, leaving Handel's works to play to empty houses. *Acis and Galatea* is sometimes called a "Pastoral," which refers to its rustic subject matter, usually involving shepherds and mythological subject matter.

The characters in Handel's drama are Acis (tenor), Galatea (soprano), Damon (tenor; can also be a high female voice), and Polyphemus (bass). In addition there is a five-part (soprano, alto, tenors I and II, bass) chorus of shepherds, which appears only a few times. The action is predictably simple. The shepherd Acis and the nymph Galatea are in love and savour to the fullest their youthful happiness in the idyllic meadows of Sicily. Their song is one of Handel's best-known melodies (Example 1).

Example 1

In the second act disaster strikes, announced by the chorus, which plays the role of observer and commentator. The mythological, one-eyed Cyclops, Polyphemus, a crude and violent giant, falls in love with Galatea and kills Acis out of jealousy. The nymph mourns inconsolably until the chorus advises her to turn her dead lover into a stream so that she will always have him flowing tenderly near her, clear and silvery. This old tale, first set down ca. 300 B.C. by the Greek poet Theocritus, the creator of pastoral poetry, formed the basis of many artistic interpretations, particularly during the Baroque and Rococo eras; its timeless, symbolic meaning probably received its most beautiful musical setting with Handel. He and his librettist, Gay, altered the legend; in the original, the drama ends not with the death of Acis, but with that of Galatea.

Esther

The masque *Haman and Mordecai* was also presented in 1720 at Cannon castle, but in 1732 Handel revised it to form the oratorio *Esther*. Because the first version was presented privately for the Duke of Chandos, it was probably relatively unfamiliar to English audiences. It is not certain whether this oratorio was composed at the same time as *Acis and Galatea* or shortly before it, but because the latter was a revision of an Italian work, *Haman and Mordecai*, or *Esther*, is often classified as Handel's first English oratorio.

The libretto, based on the Book of *Esther* in the Bible, was probably written by Handel's friends—his physician, Dr. J. Arbuthnot, and the well-known poet, Alexander Pope, although neither is named. The considerably expanded revision of 1732 used a text by Samuel Humphreys.

The cast is so numerous that we think at once of a stage production. Masque, oratorio, or pastoral—Handel's contemporaries perceived all these forms as theater, as music for the stage.

Nevertheless it is beyond dispute that both the performance at Chandos and the second one, at a private house in London, were given in concert form.

During the Babylonian captivity of the Israelites, the Jewish elder Mordecai ordered his beautiful countrywoman Esther to go to King Ahasuerus to seek protection of the Jews against the threats of his minister, Haman. Beyond all hope, the monarch received Esther sympathetically, although she had come unannounced. He heard her pleas, dismissed his unjust minister, and gave the Hebrews permission to conduct their religious celebrations. Handel consciously avoided all theatricality, using an unusually large chorus to not only observe and narrate, but also to witness and be a participant.

Deborah

This, too, is a Biblical drama with a large cast, making the designation oratorio at least doubtful. In addition, the first performance, on March 17, 1733 in the Haymarket Theater in London, was in fact staged. Handel had completed the drama shortly before, on February 21; his librettist was again Samuel Humphreys. As in *Esther*, Handel used a full Baroque orchestra: flutes, oboes, bassoons, horns, trumpets, theorbos, harp, a large string section, and organ. The chorus again had a major role.

The piece is in three parts, the action taken completely from the Book of *Judges*. The four-part overture is rich in variety; its movements—allegro, grave, poco allegro, allegro—make it almost a concerto grosso. Some scholars contend it should be interpreted programmatically, representing the contrast between the peaceful, God-fearing Israelites and the savage Canaanites. In an eight-part fugue, the unusually large first chorus ("Immortal Lord of earth and skies") constructs the image of the Jews holding fast to their faith even when oppressed by the Canaanites. In a recitative and duet, the seer Deborah prophesies the future victory of Barak, the leader of the Jews. After warlike choruses, Deborah further prophesies the death of the enemy general, Sisera.

In the second act, the two armies clash, the Israelites emerge victorious, Sisera flees and, with his last remaining strength, finds his way to the hut of the Jewess Jael, who Deborah had prophesied would be the savior of her people. Jael has accepted this omen as her sacred duty and murders the Canaanite general as he sleeps, by hammering a nail into his head.

The third act presents the victory celebration of the Jews; above the laments of the heathens is heard a tumultuous, six-part Hallelujah. Probably due to the portrayal of such cruelty the story has been frequently revised. In spite of its magnificent music it is seldom performed, either on stage or in the concert hall. This murder of an unarmed opponent by a woman who then becomes a heroine to her people is by no means unique—we need only think of Judith and Holofernes, or Samson and Dalila.

Athalia

This may be the place to take note of the weakness of so many of Handel's texts. *Athalia* was also written by Humphreys, whose dramatic sense of the material was negligible and whose poetic gifts—so important to the oratorio form since it is not staged—were unequal to the task. It could be, of course, that the Baroque era had different, which is not to say lesser, standards than we do today. But the effort to present other Handel works than the few acknowledged masterpieces comes to grief again and again thanks to the texts he used.

This is especially true of *Athalia*. It was composed at the request of Oxford University, which had invited Handel to a ceremony on July 10, 1733. We do not know when he began to compose, but he finished on June 7, 1733, and like most composers of the period, finished his scores speedily. Handel used parts of this work again, with slight revisions, in a festive cantata he composed for the marriage on March 13, 1734, of Princess Anne with the Duke of Orange—*Il Parnasso in festa*. Humphreys took the subject matter from the Biblical books *Kings* and *Chronicles*.

Athalia, who had renounced Judaism, had herself proclaimed queen of Israel following the death of her son, Ahasja. But she was haunted by a terrible dream in which she saw herself pursued and murdered by a young priest. Her dream was realized: Athalia was slain by the people who had rallied to the side of the young priest Joas.

A word on the assignment of roles, not only in *Athalia*, but in all the preceding oratorios: Following the custom of the time, Handel called for female voices to sing many male roles. This old practice—still quite common in Mozart's day—is often "corrected" today, a practice that deserves comment. In opera, costuming can solve many problems. Where the old masters called for counter tenors or castratos, a beautiful alto voice can be used today just as well, since there are few counter tenors and no castratos. But what should be done when an oratorio is performed in concert? The transcription of Handel's female roles for male voices is not always easy and can distort the balance of sound considerably.

Alexander's Feast

The remarks made earlier about the librettos Handel used do not apply to this work, which has no plot; its content is wrapped in the sonorous verse of a good poet, John Dryden. Handel composed *Alexander's Feast or The Power of Music* in 1697, in which the dazzling victory celebration of Alexander the Great is depicted. He first presents the fabled singer Timotheus, performing songs and hymns in honor of the hero, followed by St. Cecilia, the Christian patron saint of music, an anachronism intended to exemplify the commonality of the ancient and modern worlds. It is interesting to note that the scenes depicting the antique world are mostly accompanied by homophonic music, but when Christian ideals are presented, polyphony is used. This kind of historic allusion was not commonly used in the Baroque era, but it is too striking here to be accidental. Of course, Handel did not attempt to create a historically "correct" sound: undertakings of that kind were not pursued at that time. Furthermore, he knew as little of how the music of the ancient Greeks, Macedonians, and Near Eastern people sounded as we do. But there are moments in this work that conjure up images in our imagination of that antique world (Example 1).

Example 1

In the absence of a plot, Handel uses a series of tableaux: the lamentation for the Persian king, Darius, who fell in battle, is deeply moving, especially as it is sung by his victorious enemy. A savage war chant briefly intrudes upon the magical aura surrounding the feast and Alexander's love scene with the beautiful Thais, referring to Alexander's recollection of the din of battle.

The work is more than simply a series of historic tableaux—it is really a hymn to music, as the subtitle "Or the Power of Music" indicates. The original version ends with the magnificent chorus "Let old Timoteus yield the price," which is still the most satisfactory conclusion. The numbers added later—an alto recitative, a duet for soprano and alto, and a two-part chorus (using verses written by Newburgh Hamilton)—only weaken the work poetically as well as musically. *Alexander's Feast* was completed on January 17, 1736 and sung for the first time on February 19 of that year at Covent Garden in London. Each of the five successive performances for audiences numbering about 1,300 was met with thunderous applause.

Saul

This is the first of Handel's oratorios in his prime. Shortly before he had collapsed physically, due to the disappointment and overwork growing out of the last of his operatic undertakings. His almost miraculous recovery, both physical and mental, was helped by taking the baths in Aachen. He now bade farewell to the theater where he had so long sought his fortune, and turned entirely to the composition of oratorios. In the years that followed he created works whose mastery assured his fame for all time. On September 27, 1738, he completed *Saul*; on October 11, *Israel in Egypt*; from August 22 to September 12, 1741, he wrote the *Messiah*; and on October 12, 1742, he put the finishing touches to *Samson*. More followed: *Semele, Joseph and his Brethren*, the *Dettingen Te Deum, Hercules*, and *Belshazzar*. His enormous surge of inspiration went on and on.

Werner Oehlmann called *Saul* "a work of Baroque scope and profusion . . . a gigantic fresco in sound, like a Rubens painting, charged with people and events." The text was written by Charles Jennens (1700–1770), who included so many characters that it seems more like an opera. Once again, the overture is a work complete in itself, a kind of four-movement concerto with heavy emphasis on the organ but possessed of no musical or intellectual connection to the oratorio it introduces. The work opens on a victory celebration of the Israelites, orchestrated as richly as Handel's many other festive oratorio and opera scenes. The instruments are divided into three groups—woodwinds, brasses with timpani, and strings. A mighty Hallelujah forms one of the high points (Example 1).

Example 1

Hal – le – lu – jah, hal – le – lu – jah

The audience learns of the reason for the feast, as well as King Saul's jealousy of the young David, who became the hero of the battle when he met and slew with his slingshot the leader of the enemy, the giant Goliath. Tension mounts as the story is told, reflected musically in a very typical motive with octave leaps depicting the magnitude of the event (Example 2).

Example 2

David is greeted with exultation as he enters the victory celebration. He sings a song in honor of Saul, but in vain. The king's wrath is inflamed, and as one possessed he flings his spear at the young hero, who, refusing to fight his king, flees. The ruler's son, Jonathan, David's friend, intercedes and arranges that Saul give his daughter Michal to David in marriage. But Saul's amity does not last; his mania grows and, turning his weapon against his own son, he kills him. Horror grips the crowd; they think their ruler has gone mad. Frightened and in despair, Saul goes to the witch of Endor, who conjures up the shade of King Samuel, the great prophet who had anointed Saul king. The scene in which the spirit is called up is thoroughly ghostly—how few in the following Romantic century equalled it, particularly in opera! Saul then plunges into the battle with the Amalekites and falls, the enemy warrior who killed him reporting that he did so at Saul's own behest. In the funeral ceremonies for Saul and Jonathan we hear the strains of burgeoning exultation for the new king, so ardently longed for, whose name is David.

The first performance of this oratorio took place on January 16, 1739, in London. Handel had rented the Haymarket Theater for the occasion and announced that there would be no fewer than a dozen oratorio concerts during the Lenten season. The dazzling audiences, heavy attendance, and jubilant reception moved him to establish a tradition which continued successfully for many years.

Israel in Egypt

Israel in Egypt was completed on October 11, 1738, and first performed in the same season as *Saul*, on April 4, 1739, in London's Haymarket Theater. Handel himself had assembled the various Biblical passages that make up the text. He used *Psalms* 78, 105, and 106 as well as parts from *Exodus. Israel in Eqypt* differs from Handel's previous oratorios in that the six solo voices (two sopranos, alto, tenor, two basses) do not represent roles or characters but rather relate events through recitative and aria. Another difference is the heavy use of choruses. Of the 30 musical numbers four are recitatives, four arias (only one in the first section and three in the second), and 22 choruses! The dramatic events that make up the work are not represented but told—described as in a book; but the impact, the dramatic, musical force of Handel's handling of the chorus, replaces scenery for the imaginative listener and creates in his mind's eye images and visions that far and away surpass anything possible on a stage.

After a short recitative, in which the tenor reports on a new pharaoh whose overseers are cruelly oppressing the captive Israelites, the first chorus is heard describing the sufferings of the beleaguered people (Example 1).

In the first measures, Handel's skill at characterization is evident. With a few harmonies he sets the gloomy, tragic mood that pervades much of the oratorio. Then begins the description of the seven plagues that God sent to Egypt; the changing of the river waters into blood is expressed in an imposing choral fugue whose subject begins most expressively and characteristically with two descending major sevenths (Example 2).

Then, in an aria for the solo alto, comes the plague of frogs and the sickness they spread. "Hopping" violin passages here seem to be tone-painted. The next chorus describes the invasion of flies, lice, and locusts, for which Handel provides eight-part double chorus. Then the chorus tells of hail and fire falling from heaven; how darkness spread over the entire land; and finally, how all the first-born died, causing the Kingdom of Egypt to lose its power.

Example 1

Example 2

Then, in a light mood contrasting with the preceding dark horror, the chorus tells of the departure of the Israelites from the land of their enemies. "Like a shepherd" God takes his sheep home. The happy mood is maintained in the next chorus (No. 11) as the Egyptians give thanks for the exodus of the Israelites, whom they have come to fear. A chorus only eight measures long describes in majestic tones how God divided the sea so that His people could pass dry-shod. This then is elaborated in a fugal passage, the chorus now expanded to eight parts (Example 3). It becomes almost a hymn with its final words "He led them through the deep as thro' a wilderness," before the abrupt demise of the pursuing Egyptians as the waters rush together again. The first part ends with a sectional, solemn piece in which the people of Israel acknowledge God's power and renew their covenant with Him. Entrances in canon lead to a devout, monumental song of triumph.

Example 3

The solemn mood carries over into the second section: an eight-part song of praise expresses Israel's thanks for the miraculous rescue from their Egyptian captors. One must look far and wide in musical history for a choral treatment as forceful and magnificent as Handel's here. A lovely duet for the two solo sopranos is a sincere prayer of thanks which rises to heaven in jubilant coloratura. But the praises of God are not over: there is another imposing choral piece expressing adoration— a four-part, chorale-like chorus. A duet for the two solo basses follows in which God's might is praised; in plunging runs the swallowing up of the enemy armies by the waters is recalled. The memory comes to life again—in several successive pieces, the eight-part chorus praises God's miracles. A tenor and a soprano aria again describe the unforgettable event in sound, until once more a mighty chorus asks the solemn question, "Who is like unto Thee, O Lord?" They describe the awesome event yet again: "The earth swallowed them". The duet between the alto and the tenor forms a lyrical interlude. In chorus No. 25 ("The people shall hear") the neighboring lands are warned that whoever attacks Israel chooses God as an opponent, and He will destroy them as He did Egypt.

No further new subject matter is introduced hereafter, but the last numbers of the work provide a magnificent cascade of music. The entire second section is a long hymn to God, a prayer of thanksgiving and vow of allegiance, as impressive as any in the annals of music. Perhaps the work was too massive to be immediately understood by contemporary audiences. It is said that the applause was noticeably less than for Handel's other oratorios. But Handel's biographer A. E. Cherbuliez cites the contrary—an admiring, thoroughly understanding voice that found expression in the *London Daily Post* after the second performance, on April 11, 1739, a week after the first. It paid tribute to Handel's genius and called for a third performance. But true appreciation of *Israel in Egypt* only came with the appearance of Mendelssohn on the scene, who not only resurrected Bach's *St. Matthew Passion*, but also guided Handel's works to triumph and an enduring place in the hearts of music-lovers of the Western world.

Ode for St. Cecilia's Day

Handel presented the shorter *Ode for St. Cecilia's Day* in the same year as *Saul* and *Israel in Egypt*. The text is by John Dryden. Handel composed it in nine days, between September 15 and 24, 1739, and conducted it for the first time on St. Cecilia's day, November 22, of that same year at Lincoln's Inn, in London. This is the day dedicated to St. Cecilia, a Christian martyr and patron saint of music (she is said to have invented the organ, but this attribution is historically untenable). She also appears in *Alexander's Feast*, composed at the same time, an appearance that is also historically impossible, but is rather an intentional anachronism whose deeper meaning is symbolic, as previously noted. This time Dryden and Handel celebrate the patron saint of music in a work dedicated to her alone. It is a remarkable work for many reasons, not least of which is the attempt to summarize the entire history of the world, from its creation to its anticipated end.

There is a certain relationship between this work and Haydn's oratorio, *The Creation*, composed 60 years later. Handel, too, depicted in dissonant chords the chaos prevailing before the world was formed but did not find a similarly appropriate way to depict the first dawn—that eruption of light—as his successor did. We can safely say that in this context Haydn was Handel's successor, for if he had not made his trips to England, seen the production of Handel's music and witnessed the popularity of oratorios, *The Creation* and *The Seasons* probably would not have been composed.

From start to finish—or, at least, after harmony emerges from primeval chaos—the *Ode for St. Cecilia's Day* is a lovely, optimistic work, for even when death and dissolution are described, hope in the resurrection remains foremost. The instrumentation in this passage is wonderfully beautiful; the lute, seldom used, blends magically with flutes and organ. The *Ode for St. Cecilia's Day* shows the full range of Handel's imagination and the plentitude of moods his genius encompassed. Here, all is lyricism and poetry; quiet gaiety and loving meditation are the dominant moods; they give rise to images of heavenly consolation that calm the minds of searching, errant men.

L'Allegro, il Pensieroso ed il Moderato

This pastoral ode of Handel's, problematic for many reasons, has an Italian title in spite of the fact that its text was based on a work by the English poet John Milton, the famous author of *Paradise Lost*. Strictly speaking, only the descriptions of the first two character types are by Milton. Handel's friend and sometime librettist Charles Jennens compiled the text from Milton's poem, to which he added a third section of his own—il Moderato. It is not essential to the work, and Handel himself, at later performances and when the work was published, omitted this third part and substituted the *Ode for St. Cecilia's Day* as a finale if the occasion demanded a longer work.

Milton wrote his poem between 1633 and 1637, basing it on Italian Renaissance models. L'Allegro is the happy, light-hearted, easy-living bon vivant; il Pensieroso, the one who is reflective, sanguine, often deeply inclined to philosophy, even to melancholy. These are the two traditional human types, often portrayed in art and the source of many composers' musical interpretation—from Italian madrigals to Couperin's harpsichord pieces to Hindemith's *Vier Temperamente*. Jennens felt it necessary to place an intermediate type between these two extremes: Moderato, a temperate, conciliatory person who finds it hard to make decisions and who always seeks compromise. However, the addition is neither as interesting nor exciting, either musically or poetically.

Handel is probably the only significant composer who endeavored to mould this matter into a work the length of a complete oratorio. There is an enormous difference between Milton's original and Jennen's version. In Milton, the sensuous, joyful Allegro is treated in one section and the reflective, dreamy Pensieroso in another. Probably fearing that such homogeneous sections would be found monotonous in an oratorio and detract from the tension created by contrasts, Handel treats the two types side by side. Both appear in each scene—the light-hearted and the reflective. Indeed, there are fascinating, purely musical contrasts, but the continuous alternation is all too soon perceived as an inviolable rule; anticipation is dulled and the work degraded to the mere singing of arias whose mood is already known in advance. It is a surprise to no one who knows with what joy Handel undertook the work that many of the arias are particularly beautiful. He composed *L'Allegro, il Pensieroso ed il Moderato* in the very short span of 17 days, in January, 1740, and presented the piece for the first time, also during his oratorio festival, on February 27, 1740, in London. Even though Milton's poetry was then already a century old, the audience was closer to it than we are today. It seems to us rather affected in a schoolmasterly way, verbose, and weighted down with scholarly references, which is not to discount the undeniable lyric talent that distinguishes this highly esteemed poet. But the effect of Handel's music, overall and in detail, is natural even though it, too, is artistically wrought and just as Baroque as Milton's verse. Milton closes in praise of loneliness, even of a hermit's existence, whose satisfactions surpass worldly joys. Did Handel, whose combative, L'Allegro nature always seemed to put him in the thick of things, share this conviction?

Messiah

Original Title: Messiah
Original Language: English
Text: From the Holy Scriptures, compiled by Charles Jennens.
Date of Writing: August 22 to September 14, 1741, in London.
First Performance: April 13, 1742, in Dublin, Ireland.
Form: In three parts; a total of 47 musical numbers (52 in the old numbering).
Scoring: Handel left no final version of *Messiah* for he revised and adapted the oratorio again and again to suit it to changing performance conditions. For the Dublin premiere the following scoring was used: five solo voices (soprano, two altos, tenor, bass);* four-part mixed chorus (enlarged once to five parts—with sopranos divided); two oboes, two trumpets, timpani, strings, continuo with cello, contrabass, bassoon, harpsichord, and organ.
History of the Work: It seems that in the summer of 1741 Handel was deeply depressed. Perhaps the setting of the conclusion to *L'Allegro, il Pensieroso ed il Moderato*, with its glorification of the cloistered withdrawal from the world, meant more to him than was thought, or than his uninterrupted public activity might lead observers to suspect.

There is no doubt that he was in the midst of another crisis of health, though portraits of the time seem to show him bursting with health. Even though Bach is generally thought of as an introvert and Handel as the man of the world, they were probably more akin in faith and work than is usually assumed. So it was that in that dark summer of 1741, as A. E. Cherbuliez calls it, "Jennens delivered a selection of passages from the Bible intended for an oratorio, compiled by his secretary, Pooley, who was also a curate. For Handel, this form of intimate contact with the word of God was unbelievably fruitful."

These verses "summarized the essential points of the actual arrival on earth of the Messiah, long proclaimed by the prophets, and told of His suffering in this world and of the triumphant consequences of His death for mankind." We know for certain that Handel set to work on August 22, 1741; finished the first part on August 28; the second on September 6; and the third and final part on September 14. The complete, full-length work was composed of 52 sections. Such an enormous achievement could only have been accomplished by working day and night with undivided attention. A veritable storm of inspiration must have raged through him, one that did not abate when the enormous work was finished, for immediately afterward—there could have been only a few days in between—he plunged into the composition of a new work, and by October 29 had finished another great oratorio, *Samson*.

For years Handel had had a close circle of friends in Ireland (among whom was the English Viceroy) always waiting to hear his works performed. Handel was invited to Ireland and made the journey in November, arriving in Dublin on the 18th. On December 23, 1741 began a series of

---

*This scoring is also to be found in the complete works published at Halle, the most recent edition of Handel's works. But in concert practice today only four solo voices are used (soprano, alto, tenor, bass) as the duet for the two solo altos is replaced by the soprano aria "How beautiful are the feet."

eight concerts under his direction, which lasted until the end of March, 1742. The programs consisted of many of his more recent works, as yet unknown in Ireland, including the oratorios *Acis and Galatea*, *Alexander's Feast*, *Ode for St. Cecilia's Day*, and *L'Allegro, il Pensieroso ed il Moderato*. The city must have enjoyed considerable musical activity, for in the absence of a considerable body of good singers, capable choruses and orchestras, these concerts could not have been managed. In particular, the rehearsals of *Messiah*, not an easy work, would probably not have gone as well as the premiere on April 13, 1742 proved to be. It was a resounding success, and the audience was deeply moved. The public and the press were unanimous in their opinion that they had just heard for the first time one of mankind's great musical creations. In the following weeks, Handel produced his *Saul*, and repeated *Messiah* at the beginning of June.

The first London performance of *Messiah* took place at Covent Garden on March 23, 1743. Something quite memorable occurred that evening, the effects of which are still felt today: at the first measures of the mighty "Hallelujah" chorus, King George II rose to his feet to express his admiration for the piece, which by then had become quite well known. Of course, the entire audience rose with him, and to this day all English and American audiences stand for that chorus, in reverence for both the master and the work. And probably each and every one of them is capable of joining in.

Discussion of the Work: For the London premiere, the composer subtitled the *Messiah* "A new sacred oratorio"; he had never before designated a work in this way. Therefore, *Messiah* is a sacred work, although not liturgical. It begins in Handel's usual way, with a "symphony" or overture. (English usage goes back to the Italian term "sinfonia" rather than the French "ouverture.") It is in two parts: an introductory grave movement followed immediately by a fugue, allegro moderato. The sequence of movements, slow-fast, and the key relationships are typical of the Baroque sonata form. The introductory grave movement is in a slow, solemn tempo (Example 1). Then follows the allegro moderato movement in the form of a three-part fugue (Example 2). Whether this prelude expresses, as is often explained, the unrest of a world awaiting its redeemer, is a matter each listener must decide. Until quite late in the Romantic 19th century, such efforts to see extramusical, tone-painterly indications are usually incorrect. Handel's music is for the most part absolute, and except for a few instances allows of no programmatic interpretation.

The following tenor solo begins with the words "Comfort ye, my people" and repeats God's promise to send a Messiah. Handel's first aria follows this recitative; it expresses the joy at this happy prophecy with jubilant coloraturas ("Ev'ry valley") (Example 3). The exultant chorus enters: "And the glory, the glory of the Lord." The great Handel scholar Friedrich Chrysander maintains that in the *Messiah* Handel is less demanding of his choruses and orchestra than in the works he composed expressly for London, which seems to be true. *Messiah*, composed with Ireland in mind, took into account the certainly lesser capabilities of the performers. For example, the choruses only once go beyond four-part writing, whereas in many other works that were first performed in London, double choruses in eight parts are repeatedly called for. The attentive listener will also notice that the demands for high notes and other musical difficulties are noticeably lesser. This makes the effect that the composer achieved with this simpler, more accessible work all the more astounding.

With this chorus, Handel moves into the domain of A major, a bright, confident-sounding key, proclaiming joy for all people. An impressive recitative for the solo bass follows: "Thus saith the Lord," in which God announces the tremendous upheaval to be visited upon earth and mankind when the Redeemer comes. Powerful coloraturas—not often presented in the lowest voices—prepare the way for an aria that may either be sung by the bass as a continuation of the recitative or taken over by the solo alto: "But who may abide the day of His coming?"

Example 1

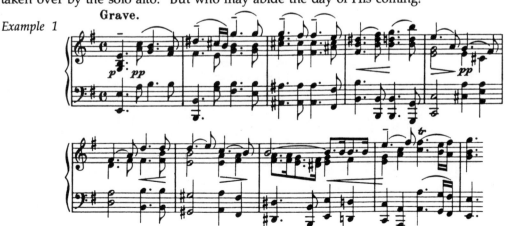

Example 2

Example 3

After a calm beginning the aria moves to a racing second section in which the orchestra's wild tremolo indicates the fearful agitation, the dread all creation experiences when confronted with the otherworldly, the incomprehensible. Gottfried Herder, the German poet and philosopher, has called this piece a "hair-raising" aria, thereby characterizing its true expression: "Who shall stand when He appeareth?" The aria alternates several times between the calm, melodic part (Example 4) and the dramatic, animated part (Example 5). A powerful choral fugue follows: "And He shall purify."

If one wanted to divide the work into several sections—which Handel himself did not do—the next one (after the "Preparation for the Arrival of the Lord") would be called the "Annunciation of the Messiah." The alto sings a solemn recitative, "Behold, a virgin shall conceive" and then launches into a joyful aria: "O thou, that tellest good tidings to Zion." The chorus takes over the aria's main melody and transforms it into a peaceful, flowing fugato, concluding in a harmonic chorale. The next part could be called "The Appearance of the Son of God on Earth." It is proclaimed by the bass, whose extended solo moves from a recitative ("For, behold, darkness shall cover the earth") to a very expressive aria ("The people that walked in darkness").

Here it does indeed seem that Handel had tone painting in mind; the description of the dark contrasts clearly with the proclamation of the light ("a great light"). In the description of darkness the harmonies are quite different from those used to describe light. The aria comes to an absolutely radiant end with the expressive coloratura of the bass voice, before the ritornello subsides once more into the darker B minor mood of the opening. But then there is light: G major, a lovely stirring in the strings like the rush of angels' wings; the sopranos of the chorus begin to proclaim the birth of Jesus ("For unto us a child is born"). It is as though the tidings were spreading: the tenors join in with the same melody, then the altos, and finally the basses. Intensity increases and the voices cry out in unison, "And his name shall be called: Wonderful! Counsellor!" (Example 6).

The next section could be entitled "The Birth of Christ." Handel begins it with an introductory orchestral section, a wonderful, pastoral sinfonia, a "Pifa." This term requires explanation. In medieval and even Baroque Italy, the term "pifari" or "piffari" referred to the playing of the shepherds' shawm, especially during the Christmas season. This was apparently a southern Italian custom, and the 12/8 time in which these melodies were usually written, as is Handel's, indicates a Sicilian origin and close ties with folk music (Example 7).

Then the solo soprano tells "There were shepherds," which is sung in two connected pieces, beginning in recitative and continuing in a melodic accompagnato. It reports the glad tidings proclaimed by an angel to shepherds in the field. The texture of the orchestral writing now is denser; gentle, broken triads in the strings sound like a gentle night wind in the trees. In this rustling the angels come near; the chorus sings praises to God, and the heavenly hosts affirm the message of salvation: "Glory to God," at first hymnlike and then in a fugue.

The next section is sometimes referred to as "The Lord and His Works." It, too, begins with a soprano aria; joy and gladness resound in the energetic bass passages and fanfarelike melodic figures ("Rejoice, rejoice") (Example 8).

After a brief recitative, "Then shall the eyes of the blind," follows one of the most beloved melodies of the *Messiah*, a solemn, dignified melody in 12/8 time: "He shall feed His flock." It exists as both a soprano aria and as a duet for soprano and alto; another lovely pastoral melody, tranquil and still, based on *Isaiah* (40:11) and *Matthew* (11:28–29).

Example 4

Larghetto

Example 5

Prestissimo

Example 6

Example 7

Example 8

Example 9

With the heartfelt words "Come unto Him, all ye who labor." it achieves the utmost expressivity. The first section comes to a close with the chorus "His yoke is easy," one of the most significant fugues of the work.

"The Suffering of the Redeemer" could be the title of what follows. A solemn, dignified chorus in G minor with a sweeping, anguished melody, introduces it: "Behold the lamb of God." The entrances follow each other in canon, and in ever denser textures the music attains ever more dramatic heights. Then the alto sings of the Lord's suffering: "He was despised," another musical number that mounts from quiet pain to an agitated description of universal suffering. The rhythmic throbbing in the orchestra, symbolizing the enduring hatred and hardened hearts of the enemy, persists until the frightening vision returns to the quiet of the beginning. Musically, therefore, it is a typical Baroque da capo aria, known to Handel from his Neapolitan teachers. The harsh dotted rhythm dominates large portions of the following chorus, "Surely, surely," whose F minor sounds unusually anguished. It is in three parts: a restrained fugue with long note values ("And with his stripes") and an animated third part in which homophony and polyphony are very effectively combined. After this long chorus, the agitated dotted rhythm appears once more as the solo tenor intones a recitative: "All they that see Him," which leads to the next chorus, "He trusted in God." This melody, a typical fugue theme, is four bars long. Introduced in the basses, it is taken over by the tenor logically at the fifth, then by the alto in its original form (as *dux*), and finally by the soprano, again at the fifth (as *comes*); but after such a powerful introduction, the development is somewhat brief and the hymnlike conclusion is quickly reached.

A lyrical interpolation, to the text of the 69th Psalm, introduces a more peaceful but no less sorrowful mood. It is sung by the solo tenor who first sings a recitative ("Thy rebuke"), adds an arioso ("Behold and see"), then moves to another short recitative, which leads to an emotional aria, "But Thou didst not leave." A radiant A major illuminates a simple folk melody. A joyful F major chorus follows ("Lift up your heads"), whose festive beginning is reminiscent of Handel's world-famous Christmas carol "Joy to the World."

The next section is devoted to the "Proclamation of the Gospel to All the World." After a few measures of a tenor recitative the chorus enters immediately in a radiant D major: "Let all the angels." This chorus, as well as the following aria, "Thou art gone up," which exists in a version for alto as well as for bass, are often omitted in performances, in which case, the work proceeds immediately to the chorus "The Lord gave the word." The tenors and basses of the chorus enter in a fanfare and are joined in exultation by the other voices. Then there is another pastoral melody, a peaceful, restrained, soprano aria in 12/8 time (Example 9).

For the Dublin premiere, Handel replaced this aria with a duet for the two solo altos accompanied by the chorus. In modern performances the version with the soprano aria is generally preferred. "Their sound is gone out" follows, an expressive piece for solo tenor, a short arioso accompanied only by the continuo. Using the same words, Handel had also composed a mighty chorus which is generally used today because of its stirring effect. The next bass aria, "Why do the nations," begins with a massive orchestral introduction; from this point on, commentators often refer to the contents as "Triumph over all enemies." This is an extremely impressive aria, from its fanfarelike ascending triad motive to its dramatic coloraturas to its majestic conclusion. Then comes the powerful chorus "Let us break their bonds." Before the second section comes to a close with the world-renowned "Hallelujah" chorus, the solo tenor is heard again, with a short recitative, "He that dwelleth in heaven" and the immediately following aria, a spectacular burst of anger: "Thou shalt break them." And then, the great "Hallelujah" bursts forth; among choruses it has few equals for power, brilliance, and popularity (Example 10).

The third part of the work, sometimes called "Death and Resurrection," is the shortest of all. It begins quietly with the emotional E major soprano aria "I know that my Redeemer liveth." The chorus replies in a four-part movement that alternates between grave and allegro, to great effect. Then the solo bass announces Judgment Day; in this aria, Handel imitates the mighty sound of the brass. The song ends on a festive, triumphant note. After a brief alto recitative, "Then shall be brought," we hear a duet for alto and tenor, "O death, where is thy sting." For both musical and textual reasons it should not be omitted, as is often done, nor should the chorus that follows immediately, "But thanks, thanks," and the unusually expressive last soprano aria in G minor, "If God be for us."

And so we arrive at the final chorus, "Worthy is the lamb." After a hymnlike opening there is a complex fugue, clearly divided into two parts. The first ends with the reiterated hope "For ever and ever"; the second is based on the single word "Amen." It extends from the deepest bass registers through the tenors and altos up into the brightest high soprano. D major, traditionally the "brightest" key of earlier times—we think of Bach's oratorios, but also of works of the subsequent

Classical period and even of the Romantic, as in the finale of Beethoven's Ninth Symphony—seems to spread a heavenly glow over the end of the work. The polyphony once more reaches enormous climaxes, rising like a Gothic cathedral into eternity. The conclusion, nothing more than a simple cadence, becomes a triumphant affirmation of faith (Example 11).

Samson

In 1741, with unparalleled, concentrated force, Handel sang his hymn of praise to the Redeemer, but when *Messiah* was finished, his inspiration, far from exhausted, flowed with such elemental power that he immediately began a new work. It was clear that it had to be another oratorio, since he was so emotionally removed from opera. But after the abstraction of the heavenly figure of the Lord, he felt compelled to return to earth, so to speak, and to portray a Biblical hero whose human foibles—all too human, as it turned out—make of him one of the most powerful figures in the Bible. Samson has often and understandably been the focus of dramatic presentations. We need only mention for comparative purposes the French opera *Samson et Dalila* by Camille Saint-Saëns, presented first by Franz Liszt in 1877 in Weimar, and subsequently repeated on opera stages around the world.

The story on which Handel's oratorio is based comes from the Biblical book of *Judges*, from which John Milton, England's leading Baroque poet, had freely adapted it for his epic *Samson Agonistes*, and which Newburgh Hamilton reworked for Handel's oratorio. He describes the betrayal, the remorse, and the triumph of the Jewish military leader Samson, whose legendary, superhuman strength lay in his hair. This hero of his people fell in love with the beautiful pagan, Delila, who, in a moment of intimacy, cut off his hair and delivered him, deprived of his strength, to his enemies, the Philistines, who blinded him and enslaved him and his now leaderless people. Samson withdrew into himself and repented, imploring God day and night to restore his former strength. The moment arrived just when the generals and priests of the Philistines were in the midst of an orgiastic, sacrificial feast in their huge temple. The blinded Samson was led by a child to the pillars supporting the temple; with his miraculously returned strength, he pulled the temple down. He was buried in the rubble together with the Philistines, but his people were freed and have since celebrated his memory as that of one of Israel's greatest saviors.

The dramatic events are told as if from memory, very sympathetically but basically in a nontheatrical way. Only in the great scene describing the downfall of the Philistines does Handel seem to have forgotten the oratorio principle, striving once more with all the means at his command, as in his opera days, for a visual effect. This music could accompany an opera scene.

The story is told by five principal characters: the tenor Samson, the soprano Delila, Samson's friend Micah (a role that according to the custom of the time is assigned to a female alto), the old Hebrew Manoa, and the Giant Harapha (a character introduced by Milton), both bass roles. In addition there are two solo sopranos (Israelite and Philistine women, Delilah's handmaidens) and a tenor (messenger and Philistine man). The choral part is extensive. The lengthy sinfonia (overture) is in solemn, stately three-four time, in which a minuet can be detected. Whether the minuet refers to Samson's role as leader or, as is sometimes maintained, a preview of the opulent, courtly manners of the Philistines cannot be said with certainty, but it is of little importance. The work opens one year after Samson has been taken captive and blinded, with the priests of the pagan god Dagon celebrating the day of their greatest victory. Micah, Samson's companion from the old days, is horrified and appeals to the hero, now a wretched man. The short aria for Samson that follows is one of Handel's most beautiful inspirations. It is reported that in his old age, and blind himself, he often played it with great emotion (Example 1).

Handel also composed *Samson* in a very short time—in five weeks in 1741 and 1742. Oddly enough, the oratorio was not performed until a year later; it received its premiere in London, on February 18, 1743, and was a great success.

Example 1

Dettingen Te Deum and Anthem

In 1743, between the two great oratorios, Handel composed his fifth Te Deum. Thirty years had passed since the *Utrecht Te Deum*, which had first been performed in London in 1713 to commemorate the victorious ending of the War of the Spanish Succession. Three similar works followed, which are seldom performed today, so only the *Dettingen Te Deum* must be mentioned.

In the War of the Austrian Succession, England sided with Austria. On June 27, 1743, British troops under the leadership of King George II defeated the French and Prussians at Dettingen, near Aschaffenburg, in the decisive battle of the war. Handel, who had held the official title of "Composer of Music to the Royal Chapel" since 1723, was commissioned to provide two sacred works to be played at the thanksgiving and victory celebrations. He began work on the Te Deum in mid-July, 1743, and soon finished it, reportedly in only a few days, as was his custom when his enthusiasm was running exceptionally high. On July 30 the second commission came, for the *Dettingen Anthem*, a setting of Psalms 20 and 21. Both compositions were performed at court on November 27, 1743, and made a deep impression.

The *Dettingen Te Deum* is considered Handel's most important liturgical work, and some of its choruses, such as the magnificent prayer "Lord, my hopes reside in thee," are among his outstanding creations.

Semele

The oratorio *Semele* was written immediately before the *Dettingen Te Deum* but was given its premiere a few months later. It is a non-Biblical work most closely related to the mythological pastoral *Acis and Galatea*. William Congreve, the noted English dramatist, wrote *The Story of Semele* in 1708, but because it lacked dramatic qualities no composer was prepared to use it. Handel decided that although it was not suitable for opera, it could be used for an oratorio. He began work on it June 3, 1743 and finished July 4 of the same year. It premiered on February 10, 1744, during the now annual oratorio festival which drew large crowds.

The piece has an unusually large cast of characters: Cadmos, the King of Thebes (bass); his two daughters Semele (soprano) and Ino (alto); the gods Jupiter (tenor), Apollo (tenor), and Somnus (bass); the goddesses Juno (mezzo soprano) and Iris (soprano); Prince Athamas of Boetia (alto); and Cupid (soprano). The text is quite muddled, but the music contains pearls of exquisite beauty. It is seldom performed today because the action, weighed down with mythology, is scarcely comprehensible to modern audiences.

Joseph and His Brethren

This drama, with text by the cleric James Miller, is another of Handel's Biblical oratorios. He began composing it in the middle of August, 1743, finishing the first act on August 26, the second on September 12, and the last probably toward the end of September, 1743. The first performance was given in London on March 2, 1744, under the title of *Joseph and His Brethren*. Once again, the cast of characters is quite long, making one think more of opera than oratorio: the Pharaoh of Egypt (bass); Joseph (alto) and his brothers Ruben (bass), Simeon (tenor), Juda (tenor), and Benjamin (soprano); the High Priest Potiphar (alto); his daughter Asenath (soprano); and the Pharaoh's servant, Phanor (alto).

The story is well known: The Pharaoh calls upon Joseph, an intelligent man who is languishing in prison, to interpret some troubling dreams. When he proves how clever he is, Joseph becomes a powerful minister; he wins the hand of the woman he loves, Asenath, and rescues his brothers. Though the text is basically primitive and not very lively, Handel's skill at creating magnificent sound images is admirable. There are relatively few choruses, compared to Handel's other oratorios. It seems that the composer made an enormous number of changes and corrections in the score, even changing voices in several roles, making performances difficult and possible only if extensive adaptations are made.

Belshazzar

The oratorios *Belshazzar* and *Hercules* were composed at the same time, in the summer of

1744. His librettist, Charles Jennens, had not delivered the new verses for *Belshazzar* on time, so Handel worked on *Hercules*, whose text had already been completed. Its author was Thomas Broughton, a cleric, and its subject matter was based on Sophocles. In the end, although *Hercules* was begun later than *Belshazzar*, it was given its premiere a few weeks before it, on March 27, 1745, in London.

With *Belshazzar*, Handel returned to the style of his great choral oratorios of earlier years. This tale, too, is quite well known. It is the story of the Babylonian king who is holding the Jews captive and who is also at war with the Persians. A mysterious inscription has appeared on the wall of his great hall, which he cannot make out. The Jewish prophet Daniel is called and foretells the king's doom: "Mene Tekel Upharsin," (weighed and found wanting). The Persians break in, kill the tyrant, and free the Jews to return to their own, much longed-for land.

Hercules

Both *Belshazzar* and the musical drama *Hercules* were composed in only a few weeks. The first performance took place on January 5, 1745, in London. This time, Handel had rented the King's Theater, where an Italian opera troupe had just completed an unsuccessful run. Handel wanted to present no fewer than 24 evenings of oratorio. At the same time he attempted to popularize his oratorios and make them more widely available by lowering ticket prices. Handel's experiment in democratizing music was a failure. The concert series was called off and Handel fell ill, retiring to Salisbury to spend the summer with good friends, the Harrises. In *Hercules*, Handel displayed the power of his music and despite a confused text composed some splendid individual numbers but not a great dramatic work.

Judas Maccabeus

Original Title: Juda Macchabaeus. An Oratorio
Original Language: English
Text: The libretto is by an English theologian, Thomas Morell; based on the Biblical account in *1 Maccabees*.
Date of Writing: July 9 to August 11, 1746.
First Performance: April 1, 1747, in the Royal Covent Garden Theater.
Form: In three parts with a total of 66 musical numbers.
Cast: Judas Maccabeus (tenor), Simon, his brother (bass), First Israelite Woman (soprano), Second Israelite Woman and Israelite Messenger (alto), Israelite Man (tenor), Eupolemus, Jewish Envoy (bass), four-part mixed chorus.
Orchestra: Two flutes, two oboes, two horns, three trumpets, timpani, strings, continuo with cello, contrabass, bassoon, harpsichord, and organ.
History of the Work: The origin of this oratorio is closely tied to the political situation in England in 1745 and 1746. A descendant of the Scottish royal house of Stuart had tried to invade England and drive out the ruling house of Hanover. Handel felt close ties to England and its king. This Scottish incursion inspired him to compose several works, including an "occasional" oratorio, which used a number of Psalms in transcriptions by John Milton and referred to the impending siege of London and its final liberation. It was performed for the first time on February 14, 1746 at which time the threat of invasion had not yet passed. Stability was only secured with the victorious battle of Culloden (April 16, 1746), the hero of which, the Duke of Cumberland, was honored in London in a great ceremony on April 1, 1747. Handel had held his newest oratorio, *Judas Maccabeus* in readiness for this outcome. Hardly any other work in the history of music is as well suited for singing the praises of manly courage, love of country, and desire for freedom. It was frequently performed; the composer is said to have conducted it nearly 40 times.

The assertion that this work decidedly reduced the always considerable number of Handel's rivals is not an exaggeration. His annual oratorio season, by then greatly augmented, became the focus of London's musical life, its most heavily attended series; and the city became the leading center of oratorio, and thereby of choral music, in the Western world.

The theologian Thomas Morell wrote the text for *Judas Maccabeus* based on the Biblical account of the Jewish war of independence under the leadership of the Maccabees in the second century before Christ.
Discussion of the Work: The two-part overture opens solemnly, but Handel's music is energetic from the very beginning as is evident even in the theme of the immediately following instrumental

fugue (Example 1).

Example 1

The drama begins with one of those scenes of mourning that Handel so well knew how to shape into impressive images. The Israelites sing their lament for their dead leader, Matathias, in C minor. After solo interludes sung by the Israelites—among them a very melodious duet between soprano and tenor—another chorus follows, whose melancholy F minor mood and dragging rhythm conveys an almost graphic image of a funeral procession (Example 2).

Example 2

Gradually, the mood of mourning changes to one of contemplation of the future: Israel is in great danger; who will save her? A chorus expresses the hope that a new leader might be able to free the people from their enemies. In a fugue, the chorus sings the praises of the one who shall come: "Grant a leader bold, and brave." Then Simon, son of Matathias and High Priest of the Israelites, steps forth. He announces (recitative and aria, fanfarelike, proclaiming victory) the will of God—that Judas, the Maccabee, will be the new leader.

The joyful mood that now prevails is expressed in the bright key of C major, in triadic themes in cheerful three-four time. Judas comes forth to provide words of hope to his people (aria in D major "Call forth thy pow'rs, my soul"). Joy erupts: the solo soprano (the Israelite Woman) represents the people and sings the praises of freedom in two successive arias; the Israelite Man replies with a recitative and aria and then the two join in a duet ("Come, ever-smiling liberty"), a folk melody in canon, which produces a lovely effect. Exulting, the people address the Maccabee: "Lead on, lead on! Judah disdains the galling load of hostile chains". He in turn addresses them in a more serious vein, recalling his dead father; against a dense orchestral backdrop, his recitative becomes an expressive arioso. A vocal trio answers, sung either by the chorus or by soloists, but composed only of the darker voices and sounding a little like the fugue in the overture.

Judas then sings an urgent admonition; it places this work not only at the highest musical level but lends it great ethical stature as well. The goal of the battle that lies before them is not victory, but peace. With a great chorus pleading for "conquest, or a glorious fall," in which the people express their calm determination, the first part comes to a close.

The second part opens with the battle over, and victory assured; a joyful chorus sings "Fall'n is the foe; so fall Thy foes, oh Lord!", a great piece of tone painting. A tenor aria (the Israelite Man) and a short recitative lead to one of the most brilliant pieces in the entire score, and in all of Handel's music: the victory chorus "Sion now her head shall raise," introduced by a duet. Handel composed this section years later and inserted it into this oratorio, well after it had become very popular (Example 3).

Example 3

The lengthy victory celebration with arias, duets, choruses, and an admonition to the Maccabees to remain humble before God who alone deserves honor for this victory, is suddenly interrupted by a messenger with disastrous news: Hostile troops from Egypt* are approaching. A soprano aria soon joined by the chorus singing the same words ("Ah wretched, wretched Israel!

---

*According to the text, the troops may have been Arabian (Syrian).

fall'n how low") depicts the Jews' dejected mood and mounting fear of the powerful enemy. Then Simon raises his voice in a rousing aria full of coloratura passages, proclaiming unshakable faith in God's miracles, which will save Israel yet again. Immediately Judas makes an ardent appeal, and the following warlike chorus shows that the people's mood has changed.

In spite of the many beautiful musical numbers that now follow in succession, we cannot escape the impression that dramatically the second part is only a watered-down repetition of the first, a judgment which must unfortunately be applied to the text of the third part as well. In general, Handel could count on little support and less talent from his authors. Many of them were simply helpless when confronted with such imposing subjects, and could not come up with more than a handful of effective mood scenes. Repeatedly it is Handel's music that raises their weak, pallid verse to immortality.

The third part celebrates yet another of Israel's great victories. After its proclamation in recitative by the second Israelite woman, one of Handel's best known melodies appears. He has the exultant boys and girls sing variations of it, after which all the people join in (Example 4). The mounting intensity of this number is something of a marvel. It is a simple song with the usual eight-bar melody and AABA form (a main theme repeated, an eight-measure middle section, followed by the first theme again). It is not surprising that this song either became a popular song or—and this is entirely possible—was already a folk song before Handel used it in his oratorio. Moreover, it was not included in the score when Handel wrote *Judas Maccabeus*, but a year later. It was composed for the oratorio *Joshua* and was only added to *Judas Maccabeus* when Handel was endeavoring to make its finale more effective. He probably also sensed that this oratorio would withstand the test of time better than *Joshua*.

Example 4

Not until it found its new home did this melody for "See, the conqu'ring hero comes!" acquire the form in which it is known today: the quiet approach of the victorious army, as if from a distance, its interruption by the two-part horn passage, its slowly increasing volume of sound achieved with darkly colored vocal passages and the full sonority of the orchestra, and finally, its full impact in a triumphant march. Peace, finally restored, is celebrated with many songs, which need not be discussed individually. The oratorio closes with one of Handel's great "Hallelujah"s, whose resounding "Amen" sends the audience on its way in a solemn mood of thanksgiving. The composer is here at the peak of his formal inventiveness, mixing polyphony with restrained, chorale-like passages—the absolute master of the principles of canon and fugue (Example 5).

Example 5

Alexander Balus

In a sense this oratorio is a continuation of *Judas Maccabeus*. Its text derives almost entirely from the Old Testament Books of the *Maccabees*, but the action has been moved to the Diadochen wars of the 3rd century before Christ. It is one of those Handelian works with such a large cast that it could almost be performed as an opera: Alexander Balus, King of Syria (alto); Ptolemy, King of Egypt (bass); Jonathan, Prince of the Jews (tenor); Cleopatra, daughter of Ptolemy (soprano); Aspasia, her betrothed (soprano); and choruses representing the various peoples. Handel is thought to have composed this three-act work in only five weeks—from June 1 to July 4, 1747; it was first performed at Covent Garden Theater on March 13, 1748. Once again, the text was by Thomas Morell.

The plot, confused and hardly profound dramatically, revolves around the love of the Syrian king for the Egyptian princess Cleopatra and their marriage—a happy one until Cleopatra's father has his daughter abducted by hired thieves. The Egyptian king tries in vain to tear Cleopatra's husband from her heart. The ending is tragic: the deaths of Ptolemy and Alexander, the suicide of Cleopatra. In the concluding chorus, Jonathan and the Hebrews praise almighty God—another occasion for Handel to display his deep faith as well as his musical inspiration in one of his "Hallelujah Amen"s.

Joshua

Upon completing *Alexander Balus,* Handel began his next oratorio, *Joshua.* He spent exactly one month on it—from July 19 to August 19, 1747. The first performance took place at Covent Garden on March 9, 1748, only a few days before *Alexander Balus.* The master, now 62 years old, was in one of his most productive periods. The singing roles are Joshua (tenor); Caleb, the High Priest (bass); his daughter Achsah (soprano); the young Hebrew Othniel (alto); an Angel (soprano); and a chorus of Jews.

A short instrumental introduction leads into the drama, once again by Thomas Morell, beginning with a feast of thanksgiving by the Israelites; they praise God for their miraculous crossing of the river Jordan. An angel appears, calling upon the leader of the Hebrews, Joshua, to take the pagan city of Jericho by storm. The people prepare for war. The siege and fall of Jericho make up the second act. The Israelites proceed around the walls of the city, carrying the Ark of the Covenant, their holiest of holies, before them. A mighty choral number describes the events: the fear of the people when they hear the trumpets blaring through a storm of thunder, the menacing tempest of elements and instruments. This leads to Caleb reporting quite objectively in a recitative, "The walls are levell'd," singing one of those typical bass arias found in almost all of Handel's scores, full of runs, embellishments, and coloratura passages. The third act brings only the joyful finale. The young hero Othniel offers to cleanse the enemy's land of the last of the heathens. Caleb awards him the hand of his daughter Achsah, who sings a beloved coloratura aria: "Oh, had I Jubal's lyre." Then we hear the beautiful chorus of girls and boys that Handel also included in *Judas Maccabeus,* here with the text "See, the conqu'ring hero comes." The finale is like many of Handel's, a chorus of praise and thanksgiving sung by the Israelites: "Hallelujah!"

Solomon

Opinions are divided as to whether *Solomon* is an oratorio or not. Its underlying theme is indeed dramatic, no matter how untheatrically it is carried out. The thread that runs through it merely connects episodes from the life of the main character, failing to provide any dramatic connection. It would be conceivable to perform each part separately, as a cantata.

But the work is exceptionally rich in musical beauty, mostly lyrical mood pieces, expressions of faith, love, goodness, and humanity. It was for this very quality that Mendelssohn, in a certain sense the discoverer of the Baroque era in the century of Romanticism (notably with his revival of Bach's *St. Matthew Passion*) was particularly devoted to *Solomon.*

The librettist is nowhere identified, but probably was again Thomas Morell. It was composed in the few weeks between May 5 and June 13, 1748, and first performed in London on March 17, 1749. The characters are Solomon, the great, wise king of Israel, originally assigned to an alto (although today it is better if the part is sung by a mid-range or deep male voice); the Queen, daughter of the Egyptian Pharaoh (soprano); the High Priest Zadok (tenor); the Queen of Sheba (soprano); a Levite, one of the priestly descendants of the Old Testament house of Levi (bass); and the Two Women who are disputing the ownership of the child (sopranos). The chorus has a large part, representing for the most part the people and the priests of Israel.

The work opens with a substantial overture in three parts. After a short, majestic beginning there is a four-part fugue with a four-bar, regal theme, answered first at the fourth, and then, strictly according to the rules, by the fourth voice at the fifth (Example 1).

Example 1

The prelude closes with a very lively third part. Then the chorus enters a cappella, the basses calling for song ("Your harps and cymbals sound to great Jehova's praise"). Soon a powerful eight-part musical setting emerges whose force and harmonic boldness form an early high point. After the Levite's aria there is another chorus, almost the equal of the first. It begins like a resounding chorale, its long notes giving it a rather hymnlike quality ("With pious heart and holy tongue"). This gives way to another fugue, whose quick, staggered entrances (within a single measure) mount in thirds: from the bass entry on G to that of the tenors on B-flat, to the altos on D, to the sopranos on F; finally the sopranos of the second chorus on A, and the basses on C—a six-part fugue for double chorus that reveals Handel's supreme mastery of this form.

Solomon is now heard for the first time. In a short but expressive arioso he calls upon the deity in a scene we should probably think of as representing a sacrificial ceremony. Immediately, Zadok, the high priest, turns to the king with a short recitative and an imposing aria, "Imperial Solomon, thy pray'rs are heard." Then there is another grand eight-part chorus with fugal and canonic elements and a generally solemn mood, carried out in long, unembellished notes, giving the impression of a chorale intercession. Solomon takes over once more, to glorify Jehovah as the source of all life and all power. Were this an opera, we would expect to see the lovely queen enter as the meditation comes to an end. Solomon turns to her with joy and listens as she sings her aria of happiness in her blissful marriage. With songs in praise of affection, loyalty, and contentment, the first act closes with a joyful chorus: "May no rash intruder disturb their soft hours; to form fragrant pillows, arise, oh ye flowr's! Ye zephyrs, soft-breathing, their slumber prolong, while nightingales lull them to sleep with their song." A lovely, gentle finale.

The second part begins with a jubilant, eight-part chorus in which the people pay homage to their king. In an aria, Solomon gives thanks once more to Jehovah as the sole source of wisdom. Immediately the opportunity arises to test the king's powers of judgment. What follows is the often-told, very dramatic tale of two women disputing the possession of a child. Solomon, in a decision worthy of his name, passes judgment based not on legal arguments but on maternal love. A joyful, lively chorus extols Solomon's wisdom, and the true mother, overjoyed, expresses her feelings of gratitude; the chorus brings the act to a close with a cheerful song.

The third part also begins with a splendid orchestral introduction. Then, in a recitative, we witness the meeting of Solomon and the Queen of Sheba. She had heard of this monarch's legendary wisdom and fruitful land and has come to become acquainted with both. The choruses set the peaceful mood with a popular-sounding chorus of greeting. But then the king orders a war song to be sung—a surprising turn of events that can only be explained if we think of the meeting of these two rulers as an occasion for a feast at which there is an artistic, vocal contest based on the most varied themes. The war chorus, in eight parts with harsh, marchlike rhythms, canonic entrances in close succession, and many realistic details, is a magnificent battle painting, which Solomon interrupts at its climax. In the sudden stillness, the king commands a new theme to be sung: the torture of unrequited love. Gravely and dejectedly, the chorus takes up the suggestion and intones an anguished lament. When it is completed, the monarch requests another theme: gentle peace. He himself gives the first words, as he had done before: "Thus rolling surges rise." The chorus develops this into a new song, taking over not only the king's lines but also his melody (Example 2).

Example 2

A musician will recognize immediately that this is a fugue theme. Handel uses it and sings of the laying to rest of the storm and of the transition to peaceful stillness in nature and in the soul. The Queen of Sheba is enchanted; "Thy Harmony's divine, great king!" In thanks she presents Solomon with lavish gifts—gold, precious stones, and incense—and declares herself completely captivated by the majesty of the temple the king shows to her. The finale of this truly heartwarming work is composed of more and more new songs of praise sung by the royal pair, alone and in duet, as well as an impressive choral hymn, "The name of the wicked shall quickly be past, but the fame of the just shall eternally last!", set for double chorus that rings out in a bright and happy D major, in solid harmonies.

Susanna

With *Solomon* finished, Handel from July 11 to August 24, 1748 worked on *Susanna*. This oratorio is quite different from his others. Its premiere preceded that of the more substantial *Solomon* and took place at Covent Garden on February 10, 1749.

The story turns on a merchant's faithful wife who is unjustly accused. She is miraculously saved from execution by the clever intercession of the prophet Daniel. The story is found in the Old Testament and in earlier times was often depicted by painters. Such a subject would be considered unsuitable for musical treatment today, although such "intimate" dramas are sometimes used as points of departure in modern music theater, for example, in Schönberg's monodrama *Erwartung* and in Britten's opera *The Rape of Lucretia*. The very "delicacy" of this subject was hardly suitable for Handel's monumental style. He wisely included only a few choral and massed numbers but a great many arias, in which a profusion of psychological nuances are expressed. But inflating the story to fill three acts detracts from its dramatic tension.

The librettist is not named. The cast consists of the married couple, Joachim and Susanna, sung by an alto and a soprano; the legendary Old Testament figure of Daniel (also a soprano); the Two Judges in Israel (tenor and bass); Susanna's Maid (soprano) and her Father (bass); and another Judge (bass).

Susanna, whose beloved husband must go on a journey, is observed, while bathing, by two lecherous old men who harass her. When she forcefully rejects their advances the men, who are judges, seek revenge. They determine to accuse her of an infidelity that they claim to have witnessed. The court judges against Susanna and condemns her to death. But Daniel intercedes, and by clever questioning traps the accusers in such a way that Susanna's innocence is upheld. The work ends with happy songs to faithful married love.

Theodora

Theodora, like *Susanna*, is little known. Handel wrote this oratorio in the summer of 1749, and presented it for the first time on March 16, 1750, at Covent Garden. The text, by Thomas Morell, is one of the weakest among all the master's works, a fact made more painful by virtue of Handel's fondness for the oratorio and the splendid music representing his mature mastery. It was never successful; at its premiere, the hall was almost empty, surprising since at that time there was no question of Handel's popularity and stature in London. His various biographers offer completely different explanations. One contends that the citizens of London, terrified by a prophecy that a severe earthquake was about to strike, were leaving the city in droves. A more objective account lays the failure to the subject matter.

It is, in fact, difficult to understand why Handel and his librettist, after relying so heavily on the Bible, chose—in Anglican England—to tell the story of a Catholic martyr.

The Choice of Hercules

The Choice of Hercules is among the last of Handel's vocal works; it is an interlude of the sort people enjoyed as part of a larger work, but also liked by itself. Handel is reported to have composed it between June 28 and July 5, 1750; it was first performed on March 1, 1751, probably to fill out a program that included *Alexander's Feast*. The author of the libretto cannot be established with certainty but it was probably based on a poem by Robert Lowth (1710–1787), a cleric and Biblical scholar. The short oratorio, or cantata, as it might also be classified, has three main characters: Hercules, and the two ways of life between which he must choose—Pleasure and Virtue. Pleasure has an attendant, and the chorus is divided evenly between attendants of Virtue and Pleasure.

It recounts the very old parable of "Hercules at the Crossroads." The worldly joys of pleasure are as enticingly described as the rewards of virtue and the serious life. The hero remains long undecided. The climax comes when the three main voices sing the trio "Where shall I go?" In the end, the winners are—and how could it have been otherwise in the 18th century?—Virtue and Duty. In this oratorio these qualities are identified with glory, bravery, and admittance to the circle of the immortal gods. The followers of Virtue sing the final chorus: "Virtue will place thee in that blest abode, crown'd with immortal youth, among the Gods a God."

Jephtha

Original Title: Jephtha
Original Language: English
Text: Libretto by Thomas Morell. The subject matter comes from chapter 11 of the Old Testament book of *Judges.*
Cast: Jephtha, Israelite judge and general (tenor); Zebul, his brother and a high priest (bass); Storge, Jephtha's wife (mezzosoprano); Iphis, their daughter (soprano); Hamor, Iphis's betrothed (alto); and an Angel (soprano).
Orchestra: Flute, two oboes, two trumpets, two horns, bassoon, strings, continuo with cello, bassoon, contrabass, harpsichord, and organ.
Date of Writing: Begun on January 21, 1751, completed after an interruption due to illness, on August 30, 1751.
First Performance: London, Covent Garden, on February 26, 1752.
History of the Work: Handel seldom mentioned his age, but at the end of the manuscript of *Jephtha* he wrote the words "aetatis 66": 66 years of age. He devoted much more time to this work than to any previous one. He began the first act on January 21, 1751, finished it on February 2, and immediately began the second act but got only as far as "How dark, o Lord, are thy decrees," the final chorus of this act. At this point, on February 13, Handel interrupted his work. To this point, he had spent almost exactly as much time on the work as he had on his earlier oratorios, an average of ten days for each act.

Handel documented this interruption with a note written in German: "biss hierher komen, den 13. Febr. 1751 verhindert worden wegen relaxation des Gesichts meines linken Auges." (Got this far, February 13, 1751; had to quit because of deterioration of sight in my left eye.) It is very curious that in the midst of an English composition, and no longer accustomed to using German, Handel wrote in his native language. By "Gesicht" he meant vision, which had deteriorated badly, in both eyes. Ten days later he took up *Jephtha* again, on his 66th birthday. He added "den 23. dieses etwas besser worden, wird angegangen." (On the 23rd it is a little better, I will resume.)

A few days later, the final chorus of the second act was down on paper, closing with these decisive words: "Yet on this maxim still obey, whatever is—is right." This sentence is not contained in Morell's original libretto, but rather "What God ordains—is right." In the libretto Handel replaced the word "God" five times with a different expression.* This, too, is not easily explained, particularly for someone whose faith in God was beyond doubt. The thought expressed here, which replaced the original wording, owes its origin to the widely read *Essay on Man* by the English poet Alexander Pope, who had died a few years before.

Months passed before Handel could finish the third act, and complete the work on August 30, 1751. His vision diminished from day to day; by the end of 1751 he was completely blind in one eye and the other was severely afflicted. Nevertheless, he appeared on February 26, 1752, at Covent Garden to conduct the premiere of this, his last great work.

> April 1752 was a gloomy month of suffering. At the beginning of May, three painful operations were performed (piercing his eyeball with a needle, without anesthetic!), one by the London eye doctor Sharp, one by the famous quack J. Taylor (who had also operated unsuccessfully on Bach), and the third by the king's personal physician, Bramfield; for a few days it seemed as though the latter had restored his sight. But he soon had a relapse and from then on lived in eternal night...**

Discussion of the Work: The overture is quite imposing. After a majestic introduction and an allegro section, Handel adds a minuet, lifting the melancholy prevailing thus far, although it, like the preceding parts, is in G minor. The drama justifies this gloom, for its mood verges on despair, but the significance of the minuet is puzzling.

---

*Johanna Rudolph, in the program notes to a performance of Jephtha at the Landestheater in Salzburg.

**Antoine-E. Cherbuliez, *G. F. Handel. Leben und Werk.* Olten 1949.

The Ammonites, enemies of Israel, have attacked west of the Jordan with a large army and threaten the tribe of Gilead living there. The people of Israel, who have renounced Jehovah and begun to serve the heathen god Moloch, realize the desperate urgency of the situation. They feel that God has turned away from them and believe all is lost. Zubul, a highly respected man, calls his brothers and fellow believers together to choose a leader, since no sign has come from Jehovah as it had in former times. Who could be more suitable than Jephtha, his brave brother? Rejected years ago because he had been born out of wedlock, Jephtha had valiantly proved himself in Gilead and had bettered his reputation so that he was widely respected. His noble heart harbored no revenge, and it would please him to lead his people if called upon. But his piety demanded that Moloch be first overthrown and that the people see the error of their ways and return to the true faith.

In the first of the great choruses that distinguish this work, Israel carries out his wish: "No more to Ammon's god and king. . . ." Jephtha rushes to the scene and declares himself ready to free his people from the Ammonite oppression of the last 18 years. He extracts one condition: If God grants him victory, he wishes to rule as a judge over Israel in the coming time of peace. Zebul swears to this condition in the name of God. In a simple, expressive aria, Jephtha accepts the mission assigned to him (Example 1). He bids a tender farewell to his wife, Storge, who sings an aria: "In gentle murmurs will I mourn." Iphis and her betrothed, Hamor, also bid each other a loving goodbye; the young man must go to war with Jephtha, Iphis's father. Gravely, the maiden calls his attention to his holy duty, for she will not be his until he returns from the war. Jephtha meditates once more before leaving for the most difficult task of his life. Wild visions beset his soul. His *recitativo secco* becomes a *recitativo accompagnato* as additional instruments enter softly; Jephtha solemnly swears a fateful oath: If God grants him victory over the Ammonites, he will sacrifice upon His altar the first person he meets at his joyful homecoming. This promise has provoked endless commentary. It represents a pagan mentality, and its appearance in *Judges* is most astonishing. Such a thing is conceivable for King Idomeneo, who, on his stormy way home from Troy promised the gods the first living being he encountered on the shores of his homeland, Crete, as retold in Mozart's opera *Idomeneo*. But for the Biblical Jephtha, such behavior is difficult to understand. Dante wrote in his *Divine Comedy* that, "Men should not play with oaths. What they swear to they must do; therefore they should not swear blindly, as Jephtha did. But it would have been better if he had said, 'I have done wrong, but I will not do even worse by abiding by my oath.'"

Example 1

Vir - tue my soul shall still em-brace, good — ness shall make me great

The chorus repeats Jephtha's oath. Storge is tortured by fearful premonitions. "Scenes of horror," her aria in a dark F minor, is a masterpiece of tone painting. Her daughter comes to soothe her; Iphis's bright manner is reflected in an aria that Handel has cast in the form of a bourrée (Example 2). Both arias, Storge's and Iphis's, are in the three-part form known as da capo aria, common in the Baroque period; after a contrasting middle section, the first section is repeated. The king of the Ammonites has arrogantly rejected Jephtha's peace offer and declared that he will fight to the last man. Jephtha calls his people to arms, and with renewed confidence the Israelites follow their leader into the field.

Example 2

At the beginning of the second act, Hamor has hurried ahead of the victorious army to proclaim the good news to his homeland: the Israelite army, led by angels who descended from

Heaven amidst thunder, has defeated the enemy in a bloody battle. After Hamor's report, in recitative, the people sing a dramatic song of victory and thanksgiving; the scene then ends with an extremely moving aria sung by Hamor. It is as though the young man were reliving the horror of battle, but also the joy of victory, which God so manifestly granted his repentant people. He also sings of his tender longing for Iphis, which gave him strength during the battle. Then the maiden commands that her wedding garments be laid out as she wants to greet her returning father joyfully, looking her most festive. She pours forth an exultant A major aria, full of gladness and anticipation: "Tune the soft melodious lute." The victors return and Jephtha praises Zebul and Hamor for their bravery in battle; they, in turn, direct all praise and gratitude to God: "His mighty arm, with sudden blow" (Example 3).

Example 3

At this point, Handel interrupts the drama with a "symphony," a lovely, restrained orchestral siciliano in 12/8 time. It immediately precedes the catastrophe: the bright G major music has hardly disappeared when Iphis, festively adorned and overflowing with happiness, goes to meet her father at the door of her house. A composer of opera would not postpone the tragedy so long. The daughter lovingly greets her returning father, now covered in glory, with a radiant gavotte: "Welcome, as a cheerful light" (Example 4). A boys' chorus pays tribute to the victor.

Example 4

Example 5

Only now does Jephtha's despair burst forth. In a recitative and aria marked with deep anguish, he seems close to collapse, which is incomprehensible to the bystanders. Jephtha discloses to them the reason for his cruel self-accusation: He has made an unholy vow that will mean death for his only child. Here, for the last time in Handel's long life, we see his strong dramatic hand at work. Storge throws herself between them; better that Jephtha himself should die, or that the whole world should perish. Hoping to spare Iphis, Hamor offers himself to be sacrificed. Zebul tries to sway Jephtha from his tragic decision, but "recorded stands my vow in Heav'n above" is all the despairing Jephtha can say. Then Iphis approaches; she has learned the reason for her father's incomprehensible behavior.

Once again Handel's music rises from recitativo secco, to accompagnato, to aria. Here poet and composer have succeeded in creating a greatly moving scene: Iphis herself asks for death, if it means that victory and peace can be assured and maintained for her people. The chorus raises its voice in gloomy anguish, singing "How dark, o Lord, are thy decrees," a fugal outcry of pain (Example 5).

But the act does not end in bottomless despair. In the finale, Handel continually stresses the line that could be thought of as the motto for the entire work: "Whatever is, is right." The third act shows Jephtha in torment, but determined; he will carry out the sacrifice. He only pleads, in an aria, that Iphis be gently carried to Heaven by angels. Iphis's farewell song is lovely, free from fear and concern, almost joyful that she will soon be in a "better world," a "kingdom of love and peace."

A chorus of priests turns to God for counsel as to whether the letter of the law is to be followed, or only its sense. Once again an orchestral piece interrupts the action; it accentuates the pleading of all in the last moments before the bloody sacrifice. An angel appears and announces God's will: Iphis shall live, but thenceforth shall serve Him as a virgin priestess. In the broadly conceived music of the ending, Jephtha, the people, Zebul, Storge, and even Hamor, deprived of the object of his love, express their thanks. In a rapture of joy, Iphis raises her song to God and finds consoling words for Hamor. All five solo voices join in a quintet, partly fugal, that merges with the choral finale. Like almost all Handel's oratorios, *Jephtha*, too, ends with "Hallelujah, Amen!"

The Triumph of Time and Truth

In 1708, during his years in Italy, years of apprenticeship and early achievement, Handel wrote an oratorio entitled *Il trionfo del tempo e del disinganno*, based on the words of Cardinal B. Panfili. Almost 30 years later, in 1737, long after he had settled in London, he took up the work again for performance. He returned to it again in his old age, in 1757. He asked his librettist Thomas Morell to make an English version that was to be called *The Triumph of Time and Truth* and made considerable changes in 20 of the musical numbers from the 1737 version and composed nine additional ones. Because he had been blind for some years, he was forced to dictate all this to his secretary, John Christoph Smith, as he did for a number of works composed in these last years. Furthermore, he could no longer think of conducting the premiere, on March 11, 1757, himself. As the name implies, this oratorio should be included among the allegorical works; the abstract concepts appearing are Time, Truth (or Counsel), Beauty, Pleasure, and Deceit. The chorus supplies commentary. Before the voices finally join in a thundering "Hallelujah," the conflict between so many, often opposing, concepts and opinions has led to the victory of Truth, which makes Time the real victor. After three acts of long, often philosophic discussion, which today's audiences would be hard pressed to follow, all, even Beauty and Pleasure, acknowledge the triumph of Truth and Virtue. Beauty, now convinced of the futility of all outward appearances, sings the last words: "Guardian Angels, oh, protect me, and in Virtue's path direct me."

The Passions

In addition to the many operas and oratorios—indeed, a total of almost 80—Handel composed a number of other vocal-instrumental works, some sacred, some secular. Two Passions should also be mentioned. The first, a *St. John Passion*, was composed in the first months of 1704 and sung for the first time in that same year, during Lent, in one of the churches of Hamburg, where Handel had lived since 1702. A year later he had met the poet and librettist Christian Heinrich Postel, who gave him a rhymed text of the Passion, based on chapter 19 of the Gospel of *John*; Postel had added texts for arias. Thus Handel's earliest oratorio came into being, some of its qualities already giving an idea of the future master. The duet "Schauet, mein Jesus ist Rosen zu gleichen" as well as the accompagnato "Weib, siehe deinen Sohn," are especially beautiful. The treatment of the chorus is very effective, with much to remind one of Bach's Passions, written 20 years later, with their wildly agitated scenes of furious mobs.

More interesting for many reasons is the so-called Brockes Passion. Its original title was *Der für die Sünden der Welt gemarterte und sterbende Jesus* (Jesus Tortured and Dying for the Sins of the World), the title of the poem written by the senator and poet from Hamburg, Barthold Heinrich Brockes. In the brief period between 1712 and 1716 alone it was set to music by Reinhard Keiser, Johann Mattheson, and Georg Philipp Telemann (and surely by others who were not as famous).

Handel composed his work based on this text (to which we can hardly relate today) in 1716. It was presented for the first time in Hamburg in 1717 while he was visiting, and before returning to London, the city he had chosen for his permanent residence.

Brockes had created a "Gospel synopsis," a compilation from all four Gospels. One of the virtues of this way of proceeding is that all seven of the "last words" uttered by Jesus on the cross are included, while in the Bible they are distributed among the several Gospels. A. E. Cherbuliez calls Handel's work "thoroughly modeled after the Italian dramatic cantata" with "a marked Pietistic flavor which caused the Bible text to be completely replaced by something in the manner of a madrigal."

Two comments might be of use here: *The Brockes* Passion seems to be Handel's only major work not composed with an eye to an upcoming performance. The Handel scholar Friedrich Chrysander (1826–1901) is even of the opinion that Handel only wanted to "test his powers" with this work, to see if he could compete with the famous masters of his time who had already set this text to music. In addition, the Brockes Passion is the last work that Handel composed in his native German. All the others are in either Italian or English.

Joseph Haydn   1732–1809

It was not until the 250th anniversary of Haydn's birth, marked throughout the world by great enthusiasm and many events, that Haydn's true greatness was acknowledged everywhere and the hoary, senseless cliché of "Papa Haydn" laid to rest forever.

This great master, born on March 30, 1732, in Rohrau on the Leitha, in Austria, was anything but a conservative or even easy-going artist. Though he was quiet, modest, and undemanding, as a composer he was a daring innovator to whom we owe a remarkable wealth of innovations. Much discussion has centered on the intellectual and musical authorship of the sonata form—the backbone of Classical instrumental music—without establishing with certainty whether it should be attributed to Sammartini from Milan, Stamitz from Mannheim, or Monn and Wagenseil from Vienna. But there is not the slightest doubt that its first true master was Haydn. It is also just as certain that chamber music, in its more modern sense, owes its origin and its first masterpieces, especially its string quartets, to him.

His role in the history of oratorio, where he was one of the most important figures, one of the path-breakers, is equally important. He wrote his first work in this genre, *Il Ritorno di Tobia*, when he was just past 40, but reached his peak only under the immediate influence of his experiences in England. Around 1796, he added choral parts to *Die sieben Worte des Erlösers am Kreuz* (The seven words of the Savior on the cross), an orchestral work composed in 1785, to make it into a sort of cantata. Following this with his *Schöpfung* (Creation) and *Jahreszeiten* (Seasons), he contributed the two most important oratorios of the Classic era. If we add Masses and other church music to the number of great choral-orchestral works, sacred works represent a large portion of his complete works. Haydn may have written 14 Masses (two of which have been lost), two Te Deums, and a Stabat mater, in addition to many smaller pieces, over a period of more than half a century. Such a large sacred output can astonish only those who are unaware of Haydn's deep religiosity which served and reassured him from childhood to his final hour, and inspired some of his greatest works.

His life divides readily into three large periods: The first his youth, confused years of apprenticeship, and first position at the castle of Count Morzin in Lukavec (Bohemia). The second comprises the 30 years he spent with Prince Esterhazy in Eisenstadt (today, the capital of Burgenland, in Austria). The third includes the years of his old age, which he spent in Vienna, with two journeys to England. It is hard to conceive of the enormous number of works he composed in his more than 50 years of creativity. This book will take leave of Haydn when he is 70, the year his *Harmoniemesse* was composed, 1802. Seven years later, on May 31, 1809, Joseph Haydn died in Vienna. The memorial service did not take place until June 15, in the Schottenkirche, because the French occupation of Vienna had upset the city's normal life. The honor guard was composed of members of both the city militia and the occupying Napoleonic troops. The Requiem by Wolfgang Amadeus Mozart was sung at this service.

The Return of Tobias

In 1771 a leading Viennese musician, Florian Leopold Gassmann, founded the "Tonkünstler Societät," a charitable society devoted to assisting poor musicians, their widows and orphans. In 1774 Haydn applied for membership from Eisenstadt, where he had been in the service of the Esterhazy family for a decade and a half. To strengthen his application, he dedicated his Italian oratorio *Il Ritorno di Tobia* to the society. The society took on the task of giving the work its premiere, which took place on April 2, 1775, in the Kärntnertor Theater where it was repeated on April 4. Both performances, conducted by the composer, were heavily attended and yielded the respectable sum of 1,700 gulden for the charity. (Nevertheless, Haydn was not accepted for membership, which led to a rupture lasting 20 years. The mistake was not made good until 1797, at the suggestion of Paul Wranitzky, a student of Haydn and secretary of the society.) On April 6, 1775, a review of the event appeared in the Imperial-Royal Most Gracious and Privileged Newspaper of the Sciences, the Arts, and Commerce, in the form common at the time. It reads:

> Once more, the famous Herr Kapellmeister Haydn has received universal applause with an oratorio set to music by himself called 'The Return of Tobias,' and has once more shown his well-known skill in its best light. The finely interwoven expressions of nature and art so permeated the work that the listener could only love the one and admire the other. His choruses, in particular, glowed with an internal fire, the like of which has heretofore been known only from Handel. In short, the entire extraordinarily large audience was enchanted, and Haydn was seen as a great artist whose works are beloved throughout Europe, where foreigners, too, recognize the original genius of this master. . . .

The choruses so emphasized in the article were really distributed sparsely throughout the work: In addition to a rather short introduction, there were only two—one at the end of each of the two acts or sections. The Old Testament text had been transcribed into verse by the Italian poet Giovanni Gastone Boccherini, originally from Lucca, but living then in Vienna.

The main characters are the blind Tobit; his spouse, Anna; his son, Tobias and his wife, Sara; the Archangel Raphael; and a four-part mixed chorus of Hebrews. The story is quite simple: Tobias returns home from a foreign land, where his father had sent him to collect a debt. His father, the blind Tobit, and his mother, Anna, have long awaited him, tormented by anxiety and fear. He brings a companion with him, a man who has loyally protected him at difficult moments along the way. However, he does not recognize that beneath the human appearance is the Archangel Raphael. Tobias had married Sara, a native of that distant land and she, too, has come home with him. The arrival of the three brings great happiness to the parents, especially since Sara immediately shows herself to be a loving daughter. Raphael now insists on curing the father's blindness with the gall-bladder of a dangerous animal killed by Tobias.

The next scene is the most important of the entire work: With the Archangel's help, Tobias tries to restore his father's sight, but the miraculous cure does not prove successful. The harsh sunlight is so blinding that Tobit, in despair, wishes he were once again in darkness, for the pain is worse than being blind. But Sara's love and patience bring the miracle to a good end: Tobit slowly grows accustomed to light. Everyone recognizes that Raphael's role in the cure was critical, so Tobit and Anna wish to pay him as well as they can. He then reveals his true identity: God has sent him "to protect you, Tobias, to see that you, Sara, are married, and to restore light to the eyes of Tobit." But he bears yet another message: Soon Israel's servitude will be at an end, "because Nineveh the proud will be destroyed and your grandchildren will look upon a dazzling Jerusalem radiant with gold and splendor, in renewed majesty, the city of the Lord!"

A song of thanksgiving sung by the quartet of soloists follows, written in Classical homophony (Example 1). It leads into the final chorus which, in good oratorio tradition, contains great fugal passages (Example 2). The fugue is resolved in a stretto, which brings the work to a jubilant conclusion—with the sopranos of the chorus twice singing high C.

Example 1

Example 2

The Seven Last Words of Christ

In March 1801 Haydn reminisced:

About 15 years ago I was asked by a gentleman from the cathedral in Cadiz to compose an instrumental work based on the seven last words of Jesus on the cross. In those days, every year during Lent it was customary to give an oratorio in the main church in Cadiz. To enhance its effectiveness, the following preparations were made: the walls, windows, and pillars of the church were covered with black cloth, and only one lamp, hung in the center, illumined the holy darkness. At noon all the doors were closed, and the music began. After a suitable prelude, the bishop mounted the pulpit, spoke one of the seven last words and then commented upon them. When he had finished, he came down from the pulpit and fell to his knees before the altar. This pause was filled by music. The bishop entered and left the pulpit a second time, a third, and so on, and each time the orchestra began to play when his remarks had ended. My composition had to be tailored to fit this ceremony. The task of writing seven successive Adagios, each about 10 minutes long, which would not weary the listeners, was not of the easiest; and I soon found that I could not confine myself to the prescribed length of time. Originally there was no text to go with the music, and it was published in this form. Only later did I have the occasion to supply a text; therefore, when the oratorio *The Seven Last Words of the Savior on the Cross* was published by Breitkopf & Härtel in Leipzig, it was a complete and, as far as the vocal music went, entirely new work. The great fondness for this work shown by discerning connoisseurs gives me hope that it will not fail to find a following among the public.

Only a few words need to be added to the composer's account of the origin. The church Haydn referred to is the Santa Cueva, in the oldest part of the Andalusian city of Cadiz, on the Atlantic. Since the earliest times it had performed the Good Friday ceremony, interestingly enough called an oratorio by Haydn; by that he meant an hour of prayer not necessarily related to music. By 1785 the Santa Cueva priests must have known of Haydn's reputation to approach him: they wanted Europe's leading master to create the music for their Good Friday ceremony. Haydn wrote an orchestral work—seven Adagios and, as a finale, a dramatic piece that he entitled "Terremoto"—the Spanish and Italian word for earthquake.

The work was performed in this form every Good Friday for many years. Almost 100 years later, in 1883, it provided a decisive musical experience for a seven-year-old boy named Manuel de Falla, an impression which remained with him throughout his life. De Falla, born in Cadiz, became Spain's leading modern composer.

The composition was written for two each flutes, bassoons, horns, and trumpets, to which were added timpani and strings. Before each of the Adagios, called sonatas, the bishop spoke one of the seven words from the pulpit and gave a brief homily.

A few years later, Joseph Frieberth, Kapellmeister of the bishopric of Passau, decided to arrange the work to use with his own choruses. On his second journey to England, in 1794, Haydn heard this version in Passau. He was fundamentally satisfied with it, but felt, justifiably, that he could create a better choral version himself, which he did in 1796, calling it an oratorio. Haydn deleted the two flutes from the score (perhaps they seemed too bright and cheerful), replacing them with two clarinets and two trombones, instruments that had recently come into use in symphony orchestras.

After a solemn orchestral introduction, the first of the seven words is heard: "Father, forgive them for they know not what they do," which the chorus sings in four parts, like a chorale. The melody is not lively and in spite of the division into four parts, is reminiscent of Gregorian chant, the earliest Christian music. This first idea is then developed in a text probably written by Gottfried van Swieten, who shortly thereafter worked with Haydn on the *Creation*. The second word is, "Truly I say unto you, today you will be with me in paradise." The third, "Woman, behold thy son and thou, thy mother!" The fourth, "My God, my God, why hast Thou forsaken me?" At this point Haydn inserted an instrumental interlude, played only by the winds. The fifth word does not begin with a chorale-like setting but immediately with a tenor solo: "Jesus called: I am thirsty!" The sixth (again like a chorale, declaimed on one note) is "It is finished!" The seventh is a chorale, with only small melodic variants: "Father, I place my spirit in Your hands!" Jesus dies.

As the Bible reports, an earthquake occurred at the moment of Christ's death, depicted in a movement Haydn headed *Presto e con tutta la forza* (very fast and with all possible vigor). Four times, each time with greater intensity, the chorus calls out "He is no more!" In its tragic vision, the movement sweeps along to the conclusion of the work: "O sun, shun and do not light this day! Break open, earth upon which the murderers stand! Graves, open up; ancestors, come up into the light! The ground that covers you is covered with blood!" Nothing auspicious here, no conciliatory finale: fierce slashes of C minor end this deeply moving work. Perhaps because it is so unusual, it has never attained the popularity of the two last, great Haydn oratorios.

The first printing, supervised by Haydn himself, bore the title *Die Worte des Erlösers am Kreuze* (The Words of the Redeemer on the Cross), but it has become the custom to refer to it as the *Sieben letzte Worte des Erlösers am Kreuz* (The Seven Last Words of the Redeemer on the Cross), a version used in most languages. In Cadiz, the city that can claim the honor of having presented it for the first time—probably on Good Friday, 1786—it is still called *Las ultimas siete palabras de Jesus en la cruz* (The Seven Last Words of Jesus on the Cross).

The Creation

Original Title: Die Schöpfung
Original Language: German
Text: By Gottfried van Swieten (based on a poem by the Englishman Lidley, who had based his work on Milton's *Paradise Lost*).
Date of Writing: 1796–1798
First Performance: Vienna, April 29 and 30, 1798, in the palace of Prince Schwarzenberg.
Form: In three sections; includes a total of 34 musical numbers.
Cast: the Angels Gabriel (soprano), Uriel (tenor), and Raphael (bass); Adam (baritone) and Eve (soprano); four-part mixed chorus.
Orchestra: Two each flutes, oboes, clarinets, bassoons, horns, and trumpets; three trombones, timpani, strings, continuo with cello and harpsichord.
History of the Work: The origin of this work can be traced to Haydn's second English journey, January 1794 to August 1795. It was suggested to the master, who was a brilliant success in London, that he compose an oratorio in the English tradition, the tradition of Handel, who had by then been dead for almost half a century. Haydn had attempted nothing in this genre since his youthful work *Il Ritorno di Tobia*, written completely in the Italian style. It was probably his impresario, Salomon, who gave him the draft of the text written by the little-known poet named Linley or Lidley, based on John Milton's *Paradise Lost*. However, Haydn's English was not sufficiently good for him to compose a full-length work in this language, so he took it with him when he returned to Vienna. It was probably toward the end of 1795 or the beginning of 1796 that his friend Gottfried van Swieten (1733–1803) came to him with the same proposal—the composition of an oratorio. Van Swieten was an important figure in Vienna's musical life. He was the son of the highly respected personal physician to Empress Maria Theresa, had been Vienna's envoy to the Prussian court at Berlin—probably the most delicate post in Austrian diplomacy—and was, when he approached Haydn, director of the Imperial Library (Hofbibliothek) in Vienna and secretary of an aristocratic musical society which presented oratorios in the great palaces of the nobility. He was himself a generous patron of the arts. Why such a splendid career bears the dark stain related to Mozart's death and burial—why van Swieten did nothing about the ignominious burial in a potter's field, in a mass grave—will probably never be explained. Did it have something to do with the Freemasons? Was it reluctance to take an active part in a mysterious, unpleasant situation?

When Haydn decided he was ready to begin the composition—his experience of how wonderfully the Handel tradition had been kept alive in London doubtless contributed considerably to his decision—and Van Swieten had translated the English draft into German and arranged it so that it made sense, he seems to have set to work with more detailed preparations than usual. Many more drafts and sketches of this work exist than for his other compositions. He was obviously in unfamiliar territory.

Many of Haydn's biographers contend that van Swieten, an extremely energetic man, had practically "ordered" Haydn to compose the work. There is no proof of this, and certainly no evidence of it in the finished score; almost none of his other works are as harmonious and joyful as this one. Karl Schumann correctly writes:

> The optimistic, interdenominational piety touched everyone's heart; one could be a believing Christian or an enlightened rationalist, a Jew or a Freemason, and still feel spoken to and inspired by this account of the creation of the world. It was composed in a time of upheaval: religious contrasts were diminishing, and rigid orthodoxy was becoming as relaxed as the belligerent faith in reason; the emancipation of Jews and the recognition of Freemasonry were making progress; the humanitarian message of the Weimar Classicists and the call for tolerance were beginning to be heard. In this revolutionary time, Handel's oratorio of universal religious feeling seemed to be a temple of impartiality, open to everyone.
>
> Haydn's *Creation* raised the world above its long-held image as a vale of tears in need of redemption; he glorified it as a well-ordered miracle, and its creator as a "busy workman" bringing meaningful order to chaos. This idea might have sounded Deistic and Rationalistic, but its composer was a simple-hearted man who took great joy in creation, a craftsman's son with both feet on the ground; he had no theological hair-splitting in mind, and went about his work with the cheerful piety and humor typical of 18th-century south Germany.
>
> This very Austrian, conciliatory quality in the music of Haydn's oratorio was understood from the beginning; the most ardent admirers of the score, which combined equal measures of the sublime and the idyllic in the simplest musical form, were in the Protestant north, where people hailed Haydn's joyful, active religiousness as the very welcome antithesis to their ancestral Pietism, which had gradually grown dreary.

Haydn himself said of the time he was at work on this enormous composition, "Never had I been so devout as when I was composing *The Creation*. Every day I fell to my knees and prayed to God to give me strength for my work." On April 6, 1798, Prince Schwarzenberg, in whose palace the first performance was to be given, received the news that Haydn had finished the composition.

As early as December 15, 1796, the Kapellmeister of St. Stephan's cathedral in Vienna, Johann Georg Albrechtsberger, wrote to Beethoven, "Yesterday Haydn came to see me; he has an idea for a great oratorio that he means to call 'The Creation'; he hopes to be finished with it soon. He played a few parts from it for me and I think it will be very good...."

In the meantime, van Swieten had found 12 men of the highest nobility to join in providing the composer with an honorarium of 500 ducats; it was under their patronage that the first performance, on April 29, 1798, was given. They were the princes N. Esterhazy, Trauttmannsdorf, Lobkowitz, Schwarzenberg, Kinsky, Auersperg, L. Lichtenstein, and Lichnowsky; the counts Marschall, Harrach, and Fries; the Freiherr von Spielmann and van Swieten himself. Many of these names later occupied prominent places in Beethoven's biography.

All sources report that the mood at that first performance was deeply emotional; the invited guests felt they were in the presence of something completely new, an art form that had transposed the Baroque oratorio of Bach's and Handel's day—a totally different kind of work—into the spirit of the new era.

The Creation spread with surprising speed to countless cities in many lands, not only in Europe but also North America. The first public performance took place in the Imperial Royal Court Theater in Vienna on March 19, 1799. The poster announced Haydn as "Doctor of Music and Kapellmeister to His Highness Prince Esterhazy." The first title came from England—Haydn had been given an honorary doctorate at Oxford—and the second was the title he had borne for the 30 years he had spent working for "his" prince in Eisenstadt, which the prince had allowed him to retain after he retired. The first Parisian performance of the *Création du monde* was set for Christmas Eve, 1800, in the Théâtre des Arts. The composer was invited to conduct but declined, purportedly out of feelings of "patriotism"; he did not want to honor the "Victor of Marengo" with his presence (six months earlier, the French had dealt the Austrians a heavy defeat at Marengo). When Napoleon Bonaparte, then the First Consul of the Republic, was on his way to the concert, someone threw a bomb at him. The attack was unsuccessful, but the future emperor of France arrived too late to hear the performance.

It is hardly possible to describe the triumphant progress of this work; it is best compared to that of the most successful operas. However, the enthusiasm that greeted this devout and honorable composition was accompanied by outbursts of indignation and misunderstanding. Many clerics felt it their duty to point out that Haydn's Creator looked suspiciously like the image of God held by the Freemasons. This accusation is not as far-fetched as it might initially sound, for Haydn was not only a believing Christian but also a Freemason, as were the Mozarts, father and son. That these two views were not in the least in conflict is best attested by the work itself. Nevertheless, church performances in many parts of Austria were forbidden at the direction of the ecclesiastical authorities. An incident in a small city in Bohemia created much attention; a rector permitted it to be sung in church, whereupon on the following Sunday the priest railed against it from the pulpit, raising the prospect of a highly embarrassing proceeding to determine whether Haydn should be called a heathen! Haydn defended himself in a letter in which he made his point with the words, "And this arousal of holy feelings" that he had tried to evoke with this work "is supposed to be a desecration of the church?" He added that if the campaign against him did not stop he would appeal to the Emperor, who, with his spouse, "listened to this oratorio with the truest emotion and was completely convinced of the value of this holy work."

Such discordant episodes did not, however, manage to slow the triumphant progress of *The Creation*. When, a few years after the premiere, Napoleon marched into Vienna with his troops, a French officer asked Haydn's permission to visit him. To the master's surprise and joy, he wished only to sing the aria "Mit Würd' und Hoheit angetan" for its creator. Early in the 19th century, Carl Friedrich Zelter, Goethe's musical advisor and director of the Berlin Singakademie, one of the leading choral groups at that time, worked long and hard to see that the work was widely performed. As a consequence hardly a leading choral society in Europe did not have Haydn's oratorio as part of its permanent repertoire. Nothing has changed today; indeed, amateur music-making has made it better known than ever.

Discussion of the Work: The story is taken from the Biblical account of creation. Haydn's art was marvelously suited to this kind of naive description—folklore at its best. It all flows so naturally, so artlessly, in its simple faith and love of nature and its creatures that hardly a more ideal subject could have been wished or indeed imagined by him. Leopold Nowak, in his seminal Haydn biography, wrote:

> The master was faced with a multicolored profusion of details from the heavenly and earthly order: chaos, the stars, plants and animals, mankind, and all under the hand of God. His vision encompassed the cosmos yet could depict the little things: the murmur of a brook, the charming beauty of plants, the movements of animals. The way he mastered the contrasts, the way he described the heavenly and the earthly is inimitable and unique. In Haydn's day, some voiced displeasure over many of these points and even found fault with the music. Some held it a degradation of art to use it to the end of imitating the movements of tigers or worms. This was the view of Rationalism, intellectual and constricted. If, however, one reads the simple, unadorned language of the creation story in light of van Swieten's interpretation, one sees it as a sort of Gothic panel painting. Crowded together in a small space one sees a multiplicity of things, almost a confusion of lines and colors of every hue. Nevertheless, it is all simple and direct. The observer readily understands that he is in the presence of a work of great art. So is it with *The Creation*. It is a musical picture book written for all ages. The origin of the world, with its stars and tides, plants and animals, as well as the dignity of mankind in paradise are described in a unique way.

The work begins with the "Representation of Chaos;" of the oratorio's many beauties, this is perhaps the most miraculous. In order to fully grasp its meaning, one must understand its development. It begins with a forceful orchestral stroke of only a single note, C, running, long sustained, through several octaves. The dawn of time could not be expressed more magnificently—nor more simply. The Biblical version is expressed exactly as the modern "Big Bang" theory—of which Haydn knew nothing—might be. It is, so to speak, "the Void" and yet the source of all being, an indefinable something, a mysterious force. Then, very softly, nebulous developments begin: strained chords, dissonances—for 59 bars Chaos reigns. The harmonies are somewhat vague, even though they do not go much beyond the understanding and custom of the time, which may be regarded as a period of transition from the Classic to the Romantic. There is an aura of holy mystery about these eons which surpasses man's comprehension (Example 1).

Then a voice is heard. The Archangel Raphael recites the famous words "Im Anfange schuf Gott Himmel und Erde . . ." (In the beginning, God created heaven and earth). Haydn has the voice sing alone, as if suspended in the air; the orchestra only weaves a soft tissue between the lines. Then the sound becomes denser, a delicate background against which the chorus announces, timorously, as though witnessing a great mystery, "Und der Geist Gottes schwebte auf der Fläche der Wasser..." (And the spirit of God was upon the face of the waters...). Once again the orchestra pauses and we hear "und Gott sprach" (and God spoke) and "Es werde Licht" (Let there be light). And this is what is called the miracle—the miracle worked by God, without which there would be no life. To depict this miracle, Haydn created a reverent, humble, musical miracle: the gigantic outburst of sound at the word "Licht" (light): "Und es ward Licht" (and there was light). This passage has been called the "sacrament of tonality." It is no more than a C major chord, the simplest known to a musician, but, as it breaks forth from the long "chaos" of tangled dissonances, its effect is stunning; so must the first light have dawned, unseen by human eye, after millennia of darkness (Example 2).

Once more objective, Ariel declares in a recitative "Und Gott sah das Licht, dass es gut war, und Gott schied das Licht von der Finsternis" (And God saw the light, that it was good, and divided the light from the darkness). The first aria then interrupts the Biblical account: "Nun schwanden vor dem heiligen Strahle des schwarzen Dunkels gräuliche Schatten..." (Now the gray shadows of black darkness disappear in the holy radiance). These are van Swieten's words, and it would be unfair to demand "great poetry" from him. He writes as a sensitive and intelligent man attuned to the primal mystery of the creation, as well as a man who lived in a "folklike time." Van Swieten and Haydn represent an era that in its artistic strivings for "innocence" sought a return to the artlessness of folklore; a far cry from Baroque elaboration.

Uriel's aria is of the same stuff, a joyful hymn to the first day of light. The chorus joins in and sings of the final plunge of Hell's evil spirits into the depths of night. Then, in recitative No. 3, Raphael speaks of the division of the waters; Gabriel tells how the angels sang "the praises of the Creator." A curious point of contention arose here: In the English original, which Haydn brought home from England, "the glorious hierarchy of heav'n" is written, referring to God's attendants—archangels, angels, and perhaps other high beings. Van Swieten, a child of his time, who—even in imperial Austria—had been influenced by French Revolutionary thought, translated it as, "der Himmelsbürger frohe Schar" (the merry crowd of heavenly citizens). This must surely have sounded revolutionary to many a supporter of the Ancien Régime. Haydn probably failed to notice this difference in meaning, so direct and sincere was his most natural attitude to all matters of religious faith and secular power.

The chorus and the solo soprano sing, forte, the joyful praise of God, "das Lob des zweiten Tags" (the praise of the second day). In recitative No. 5, Raphael continues his description: On the third day God divided the land from the waters, and the Archangel sings of the ocean in a majestic aria. The key (D minor) and the syncopation remind one of Mozart, and dramatic characteristics of Beethoven can be heard: "Rollend in schäumenden Wellen bewegt sich ungestüm das Meer..." (the tempestuous ocean, rolling in foaming waves). Gabriel reports, in recitative No. 7, the next act of creation, the miraculous coming into being of trees and grasses: "Und Gott sprach: Es bringe die Erde Gras hervor" (And God said, let the earth bring forth grass). How joyous is the aria "Nun beut die Flur das frische Grün" (Now the meadow freshens green) (Example 3); it is almost as if we already see the fields of ripening grain, as if the colorful flowers had emerged beneath the beneficent rays of the sun. The music is as simple and artless as a folk song, and just as sincere.

After Uriel's short recitative (No. 9) comes the exultant chorus "Stimmt an die Saiten, ergreift die Leier" (Tune up the strings, take up the lyre), which becomes a fugue in the second part: "Denn er hat Himmel und Erde bekleidet..." (He adorned heaven and earth). Strict Baroque forms are more relaxed; compared to Bach's and Handel's models, all is charming, somehow more earthly. No. 11 is again a recitative: Uriel relates how God creates the stars. He continues in the next recitative, No. 12, which, however, develops into much more than a simple speech-song.

It reminds one of the previous eruption of light out of chaos: this number, too, begins on a single tone from which the voices multiply and tension builds. But the development is gradual, until it reaches the brightest D major, fortissimo, after which Ariel's voice enters: "In vollem Glanze steiget jetzt die Sonne strahlend auf..." (In total brilliance rises the radiant sun) (Example 4).

A booming chorus comes next, to a text that has often been set to music. The most famous is Beethoven's version, whose German words are much the same as Haydn's: "Die Himmel rühmen des Ewigen Ehre" (The heavens are praising God eternal). In Haydn's composition, this confession of faith is equally impressive (Example 5).

The solo voices of the three angels are interwoven with the choral passages. It is all shaped so simply—C major for the day, C minor for the night—and yet is so effective, without the slightest loss of musical worth! With the bright, joyous praise of God, the first part comes to an end.

The division of this oratorio into parts must be considered only a practical necessity since the telling of God's creation proceeds without interruption. A somewhat natural division occurs at the fifth day of creation, for living creatures appear on the scene, but this criterion is hardly above

Example 6

criticism as trees and flowers are also living organisms. All things taken together a performance without pause is most desirable if the endurance and powers of concentration of the participants permit and the audience is prepared to share the joy of this pleasing, cheerful music in a continuous presentation.

In recitative No. 14, Gabriel tells of the creation of fish and birds, and in the related aria (No. 15), the poetic and musical elaboration continues. The key of F major was often chosen by Classical and Early Romantic composers for realistic descriptions of nature. For example, a few years after Haydn's *Creation*, his student Beethoven used it as the basis of his sixth symphony, the *Pastorale*.

A lengthy orchestral prelude depicts the new liveliness apparent everywhere: "Auf starkem Fittiche schwinget sich der Adler" (The eagle soars on powerful wings) and "Den Morgen grüsst der Lerche frohes Lied" (The lark greets morning with a joyful song). Then another new element appears in creation: love. Mankind has not yet appeared, but Haydn found moving music for this word, which hints at the throb of loving hearts, nervous with excitement (Example 6).

Raphael dedicates a line to the "grossen Walfischen" (great whales) in the following recitative (No. 16) and sings an expressive arioso on God's command: "Seid fruchtbar alle, mehret euch!" (Be fruitful and multiply!). After a short recitative (No. 17), the angels sing "die Wunder des fünften Tags" (The miracles of the fifth day); Gabriel, Uriel, and Raphael join in a thoroughly melodic—and once again, almost folksonglike—A major trio, "In holder Anmut steh'n, mit jungem Grün geschmückt, die wogigten Hügel da..." (The fair and graceful rolling hills, newly bedecked with green...). They stand amazed before God's innumerable works: "Wer fasset ihre Zahl?" (Who can count them?), their song leading into the exultant outburst of the chorus (No. 19) which sings an overpowering, four-part ensemble—in all, seven jubilant voices (Example 7).

But all sorts of creatures are still missing from creation. Raphael continues in recitative No. 20: "Es bringe die Erde hervor lebende Geschöpfe nach ihrer Art, Vieh und kriechendes Gewürm und Tiere der Erde..." (Let the earth bring forth living creatures each after his kind, cattle, and creeping things, and beasts of the earth...). Librettist van Swieten puts it this way: "Gleich öffnet sich der Erde Schoss, und sie gebiert auf Gottes Wort Geschöpfe jeder Art, in vollem Wuchs und ohne Zahl. Vor Freude brüllend steht der Löwe da, hier schiesst der gelenkige Tiger empor..." (Immediately at God's command the earth opened up and bore creatures of all kinds, full grown and too numerous to count. Here stands the lion roaring with joy, there springs the supple tiger...).

Tone painting, a favorite device in the Rococo era, gives the late-Classicist Haydn the opportunity to depict each animal with its own rhythms, melodies, and typical sounds: the lion's roar; the tiger's litheness; the deer's light-footedness; the noble horse's joy in life, "voll Mut und Kraft" (full of courage and strength); the peacefully grazing cattle and the gentle sheep; but also "das Heer der Insekten" (the swarms of insects) in a whirring tremolo in the strings; and "das Gewürm" (the reptiles), with their undulating movement over the ground.

Hard upon the heels of the realism used for the zoological descriptions, Raphael turns once more to more abstract matters in his aria (No. 22) "Nun scheint in vollem Glanze der Himmel, nun prangt in ihrem Schmucke die Erde..." (Now heaven shines in all its glory, now earth goes forth resplendent in its finery). Tone painting is used here, too, in part in anticipation of the next and final act of creation, which Uriel's recitative (No. 23) announces. "Und Gott schuf den Menschen nach seinem Ebenbilde..." (And God created man in his own image...) sings Uriel, his aria rising to an ecstatic hymn of thanks (Example 8). The enormous work of creation is now complete, "und der himmlische Chor feierte das Ende des sechsten Tages mit lautem Gesang" (and the heavenly choir celebrated the end of the sixth day with rousing song), sings Raphael, in recitative No. 25. The chorus bursts forth joyfully (No. 26), and in fugal passages rises to exultation. A meditative trio of the three angels follows (No. 27, "Zu Dir, o Herr, blickt Alles auf"—All creation looks to you, Oh Lord); for the first time the subject is not the miraculous being and becoming, but its natural consequence, death and dissolution. The gloomy prophecy is reserved for the bass, Raphael: "Du wendest ab Dein Angesicht: da bebet Alles und erstarrt. Du nimmst den Odem weg: in Staub zerfallen sie..." (You turn Your face away: all creation trembles and is still. You take the breath of life away: they turn to dust...) (Example 9).

The music has darkened, too, moving from E-flat minor and A-flat minor to C-flat minor, in actual sound really a not so rare B minor. Even the score looks gloomy and quite un-Haydnlike with its double-flat signature. Then the mood brightens again with the assurance that life is an unbroken cycle of birth, death, and rebirth: "Verjüngt is die Gestalt der Erd' an Reiz und Kraft. Und neues Leben sprosst hervor..." (Earth is made young again in charm and strength. And new life sprouts...). Now we hear the choruses "das grosse Werk vollendet" (the great work is complete) (No. 28); "Alles lobe Seinen Namen" (All creation praise His name) and "Denn Er allein is hoch erhaben" (For He alone reigns on high). The last two furnish the themes for a double fugue, the development of which leads magnificently to the end of the second section of the work.

In the third section, cosmic and creative events develop within a human dimension. A bright, wonderfully earthy orchestral prelude in E major leads off, after which Uriel observes life stirring on earth and describes in a melodic, yet recitativelike song how "vom himmlischen Gewölbe strömt reine Harmonie zur Erde hinab" (from the vault of heaven pure harmony streams to earth). His voice now symbolizes the shift of attention to the earthly domain. The first humans walk along hand in hand, united in love, giving thanks to their creator. We are in Paradise, before the fall from grace. The duet with chorus (No. 30) is full of cheerful sonority in which the voices of Adam and Eve join with those of the choir of angels. As in a great opera finale, Haydn structurally unites various elements—ariosos with choral parts, the lyrical with the dramatic—until the piece reaches its climax in a hymn of praise: "Heil Dir, O Gott, O Schöpfer, Heil!" (Hail to Thee, God the Creator, Hail!).

Up to this point we have looked upon the human scene taking place in Paradise, but recitative No. 31 points to an earthly, human bond between Adam and Eve: "Erkennen sollst du dann, welch unaussprechlich Glück der Herr uns zugedacht... Komm, komm, folge mir! Ich leite dich!" (Know then what inexpressible happiness the Lord has prepared for us... Come, come, follow me. I will lead you.). Eve answers, "O du, für den ich ward! Mein Schirm, mein Schild, mein All! Dein Will' ist mir Gesetz..." (You, for whom I was created. My shield, my shelter, my all. Your will is my law...). This relationship is lovingly expressed in the duet (No. 32): "Holde Gattin..." (Beloved wife...). In a folklike melody, simple and sincere, the first two humans sing of their deep sense of belonging to each other, their heartfelt happiness, and their everlasting bond. A short recitative sung by Uriel precedes the solemn choral finale with soloists, which depends upon much fugal material and increases powerfully in force but is without Baroque pathos. With immense dignity and exaltation, overflowing with happiness and deep thankfulness to God, *The Creation* comes to its radiant conclusion.

The Seasons

Original Title: Die Jahreszeiten
Original Language: German
Text: By Gottfried van Swieten based on the English poem *The Seasons* by James Thomson.
Date of Writing: 1799–1801
First Performance: Vienna, April 24, 1801, in the palace of Prince Schwarzenberg.
Form: In four parts:
    1. Spring
    2. Summer
    3. Autumn
    4. Winter
a total of 44 musical numbers.
Cast: Simon, a tenant farmer (bass); Hanne, his daughter (soprano); Lucas, a young peasant (tenor); four-part mixed chorus.
Orchestra: Two each flutes, oboes, clarinets, bassoons; one contrabassoon; four horns; two trumpets, three trombones; timpani, strings, continuo with cello and harpsichord.
History of the Work: Accounts written at the time report that *The Seasons*, like *The Creation* but even more so, owed its genesis to van Swieten's considerable moral suasion. However, we can probably assume that following the enormous success of *The Creation*, it was not overly difficult to convince Haydn of the wisdom of continuing on this path, one that had earned him the love and admiration of such large numbers of people in such a short period of time. Only his advancing age—he was close to 70—and the great weariness he had felt when *The Creation* was finished, may have aroused some misgivings. But they vanished when this work turned out to be a joyful one in every respect. He had long been considered the greatest instrumental composer of his time, and the spread of his fame in a new genre—a genre which at that time did not enjoy a place of any significance in the repertory of Central Europe but had, thanks to the success of *The Creation*, quickly gained great popularity—understandably brought him great joy. The material aspect of the commission for the composition was once more arranged by van Swieten, on very generous terms. A group of prominent aristocrats undertook to guarantee an honorarium worthy of the master and also took charge of presenting the premiere, enlisting the best musical forces under the most agreeable conditions.

The premiere took place on April 24, 1801; its enormous success leading immediately to two more performances, on April 29 and May 1. *The Allgemeine Musikalische Zeitung* waxed enthusiastic over the event: "The audience responded by turns with rapt attention, astonishment, and loud enthusiasm; the mighty onslaught of colossal visions, the endless profusion of felicitous ideas, surprised and overwhelmed the boldest imagination. . . ." The work marked a significant turning point in Haydn's life. He wrote that it was composed sometimes at the cost of great effort, though not a single measure reflects it. *"The Seasons* really did me in; I should not have written it. I had to struggle for days at a time with the smallest details." He clearly felt that it was to be his last great composition, for a few days after the successful series of first performances on May 5, 1801, he began the complex and exacting task of drafting his first will.

Discussion of the Work: Oratorios composed in Vienna prior to Haydn's day invariably had followed the tradition of Italian oratorio; Haydn's *Il ritorno di Tobia* was no exception. But *The Creation* and *The Seasons* were clearly based on the Handel model, although they neither aim for nor equal Handel's sense of drama. *The Seasons,* in particular, can rather be taken as a connected series of colorful, lyrical images, admirable for its diversity provided by the changing seasons of the year.

Of course, this concept had occasionally been tried before. Telemann wrote a cantata called *Die Tageszeiten* and his contemporary Vivaldi composed the violin concerto cycle *Le Quattro Stagioni* (The Four Seasons). The latter is still well known and often performed. It too describes the course of the seasons in a marvelous way, with many tonepainterly details. A similar setting informs the cantata, *Les quatres saisons,* now long forgotten, written by the French composer Joseph Boismortier in 1726.

The theme is an obvious one, with meaning for everyone; it has been treated by countless poets of all times and in all languages. It would be an exaggeration to say that the Englishman James Thomson's version is particularly successful or worthy. Nevertheless, in the version by Gottfried van Swieten, that cultured, sensitive Viennese patron of the arts, it provided an ideal framework for Haydn's talents, who turned it into a masterpiece: the "popular oratorio." Not the slightest musical knowledge is necessary to understand it; it speaks to everyone, the melodies are as simple as folk songs, and the setting, carried out with the greatest skill, is direct and easy to comprehend; the work is personal, humorous, and touches the hearts of all who hear it.

The first part describes spring. The orchestral introduction, perhaps not quite as magnificent as that of *The Creation,* depicts, according to Haydn, "the transition from winter to spring." The first measures seem to describe a world frozen in snow and ice (Example 1). But the first rays of the sun soon cause a stirring, developed in a lengthy orchestral piece full of picturesque details. Imaginative listeners can easily visualize that which Haydn's heading describes: melting snow, the first green shoots, spring breezes, the struggle as cold gives way to the first warm rays of the sun, the awakening songs of birds.

While all of these images are indeed contained within this symphonic piece, Haydn is too much of a Classicist to compose music that is purely programmatic. It is true that the sonata form is not as strictly adhered to as, for example, in his earlier quartets and symphonies, but it still determines the way in which the themes are developed. Finally, the orchestra concentrates its forces, and in a great fortissimo the last of the winter storms rolls over the land.

Simon, the farmer, observes the struggle between the elements. The first words of the work are "Seht, wie der strenge Winter flieht, zum fernen Pole zieht er hin, ihm folgt auf seinen Ruf der wilden Stürme brausend Heer mit grässlichem Geheul . . ." (See how harsh winter flees to the distant pole; at his call, the raging storms follow him with their dreadful howling). The young peasant Lucas watches as the snow melts, Hanne feels the first gentle winds of spring; here, the orchestral accompaniment is truly painterly, and the listener, deeply moved, experiences the annual miracle of nature's rebirth. The chorus enters with a lovely melody (Example 2): "Komm, holder Lenz . . ." (Come, sweet springtime).

The piece is in three parts: Between the main melody and its repetition at the conclusion, a splendid antiphonal exchange between the male and female voices is used. The male voices warn against celebrating too soon—winter could return at any time, destroying blossoms and sprouts. Nevertheless, this enchanting piece, one of Haydn's most popular, comes to a close in joy and confidence. After a short recitative (No. 3) Simon enters in his first aria (No. 4), with a clear folk song quality: "Schon eilet froh der Ackersmann zur Arbeit auf das Feld" (Already the ploughman hurries to work in the field) (Example 3).

As the peasant follows his plough, probably whistling (the score says "flötend"—playing the flute), Haydn gives him a melody that audiences of those days almost all recognized: the Andante, the second movement from his Symphony No. 94, the *Surprise* Symphony. This was one of those little jokes which the master so often played; the listeners' expressions must have brightened into amused smiles when they heard it.

In recitative No. 5 and the connecting trio with chorus (No. 6), the mood becomes more serious: A song of prayer begs for grace and blessing from Heaven (Example 4). This eloquent

Example 1

Example 2

Example 3

Schon ei — let froh der Ak — kersmann zur Ar — beit auf das Feld

Example 4

Sei nun gnä dig mil der Him mel!

Example 5

E — wi—ger, mäch — ti — ger, gü — ti — ger Gott

piece ends with a choral stretto in the form of a fugue. Recitative No. 7 tells that the prayers have been heard: the longed-for rain falls and the luxuriant meadows bloom with color. Now we hear a song of joy in several parts (No. 8). The chorus of young people joins in as Hanne and Lucas sing a cheerful duet.

Descriptions of nature are included, as in *The Creation*, but in *The Seasons* they reflect human reactions and are experienced happily and thankfully: "Alles lebet, alles schwebet, alles reget sich " (Everything is alive, even the air, everything is astir) sings Lucas; the springing lambs, the streams teeming with fish, the swarming bees, the fluttering of birds—all fill Hanne with gladness. "Welche Freude, welche Wonne schwellet unser Herz, süsse Triebe, sanfte Reize heben uns're Brust!" (What joy, what bliss fills our heart; sweet desire, gentle sentiments gladden our heart!) sing the young people in exultation. Simon interprets it all as the will of God, whereupon a great song of thanksgiving unfolds (Example 5).

After this very solemn chorus, the three soloists express their thanks, and "Spring" comes to an end with a powerful, multipartite choral fugue, radiant and devout—the kind Haydn so loved.

"Summer" begins with a short but expressive orchestral introduction intended by the composer to depict daybreak. In this second part of his oratorio, Haydn gives a portrait of a single summer day. After the first reddening of the sky we hear a wakening call from the oboe. Is it the cock that summons the peasants to a new day? It calls out three times, each time musically more intense. Then the spirited horn resounds (No. 10), announcing the day. In an aria, Simon sings of the shepherd leaving with his herd, and this pastoral music shines with a true folk quality. Hanne describes the spread of dawn across the heavens and its setting the mountains alight with a golden fire. A trio with chorus (No. 11) sings of the new day—a hymn to the wonders of nature and to the sun, "des Weltalls Seel und Aug', der Gottheit schönstes Bild" (Eye and soul of the world, finest of God's creations).

In recitative No. 12 Simon describes the harvest. Lucas (No. 13, called a cavatina) notes the hot noonday sun and a scene of weariness: the meadows dry out and people weaken from "der Hitze Wut" (the heat's wrath). In recitative No. 14 Hanne summons all to the coolness of the grove, where old trees spread their shade and the stream trickles over soft moss. While her recitative is very melodious, her aria, No. 15, is a beautiful, full-blown song: "Welche Labung für die Sinne! Welch' Erholung für das Herz!" (What refreshment for the senses! What healing for the heart!); a lively second part follows. Then Simon observes (recitative No. 16) the approach of a storm; Lucas and Hanne describe the dark clouds drawing near while all Nature seems to wait. The first lightning strikes (in the flutes), and thunder cracks in the orchestra with a fortissimo C, in unison. The choruses (No. 17) and instruments, now in a frenzy, produce one of the most magnificent pieces of storm music in all the literature. It gradually dies away, and silence returns. The three soloists then sing (No. 18) of the peaceful evening, the gentle mood, as animals and people return to their dwellings. Once again Haydn "paints" in sound: the chirping of crickets, the croaking of frogs. The evening bell rings out, the first star winks from the firmament. Peacefully, with warm sonority, the summer day comes to an end.

Van Swieten and Haydn wrote above the beginning of the third part, "Autumn": "The introduction depicts the peasants' joy in a rich harvest." No. 20 is an extended piece of music in which the chorus and soloists sing of diligence and hard work. In spite of all its technical mastery, perceptible in every measure, this vocal ensemble is one of the least inspired in the work. Haydn often said about himself, "I have always been a diligent, hardworking person, but I have never been able to set this quality to music." And this piece lacks that magnificent originality and naiveté typical of the work. Handelian sounds, reminiscences of the Baroque, full of power and strength, are not well suited to this simple description of three ordinary people, which is really what *The Seasons* at its most charming is. In the following recitative (No. 21), the three soloists report in rapid speech-song their observations of small things: picking walnuts and hazelnuts, harvesting fruit. Then we hear a duet (No. 22) sung by the two young people, Hanne and Lucas, a love duet with a folklike melody (Example 6).

Here, too, Haydn is somewhat conventional; overly formal and lacking in warmth. Van Swieten has, influenced by the pastoral poetry of his Rococo era, made the artless, wholesome country maid into a "lady of the city," and the faithful peasant lad a "young gentleman."

In many of his operas Haydn had composed love scenes—but this was long before; then they were more genuine, more passionate, even though never, either in life or in art, as passionate as those of his contemporaries Mozart and Beethoven. Sincere emotion is not really perceptible until the two voices finally join in a true duet: "Lieben und geliebet werden ist der Freuden höchster Gipfel, ist des Lebens Wonn' und Glück..." (To love and be loved is the highest form of joy, it is life's happiness and bliss).

Example 6

Example 7

In No. 23 (recitative) and No. 24 (aria) Simon sings of the hunt, with much tone painting—the firing of the guns, the starting up of hunted birds—a theme which Lucas carries on in recitative No. 25, where a hare is the victim. Finally, the chorus of hunters (No. 26) reports on the deer hunt, where neither speed nor cunning could save it from its killers. It is difficult to understand how a nature lover like Haydn could write a chorus rejoicing over the misery of innocent creatures, hunted down. No. 27 (recitative) and No. 28 (chorus) are dedicated to the grape harvest. A resounding drinking song with triangle and tambourine ends in rollicking gaiety.

The introduction to the fourth and last part is headed by the author: "describes the thick fog with which winter begins". Here Haydn has once again composed great, significant music for this piece. His orchestration possesses a wealth of color almost never before heard. The year draws to a close. Simon's recitative is serious and a little sad, to which Hanne adds her melancholy cavatina (No. 30): "Licht und Leben sind geschwächet, Wärm' und Freude sind verschwunden..." (Light and life have diminished, warmth and joy have disappeared). Then Lucas completes the image of winter (recitative No. 31 and aria No. 32), creating a Schubertian image of a traveler lost in the dark and cold, walking in circles until a light shining from a hut sets him in the right direction. The villagers gathered in the hut weave, spin, and tie nets; they sing of their work. Haydn chose for this scene a text by Gottfried August Bürger: "Knurre, schnurre, knurre, schnurre, Rädchen, schnurre!" (Hum and rumble, little wheel) (Example 7).

The rocking rhythm of the spinning wheel is in six-eight time; the music anticipates later spinning songs, such as Schubert's *Gretchen am Spinnrad* to a poem by Goethe, and Wagner's spinning song from *Der Fliegende Holländer*.

No. 36 is a curious piece: Hanne adds spice to a winter evening with a short, humorous ballad, joined by the chorus at the refrain. She tells of how a country maiden pokes fun at a nobleman who has chased after her and holds him up to ridicule. The mood then becomes serious once more; Simon looks back meditatively over the dying year—a symbol for the passing of life: "Wo sind sie nun, die hoh'n Entwürfe, die Hoffnungen von Glück..." (Where are they now, the great plans, the hopes for happiness). But the work does not end in melancholy. The chorus, divided into two groups, and the three soloists raise their voices in a great solemn song on the meaning of human life, in which one must do good and noble deeds to reap the reward of eternal life. Moving into an almost liturgical mood, the poet and the musician create an image of the greatest, deepest joy; no one is surprised when this oratorio, a totally secular work, ends with a twice-repeated "Amen."

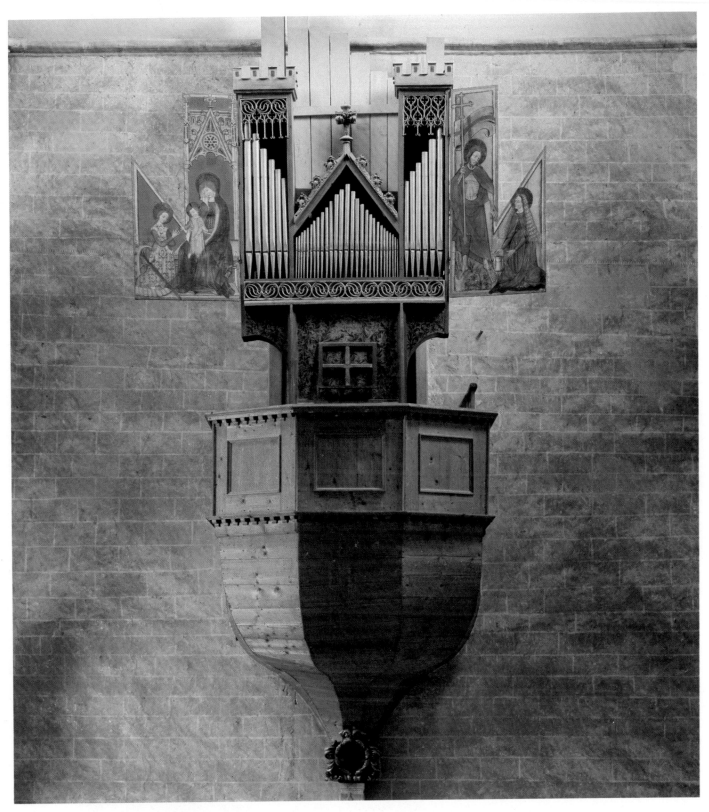

1. One of the oldest organs still
playable: the "Swallow's Nest
Organ" in the church of Notre
Dame de Valère (Sitten, canton of
Wallis, Switzerland). From the
beginning of the 14th century.

2

3

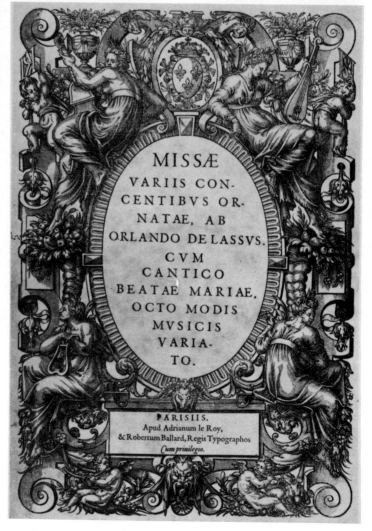

MISSÆ
VARIIS CON-
CENTIBVS OR-
NATAE, AB
ORLANDO DE LASSVS.
CVM
CANTICO
BEATAE MARIAE,
OCTO MODIS
MVSICIS
VARIA-
TO.

PARISIIS.
Apud Adrianum le Roy,
& Robertum Ballard, Regis Typographos
Cum priuilegio.

4

5

2. Solemn Mass with choruses and instruments (left). The parts have not been handed out individually: instead a large manuscript is placed on a high lectern in front of the performers. Engraving from 1595.

3. Winds, organ, and vocalists performing church music. Above right, the organ bellows. From *Spiegel der Orgelmaker* The Organ Maker's Mirror), printed in 1511 in Mainz.

4. Title page from an edition of Masses by Orlando di Lasso, printed in Paris in 1577. (Austrian National Library, Vienna.)

5. Heinrich Schütz, whose name was often Latinized as in this portrait, Heinricus Sagittarius, in 1670, when he was 85 years old.

6. Title page of a *St. Matthew Passion* by Johann Sebastiani, Königsberg, 1672 (Denkmäler deutscher Tonkunst).

7. Heinrich Schütz standing in the midst of his "Kapelle" (musicians) in the Alte Schlosskirche in Dresden (Title page of Christoph Bernhard *Geistreiches Gesang-Buch*, 1676.)

8. An "oratory" (prayer room) in the Roman palace of Cardinal Pietro Ottoboni, probably with set for performance of a Passion by Alessandro Scarlatti.

9. Musical scene in a church in Jena, Germany (1665): singers and instrumentalists on two balconies; the organ in the background, and in the center, the Kapellmeister with baton and score.

10. Title page of Emilio de Cavalieri's *Rappresentatione di Anima e di Corpo*, Rome, 1600.

11. Title page of the libretto of Alessandro Stradella's *San Giovanni Battista*, for a performance in Modena, 1688.

8

9

RAPPRESENTATIONE
DI ANIMA, ET DI CORPO

Nuouamente poſta in Muſica dal Sig. Emilio del Caualliere,
per recitar Cantando.

Data in luce da Aleſſandro Guidotti Bologneſe.

Con Licenza de'Superiori.

IN ROMA
Appreſſo Nicolò Mutij l'Anno del Iubileo. M. D C.

SAN
GIOVANNI
BATTISTA
ORATORIO
MVSICA
D' ALESSANDRO
STRADELLA.

IN MODONA, M.DC.LXXXVIII.
Per gli Eredi Soliani Stampatori Ducali.
Con Licenza de' Superiori.

12. The Chiesa Nuova in Rome; to its left, the "oratorium" that was added. At the end of the 16th century, it was the headquarters of the "Congregation of Oratorians" (see Introduction).

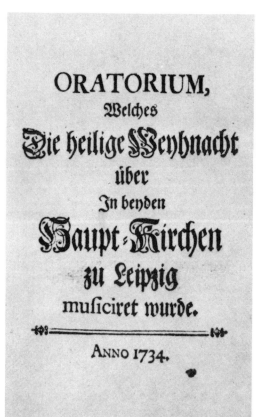

12

ORATORIUM,
Welches
Die heilige Weyhnacht
über
In beyden
Haupt-Kirchen
zu Leipzig
musiciret wurde.

ANNO 1734.

13/14. Title page and original printed text of Johann Sebastian Bach's *Weihnachts-Oratorium* (Christmas Oratorio), Leipzig, 1734.

15/16. Two autograph scores by Bach: left, the beginning of *St. Matthew Passion* (1729); right, from the *Weihnachts-Oratorium* (1734).

Am isten Heil. Weyhnacht-
Feyertage,
Frühe zu St. Nicolai und Nachmit-
tage zu St. Thomæ.

Tutti.

Jauchzet! frohlocket! auf! preiset
die Tage,
Rühmet, was heute der Höchste ge-
than,
Lasset das Zagen, verbannet die Klage,
Stimmet voll Jauchzen und Frö-
lichkeit an:
Dienet dem Höchsten mit herrlichen
Chören
Laßt uns den Nahmen des Höchsten
verehren.

Da Capo.
A 2   Evan-

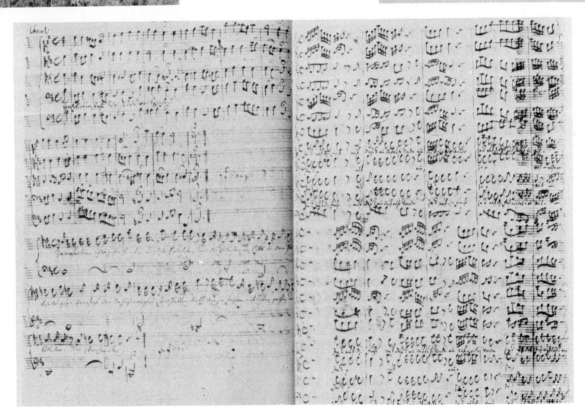

17. Title page for *St. Matthew Passion*, written in Bach's hand.

18. First edition of the text by Christian Friedrich Henrici (Picander) for the *St. Matthew Passion*.

19/20. Autograph pages from Bach's *St. John Passion* (1721/24).

Passio Domini nostri
J.C. secundum Evangelistam Matthæum

Poesia per Dominum Henrici
alias Picander dictus

Musica di G.S.Bach.

Prima Parte.

※) 101 (※

Es ist kein Sterblicher nicht schlimmer, auch nicht besser,
Wenn sie der Tod begehrt, der unerbittlich ist.
Wir haben einen Weg die Stunde geht zu Ende,
Das Schicksal hat allein den Zeiger in der Hand,
Der eine hält sich auf, der andre stirbt behende,
Und endlich decket uns ein allgemeiner Sand.

XI.

Texte zur Paßions-Music, nach dem Evangelisten Matthäo, am Char-Freytage bey der Vesper in der Kirche zu St. Thomä.

Vor der Predigt.

Die Tochter Zion und die Gläubigen.

Aria.
3. Kommt, ihr Töchter, helfft mir klagen,
Seher! Gl. Wen? 3. den Bräutigam.
Seht ihn; Gl. Wie? 3. als wie ein Lamm.

Choral.
O! Lamm GOttes, unschuldig
Am Stamm des Creutzes geschlachtet,
3. Seher; Gl. Was? 3. Seht die Gedult.
Allzeit erfunden gedultig,
Wiewohl du warest verachtet,

G 3   3. Seht;

21

21/22. The churches of St. Nicholas (21) and St. Thomas (22) in Leipzig: colored engravings from 1749, one year before Bach's death. He was in charge of the music in both churches. When he first took up his duties in Leipzig, his "debut" cantata was performed in St. Nicholas church on May 30, 1723.

23 (facing page). The interior of St. Thomas church in Leipzig; it has not changed much since Bach's day.

22

24. The Vienna Court Chapel during a solemn *Te Deum* in honor of Emperor Joseph I, who was in attendance. Engraved in 1705 by J. A. Pfeffel and C. Engelbrecht.

SAMSON.

AN

ORATORIO.

As it is Perform'd at the

THEATRE-ROYAL in Covent-Garden.

Alter'd and adapted to the Stage from the SAMSON
AGONISTES of *John Milton*.

Set to Muſick by GEORGE FREDERICK HANDEL.

LONDON:
Printed for J. and R. TONSON in the *Strand*.

MDCCXLIII.

[Price One Shilling.]

25

25. Title page of the first edition (1743) of the oratorio *Samson,* by George Frideric Handel.

26. Handel's tomb in "Poet's Corner" of Westminster Abbey in London.

27. Ticket for performance of Handel's *Hercules*, Friday, February 21, 1751, at the King's Theater in London.

26

27

28

29

30

28. Joseph Haydn's last public appearance: on March 27, 1808, he attended a performance of his *Creation* in the ceremonial hall of the old Vienna University. Watercolor by Walter Wigand, in the Historical Museum of the City of Vienna.

29. The "Theater an der Wien" in Vienna; important site of opera, oratorio, and concert premieres in the Classic era.

30/31. The archabbey of St. Peter in Salzburg, where Mozart's *C Minor Mass* was first performed. View towards the high altar; below, the organ, built in 1620.

31

32. Handel's autograph score for the first bass aria from the *Messiah*.

33. The Foundling Hospital in London. From 1750 on, an annual benefit performance of the *Messiah* was given here in the chapel (center).

34. Handel's autograph score of the beginning of the "Halleluja" chorus from the *Messiah*.

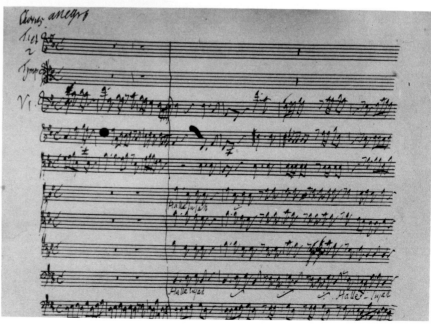

35/36. Continuation of the Handel tradition after his death: An imposing mass performance of his *Messiah* in Westminster Abbey in London, 1784. Below: the floor plan for the positioning of chorus and orchestra for a Berlin performance of the same work, conducted by Johann Adam Hiller in 1786.

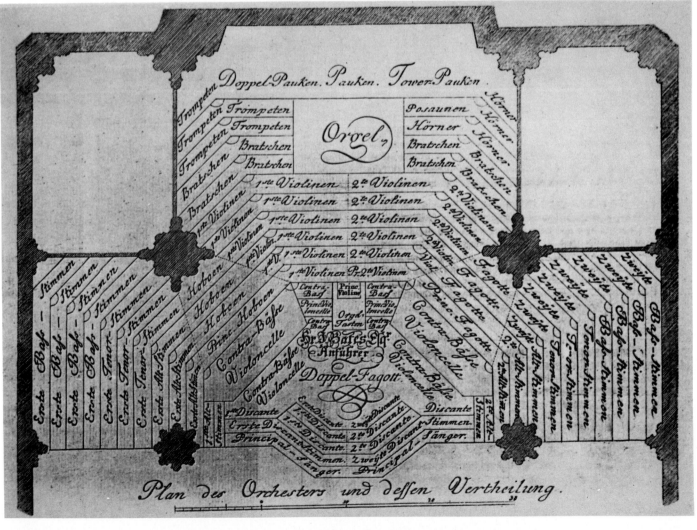

37. Title page of G. B. Pergolesi's *Stabat mater* in an early English edition, John Walsh, London, 1749.

38. Coronation of Louis XV on October 25, 1722, in Rheims. In the foreground, four drummers and the 12 oboists of the royal ensemble. For the coronation ceremonies, 52 vocalists and instrumentalists performed a *Te Deum* by Colin the Younger and several sacred works by de Lalande.

39. Transept of St. Mark's church in Venice during High Mass. Pen and ink drawing by the landscape painter Antonio Canale, called Canaletto (1697–1768).

40. Title page of the first edition of Haydn's oratorio *Die Jahreszeiten* (The Seasons), 1801.

41. The beginning of the "Kyrie" of Haydn's *Kleine Orgelmesse*, 1778.

40

41

42

42–44. Three documents relating to Haydn's oratorio, *Die Schöpfung*, (The Creation) (1799): (Top) The announcement of the public premiere for Thursday, March 19, 1799, in the Imperial and Royal Court Theater next to the palace in Vienna, with Haydn's titles, "Doctor of Music" and "Kapellmeister to His Highness, Prince Esterhazy", and a lengthy announcement. (Center) Entries of subscribers' names in his notebook, most of them from the high nobility; (Below) Sketches for the "eagle aria."

43

44

45. Autograph score of the beginning of Mozart's *Requiem*.

46. The last notes Mozart ever wrote: The opening bars of the "Lacrymosa" from the *Requiem*.

47. First edition of Beethoven's *Missa solemnis* with the prominent dedication to his student, friend, and patron, Archduke Rudolph von Habsburg, the Emperor's brother.

48. The first page of the *Missa solemnis* (Kyrie) in Beethoven's hand, with the now famous words, "Von Herzen—möge es wieder—zu Herzen gehn!" (May it go from heart to heart).

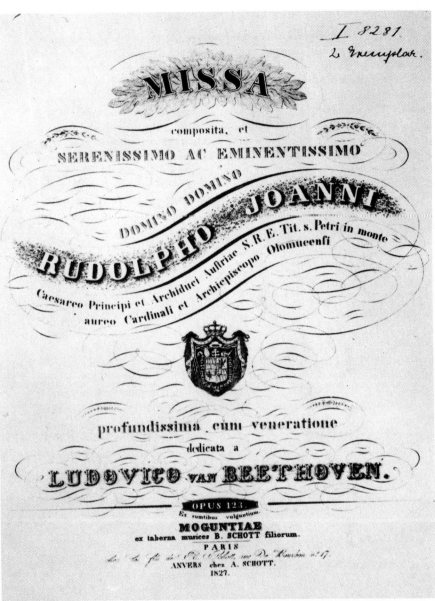

47

48

49. The console of the organ in the Liechtenthal church in the Vienna suburb (at that time) of the same name, where Schubert performed his first Mass. Austrian National Library.

50. Schubert's manuscript of this Mass, in F Major, with his dating: May 30, 1814.

51. The house in Leipzig where Mendelssohn lived for many years.

52. Mendelssohn's diary from his wedding journey (1837), in which he drew a picture of himself in the Heiliggeist church in Heidelberg, "conducting," according to the note by his wife, Cecile.

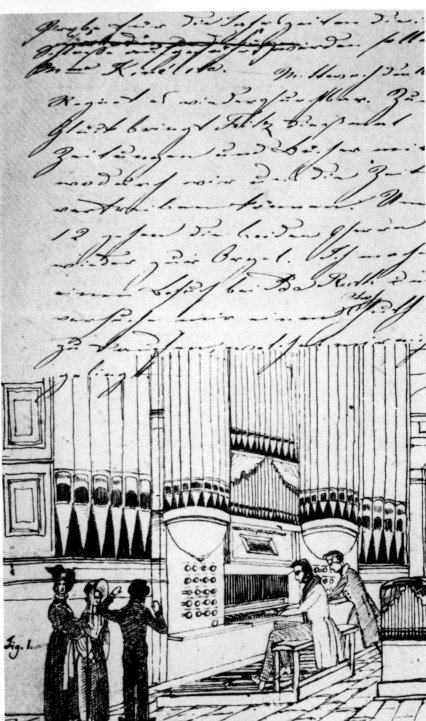

53. The interior of the Marien-
kirche in Lübeck during a concert of the first North German
Music Festival (1839), at which
Handel's *Samson* and portions of
Hadyn's *Creation* were
performed.

54. Franz Liszt, in the robes of an
abbé, conducting a performance
of his *Legend of St. Elizabeth*,
Budapest, 1865.

55 (above). Three great masters of music who never met; Beethoven, with Wagner to his right, and behind them, Brahms. Ceiling fresco in the Zürich Tonhalle, dedicated in 1895, in the presence of the guest of honor, Brahms. (Beethoven died in 1827, Wagner in 1883.)

56. Title page from the first edition of Liszt's oratorio *Christus*.

57. Beginning of the second movement of the autograph score of Brahms's *Ein Deutsches Requiem*: "Denn alles Fleisch, es ist wie Gras." Austrian National Library, Vienna.

56   57

58. The church of St. Mark in Milan, site of the first performance of Verdi's *Requiem* on May 22, 1874, conducted by the composer.

59. The "Bruckner Organ" in the beautiful St. Florian abbey church near Linz, in Upper Austria—the composer's spiritual home.

58

59

60

60. Page of the autograph score
of Arnold Schoenberg's oratorio
Gurrelieder (detail).

61. *Oedipus Rex* by Stravinsky, in a
performance at the Warsaw
Opera, 1962.

62/63. *Jeanne d'Arc au bûcher* (Joan
of Arc at the Stake), oratorio by
Arthur Honegger, text by Paul
Claudel, in a performance at the
Zürich Opera, 1983. In the title
role, Christine Ostermayer; Frère
Dominique, Rudolph Bissegger.

61

62

63

64. *Carmina burana* by Carl Orff (1937) in a performance at the National Theater in Munich.

65. Title page of the *Buch mit sieben Siegeln,* one of the most significant oratorios of the 20th century, by the Austrian composer Franz Schmidt.

66. Page from autograph score of Frank Martin's *In terra pax,* 1944.

67. The church opera *The Burning Fiery Furnace,* by Benjamin Britten; performance by the Zürich Opera in the Grossmünster, 1983.

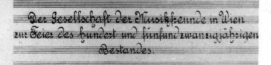

68. Leonard Bernstein's *Mass* in a
1981 performance in Vienna. In
the leading roles, Franz Wächter
and Donna Wood.

69

69/70. *Das Spiel vom Menschen,* by
Cesar Bresgen; 1983 premiere at
the Carinthian Summer Festival
at Ossiach-Villach.

70

71. A performance of
Monteverdi's *Vespro della Beata
Vergine* in the Fraumünster
church in Zürich. The choir
windows by Marc Chagall in the
background.

72

73

72/73. Performances of sacred music: (Above) The New Phil-harmonic Orchestra and Chorus in St. Michael's Cathedral in Ghent; (Below) The Academy of Ancient Music in St. Martin-in-the-Fields in London (rehearsal).

74. Emilio de Cavalieri's *Rappresentatione di anima e di corpo* in a Salzburg Festival performance, University Church, 1972. Directed by Herbert Graf; conductor, Ernst Märzendorfer; stage design, Veniero Colasante.

75. *Il Sant'Alessio,* by Steffano
Landi, at the Salzburg Festival,
1977. Director, August Everding; conductor, Peter Maag; stage
design, Jean-Pierre Ponnelle.

76. *Juditha Triumphans* by Antonio Vivaldi, with Carmen Gonzalez and Stella Silva. Performance in the Ossiach church at the Carinthian Summer Festival, 1976.

77. Handel's *Belshazzar* at the German Opera in West Berlin, April 1959, for the 200th anniversary of the composer's death.

78. Scene from Handel's *Saul* in a
performance at the Zürich
Opera, 1983. Director, Claus
Helmut Drese; conductor,
Nikolaus Harnoncourt; stage
design, Josef Svoboda.

79. Staged performance of
Handel's oratorio *Jephtha* in the
University Church in Salzburg,
1983, directed by Federik
Mirdita; musical director, Ralf
Weikert.

Haydn's Masses

Haydn composed a total of 14 Masses. Two, composed during his youth, have been lost. The remaining 12 are uneven, containing many beautiful parts but also some of notable weakness. Only in England and Vienna—Haydn's two early strongholds—has his sacred music been regularly performed, whereas appreciation has long declined in Germany and Italy.

In this respect, Hermann Kretzschmar's important encyclopedia, whose origin and spirit place it securely in the 19th century, and which served for many decades as the standard treatment of concert music, makes interesting reading. He had this to say about Haydn's Masses:

> .... Indeed, great exultation and deep reverence are not part of Haydn's happiness in God. At best, he varies the tone of the choruses of *The Creation*, and its arias are even quoted. But he was never so unequal to the task as here, as so often when dogmatically profound and moving passages were to be rendered: How shallow is the counterpoint in the "Qui tollis" of the *Mass in Time of War* and in the Theresienmesse! What a superficial "Et incarnatus" here and in the *Nelson Mass*! The Haydn who composed the *Seven Last Words* and such beautiful motets as "Insanae vanae curae" can hardly be recognized in the Masses. We have to take him at his word when he assured his biographer Griesinger that the writing of Masses touched him deeply and that he considered writing them a task of the highest order. We must take pleasure in the parts that are successful, the touches of genius, just as in architecture we appreciate the marvelous structure of the [Venetian] Cathedral of St. Mark. But just as that edifice is never taken as a model for a Christian house of God, we must also grant that Archbishop von Hohenwarth was correct, and praise him for his decision to forbid the performance of Haydn's Masses in Vienna's churches!

Since then, much in this way of thinking has changed, and some of Haydn's Masses now seem ideal examples of deep, although perhaps "naive" piety. A few words in explanation must be given here.

The first Mass, the Missa brevis in F major, was probably written around 1750, and is therefore the work of an 18-year-old who had not yet learned much about the technique of composition. He wrote it in Vienna for four-part chorus, two solo sopranos, two violins, bass, and organ. Late in life he added winds to the orchestration; in 1806 he found "the melody and a certain youthful fire" in this composition still so vital that he wished to enlarge upon it.

In Eisenstadt, where, beginning in 1761, Haydn spent almost 30 years in the service of Prince Esterhazy, and where he found his true home, he wrote the so-called "Great" Organ Mass in E-flat major, originally entitled *Missa in honorem Beatissimae Virginis Mariae* (1776). In addition to organ and the usual strings, it called for two each of English horns, horns, trumpets, and timpani.

Haydn probably composed the *Missa Sancti Nicolai* in G major in 1772. The *Missa Sanctae Caeciliae* in C major is not as easy to date, but it is thought that it was written between 1769 and 1773. This Mass, Haydn's longest and most important, was dedicated to the confraternity of St. Cecilia, a religious music society in Vienna. Every year it celebrated the day set aside to honor the martyr Cecilia (later canonized and named patron saint of music) with a High Mass, usually in the cathedral of St. Stephen.

Haydn dedicated his *Missa brevis Sancti Joannis de Deo*, called the "Little" Organ Mass in B-flat major (along with a Salve Regina), composed between 1775 and 1778, to the Order of the Brothers of Mercy in Eisenstadt, with whom he was on friendly terms. It is said that he played the organ for the first performance in the abbey church.

Between April and June 1782 Haydn must have composed the *Missa Cellensis* in C major; it was possibly commissioned by his friend Anton Liebe von Kreutzner. It seems that the newly ennobled Liebe offered it to the Virgin Mary as a token of thanks for his appointment. This "Mariazellermesse" concluded Haydn's first period of Mass composition, for he produced no others during the next 14 years.

Haydn's service at Eisenstadt came to an end when the old prince died and the orchestra was dissolved by his successor. With a good pension and the honorary title of Kapellmeister provided by the new Prince Esterhazy, the master went to live in Vienna. Upon his return from the second triumphal journey to England he received an invitation to return to Eisenstadt, where another new prince, Nicolaus II, wished to reestablish the former musical glory. But the aging master could do no more than make frequent visits and compose some works for the prince and the church in Eisenstadt.

Haydn composed a Mass almost every year from 1796 on. In 1796 he wrote the *Missa in tempore belli* in C major, meaning a Mass in Time of War, also often called the *Paukenmesse*. Did the kettle drums that gave the Mass its name have to do with the warlike sounds issuing from France, which threatened to spread across Europe? Did they represent the "hearts of the people, beating fearfully at the thought of war and destitution," as Leopold Nowak postulates in his biography of Haydn?

In this Mass, Haydn called for clarinets for the first time in his sacred music. The instrumentation now was much richer, probably due to his experience with his last symphonies. But beyond that, his mastery of vocal style was at its peak. The *Paukenmesse* was composed in Eisenstadt and performed there for the first time on September 13, 1796.

It seems that Haydn began the *Missa Sancti Bernardi de Offida* in B-flat major, the so-called *Heiligmesse*, in the same year, the Mass being performed in 1797. The choral parts make the *Paukenmesse* so remarkable, while parts for the four solo voices distinguish the *Heiligmesse*. After a canon-like introduction in the "Et homo factus est," three voices join in a deeply felt, harmonically intense "Et incarnatus est." For the wonderfully expressive "Crucifixus" Haydn used one of his secular canons. Since he had not included it in the collection of canons, he had probably considered it a preliminary model for an essentially "higher" use in the *Heiligmesse*. We can only marvel at how the same melody, set to a completely different text, transposed into another key, and used for a quite different purpose, can take on such a fundamentally different character. Examples of this same sort turn up more than once in the work of great composers, especially those of the Baroque and Classical eras.

The *Missa in angustiis* in D minor was probably composed in 1798 and performed for the first time on September 23 of that year in Eisenstadt. It probably did not receive its popular title, *Nelson Mass*, until two years later, when Lord Nelson paid a ceremonial visit to Prince Esterhazy, at which time the work was performed once more. The distinguished guest, much admired for his role in the defeat of France, was greatly impressed. It is said that Admiral Nelson asked to have the pen with which Haydn had composed the work, for which he gave the composer a valuable gold watch in return. This Mass has an unusual strength and lofty earnestness about it; Haydn himself called it *Missa in angustiis*; one wonders in what "fear and trouble" had he composed it? How variously its character can be judged is illustrated by the fact that in England it is known even today as "The Imperial."

A year later, in 1799, Haydn wrote the *Theresienmesse* in B-flat major. There is much doubt about how it got its name. It does not seem, as often postulated, that it was written for Maria Theresia, the Empress of Austria, but rather for the name day of Princess Maria Hermenegild von Esterhazy, a much celebrated event in Eisenstadt. Many commentators think it the richest in contrast of all Haydn's Masses because it combines seriousness and joy with the most consummate beauty. The instrumentation of this work was that of the small ensemble Haydn had at his disposal in Eisenstadt: two each of clarinets, trumpets, and timpani, and the usual strings.

In November 1799, Haydn offered the publishers Breitkopf and Härtel in Leipzig four Masses, but the offer was turned down—an astonishing decision, all the more so since this publisher had accepted and published practically everything Haydn had written. Was Haydn's sacred music, especially the Masses, too "Austrian" or too Catholic? It has been claimed that in January of 1801, the composer offered the *Nelson Mass* to the publisher as a gift, but it came to nothing.

On September 13, 1801, the *Creation Mass* in B-flat major was heard for the first time in Eisenstadt. We know that the composition was not begun until July 28: What an astonishing achievement for Haydn, then almost 70 years old! The name of this Mass, written for Princess Esterhazy's name day, relates to its "Qui tollis peccata mundi," the melody for which came from duet No. 32 ("Der tauende Morgen") in *The Creation*. It has never been established that Haydn consciously quoted it; the theme is neither developed nor repeated. Leopold Nowak, in his biography of Haydn, speculates on whether the cheerful, relaxed mood of this Mass, with its peaceful atmosphere, reminded the master of the satisfying and rewarding period when *The Creation* was composed—perhaps the genial theme unintentionally flowed from his pen.

Haydn's life's work had begun with a Mass (Missa brevis in F major) in 1750; it came to an end with a great Mass: on September 8, 1802, the magnificent *Harmoniemesse* in B-flat major (like the two previous Masses, it was in Haydn's favorite key for this genre) was heard in Eisenstadt. It is the most richly instrumented of all the master's sacred works, calling for one flute, two each of oboes, clarinets, bassoons, horns, trumpets, and timpani, and the usual strings. The musically literate Prince Ludwig Starhemberg, who heard it performed, wrote in his diary, "A sumptuous Mass, a new and excellent piece of music from the famous Haydn, and directed by the master himself (he still is in the service of the prince). I cannot conceive of anything more beautiful or better executed."

Nowak summarized his view of Haydn's Masses this way:

From the *Paukenmesse*, with its still varied moods, [Haydn's Masses develop] through the unity of the *Heiligmesse* to the dramatic strength of the Nelson Mass.

In the *Theresienmesse*, a definite quality of deep affection appears, tempering the impact without eliminating it, and leading the flow of musical thought toward the harmonious joy of the *Creation* Mass. Then came the step toward perfection. The *Harmoniemesse* is the master's last complete work.

Michael Haydn   1737–1806

Not only is it difficult to be the son of a famous father—Wilhelm Friedemann Bach and Siegfried Wagner had some painful experiences along these lines—but it is just as trying to be the brother of a genius, working in the same field as he. This was the lot of Johann Michael Haydn, an outstanding musician and important composer who never quite measured up to the genius of his brother, Joseph. He was born on September 14, 1737, in the same small house in Rohrau, in southern Lower Austria where Joseph had been born five years earlier. When Michael's unusual musical gift began to make itself apparent, he did exactly as his brother had done and joined St. Stephen's in Vienna as a choir boy. He remained there for 10 years, at the same time his brother was working there on his own, desperately trying to keep his head above water.

Then Michael became Kapellmeister for the bishop in Grosswardein, then in Hungary*. In 1762 he moved to Salzburg, where he remained until his death, 44 years later. He quickly climbed the ladder of musical success, finally attaining the highly respected position of concert master and organist in the Cathedral.

Michael Haydn was a close colleague of Leopold Mozart and witnessed the amazing career of his son, Wolfgang. There is a story that Wolfgang once helped Haydn in an emergency; Haydn was not going to be able to deliver a composition on time so Wolfgang, without a moment's hesitation, took on the task himself. The story goes on to say that Michael Haydn could not deliver the music because he was "sick," which was about the same as saying that the highly respected Herr Cathedral Organist was "under the influence." Modern psychology may offer an explanation for Michael Haydn's occasional lapses into apathy and alcohol, and even his bouts of outright physical illness: Was it that within his outwardly even-tempered soul lay an unacknowledged jealousy of his much more famous brother, a man pampered by all the world? Michael Haydn's compositional accomplishments are admirable, particularly in the area of sacred music: he wrote 24 Latin and 4 German Masses, 2 Requiems, 114 Graduals, 67 Offertories, and in addition Vespers, litanies, cantatas, choruses and a few oratorios. Michael preceded his brother in death by about three years; he died in Salzburg on August 10, 1806, 15 years after Mozart, who in his youth had been his friend, and in his adulthood in Vienna, Joseph's friend. Music history is replete with accounts reporting the mutual respect Mozart and Joseph Haydn had for each other. And was it not also a sign of great respect that Mozart once copied a Michael Haydn Te Deum note for note, without the slightest misgiving, and included it in one of his Masses?

Requiem

Original Title: Missa pro defuncto Archiepiscopo Sigismundo (Mass for the deceased Archbishop Sigismund)
Original Language: Latin
Text: Mass for the Dead from the Catholic liturgy (Missa pro defunctis).
Date of Writing: During the last two weeks of 1771.
Scoring: Four solo voices (soprano, alto, tenor, bass), four-part mixed chorus; two trumpets, two clarini, three trombones (used in the "Dies irae"), timpani, bassoon, strings, and organ.
History of the Work: The year 1771 was fateful in the life of Michael Haydn. In December, the Prince-archbishop of Salzburg, Sigismund, Count Schrattenbach, died. The city's culture owed much to him, and he had been especially supportive of music. Mozart had him to thank for his staunch sup-

---

*Now Oradea Mare, in Romania

port, especially the generous permission to travel repeatedly, which made Mozart's world fame first possible.

Michael Haydn enjoyed the Archbishop's special respect and justified it by fulfilling his duties with great enthusiasm and providing a large number of compositions. So it was that the death of this benevolent employer deepened the wound Haydn had sustained in the same year and from which he never apparently recovered. Close colleagues reported that even at his death he had never really gotten over the loss of his small daughter—the only child born to his very happy marriage. Clearly, the state of the soul necessary to compose a Requiem was already prepared when the death of the prince plunged him and all Salzburg into deep mourning. Haydn seems to have set to work immediately and to have composed at a fevered pace. The manuscript bears the completion date "Salzburg, December 31, 1771."

Discussion of the Work: From the very beginning—the first notes in the orchestra, then taken over in fugal form by the voices—the work has all the qualities of greatness (Example 1).

Example 1

The movements are in the usual order: After the first movement—Requiem and Kyrie—comes the "Dies irae" where Haydn holds to tradition and places dramatic accents only in the "Mors stupebit," which expresses the fear of all creation when faced with the inevitability of death. After countless "Amen"s, the melancholy key of C minor, which had dominated from the beginning, brightens to the major near the end of the second movement; it is as if thick clouds were penetrated by a single ray of light. But the following "Domine Jesu Christe" is once more in minor, this time G minor. The "Quam olim Abrahae" is also in this key, and here, too, Haydn hews to tradition, as it is in the form of a fugue. The "Hostias" offers the solo alto an opportunity to display her skill, before the choral fugue is repeated.

It should be emphasized here that in those days, the division between solo and choral voices was usually indistinct and left to the wishes of the performers. The Sanctus leads back to C minor, the key in which the Agnus Dei begins. It, in turn, yields to a great choral fugue, "Cum sanctis tuis," which is interrupted only briefly by the slow, calm "Requiem aeternam," before, brightening once more to the comforting major, it proceeds to the conclusion of the work. At the end, Haydn wrote the customary sentence, used by Bach and many other composers of sacred music: SDHetG (Soli Deo Honor et Gloria—Glory and Honor only to God). Charles H. Sherman, the man who rediscovered Michael Haydn, correctly said of this work: "The Requiem clearly testifies to Haydn's genius and in fact establishes his right to be counted among the best composers of his time."

Hieronymus Mass

Original Title: Missa Sancti Hieronymi
Original Language: Latin
Text: The five parts of the Ordinarium Missae.
Date of Writing: The notation at the end of the score reads "Salzburg, September 14, 1777".
First Performance: On November 1 (All Saints' Day), 1777, in the Salzburg Cathedral.
Orchestration: Several oboes (can be used soloistically as well as in the orchestral tutti), bassoons, trombones, and strings (partly ad libitum).
History of the Work: The warm relationship Michael Haydn and other Salzburg musicians enjoyed with the Prince-archbishop Count Schrattenbach, who died in 1771, did not continue with his successor, Hieronymus, Count Colloredo. Perhaps it was in order to extricate himself from the tense situation that in 1777, after a lengthy hiatus, Michael Haydn composed a great work, a Mass, which not only precisely conformed to the prince's wishes and stipulations but was dedicated to his patron saint, St. Hieronymus.

We have an estimable witness of its first performance on All Saints' Day, 1777: Leopold

Mozart was present and reported it in a letter to his son, Wolfgang, who was away on another journey—this time to Mannheim.

> I have just this moment come from services in the Cathedral. It was the oboe Mass by Haydn; he conducted it himself. . . . I was extraordinarily well pleased with it because there were six oboists, three contrabasses, two bassoons, and the castrato, who has been hired for six months at 100 gulden per month. . . . What I especially liked was that since oboes and bassoons are so close to the human voice, the tutti seemed to be a heavily scored piece of vocal music, in which the soprano and alto voices, augmented by the oboes and the alto trombone, maintained the correct balance with the mass of tenor and bass voices, and the tutti was so majestic. . . . The whole thing lasted an hour and a quarter, and was too short for me since it was really excellently written. Everything flowed so naturally, the fugues—especially the "Et vitam" in the "Credo" and the "Dona nobis" . . . are developed in a masterful fashion. The themes are natural, with no exaggerated modulation or overly abrupt transitions. . . . If I can get a copy of the Mass sooner or later I will certainly send it to you . . .

Discussion of the Work: The best description has already been given by an extremely knowledgeable contemporary. If Leopold wanted to send this Mass to his son as soon as possible it can mean only one thing: He could learn something from it—father Mozart did not send Wolfgang scores for fun. It is in fact an outstanding work of its kind.

Missa Hispanica (The Spanish Mass)

Original Title: Missa a due cori
Original Language: Latin
Text: The five parts of the Ordinarium Missae
Date of Writing: Possibly as early as 1786 (in the handwritten parts found in Kremsmünster, there is a note "Composuit 4. August, 1786").
First Performance: The earliest known performance took place on June 24, 1792, in the abbey at Kremsmünster, in Upper Austria, conducted by the composer. The question of why six years passed before it was performed must remain unanswered. The first performance in Salzburg is said to have taken place four years later. It has thus far not been learned whether the very first performance might have taken place in Spain (cf. History of the Work).
Scoring: Four solo voices (soprano, alto, tenor, bass), two four-part mixed choruses; two each of oboes, bassoons, horns, and trumpets, and timpani, organ, and strings.
History of the Work: We can no longer ascertain upon what fact or supposition the belief that Michael Haydn was commissioned to compose this work by the Spanish Court of Madrid rests. His brother Joseph wrote an orchestral work in 1785 for a church in Cadiz (*The Seven Last Words*). It is difficult to conceive of any relationship between Joseph's commission and that of Michael for a Mass, all the more so in that the requests came from totally different sources and only by chance in the same country. Nevertheless, it was said in Salzburg that the very popular cathedral organist had composed a great work for Spain, and so it was that it received the subtitle still in use today, *Missa Hispanica,* the Spanish Mass.

As noted earlier, the date of its writing is not at all clear. The musical records of the abbey at Kremsmünster reported the first performance (?) was "to celebrate the abbot's golden jubilee" on June 24, 1792. (By way of a hunch: in 1792 Spain was celebrating the 300th anniversary of Columbus's journey to and discovery of America. Certainly a solemn Mass by a great composer would have been appropriate for the occasion.) Four years later, the work was heard in Salzburg. A copy owned by the Archbishopric of St. Peter bears the following notation[*]: "This Mass was performed for the first time on Friday, June 3, 1796, at four o'clock in the afternoon at the University Church in Salzburg." The chronicles of the abbey go on to say that

> The local concert master, Michael Haydn, presented a new Mass composed by him for Spain, which called for up to 60 musicians, including the three choruses. Music lovers took up a collection to defray the costs of the two rehearsals and today's performance. The large audience greeted the work with general applause.

Discussion of the Work: This Mass for double chorus, soloists, and orchestra is probably not only

---

[*]Cited from the foreword written by Charles H. Sherman for the published score (1966).

Michael Haydn's largest, but also his most significant work. Its radiant, festive character is apparent from the beginning and is emphasized throughout by the double chorus, to great effect.

Against the almost uninterrupted exultation and rejoicing there are only a few lyrical passages, the most impressive of which probably is in the "Agnus Dei"; the "Dona nobis pacem" follows, in the form of a powerful fugue, which brings the work to its conclusion.

Anton Heiller   1923–1979

Heiller was born in Vienna on September 15, 1923, and died there on March 25, 1979. He was one of the leading organists of his time and as teacher of organ performance, in the sacred music department of the Musikhochschule in Vienna, played a significant role in organ pedagogy. The majority of his compositions were sacred, with at times a strong Austrian folk flavor. Among his most important works are *Vesper zum Vorabend des 1. Adventsonntages* (Vespers for the evening before the first Sunday in Advent), a work commissioned for the 850th anniversary of the city of Graz; a *Stabat mater*; many Masses; as well as the cantata *In principio erat verbum* (In the Beginning was the Word). When on May 6, 1965, this work was performed for the first time, in a Berlin radio broadcast on the occasion of the 18th Heinrich Schütz Festival, Heiller had this to say:

> The text is taken from the Gospel of St. John (I:1–14). Until recently it was read as the concluding gospel of the Catholic Mass; the responsorium that followed, "Deo gratias," was also included in my cantata. Basically, this text treats the incarnation of the Son of God as the "Word of God," source of all existence, life, and light.... I tried to subordinate the music to the intrinsic as well as to the extrinsic content of this text. Several twelve-tone rows, the most important of which sound in unison at the beginning of the work—a likeness, as it were, of the "primeval magma" of our music—are transposed several times by inversion, retrograde, and retrograde inversion, but are not developed in consistent twelve-tone technique. They are rather the thematic material for a free tonal structure.... Experimental elements, which in my opinion go against the grain of this text, were consciously avoided; my efforts were primarily directed toward a musical interpretation of this unique Gospel that would be comprehensible to the ears and hearts of music lovers.

Hans Werner Henze   1926–

Future writers of musical history will puzzle long and hard when judging Hans Werner Henze. He was born July 1, 1926, in Gütersloh, in Westfalia, and was a student of Fortner. He went through all kinds of "systems" and "techniques," which he at first subordinated to his pleasure in making music. Early operas show him as one intoxicated with sound, and some of his stage works were immediately successful. But as time went by, his style changed appreciably. He also adopted a strong political bent and tried his hand as a composer of the Marxist doctrine of class struggle. He left Germany to settle in Italy, devoting himself exclusively to composition, occasionally conducting his own works. These became increasingly complex and finally presented such difficulties for performers as well as listeners that only the most musically educated could cope with them. This is particularly true of the oratorio *Das Floss der Medusa* (The Raft of the Medusa).

Some of his earlier compositions tended toward the cantata form: *Five Madrigals* based on texts by François Villon (1947); a *Chor gefangener Trojer* (Chorus of Captive Trojans); verses from *Faust II*, after Goethe (1948); *Wiegenlied der Mutter Gottes* (Cradle Song of the Madonna) after Lope de Vega (1948); as well as the important *Novae de infinito laudes*, based on lines by the philosopher Giordano Bruno, who was burned at the stake in 1600. After other, less noticed compositions for various types of ensembles—among them *Lieder von einer Insel* (Songs from an island) written for chamber chorus, trombone, two cellos, contrabass, organ (portative), timpani, and percussion, and settings of poems by Ingeborg Bachmann—came the full-length oratorio *Das Floss der Medusa*, in 1968.

It is one of Henze's most passionate and most controversial works. The libretto, by Ernst

Schnabel, retells the tragedy of the army dispatched by the French king Louis XVIII to Senegal to recapture this former colony from the English; the story has become a cruel legend of Realism. Shortly before arriving at her destination, the flagship "Medusa" struck a reef and had to be abandoned. Officers and passengers took to lifeboats, but the soldiers and crew, with women and children, were given a raft which was towed by the lifeboats. Then one night, in order to save the lifeboats, the commander-in-chief ordered the towrope cut. For many days and nights, the raft drifted aimlessly at sea, its 150 occupants doomed to a brutal death from heat, thirst, hunger, and madness. This incident aroused great outrage when it became known, but like all horrors, it was soon crowded out of the minds of the living.

But it was revived by Théodore Géricault in his famous painting, hanging in the Louvre: "Le Radeau de la Meduse" (The Raft of the Medusa). A few wretched planks crowded with exhausted, dying people drift on an endless, turbulent sea under the gloom of a stormy, evening sky. A man stands erect and in utmost despair waves a red rag to signal a ship off in the distance. When this ship, the "Argus," finally sighted the raft, on July 17, 1816, only 15 people remained alive, 5 of whom did not survive their ordeal. Géricault's painting, the beginning of a "romantic Naturalism" (Delacroix was to become the leader of this movement), was the sensation of an 1820 exhibit in Paris, both because of its subject, which dredged up old memories, and the consummate skill with which it was painted.

Henze provided the story in outline, which Ernst Schnabel then adapted. The poetic quality of the libretto is remarkable; the descriptions of the numerous scenes are of extraordinary visual force. Although *Das Floss der Medusa* is conceived of as a pure oratorio and is subtitled "Oratorio volgare e militare" (a curious, questionable label), limited movement is called for during a performance. As indicated by the authors: The "Chorus of the Living," stands on one side of the stage, the "Chorus of the Dead" on the other. As the drama progresses, singers from the side of the living move one by one over to the side of the dead. The disappearance—the rescue—of the "Privileged" is also depicted. Two solo roles are among the most difficult ever assigned to vocalists: Death, a very high female voice, and Jean-Charles, the mulatto who survived the experience, a baritone, who must also penetrate the highest registers. They are joined by a narrator, the Speaker, symbolically named Charon, the legendary boatman of Greek mythology, who ferried the dead to the other world.

It is impossible here to discuss this work in detail. Henze uses all the means of producing sound available to the mid-20th century in a concentrated, ingenious way. The chorus sings almost without interruption in such polyphonic profusion that it is utterly impossible to hear intervals, but is sound painting of terrifying realism. The huge orchestra includes four flutes (with piccolo and alto flute), four oboes (with oboe d'amore, English horn, and heckelphone), four clarinets in different keys, two saxophones, three bassoons (with contrabassoon), four horns, three trumpets in different keys, two ophicleides (low brass), various tubas (bombardon, Wagner tuba, bass tuba), timpani, two harps, piano, electric guitars, electronic organ, 12 violins, eight violas, six cellos, four contrabasses. In addition the percussion includes: bongos, cymbals, wood blocks, drums (military, Basque and Indian), tam-tams, chains, maracas, shell bells, bells, vibraphone, marimba, and others. The score itself presents even the most experienced conductor with almost insoluble problems. Visually it is an enormous tableau of the entire musical knowledge of the age; technically, it surpasses anything that has gone before.

But—and this is the burning question in 20th-century music—what of all this enormously ingenious and complicated music reaches the ear of the listener? *Das Floss der Medusa* is intended as a revolutionary work, one planned to stir up its listeners, as expressed in its final words: "Die überlebenden kehrten in die Welt zurück, belehrt von Wirklichkeit, fiebernd, sie umzustürzen" (The survivors, having learned from reality, return to the world with a burning desire to topple it). Such a statement could have come from the pen of Brecht; but it is one of the few sentences in the entire work that is clear and simple, as such messages should be, and so can be understood by the audience as it is recited. Hardly a sentence in the rest of the text can be grasped due to the enormous sound apparatus employed and exploited to the fullest. The work is dedicated to Che Guevara, the almost legendary South American revolutionary who left a ministerial post in Cuba to fight social injustice as a guerilla in the Bolivian jungles, where he was later captured and shot.

The premiere of Henze's *Das Floss der Medusa*, a work commissioned by the North German Radio Network in Hamburg, took place in a radio broadcast on December 9, 1968, and was conducted by the composer. Edda Moser sang Death, Dietrich Fischer-Dieskau sang Jean-Charles, the mulatto, and Charles Regnier the Speaker (Charon). The public performance planned for the same time was cancelled due to huge demonstrations and rioting by the public.

Paul Hindemith 1895–1963

Hindemith was a controversial personality—and not only during the revolutionary time of the early 20th century—but a strong personality nonetheless. More than that, he was a genius whose effect on his times—times of turmoil and upheaval—were unequalled. He was born in Hanau (Main) on November 16, 1895, played viola in the Frankfurt orchestra, became the moving spirit of an outstanding chamber ensemble (the Amar-Hindemith Quartet), and from 1927–1934 taught composition at the Musikhochschule in Berlin, probably the most important institution in Central Europe at the time. He directed countless "music days" throughout the German-speaking world, which attracted many forward-looking young people who sang, made music, improvised, and performed new music by forming ad hoc choruses and orchestras. He could play virtually every instrument, invent canons in an instant, and kindle enthusiasm wherever he appeared. He played a more significant role in the development of music than, for example, his much honored colleagues Fritz Jöde and Walter Hensel, who remained in the field of youth and amateur music, whereas Hindemith became one of the century's leading composers.

Early on, Hindemith achieved sensational success with his song cycle *Marienleben* and the opera *Cardillac*. The Nazi regime labeled him a "degenerate" artist, and so, in 1934, he shared the fate of countless German creative artists who went into exile. He spent those years in the United States, teaching at Yale and Harvard universities. After the war he divided his time between Zurich and the United States, until in 1953 he found a beautiful home at last in Blonay, near Lake Geneva. He died on December 28, 1963, in Frankfurt am Main in St. Mary's Hospital, to which he had been admitted a few days earlier.

He is included here primarily for his oratorio *Das Unaufhörliche* (The Never-ending). It should be mentioned, however, that subsequent to this important work, composed in 1931, other compositions for voices and orchestra followed: *When Lilacs Last in the Dooryard Bloom'd*, (*A Requiem For Those We Love*), for two solo voices (mezzo soprano and baritone), mixed chorus, and orchestra, based on poems by Walt Whitman (1946); the choral work *Apparebit repentina dies*, based on a medieval text and accompanied by 10 brass instruments (1947); the three-part cantata *Ite, angeli veloces* to a text by Paul Claudel (composed for UNESCO between 1953 and 1955); and finally, the *Mainzer Umzug* (Procession in Mainz) for three solo voices (soprano, tenor, baritone), mixed chorus, and orchestra, an homage to his homeland (1962). He wrote many choral works and also works he called "Spielmusik" (music for the theater), of which *Wir bauen eine Stadt* (We Build a City), a play for children, deserves special notice.

The Never-Ending

Original Title: Das Unaufhörliche
Original Language: German
Text: Gottfried Benn
Date of Writing: 1931
First Performance: November 21, 1931, in Berlin, directed by Otto Klemperer.
Scoring: Four solo voices (soprano, tenor, baritone, bass); a two-part boys' chorus, a three-part female and a three-part male chorus, and a four-part mixed chorus; two flutes (one piccolo), two each of oboes, clarinets, and bassoons, three horns, two trumpets, two trombones, bass tuba, timpani, percussion, strings, contrabassoon, and organ ad libitum.
History of the Work: Like so many other musicians, Hindemith took an active part in the extremely turbulent events of the 1920s and 30s in Germany. Polarization had begun: The liberal middle class, which had continued to play an important role in theater, music, and art and tried to mediate between the political and intellectual extremes which had developed, dwindled from day to day. Everything became politicized, down to the smallest aspect of life, and violent confrontation between Left and Right loomed, unavoidable and relentless. Hindemith's sympathies were with the Left, for he looked to this side of the spectrum for the progress, the possibilities needed to create the new musical world he so longed for. He met several times with one of the leading figures of the intellectual Left, the dramatist Bertolt Brecht, whose writings not only played a role in the political arena but also had been set to music countless times. But with the exception of a minor composition—*Lehrstück* (1929)—they never collaborated, which was probably more than simply accidental. In spite of many affinities, Hindemith's artistic thought moved on a different plane; irreconcilable differences separated him from Kurt Weill, Paul Dessau, and Hans Eissler. Certainly,

at the time, many people—politicians as well as those of cultural inclinations—looked for a joint work from Brecht and Hindemith, but it never came.

Andres Briner wrote in his biography of Hindemith:

> As early as 1929, Hindemith had come across Benn's poems.* The next year he composed three works for male chorus with texts by Benn; they seem close to Brecht in their mixture of enigma and linguistic directness, but they were really worlds apart. Hindemith's sense of poetry was not formed by academic, critical examination and stylistic analysis, yet his powers of judgment were entirely correct in this instance, too: Benn was the right man to compose the oratorio text Hindemith was looking for. He was able to put together a libretto capable of standing in the face of the confrontational, polemic writings of the time; a man who could view human existence in that wider context so lacking in the works of "involved" writers. Benn's sense of the endless, incessant transformation of human symbols, ideals, and ways of living corresponded to Hindemith's own. Benn's unsentimental reference to the timeless confirmation not of technological, but human achievement was a most welcome confirmation of the values Hindemith saw as disappearing. Hindemith and Benn shared a sense of the urgency with which these larger matters had to be addressed.

The first performance of the oratorio *Das Unaufhörliche* took place in Berlin and was conducted by the already prominent Otto Klemperer, the director of the "Kroll Opera" and one of the most effective champions of modern music.

Stravinsky heard the work shortly after and noted in his *Chronique de ma vie:*

> Not only because of its large scope, but also because of its character and the variety of its movements, this work offers an excellent means for becoming acquainted with the personality of the composer and for enjoying his magnificent talent and outstanding mastery. Hindemith is an important phenomenon in the musical life of our time; he represents a healthy principle that shines like a light through the murk of contemporary work....

Discussion of the Work: The work opens with the words "Das Unaufhörliche. Grosses Gesetz" (The Unceasing—The Great Law), and then continues: "Das Unaufhörliche! Mit Tag und Nacht ernährt und spielt es sich von Meer zu Meer (The Unceasing! Nourished by day and night, playing itself out from sea to sea.) These words, almost incomprehensible initially, become completely unintelligible by being unevenly distributed rhythmically among the four parts of the chorus. The work is characterized by a dark mysticism. Did Hindemith, a musician who had always tended to clarity, whose works in general were often of an astonishing directness, take pleasure in this setting? Had he perhaps so much music in him that the text he clothed could have no decisive influence on him? Or did he take to heart the harsh and often malicious charges that he was only a "composer of the moment," an opportunist, a worshipper of the crassest materialism? In fact, it seems that at that time Hindemith was in a particularly introspective period; he had turned towards higher ideals, and away from many earlier would-be revolutionary ideals. These new ideals and visions reached their purest expression in the opera *Mathis der Maler*, the ballet *Nobilissima visione*, and similar works.

What attracted him to Benn's obscure texts was probably exactly the idea that led him to his about-face: the recognition of the "futility of technical advances, which means nothing in the eternal scheme of historical events" and of "personal accomplishment, the consciousness of which remains imprinted in us, of the powers of order and individual renunciation." How different this sounds from the lines Hindemith wrote in his "Sturm und Drang" period a few years earlier! The music of this oratorio also indicates a new creative direction. Nothing of his free tonality (what really are long passages of atonal music), had changed, but we now feel a striving toward a new kind of lawfulness and organization leading to a new formal order.

A Requiem For Those We Love

Original Title: When Lilacs last in the Dooryard Bloom'd (A Requiem for Those We Love).
Original Language: English
Text: By Walt Whitman (1819–1892)

---

*Gottfried Benn (1886–1956) was a German physician and writer, one of the leading Expressionists.

Date of Writing: In the first months of 1946; the piano score completed on March 20; the full score, on April 20, 1946, in New Haven, Connecticut.

First Performance: On May 5, 1946, in New York, with Robert Shaw conducting his chorale.

Scoring: Two solo voices (mezzo soprano and baritone), four-part mixed chorus, and medium-sized orchestra.

History of the Work: Andres Briner, Hindemith's Swiss biographer, recalls that in his youth, Hindemith came across a German translation by Franz Blei of Walt Whitman's poetry and felt that he wanted to compose some. His attachment increased with time, and during Hindemith's stay in the United States, he came to fully appreciate the poet's extremely personal, powerful style — poems written predominantly in free rhythm and overflowing with vitality. The death of President Franklin Delano Roosevelt, who died a few weeks before the Allied victory in Europe, but in the unshakable certainty of victory, called up in Hindemith

> . . . the image Whitman had found for Lincoln's death. Whitman's text symbolizes a striking parallel—not of time, but of psychological mood—to the end of the war in 1945: It dealt with the death of President Lincoln assassinated in 1865, and those who had died in the American Civil War. Hindemith dedicated his Requiem not only to the memory of Roosevelt but to the dead of World War II as well.*

Hindemith wanted, as he himself said, to compose a hymn to peace, to the brotherhood of former enemies, after which a reconciliation of the whole world would follow. The first performance of the work was not received with much enthusiasm; this completely secular Requiem gained favor only very slowly. It finally did came into its own, usually with Hindemith on the podium. Within a few years he conducted the work in Perugia, Hamburg, Berlin, Rome, Washington, New York, and twice each in Vienna and London.

Discussion of the Work: Over a very long C-sharp pedal point a solemn four-note motive (a-c-f-e) stands out and is repeated nine times; it reminds us of the slow steps of a funeral procession (Example 1).

Example 1

A second motive is composed of a muffled chain of trills rising from the depths, which mounts to a high point before it and the first motive bring the prelude quietly to a close. A baritone solo begins a series of solo numbers, which from the outset present an abundance of varied moods. Hindemith follows each as if he had never been an anti-Romantic iconoclast who marched at the head of the "Modernists" during the '20s. The same turning back to make a connection with a sound tradition is also evident in the programs of concerts he directed at the time.

Whitman's verses (difficult to translate) are inexhaustible in their vision, and Hindemith follows them with deep sensitivity. They return repeatedly to the theme of death, but against this background rises a hymn to life, to spring, to nature's eternal renewal, but—oddly enough—also to the great cities:

> With ranging hills on the banks, with many a line against the sky, and shadows, and the city at hand with dwellings so dense, and stacks of chimneys, and all the scenes of life and the workshops, and the workmen homeward returning. Lo, body and soul—this land, my own Manhattan with spires.

This is the American pioneer spirit of "God's own country," which Whitman felt pulsing through his veins, bursting with vigor and sure of success; Hindemith set it all to music, in thanks to a land that seemed to him and thousands of others to be a guiding light during a black hour in the history of the world. "And the far-spreading prairies cover'd with grass and corn, the varied and ample

*A. Briner, Paul Hindemith, Zurich, 1971. [no page given—ed.]

land, the South and the North in the light . . . Missouri, Ohio's shores . . . Lo, this land!" Here, across a distance of almost a century, the two men met, both intoxicated with life, Hindemith hardly less than Whitman.

Then death and life are interwoven. In the score the words appear, "Hymn to those we love." It is a funeral march, full of strident harmonies and yet "tonal." Is it a procession of the living or of the dead? A commemoration of the living, or the dead? Oddly enough, the one is the other and remains so even when "in noiseless dreams hundreds of battle-flags . . ." wave and visions of legions of youth fallen in rubble and dust appear. But, "they were not as was thought, they themselves were fully at rest, they suffer'd not . . . The living remain'd and suffer'd. . . ." Before the finale, an orchestral interlude is heard in which a distant bugle sounds "the great roll call" (as Gustav Mahler composed it). The finale begins with the words of the baritone,

> Passing the visions, passing the night, passing, unloosing the hold of my comrades' hands, passing the song of the hermit bird and the tallying song of my soul. Victorious song, death's outlet song, yet varying ever-altering song, as low and wailing, yet clear the notes, rising and falling, flooding the night, sadly sinking and fainting, as warning and warning, and yet again bursting with joy . . . as that powerful psalm in the night I heard from recesses. Passing, I leave thee lilac with heart-shaped leaves, I leave thee, there in the door-yard, blooming, returning with spring.

The last word of the work is "bloom'd"—the finale speaks of life, quite the reverse of what is found in every other Requiem.

Gustav Holst 1874–1934

Holst, born on September 21, 1874, in Cheltenham, a health resort in the English county of Gloucester, was one of the most interesting composers of his generation. He was a genius who, outside his native land, is known almost exclusively for his stirring orchestral suite *The Planets*, Op. 32. The descendant of Swedish immigrants, trombonist and brilliant pedagogue, he embodied "the very English mixture of greatness and spleen, ingenuity and eccentricity." Holst's place in this book derives largely from a handful of works for chorus and orchestra: *Choral Hymns* from the *Rig-Veda*, Op. 26 (1912); *The Cloud Messenger*, Op. 30 (1910); and *Hymn of Jesus*, Op. 37 (1917). In addition, his Choral Symphony, Op. 41 (1924) must be mentioned. His most important work in this genre, however, is his *Ode to Death*, based on a poem by Walt Whitman. This work, based on the powerful words of the North American poet, is one of the English composer's most impressive but is unfortunately seldom performed. From 1903 on, Holst taught music in secondary schools in London, and later also at Harvard University. A nervous breakdown in 1924 compelled him to devote himself to composition only, which he did, in London, until his death on May 25, 1934.

Arthur Honegger 1892–1955

Shortly after World War I, several young Parisian musicians formed a group called "Les Six," although their ideas of composition had little in common; they had simply come together by chance through performances of their earlier works. Their names are Darius Milhaud, Francis Poulenc, Georges Auric, Louis Durey, Germaine Tailleferre, and Arthur Honegger.

Honegger was born on March 10, 1892, in Le Havre, son of German-Swiss parents. He studied first in his native city, then (from 1907–1909) in Zürich, and finally at the Paris Conservatory. During the war years spent in Paris, he wrote a few pieces for piano, a violin sonata, songs, and the symphonic poem *Le chant de Nigamon*. The beautiful, appealing *Pastorale d'été*, composed in Impressionistic colors, was first performed in 1920 by Vladimir Golschmann; causing a sensation and winning the *Prix Verley*. Shortly thereafter the casual association of "Les Six" came about; it was to play an important role in the musical history of those revolutionary years, in association with two other brilliant Parisian figures: the writer Jean Cocteau and the musical eccentric Eric Satie.

In 1921, Honegger achieved his first international fame with the oratorio *Le roi David*. From that time on, his works were seen as blazing entirely new trails in music. Together with Stravinsky, Bartok, Prokofiev, Hindemith, and his associate Milhaud, he was one of those who paved the way to modern music, the distinguishing characteristic of which was more than anything else the loosening and virtual dissolution of the bonds of tonality. Honegger soon created another international success with his "machine piece" about a locomotive, *Pacific 231*. This work while entirely consonant with one of the themes of the time (Prokofiev, *Pas d'acier*; Carlos Chavez, *HP*; Alexander Mossolow, *Iron Foundry* and others), was fundamentally of a late-Romantic character. He composed other works in praise of sports (Rugby); five fine symphonies; he wrote operas (*Antigone, Judith*), and reached new heights with *Jeanne d'Arc au bûcher*, (St. Joan at the Stake), probably the most important work of his life. Performed both as an oratorio and staged, *Joan* is one of the great works of this century. Few modern composers have succeeded as well as Honegger in creating a work possessing such a comprehensive and unified overview of contemporary concerns and hopes, and one that is, moreover, accessible and well received by audiences.

He lived out World War II in occupied Paris, where he occasionally worked as a music critic. Thereafter he spent a good deal of time at the home of the Swiss conductor and patron of the arts, Paul Sacher, for whose chamber orchestra in Basle he wrote a number of significant works. Despite his successes and the esteem in which he was held everywhere, Honegger's outlook on life and perception of mankind became perceptibly more pessimistic; a view which he explicated in his book *Je suis compositeur* (I am a Composer). Following a long illness, Arthur Honegger died in Paris on November 27, 1955, "an example of humanism and universality" (Walter Labhart).

King David

Original title: Le roi David
Original Language: French
Text: René Morax (1873–1963), based on the Bible.
Date of Writing: First version: February 25 to April 28, 1921; the revision to a symphonic psalm, during the summer of 1923.
First Performance: First version (as theater music for a play of the same name) in the Théâtre du Jorat at Mézières, near Lausanne, on June 11, 1921. As symphonic psalm in German, translated by Hans Reinhart, on December 2, 1923, in Winterthur, Switzerland.
Form: In the first version, concise, individual pieces; incidental music for the stage play of the same name. In the second version, a symphonic psalm, or oratorio.
Cast: A male or female narrator, who also recites with orchestral accompaniment (melodrama); solo roles for soprano, alto, and tenor voices; and four-part mixed chorus.
Orchestra: First version (1921) for 17 instruments: two flutes, one oboe, two clarinets, one bassoon, one horn, two trumpets, one each trombone, contrabass, piano, harmonium, celeste, gong, and tam-tam; a pair of timpani. Second version (1923) for large orchestra: two flutes, two oboes, one English horn, two clarinets, two bassoons, four horns, two trumpets, three trombones, tuba, harp, percussion, celeste, organ ad libitum, and strings.
History of the Work: In 1908, the poet René Morax, from the canton of Vaud in western Switzerland, founded an open-air theater in the Greek style, in Mézières, a village near Lausanne. The idea had come from a friend of his, the great French writer Romain Rolland. While on a journey in Asia, Morax made plans to write a Biblical drama which took the form of the play *Le roi David*. The author had always conceived of the play as having a major musical component which he solicited from two different composers, both of whom turned him down. The prominent conductor Ernest Ansermet then suggested the 29-year-old Honegger, who gladly accepted the commission although little more than three months remained before the planned premiere. Honegger tells in his memoirs that he turned for advice to Stravinsky, who was then living on the shores of Lac Léman. Stravinsky, 10 years older than Honegger and long since well established, helped him with his dilemma: how to compose music for a chorus of 100 voices and an instrumental ensemble of only 17, the capacity of the small orchestra pit. His advice was simple and clever: "Compose as if 17 instruments were all you wanted in the first place!"

The premiere of *Le roi David*, conducted by Honegger, took place on June 11, 1921, and was a great success. He soon wished that the music might be used for more than just performances of the Mézières play. The choral director at Wintherthur, Ernst Wolters, was interested in performing it, but space considerations ruled out a stage production. Thus the idea to join the musical numbers together with a recited text, one that would relate the story in condensed form, was formed. Hans Reinhart wrote the German version of the oratorio, which, after the Winterthur premiere on

December 2, 1923, traveled around the world.

Later, as Peter Aistleitner reports, Honegger lamented the transformation of his work:

> I am sorry that I made oratorios out of *King David* and *Judith*. When all is said and done, it is really theater music, not concert music. The speaker cannot replace the stage. It would have been better to have made a purely musical suite from it, without referring to the stage at all, or perhaps a true opera.

Discussion of the Work: David is represented by three voices who sing his text, taken from the Bible. The words sung by the chorus of the people were written by Morax. The work, about an hour and a quarter long, is composed of 27 short musical numbers which provide a wide variety of moods within the tightest conceivable framework. Honegger created impressive sounds for rustic as well as battle scenes, for dances as well as for elegies; he is as comfortable with impressionistic dreaminess as with harsh dissonances.

The work unfolds in the course of the following musical numbers: Introduction; David's shepherd song (alto solo); psalm "Praised be the Lord" (unison chorus); fanfare and entry of Goliath; victory song (mixed chorus); military procession; psalm "Fear nothing!" (tenor solo); psalm "Ah! If I had the wings of a dove!" (soprano solo); song of the prophets (male chorus); psalm "God have mercy upon me!" (tenor solo); Saul's encampment (orchestral number); psalm "The eternal God is my infinite light" (mixed chorus); incantation of the witch of Endor (melodrama, speech with orchestral background); the march of the Philistines (orchestral number); Guilboa's lament (soloists and female chorus). These numbers conclude the first part, which describes David's rise from shepherd boy to king, his victory over the giant Goliath, and his assumption of his kingly rank after much confusion.

In the second part, we witness a ceremony (ceremonial song with solo soprano and female chorus) as well as the orgiastic dance before the Ark of the Covenant, the people's rejoicing and the high point of David's life (expressed in solos and choruses). The third part, dedicated to his decline and fall, and his guilt and atonement, includes the following musical selections: "Song springs from my heart" (unison chorus); the song of the serving maid (alto solo); psalm of expiation (mixed chorus); psalm "I was conceived in sin" (mixed chorus); psalm "I lift up my eyes to the mountain" (tenor solo); song of Ephraim (soprano solo and female chorus), march of the Israelites (orchestral); psalm "I love you, Lord, with a tender love" (mixed chorus); psalm "In thy wrath" (unison chorus); coronation of Solomon (melodrama); and David's death (soprano solo and mixed chorus). The second and third parts both close with an impressive Hallelujah. The final musical numbers seem transfigured; a shining vision—like the announcement of the coming of a redeemer—seems to illuminate David's end, an interpretation which certainly possesses a deeper meaning for so devout a musician as Honegger.

Joan of Arc at the Stake

Original Title: Jeanne d'Arc au bûcher
Original Language: French
Text: Paul Claudel (1868–1955)
Date of Writing: 1935–1937
First Performance: The concert version was first performed on May 12, 1938, conducted by Paul Sacher in Basel. The first staged productions were given in Orléans (at the Jeanne d'Arc Festival) in May, 1939, and in the Zürich Stadttheater on June 13, 1942.
Form: Staged oratorio (can also be produced in concert) in 11 scenes.
Cast: Joan of Arc, Brother Dominic, the Kings of France and England, Regnault de Chartres, Guillaume de Flavy, the Dukes of Bedford and Burgundy, Jean de Luxembourg, Perrot, Mother of Barrels, Grinder Trusty, a Priest, symbolic figures such as Folly, Pride, Avarice, Lust—all either speaking or (when staged) dance roles; the Holy Virgin (soprano), St. Margaret (soprano), St. Catherine (alto), Porcus the Swine (tenor), Asinus the Donkey (tenor), two Peasants (tenor and bass), two Heralds (tenor and bass), a child's voice; mixed chorus; children's chorus.
Orchestra: Two flutes (one piccolo), two oboes, two clarinets, one bass clarinet, three saxophones, three bassoons, contrabassoon, four trumpets, three trombones, bass trombone or tuba, two pianos, timpani, percussion (two performers), celeste, Ondes Martenot (electronic instrument), strings.
History of the Work: The well-known French dancer and actress Ida Rubinstein suggested to Honegger in 1935 that he set to music a work on Joan of Arc written by the great French literary

figure Paul Claudel, to be a vehicle for her talents. Thus came about the fruitful collaboration between the Catholic mystic and the Protestant musician, which yielded, in addition to *Jeanne d'Arc*, a *Dance of the Dead*. Honegger's friend Paul Sacher, a conductor and patron of the arts living in Basel, gave the work (a very different one from Schiller's play *Die Jungfrau von Orleans*) an impressive concert performance on May 12, 1938. A year later, in the course of celebrations in honor of the French national heroine and saint, a partially staged presentation was given, and then in the midst of the war, when France could have used a new Jeanne d'Arc, the fully staged version was premiered on June 13, 1942 in Zürich.

Discussion of the Work: This is a large, colorful portrait of the time, in which the historical mingles with the supernatural. Voices ring out from darkness and come down from Heaven, but in the gloom of night all is very eerie. Gradually we see that Joan stands at the stake awaiting her doom. Slowly the stages of her life pass by. Brother Dominic comes to comfort her, holding in his hands a large book in which Joan's earthly deeds are recorded. In the third scene she sees once again the trial that resulted in her condemnation to death. Angry voices, a bawling mob, scolds her, accuses her. Are these the same people who only recently acclaimed her? Who dares to judge Joan? The tribunal was not human: indeed, a fox, a tiger, and a snake declined to serve, but a swine was found to preside over the sheep, and a donkey offered to serve as scribe. Voices from Hell are heard. Joan wonders how she, a simple, peasant maid from Domrémy, in Lorraine, could arouse such hatred? Brother Dominic explains that the world is run by madmen, an insane king invented a card game that is the rage among all who have power. It is all backwards: the one who wins, loses, and the reverse. One of the kings in the game is Death: he is the most powerful, but no one pays any attention to him. Two bells begin to chime, and in their chiming Joan recognizes the voices of the two saints, Catherine and Margaret, who first summoned her from the fields at home. She is once more the girl who follows the call, which can only have come from God. The sympathetic Dauphin reappears; she speaks to him, but he does not understand her. Then she takes charge, unites France once again, and crowns the Dauphin as its king. Scenes of war terrify her. But suddenly a child is singing—is she back home once more? She hears the old song she used to sing with the children, "the month of May, the pretty month of May"; she calls it "Trimazo" (Example 1). *

An unknown priest comes to her and brings her back to reality. She must recant her "lies," and if she does so she will not be burned but rather imprisoned for the rest of her life. She refuses, she has never lied, and her voices came from God. The pyre is set aflame and the crowd rages and screams. She hears Catherine and Margaret, she hears the Holy Virgin who is waiting for her. "Pain

Example 1

*Simplified accompaniment by Kurt Pahlen

is brief and joy is eternal", Schiller said of these greatest final moments. Claudel, too, found poetic, gentle, consoling words for this dark hour in Western Christian history: "There is no greater love than to lay down one's life for the object of one's love."

Honegger has created sublime music; it follows Claudel's text faithfully, and we understand his assertion that the greatest gift of his life was to have found a poet so blessed. Words and music depict the material world and the transcendental, children's song and the dance of death, the evil ways of the world and purity of heart. Honegger's resources are inexhaustible, from the simple triad to the first use of an electronic instrument—the Ondes Martenot; from ancient Christian chant to jazz: it is all in the score of *Jeanne d'Arc au bucher*.

Alan Hovhaness 1911–

Alan Hovhaness may well emerge as the most prolific composer of the 20th century. Over 400 compositions comprise the corpus of his known works. As he destroyed a large number of completed compositions at different points in his career, the actual number of works could be twice that amount.

His interest in composition surfaced at the age of four and continued through his early years. After a brief period of study at Tufts University, a two-year scholarship at the New England Conservatory enabled him to study with Frederick Shepherd Converse and launched his career as a composer. During the '30s, the music of his father's homeland, Armenia, captured his imagination and led to a surge of interest in all Eastern music, including Indian and Japanese. These influences caused radical changes in his style.

Well over 75% of his output is instrumental. All but a scant few choral works are on sacred texts, most of these being shorter works, cantatas and motets. Among the few large works, *The Way of Jesus* aligns reasonably with the dramatic oratorio tradition. One noted source erroneously classifies this work as a "folk mass", perhaps misled by the call for guitars in the instrumentation. The texts for the 23 individual numbers of this work have no relation to the liturgical Mass nor any modern adaptation of it.

The Way of Jesus, Op. 279

Original Language: English
Text: Selected excerpts from the New Testament and the composer's own poetry, which focus on the ministry, passion and resurrection of Jesus.
Date of Writing: 1974
First Performance: February 23, 1975, at St. Patrick's Cathedral in New York.
Form: No major sections are delineated, yet the text clearly divides into two large, almost equal parts. Each has dramatic coherence within itself, yet both are complementary in the spiritual sense, pointing out the "way of Jesus." There are 23 individual numbers. Performance time is approximately one hour, 26 minutes.
Scoring: Solo soprano, tenor and bass; mixed chorus, baritone chorus, three guitars, orchestra including timpani, percussion, harp, strings.
Discussion of the Work: Numbers 1–12 form the first part. They single out events in Jesus' life, mainly miracles, and illuminate key teachings in Christianity. Christ's identity and the purpose of his ministry are made clear at the opening: "And He began to teach them, that the Son of Man must suffer many things, and be rejected, and be killed, and after three days must rise again." This text accounts for the composition's title.

Three of the four miracles in the first part serve to affirm Jesus' divine powers over the elements and over death itself. The other, "the feeding of the five thousand," symbolizes His compassion for humanity. The Biblical quotations chosen to exemplify Jesus' teachings emphasize the Kingdom of Heaven and the Great Commandment—Thou shalt love thy neighbor as thyself. The remainder of the work, numbers 13–23, capsulize the story surrounding Jesus' betrayal, crucifixion and resurrection.

Following a brief, 14-measure introduction, the baritone chorus in unison sings "Behold, the Lamb of God," and the full chorus follows with "And He began to teach them." This excerpt typifies the simple rhythmic character of the choral writing in *The Way of Jesus*. Also, it suffices to illustrate the theoretical basis for understanding this composer's harmonic style, namely; common-tone connection of chords (Example 1). [Musical examples copyright 1974, 1979 by Peer International Corp. Used by permission.]

Example 1

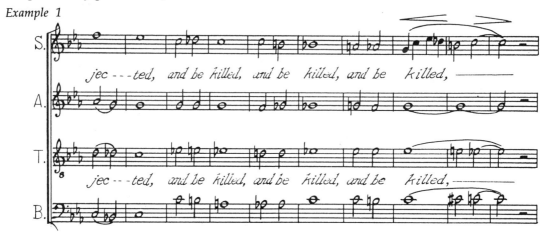

Example 2

The baritone soloist acts as a narrator, taking only, but not all, narrative texts. He begins No. 3, "The Raising of Jairus' Daughter," with the father's words, "My little daughter lieth at the point of death." Chorus and narrator alternate in short passages, the chorus singing the words of Jesus. This section ends with two aleatoric passages for women's chorus. In the first, the chorus divides into eight parts, each having a melodic fragment distinct from the others in length, but using the same words—"wept and wailed greatly." At the appropriate time—under the direction "senza misura" (unmeasured)—the voices begin repeating the assigned lines in an individually expressive manner. Only the termination of the passage is under the conductor's control (Example 2). The second aleatoric passage uses the words "And they laughed him to scorn." The manner in which narrator, chorus and the aleatoric style are used in this passage is common to several sections of this work. Hovhaness uses aleatoric lines frequently as accompaniment for solo vocal passages with telling dramatic effect, further confirming this technique as a marked feature of his style (Example 3).

Example 3

Homophonic sections have little text repetition, in contrast to the contrapuntal passages. In the final chorus of this part, "This is my commandment, that ye love one another," however, the words "love one another" are repeated 12 times before the final cadence is reached, with spaces of three to five measures between each. In the last six repetitions the chorus sings in unison, pianissimo. This passage reflectively expresses these words and also symbolizes Christ at the Last Supper, admonishing each disciple, individually, with this benediction.

The soprano soloist sings two arias, one in each part. Both are reflective. The disciple Peter (tenor) is heard incidentally in Part One, during the scene depicting Christ walking on the water. He assumes a major role in Part Two. In this truncated account of Christ's passion Peter's denial of Christ is spotlighted immediately (No. 13). Peter, narrator and chorus join to portray this scene. The chorus sopranos expose Peter's denial with a taunting sing-song melodic line in jaunty 6/8 meter (Example 4). A solo trumpet imitates the crowing of the cock. Peter weeps, as he remembers the words Jesus had spoken to prophesy this event, and sings a lament, "I am alone with God" (No. 14), text by the composer.

The next three sections (15, 16, 17) are for full chorus, baritone, and full chorus, respectively. The texts are meditative, "Greater Love Hath No Man"; "Lamb of God, O Come to Me"; "He was led as a Sheep"; all anticipating the death of Jesus. With number 18, "Now from the Sixth Hour there was Darkness," the dramatic action resumes. A violent "senza misura" instrumental passage, marked triple-forte, imitates the earthquake at the moment of Christ's death. The chorus carries the Centurion's response, "Truly this was the Son of God," in typically simple rhythms, but with a clear—and now unexpected—tonal orientation to the scale of G minor. A soprano aria, "Mary Stood by the Cross" (No. 19), follows, completing the passion narrative.

Example 4

Example 5

In the closing four numbers, "As it Began to Dawn"; "Christ is Risen"; "Behold, the Lamb of God"; and "Hosanna," the oratorio is carried to a triumphant conclusion. It is in these sections particularly that one senses a near-eastern flavor. These full, majestic parallel harmonies which follow the proclamation that "Christ is Risen," surely have their roots in the composer's ancestral homeland (Example 5). The final chorus rings with "Hosannas" in an unbroken fugal style, the polyphonic trademark of this composer. Once all voices have entered, the counterpoint moves relentlessly in all parts, without rests, until it erupts with rhythmic abandon into the closing "shouts" of victory over death.

Following the first performance Robert Sherman of *The New York Times* wrote:

The Way of Jesus is a glowing, deeply expressive, often eloquent testament of faith and love. It is complete enough to suggest that further hearings will reveal new dimensions, sufficiently clear and emotionally direct to be entirely accessible on the first encounter.

—Thurston Dox

Johann Nepomuk Hummel   1778–1837

Everything a youth could learn from a teacher who was also a genius, Hummel, born on November 14, 1778, in Pressburg (today Bratislava), learned from Mozart. He studied with the master for two years and by the age of 12 was one of the best pianists of the time. Creative genius can, however, neither be learned nor taught. Hummel composed much and easily, but his many works both large and small were soon forgotten. He succeeded Haydn in Eisenstadt, and was later Kapellmeister in Stuttgart and Weimar, but never gave up his triumphant concert tours as a virtuoso pianist. He died in Weimar on October 17, 1837.

With an extremely large and varied musical offering from many centuries available to today's interested listener, Hummel's compositions are receiving more attention, particularly his chamber music and virtuoso piano concertos. His great Mass in E-flat major, Op. 80, which can still speak to us, is occasionally performed. It recalls the writing of Mozart and Beethoven, expressing a deeper feeling we would hardly expect from this "elegant," successful musician.

Carlos Alberto Irigaray   1916–1987

Irigaray, born on May 2, 1916, in Montevideo, the capital of Uruguay, was one of the foremost authorities on the folklore of his South American homeland. He used this material again and again in his compositions. Most of them were not heard much beyond the Rio de la Plata region; only his *Navidad criolla* (Creole Christmas) won broader attention. This hour-long work for a narrator, three vocal soloists (soprano, mezzosoprano, baritone), small instrumental ensemble, mixed and children's choruses, and organ, is an unpretentious but pleasing work, one that touches the heart. It can be considered a folk-Christmas work. The narrative for which the composer himself wrote the texts, follows the Bible. Each musical number is in a different folk rhythm, and the concluding Hallelujah, a rousing piece, is in the style of a Black native dance ("Candombe"). It should be remembered that in the composer's native land Christmas falls in mid-summer and is celebrated, as in all southern lands, as a feast of joy—a completely justifiable, in many ways even quite felicitous, interpretation.

Leos Janacek   1854–1928

A man whose life was in many respects odd, difficult to categorize, one who could almost be called an eccentric but who was nevertheless a completely winning person of a most original genius: that was Leos Janacek. He was born on July 3, 1854, in Hukvaldy (then Hochwald in the border region of Moravia and Silesia, in the former Austrian province of Bohemia, now Czechoslovakia). He became the third of the Czech classicists, following Smetana and Dvorak. His biographers portray a life full of drama, but one which in spite of all the hardship and bitterness, all the struggle and loneliness, had a consoling, even happy ending. After an endless series of bitter experiences in his personal as well as artistic life, the sun finally shone on this aging man and bestowed upon him fame and affection. Indeed, in both aspects of his life, the personal and the artistic, he was a late bloomer: he was almost 50 years old when he finished his first undisputed masterpiece, the opera *Jenufa*. And it was not until 1918, when the work was successfully performed in Vienna, that he received his first break, which in turn led to a period of great creativity. The operas *The Excursions of*

Mr. Broucek (1920), *Katja Kabanowa* (1921), *The Cunning Little Vixen* (1924), *The Makropoulos Affair* (1926), and *From the House of the Dead* (1928), works composed by a man 70 years old and more, received international attention for this quiet, modest man, who lived with his music in Brno, Czechoslovakia, apart from the world. He died in Moravia on August 12, 1928. The essence of his being is found in his sincere compassion for all God's creatures.

Glagolitic Mass

Original Title: M'sa glagolskaja
Original Language: Liturgical Old Slavic (in Glagolitic script).
Date of Writing: August 5 to October 15, 1926
First Performance: December 5, 1927, in Brno.
Form: In eight parts:
  1. Uvod (Introduction)
  2. Gospodi pomiluj (Kyrie)
  3. Slava (Gloria)
  4. Veruju (Credo)
  5. Svet (Sanctus)
  6. Agnece Bozij (Agnus Dei)
  7. Varhany Solo (Organ solo)
  8. Intrada

Scoring: Four solo voices (soprano, alto, tenor, bass), four-part (sometimes subdivided) mixed chorus; four flutes, two oboes, English horn, three clarinets (with bass clarinet), three bassoons (with contrabassoon), four horns, four trumpets, three trombones, tuba, timpani, percussion, two harps, celeste, organ, and strings.

History of the Work: Janacek composed relatively little religious, let alone liturgical music. In 1901 he adapted Liszt's *Organ Mass* for mixed chorus with organ, but the work enjoyed little success. In 1908 he began a Mass in E-flat major for the same scoring but finished only a few sections of it. At different times he wrote smaller works such as the cantatas *Lord, Have Mercy* (1896), *Our Father* (1901), and *The Eternal Gospel* (1914), which also fell on deaf ears.

Only the *Glagolitic Mass* entered the ranks of important religious choral works of the 20th century. The first question that must be asked in connection with this work has to do, of course, with the composer's religious outlook. The answer is no easier to come by than in the case of Beethoven, Schubert, and many other great composers. Janacek understood God not in any churchly or denominational sense but rather as an all-embracing being or essence. He could almost be called a pantheist; his deep, warm ties with nature and all its creatures support such a conclusion.

He has expressed himself several times on the subject of his faith, or better yet, his convictions, once in relation to the *Glagolitic Mass*. Upon its appearance in 1926, the Czech critic Dr. Ludvik Kundera called the composer—not maliciously, we assume—a "religious old graybeard." Two years later, on March 8, 1928, an interview with Janacek appeared in the *Literarni Svet* (Literary World) in which he was asked about this Mass. His answer was:

> The Old Slavic Mass? Don't you remember what was written at the time—"a religious old graybeard"? I was quite upset then and would like to say today: O.K., young fellow, first, I'm not an old graybeard—and religious? By no means, by no means. Not until somebody convinces me! Do you know what's missing in this year of 1928? The Cyril-Methodios atmosphere, that's what's missing, and so I want to relate my work to this year. But it has been in existence since 1926. It was in Luhacovice; it was awful there, it rained day after day, and every evening I sat down and prepared my music paper and was finished in three weeks. I wanted to express my belief in the durability of the Slavic peoples, not for religious reasons but for their decency, their strength, which calls upon God as its witness.

There is much of importance in these words, beyond the fact that the *Glagolitic Mass* was composed during a few weeks Janacek spent in the Czech town of Luhacovice. The reference to the Cyril-Methodios atmosphere has to do with the two Slavic apostles, Cyril and Methodios, brothers who in the 9th century introduced the Slavic language into religious services and thus became the founders of Slavic literature. Janacek's idea of composing a Mass in Old Slavic was, like much else in his life, basically a patriotic deed having to do with Slavic culture.

The composition was completed in the extremely short time span of about 10 weeks. The work first achieved international stature in 1929, after Janacek's death, when it was performed at the Festival of the International Society for Contemporary Music (ISCM) in Geneva.

Discussion of the Work: A dominant motive based on fifths marks the orchestral introduction, Uvod (Introduction, No. 1), which establishes a kind of instrumental ascendancy over the voices. It is difficult to describe or explain Janacek's sound, for he created a completely idiosyncratic tonal language, one that can scarcely be reproduced in a piano reduction and for which there is no real definition. He used tonality expanded to its furthest limit. His precursors were Mussorgsky and—remarkably—Debussy, making his music reminiscent of both Realism and Impressionism.

In the Kyrie (Gospodi pomiluj, No. 2) we hear the main motive first in the cellos and then in the chorus, as it enters. But before this occurs, the composer interrupts the calm, resolute course of the music with a presto passage that plunges suddenly from the heights only to fade away again, yielding to the main motive. What are we to make of this short interruption? It cannot be explained in terms of form, nor does anything justify interpreting it as tone painting.

The treatment of the chorus is completely harmonic; there are very few contrapuntal passages in this work. The words "Christe eleison" are sung three times by the solo soprano, after which the chorus enters, supporting the solo with difficult chords—second intervals between sopranos and altos with augmented progressions. At the conclusion, the main motive returns. The solo soprano introduces the Gloria (Slava, No. 3) but pauses in several places for orchestral interludes, some longer than others, which are extremely expressive, even ethereal. Finally, the chorus brings the majestic section to an end; what follows is a fast and lively piece, whose rhythms place high demands on the performers. Choruses alternate with solos; entrances on high notes (B-flat, B) are demanded of the tenor. The movement is full of changing moods, but tension is sustained, and there is much that is beautiful and deeply moving. The Credo (Veruju, No. 4) begins with a characteristic orchestral motive (Example 1). It furnishes the thematic material for this movement, both in single motives and as a whole. A very meaningful and often passionately agitated orchestral interlude occurs in the middle, which leads into the "Et resurrexit." At this point, a new motive dominates (Example 2).

Example 1 **Con moto**

Example 2

Extensive choral sections rest on a carpet of sound woven of pianissimo trills in the orchestra, creating the effect of a capella singing, yet with a pronounced, but indefinable timbre. Then, toward the end, the main motive (No. 1) reappears. The eventful movement comes to a close with a tenor solo (again very high), a bass solo, and powerful choruses of "Amen."

In the "Sanctus" (Svet, No. 5), soloists and chorus are very lively, but here, too, imposing interludes are played by the orchestra. The last vocal section, the "Agnus Dei" (Agnece Bozij, No. 6) is tranquil and relatively short. Once more the four soloists intervene, and finally the chorus, singing the quiet "Miserere nobis" without accompaniment, and a short orchestral postlude bring the movement to an end. The mood, at this point, is one of excitement—the reason, perhaps, that even though the Mass itself has ended, the composer felt he had to add an organ movement (No. 7). Here, for the first and only time, he follows a traditional musical form: an endless repetition of a two-bar ostinato motive (Example 3) leads to an organ fantasy on a grand scale. But even then the composer felt compelled to conclude the work with an orchestral piece, which he entitled Intrada (No. 8), a name that in earlier times indicated the opening of a musical work, not its ending. Whether this was an oversight on Janacek's part—perhaps he did not know the original meaning of the term—or whether it has a deeper significance cannot be determined.

Example 3

Josquin des Préz ca. 1445–1521

Josquin des Préz (Déprés, De Près) was a student of Ockeghem and one of the greatest masters of the Netherland School, indeed of all of Medieval and early Renaissance music. He was born in Hainault, in Picardy, near Amiens, between 1440 and 1450. After 1474, he sang in the choir of the Milan cathedral and 10 years later, in the papal chapel in Rome. After 1494, it seems he directed the choir of the Cathedral at Cambrai, one of the most important musical centers of the time. In 1499, we find him in Modena, then probably in Paris, in 1503 in Ferrara, and finally in his native Condé, which he ultimately preferred to all the enticing court positions offered him in France, Spain, Austria, or the Netherlands. He was renowned far and wide. Luther called him "Master of the notes."

His Masses were sung everywhere. About 20 of them have come down to us, of which probably the best known is *L'homme armé* (with a popular folk song of the time serving as its main theme) and *Pangue lingua*, based on the Gregorian melody "Pange lingua gloriosi corporis mysterium." Lovers of old music are urged to take note of des Préz's Masses; their sounds draw the listener into a strange, distant, and enchanting land. They use practically no harmony in the modern sense; all the vocal parts move contrapuntally in a simple, clear polyphony. The question of instrumental accompaniment is vexed. It is likely that at that time instruments, especially those of the lower registers, played along with the main voices, chiefly the bass; stylistically it would be appropriate to use a trombone today. Compared to the music of Guillaume de Machaut (discussed in this book), who lived a century and a half earlier, Josquin's is livelier, freer, and "more melodic" in our sense. His Masses follow the usual division into five parts: Kyrie, Gloria, Credo, Sanctus, and Agnus Dei. The *Missa Pangue lingua* seems to have been one of his last, for the composer displays such mastery over the musical means of his time that it could only have emerged from long experience. Josquin died in the Condé, possibly on August 27, 1521.

Zoltán Kodály 1882–1967

The 20th century bestowed two very important musicians on Hungary, two men who were among the leaders of their time and who have greatly influenced the direction of music: Bela Bartók, born in 1881, and Zoltán Kodály, born on December 16, 1882 (making him one year younger) in Kecskemét. Kodály spent his youth, from 1885–1892, in Galanta, and passed his secondary school examinations in 1900 in Nagyszombat, both towns in Czechoslovakia today. From that time forward he lived in Budapest, where he attended the Academy of Music and the University, receiving diplomas from both. In 1905 he made his first journey through the Hungarian countryside to record folk songs, a pursuit which he sustained throughout his life and which was a fundamental aspect of his work. Often in the company of Bartók, he roamed the Balkans, recording countless melodies of the many ethnic groups living there. He put them to good use in the other two major areas of his life's work: composition and music pedagogy. The short-lived Republic of Councils appointed Kodály, long a teacher, Deputy Director of the Academy of Music in Budapest. After the government fell, he was subjected to intense criticism which continued until 1921 when he was officially found "guiltless of legal violations." Despite these difficulties international recognition of his work grew.

In 1923, the *Psalmus hungaricus* appeared, now widely performed, and his *Te Deum* followed in 1936. Whereas Bartók emigrated just before World War II, Kodály spent those difficult years in his own land, for a time as a fugitive in a monastery. After the war his fame spread widely and many musical honors were bestowed on him. The theory of music pedagogy (the Kodály Method) which he developed is now widely employed and, like Orff's, has made a powerful contribution to the schooling of young musicians. The Kodály method is largely based on the singing of folk songs. Heaped with honor and recognition, Kodály died in Budapest, on March 6, 1967.

Psalmus hungaricus

Original Title: Psalmus hungaricus, op. 13
Original Language: Hungarian
Text: The 55th Psalm in a Hungarian version translated in the 16th century by Mihály Vég.
Date of Writing: 1923, commissioned for the 50th anniversary of the joining of Ofen (Buda) and Pest to form the city of Budapest.
First Performance: 1923
Form: A cohesive cantata composed of several sections.
Scoring: Solo tenor, mixed chorus (further subdivided into eight parts), children's chorus, recommended by the composer to reinforce the female voices of the main chorus; three flutes, two oboes, two clarinets, two bassoons, four horns, three trumpets, three trombones, timpani, cymbals, harp, organ ad libitum.
History of the Work: In spite of the very difficult time it had weathered—one of great political turmoil and much bloodshed, almost a civil war—Hungary wished to celebrate the 50th anniversary of its capital, Budapest. The city had been formed in 1873 from two half-cities that had grown together. Several leading Hungarian composers were asked to contribute to the celebration. Thus, Bartók wrote his *Dance Suite,* and Ernö von Dohnanyi, a *Festival Overture.* Kodály composed what was to become one of his major works, the *Psalmus hungaricus*—a rare distinction for a commissioned work. It was the first to bring Kodály to the attention of the international music community, as he himself noted late in his life.
Discussion of the Work: Following an orchestral prelude (andante molto appassionato), the low voices of the chorus (alto and bass) enter, a cappella and in unison, peacefully relating how at a time of suffering, King David prayed to God. Then the solo tenor, who represents David, accuses not his enemies, against whom he can well defend himself, but his false friends; their greed, duplicity, and immorality are leading to the downfall of Jerusalem, and more seriously they mock and profane the name of God. The narrative lines of the chorus return again and again in all sorts of variations, like a Leitmotif. David prays that the man he had trusted above all others be punished, for his friend had turned away from him because David had spoken the truth in all matters.

Like a message from Heaven, an adagio interlude with violin and harp restores David's confidence and peace of mind. His song, which follows, is full of hope: "You, my heart, be glad and fear not; God will comfort you, God is the sunlight of your days, He takes away all the soul's earthly cares."

The final chorus is also full of confidence, taking on the character of a hymn, but the work does not end on a note of triumph. The early sounds fade away, and the chorus, now in four parts, intones these words, the first measures sung once more in unison: "Thus says the Bible, thus wrote David, thus do we read it in the 55th Psalm, how a pious man, sick at heart, devised this song of consolation. . . ." It is as if the chorus were summing up David's passionate testimony, the unshakable faith in God.

The *Psalmus hungaricus* fades quietly away on an open fifth—neither tonal nor atonal, for the work is at home in both realms. In contrast to most of Kodály's compositions, this piece has nothing folkloric about it, yet nearly every measure possesses a hard-to-define Hungarian quality.

Te Deum

Original Title: Budavári Te Deum
Original Language: Latin
Text: Ambrosian song of praise "Te Deum laudamus" from the 4th century.
Date of Writing: 1936
First Performance: Budapest, on September 2, 1936.
Scoring: Four solo voices (soprano, alto, tenor, bass), four-part mixed chorus (further subdivided into as many as nine parts); two each of flutes, oboes, clarinets, and bassoons, four horns, three trumpets, three trombones, tuba, timpani, strings and organ ad libitum.
History of the Work: Between 1541 and 1686, the city Buda (then called Ofen) was the seat of Turkish pashas of the Ottoman Empire who ruled the Balkans almost as far north as Vienna. A decisive battle at the very gates of that city, in 1683, brought an end to the Turkish domination in south-eastern Europe. In 1936, the modern city of Budapest celebrated the 250th anniversary of this battle, for which Kodály wrote his *Te Deum.*
Discussion of the Work: Festive trumpets open the work, and the mighty chorus enters, at first in unison, with "Te Deum laudamus, Te Dominum confitemur." Here, Kodály's style is best described as one of free tonality and polytonality, but again and again, at decisive moments and high points, he returns to pure tonality, to classic harmony. Thus at the beginning of the radiant "Sanctus," the music shines out in the brightest C major before embarking on a path of modulation and deceptive cadences leading to D-flat major and finally breaking off on its chord of the seventh. Such a sequence could almost have been used a few decades earlier in the Romantic era by Kodály's great Hungarian forebear, Franz Liszt.

A fugue follows (Example 1), very clear in structure and almost classic in tonality. The voices and the winds then join in a chorale-like piece: "Te gloriosus Apostolorum chorus..." Only here, notably late in the piece, do the soloists enter with "Tu Rex gloriae," a three-voice fugato (bass, tenor, soprano) with a very pronounced rhythm whose origin is probably to be found in Hungarian folk music (Example 2).

The great, multipartite choral number "Tu ad dexteram Dei sedes" repeats the previous "Sanctus" motive, now modulated to E major. After a lengthy, contemplative general rest, the imposing conclusion begins to take shape. In the adagio, the tenors and three-part basses (the latter singing in A minor) whisper their "Te ergo quaesumus," lent a curious agitation by accents in the brasses. The altos and finally, the sopranos, join in, while a lamenting solo oboe is heard. Against this background a masterfully constructed fugal passage ("Quos pretioso sanguine") for the vocal soloists stands out, beneath which the murmuring chorus spreads a carpet of sound.

Example 1

Example 2

With "Aeterna fac" the chorus once more comes to the fore; the tempo, previously moderate, speeds up, while the expression becomes more intense, frequently through those unison passages for the voices which Kodály repeatedly used to create a sense of great tenderness and intimacy. The master of folk song is quite evident here. With "Per singulos dies" the work returns to its beginning, but the intensity mounts as the solo soprano and solo tenor enter. With the "Miserere" the piece reaches a stirring climax of whispered prayer and despairing outcry. The sequence of keys is of unusual clarity and strength; the high point of the "Miserere" at the sudden appearance of A major is like a blinding ray of light. Another urgent fugue with a lengthy theme ("In te Domine speravi") contracts to a resounding outburst in unison—"Non confundar in aeternum." From this point on the work becomes quieter, slower, more comforting. "In aeternum" repeat the solo soprano and the chorus, until sound dies away. The purest A major seems to point toward Heaven, wide and open. The conclusion of Gustav Mahler's *Das Lied von der Erde*, composed a quarter of a century earlier, comes to mind, with its fading "Ewig, ewig..., ewig...."

Rafael Kubelik 1914–

Rafael Kubelik, son of the prominent violinist Jan Kubelik, was born on June 29, 1914, in Bychory, near Kolin (then in Bohemia, today in Czechoslovakia). He has had a brilliant career as a conductor: for many years he was director of the excellent orchestra of the Bavarian Radio Network in Munich. But few know him as a composer, since he has modestly refrained from drawing attention to this aspect of his career. In the 1950s, after Kubelik emigrated from his homeland, he composed a *Libera nos*, which took its place beside his other large works (operas, symphonies).

The death of his wife June 23, 1961, led him to compose an intense, pain-filled *Requiem pro memoria uxoris* (Requiem in Memory of my Wife), a work more than a half-hour long, whose score bears the completion date of September 24, 1961. The following summer, on August 25, 1962, it was performed for the first time at the Lucerne Music Festival. "In this Requiem, Kubelik expresses forthrightly and modestly what he feels deep in his heart," wrote Joachim Kaiser at the time, thereby putting his finger on the fundamental mood of this deeply affecting work. It calls for a solo baritone, mixed chorus, children's chorus, and an unusually extensive orchestra, (including English horn, bass clarinet, four Wagnerian tubas, bass tuba, five percussionists, celeste, and one or two harps. It is a deeply introspective, confessional work of great beauty, and unusually melodic, but one that places great demands on the performers.

Michel-Richard de la Lande   1657–1726

De la Lande was one of the most highly ranked (a protégé of the king) most honored, and best loved musicians at the most brilliant court of the Baroque era, that of the Sun King, Louis XIV. It is astonishing that his work virtually passed into oblivion until the recent revival of interest in Baroque music. Only recently has the value of some of his works been reestablished.

La Lande (or Lalande, or Delalande), born in Paris on December 15, 1657, followed the usual musician's career: choir boy, instrumentalist in ensembles, and organist in several churches. He then was called to Versailles where he taught harpsichord; in 1683 he became one of four assistant music directors; in 1685, court composer; in 1695, director of the royal chamber music and court composer. He, like Marc-Antoine Charpentier, knew how to please the musical taste of the King and his court. He succeeded Jean-Baptiste Lully, who died in 1687, taking over Lully's positions one after the other. The several hundred instrumental pieces with which La Lande embellished the almost daily festivals and ceremonies at Versailles, while of great merit, are of lesser import for this book than the more than 70 motets he contributed to the sacred music of the era. Most are choral works, accompanied by organ and orchestra. Among them are works for specific feast days, for example, *Symphonies des Noëls* for Christmas. In addition, his secular works, performed at the *Concerts Spirituels*, one of the oldest concert institutions in Europe, are of considerable interest. La Lande died on June 18, 1726, in Versailles, after having spent more than a decade in the service of King Louis XV, who esteemed him no less than his predecessor.

Steffano Landi   1585?–1639

Steffano Landi, together with Emilio de' Cavalieri, Giacomo Carissimi, and other Italian masters writing at the beginning of the 17th century, is today slowly emerging from the shadows of history. His age when we first learn of him in 1595, when he was studying at the German Jesuit seminar in Rome, is not known. He was a boy soprano, then studied at the Jesuit seminar, from which he graduated in 1607. It seems then he turned his attention completely to music and became music director at the court of Cardinal Marco Cornaro, in Padua. He wrote madrigals as well as his first opera, *La morte d'Orfeo* (1619) while there. About 1620 he returned to Rome where he was organist and musical director at the church of Santa Maria ai Monti. He must have sung well, for in 1629 he joined the choir at the Sistine Chapel as an alto. In time, Landi devoted increasing energy to composition. Probably his most important work was the sacred opera—the term oratorio had not yet come into use and no absolute distinction between opera and oratorio had been made—*Il Sant'Alessio* (Saint Alexis). Although Landi had taken religious vows, he composed secular as well as sacred works during the last years of his life. He died in Rome on October 28, 1639, and was buried in the common grave for Papal singers in the church of Santa Maria in Vallicella.

The text for *Sant'Alessio*, called a "dramma musicale in tre atti," was written by the Marquis and Prince Giulio Rospigliosi (Ruspigliosi) (1600–1669), an extremely interesting man, important in the musical circles of his time, especially in Rome. He not only rose to the highest positions in the church—Papal Nuncio in Spain, Cardinal, and in 1667, under the name of Clement IX, Pope—but played a leading role in the early history of opera as librettist, promoter, and patron. Like so many works of the time, *Il Sant'Alessio* represents an intermediate form (sometimes revived in our own day) between opera and oratorio. Paradoxical as it may seem, it is best performed in costume, with entrances and exits, but can also be performed in concert.

The story of St. Alexis is characterized by an almost total lack of movement, such that a stage play would not do it justice. Its deeper meaning lies in the saint's freely choosing the inner life. It reflects a concept closer to Eastern mysticism than to the Western sense of the duty of the Christian in the world. The legend from which it is derived originated in Syria in the 5th century; it is to be found in accounts written a hundred years later in Greece, and spread from Byzantium to Eastern and Western Europe. It appeared in Rome in the 10th century in various adaptations at first literary and later musical. In the 17th century, Rospigliosi probably knew that the theme he dramatized was widely known.

Alexis was the scion of a noble Roman family, and, according to tradition, a marriage to the daughter of another noble family had been arranged. However, on the wedding day he left his bride and his homeland to follow the call of God. Friends and family gave him up for dead as nothing had been heard of him for years. He returned to Rome as a squalid beggar and, unrecognized, knocked at the door of the house of his youth. He was given a corner in the courtyard where he lived out his life supported by alms for which he begged. He never revealed himself to those who had once been his near and dear. Only after his death did his identity come to light.

The first performance of Steffano Landi's *Sant' Alessio* took place on February 21, 1632, in the private Barbarini theater in the Palazzo ai Giubbonari, in Rome. It was produced for the festivities held in connection with the visit of Prince Eggenberg of Styria, in southeast Austria. It was repeated two years later, in 1634, in the same theater, probably in the same form, again to honor a princely visitor. When the work was revived at the Salzburg Festival of 1977 the program notes prepared by Silke Leopold (Rome) contained a good deal of information about those two 17th-century performances.* They include an eyewitness report on the first one by Jean-Jacques Bouchard and engravings of stage sets from the second. Virtually all the important roles were taken by singers from the Sistine Chapel. Castratos sang the two soprano roles, since it was then unthinkable for women to appear in performances of sacred works. Boys from the chorus of St. Peter's sang the roles of pages. The production was absolutely elegant with costumes of gold and silver fabric; the costume of Demonio, the devil, is described as having been particularly impressive: red and yellow flames had been sewn to his black gown. The always astounding machinery of the Baroque theater was all in place; Religione (Faith) floated among heavenly clouds, and the earthly scenes were full of pomp and splendor. The lavish setting made the appearance of the completely unadorned Alexis in his sackcloth monk's robe doubly impressive. Rospigliosi embellished the original tale, an extremely simple one, by adding numerous other characters, some real, some symbolic, as was expected at the time. The church victorious and the defeat of the Devil are the overt themes of the drama, while the spiritual transformation of one who lived in the "vanity" of the world is the inner meaning of the work. The music is largely in the recitative style of the earlier, Florentine opera, displaying a relationship to Monteverdi but without attaining the degree of excitement he created. At the dramatic points we hear the beginnings of arioso, but not yet aria. This is an early work in the genre, which, in light of its revival at Salzburg, deserves inclusion in this book. But I do not want to assign too great an importance to either its content or artistry.

Orlando di Lasso   ca. 1530–1594

This "Prince of Music," as his contemporaries saw him, cannot be omitted from a book treating the large forms of choral music, secular and sacred. He composed no oratorios, and his Masses are not as well known as those of his contemporary, Palestrina; but in the genre of the motet he was the leading master in his time, his century, and indeed the period of the Renaissance. His Psalms were also regarded as the finest examples of high polyphony (*Septem Psalmi Davidis poenitentiales*—David's Seven Penitential Psalms—is the title of the best known collection).

Orlando di Lasso, also known as Orlandus Lassus or Roland de Lassus, was born in Mons, in Hainault. He was the last great master of the Netherland school—the "Golden Age of Polyphony"—which dominated European music for more than a century. The date of his birth is uncertain: various chronicles place it any time between 1523 and 1532. It is certain that he was a choir boy, but he seems to have performed in this capacity in several places—whether due to his own choice, his parents' wishes or to forcible abduction, instances of which are often reported in tales of the time, we do not know. It is said that in 1553 he sang in the Vatican choir under Pope Julius III; there is evidence that he spent time in Antwerp later. From 1555 on he was active in Munich, rose to the post of Kapellmeister, and turned the court ensemble, which consisted of chorus and orchestra, into what was probably the best in all of Europe. The number of his works is legion, and his style, whether sacred or secular, is brilliant. He was a much-traveled man, a guest at many princely courts, and the recipient of many honors, distinctions, and decorations. Both confessions, Catholic and Protestant, bitter enemies at the time, paid him equal honor. His mood appears to have darkened during the last years of his life. There are reports of melancholy and depression for which his high place could not compensate. Among his more than 2,000 works there are 500 motets, of which several are in the active repertories of choruses and societies of ancient music today. Lasso died in Munich on June 14, 1594.

---

*The idea of presenting early works (church operas, spiritual plays, etc.) at the Salzburg Festival came from Bernhard Paumgartner. The following people were instrumental in the revival: Hans Ludwig Hirsch (musical adaptation), Peter Maag (conductor), August Everding (production), Jean-Pierre Ponnelle (stage design), Pet Halmen (costumes).

Rolf Liebermann   1910–

The Swiss composer Rolf Liebermann was born on September 14, 1910, in Zürich. During the active years of his career he held many important positions in the European musical world; his dynamism contributed much to the development of contemporary music. His early environment, his teacher Wladimir Vogel, and his own intellectual and speculative inclinations led him to a profound understanding and development of Schönberg's twelve-tone system, which he used to great effect in sophisticated but lyrical stage works and some unusual concert pieces. From the 1960s on, his ceaseless activity—as farsighted organizer and energetic manager of the music department of the North German Radio Network, of the Hamburg and then Paris operas, and of the summer courses at the Salzburg Mozarteum—increasingly impinged upon his compositional activity. The work warranting attention in this book—*Streitlied zwischen Leben und Tod* (Quarrel between Life and Death)—was composed in 1950, first performed by Radio Zürich and heard frequently since then.

In this work, Liebermann composed a "dramatic cantata" to a text of his own writing. It calls for four soloists (a high soprano, mezzosoprano, tenor, and bass), mixed chorus and orchestra. Its late Romantic text is in sharp contrast to its dodecaphonic music, but it remains tight and consistent. Following a brief introduction in the woodwinds, the two female solo voices announce "So spricht das Leben: die Welt ist mein!" (Life says, "The world is mine!"). An orchestral interlude follows, marked "concerto grosso," which, in its use of the introductory theme as the main element that recurs in various transformations, is akin to the Baroque musical form given that name. The soprano continues: "Mich preisen die Blumen und Vögelein, ich bin der Tag und der Sonnenschein—die Welt ist mein!" (Flowers and birds sing my praises; I am the day and the light of the sun—the world is mine!). Then Death arrives with a vehement, harshly accented, wildly boastful theme, to which the murmuring chorus provides an eerie contrast: "So spricht der Tod, so spricht der Tod . . ." (This is what Death says). The solo bass, as Death, announces: "Die Welt ist Mein! Dein Leuchten ist nur eitel Pracht, sinkt Stern und Mond in ew'ge Nacht! Die Welt ist mein!" (The world is mine! Your shining is but vain splendor; stars and moon sink into eternal night! The world is mine!). The orchestra begins an intentionally "kitschy" waltz ("a la valse" writes the composer in the score and calls this passage "Totentanz"—dance of death). The solo bass part contains such directions as "mephistophelian" and "even more ironic," as it combines a lilting melody with the previous text. The mezzosoprano replies, "So spricht das Leben: die Welt ist mein! Und machst du Särge aus Marmorstein, kannst du nicht sargen die Liebe ein!" (And Life says, "The world is mine! And even if you make coffins out of marble, you cannot entomb love). The chorus joins in, and in a solemn, chorale-like passage underscores the words Life has spoken. A "military march" is heard, and the solo tenor announces "radiantly": "So spricht der Tod: die Welt ist mein! Ich habe ein grosses Grab gemacht, ich habe die Pest und den Krieg erdacht . . ." (Death says, "The world is mine! I have dug a huge grave; plague and war are my inventions.) A lengthy orchestral interlude leads step by step from the stirring drum beats of Death back to the sunny fields of Life, which now speaks through a duet of the two female solo voices (the soprano frequently reaches high C-sharp). The form here is recognizable as a sort of reprise: the Life and Death themes from the beginning exposition are repeated, and the two engage in another struggle. Finally, Life, in a great apotheosis, is victorious: "Ein jedes Grab muss ein Acker sein, mein ewiger Samen fällt hinein!" (Every grave must be a fertile field upon which falls my eternal seed!) The impression is powerful yet ambiguous.

The text sounds archaic, medieval in its primitive, yet poetic way of speaking, but the music, almost completely devoid of any harmonic quality, is constructed on twelve-tone combinations, and is typical of much 20th-century music. Can such opposites be combined in a piece of music? *Streitlied* seems to answer in the affirmative. At times we even have the impression that this music is not only modern but reaches back into the earliest European sound-world and is thus well suited to depict the simple images, chiseled like woodcuts in the text. It is an extremely interesting and novel idea, typical of Lieberman's creative instincts.

György Ligeti 1923–

Ligeti was born in Tirnaveni, Hungary, on May 28, 1923. After the uprising of 1956 he settled in Vienna and soon rose to become one of the leading composers of the avant garde. His earlier technique of sound planes or surfaces created a magical atmosphere but, like Debussy's Impressionism, threatened to become a dead end. Ligeti has since developed his musical language further and composed a number of works considered by aficionados of new music to be pioneering. Among the most important is doubtless the *Requiem*, commissioned by the Swedish Radio and completed in 1965. Its liturgical content consists of a fragment of the Missa pro defunctis, the Mass for the Dead, and is composed of four movements: Introitus, Kyrie, De die judicii sequentia, and Lacrimosa. The work is scored for two solo voices (soprano and mezzosoprano), double chorus, and large orchestra. It exceeds in difficulty of performance almost anything ever demanded of voices, instruments, and the perfecting of their combined effects. If there is any tie to tradition at all, it lies in the fact (determined by the text) that the "Dies irae" of the third movement (for that is what that lengthy title actually means) depicts the "Day of Terror" with all available means of creating terror, exactly as Verdi did almost 100 years before, and that the last section, the "Lacrimosa," is a quiet refrain.

Franz Liszt 1811–1886

Franz Liszt (called Liszt Ferenc in Hungary) was born on October 22, 1811, in Raiding, a small village in what is today the Austrian province of Burgenland, which borders on Hungary. He was close to being a religious mystic throughout his life. Long before he took minor orders and donned the cassock, his thoughts and sensibilities were markedly religious, which by no means led him to naive, unrealistic, or narrow-minded positions. Nor was he disinclined to savor worldly pleasures. He understood his faith to be the secure basis for understanding life and art; it provided a moral standard and was the powerful impetus to his creativity. And so, many of the works by this man, a brilliant figure among the musicians of his time, or indeed of all time, are sacred works—many more, in fact, than the layman, who thinks of Liszt as a master pianist and as a creator of symphonic music, is usually aware of. His most important sacred works, which began to appear in the 1840s, are the *Missa solemnis* (1855), composed for the consecration of the basilica in Gran (*Graner Festmesse*), the oratorio *Die Legende von der heiligen Elisabeth* (The Legend of Saint Elisabeth) (1862), *Christus*, the *Hungarian Coronation Mass* (both of 1867), and the *Requiem* (1868).

It is impossible to recount Liszt's career in a short space. As "king of the pianists" his concert tours encompassed virtually all of Europe and are replete with worldly laurels—popular acclaim, honors, and experiences of all kinds. His rise began very early: When only nine years old he first played in concert after which he was immediately sent by a group of wealthy, influential Hungarians to study piano with Karl Czerny and composition with Antonio Salieri in Vienna. Beethoven attended a concert there, given when Liszt was 12—but how much the master actually heard is hard to say, since he had long been almost totally deaf. The next years led him to Paris, where he formed a fast friendship with Chopin, a year older than he. His career as a virtuoso had begun. Yet at the age of 18 he settled for a short time on the notion of entering a monastery, probably inspired by an affair of the heart. The wish was to be a recurring theme throughout his long life. At his mother's request, however, he gave up the idea and plunged into the burgeoning concert life of the era. He was soon showered with wild acclaim and lionized wherever he performed. In 1835 he began an affair with the French countess Marie d'Agoult and became a teacher at the Geneva Conservatory. But in 1839 he decided upon the itinerant life of a virtuoso performer, which brought him endless triumphs and quickly earned him a place among the most famous musicians of his time, Paganini and Rossini, to name two. After his separation from Marie d'Agoult, who had borne him three children (one of whom was Cosima, later the wife of Wagner), he formed a relationship with the Russian princess Caroline von Sayn-Wittgenstein. The pair settled down in Weimar, where he directed the musical life of that small princely establishment, leading it to the highest musical brilliance, as Goethe and Schiller had once done for literature. Most of his great compositions were conceived there. He repeatedly undertook to legitimize his relationship with the extremely intelligent and mystically inclined princess, but there were always legal or churchly difficulties, and the effort came to nothing. The obstacles gradually led to the separation of the lovers. Liszt then moved to Rome for a time, and when he was getting on in years, moved to Bayreuth, where his daughter Cosima was then living, married to his friend of long standing, Richard Wagner. Liszt had once had a falling out with Wagner over this relationship, but now, full of admiration for the man, was reconciled to it. Wherever he went Liszt was followed by throngs of sometimes brilliant students and countless admirers. On July 31, 1886, in the town that was soon to became world famous for his son-in-law's music festival, he finally closed his weary eyes. Wagner had preceded him in death in 1883. He was buried in Bayreuth on August 3 of that year, not to his own music but to Wagner's, which Anton Bruckner played on the organ.

The Legend of St. Elisabeth

Original Title: Die Legende von der heiligen Elisabeth
Original Language: German
Text: By the poet Otto Roquette, of Poznan, Poland; inspired by frescoes depicting the life of St. Elisabeth painted by Moritz von Schwind in the great hall of Wartburg castle, near Eisenach.
Date of Writing: From the beginning of 1857 to 1862, in Weimar.
First Performance: August 15, 1865, in Budapest, conducted by the composer, with a Hungarian translation of the text done by Kornel Abrányi. The first German language performances, conducted by Hans von Bülow, took place in Munich on February 24, March 1, and May 10, 1866, in Prague in the fall of 1866, under the baton of Smetana; and on August 28, 1867, the 800th anniversary of Wartburg castle, in its great hall.
    Form: In two parts;
    Part 1: 1. Elisabeth's arrival at Wartburg castle
            2. Landgrave Ludwig
            3. The Crusaders
    Part 2: 4. Landgravine Sophie
            5. Elisabeth
            6. Solemn burial of Elisabeth
Cast: St. Elisabeth (soprano), Landgrave Ludwig, her husband (baritone), Landgrave Hermann of Thuringia, his father (bass), Landgravine Sophie (mezzosoprano), a Hungarian merchant (baritone), the Steward (baritone), Emperor Frederick II von Hohenstaufen (bass). The last three roles may be performed by the same singer, a low baritone. Mixed four- to eight-part chorus.
History of the Work: On December 26, 1856, Liszt opened the opera season in Weimar with Wagner's *Tannhäuser,* but felt weak due to a lingering illness. He used the period of convalescence to advance his plans for composition. During this period he composed the two symphonic poems *Die Ideale* and *Die Hunnenschlacht* as well as the final chorus of the *Faust Symphony,* and began *Die Legende von der heiligen Elisabeth.* Elisabeth, later canonized, (not to be confused with the almost contemporary queen of Portugal, her country's patron saint) was a Hungarian princess, born in Sárospatak in 1207, daughter of the Magyar king Andreas II. When very young she married Landgrave Ludwig of Thuringia—the wedding took place in Wartburg castle—and was widowed early, in 1227, when the Landgrave died on the Fifth Crusade. Robbed of her possessions by his relatives, Elisabeth fled to Marburg where she devoted herself to caring for the poor and sick. She died in 1231 and was canonized in 1235. Liszt, who never forgot his ties to Hungary, felt very close to this figure out of Hungarian legend.

    Since Weimar was close to Wartburg castle, where part of her story was played out, Liszt proceeded with an idea he had had in mind for some time, of creating a musical setting of the Elisabeth story. This, his first great oratorio, was not finished until five years later, in 1862. Several eventful years passed for Liszt before it was given its premiere. At the end of 1865 he took minor orders. It was as an abbé that he traveled to Budapest, where, on August 15, 1865, wearing a cassock, he conducted his oratorio, which had been translated into Hungarian for the occasion. It was a smashing success and was performed again a few days later. Liszt was enthusiastic about the zeal and capabilities of his performers, as he reported to Princess Caroline in Rome. Disgusted and sickened by the animosity of the press, however, Liszt was all for giving up further performances of his works in Central Europe. Yet this oratorio continued to be a success. Hans von Bülow conducted it three times in Munich; on August 28, 1867, the composer conducted a performance in the great hall of Wartburg castle, to enormous acclaim—Liszt was somewhat mollified.
Discussion of the Work: Die Legende von der heiligen Elisabeth, dedicated to King Ludwig II of Bavaria, is not really a drama but has a powerful dramatic quality; it mounts to a climax and has a resolution. Six quite different scenes are grouped in two sections, in a logical way. The orchestral introduction

is based on a folklike hymn sung at festivals honoring St. Elisabeth at least as early as the 16th century. The first scene describes the arrival of the Hungarian princess who, as was the custom in those days in princely houses, had been promised as a child to the son of the Landgrave of Thuringia at Wartburg castle.

The chorus sings a song of welcome and the reigning Landgrave, Hermann, greets the bride warmly. Then a Hungarian rhythm is heard, and a grandee, who has accompanied the young princess, hands over "dieses teure Pfand, des Ungarlandes holde Blüte, vertrauensvoll" (this priceless pledge, sweet, trusting flower of Hungary) to the Landgrave. Next the heir to the throne, Ludwig, faces his bride: "Sieh um dich! Was dein Aug' erschaut, wird dein und mein einst." (Look around you! Whatever your eyes see will one day be yours and mine.). Elisabeth replies happily, "Wie ist das Haus voll Sonnenschein!" (How filled with sunlight is this house!). A group of girls dances playfully around Elisabeth. The cheerful scene ends with more songs of greeting sung by the chorus.

The young Landgrave is the focus of the second scene, which begins as a hunting scene. On the way back to the castle, Ludwig encounters Elisabeth, who is obviously frightened by this meeting, which Ludwig does not understand. The husband discovers that his beloved wife is keeping a secret from him. Elisabeth maintains that she was picking roses deep in the forest and lost her way, but she refuses to show him the flowers. Ludwig is so puzzled and full of dismay that Elisabeth confesses her mission: Against his wishes, she had gone, as she had often done, to the huts of the poor and sick to ease their misery and console them. Her basket does not contain roses but bread and wine. She turns back the cloth but a miracle has happened: The basket is full of roses.

Frightened, the Landgrave realizes his wife's mission and believes he sees her head transfigured in an otherworldly light. The chorus sings the praises of the "miracle of the rose" performed by St. Elisabeth. The third and last scene of the first part is called "The Crusader." Warlike sounds introduce it; the male chorus describes the setting off on the Crusade, bravely facing the prospect of war and hoping to free Christ's tomb from the hands of the Saracens. The troops, under the command of Landgrave Ludwig, intone again and again the war cry, "Gott will es!" (God wills it!). Sad but resolute, Ludwig bids farewell to Elisabeth, who is filled with forebodings of evil. In vain she pleads with her husband to remain with her and their children, as the battle songs exhort the men to leave. The orchestra plays a military march, but with a lyrical intermezzo, to accompany the procession of Crusaders, who, singing, depart for the Holy Land.

The second part of the work opens on the sad news of the death of Landgrave Ludwig in a battle with the "Infidels." When Elisabeth collapses in despair, Landgravine Sophie, widow of the previous Landgrave, Hermann, seizes control of the castle and full of hatred, turns Elisabeth out. In vain Elisabeth implores to be allowed to spend one more night under the sheltering roof that has become her home, due to a terrible storm which is breaking. The Steward pities the exiled princess but is threatened with the same punishment when he pleads her case. He is forced to acquiesce and so casts the young princess out into the threatening darkness. As the elements rage, a bolt of lightning sets the castle on fire.

In the fifth scene, Elisabeth is living among and caring for the poor and the outcast. In spite of her youth, she feels her final hour is at hand and commends her children to God's care, praying that He will protect them far from her and make them worthy of their father. Then she thinks of her native land, distant Hungary—and here we virtually share Liszt's own fervor as he set these words. Throngs of poor from far and wide draw near to sing her praises and receive their last alms from her hands. Her farewell from the world is easy: "Das ist nicht Erdennacht! Ein seliges Gefühl durchströmt die Brust, als wär' ich neu erwacht. Die Erdenbürde weicht, es heben weh'nde Schwingen leicht mich hoch empor." (This is no earthly night! A blessed feeling courses through my breast, as if I were newly awakened. Earth's burdens fall away, gentle wings lift me on high.). Gently she falls asleep, transfigured, as the weeping needy pray.

The sixth and final scene depicts Elisabeth's apotheosis. Emperor Frederick II has arrived to pay homage to her memory; the mighty ones of the kingdom have gathered, to festive but solemn music. "Die Räuber ihrer Habe sind verfallen des Himmels Strafe und des Reiches Acht" (Those who have stolen her possessions have been punished by Heaven and banned from the kingdom), announces the monarch, "indessen sie nach ihrer Leiden Nacht Fürbitterin uns ward im ew'gen Licht" (while she, after her night of suffering, interceded for us with the eternal light). The work ends with Latin chorales sung by the Hungarian and German clergy and by powerful choruses.

Christus

Original Title: Christus
Original Language: Latin
Text: From the Bible and the Latin liturgy.
Date of Writing: 1862–1866
First Performance: After partial performances (at the end of 1866 and in 1867 in Rome, in 1871 in Vienna), *Christus* was heard for the first time in its complete form on May 29, 1873, in the Herder Church in Weimar, conducted by the composer. On November 9 of the same year Hans Richter conducted a performance in Budapest.
Form: Oratorio for six soloists, chorus (subdivided into as many as eight parts), and orchestra; in three main sections with a total of 14 musical numbers:
1. Christmas oratorio
2. After Epiphany
3. Passion and Resurrection

History of the Work: In 1853, Liszt conceived the idea of composing a sacred oratorio in collaboration with the poet of revolution, Georg Herwegh. In those years Herwegh was in close contact with Liszt and Wagner; the three often met in Switzerland, where Wagner was in political exile. At the time, however, nothing came of the plan. The wish to compose a religious oratorio apparently occurred to Liszt a second time when he conducted Berlioz's *L'enfance du Christ* in Aachen, in 1857. He asked his companion, Caroline von Sayn-Wittgenstein, to sketch out such a work, and a friend, the young composer Peter Cornelius, who had a fine flair for poetry, was to write the verses. But once again Liszt's plans came to naught. It was not until 1862 that he finally undertook its composition. He had completed *Die Legende der heiligen Elisabeth*, his first oratorio, and felt himself sufficiently seasoned to take on the highest task, that of a work dealing with the life, miracles, death, and resurrection of Christ.

Countless composers have considered the idea. All have assumed from the outset that a dramatic representation, in which Jesus appeared on the stage, was out of the question, even though many an opera had come close to doing so. In his youth, Wagner had planned a music drama entitled *Jesus von Nazareth*, in which Jesus was to have had a prominent role, less as the redeemer, it seems, than a social revolutionary. He dropped the idea.

While the suffering and salvation of Christ has often been described in orchestral pieces, the oratorio proved to be a better medium from its beginning, or certainly from the time of Handel's *Messiah*. It was only natural that Liszt, who was a religious mystic and felt Jesus as a living presence, would compose such a work.

Shortly after the completion of *Die Heilige Elisabeth* he suffered a severe blow: his daughter Blandine, still young and happily married, was carried off by death. She had been very attached to her father, perhaps more than Cosima, and had always idealized him. She was the second of Liszt's children to die—he had earlier lost a son, Daniel. Her death quite likely was the immediate impulse which set him to work on the *Christus* oratorio.

The bulk of the music was composed in Rome to which he now invariably returned after long concert journeys. From October 18, 1864, he had lived in a plain cell in the monastery Madonna del Rosario, where, far from the hustle and bustle of the world and any social engagements, he devoted himself entirely to composition. It was here that he prepared himself for the clerical orders. Step by step, in the months that followed, he took the minor vows to become an abbé which obligated him to hear Mass and read the Breviary daily. These vows, did not, however, confer the status of active priesthood but rather, as we read in Paula Rehberg's biography, that of a secular cleric.

Into the growing score of the *Christus*—sections of which had occasionally been performed in Rome by musician friends—Liszt inserted short choral works that he had written at various times, such as *Les Béatitudes*, based on a text from the Gospel of *St. Matthew*, and a *Pater noster*. Liszt made no effort to have it performed in its entirety. "It is of absolutely no concern to me when and where it is performed. Composing is an artistic necessity for me; I am completely satisfied to have written it," he wrote in a letter to Carl Gille dated October 23, 1866. A month later, he wrote to Agnes Street, "*Christus* can wait . . . perhaps until after my death." In 1867, the first section was performed in Rome as a "Christmas Oratorio" to celebrate the 1800th anniversary of the martyrdom of Peter. The entire work was performed for the first time in the Protestant Stadtkirche in Weimar on May 29, 1873, with Liszt conducting. Among many prominent guests, Wagner and his wife Cosima, who had by then settled in Bayreuth and were preparing for the first music festival in their own theater, were probably the most important. Shortly before, the two great musicians had settled their quarrel and taken up their former close friendship and mutual admiration. In November of that year, a Liszt festival was presented in Pest, the high points of which were a tribute by Liszt to Hungary ("I am yours—my talent belongs to you—I belong to Hungary as long as I live!") and a magnificent performance of *Christus* directed by the great conductor Hans Richter. The road to triumph for Liszt's perhaps greatest work had begun.

Discussion of the Work: The theme for the oratorio comes from a letter by the Apostle Paul to the *Ephesians* (4:15): "Veritatem autem facientes in caritate, crescamus in illo per omnia qui est caput: Christus" (We would rather hold to truth in love, in all things grow toward him who is the head: Christ).

The first section, the "Christmas Oratorio," begins most delicately, in unison at first. Here Liszt quotes, almost as a Leitmotif, the old Gregorian melody for the words of Isaiah, "Rorate coeli de super et nubes pluant justum: aperiatur terra et germinet Salvatorem" (Let the heavens open and rain fall upon the righteous; and let the earth open up and bear the Savior). It is an extended, deeply meaningful orchestral piece. A mood of gentle transfiguration lies over the music, which seems to descend from Heaven. A close relationship to Wagner's prelude to *Parsifal*, written later, cannot be denied; both works treat the subject of Redemption (Example 1), albeit in different ways. The mood of transfiguration passes to one more earthly; a lovely, bucolic pastorale follows, in the rocking twelve-eight meter usual for such shepherds' songs. Musical evocations of Hungary are clearly discernible (Example 2).

Example 1 Andante sostenuto

Example 2

Then the music becomes chorale-like; as if from afar, with gentle quotations from the "Rorate coeli" theme, the wondrous mood that has taken the listener to another world leads into the second section: "Pastorale and the Angel's Annunciation." The solo soprano sings an unaccompanied Gregorian melody as both narrator and herald: she announces the arrival of the Savior. "Angelus Domini ad pastores ait: Annuntio vobis gaudium magnum." (The angel of the Lord spoke to the shepherds: I bring you tidings of great joy.). Against the sparest of orchestral backdrops, the female voices of the chorus intone a gradually rising Hallelujah. The song of praise swells; with the words "Gloria in excelsis" the tenor enters, then the mixed chorus (the heavenly host), leading the movement to a hallelujah chorale, to which the orchestra adds a delicate, heartfelt conclusion.

The following "Stabat mater" (No. 3) is a choral movement composed in stanzas, a very simple, pious chorale. After long a cappella passages it is lightly underscored by the orchestra. No. 4 is entitled "The Shepherds at the Manger" and carries on the rustic scene of Christ's birth among shepherds and angels with a very long, moving orchestral piece. At one place, where the music seems to become more worldly, Liszt wrote in the score, again like a motto, the words of *Matthew* (2:11), "Apertis thesauris suis, obtulerunt magi Domino aurum, thus et myrrham" (The wisemen opened their treasures and gave the Lord gold, incense, and myrrh). The mood again fades away in a long orchestral postlude. By the end of this first section the fundamental structure of the work is clear: the chorus and the orchestra balance each other in a way seldom found in oratorios. The orchestra performs a truly symphonic function and is an equal partner with the chorus. The choral sections are in the most varied styles, from Medieval to Romantic. Liszt's opponents—and he, like all great men, had his share—held this against him, but posterity has recognized this quality as being one of the principal virtues of the work.

The second section, "After Epiphany," begins with the "Beatitudes," introduced by the orchestra again with the "Rorate coeli" melody. The voice of the baritone now represents Christ, singing "Beati pauperes spiritu quoniam ipsorum est regnum coelorum. . . ." (Blessed are the simple in spirit, for theirs is the kingdom of Heaven). Again and again, the voice of Jesus enumerates the "blessed ones," those who will share Paradise with Him, while the mixed chorus repeats or supplements his words. Rather far along, the orchestra enters, its simple harmonies providing a scarcely noticeable foundation; only when the chorus bursts out joyfully, singing of the magnificence of "regnum coelorum" (the kingdom of Heaven), does the orchestra come to the fore momentarily.

The next number, "Pater noster" (Our Father) (No. 7), was first composed as an independent piece and only later incorporated into the *Christus* Oratorio. It is sometimes omitted from performances, just as is the "Pastorale" of the first section and the "Stabat mater dolorosa" of the third. The "Pater noster" is a choral movement without soloists, with only light accompaniment by the orchestra.

No. 8 is called "The Founding of the Church." Here, the male chorus—does this unwittingly (or perhaps not) point to the male dominance of the Catholic Church?—proclaims, "Tu es Petrus et super hanc petram aedificabo ecclesiam meam et portae inferi non praevalebunt" (You are Peter, and upon this rock will I build my church, and the gates of Hell shall not prevail against it), from the Gospel of *St. Matthew*, 16:18. A verse from the Gospel of *St. John* follows (21:15) sung by the chorus: "Simon Joannis, diliges me? Pasce agnos meos! Pasce oves meos!" (Simon John, do you love me? Graze my lambs! Graze my sheep!) Liszt emphasizes the words addressed to Peter with unshakable firmness at the beginning and end of the movement, making them stand out from the lyrical middle section. He has created tender, loving music for the words "amas me, diliges me" (do you love me?) and the scene of peaceful pastures. No. 9, entitled "The Miracle," begins once more with a Latin motto: "Et ecce motus magnus factus est in mari, ita ut navicula operietur fluctibus" (A great storm arose on the lake and the boat was awash with waves). The storm is then depicted by the orchestra in realistic tone painting. Above a point where the music suddenly becomes calm, Liszt wrote, as if wanting to correlate it with the Biblical narrative: "Ipse vero dormiebat" (But He was asleep). Once more the orchestra rises in a veritable symphony of storm and sea until the male chorus of the Disciples, now terrified, awakens Jesus: "Domine, salva nos" (Lord, save us). Christ turns to them calmly and says, "Quid timidi estis, modici fidei!" (How fearful you are, you of little faith!)

In an andante interlude, the orchestra describes how, upon Christ's entreaty, the sea calms, and the astonished Disciples sing of the miracle, "Et facta est tranquilitas magna" (And a great stillness came upon it). The movement continues in the orchestra, calmly and comfortingly, to its closing in C-sharp major, a key very seldom used in those days, one of gentle transfiguration. The second section ends with "Entry into Jerusalem" (No. 10). Once again extensive tone painting in the orchestra introduces the scene: We can almost see the city streets thronged with people, feel their mounting excitement as they greet Christ with rejoicing and exultation, singing "Hosanna qui venit in nomine Domini" (Hosanna, blessed is he who comes in the name of the Lord). Now, as the tempo becomes calmer, the solo mezzosoprano, aided by the chorus, intones "Benedictus," but then for long passages only reinforces the soprano melody in the chorus. What did Liszt have in mind when he gave the soloists—except for the baritone, the voice of Jesus—relatively unimportant roles? The second section closes with choruses of rejoicing. No. 11, the beginning of the third section, is entitled "Tristis est anima mea" (My soul grieves). Jesus, the solo baritone, sings these words, while the orchestra pauses intermittently, only to resume after his last words with a long, intense interlude. The strongly modulating, sometimes fully instrumented and passionate section leads back to the almost unaccompanied voice of Jesus, who calls upon his Father: "Pater, si possibile est, transeat a me calix iste." (Father, let this cup pass from me). The pleading in his voice reaches a dramatic outburst on high notes: "sed quod tu . . ." (but Thy will be done). Here we have Liszt's personal confession of faith, expressing the despair he seldom expressed, the desolation of humankind in this earthly existence, which even he, one of the most fortunate of men, experienced (Example 3).

The "Stabat mater dolorosa" (No. 12) which follows, is often omitted to shorten performance time. It is a fully developed cantata for five soloists (soprano, mezzosoprano, alto, tenor, and bass) and chorus. They sing of the crucifixion of Christ and the moving lament of His mother. The "Easter Hymn" (No. 13) follows: "O filii et filiae" (O children of men); the joyous message of the resurrection is sung by a chorus of women's voices with only soft, sensitive support in the orchestra. The last piece (No. 14, "Resurrexit") is one of the most powerful of the entire work. Here the soloists come brilliantly into their own, and Liszt shows himself a musician well versed in poly-

Example 3

phony. There is a choral fugue with an eight-bar theme, "Christus vincit, Christus regnat." (Christ is victorious, Christ reigns) and a fugue for the four soloists (not classical in its tonality): "Christus vincit," also with an eight-bar theme and sustained by the chorus. After the long, radiant repetition of "Hosanna," Liszt inserts a tense pause. With great impact the orchestra in full vigor returns to the main theme, the "Rorate coeli," no longer Gregorian but Romantic, splendidly proclaiming "Amen, amen!"

The Masses

Even though Liszt's Masses remain under-appreciated in both church and concert circles, and have been regrettably neglected by historians, I include two here: the *Missa solemnis* ("Graner Festmesse") and the *Hungarian Coronation Mass*.

Liszt composed the *Missa solemnis* for the dedication of the huge basilica of Gran (Esztergom, in Hungarian), impressively set on the banks of the Danube and considered to be that country's greatest national shrine. Liszt was asked by a friend, acting for the Hungarian Cardinal Primate, to compose this work, which he longed with his whole heart to do. On May 2, 1855, he wrote to Wagner in Zürich, "The last few weeks I have been completely taken up with my Mass, and yesterday I finished it. I do not know how it will sound but can say that I did more praying than composing"—a sentence that must have thoroughly astonished his friend.

Scarcely finished, the work met with unsuspected difficulties. There must have been intrigues against the author and the work; letters were exchanged between the musician and the Cardinal, which never exceeded the bounds of good manners but reveal that Liszt, at least, was very upset when he wrote them. Not until April 24, 1856, did everything finally seem to be arranged, but shortly thereafter the Church's affirmative decision was withdrawn. Liszt intervened heatedly.

Permission was finally granted on July 27, 1856, shortly before the church was to be consecrated. On August 31 the work was performed at the magnificent inauguration celebration attended by Emperor Franz Joseph I. A few years later he bestowed upon Liszt one of the Empire's highest distinctions, the Order of the Iron Crown, which carried with it patents of nobility and knighthood in perpetuity. The "Graner Festmesse" soon became widely known, but critics were never silenced; their objections were basically liturgical, not musical.

Unexpected difficulties also beset the performance of the *Hungarian Coronation Mass*, composed 12 years later. The coronation of Emperor Franz Joseph I and his wife, Elisabeth ("Sissy") as king and queen of Hungary had been set for May 9, 1867, in Budapest. A solemn Mass was to accompany the religious ceremony. However, the church of St. Matthew in the Hungarian capital was not large enough to contain the great musical forces called for. Liszt had to be satisfied with a small orchestra, a male chorus composed of four each of tenors and basses, and 10 choir boys as a substitute for the female voices. They all came from Vienna and were directed by the assistant Kapellmeister there, Gottfried Preyer. The court had stipulated that on such a solemn occasion

"Court etiquette" was to be observed. As a consequence no Hungarian musician would be allowed to conduct the festival Mass nor compose it. After lengthy skirmishing at least the second of the two conditions was dropped, but the final decision to perform a Mass by Liszt was not made until May 1. Luckily, he had begun the composition a year before in hopes of obtaining the commission.

Then followed a second insult: Liszt was not invited to the ceremonies. But he secretly joined the musicians and at the first performance of his Mass was at least able to sit in the choir loft. Incidentally, he had never thought it a good composition, as we learn from a letter he wrote on August 9, 1868, to Princess Caroline von Sayn-Wittgenstein:

> From a musical point of view the work is fairly weak. The necessity imposed upon me of providing as short a musical piece as possible, so as not to lengthen an already very long coronation ceremony, prohibited the use of thematic development, episodes, interludes, and details normally used by great masters in great works. Nevertheless, I think that within these narrow limits the Coronation Mass is rather more concentrated than jammed together, and that in it the two basic elements, Hungarian nationalism and Catholic religious faith, assert themselves and act in harmony from the beginning to the end....

Lastly, Liszt's *Requiem* should be mentioned. He composed it for the 20th anniversary of the death of his friend Chopin. It calls for two tenor and two bass soloists, four-part male chorus, and organ. He presented it in Lemberg, a border city of the old Kingdom of the Danube (today, Lwow in the Soviet Union), noted for its music-loving citizenry composed of Germans, Jews, Poles, and Russians.

The music played at Liszt's funeral 18 years later was composed by someone else. This irony was in a certain sense typical for Liszt, a man who had achieved the greatest international fame and almost legendary popularity as a virtuoso, but who had never "pushed himself" as a composer. Although the music was not his own, it was that of a friend, one could even say a "relation": Bruckner improvised on themes from Wagner's *Parsifal* on the organ.

Guillaume de Machaut   ca. 1300–1377?

Only a few years ago, inclusion of Guillaume de Machaut (or Machault) in a book devoted to oratorios would have had only academic value; save for a few experts, no one knew anything about this great 14th-century master, who—together with Philippe de Vitry—has been called the founder of the French Ars Nova. However, in recent years many Medieval works have been rediscovered and music societies formed to perform "ancient music" in an authentic way, thus pushing the limits of our musical repertory back from the Baroque era some 300 years.

Guillaume was probably born around 1300 in the village of Machaut in the Ardennes. His career followed that customary for a cleric, but one which brought him fame, honor, and considerable wordly wealth. He served King John of Bohemia as well as Charles V of France, for whose coronation he probably composed the *Messe de Nostre Dame*, which appears to be the first complete setting of the Ordinarium Missae undertaken by a single composer. The slightly older *Messe de Tournai* seems to be a composite of works by various composers. The Mass by Machaut presents not only the five parts of the Ordinarium Missae, which became the customary musical components of the Mass, but added at the conclusion an "Ite missa est," the words with which the Priest dismisses the faithful after the Mass: Go home, the Mass is over.

Machaut's style is simple, lapidary. Often it is *punctus contra punctum*, note against note, in the style of music around the year 1000, the time when polyphony and counterpoint first made their appearance. Thus we hear archaic sounds, music as if from another, long-forgotten world. We sense not only the strength and purity of belief, but also the struggle to find the means of musical expression, in a world in which so much was yet to be discovered.

Frank Martin   1890–1974

Frank Martin, of western Switzerland, was born on September 15, 1890, in Geneva. He studied in his native city, then in Zürich, Rome, and Paris, and thereafter worked for many years with Jaques Dalcroze, who made a great contribution in our time with his revival and teaching of rhythm. Martin held several positions before retiring in 1946 to the little Dutch town of Naarden, where he was able to compose an unusual number of valuable works and where he died on November 21, 1974. He was one of the most important composers of the 20th century. There is nothing forced or artificial in his music. Its modernity is natural and genuine, has nothing to do with revolution, and is spiritually in tune with the turbulant epoch it was his fate to live in. While tonality is stretched to its limits it is never in question; feeling retains a central role set within a crystal-clear understanding of form. Of all the genres in which he worked, the oratorio, in the most varied forms, was probably the most important. In 1922 he wrote a Mass for male chorus; in 1941, *Le Vin herbé* won him his first recognition, which increased following World War II. After a few works better described as vocal pieces with orchestra (*Die Weise von Liebe und Tod des Cornets Christoph Rilke, Monologe aus* Jedermann), *In Terra Pax* and *Golgotha*, clearly oratorios, appeared. To them he added later *Le Mystère de la Nativité, Pilate*, a *Requiem* (1972), and the chamber cantata *Et la vie l'emporta*. Despite not inconsiderable difficulties of performance, several have already entered the permanent repertory of large concert organizations, whereas *Le vin herbé* has found its way to the stage, a form of performance for which it was not originally intended, but one that is thoroughly defensible. Many of these works, as well as others, were composed in his retirement. He worked only seven years, from 1950 to 1957, as professor at the State Academy of Music in Cologne; the last 17 years of his life were devoted to composing.

In Terra Pax

This "Oratorio breve," first performed in Geneva in 1945 by Ernest Ansermet and the Orchestre de la Suisse Romande, was composed in the last years of World War II. Though, living in Switzerland, Martin was spared the ravages of the war, he was nevertheless greatly moved by its cruelty. He set passages from *Revelations of St. John* in verse to form the basis of a work for five solo voices (soprano, alto, tenor, baritone, and bass), two four-part choruses, and large orchestra. The orchestra is composed of two flutes (with piccolo), two oboes (with English horn), two clarinets (with bass clarinet), two bassoons, four horns, two trumpets, three trombones, tuba, timpani, percussion, celeste, two pianos, and the usual strings. The term "short" oratorio is only relative, for the composer noted that the work takes about 45 minutes to perform. Martin follows the form of the "classical" oratorio, in which narrative passages reporting events alternate with passages describing experiences and spontaneous impressions.

The work begins with a long description by the solo baritone, who sings the role of the Evangelist—the old Italian Testo—with words from the *Apocalypse*: "Lorsque l'agneau rompit...." (When the Lamb broke the first seal, I looked up and saw a white horse appear. The figure on its back carried a bow, a crown was given to him, and he took off like a hero, to conquer.) The voice parts steer a middle path between pure declamatory recitative and expressive melodic intonation. The lamb breaks the second seal of the secret book, whereupon a red, a black, and a pale horse appear, their riders proclaiming war, Hell, famine, and plague. The sun grows dim, the moon turns the color of blood, the stars fall from the sky: "Le grand jour de la colère est venu" (The great day of wrath has arrived). The baritone concludes his recitative with "Et qui donc pourrait subsister?" (And who, then, will survive?), after a choral interruption expressing man's fear, almost in a shriek. Then, in three parts (soprano, alto, and tenor) comes the plea, "Mon Dieu, pourquoi m'as-tu abandonné?" (My God, why hast Thou forsaken me?), the words of the crucified Jesus. The chorus sings them in unison, expressive as a litany, while the orchestra plays piercing dissonances in recurring strokes, as in inescapable despair.

Here begins the first large aria, sung by the solo bass: "Malheur au peuple chargé de péchés!" (Woe to those who have sinned!). Violent choral entries in all four parts are interwoven in the largo cantilena of the bass—is this the voice of God? "Je punirai le monde pour sa malice" (I will punish the world for its malice); powerfully, now, the voice stands out and, accompanied by mounting intensity in the orchestra, rises to a climax, first alone and then with the chorus. How clearly the harmonies shine! Their progression may be unorthodox—D, F-sharp, C, E, G-sharp (A-flat), but there is a magnificence in it somewhat like that in Haydn's *Creation* when light breaks through the gloom and chaos. (Here, too, the luminous C major chord appears at the climax [Example 1].

Could this have been a coincidence?)

Example 1

The first part ends with a lengthy vocal passage alternating between soloists and chorus. It establishes B minor as a basic key, but contrary to its several earlier appearances, here there is no complete chord but only the B/F-sharp fifth, without the third. Might it suggest the brighter mood of B major?

The tenor solo opens the second part, accompanied only by a dense tremolo on a single note. The first chorus enters in four parts, the second with only the male voices; they sing a song of repentance, praying for grace and mercy. Then the baritone proclaims, "Mais les ténèbres ne regneront pas toujours" (But darkness will not always reign). A radiant light dawns. The solo soprano continues, telling how the mountains glow where the herald, who has come to announce peace on earth, has trodden. The soprano and the tenor sing antiphonally, welcoming the salvation that is to come. Now there is a joyful chorus, but Martin does not develop it like a chorale but rather has both choruses sing very expressively in unison, antiphonally. This seldom-encountered unison singing of many voices takes on a new, or really, an ancient meaning: that of a group acting in consort, not individually. Even Bach set his chorales for four parts, polyphonically. Martin achieves a great effect with homophony, which then returns to polyphony when the two choral melodies come together toward the conclusion of this number. The second part ends with an unusually tight four-part fugue: "Poussez vers Dieu des cris de joie" (Raise a joyful cry unto the Lord). This Medieval art form, wielded by a master, never fails to have stunning effect (Example 2).

Example 2

A lyrical melody—also unaccompanied and in unison—introduces the third part. The alto soloist sings, "Voici mon serviteur, mon élu" (This is my servant, my chosen one). Once again we are reminded of ancient music: the homophonic melody of the beginning is taken up by the solo alto—it is quite striking in its eighth-measure phrase—and, in all kinds of transformations, also serves as a building block for the rest of this extended number; we are reminded of the passacaglia (or toccata) form. The following text, from the Beatitudes, is sung by the solo tenor, "Heureux les affligés car ils seront consolés" (Blessed are those that suffer, for they shall be comforted), accompanied by only a few sustained chords.

Then the choruses pray the Our Father: "Notre Père qui es aux Cieux" (Our Father who art in Heaven). Here, Martin has borrowed from speech inflection: the words sound as if they were spoken but have the intensity of a song; it hovers around one main note—the central B-flat—and the few steps taken by the melodic line sound precisely like a prayer (Example 3).

Example 3

The accompanying chords repeat one harmonic sequence over and over, giving the listener the impression of a congregation at prayer; it is as if one were standing in the half light of a cathedral, hearing the murmuring of hundreds of people on their knees. Once again, by having the large chorus sing in unison, Martin has achieved a most impressive piece.

With the fourth section of the work we return to the *Apocalypse*. The baritone reports: "Puis je vis un nouveau ciel" (Then I saw a new Heaven). Destruction and Judgment Day have thundered by, and the vision of a new life on earth has been born: "Voici le tabernacle de Dieu . . ." (Here is God's tabernacle . . . now they will be His people, and God Himself will be with them). In a long crescendo the music reaches a peak of intensity; the solo bass has replaced the baritone as the narrative becomes a radiant prophecy. In a mighty gathering of forces, the choruses and soloists acknowledge Almighty God: "Saint! Saint!" (Holy! Holy!) rings out ever more powerfully like a rousing hymn, and finally all the voices flow together to conclude on a single D. The orchestra, too, after strongly polytonal changes, now converges on a D major chord—the bright, jubilant, victorious key of Johann Sebastian Bach and his great Christian messages.

At the end of Martin's handwritten score is the date: August to October, 1944. Perhaps we must imagine ourselves back in that time if we are to fully appreciate this cry for peace: the invasion of the "Fortress Europe" had already taken place, and the bloody struggle, one whose cruelty had no equal in human history, was nearing its end. Frank Martin's *In Terra Pax* will forever be associated with that period.

Golgotha

Soon after *In Terra Pax* was completed, Martin began work on a new oratorio that was to occupy him for more than three years. He began it in Geneva in 1945 and finished it at Naarden, his final residence in the Netherlands: "June 8, 1948, Amsterdam" is noted on the score. The work was first performed in 1949 in Geneva by the Orchestre de la Suisse Romande conducted by Samuel Baud-Bovy.

The score calls for two flutes (one piccolo), two oboes (one oboe d'amore ad libitum and an English horn), two clarinets, two bassoons, four horns, two trumpets, three trombones, timpani, percussion, organ, piano, and strings. The duration of the work is 85 minutes, divided into 45 for the first section and 40 for the second. The chorus is divided into as many as eight parts (two each in each register). The solo roles for soprano, alto, tenor, baritone, and bass repeat the arrangement that had worked quite well in the earlier work.

The text was compiled by the composer from the Gospels and the writings of St. Augustine. The content is indicated by the title: it is a Passion—a description of the crucifixion and death of Christ.

The first piece was taken from the *Confessions* of St. Augustine. It presents an invocation of God and an image of Jesus, sacrificed by his Father for love of mankind. The actual story begins in the second section, with the solo bass singing the role of the Evangelist: "Comme Jesus cheminait approchant de Jérusalem" (As Jesus made his way toward Jerusalem). The chorus now becomes the crowd of people who greet Jesus on his entry into the holy city with joyful cries of "Hosanna!" They strew his path with greenery and wave palm fronds in his honor, singing "Béni soit le roi" (Praises to the king who comes in the name of the Lord). Joyfully the soloists join in the greeting and welcome the kingdom that is at hand: "Gloria in excelsis!" The texts are from the gospels of *St. Matthew* (21:2–9) and *St. Mark* (11:8–10).

A few brief words by the tenor, who now takes up the role of the Evangelist, prepare the way for Jesus' address, sung by the solo bass. It is calm, clear, and plainly spoken, for it is recitativelike in style and underscored by only a few long, quiet chords in the orchestra. Mysteriously now, and as from afar—first in unison and then in open fifths—the people hear a call from Heaven, and Jesus explains that this is a sign to the world that it will now be judged: "Et pour moi, quand j'aurai été élevé de la terre . . ." (And as for me, when I have been raised from this earth . . .) A slow, solemn chorus replies, a portent of the coming miracle, singing a text from the *Meditations* of St. Augustine, VII.

The following piece is entitled "The Disputation in the Temple" again after Augustine, Chapter 41. Jesus' voice becomes heated as he begins a terrible accusation of the scribes and the pharisees, hypocrites who do not practice what they preach. "Jérusalem, toi qui tues les prophètes" (Jérusalem, killer of prophets, who stones those sent to you): With these words, so often set to music, Jesus' speech in the temple reaches its climax.

It is not the people who answer, nor those who have been attacked, as would be expected in an opera; rather, the voice of the solo soprano rises softly, referring to Jesus' prophecy that he will soon disappear from the eyes of men until that day when all will honor him: "Quand serai-je assez heureuse pour voir ce jour béni?" (When will I be fortunate enough to see that blessed day?) This female voice, so fervent and sincere, speaks for the people; she expresses with St. Augustine's words the faith of all those in the temple when Jesus appears.

"The Last Supper" follows. The tenor sings the role of the Evangelist, combining the words of Jesus from the Gospels of *St. John* (23:1–2 and 21–30) and *St. Luke* (22:19–20 and 39), in which we experience the prelude to Judas' betrayal and the sharing of bread and wine. The next part (No. 5) is called "Gethsemane." Here, the role of the Narrator is doubled by the alto; the words are repeatedly interpolated, bringing that last evening with the Disciples to life. Three times Jesus finds them asleep and warns them. He knows his last hour is at hand and prays, "Let this cup pass from me, but not as I will but Thy will be done!"

Judas' betrayal is reported by the Narrator, now the solo bass. The seizure of Jesus is also only described; the solo alto and solo tenor have the last words: "Alors les disciples l'abandonnèrent et s'enfuirent" (Then the Disciples abandoned him and fled), as in the versions of *St. Mark* (14:32–43, 45–46, 48–50) and *St. Luke* (22:53). The first section closes with a large ensemble of soloists with chorus. St. Augustine's words (*Meditations* V) on the Savior, who is an innocent man victimized, march by in a broad, polyphonic movement.

At this point, a completion date in Martin's original score is noted: January 5, 1946. The first part was clearly finished in a much shorter period of time than the second. The second section begins with a bassoon solo against a soft background of strings. The lamenting voice of the solo alto enters and the chorus answers, almost in a murmur, with the beautiful words of the Psalm, "I lift up mine eyes unto the hills. . . ." Now the alto and the chorus, here divided into eight parts, sing a complex piece of great intensity based on Augustine, *Meditations* XLI.

No. 7 is called "Jesus before the High Priest." Martin again draws a clear distinction between oratorio and opera; as dramatic as this scene is musically, it remains untheatrical. The male chorus assumes the role of Narrator, describing the course of the accusations against Jesus. Only the High Priest's question to Jesus is given to a soloist—the bass: "Ne réponds-tu rien?" (Do you have nothing to say to those who testify against you?) As the scene develops we experience the first dramatic encounter: the bass, as the Priest, entreats Jesus to say if he is the Son of God, the promised Savior. Then Jesus speaks for the first time: "Tu l'as dit: je le suis." (You have said it; I am he.) Now he announces his destiny: he will soon ascend into Heaven and sit on the right hand of the Almighty.

The music now becomes greatly agitated. The solo tenor describes how the High Priest tore his garments, and the bass repeats his indictment and pronounces the verdict. The four-part male chorus supports him in his savage accusation, and then reviles Jesus and spits upon him. Martin enlarges this scene until it becomes an actual tribunal: committed to the defense, the female chorus counters the furious male voices, and the opposing positions clash mightily. Only slowly does the excitement of the ensemble (sometimes in 12 parts) abate. Feelings of remorse overcome the people. This powerful scene ends in reconciliation, on the text of Augustine, *Meditations* VII.

"Jesus before Pilate" is the title of the next scene. The bass is once again the Narrator, while the tenor sings the words of Pilate as he addresses the crowd that brings Jesus to him. The people demand that Pilate judge him because their law forbids the death penalty. The exchange between Pilate and Jesus, between the solo bass and solo tenor, is fit material for an opera.

In the following scene, the people angrily reject Pilate's counsel to set Jesus free to honor the Passover festival and demand instead the freeing of the murderer Barrabas. All of this is portrayed with great realism—no oratorio composer has ever passed up this splendid opportunity. The sense of realism continues as the choruses, in eight parts, demand that the captive be crucified, upon which soldiers mock him by placing a crown of thorns upon his head and clothing him in a purple garment.

The scene ends in a narrative drawn from the Gospel of *St. John* 18:28–31 and 33–40; and 19:1–7 and 15–16. The solo bass reports that Pilate has given way to the demands of the people: "C'était la veille du Sabbat de Paques, environ la sixième heure" (It was the eve of Passover, around the sixth hour). The conclusion on Golgotha is in two scenes. The chorus, without sopranos, becomes the Narrator. Jesus interjects only his final few words into the description: "Femme, voilà ton fils!" (Woman, behold your son!), "Voilà ta mère! (Behold your mother!), "J'ai soif!" (I am thirsty), "Tout est accompli!" (It is over!), as found in the Gospel of *St. John* (19:17–19, 23–30). Then, exactly as Bach had done, a contemplative tenor aria is inserted, based on the words of St. Augustine, *Meditations* VI: "O mon Seigneur et mon Dieu...." (O my Lord and God....).

The final chorus is nothing less than a masterpiece of modern vocal music. It is in free tonality. Sometimes the harshest dissonances are heard, but the progression of each separate voice is logical. "O mort, où est ton aiguillon?" (Death, where is thy sting?) begins the hymn of consolation, words intoned over and again by the faithful for almost 2,000 years, for they announce the conquest of death and Hell by hope and eternal life. In a lengthy movement, the female voices stand alone against the wrath of the chorus; then a short orchestral interlude leads to the chorale-like entry of many solo voices in unison, a device Martin uses repeatedly and most effectively. The conclusion, again in D major, as in *In Terra Pax*, is both a hymn and a chorale, triumph and veneration: "Lumière essentielle et souveraine!" (Essential, sovereign light!) on the text "Exsultet" (office of Holy Saturday) and *Meditations* of St. Augustine, XV and XVIII.

Pseaumes (The Geneva Psalms)

When Frank Martin was awarded an honorary doctorate by the University of Geneva, coincidentally with its 400th anniversary, he obliged with a composition. It is a little over 20 minutes in length and calls for mixed four-part chorus, unison children's chorus, organ, and orchestra (four oboes, of which two play English horn; two bassoons; two trumpets; three trombones; timpani; cymbals; and the usual strings, in five parts).

The Psalms used are Nos. 127 (On a beau sa maison bâtir—Except the Lord build the house), 8 (O notre Dieu et Seigneur aimable—O Lord our God), 38 (Las! En ta fureur aigue—Rebuke me not in Thy wrath), 57 (Aye pitié de moi—Have pity on me), 55 and 51 (Exauce, ô mon Dieu—Grant me, O Lord), and 68 (Que Dieu se montre seulement—Let God arise) as set in French by Clément Marot and Théodor de Bèze.

The melodies used derive from the time of the founding of the University and were composed by Loys Bourgeois (1510–1572) and Matthieu Greiter (?–1550). The piece is actually a modernization of a work composed in 1565 by the renowned French church master Claude Goudimel. It is a beautiful, grateful evocation of an early age, easier and simpler to perform than Martin's works previously discussed.

Bohuslav Martinu 1890–1959

Martinu was born on December 8, 1890, in Policka, in Bohemia. Only one work of this extremely inspired but difficult-to-classify Czech composer calls for mention in this book: *The Epic of Gilgamesh*, composed in 1957. It is one of the composer's lesser works for his best composition is in the area of music theater and symphony. In these genres much of his music has entered the standard repertory, where it is likely to remain for some years. It is fresh, uncontrived, and often happily reminiscent of its origin in the most music-saturated soil of Europe. His career was checkered: he wandered through many countries, sometimes out of choice, sometimes because he was homeless. After playing for 10 years in an orchestra in Prague he went to Paris in 1923, where he gravitated to the group of composers then working there: Milhaud, Honegger, Ravel, Roussel. He quickly made a name for himself, but when war broke out in 1940 he fled to the United States. He taught at Princeton from 1948–1951. In 1957, with support from the Swiss patron of the arts Paul Sacher, he settled in Liestal, near Basel, where he died on August 28, 1959.

The *Gilgamesh Epic* is one of the oldest poems known to man. In it, the Babylonians described a legendary king of the city of Urk, by the name of Gilgamesh, and his exploits. Several versions have been preserved, all of which tell of his mythic origins, his fabulous deeds and his close friendship with Engidu, or Enkidu, a creature half man, half bull. Was Gilgamesh a man or a demi-god? One of the versions preserved on clay tells of a great flood to which some scholars attribute the origin of the Biblical flood.

The epic is permeated with the anxious question that from the very first has preoccupied mankind more than any other: the question of death. A man who has been saved from the flood, somewhat like Noah in the Bible, shows Gilgamesh the path to immortality. But this "superman"— there is an alabaster statue of him almost 15 feet high in the Louvre; he holds a lion to his chest as if it were a lapdog—forfeits this path, suited only for the gods.

Almost none of the material in this heroic tale is used by Martinu. Moreover, the text never really comes to life and hardly touches the listener. There are a few very effective passages, but most of it is made up of long stretches of fast recitative on specific pitches and attains lyrical verve only in solo passages for soprano, tenor, or bass.

The date of composition, 1957, as well as the dedication inscribed in the score—to Maja Sacher, wife of Paul Sacher—leads me to believe that this is perhaps a "thank you" for help offered to the ailing composer, which spared him material concerns at the end of his life.

Johann Mattheson 1681–1764

With the renewed interest in the Baroque, music by many contemporaries of Bach and Handel is again being heard. Among the most important German musical figures of that time was Johann Mattheson. He was born on September 28, 1681, in Hamburg, and died there on April 17, 1764; he never left the city except to travel. He was a singer, conductor, composer, chronicler, and clever theoretician, all in one.

Of concern here are 24 oratorios and cantatas: a Passion, to a text by Brockes, who also wrote librettos for Handel; and a Mass. Hermann Kretzschmar commented on Mattheson's oratorios, in his *Guide to the Concert Hall*:

> *Der reformierende Johannes* (written for the 200th anniversary of the Reformation, on October 31, 1717), the most important of Mattheson's sacred oratorios, begins with conversations between a "Lutheran man" and various allegorical figures which lead to observations on the meaning of the Reformation. The Lutheran congregation joins in, singing a chorale. The assertion, voiced by some, that Luther was a *Johannes redivivus*, provides the occasion to move on to John the Baptist and the Messiah, whose figures suddenly appear before us right in the middle of things, as if from a magic mirror, and are led from image to image by the explanatory words of the "Lutheran." *Der siegende Gideon*, with which Prince Eugene's victory at Belgrade was celebrated on September 26, 1717, begins with a splendid trumpet symphony. Then a Herald appears singing "Victoria," followed by "Germania" singing the aria "Welcome Sound," and finally a joyful chorus, about which Mattheson goes out of his way to observe that he has artfully used four themes.

Felix Mendelssohn 1809–1847

If one is looking for the very picture of a man of many talents, one graced with genius, with a well-rounded education, highly cultivated in the Classical sense, one with a cheerful, noble, and sunny disposition in spite of Romantic sensibilities, one could hardly find a better example than Felix Mendelssohn. The expression "darling of the gods" suits him perfectly, not only because he lived as a happy man and one who made others happy, but also because he died an early death, the fate of such chosen ones. Darling of which god? The question is completely without meaning in the case of Mendelssohn. He was born to a Jewish family; his grandfather Moses Mendelssohn was one of the leading philosophers of his time. His father, a wealthy Hamburg banker, cosmopolitan and open-minded, converted to Protestantism with his family. Fanny and her brother Felix, inseparable from childhood, grew up as Christians and in the best traditions of the German upper middle class. The family was unquestionably fully integrated into the national culture, to the European ideal of humanism, and that liberalism for which religion was a private matter having nothing at all to do with native land or even race. Mendelssohn composed German folk songs ("Wer hat dich, du schöner Wald; O Täler weit, o Höhen; Es ist bestimmt in Gottes Rat) in the company of Silcher, Schumann, and Brahms, yet could compose thoroughly devout religious music, whose texts he took from both the Old and New Testaments without seeing any conflict in doing so. His *St. Paul* stands side by side with *Elijah*. A quote from Luther is used as a motto for his *Lobgesang*, based on texts from the Psalms. Religion and belief were never a problem for his broad-minded way of thinking and viewing the world. Though secular compositions quantitatively dominate his life's work, his oratorios were specially important. They are not only among the most important of his own works but occupy a prominent place in the history of music.

Felix Mendelssohn—he liked to add to this name that of one of his uncles and called himself Mendelssohn-Bartholdy—was a child prodigy almost on the order of Mozart. He was born on February 3, 1809, in Hamburg, and was a mature pianist and serious composer at the age of 11. The overture to Shakespeare's *A Midsummer Night's Dream*, composed at the age of 17, surely places him in the ranks of genius. When he was 20 he undertook the quite remarkable venture for which alone music must forever honor him: the rediscovery and performance of Bach's *St. Matthew Passion*, which had slumbered undisturbed in the archives for a century. He founded the Leipzig Conservatory, soon to be recognized as an excellent school of music; leading figures including his friend Robert Schumann, whom he helped when he could, were invited to teach there. Mendelssohn was one of the first conductors in the modern sense, a true pioneer in the then emerging orchestral art. He was a much sought after musician throughout Europe, particularly in Germany and England. He travelled frequently, not only to fulfill professional engagements but because he was also passionately devoted to becoming acquainted with other lands and their peoples. On his journeys he not only composed but always carried a sketch book and water colors. His eye was as sharp as his ear and equally open to beauty. The letters he wrote of his experiences—at first to his parents and later to his sister—are full of subtle observations. Following Fanny's sudden death, his own life came swiftly, surprisingly, to an end on November 4, 1847 although he displayed no signs of ailing health. He had been happily married to a beautiful, highly cultivated woman of French Huguenot descent. His unflagging creativity was marked by an unusual lightness of spirit as well as of hand; his composing had never been "work" for him but always a joy, bringing joy to all mankind.

St. Paul

Original Title: Paulus, op. 36
Original Language: German
Text: Passages from the Holy Scriptures, compiled by Julius Schubring.
Date of Writing: Plans and first drafts 1832, composed in 1834, 1835, and the first months of 1836.
First Performance: May 22, 1836, at the Rhenish Music Festival in Düsseldorf.
Form: In two sections with a total of 45 musical numbers.
Scoring: Soprano I, soprano II (or alto), tenor (in the roles of Ananias, Stephen, and Barnabas), bass (in the role of St. Paul); two False Witnesses (two basses); four-part mixed chorus.
Orchestration: Two each of flutes, oboes, clarinets, and bassoons; four horns, two trumpets, three trombones, timpani, organ (ad libitum), and strings. In addition, the original score lists "serpents," medieval wind instruments long out of use in Mendelssohn's day; he probably meant contrabassoon.
History of the Work: Mendelssohn began to compose *St. Paul* in Düsseldorf, where he battled with a very inept, perhaps also unwilling orchestra. (Years later Schumann suffered the same lot, which led to his final mental breakdown.) In 1835, Mendelssohn was appointed conductor of the renowned Leipzig Gewandhaus concerts, ushering in one of the happiest periods of his life.

However, death soon cast its shadow: In November of that year his father, to whom he was very close and for whom he felt profound gratitude, died. Much of Mendelssohn's work seemed to be devoted to proving to his father that he was worthy of all the encouragement and advantages bestowed upon him. Thus, in great anguish, he wrote to the Dessau councillor Julius Schubring, whom he had commissioned to assemble the text for *St. Paul*, "I feel I must now devote all my efforts to finishing *St. Paul* as well as I can, and then imagine that he will hear it."

Unfortunately, Schubring was not the best author to carry out such a task. In spite of a text whose verses were often very shabby as well as dramatically clumsy, Mendelssohn's first oratorio proceeded as fast as the busy young Kapellmeister's life would allow. When it seemed likely that the work could make its first public appearance (in May, 1836, at the Rhenish Music Festival in Düsseldorf), Mendelssohn tried his best to have it ready on time.

The first performance, on May 22, 1836, was an unqualified success. Schumann, always an enthusiastic devotee of his friend's work, spoke of a "modern day jewel." Mendelssohn, however, **as so often, was less satisfied and shortly after the premiere wrote to a friend: "I learned a lot from all this and hope to do better if I compose another oratorio...."**

He was right. Most connoisseurs and music lovers consider *Elijah*, composed 10 years later, a significant improvement over *St. Paul*. Nonetheless, the latter contains a wealth of wonderful music, the four chorales deserving special mention even though they have been severely attacked for reasons of both religion and form. One of the leading critics of oratorio, Hermann Kretzschmar, wrote just a century ago:

> On December 23, 1832, the young composer sent Schubring his own outline for a text that was to be divided into three parts, in the Handelian manner. He also asked that some chorales be inserted and wanted "the arrangement to be just as in the Bach Passions." Undoubtedly Mendelssohn had set his sights high... The influence of the earlier sacred oratorios of Mattheson and other musicians of Hamburg and Northern Germany had obviously not yet waned. Of course, their compositions had only used brief stories, not much more than extended scripture lessons subdivided and expanded to roughly the length of a substantial cantata... Naturally, it had to contain chorales so that the congregation could sing along. But things are different, quite different in the case of an oratorio like *St. Paul*. It is fundamentally unacceptable to the Protestant church since saints are not honored. It will remain a concert oratorio, in which case the presence of chorales, simply in imitation of practices used in religious services, is disrupting.

Today we are more tolerant in these matters.

Discussion of the Work: At the time of its planning only a few years had passed since Mendelssohn had rediscovered Bach's *St. Matthew Passion* and given it a very effective, widely acclaimed performance. *St. Paul* is characterized not only by the inclusion of four Protestant chorales, which ties it as closely as possible to Bach, but one of these chorales ("Wachet auf, ruft uns die Stimme") actually serves as a Leitmotiv for the work, beginning with the overture where it appears in the low winds and strings (Example 1).

Example 1

In a fugal, very melodious middle section in minor, the chorale theme, now in minor, is heard over and over like a distant signal. The music then returns to A major, hymnlike, bringing the long, substantial prelude to its conclusion.

The first section also begins in A major, a "bright," even joyful—or devout—key. The chorus describes the situation: "Herr!... Die Heiden lehnen sich auf wider Dich und Deinen Christ. Und nun, Herr, siehe an ihr Droh'n, und gib Deinen Knechten mit aller Freudigkeit zu reden Dein Wort!" (Lord!... The heathens are rebelling against You and Your Christ. And now, Lord, see how they threaten; speak joyfully to Your soldiers!) The first chorale follows: "Allein Gott in der Höh' sei Ehr' und Dank!" (Honor and thanks only to God on high!) Then, in recitative, the solo soprano reports that Stephen* "Wunder tat vor dem Volk, und die Schriftgelehrten vermochten nicht zu widersteh'n der Weisheit und dem Geist, aus welchem er redete" (Performed miracles before the people, and the scribes could not resist the wisdom and the spirit by which he spoke).

In a short andante, the two solo basses slander Stephen: "Wir haben ihn gehört Lästerworte reden." (We have heard him blaspheme.). The soprano goes on to tell how the people, stirred up

---

*St. Stephen was the first Christian martyr and is remembered in the Christian calendar on December 26. He was stoned to death in Jerusalem sometime between A.D. 32 and 37.

against him, captured Stephen and took him before the council. In a chorus (No. 4), the people now attack him: "Dieser Mensch hört nicht auf zu reden Lästerwort wider Moses und wider Gott... denn wir haben ihn hören sagen: Jesus von Nazareth wird diese Stätte zerstören und ändern die Sitten, die uns Mose gegeben hat." (This man never ceases blaspheming Moses and God... we have heard him say: Jesus of Nazareth will destroy these holy places and change the law that Moses has given us.). Stephen defends himself and his teachings before the High Priest (tenor solo, No. 5): Did not the Jews, too, once deny God who saved them? Had they not thrust Moses from them, who spoke to them in His name? Indeed, Solomon had built Him a wondrous dwelling—the great temple of Jerusalem. But God needs no house of stone; Heaven is His throne and earth, His footstool. His speech becomes more and more urgent: "Ihr Halsstarrigen! Ihr widerstrebt allezeit dem Heil'gen Geist!" (You obstinate people! You always resist the holy spirit!).

Then the crowd bursts out in a frenzy, "Weg, weg mit dem! Der soll sterben!" (Away with him! He must die!) The music becomes powerfully strident. As the tumult reaches its highest pitch it breaks off, with the martyr's voice still heard above soft, drawn-out chords; he does not cry out in fear of death, he does not accuse, nor does he despair: "Ich sehe den Himmel offen und des Menschen Sohn zur Rechten Gottes steh'n" (I see the Heavens open and the Son of Man standing at the right hand of God).

At this point, the flow of this intense drama is interrupted by the solo soprano singing an unworldly melody to softly beating rhythms in the wind instruments: "Jerusalem, die du tötest die Propheten, die du steinigst die zu dir gesandt." (Jerusalem, slayer of prophets, you who stone those sent to you). These are the kinds of moments that only oratorio and no other art form can offer: the breaking off at a dramatic high point to withdraw into the world of contemplation, the stillness of reflection. Scarcely has the soloist finished, however, than fate intervenes: the frenzied masses drag Stephen outside the city and stone him. They see and hear nothing, wanting only their victim. Here Mendelssohn's music is of the most gripping realism.

Oddly enough, the recitative that follows is not given to the soprano who has been reporting, but to the tenor, who sings the martyr's last words. Is this a mistake? If so, these first lines should be assigned to the soprano: "Und sie steinigten ihn, er kniete nieder und schrie laut" (And they stoned him; he fell to his knees and cried aloud). Then the words of Stephen would be all the more effective: "Herr, behalte ihnen diese Sünde nicht! Herr Jesu, nimm meinen Geist auf!" (Lord, do not hold this sin against them. Lord Jesus, take my soul). And then the soprano should finish with, "Und als er das gesagt, entschlief er" (And when he had said that, he passed away).

The respite provided by the chorale "Dir, Herr, Dir will ich mich ergeben." (To You, Lord, will I surrender) is dramatically well placed, as it signifies a profound relaxation of tension. At this point the actual story of Saul, who became Paul, an Apostle of Christ, after supernatural experience on the road to Damascus, is taken up. He preached the Gospel for 30 years and founded the Christian church in the West. He was beheaded in Rome around A.D. 67. He was a fairly young man at the time of the stoning of Stephen and a zealot for the Jewish faith; he condoned the deed, possibly even participated in it. The Narrator tells of this (recitative No. 9) and adds that Saul and his co-religionists were then witnesses to the very moving lament by a group of Christians who gathered around the body of the slain Stephen. Above the soft arpeggios of the violins a gentle, noble melody arises in the cellos and violas, colored by the melancholy sound of a bassoon (Example 2). It depicts the beatification of the martyr, "for even though the body dies, the soul lives."

Example 2

Angrily, Saul goes among the believers in the new faith, whom he views as defectors from the true law of God. In his powerful bass, he counters their funeral song with an aria of frenzied rage (B minor); his words and the musical idiom mark him immediately as a strong personality and entirely sure of himself: "Vertilge sie, Herr Zebaoth, wie Stoppeln vor dem Feuer! Lass Deinen Zorn sie treffen, verstummen müssen sie!" (Exterminate them, Lord Zabaoth, as stubble before a fire! Show them your wrath; they must be silenced!)

The narrative continues with a solo for the alto, who otherwise has little to do in this work. She tells of the mission given Saul by the high priests: He is to go to Damascus and with the help of a small detachment of soldiers bring all those in that city who have fallen away from the old faith back to Jerusalem in bonds.* As if she could foresee the miracle, the alto sings a sonorous arioso,

*Damascus, today the capital of Syria, then belonged to Israel; there was a particularly large number of Christians living there.

full of hope (Example 3): "Doch der Herr vergisst der Seinen nicht" (But the Lord does not forget His own). The miracle itself is described in a recitative with chorus that becomes increasingly excited (No. 13). This time it is the solo tenor who reports, "Und als er auf dem Wege war und nahe zu Damaskus kam, umleuchtete ihn plötzlich ein Licht vom Himmel, und er fiel auf die Erde und hörte eine Stimme, die sprach zu ihm" (And as he was on the road to Damascus, he was suddenly surrounded by a light from Heaven, and he fell to the ground and heard a voice, which spoke to him). At this point the tremolo in the strings, which has accompanied the vision, attains its peak of intensity and greatest harmonic tension: it is "only" a diminished chord (F—G-sharp—B—D), but its effect in this context is thoroughly startling.

Example 3

The dissonance is resolved in a pure A major chord in the winds, which seems to dispense light from Heaven. The voice Saul hears is not assigned to a soloist but rather, in the manner of early motets, is sung by a female chorus in four parts, perhaps to symbolize its all-encompassing greatness. They sing, "Saul! Saul! Was verfolgst du mich?" (Saul! Saul! Why do you persecute me?) In answer to the astonished question received in reply, the vision responds with, "Ich bin Jesus von Nazareth, den du verfolgst!" (It is I, Jesus of Nazareth, whom you persecute). As Saul stands in fear and trembling, the mission he accepted in Jerusalem is changed: "Stehe auf und gehe in die Stadt, da wird man dir sagen, was du tun sollst" (Get up and go into the city; there you will be told what to do).

After such a miracle, the narrative cannot proceed, so strongly does the excitement linger. Schubring and Mendelssohn insert here one of the most important choral pieces in the entire work. Just as the manifestation lingers in Saul's heart, the sharply dotted rhythms do not leave the listener in peace for a long time. "Mache dich auf, werde Licht! Denn Dein Licht kommt und die Herrlichkeit des Herrn gehet auf über dir!" (Arise, it is daylight! Your light comes and the majesty of the Lord enfolds you).

This is a long piece, divided in several parts; more than once the great shadow of Bach is conjured up, and not in an unworthy way. The fugue "Denn siehe, Finsternis bedeckt das Erdreich...." (Behold, darkness covers the earth....) could only have been composed by a great master who not only was completely versed in the musical forms of the Baroque but also knew how to use them in the spirit of his own time without sacrificing their vitality (Example 4).

Example 4

As Bach taught, Mendelssohn does not reduce the tension he has built in the mighty chorus and brought to a climax, but extends it in the artful chorale adaptation of the Leitmotivic "Wachet auf, ruft uns die Stimme" (see Example 1). Here the call to awaken is not only symbolic, is not only a call to take up the divine mission: the horns, trumpets, and trombones blare forth a genuine, often repeated fanfare, as if to awaken all the sleepers on earth.

Only then does the solo tenor continue the narration: the astonishment of Saul's companions, who in fact did hear the voice but saw nothing; the three-day blindness suffered by Saul, who saw the supernatural light. His conversion is the subject of the following piece (No. 17), also one of the most important in the work. In a very solemn tempo (adagio) Saul prays for God's grace, that he may be worthy of this overwhelming experience: "Gott sei mir gnädig nach Deiner Güte und tilge meine Sünden nach Deiner grossen Barmherzigkeit" (God be gracious unto me according to Your goodness and forgive my sins in Your great mercy) (Example 5).

Example 5

Such an extensive piece must necessarily be divided into parts, and this one is in three. The middle section is a lively recitative; the last returns to the calm, flowing tempo of the beginning, repeated in considerably shortened form. Then this piece is interrupted, and the tenor, narrating once more, tells of a disciple named Ananias. The voice of God—here the solo soprano, much less mystical but with musical quotations from Saul's vision—commands him to tell Saul of his calling and his future suffering. Here the voice of the now chosen one enters again; against a choral backdrop he gives thanks to God.

The chorus—no composer since Beethoven had shown such expressive power with choral entrances, none since Schubert had used the human voice so wonderfully, naturally and with such intimacy—now consoles: "Der Herr wird die Tränen von allen Angesichtern abwischen." (The Lord will wipe the tears from all faces.). Now the solo soprano continues telling of how Ananias calls on Saul, lays his hands upon his head as a sign of blessing, and addresses him (sung by the solo tenor): "Lieber Bruder Saul, der Herr hat mich gesandt." (Dear brother Saul, the Lord has sent me.). A short orchestral interlude, probably to accompany the act of baptism now performed, develops into an ascending fugato and builds to an agitated climax. It then leads to an expressive soprano recitative: "Und alsbald fiel es wie Schuppen von seinen Augen." (And immediately it fell as scales from his eyes), words that have become a familiar quotation. Saul's new life begins; he discards his Jewish name and calls himself Paul, and devotes himself to preaching the teachings of Christianity. An important chorus (No. 21) closes the first section of the work, as if God, well pleased, was observing the transformation (Example 6). The people join in their praise: "Ihm sei Ehre in Ewigkeit! Amen!" (Eternal honor to Him).

Example 6

O welch ei — ne Tie — fe des Reich — tums, der Weis.— heit und Er — kennt — nis Got — tes

The second section of the oratorio tells how Paul, filled with the sense of his holy mission, undertakes his missionary travels, and of the persecutions he endures. The first chorus of this section (No. 22) is expanded by dividing the sopranos into five parts. The introduction is slow and solemn (grave): "Der Erdkreis ist nun des Herrn." (The earth belongs now to the Lord.). Lively and vivacious, with fugal entrances, it continues, "Denn alle Heiden werden kommen und anbeten." (For all the heathens will come and worship.).

In the following recitative (No. 23) Paul is joined by Barnabas, and together they set off. "So sind wir nun Botschafter an Christi Statt." (Thus are we now messengers in Christ's name), they sing in the duettino No. 24; the following chorus sings, "Wie lieblich sind die Boten, die den Frieden verkündigen." (How dear are the messengers who proclaim peace.). The solo soprano tells of their journey by ship; are there distant peoples to be converted to the teachings of Christ? She continues in an expressive arioso, temporarily surrendering the role of narrator: "Lasst uns singen von der Gnade des Herrn ewiglich!" (Let us sing of the grace of the Lord forever!). The narrator's role is now taken by the tenor (No. 27), who reports how the Jews turn against Paul when they see multitudes rushing to hear him preach. Their chorus (Nos. 27 and 28) first observes, "So spricht der Herr, und ist ausser mir kein Heiland" (Thus says the Lord, except for Me there is no Savior). They set out to kill him.

The second choral entry introduces another of the dramatic numbers. The Jews recognize Paul as a dangerous enemy bent on converting their people; their song of hate mounts from a whisper to a furious outbreak of wrath. The accusations earlier directed against Stephen are now repeated, sometimes word for word. A quartet of the four solo voices opposes them with a deeply felt Adagio. The Christians plead with God: "O Jesu Christe, wahres Licht, erleuchte die Dich kennen nicht, und bringe sie zu Deiner Herd', dass ihre Seel' auch selig werd'" (O Jesus Christ, true light, enlighten those who do not know You and bring them to Your hearth so that their souls, too, shall be blessed). It is a chorale, accompanied by delicate figures in the wind instruments, which is then continued in a second verse by the softly singing chorus.

In recitative No. 29, the tenor reports further on Paul and Barnabas preaching openly to the Jews; they then announce their intention to take the teachings of salvation to the heathens because their own people pay no attention to them. In duet No. 30 the missionaries (tenor and bass) sing, "Denn also hat uns der Herr geboten: Ich habe dich den Heiden zum Licht gesetzet." (The Lord has commanded us to take the light to the heathen). Recitative No. 31 tells of Paul healing the cripple from Lystra, while the following chorus of heathens sees Paul as a god.

The solo soprano takes over the narration once more: the heathens, thinking Barnabas is the Roman god Jupiter and Paul the god Mercury, gather offerings to bring to them. In chorus No. 34 the people raise their voices in praise: "Seid uns gnädig, hohe Götter!" (Have mercy upon us, great gods!) The missionaries thrust this offering from them with abruptly ascending orchestral strokes. Paul speaks to the heathens, angrily at first, then in a more conciliatory tone: "Ihr Männer, was macht ihr da? Wir sind sterbliche Menschen gleich wie ihr und predigen euch das Evangelium, dass ihr euch bekehren sollt." (What are you doing? We are mortal men like you and preach the Gospel to you so that you will be converted.). At the last, his urgent recitative becomes an aria (Example 7).

Example 7   **Allegro assai moderato**

Wis – set ihr nicht, dass ihr Got – tes Tem – pel seid

In the second section of the aria the chorus enters with a solemn, four-part fugue: "Aber unser Gott ist im Himmel." (But our God is in Heaven.). This utterance upsets the people, Jews as well as heathens (soprano recitative, No. 36), and stirs them against both preachers. Angrily the chorus (No. 37) confronts them: "Hier ist des Herren Tempel!" (This is the Lord's temple!) The following tenor recitative tells of the persecution of Paul and his protection by God. The same voice then intones (No. 39) the deeply devout cavatina (Example 8).

Example 8

Sei ge–treu bis in den Tod, so will ich dir die Kro–ne des Le–bens ge–ben

In recitative No. 40, Paul bids farewell to Ephesus: "Ich fahre hin gen Jerusalem, Trübsal und Bande harren mein daselbst—ihr werdet nie mein Angesicht wieder sehen" (I am going to Jerusalem, affliction and shackles await me—you will never again see my face). The people seek to hold him back (chorus No. 41): "Schone doch deiner selbst!" (Save yourself, then!) sing first the solo voices, then the sorrowing multitudes. Paul, deeply moved, replies, "Was machet ihr, dass ihr weinet und brechet mir mein Herz?" (What are you doing, weeping and breaking my heart?) The narrator continues, "Und als er das gesagt, kniete er nieder und betete mit ihnen allen, und sie geleiteten ihn in das Schiff und sahen sein Angesicht nicht mehr" (And when he had said that, he knelt and prayed with them, and they accompanied him to his ship and never saw him again). Their thanks and deep faith are expressed in chorus No. 42.

In the concluding chorus (No. 44), the thanks given to Paul are extended to include all those who suffer and die for their faith. It rises to a song of praise with the last Allegro vivace, "Lobe den Herrn, meine Seele, und was in mir ist, seinen heiligen Namen, lobe den Herrn!" (Praise the Lord, my soul, and what is in me, His holy name, praise the Lord!) The work ends in a festive, radiant D major, a great chorus of religious faith and certainty of eternal life.

Lobgesang, Op. 52

The city of Leipzig had planned a great festival for the summer of 1840 to celebrate the 400th anniversary of the art of printing (whose beginnings actually should be put a few years after 1440, according to more recent findings). It was moved to stage such a festival because it rightly considered itself a "city of books," as the most important German publishers were located there. There was also no question but that they should call upon Felix Mendelssohn to compose some music for this festive occasion, as he was the Kapellmeister of their Gewandhaus, an institution highly esteemed throughout Europe.

Mendelssohn contributed two compositions: a *Festgesang*, played for the first time on June 24, 1840, on the market square, for the dedication of a statue to Johannes Gutenberg, the inventor of printing with movable type; and the *Lobgesang*, given its premiere the next day, June 25, 1840, in the historic St. Thomas Church, where in the previous century Bach had worked for years and where, on Good Friday, 1729, he had conducted his *St. Matthew Passion*.

We have a detailed description of the event, written by Robert Schumann for his *Neue Zeitschrift für Musik*. He remarks on the magnificent effect of this concert, with its 500 participants. In addition to Mendelssohn's *Lobgesang*, it included Weber's *Jubelouverture* and Handel's *Dettingen Te Deum*. Schumann, who admired Mendelssohn greatly, was enthusiastic about the new work, one of Mendelssohn's best, he thought. He opined that the work was the result of a happy union of two very different elements: a symphony and a cantata, which probably originally had no relationship to each other.

Schumann was the first to draw a comparison between this work and Beethoven's Ninth, the *Choral Symphony*, even though the latter is predominantly instrumental and Mendelssohn's work predominantly vocal. What is even more striking is that when the work was to be printed, Schumann recommended that the two components again be separated. Had he discovered a flaw in it?

The story of the writing of the *Lobgesang* seems to confirm the view that Mendelssohn had been first thinking of a new symphony, of which three movements were already either sketched or even completed, when he received the request to contribute a work for chorus and orchestra. He then oriented the composition in progress to the particular demands of the Gutenberg Festival. Several of Mendelssohn's letters from 1838 and 1839 seem to support this contention, for in them he spoke of a symphony he was thoroughly pleased with. Not until May 15, 1840 did Schumann, who was very familiar with his friend's life and work, write that Mendelssohn was working on "something from the Psalms." The subtitle the composer gave the *Lobgesang* also speaks for this double origin: "Eine Symphonie-Cantate nach Worten der Heiligen Schrift" (A symphony-cantata based on passages from the Holy Scriptures).

The length of the work—roughly 75 minutes—as well as the musical forces are surely those of an oratorio. The orchestra is composed of two each of flutes, oboes, and bassoons; four horns, two trumpets, three trombones, timpani, organ, and strings. The voices include two soprano and one tenor soloist, and a large mixed chorus, which at the climax is divided into eight parts. Mendelssohn set a passage from Luther at the head of the work, which he also placed on the title page as a motto: "Sondern ich wöllt alle künste, sonderlich die Musica, gern sehen im dienst des der sie geben und geschaffen hat!" (I wanted to see all art, especially music, in the service of the One who had given and created it).

It is debatable whether a close description of the work is necessary or even advisable today, except in scholarly analyses. There are a number of modern concerns which would preclude the widespread acceptance accorded the *Lobgesang* in the 19th century. The undisputed esteem which Mendelssohn enjoyed during his lifetime, and which extended for decades after his death, has yielded to a more objective evaluation.

There have been objections to the "all too facile skill" and the occasional "lack of depth" in many of his works, to the often undeniable "slickness of execution" and "elegance of form" causing some observers to doubt whether Mendelssohn should be given a place among the great masters. Such charges are completely unsupportable with respect to works like *St. Paul* and *Elijah*. The *Lobgesang* is more debatable.

As with many of Mendelssohn's compositions, his strong following in England contributed greatly to the contemporary popularity of the *Lobgesang*. After some preliminary difficulties, the work was performed as *Hymn of Praise* on September 23, 1840, in Birmingham, under the direction of the composer. The rehearsal the day before was reported to have lasted "from morning to midnight." Mendelssohn was dissatisfied; the fact that all participants were probably overly tired (the concert took place in the morning, i.e., after only a short pause after the "exhausting" rehearsal) was not the only reason. He revised parts of it at least twice. In its new form, the *Lobgesang* was performed for the first time on December 8, 1840, in Leipzig, at a benefit concert for aged and infirm musicians. The first English performance of the final version took place in 1841 at the Gloucester Music Festival, where it was called "a new sacred oratorio."

The *Lobgesang* is in 11 parts. The very long overture has three movements, slightly reminiscent of the first three movements of Beethoven's *Choral Symphony*: after a peaceful but animated movement comes a sort of Scherzo and then a slower, very lyrical section, which Mendelssohn headed "Adagio religioso." The "cantata" begins with the choruses singing "Alles was Odem hat, lobe den Herrn!" (All who have life and breath, praise the Lord!), which becomes a sort of Leitmotif of the work.

A soprano solo follows ("Lobe den Herrn, meine Seele"—Praise the Lord, my soul) with choral insertions, succeeded by a solo tenor recitative and aria ("Er zählet unsre Tränen in der Zeit der Not"—He counts our tears in times of want), another chorus ("Sagt es, die ihr erlöset seid"—Say it, you who are saved); a duet for two solo sopranos ("Ich harrete des Herrn"—I awaited the Lord) with choral accompaniment; a multipartite tenor aria ("Stricke des Todes hatten uns umfangen"—the bonds of death had surrounded us); the very substantial and dramatic chorus "Die Nacht ist vergangen" (The night is over); and finally, the quiet counterpart of the famous chorale "Nun danket alle Gott mit Herzen, Mund und Händen" (Now thank we all our God, with hearts, mouth and hands)*, which is sung a cappella in seven parts. Mendelssohn leads the chorale into a lively choral movement ("Lob, Ehr'und Preis sei Gott!"—Praise, honor and glory to God),

---

*Very popular in all Reformed, Lutheran, and Protestant areas of German-speaking countries and usually referred to as the "Old Netherlandish Prayer of Thanksgiving."

followed by a duet between the tenor and the soprano soloists ("Drum sing' ich mit meinem Liede ewig dein Lob"—Therefore shall I sing thy praises forever), and crowns the work with the final chorus "Ihr Völker! Bringet her dem Herrn Ehre und Macht!" (You, people! Bring the Lord honor and power!). The last solemn bars belong to the Leitmotif: "Alles was Odem hat, lobe den Herrn!" with all the splendor of the combined chorus and orchestra.

Die erste Walpurgisnacht

This composition occupies a curious position, not only in Mendelssohn's works, but in the history of music as well. Here we have a devout Christian writing a work that is fundamentally anti-Christian. The text which supplies the basic idea was written by no less an author than Goethe. When Walpurgis night is mentioned, most people think of *Faust*, where the Walpurgis night scene plays an important part: The Witches' Sabbath, the orgy of spirits in the kingdom of Mephistopheles. But few know that in addition to this Walpurgis night, Goethe wrote a text of the same title for a cantata, with the express purpose of having it set to music. Although music did not play a large role in his life, Goethe had become acquainted with two musical child prodigies: When 14 he had heard the 7-year-old Mozart, and as a mature master, the child prodigy Mendelssohn. The latter profoundly impressed him, whereas all he could recall of his youthful encounter with Mozart was the fancy dress coat and a little sword the celebrated Salzburg child wore.

Goethe hoped that Carl Friedrich Zelter, his friend and musical advisor, might compose music for his pagan ballad. But when Zelter received the poem in 1799, he did not know what to make of it. He took it up once more in 1812 before giving up entirely on the idea of setting it to music.

In 1830, Mendelssohn, then 21 years old, took up the poem. What attracted him to it? To say that he admired Goethe does not get to the heart of the matter. It is more likely that his fascination grew out of his wide-ranging interests, for he was truly a man of the Enlightenment who saw all things in a broad, historical perspective. Furthermore, he loved stories of ghosts and goblins, as his music for *A Midsummer Night's Dream* clearly indicates. And lastly, given his strong sense of justice, he saw in it a vehicle to champion the cause of the oppressed.

As is clearly evident today, Goethe's seemingly ironic, mocking poem was written against a backdrop of political reality. He takes up with great sympathy the cause of an oppressed people, those living in an occupied land. The irony arises out of his portrayal of the occupying force as Christians and the oppressed as "heathens."

The text turns on the ingenious plan devised by the pagan Druids whose traditional rites celebrating the arrival of spring have been forbidden by the conquering Christians. The Druids gather secretly in the forest, where their priests urge fearless defiance but other voices counsel caution so as not to incite the army of occupation to even harsher measures. The priests warn: "Wer Opfer heut zu bringen scheut, verdient erst seine Bande" (He who flees sacrifice today deserves his chains)—counsel as meaningful and profound in the 20th century as in the 18th, or any other century.

But no mortal conflict, no tragedy, as in so many similar instances, follows. Goethe finds an ironic, much more amusing and inspired resolution. A "Druid watchman" proposes an absolutely ingenious plan: "Diese dumpfen Pfaffenchristen, lasst uns keck sie überlisten! Mit dem Teufel, den sie fabeln, wollen wir sie selbst erschrecken!" (Let us outsmart these stupid priest-ridden Christians! We can defeat them with their own Devil!) And then begins a masquerade, brilliantly described by Mendelssohn: "Kommt, Kommt, Kommt mit Zacken und mit Gabeln und mit Glut und Klapperstöcken lärmen wir bei nächt'ger Weile durch die engen Felsenstrecken." (Come, Come! Come! with spikes and forks and with live coals and with rattling sticks to make a frightful racket in the night as we course through the narrow, rocky passes).

A ghost scene follows, a frenzy of phantoms reminiscent of the Wolf's Glen scene in Weber's opera *Der Freischütz*. Mendelssohn's music very cleverly describes this wonderful scene of undulating processions of spooks. The plan is an overwhelming success. The occupying Christians, terrified because they believe in the Devil, flee before this masque, leaving the heathens free to mount their ancient celebration of spring, a joyous ceremony the world around. The "heathens" praise the sun while the Christians cower before the Devil, whom they believe to have seen in the flesh. First performance: Leipzig, February 2, 1843.

Elijah

Original Title: Elias (*Elijah* at the first performance)

Original Language: German (English at the first performance).

Text: Based on Bible passages, mainly from *Kings* I:17–19, and *Kings* II:1 and 2, compiled by Mendelssohn with help from Julius Schubring and Karl Klingemann.

Date of Writing: Planned during the summer of 1836; composed in 1845–46.

First Performance: August 26, 1846, in Birmingham. Mendelssohn conducted and the world-famous Jenny Lind sang the soprano role.

Form: Oratorio, in two parts with a total of 42 musical numbers, plus an introduction and an overture.

Cast: The Widow (soprano), the Youth (soprano), the Angel (soprano), an Angel (alto), the Queen (alto), Obadiah (tenor), Ahab (tenor), Elijah (bass); four-part mixed chorus.

Orchestra: Two each of flutes, oboes, clarinets, and bassoons, four horns, two trumpets, three trombones, one bass tuba, timpani, and strings.

History of the Work: Mendelssohn worked on his second great oratorio for 10 long years, at least in thought. The performance of *St. Paul* at the 1836 Rhenish Music Festival in Düsseldorf left a deep impression on the audience. With one stroke it had made him one of the masters in this musical genre and its greatest living representative. All of this led Mendelssohn to immediately consider composing a similar work. As early as August 12 of the same year he wrote to Karl Klingemann, a life-long friend since his youth who lived in London, to tell him of this plan. He had not yet formed a fixed idea for the work; he considered various Biblical figures such as Elijah or Peter, "or for all I care it could be Og of Basan," as he good-humoredly wrote, to indicate it could be any Biblical figure whatsoever, as long as the subject was sufficiently compelling.

In his excellent program notes for a performance of the work at the 1984 Salzburg Festival, Friedrich C. Heller pointed out the significance of the fact that Mendelssohn turned first not to Schubring, but to Klingemann. He envisioned a work which differed completely from *St. Paul*. Heller quoted two passages from a letter Mendelssohn wrote dated April 30, 1837, addressed to Klingemann: "At the moment the choral society is in good form and longing for something new; I'd like to give them something that I like better than my previous oratorio." And ". . . for that reason, I would really like to write something in the church style soon, since an opera does not seem to be in the offing."

One external factor surely led to the decision to compose *Elijah*. Opera was probably the only unrequited love in his life. His efforts in this genre turned out poorly: Neither *Die Hochzeit des Camacho* nor the Singspiel *Die Heimkehr aus der Fremde* achieved real success, and *Lorelei* remained a fragment. It is understandable, then, that there was no opera "in the offing," in spite of the fact that every other Mendelssohn premiere caused a sensation. But it was not only the failure of his operatic ventures that led the composer, at the peak of his creativity, to turn once more to the composition of a religious work; he must have felt compelled to do so.

Interestingly he finally opted for Elijah rather than Peter. This Old Testament zealot, whose unflagging efforts kept the Children of Israel from defecting to the idols of their neighbors, appeared in the 9th century before the Christian era. He was a mighty figure whose meaning remains with us today. (Richard Strauss in his opera *Salome*, based on a text by Oscar Wilde, presents a heated discussion of the theological question as to whether "anyone has seen God since the time of the prophet Elijah".)

Perhaps Mendelssohn thought first of a dramatic work, a sort of "pseudo-opera" (Heller), making his choice of Klingemann quite natural, since he had often discussed such plans with him. But other events played a part in the selection of *Elijah*. Klingemann was unable to devote any time to artistic activity due to financial difficulties connected with the accession of Queen Victoria to the throne in England. When Mendelssohn was in London for two weeks in 1837, however, they did work out the basic design of the oratorio.

At about the same time, the composer reestablished contact with his "theological advisor," a cleric from Dessau named Julius Schubring, without, however, at first telling him anything about *Elijah*, though they had discussed the idea of a *Peter* oratorio. It was only a year later, when Klingemann had to suspend work on *Elijah*, that Mendelssohn turned to Schubring.

Schubring found Klingemann's outline unacceptable. There was practically nothing in the first section that conformed to his own view. Among other things, Schubring wanted it made clear that Christ was the fulfillment of Elijah's prophecies, and wanted an appearance by Christ; Mendelssohn, it seems, did not agree. These fundamental differences of opinion led to breaking off the joint undertaking.

Mendelssohn did not return to the project until 1845 but he had never stopped thinking about it. And just in time, too, because shortly thereafter he was invited to a music festival in the English city of Birmingham, accompanied by the request that a new composition conducted by him would be most welcome. Schubring, who sincerely admired Mendelssohn and was always ready to help, was asked to complete the text; since time was so short, there were probably no discussions of theological issues.

When the orchestra for the Birmingham Music Festival was being put together, an event that provides insight into Mendelssohn's character occurred. During a rehearsal of the London Philharmonic, a few of the players took issue with him in a most unseemly way. Ignaz Moscheles, a student of Beethoven who had became a leading musical figure in London, was in charge of choosing the musicians for the festival. He advised Mendelssohn that none of those who had taken part in the argument would be included in the orchestra. Mendelssohn's reply from Leipzig counseled against such a course of action; he explained that he bore them no ill will and thought he could rely on their loyal cooperation in the future.

This music festival was a high point in Mendelssohn's life. His oratorio was performed in the company of some of the greatest choral works of all time: Handel's *Messiah*, Haydn's *Creation*, and Beethoven's *Missa Solemnis*. Of these, *Elijah* was the only one to have its premiere in England (the *Messiah* had been performed for the first time in Dublin; the *Creation*, in Vienna; and the *Missa solemnis* in Petersburg). England had became the world's center for the art of oratorio. From the time of Handel, the oratorio had been cultivated by numerous first-rate British choruses.

The premiere of Mendelssohn's *Elijah* in Birmingham on August 26, 1846, was an event of signal significance in music history.

It is useless to argue whether Mendelssohn's oratorios are church music or not. It is not usage that turns a musical work into a piece of religious music, but rather its capacity for creating a sense of spiritual community in the audience. This has certainly often been the case with *St. Paul* and even more so with *Elijah* (F. C. Heller).

The form in which *Elijah* was first performed was considerably different from its later, final one. Mendelssohn created a number of additional pieces and made other important revisions in the version printed in 1847. The result was a "great" work in every sense of the word, one that was effective in a church as well as in a concert hall. It is true that it reflects the 19th-century bourgeois concept of art and the cultural sensibilities of the Romantic era, but the composer's genius created something timeless, a work that even today enthralls people in every walk of life, in every land, of every religious faith.

Discussion of the Work: Elijah begins in a highly unusual way: Before the overture, Mendelssohn sets a short, very expressive recitative by the prophet (Example 1). Another unusual feature is the use of the tritone interval, which appears in the seventh, eighth, and ninth bars. This melodic step of the diminished fifth (or augmented fourth) was considered to be the "diabolus in musica," the devil in music, in the Middle Ages and into the Classical era. Mendelssohn uses it twice in the vocal parts (the downward leap from C to F-sharp and from G to C-sharp) as well as in the following measure in the instruments: D/G-sharp. Do these unusual melodic steps represent tone-painting? Do they express the harshness of the prophecy?

The following overture is in a fugal style: a four-measure theme in D minor (the principal key, right from the beginning) runs through several voices and appears repeatedly in variation, without ever becoming a true fugue. This piece has not been lacking for interpretations; some say they hear the "withering of nature" or the "desperate situation of the people" in it. But the massive climax as the end draws near contradicts these views.

The chorus bursts forth immediately thereafter with "Help, Lord!" After the pleading cries—with full orchestra and voices fortissimo—Mendelssohn again introduces a fugato; in the sequence tenor-alto-soprano-bass the voices lament, "The harvest now is over, the summer days are gone, and yet no power cometh to help us" to the same melody, which is paraphrased by the other parts. The people from the depths of their souls bewail the terrible deprivation into which they have been plunged; it is dramatic music, confronting the listener with the untenable plight of the Israelites.

The lament becomes accusatory: "Will then the Lord be no more God in Zion?" This is not only despair speaking, but also rebellion. The voices subside as if they are drying up. A choral recitative continues, again in an unusual form. The chorus laments, no longer individual voices pleading for help, but all the people: "The deep affords no water, and the rivers are exhausted!" While the chorus is still calling for help, two solo sopranos raise their voices in an almost folk-songlike, A minor lament (Example 2).

The chorus continues to support the two melodious voices singing of Zion's misfortune, but their anguish is mixed with faint hope. Obadiah's recitative and aria (Nos. 3 and 4) are magnificent; he warns the children of Israel: "Ye people, rend your hearts, and not your garments!" The aria begins with God's words: "If with all your hearts ye truly seek Me, ye shall ever surely find Me" (Example 3), sung in a widely arched, strongly emotional melody.

The chorus replies with great vigor: "Yet doth the Lord see it not: He mocketh at us." Fear and despair speak out in this number (No. 5), which begins in C minor and uses all means of choral expression: lashing sforzato strokes in the orchestra, fugal entries in quick succession. It should be noted that within the agitated melodic line the tritone interval is again distinctly and harshly repeated several times. This motive connects Elijah's opening recitative with this choral number—and it will not be the last time that such a motivic connection occurs.

The chorus, which entered so dramatically, fades away quietly. C minor, with the agitated, frenzied string tremolo and harsh accents, resolves to a bright C major, and the notes become longer, more peaceful, as in a confident chorale; God promises "His mercies fall on all them that love Him." In recitative No. 6, an angel speaks to Elijah, announcing God's wish that the prophet leave the land and take shelter by the brook Cherith, where a raven will bring him bread mornings and evenings.

The following number, sung by a double quartet, is very important to the development of the theme. The angels—two in each voice register—give God's message to Elijah in a poetic, bright and peaceful piece, full of gentle hope and infinite trust in God. But scarcely has the piece faded away pianissimo than the voice of the angel is heard again telling Elijah that though the brook has run dry God continues to watch over the prophet. He is now to go to Zarephath, where a widow will care for him until the terrible drought, God's punishment, has finally ended.

The duet No. 8 is a dialogue between the widow and Elijah, who through prayer has restored her dead son to life. The scene is described almost theatrically; from the widow's lament, the miracle of the raising from the dead accomplished in the name of the Lord, to the woman's exultation, which joins with the prophet's gratitude to become a prayer.

Example 1

This leads into a chorus (No. 9): "Blessed are the men who fear Him." The voices enter in a fugato: first the soprano, then the tenor in the same key, and finally the alto and the bass in close succession and on the fifth.

The expressive middle section continues with sweeping melodies: "Through darkness riseth light," once more with fugal entries, in which "classical" key sequence is not observed. Instead, the last tone of each melody becomes the first one of each new entry (Example 4).

Unshakable faith, confidence, and hope are the hallmarks of this music; its bright G major is unclouded by doubt and no agitation shakes it. All the more effective, then, is the following section: In E-flat major trumpets and trombones blast out the same chords with which the work opened, in a slightly altered progression. And with the same dramatic melodic sequence the voice of Elijah begins, announcing that he must go to the king, for the drought is nearing its end.

Once again, the tritone appears in his words—although only once this time (in contrast to three times at the beginning), suggesting that this striking interval is connected with the prophet Elijah and the transcendental world he embodies.

Example 2

A powerful scene follows: Ahab, the king of Israel, accuses the prophet: "Art thou Elijah? Art thou he that troubleth Israel?" The people angrily join in the indictment: "Thou art Elijah!" With equanimity the prophet replies in a recitative, his first words again in a descending tritone interval: "I never troubled Israel's peace: it is thou, Ahab," for it was Ahab who had turned to the pagan cult of Baal, calling down all misery upon Israel. Elijah requests the king to assemble the people and the priests of Baal on Mount Carmel, where God will prove He is the true Lord of Israel.

Again, we seem to find ourselves almost in an opera; the scene is extremely dramatic in both words and music; one can imagine it successfully staged. Elijah proposes that a burnt offering be prepared. The priests of Baal should prepare theirs, and he, the last true believer in Jehovah, will do the same. "The God who by fire shall answer, let him be God." The people quietly but resolutely acclaim the decision. Elijah continues: "Call first upon your god: your numbers are many."

Now the priests of Baal raise their voices in a solemn male chorus (No. 11); the female voices repeat the call exactly, until a grand eight-part choral setting is formed. Mendelssohn's heart is of course on the side of Elijah and his God; but he recognizes that the people, led by their priests, are in truth faithful to Baal. So it is that this chorus is one of the more impressive numbers in the work.

Example 3

It is in two parts: First, an Andante, more specifically described as a Grave e maestoso (solemn, majestic); and then an Allegro non troppo in a lively three-four rhythm: "Hear us, mighty god! Let thy flames fall and extirpate the foe!" The chorus ends suddenly, very softly backing down, after the orchestra has already stopped, also very softly: an odd turn for a pagan prayer of a religion distinguished by noisy festivals and orgies. Is a psychological point being made here? Or does it signify a spreading loss of certainty as no flame appears in the sky?

In a recitative, delivered slowly and distinctly so that every word is understandable, Elijah jeers: "Call him louder! For he is a god. He talketh, or, he is pursuing, or, he is on a journey, or, peradventure, he sleepeth; so awaken him. Call him louder!" Now in a frenzy the priests of Baal enter, the throbbing, fanfarelike blasts of their voices rising in a fierce fugato: "Hear our cry, O Baal! Now arise! Wherefore slumber?" Ever more certain of victory, Elias mocks them again: "Call him louder! He heareth not. Cut yourselves with knives, jab yourselves with awls the way you do!

Example 4

Shuffle around the altar you made!" With renewed intensity, now presto with tempestuous runs in the strings, as if a hurricane were sweeping the earth, the raging voices rise to the silent pagan god: "Baal! Baal! Hear and answer!", followed by an anxious pause. The calls ring out, unanswered.

Then Elijah steps forward: "Draw near, all ye people, come to me!" There is a gentle, expressive prelude before his aria (No. 14), which introduces the solemn melody with which his prayer now begins (Example 5).

We have arrived at one of the most sublime moments in the work. To prolong the mood of Elijah's prayer, Mendelssohn follows it with a chorale-like quartet of the soloists, a warmhearted, deeply felt piece: "Cast thy burden upon the Lord." At this moment, Mendelssohn's melody takes on a true folk sound. The orchestral accompaniment is spare, and the harmony, bold as it was elsewhere, here never exceeds the bounds of the simplest tonality.

After this meditative pause, the prophet begins to speak again: He pleads with God to send

His angels as flames from Heaven. At once the miracle comes to pass. Because there is no stage, the listener experiences it only vicariously; the masses cry out in exultation, "The fire descends from heav'n!" Interestingly enough, the melody leaps upwards a tritone; does this interval signify the miracle, the supernatural strength of the prophet in God's name?

The excitement abates only slowly until, at the end of the piece, there is a contemplative chorale accompanied by the full orchestra—slowly, almost solemnly, as if a great truth were dawning. But Israel's God is a "jealous" god, a God of punishment as well of reward, a God of vengeance. Hardly has the miracle passed and the people have returned to their faith in Jehovah, when Elijah demands that none of the priests of Baal be allowed to escape. "Bring them down to Kishon's brook; and there let them be slain." The people follow his instructions, singing, "Bring all and slay them!" Then Elijah reiterates his demand in a frenzied aria (No. 17), in which we again hear the tritone—this time ascending—at certain points of emphasis. It is a piece that places extreme demands upon the bass, calling for many high notes and at the end, sung unaccompanied, ranges over an octave and a half.

Example 5

10188

An arioso by the solo alto takes us from this dramatic episode back to a meditative mood. An alto voice: we are reminded of Bach's great Passions. Herein lies the strength of the oratorio form: in the midst of the liveliest action meditative pauses can be inserted; in a single moment the course of the action passes from external events to inner spirituality, whereupon peace vanishes once again and the action proceeds.

Obadiah asks Elijah for a second miracle: Let God intercede to bring rain. First in a recitative, then in an arioso, Elijah prays to God, and the chorus joins in. The prophet sends a youth to look out to sea, to see whether God has heard the prayer. Three times the boy answers in the negative, while an oboe plays a long, drawn-out note symbolizing the tension. Three times Elijah prays, each time more fervently, and then the boy announces that a tiny cloud floats above the ocean.

A brisk wind springs up and the cloud grows swiftly—Mendelssohn, the tone painter, now describes the rush of the oncoming storm as the cloud grows to enormous size. Then the chorus breaks out with rejoicing: "Thanks be to God!", and Elijah takes up the word, again with a falling tritone, and leads into the great choral finale of the first section, the people's wholehearted, rising song of thanksgiving: "Thanks be to God! He laveth the thirsty land."

Example 6

The second part dramatically is less unified. It begins with a contemplative soprano aria "Hear ye, Israel, what the Lord speaketh" (Example 6), a lovely piece, with more powerful accents only in its second part. The following chorus is very similar (No. 22): "Be not afraid, saith God, the Lord."

After its melodious, quiet beginning comes a more animated middle section with fugal entries and lively movement, from which a third part—a repetition of the first in variation—returns to the tranquil tempo. Solemnly, in long, choralelike notes, the piece comes to an end: "Be not afraid, thy help is near, saith God the Lord."

Then Elijah stands once more before Ahab, King of Israel, and charges him with worshipping idols. The queen replies and stirs the people up against him. Threats are uttered against the prophet and, growing increasingly violent, the crowd demands his head. From the queen's recitative with its short choral inserts grows the dramatic choral number (No. 24) "Woe to him, he shall perish!" Once again we hear the excited fugal entries of the voices: "Let the guilty prophet perish!" Obadiah speaks to Elijah and tries to convince him to flee: God will be with him.

Example 7

10188

Sorrowfully, Elijah bids him farewell; his path leads into the wilderness. His aria No. 26 is one of the most beautiful selections in the work. With touching tenderness the cello plays the melody that Elijah then takes over: "It is enough." (Example 7).

It is a powerful piece of music, full of pain and renunciation, which, after a moving middle section, returns at the end to the resigned melody of the beginning: "Now, let me die, Lord!" In the following tenor recitative we learn that Elijah sleeps under a juniper tree, watched over by angels. This leads to No. 28, the angel trio, probably the best known piece in the entire composition and one of the most often sung, not only in the oratorio literature. In the second half of the 19th century, all German and English school children learned this song (Example 8).

The melody "Lift thine eyes," sung to the Psalm text, can justifiably claim the stature of a folk song. Three solo voices, without accompaniment, join in a beautiful, simple, partly harmonic, partly polyphonic movement in three-part song form.

The mood of the following chorus (No. 29) is also lyrical: "He, watching over Israel, slumbers not nor sleeps." Its form can be described as canon- or fuguelike; in any event, it is pure Mendelssohn, in a noble, lively style and Romantically relaxed texture.

Then the angel comes to Elijah, saying, "Arise, Elijah, for thou hast a long journey before thee." Elijah is filled with self-doubt and feels unworthy of future missions. In mounting despair he calls out to God: "O that Thou wouldst rend the heavens, that Thou wouldst come down." The orchestra, which has accompanied the angel's voice with quiet chords, in a frenzy of ascending interjections now depicts the prophet's fierce agitation. "Make thy Name known to thine adversaries through the wonders of thy works." God speaks through the angel (alto) in aria No. 31: "O rest in the Lord, wait patiently for Him." Gentle consolation seems to flow from Heaven, and the beginning is once again folklike (Example 9).

The following chorus (No. 32) has characteristics of a chorale: "He that shall endure to the end shall be saved." It is one of those contemplative pieces that are the essence of oratorio—devout meditation, immersion in religious faith.

Example 8

But the work does not end in such a mood. Recitative No. 33 shows Elijah in fervent prayer to the Almighty: "Night falleth round me, O Lord! Be Thou not far from me! My soul is thirsting for Thee, as a thirsty land." What more can man long for than to see God? And God does as His servant prays: in His name, the angel announces, "Arise now! Get thee without! Stand on the mount before the Lord: for there His glory will appear, and shine on thee!" But no mortal may look upon God. Therefore, "Thy face must be veiled, for He draweth near." A rushing sound fills the air and mounts to a peal of thunder; the chorus (No. 34) tells what happened: "The Lord passed by."

There is good reason to consider this chorus the midpoint or climax of the work. It is a musical piece of enormous spirit and overwhelming vision. It depicts the cliff-splitting storm, the raging sea, the cracking earth, the consuming fire. But the Lord is in none of these. The furious elements pass, and a wondrous stillness is at hand. Above the E major pianissimo of the now murmuring orchestra the chorus whispers: "And after the fire came a still small voice, and in that still voice onward came the Lord." Mendelssohn continues his climax. A short alto recitative leads to prayer: "Holy, holy, holy is the Lord God." To the four-part chorus are now added four solo

Example 9

voices; the key of C major, always a symbol of clarity, the brightest of lights, underscores the confession of faith. Then voices speak to Elijah—tenors and basses, joined in the last measures (of the choral recitative No. 36) by the female voices, tell him to descend the mountain and to appear before the "seven thousand in Israel" who have not knelt before Baal.

Strengthened by his miraculous vision of God, the prophet does as he is bidden. In an arioso, he again takes up the task of securing the holy bond between the Eternal One and His people. The chorus describes (No. 38) the events in dark F minor: "Then did Elijah break forth like a fire; his words appeared like burning torches." He rages ferociously in the name of God against the unbelievers and the apostates. Suddenly there is light, with chorus and blaring trumpets: God takes Elijah to Him. A chariot of fire drawn by flaming horses takes him to Heaven, removing him forever from earthly events; he has fulfilled his mission.

After this dramatic coda, it is difficult to listen to the balance of the work with the same kind of attention. A tenor aria (No. 39) provides a glimpse of the future, when "the righteous shall shine forth as the sun in their heavenly Father's realm." The last pieces (Nos. 40, recitative; 41, chorus and quartet; and 42, final chorus) proclaim the coming "great and terrible day of the Lord," the day of the Last Judgment and the appearance of the Messiah, whose way Elijah had been sent to prepare. "Lord, our Creator, how excellent Thy name is in all the nations!"

Was this glimpse of the redemption of the world Mendelssohn's wish? Would this work, probably his greatest, have been even greater had he concluded with Elijah's departure in the fiery chariot to be with God? Is the "Christian" conclusion at the end of an Old Testament work warranted, advisable, advantageous, theologically or musically justified? It doubtless corresponds to one of Mendelssohn's deepest desires, for he was devout in the Christian faith and consequently regarded the Old Testament only as the prelude to the New, but they were indivisible in his eyes.

Christus

Toward the end of his short life Mendelssohn thought of composing a third, great, sacred oratorio with Jesus as its main character. He planned, it seems, to divide the oratorio into three parts; the dramatic action would include the entire story of the Savior from birth to Ascension. Death interrupted the work, leaving us only a few completed portions from the first and second sections—beautiful, but of only limited performance potential. In the catalogue of his works they were later given opus number 97, but most likely much in them would have been changed if he had completed the composition.

We have from the first section a recitative for solo soprano describing the arrival of the Wisemen from the East at the manger where the infant Jesus lies; a short trio for the three Wisemen (one tenor and two basses); a four-part mixed chorus whose content is prophetic ("Es wird ein Stern aus Jakob aufgeh'n und ein Szepter aus Israel kommen. . . ."—A star from Jacob will rise and a scepter will come out of Israel), which becomes more dramatic: "Der wird zerschmettern Fürsten und Städte" (He will shatter princes and cities), before it grows more spiritual with lyrical contemplation: "Wie schön leuchtet der Morgenstern." (How beautifully shines the morning star).

From the second section, which was to describe Christ's suffering, a short tenor recitative remains ("Und der ganze Haufe stand auf"—And the multitude arose) as well as the following accusatory chorus: "Diesen finden wir, dass er das Volk abwendet . . . und spricht, er sei Christus, ein König." (We find that he has turned the people away . . . and says he is the Christ, a king). The scene continues with a solo for the tenor, who plays a role something like that of the Evangelist in Bach's oratorios: "Pilatus sprach zu den Hohenpriestern und zum Volk" (Pilate spoke to the High Priests and to the people), whereupon the people's anger bursts forth: "Er hat das Volk erregt damit, dass er gelehrt hat . . ." (He has disturbed the people with his teachings). Once again the tenor has a narrative recitative: "Pilatus aber sprach: Ich finde keine Schuld an ihm." (But Pilate said, I find no blame in him), and again, even more violently, the chorus demands freedom for Barrabas.

Then the tenor has a few words, having to do with justice and seeking Jesus' release, but the people, now infuriated, rage: "Kreuzige, kreuzige, kreuzige ihn!" (Crucify him!)—a powerfully passionate number, one that can stand alongside similar pieces by Bach. In strict accordance with the Gospels, Pilate now hands Jesus over to the Jewish people, who plan to kill him: "Wir haben ein Gesetz, und nach dem Gesetz soll er sterben!" (We have a law according to which he must die), expressed in a fugue. The narrator continues, saying that a "grosser Haufe Volks und Weiber, die klagten und beweineten ihn" (a great crowd of people and women, weeping and lamenting) follow Jesus as he is taken away.

The last of the remaining pieces is a lament, an elegiac dirge: "Ihr Töchter Zions, weint über euch selbst und über eure Kinder...." (Daughters of Zion, weep for yourselves and for your children). The last complete fragment is a chorale for four-part male chorus accompanied only by the low instruments (bassoons, violas, cellos, and basses): "Er nimmt auf seinen Rücken die Lasten, die mich drücken bis zum Erliegen schwer...." (He bears on his own back the burdens that weigh upon me so).

The bridge to Bach is complete: it is not incorrect to call Mendelssohn a "Classical Romantic" or a "Romantic Classicist"; but the bridge he built has a greater span than that: He begins with Bach, bridges Mozart and ends in the High Romantic idiom. Still, perhaps we should not speak of "arcs" and "ends" but of a circle without beginning and end, for in his works Mendelssohn joined epochs, styles, and extremes in ways hardly matched by any other great master.

Claudio Monteverdi   1567–1643

The Monteverdi renaissance of the 20th century, whose main thrust emanated in the 70s from the Zürich Opera, has brought the works of this ancestor of modern music—he deserves this title as much as Bach—to the attention of a wide public. Not only are his operas being revived but also many of his other works (many, unfortunately, have been lost), putting his music to the test once again after so many centuries.

Monteverdi's birthdate is unknown, but the entry in the baptismal records of the city of Cremona was made on May 15, 1567. When 15 years old, he published his first sacred work (as a student of Ingegneri); in 1590 he went to the court at Mantua, where he became *maestro di capella* in 1602. On August 19, 1613, he was chosen to be musical director of St. Mark's Cathedral in Venice, where he worked until his death. Many of his manuscripts were kept in the duke's palace at Mantua, which was plundered along with the rest of the city in 1630, and partially destroyed. In September 1610, while in Rome, Monteverdi dedicated his *Missa in illo tempore* and the *Vespro della Beata Vergine* to Pope Paul V. In 1624 he performed his setting of the Torquato Tasso poem *Il combattimento di Tancredi e Clorinda* for the first time in Venice, and in September 1638, the Eighth Book of Madrigals appeared, in which theater pieces were included, such as *Combattimento* and the much earlier *Ballo delle ingrate*. It was earlier maintained that his songs went beyond the concept of the madrigal, but it must be remembered that his epoch was a time of great change in all aspects of music: style changed from polyphony to harmonically accompanied melodies, new forms such as opera and oratorio together with related hybrid forms arose. Monteverdi's most important choral works surely deserve a place in this book. Monteverdi died in Venice one year after the first performance of his last opera, on November 29, 1643.

Il ballo delle ingrate was composed in 1608 in Mantua, the same year as the opera *Arianna* (almost all of which has been lost) and one year after the sensational *Orfeo*, the first "classic" of opera literature. Ottavio Rinuccini, who may be called the literary father of opera, and who spent the years from 1601–1605 at the Parisian Court, wrote the libretto for *Ballo*. At about the same time, in 1599, Monteverdi had accompanied the duke of Mantua on a journey through France to Flanders. As a consequence some French influence in *Ballo* is probable. The French ballet de cour was an art form very similar to the English masque in that it combined vocal, instrumental, and dance elements. In "The Dance of the Thankless Women" Venus and her son, Cupid, lament the decline of love in the world. They then ask Pluto, lord of the underworld, for the souls of all those "ingrates" who did not know how to truly love when they were on earth and who must now endure eternal torture. They appear and perform a dance of remorse and sadness, before they must once more descend to the dark kingdom.

Sixteen years later, for the carnival of 1624, Monteverdi presented *Il combattimento di Tancredi e Clorinda* in the Mazzenigo Palace in Venice. It is an extremely forceful, unusual piece of music, best described as danced drama with sung narrative. A *Testo* (the narrator in oratorios) sings the famous text from *Gerusalemme liberata* by the great Torquato Tasso, which describes the tragic encounter between the Italian crusader Tancred and the beautiful Saracen Clorinda; during the siege of Jerusalem, they meet one night outside the city gates in a bitter duel. Tancred, who loves Clorinda passionately, does not recognize her in her knight's armour and kills her; as she lies dying, she opens the visor of her helmet and asks her opponent to baptize her. Only then does the despairing Tancred comprehend his error.

The two sacred works dedicated to Pope Paul V in 1610, *Missa in illo tempore* and the *Vespro della Beata Vergine* are in different, even opposing styles: the *Mass* is "in the old style" of a cappella polyphony, which in those years was slowly approaching its end, whereas the *Vespers* looked boldly into the future. Monteverdi had not only completely mastered both techniques of composition, he wrote knowledgeably about them, legitimizing them as "prima prattica" and "seconda prattica," and defended them against the polemic attacks of the musical theorist Giovanni Maria Artusi. Many music lovers find the *Vespro della Beata Vergine* to be one of Monteverdi's supreme accomplishments, perhaps his most beautiful work. We should further note that today, since we have many of the original versions of these works, it has become senseless to perform transcriptions as was once done. Nor need new instrumentation be provided as we have Monteverdi's exact instructions. It is true that over the centuries, many of the old instruments called for have fallen into disuse, but they can be copied quite accurately, and their use assures that "ancient," inimitable orchestral sound suitable for these compositions. No female voices are used in the Mass, the Vespers nor in the two superb settings of the Magnificat that have been preserved. The church stipulation that only male voices could participate in the liturgy, with high voices sung by boys, was still in force.

Wolfgang Amadeus Mozart   1756–1791

That Mozart was at one time a bone of contention for music scholars, the target of all kinds of charges seems inconceivable to us today. Yet in our own time new aspects of his life and work still turn up, furnishing grist for the mills of speculation. And more alarmingly the media have dealt with this illustrious figure in the most startling and often indefensible ways but without, fortunately—and a point of great importance—ever managing to cast doubt on the artistic worth of this wide-ranging, most universal of geniuses in music history. Many of the objections, raised posthumously by purists of other epochs, concern his sacred music. They viewed it as being too worldly, or dependent upon the style used in his operas. Eric Blom's biography of Mozart notes that the Kyrie of the C major Mass, K 317 (*Coronation Mass*) was used again 11 years later in Fiordiligi's aria in the opera *Così fan tutte*, and the Agnus Dei of the same work, as an aria for the Countess in *Le Nozze di Figaro*. Much can be said about this complex subject. One might point out that a composer who, at a conservative estimate, wrote 5,000 melodies during his short life could not possibly recall all of them in the heat of creativity, at the moment of inspiration. This is particularly true when similar moods were to be reflected in different genres. In the examples put forward the correspondences are not absurd: both come from opera, an art form never completely respected by the purists—they thought it "frivolous." But in both situations, that of Fiordiligi and the Countess, the music is completely serious, dignified, and deeply affecting. By no stretch of the imagination can it be held that the music is degraded or blasphemous. Moreover, it must be understood that all composers in all times, develop a style which forms the basis of their works and is effective in all genres. How else should late-18th-century sacred music have been composed? The reigning style was that of the Rococo, which to modern ears sounds playful, lacking seriousness and representing the superficiality dominating public life at that time. But it would be absurd to claim that these characteristics dominated the inner nature of all people living then, as illustrious examples of the time prove—not the least of whom was Mozart.

Another salient point must be raised: When Mozart was dismissed from the service of the Prince Bishop of Salzburg and entered the musical life of the great city of Vienna, the number of his sacred compositions dropped abruptly. By way of explanation, we must look to the times and beyond that, to Mozart's own life. He was to a substantial degree a musician who wrote on commission, as was usual at the time. His job in Salzburg was to compose sacred works, but since he held no post in Vienna he accepted whatever commissions he was offered. Probably the two most beautiful and important of his sacred compositions, both written in Vienna, were composed for specific occasions: The *C minor Mass* was the result of a vow, while the *Requiem* was commissioned. The number of his works belonging in this book is small when compared to those in other genres, but their importance cannot and should not be underestimated. If Masses, individual Mass movements, offertories, antiphons, vespers, and the many akin compositions are taken into account, they far outnumber his 17 operas and other compositions for the stage.

Little will be recounted here of Mozart's brief 36 years. After a truly amazing childhood, for which the term "child prodigy" in its fullest sense barely suffices, came an adolescence marked by the full development of his most wonderful gifts. His material existence, however, was marked by a continuing decline, hard to fathom, even harder to explain. Forced to rely upon imperial commissions for operas; subscriptions by the nobility for the printing of his chamber works; the organization of "academies" (concerts); taking on students, Mozart's circumstances during his last 10 years, the Vienna years, steadily worsened. His genius seemed purely musical and of no help in controlling his personal affairs. Or alternatively his character may have been ill-suited to cope with such matters. Whether a love of gambling was to blame, or a tendency to pursue the good life, or his inability to maintain friendships with the powerful people in his environment—an ability highly developed without making concessions by Beethoven—will probably never be established with any certainty. Mozart was from childhood on a practicing Catholic, but more importantly, he was a man of the Enlightenment, which in turn led him to become a committed Freemason. He saw no conflict or incompatibility between the Church and Freemasonry: his religious music is as sincere and deeply felt as the music he created and performed for his masonic lodge. Oratorios make up only a small part of his total output; those requiring mention here are: the setting of the Metastasio text *La Betulia liberata*; four cantatas (*Dir, Seele, des Weltalls*; *Davidde penitente*; *Die Maurerfreude*; and *Kleine Freimaurer Kantate*); a youthful work, *Grabmusik*; and his arrangements of four of Handel's oratorios, among them the *Messiah*, with new instrumentation.

Mozart's Masses

All Mozart's Masses, with the single—and most important—exception of the *C minor Mass*, K 427, are works of the early Salzburg period, the first 25 years of his life, which came to an end when he was unceremoniously dismissed from the service of the Prince Archbishop on May 9, 1781. Mozart had secretly longed for this termination, which he had to a large extent provoked, but had not expected it would come about in this way. From those Salzburg years, the following Masses have been preserved:*

Missa Brevis in G major, K 49 (1768)
Miss Brevis in D minor, K 65 (1769)
Missa in C major, K 66, *Dominicus Mass* (1769)
Missa brevis in C major, K 115 (only a fragment, the Sanctus, remains) (1773)
Missa brevis in F major, K 116 (fragment) (1771)
Missa solemnis in C minor, K 139, *Orphanage Mass* (1771/72)
Missa in honorem SSmae Trinitatis in C major, K 167, *Trinity Mass* (1773)
Missa brevis in F major, K 192 (1774)
Missa brevis in D major, K 194 (1774)
Missa brevis in C major, K 220, *Sparrow Mass* (1775)
Missa brevis in C major, K 257, *Credo Mass* (1776)
Missa brevis in C major, K 258, *Spaur Mass* (1776)
Missa brevis in C major, K 259, *Organ Solo Mass* (1776)
Missa longa in C major, K 262 (1776)
Missa brevis in B-flat major, K 275 (1777)
Missa in C major, K 317, *Coronation Mass* (1779)
Missa solemnis in C major, K 337 (1780)

From this imposing list of 17 Masses, of which two have come down to us only as fragments, possibly because Mozart never finished them, two call for detailed description here: The Missa brevis in C major, K 220, of 1775, called the *Sparrow Mass* because of a "twittering" violin figure in the Sanctus (Example 1); and the Mass in C major, K 317, which became known and popular under the name *Coronation Mass*.

Mozart's Mass in C major is one of his most attractive sacred works. He wrote it in 1775 in Munich, where he had journeyed for the first performance of his opera *La finta giardiniera*. The Mass was originally bound with four others, all in C major, in a single volume on which his father Leopold had written, as he had done when Mozart was a child (although "the child" was 19 years old): the title "V Missa in C". (The Latin is incorrect, surprising for a trained and educated musician.)

Though called "short Masses," these are festive works by virtue of the instrumentation, calling as it does for trumpets and timpani. The brevity of the *Sparrow Mass* and the other four written at the same time can be ascribed to an edict by the Prince Archbishop of Salzburg of whom Mozart wrote to his esteemed Italian teacher, Padre Martini, on September 4, 1776: "A Mass . . . even the most solemn, when the Archbishop officiates, may not last longer than three-quarters of an hour and must be scored for all the instruments, trumpets and timpani."

We do not know the reason for the title *Coronation Mass*. Mozart never used it and probably had never heard of it, which leads us to believe that it was coined after Mozart's death. It was long believed that it had something to do with its composition for an annual feast day in the pilgrimage church Maria Plain, near Salzburg, during which an image of the Virgin was crowned. Mozart scholar Karl Pfannhauser (in the *Mitteilungen der Internationalen Stiftung Mozarteum*, Salzburg, 1963) writes that immediately after Mozart's death this Mass became the one preferred at the Vienna Hofmusikkapelle for the religious services performed at the coronation of emperors and kings. It was used for the first time for the coronation ceremonies for Emperor Francis II. The designation *Coronation Mass*, originally used as a title by the court chapel for its own internal records, soon came into general use.

We know exactly the day on which Mozart finished the work: March 23, 1779. We also know that he had only shortly before returned from his journey to Mannheim and Paris, a journey critical in many ways to his career. In Mannheim, the first true love of his life, the very talented singer Aloysia Weber, who "was not meant for him" (to use Schubert's term), rejected his attentions. In Paris, his mother, who had accompanied him, died. These events moved his sensitive heart to compose a sacred work. Despite his personal losses it is not a "sad" work but rather overflows with melody. The orchestral part is surprisingly well developed, employing both sonata and rondo forms. This is one of Mozart's works most persistently charged with being too worldly. The French commentator Bernard Gavoty refuted this charge marvelously in the *Almanac* for the Salzburg Easter Festival of 1973:

> Mozart saw no division between the human and the divine, between nature and the supernatural. Everything spoke to him *of* God, but he spoke *to* God. A bird sings the same song, for a prince or for a beggar. Before God and before man, Mozart sings the same tune.

And Mozart's English biographer, Eric Blom, further illuminates the matter: "The most natural genius, Mozart was born into the most artificial time."

Example 1

Mass in C minor, K 427

Original Title: Missa C moll
Original Language: Latin
Text: From the five parts of the Ordinarium Missae
Date of Writing: 1782/83
First Performance: August 25, 1783, in St. Peter's church in Salzburg.
Form: The Mass was never completed: of the five parts of the Ordinarium Missae, Mozart set completely only the Kyrie, Gloria, and the Sanctus with its Benedictus. The Agnus Dei is lacking entirely; and the Credo was completed only to "Et incarnatus est." The composition is in four parts and includes a total of 12 musical numbers.
Scoring: Four solo voices (two sopranos, tenor, bass), four- to eight-part mixed chorus; flute, two oboes, two bassoons, two horns, two trumpets, three trombones, timpani, strings, and organ.

Discussion of the Work: Although uncompleted, this Mass is Mozart's most famous work in the genre. As with Schubert and his *Unfinished Symphony,* so with Mozart; it is not that death had taken the pen from his hand; that occurred nine years later, with the *Requiem.* As with Schubert, the question then arises: Why did he not finish it? No one knows the answer, for he said never a word about it. There are many such instances in both art and music history. But only rarely has a composer given such a torso a premiere.

We know something of what led up to this performance. During the summer of 1782, the romance between Mozart and Constanze Weber—a sister of his once-beloved Aloysia—flowered, and they talked of marriage. But Wolfgang suspected, in fact knew, that he could not count on his father's permission to marry "one of those Weber girls." He was still a good and dutiful son, for Leopold had planned and guided his entire upbringing, including his musical education; had led him in triumph across half of Europe; and was in all important matters still his mentor. "After the good Lord comes Papa" Wolfgang once remarked.

In this terrible dilemma, Mozart made a vow that he would compose a Mass if the situation worked out as he hoped, meaning that he could marry Constanze without damaging his relationship with his father. It did work out, although his relationship with Leopold, already hard hit by the death of his wife, was never again as close and warm as it had once been. Wolfgang set to work. Easy going as he may have been in many respects, a vow was a vow. He wrote a Kyrie, a Gloria, a Sanctus with Benedictus, and parts of a Credo, specifically the first article of faith "Credo in unum Deum" and the following "Et incarnatus."

How far he got with it in 1782 is unknown; it seems that he continued work on it until May 1783. By the end of July of that year the time had come for the married couple to visit his father in Salzburg. Mozart had already sent his father some of the completed portions, and now he brought the rest. What kept Mozart, who composed so swiftly, from finishing the missing parts in a few days?

However, he arranged for it to be performed on August 26, 1783, in the beautiful old monastery church of St. Peter in Salzburg. He knew the place well; it stands next to both the cathedral and the archbishop's *Residenz,* two places where in his Salzburg days he had made music countless times. We learn more about this first performance from his sister, Nannerl. She wrote in her diary that "all the court musicians were there" and that her sister-in-law, Constanze, "sang the solos." And they were by no means easy; either Constanze was a good singer, or the young, loving husband closed his ears (difficult to imagine considering how sensitive he was to singers). It seems, however, that on that August 26, Constanze transposed her solos slightly lower. She may never have received greater proof of her husband's love.

But these facts do not clear up the most important question: In what form was this first performance given? For liturgical reasons it seems unthinkable that only the finished parts were sung. Did Mozart fill in with parts from other works? Had he perhaps actually finished this Mass and later lost the parts that are missing today? The first supposition is the more likely: driven by necessity, he took the corresponding parts from earlier Masses. This was not a satisfactory solution because although Mozart's earlier sacred music contained many splendid pieces, the C minor Mass stands head and shoulders above anything of this kind he had ever written, as posterity recognized after decades of neglect.

Its annual performance at the Salzburg Music Festival, in the same city in which it was first performed, is due in part to the efforts of the great singer Lilli Lehmann. She had first urged regular performances of the *Requiem* at an earlier Mozart Festival in Salzburg, mounted in the 19th century. For whatever reasons, this proved unworkable, and the *C minor Mass* was substituted, first in 1904 and then regularly since 1927, thanks to Bernhard Paumgartner, the noted Mozart scholar, conductor, and long-time president of the Festival.

Attempts to complete the work were not lacking. Performances after 1901 were done with additional material by Alois Schmitt, who used parts of Mozart's other sacred works. In recent years, however, it has been concluded that this composition, like Schubert's *Unfinished,* needs no additions. Unless it is to be performed as part of a liturgical service, the original score is usually followed in concert performances.

We should also mention that two years later Mozart used large parts of this Mass in his cantata *Davidde penitente,* composed in 1785 under tremendous time constraints. The Kyrie of the Mass became the opening chorus of *Davidde penitente* ("Alzai flebili voci al Signor").

The C minor in the Kyrie becomes C major in the Gloria, a modulation also used in the cantata ("Cantiamo le glorie e le lodi").

The chorus then bursts forth with "Gloria," turning into a fugue on the words "in excelsis Deo," but continuing in a free form. The "Laudamus te" of the Mass (a soprano aria in the cantata) is a very long soprano solo with many coloratura passages, again with a broad range, covering two octaves. Did Constanze's voice have such a range?

The third part of the Gloria, the "Gratias agimus tibi," is for five-part chorus, the soprano section being divided into two; it, too, was taken over in its exact form for the cantata ("Sii pur sempre benigno"). The following "Domine Deus" is an expressive duet in D minor for the two solo sopranos (exactly the same music is used in the cantata, with the words "Sorgi, o Signore") (Example 1).

At this point, Mozart inserted a tenor aria into the cantata, which is not found in the Mass. There follows the "Qui tollis" sung by eight-part double chorus (taken over just as it is by the cantata: "Se vuoi, puniscimi?"). The orchestral backdrop is distinctly rhythmical, with trumpets and timpani; its relation to the Mass text here is not altogether clear. The following "Quoniam" (a terzetto in the cantata) brings the two solo sopranos together with the solo tenor. The whole piece is built upon fugal entries and shows Mozart's facility in the "ancient" polyphonic style, more evident in the important fugue of the "Cum Sancto Spiritu," which follows the brief "Jesu Christe" (Example 2).

The seven-bar theme, unusual for the Classic era, sounds like a cantus firmus of the Middle Ages. (The fugue does not appear in the cantata.) After this last part of the Gloria, the chorus, again in five parts, begins the Credo, which has a festive, majestic ring—and sounds quite secular.

All the more lovely, though hardly more spiritual, is the "Et incarnatus est." Is this folklike melody (Example 3) related to the rustic birth of Jesus? Do the piping sounds represent the shawms of the shepherds who stand before the manger amazed? A beautiful soprano voice can make this solo fit for an angel, which would be quite suitable at this point. This brings the Credo to an end; as with the Gloria, Mozart had probably envisioned a movement of greater scope.

Once more back in C major—after the previous bucolic F major of the solo soprano—the double chorus announces its very solemn, dignified "Sanctus." With "Osanna" the choruses launch into the most complex fugue of the whole work, ending with the jubilant "in excelsis, in excelsis." The solo quartet intones the "Benedictus," also very polyphonic, and finally merges with the virtuoso double chorus again singing "Osanna," with at one time or another all the voices except the basses singing God's praises in sixteenth notes, supported by the rejoicing full orchestra, with brasses and timpani. Here the fragment ends, just as, it seems, Mozart left it.

Example 1

Allegro moderato

Example 2

Example 3

Andante

Requiem, K 626

Original Title: Requiem
Original Language: Latin
Text: Mass for the Dead from the Catholic liturgy (Missa pro defunctis).
Date of Writing: June or July to December 4, 1791
First Performance: December 14, 1793, in the Neuklosterkirche in Wiener Neustadt.
Form: As completed by Franz Xaver Süssmayr, the work is in eight parts and contains 14 musical numbers.
Scoring: Four solo voices (soprano, alto, tenor, bass), four-part mixed chorus; two basset horns, two bassoons, two trumpets, three trombones, timpani, strings, and organ.
History of the Work: In 1826, 35 years after Mozart's early death, the musicologist and jurist (Jakob) Gottfried Weber (1779–1839) in his musical journal *Cäcilia* first raised the question of the authenticity of the then known manuscript of Mozart's *Requiem*. Since then such a mass of legend, supposition, rumor, speculation, and fantastic embellishment has appeared that the whole truth will probably never be known. Mozart and Constanze were to journey to Prague, where his opera *La clemenza di Tito*, commissioned on such short notice, was to have its premiere. Shortly before their departure at the end of August—so the usual story goes—a mysterious "messenger" came to him asking if he could compose a Requiem and how long it would take. The name of the man, who turned out later to be perfectly harmless, was Leutgeb, acting on behalf of Count Franz von Walsegg-Stuppach. Later authors enlarged upon suspicions rumored at the time that he appropriated other people's works as his own, and wanted to perform Mozart's *Requiem* in his palace on the first anniversary of his wife's death, passing it off as his own. Whether Leutgeb was dressed "all in gray" on the day he visited Mozart, we do not know, but Mozart, in telling Constanze of his premonitions of death, incorporated the vision of a messenger all in gray who came from the next world to tell him of his impending death.

Looked at objectively, the matter was quite straightforward, witness the fact of the contract Walsegg had drawn up by the Vienna notary Sortschan for the work.

That Leutgeb acted "mysteriously" and requested Mozart to refrain from inquiring after the person commissioning the work is understandable: Count Walsegg's intentions were obviously not the most honorable. It is equally understandable that Mozart, in the extreme hypersensitivity of his final weeks, when his illness—whatever it may have been—progressively weakened and frightened him, would develop premonitions of death, which might well have become associated in his mind with a "man in gray."

Among the hundreds of rumors relating to Mozart's death one holds that the Freemasons poisoned him. The many unusual circumstances surrounding his death have led to a chain of suspicions, in which the role of the "gray messenger" was to give notice of the crime. Entirely apart from the fact that the Freemasons had not the slightest reason to do away with their dear and faithful brother, such an assumption (which is as absurd as the version claiming that Salieri murdered him) is confounded by the fact that Mozart's last venture from his house was to attend a mid-November function at his lodge. He did so to perform a composition dedicated to the Freemasons. Would he have willingly gone to the house of his murderers when he had been forewarned by the "gray messenger?"

The death premonition and its "announcement" by the "messenger" seems to be confirmed by a letter published by Lorenzo da Ponte, the librettist for *Figaro, Don Giovanni,* and *Così fan tutte,* in his memoirs. He claimed to have received the letter from Mozart when the master was deathly ill. It speaks of the "messenger in gray": "I see him ever before me. He asks me, he urges me, he demands the work from me.". The poet, who had meanwhile grown old, and was never viewed as a "serious" person, tried to prove that he had in 1791 offered to take Mozart to London to obtain help. In the same letter, Mozart supposedly declined the offer, saying "it is too late." Later research has proved the letter to be a forgery:

Let us return to the incontrovertible facts. In the fall of the year of his death, Mozart worked feverishly, although often intermittently, on the *Requiem,* even when confined to bed. A few days before his death on December 4, 1791, he showed the finished pages of the work to visiting friends: his brother-in-law Hofer, Benedikt Schack, and the singer Franz Gerl who was singing the role of Sarastro in the *Zauberflöte* in the nearby Theater auf der Wieden. They sang from Mozart's manuscript while Mozart, weak as he was, hummed along and gave the beat. Which part of the *Requiem* could that have been? Did they see rough drafts, or were these finished pages of the score?

Immediately after Mozart's death, on December 5, 1791, efforts to complete the Requiem began. Joseph (von) Eybler (1765–1846), a good musician who later became Hofkapellmeister, was the first asked. He orchestrated the "Dies irae" as far as the "Lacrimosa"; then he stopped working on it. Constanze then contracted with Franz Xaver Süssmayr (1766–1803) to finish it, which he did. Most contemporary performances of the *Requiem* include his supplements to Mozart's original composition. Again and again, and for good reason, the extent of Süssmayr's work has been debated. Some of the issues raised include: Which autograph or manuscript was picked up immediately after Mozart's death and apparently delivered? Which manuscript was supposedly paid for by one Baron Jacobi on March 4, 1792, a quarter of a year after Mozart's death? Did he pay, as was agreed upon, only that part of the honorarium still outstanding after the payment that had been made directly to Mozart in the summer of 1791? Did the clarinetist Maximilian Stadler (who managed to extract "loans" from his "friend" Mozart, deeply in debt himself, and never pay them back) in his various statements about the origin of the *Requiem* tell the truth or, as is more generally assumed, lie? Did Constanze really know everything about this work, as she apparently assured her second husband, the Mozart biographer Georg Nikolaus von Nissen?

Constanze, to be sure, never maintained that at the time Mozart died there was a completed manuscript. Ignaz von Seyfried wrote on October 16, 1825: "That a complete manuscript was delivered to the mysterious unknown person is only a myth, which the widow never claimed was true."

Süssmayr was surely the closest of Mozart's friends and assistants. Mozart had taken him to Prague to work out the secco recitatives for *Tito*, for which he himself had no time. He knew Mozart's style better than anyone and was familiar with his way of composing. But in all of his own works—and there are many, most of them operas—there is nothing that can compare with some of the passages he supposedly wrote to complete Mozart's Requiem.

Was it that the master's spirit so influenced him that in this one effort he outdid himself? Or had he perhaps only fleshed out sketches Mozart had already written? As fate would have it, his handwriting is so similar to Mozart's that in many places the calligraphy cannot be distinguished.

In any event, Mozart certainly composed the first two parts of the *Requiem*—the Introitus and the Kyrie—as well as their instrumentation right down to the last detail. All the music in the third part, the Sequence, with the exception of the last number, the "Lacrimosa," is also by Mozart; he had, however, notated only the vocal parts and the figured bass but not the individual instruments. Of the "Lacrimosa," the first eight measures are by Mozart; Süssmayr composed the continuation from measure 9 and in addition, the instrumentation for the preceding numbers of the Sequence. The next part, the Offertorium (with the two numbers "Domine Jesu Christe" and "Hostias") comes once more from the hand of Mozart. Here, too, he only notated the vocal parts and the figured bass; Süssmayr provided the orchestration.

Of the three following numbers—Sanctus, Benedictus, and Agnus Dei—there is no evidence in Mozart's own handwriting. We must, as a consequence, regard these parts as Süssmayr's compositions. Although Mozart had written nothing for the closing Communio, the last part of the *Requiem*, Süssmayr composed nothing; but instead he returned to the beginning of the work and used parts of the Introitus and the Kyrie, both composed completely by Mozart. Süssmayr used it with the text of the Communio: "Lux aeterna luceat eis."

Discussion of the Work: The first movement begins in a melancholy D minor; it may symbolize not so much eternal rest ("Requiem aeternam") but the inner unrest of a man who feels his final hour approaching. The syncopated effect (melodic and theme entrances on the unaccented beats, suspensions, the consequent shifting of emphasis from the beginnings of measures, and so on) is lessened by the slow tempo (adagio) and robbed of its harshness, yet gives the whole movement the impression of only slightly suppressed restlessness.

We are reminded of the special meaning of D minor in Mozart's works; it is not only the key of *Don Giovanni* (which alone suffices to bring to mind inner conflict and intervention by supernatural powers, the mysterious presence of death and struggle for salvation) but of several other works which seem to have a special aura about them.

Dark colors predominate in Mozart's *Requiem*: there are no high parts in the wind instruments but only low, often melancholy sounds. The first melodic entry is heard in the bassoon, and the second—at the fifth, as in a fugue—in the basset horns, those early clarinets with the deep, golden tone, which Mozart liked to use toward the end of his life (they may have been invented in the 1770s) and which characterize the mood of *Die Zauberflöte* as well the *Requiem* (Example 1).

The voices of the chorus enter fugally, at brief intervals—bass, tenor, alto, and soprano—with the theme already presented in the prelude, but freely treated. The texture remains polyphonic until "et lux perpetua," at which point the voices come together in chords. Shortly thereafter the solo soprano begins the "Te decet hymnus," but after a few measures yields to the chorus, whose sopranos take over the soloist's melody. After a brief orchestral bridge passage, the choral basses resume the opening "Requiem aeternam", but Mozart shapes it somewhat like a double fugue, announcing things to come. The main theme in the basses is accompanied contrapuntally by the altos, whereupon the tenors and the sopranos appear in the same way, also sharing the theme (Example 2).

Again the voices come together in harmony at "Et lux perpetua" and reach a pause and half cadence on the dominant, with an A major chord (fifth scale step in D minor). Then Mozart leaves

Example 1

Example 2

the slow tempo to begin a lively allegro, a mighty double fugue in which the entrances of the first theme (in the basses, then the sopranos) are sung to "Kyrie eleison," those of the parallel second theme (in the altos, then the tenors) the "Christe eleison" (Example 3).

Example 3

Example 4

Every composer of a Mass for the Dead wanted to construct the *Dies irae* sequence so as to present a terrifying image of fear, retribution, and destruction. Here Judgment Day bursts forth (Example 4) allegro assai, at a driving tempo; the chorus, entering powerfully in D minor, seems to see a fearful vision of the end of the world before its very eyes.

In a raging whirlwind the nightmare roars by. Mozart, who very seldom used tone painting, here describes three times the quaking and trembling that seizes mankind (Example 5). And he stays with tone painting: the next number, the "Tuba mirum," begins with a trombone solo, whose majestic, resounding call to Judgment Day vividly expresses in sound what the text says with words (Example 6).

Example 5

Example 6

Above a soft throbbing in the strings, the tenor sings his "Mors stupebit," and then, a little more gently, the solo alto sings "Judex ergo," taking over a phrase the tenor has used in which an augmented second interval is prominent; since time immemorial Western music has used this interval to symbolize pain, sorrow, heartache, and deep emotion. With the entry of the solo soprano ("Quid sum miser") the minor keys that have dominated until now brighten to B-flat major, but the soprano, too, takes over the phrase with the augmented second, before the movement comes to an end in a mood of confidence.

The following movement is overpowering in its magnificence: The thrice repeated call "Rex! Rex! Rex!" to a majestic orchestral accompaniment gives a vision of omnipotence scarcely imaginable by man. The awesome power of the "King in terrible majesty" has probably never been more convincingly described than here. The effect is magnified as mankind begins to plead for itself: first, in quiet reverence, the female voices and then the male, sing "Salva me;" then all together repeat this heartfelt supplication, "Salva me, fons pietatis" (Save me, source of all compassion). The final harmonies move from the more serene, hopeful E-flat major back to D minor (although the piece began in G minor). Is this meant to depict despair?

The following "Recordare," in F major, is wonderfully tender; it is sung like a prayer by the four solo voices and in a deeply affecting, one might almost say Romantic, polyphony. The next movement, the "Confutatis," is more dramatic. The male chorus, supported by menacing trombones, is set against the gentle, hopeful female chorus "Voca me cum benedictis!" The "Lacrimosa" follows, during the writing of which Mozart laid down his pen forever. Is it the other-worldly purity of the melody or the knowledge of its significance in musical history that makes the listener, upon hearing this work, aware of the full power of music and of Mozart's incomparable genius (Example 7)?

This movement proves that when all is said and done, any argument as to whether Süssmayr was "qualified" to carry out Mozart's musical testament is senseless. Even a composer greater than he could hardly have written anything more appropriate here, nothing that could have fitted so seamlessly into Mozart's whole design, without betraying a foreign hand.

"Domine Jesu" and "Hostias," the two parts of the Offertorium, lead to the same fugue, "Quam olim Abrahae," which proudly conjures up the greatness of its own long history (Example 8).

Example 7 Larghetto.

Example 8 Andante.

The following parts, the "Sanctus" and the "Benedictus," are probably completely attributable to Süssmayr, unless we assume that Mozart had already quickly sketched out the whole work and that Süssmayr had then destroyed these sketches after he had incorporated them into the work. The first melody of the solo alto in the "Benedictus" and the response to it by the solo soprano are so full of Mozartian nobility, so completely beautiful, that it is difficult to conceive of someone other than Mozart composing them (Example 9).

The concluding fugue of this movement is quite short, more a fugato, since its brevity does not permit further development. If it is Süssmayr's work, it is proof that even then, almost half a century after the end of the Baroque era, every good musician was still capable of composing an honest, four-part fugue.

Süssmayr's "Agnus Dei" moves from the broad lyrical prayer to the Lamb of God immediately to the last part, the Communio, for which he returns to the soprano solo of the beginning.

Example 9

Perhaps this was Mozart's idea, one he had been able to share with his student, friend, and confidant before his death. Süssmayr faithfully carried out the task entrusted to him—more by fate than by Mozart or his heiress Constanze. Permeated with the dead man's spirit and conscious of the importance of his undertaking, he created a work that is by far his greatest.

Ave verum

Of Mozart's many sacred works, this one motet has been selected simply because it is so beautiful. One of Mozart's most generous friends in his later years was the choir director of a church in Baden near Vienna, Anton Stoll. At Mozart's behest he did many favors for Constanze when she was taking the cure there; Mozart even asked him to find her a suitable place to live during her visits, a task this conscientious man and good musician dutifully carried out.

To thank him for such courtesies, and also for performing his Masses, it seems that Mozart composed this motet in 1791 for Corpus Christi Day. It calls for four voices, strings, and organ, and its number in the Köchel Catalogue, 618, is close to that of the Requiem—626. The relatively brief work is arranged in two stanzas. This composition is so permeated with deep, pure faith that all the negative judgments directed at Mozart's sacred music are left without foundation. Our chapter on Mozart could not end with a truer, more tender melody than the one introducing this small but great work (Example 1).

Example 1

Johannes Ockeghem   ca. 1430–1495?

This musician, one of the great figures in music history, is now, 500 years later, not only a familiar figure to scholars, but also a composer whose works are occasionally performed. He spelled his name in various ways: Okeghem, Okehem, or Ockenheim, and the facts of his life are just as hazy: Of Flemish extraction, member of the boys' chorus at the cathedral in Antwerp, royal musician at the court in Paris, and active after 1459 in Tours, where he may have died. He is included in this book for the many Masses he wrote (11 have been authenticated) and a 36-part "Deo Gratias," quite famous at the time, though not all authorities consider the manuscript of this work authentic. His works were apparently all sung a cappella and reflect the highest mastery of compositional technique. Thanks to the great number of specialized choruses in existence today, much of the music of the Flemish school has again become "living" music. It includes the Masses *Serviteur, Ma maistresse* and *Caput* by Ockeghem. The names of the first two come from secular songs—well-known melodies that were often used by composers of sacred music as a cantus firmus. Our interest in old music has made possible the revival of the great Netherland masters. Though their music may be technically difficult, and sound unfamiliar, it is one of the great flowerings of Western culture. In many ways it was the basis of all later European music, preparing the Baroque and Classic eras. Furthermore, many a 20th-century composer has been inspired by those austere sonorities that preceded the establishment of tonality, and which dominated musical practice for hundreds of years.

Carl Orff 1895 1982

No other German musician of his generation evoked such intense, international interest as Carl Orff. Nor is there another quite as controversial as this innovator of music theater. How different opinions of his early work were can be illustrated by excerpts from critical accounts which range from "relapse into primitivism," "the dreariest lack of harmony," "nerve-wracking hammering of the most inartistic phrases," "the very antithesis of music," to "gifted creator of a true music theater," "most valued rediscoverer of Antiquity," "apostle of a new feeling for life," "enthralling creativity." One either loves Orff's works or rejects them out of hand—and with great intensity—but it is difficult to remain indifferent. Orff's style is so completely his own that it is recognizable from the first measure of any of his works. It is not just by chance that a work like *Carmina Burana* made such a great hit with hundreds of thousands of people around the world. It is the most performed work of its kind of our time, and not only in concert halls but (of greater consequence) in countless schools and universities, giving boundless pleasure to performers and audiences alike.

Orff was born on July 10, 1895, in Munich. He studied at the Academy of Music in his native city, becoming assistant conductor and then Kapellmeister in Munich, Mannheim, and Darmstadt. But then he broke out of the typical musician's path by founding an experimental school of movement and dance in Munich. Here he developed the concepts of the basic rhythmic elements employed in music of all kinds, which in turn served as the foundation of his *Schulwerk*, a pedagogical approach based on the connection between gesture, speech, and music. Its importance to both pedagogy and psychotherapy has been enormous. Then his cantata *Carmina Burana* (1937) suddenly burst on the scene, and it was a bombshell. The name of this hitherto unknown composer was widely recognized virtually overnight. Then 42 years old, Orff began turning out work after work. With the additions of *Catulli carmina* and *Il trionfo di Afrodite, Carmina Burana* was enlarged to form a triptych called *Trionfi.* In addition to these works, intended mainly for the concert hall, Orff also created several works which are at the core of contemporary music theater: *Der Mond* (1939); *Die Kluge* (1943); *Die Bernauerin* (1947); *Antigone* (1949); *Oedipus der Tyrann* (1959); *Prometheus* (1968); and *De temporum fine comoedia* (1973).

Trionfi

I. "Carmina Burana"
Original Title: Carmina Burana
Original Languages: Distorted medieval Latin and Middle High German.
Text: By Carl Orff, based on medieval sources.
Date of Writing: 1937. "Carmina Burana" was later made part of the triptych *Trionfi.*
First Performance: June 8, 1937, in Frankfurt am Main.
Scoring: One soprano, one baritone; a few male voices in short solos; a large and a small chorus, children's chorus, orchestra.
Discussion of the Work: A collection of poems and songs, some written by itinerant scholars and clergy, had lain in the Benedictine abbey at Beuron since the 13th century. Their authors, called Goliards, wrote in very corrupt Latin or in Middle High German. They were first published in the middle of the 19th century under the title of *Carmina Burana* (Songs from Beuron). Orff found in them a rich source of material for a production combining dance and song, a form for which there is no exact term, but "cantata" is the closest. The work can be performed either in concert or on the stage, with ballet and an eurhythmic chorus. The theme running through the work is the wheel of

Fortuna, the goddess of fate. It is she who rules our lives, who causes spring to burst forth with its elemental power, awakening love and longing. The work is really one long hymn to the pleasures of life, youth and beauty. It plays itself out lightheartedly, grasping, whirling, holding, and letting go, all fatefully intertwined and, like spring, like love, like everything that lives, ever regenerating.

The first chorus is a call to Fortuna (in Latin); its subject is eternal transformation: "O Fortuna, your moods change like the phases of the moon." A male chorus then laments the wounds that fate inflicts upon us. A song in praise of spring begins. Catchy melodies in simple song forms (Example 1), alternating with others reminiscent of early Christian Gregorian chant, dominate the work. There are no modulations; all is primitive and compellingly logical. The most important sound colors and nuances are provided by the orchestra, employing an extremely complex percussion section which plays a critical role in the presentation. The sixth piece is purely instrumental and bears the Middle High German title "Uf dem anger" (In the meadow) (Example 2). It is a happy, lively dance with a medieval crudeness about it; its rhythmic interest results from the alternation between quadruple and triple time. Then the maidens sing, calling to their friends and lovers. The forest is in bloom, everything is coming alive and greening in the spring sunshine. "Floret, floret, floret silva"—first in Latin, then in Middle High German: "Gruonet der wald allenthalben."

The maidens appeal to the shopkeeper (in Middle High German), asking him to sell them powder to redden their cheeks so that the young men will come running faster ... A round dance follows and then an enchanting, tender lovesong: "Chume, chum, geselle min" (Come, come, my love) (Example 3). With a jubilant "Were diu werlt alle min" (If all the world were mine), the first part comes to a close.

The second scene takes place "In Taberna" (In the tavern), using only male voices. It consists of a series of drinking songs, which in often quite crude, rollicking texts, enumerate life's pleasures, including sexual and culinary joys. A tenor sings ironically of roast swan, a baritone sings a mocking song about the abbot of "Cucanienis" (roughly translated, "land of the Cuckoo").

The third part takes us back to the kingdom of love: "Amor volat undique" (Cupid flutters everywhere) is the first song. There is a charming soprano solo, and a passionate suitor's song for the baritone. The choruses become more and more orgiastic as youths and maidens find each other. The call to Venus "Ave formosissima" (Greetings, most beautiful one) leads to the last song, which repeats the hymn to Fortuna with which the work began. It is impossible to convey in words the effect of this scenic cantata. Orff's music lifts the old songs to a magical atmosphere, now

Example 1

Example 2

Example 3

rapturous with the joy of life, now tender and heartfelt, inspired by inexhaustible rhythmic inventiveness and possessing a primitive force resulting from a technique he often uses—repetition of a single nucleus of sound and rhythm. Much of what was to be characteristic of his style is already clearly evident in this, his first important work.

Orff's thoroughly new way of using the extensive percussion section provides an unheard-of wealth of nuance. The total union of word and tone by which one gives rise to the other in a completely natural, seamless way; the related melodies of speech and song; the primacy of rhythm, from which, in a certain sense, everything else is born; the chiaroscuro quality resulting from the absence of dynamic transitions, wherein contrasts follow each other directly, in the old manner—all these are characteristics that since *Carmina Burana* have been called "typical Orff." His manner is always direct and hard-edged, like a woodcut; yet everything lives and moves, and its seeming monotony is replete with fascinating diversity.

II. "Catulli Carmina"

Several years after *Carmina Burana*, Orff created the scenic work (it might also be called a "madrigal cantata" or even "madrigal opera") entitled "Catulli Carmina," meaning "the poems (songs) of Catullus." It is related in some ways to "Carmina Burana" but is shaped completely differently. The structure is provided by a group of old men who, using as an example the disappointment in love suffered by the famous Latin poet Gaius Valerius Catullus, counsel of the perils of love. The scene then moves to Catullus and the patrician Clodia (who became legendary under the name of Lesbia) who sing of their love. Their romance comes to its end with Clodia's unfaithfulness and Catullus' painful resignation. But this example does not turn the young people (here the chorus; only the lovers sing solo roles) away from the toils of romantic love. The story is largely acted out by two dancers, singers and orchestra being placed in the orchestra pit. Orff joined this work to the *Carmina Burana* and later added a third section to form the triptych, *Trionfi*. (First performance: November 6, 1943, in Leipzig).

III. "Il Trionfo di Afrodite"

Orff sings here for yet a third time of love but this time in an ecstatic, magical, ritual way—like almost nothing ever written before. The texts used come from Catullus, Sappho and Euripides. Greek words are mingled with the Latin text, giving substance to Orff's view that all languages share a common structure—a concept that informs both his music and writings. The orchestral forces called for are extremely large and use many unusual instruments (three pianos, guitars, bells, marimba, rattles, and others). The rhythm has a primitive strength and the pounding melodies are brief. It is an orgiastic, frenzied work which, like its predecessor, is not an opera, but neither is it a "scenic cantata," nor a "scenic concert," nor indeed any other term in any musical dictionary.

Orff wrote *Trionfo di Afrodite* more than a decade and a half after *Carmina Burana*, but made a cycle of it by coupling *Catulli Carmina* and *Trionfo di Afrodite* with it, entitling the cycle *Trionfi*, a common term in Baroque theater and its medieval predecessors. Each in its own way describes the power and triumph of love indomitable. The first performance of *Trionfo di Afrodite* was presented at La Scala in Milan, on February 13, 1953; three weeks later, the work was performed in concert in Munich, and on March 10 it was staged in Stuttgart.

John Knowles Paine 1839–1906

Public recognition for an American composer in the 19th century was a hard-won victory. John Knowles Paine achieved it, not only for himself, but for American musicians in general. The composer of almost 100 known works for orchestra, small ensembles, organ, piano, chorus and the stage, and the first American to have a work performed abroad (Mass in D, 1867), Paine drew the musical world to respect the American composer as more than an imitator. As an organ virtuoso he was attracted to the Bach revival and was instrumental in bringing more of Bach's music to America. As the teacher of Carpenter, Converse, Foote and many others he encouraged the growing spirit of nationalism in younger American composers. Finally, as the first professor of music in this country (Harvard University, 1873) he fought persuasively to establish a place for music in the liberal arts curriculum, worked to establish college departments of music, and introduced the American concept of "composer-in-residence." His eminent position as a musical leader in 19th-century America is widely recognized.

St. Peter

Original Language: English
Text: Except for the three chorales, all the text is scriptural, drawing heavily on the New Testament.
Date of Writing: 1872
First Performance: June 3, 1873, in Portland, Maine.
Form: In keeping with tradition the oratorio is in two parts, each having two dramatic subdivisions—a total of 39 individual numbers.
Cast: Of the soloists, one tenor serves as the chief narrator; the other acts the role of Jesus. St. Peter is sung by the bass. Soprano and contralto soloists carry narration text at times, have occasional arias, and fill minor roles as servants during the "denial" scene.
Scoring: At least five soloists, full orchestra and chorus.
History of the Work: The year 1873 was not only the year of Paine's historic appointment at Harvard, but also saw the premiere of his full-length romantic oratorio, *St. Peter.* Only a scant few choral works of this magnitude had been attempted before by American composers. *St. Peter* is openly in the Germanic tradition, modelled on the great works of Mendelssohn and Spohr—expected in light of Paine's extensive study in Europe. The premiere of *Saint Peter* was given in Portland, Maine on June 3, 1873, with the composer as conductor. The following day, a reviewer for the *Portland Press* was moved to record these observations:

> The oratorio performance of last evening was a brilliant, important and entire success, which will greatly increase the musical reputation of our city. . . . It is only within a few years that music and the immortal works of the great masters have been listened to with ever-increasing enjoyment and satisfaction. Nothing could more distinctly indicate the great progress made, than the successful attempt by a native composer in the high and austere department of the oratorio; and its intelligent and adequate performances and cordial reception in his native city.

Discussion of the Work: A brief orchestral introduction leads directly into Part One, beginning with eight numbers grouped under the heading *The Divine Call.* In the opening chorus, the words of John the Baptist announce, "The time is fulfilled, the Kingdom of Heaven is at hand. Repent and believe the glad tidings of God." Paine immediately shows his consummate skill in manipulating all manner of rapidly changing harmonic and contrapuntal textures, equal to that of his best European contemporaries. His harmonic vocabulary draws from the common practice of the mid-19th century, but there is no tendency toward ultra-chromaticism. Word painting receives discreet attention. In this chorus, the word *repent* is repeatedly associated with the "sinful" sound of the diminished-seventh interval, but is always repeated on the next beat to a "cleansing" perfect fifth ascending, in another voice (Example 1). Except for the homophonic statement of the opening words, the texture remains contrapuntal. A pseudo-ternary design results when the initial text returns to mark the closing section. Joyful ascending melodic arches accompany the words "the glad tidings," and the rhythmically insistent repetition of the word *repent* leads into a meditative pianissimo coda on the text "believe the glad tidings of God." Many choruses follow a similar design.

Example 1

The scene shifts to the Sea of Galilee, where Jesus calls the 12 disciples to "preach the kingdom of God." An aria of consecration ("The Spirit of the Lord is upon me") is followed by a chorus of twelve men representing the disciples: "We Go Before the Face of the Lord, to Prepare His Ways." The first of three chorales, "How Lovely Shines the Morning Star," comes at this point. It is of historical interest that a lengthy footnote in the published score justifies in detail the use of these chorales, apparently for the benefit of the uninitiated American performers. In recitative, Jesus questions Peter, "But who say ye that I am?" Peter's seemingly immutable reply, "Thou art the Christ," opens the way for Jesus to proclaim the founding of His Church. Peter responds in a flowing, ternary aria on a text from Psalm XVI, "My Heart is Glad." In the closing number for this section, the chorus brings all these events into focus with its initial proclamation "The Church is built upon the foundation of the apostles and prophets." Confirmation comes in the final phrase (Example 2).

Example 2

The second section, *Denial and Repentance*, begins with the scene at the Mount of Olives during Holy Week and deals with Peter's denial of Christ. In accompanied recitative, Peter enters into dialogue with Jesus and doggedly affirms his allegiance. Jesus divines Peter's fragile faith and predicts denial. The biblical account is interrupted here and Jesus sings the oft-quoted words of comfort from John's gospel "Let not your heart be troubled." This aria is in a modified strophic-ternary design. There are three musical sections and two units of text: the first unit is reused for the final section, as in a da capo aria. The opening phrase, quoted above, begins each section, but the musical resemblance ceases after the first cadence, and only a pretense of ternary form remains. The entire vocal ensemble now joins in a lengthy chorus "Sanctify us Through Thy Truth." These two numbers are not lacking in beauty, but do exemplify certain weaknesses in the libretto. Judas betrays Jesus and the chorus, in retreating phrases, reflects the shame and guilt of the faint-hearted believers (Example 3). For the scene of Peter's testing the chorus represents his accusers (Example 4). Unlike many composers who have treated this scene, Paine did not choose to imitate the crowing of the cock after Peter's final denial. Three ominous notes by the horns symbolize the prophetic words of Jesus "Thou shalt deny me thrice." An anguished orchestral lament, glimpses of which appear in the overture, depicts Peter's intense remorse (Example 5). Again Peter turns to the psalms for comfort in his poignant aria "O God, My God, Forsake Me Not".

This moment of penetrating reflection on Peter's faithless action leads into the three closing numbers of Part One: the chorus "Remember From Whence Thou Art Fallen, and Repent", a contralto aria "The Lord is Faithful and Righteous to Forgive Our Sins," and the chorus "Awake Thou that Sleepest." These numbers stand apart from the narrative. Drawn from the biblical narrative, their purpose is spiritual edification for the listeners, like a sermon. Their presence, mid-point in this work, is well aligned with the Romantic oratorio tradition.

Example 3

Example 4

Example 5

The subjects of Part Two relate to two major events in the life of the early Church which directly involved Peter: Ascension and Pentecost. A brief account of Jesus' trial, crucifixion and resurrection is condensed into the highly expressive opening chorus. Each event has an individual emotional quality. The brief reference to the trial is delivered by the chorus in unison—a rare but effective choral technique for this work. Four repetitions of the text "He was crucified" suffice to portray Christ's death on the cross. A transition to the resurrection passage leads into the triumphant phrase picturing the risen Christ (Example 6). This towering soprano line later becomes the subject for short fugal expositions. A chorale follows, "Jesus My Redeemer Lives," allowing for a moment of contemplation, as in the great Passions. Now the scene moves quickly. Jesus appears to the disciples and after dialogue with Peter—"Simon, lovest thou me?"—issues the *great commission* in a brief arioso: "Go ye and Teach." Christ's ascension follows with appropriate upward-moving arpeggios in the orchestra: the chorus sings "If ye be Risen with Christ." Peter's spiritual strength and determined zeal are extolled in the soprano aria which follows, "O Man of God." This setting is harmonically, melodically and formally simple, but no musical structure could express more effectively the determined zeal of Peter the Apostle—the rock upon whom the Church was built. This aria stands majestically at the center of the oratorio (Example 7). Unlike the other three sections, this one concludes with a solo quartet. Its text, "Feed the Flock of God," passes gently over the disciples as they prepare to spread the Gospel. A flurry of winds and brass in the orchestra abruptly announces the opening text for the final section—"And when the day of Pentecost was fully come." The narrator continues, as violent tremolos in the strings propel the "mighty rushing wind." Darting broken chords throughout the orchestra picture the "cloven tongues of fire" and finally "they were all filled with the Holy Ghost" (Example 8). A lengthy syllabic commentary from the chorus follows, "The Voice of the Lord Divideth the Flames of Fire." Multitudes gather, speaking in tongues. Peter quotes the prophet Joel in the driving, energetic aria "Ye Men of Judah," explaining how Joel's prophecy is being fulfilled here: "In the last days, saith God, I will pour out my spirit upon all flesh". In the succeeding aria Peter preaches about Christ's life and ministry and the significance of this Pentecostal "outpouring of the Holy Spirit." Speaking for the multitudes, the chorus asks: "What Shall we do to be Saved?" Peter and the disciples reply: "Repent, for the promise is to you and your children."

An exceptionally well-constructed polyphonic chorus follows, "This is the witness of God which He hath testified to his Son," in the imitative style associated with Handel and Mendelssohn (Example 9). In this chorus, the theological foundation of the incipient church is affirmed and the path for Peter's ministry opened. A third chorale, "Praise to the Father," appropriately captures the spiritual mood.

Example 6

Example 7

Example 8

Example 9

Peter's departing words to the disciples "Go and tell these things to the brethren" leads to the most elaborate and extensive chorus in the work, "Beloved, Let Us Love One Another." The 12 disciples, a four-part male chorus, the full chorus and Peter join in an extended interplay of choral phrases, always in response to the dominating voice of the Apostle, exhorting the faithful to "love one another." The closing two numbers, a duet for soprano and tenor "Sing Unto God" and the massive final chorus "Great and Marvellous are Thy Works," witness to the story of the church's beginning—a mood of resounding praise to God.

—Thurston Dox

Horatio William Parker   1863–1919

In his lifetime, Horatio Parker was America's leading composer. After extended study in Europe during his early years, he rose to prominence as a church musician and teacher in New York. His appointment as Professor of Music at Yale University in 1894 and subsequent life-long tenure, placed him in a position of national leadership and influence.

Parker's ebullient, romantic style is anchored in the Wagnerian chromaticism of his time and he never saw cause to progress from that position. He wrote for orchestra, for organ and for the stage, including two prize-winning operas. The largest portion of his oeuvre, however, consists of solo songs and choral works. Among the many large works for chorus and orchestra, two are outstanding: *Hora Novissima* (1893) and *The Legend of St. Christopher* (1897).

Hora Novissima

Original Title: Hora Novissima, Op. 30
Original Language: Latin
Text: Verses reflecting on eternal life, drawn from portions of "De contemptu mundi," a lengthy poem on spiritual life by the 12th-century monk Bernard de Morlaix.
Date of Writing: 1893
First Performance: May 3, 1893, in New York.
Form: Its two major divisions are subdivided into 11 units, perfectly balanced in a number of ways. First, sections one and two (chorus and quartet) and the closing two choruses (ten and eleven) act as a formal frame. Then, beginning with section three, four arias alternate with three choruses, providing a balanced middle group. Chorus six stands majestically in the center, a summary of material from the first chorus, symbolizing spiritual and musical unity. The proportions are symphonic. Also, each soloist sings one aria only, the lowest voice first, then the highest (soprano), followed by tenor and alto. A subtle balancing results from this ordering of the solo ranges.
Scoring: Full orchestra, solo quartet and chorus.
History of the Work: Hora Novissima was premiered in New York on May 3, 1893, by the Church Choral Society. It was warmly received. A reviewer for *The New York Times* observed that it took rank immediately "among the best works written on this side of the Atlantic." He commented on its "remarkable command of variety in style" and felt it would "bear comparison with the productions of foreign composers." In September, 1899, the European debut of *Hora Novissima* took place at the Three Choirs Festival in Worcester, England. The critic of *The Pall Mall Gazette* gave an honest appraisal when he accorded it a place among the respected works of the day.

> Sometimes his thoughts were other men's thoughts. There are many places, here and there, when it is wonderfully easy to say, "Rossini passed this way." "Gounod caught that bird." "Mendelssohn picked that flower," and so forth. But that comes in as part of the essential situation. ... The man was full of ideas and imagination, and, perhaps with lack of stern criticism and careful sifting, but certainly with perfect gaiety, good humor and courage, he set them all down in due order. To deny the thing originality is to avoid the work altogether. It has the best originality in the world, that of being alive in itself, of possessing liberality, freedom, extraordinary openness of sentiment. I do not know where else to look in quite recent music for just these qualities.

Discussion of the Work: Prior to the recent resurgence of interest in America's musical past, *Hora Novissima's* imposing stance as the earliest American choral work of stature was undisputed. It was considered America's *only* oratorio. In fact, this monumental composition, which earned respect abroad at the Three Choir Festival in England (1899) and received many performances over the years, is not aligned with historical oratorio form in the strictest sense. It does not have a narrative dramatic libretto and its soloists do not fill character roles.

Throughout the work there are clear indications of thematic transformation, modification and reuse, as well as developmental passages and choral recapitulations. These factors are decisive enough to characterize the work as a choral symphony. The orchestral introduction contains the germinal theme (Example 1). This stately melody strides majestically through the opening chorus. It is literally reused in chorus six and becomes the intervallic source of several themes in other movements. A second equally important unifying factor is the rhythmic organization of the theme's motive—two notes of longer value framing shorter notes. This feature is common to a large number of melodic units.

Example 1

Due to these pervasive factors, vivid contrast in mood between the 11 sections is not present to the same degree as in so many other large choral works (*Requiem*, Berlioz; *Elijah*, Mendelssohn). There are good reasons. The subject matter in each section is similar—a poetic view of heaven as God's "celestial country." The verses themselves are variants of the same poetic theme. Secondly, there are no scene changes to call for striking shifts of character and mood in the music. However, constantly changing textures do accommodate shifting emphases within the verses.

A brief but dramatic introduction moves directly into the opening chorus, "Hora Novissima" (The Final Hour). This chorus actually resembles a sonata in form, having two themes, a pseudo-development, a recapitulation and even a short coda. Re-statements of the main theme, fughetta passages and brief expressive textures add interest. This kind of formal clarity and organization brings a sense of classic stability to the movement. In the solo quartet "Hic Breve Vivitur", No. 2 (Her life is quickly gone), a series of brief imitative passages using different motives and blocks of homophony create a modified 16th-century motet style. Textures change rapidly to enclose particular portions of text in more expressive settings. The questioning inflection on the word "Qualia?" (what are they) is immediately followed by measures of slow, descending half notes on the word "Plena"—like a gentle blessing (Example 2). The bass aria "Spe Modo Vivitur" (No. 3) is in a straightforward ternary form. Throughout the work phrases are generally two measures in length. The dark shades of a D-minor tonality and stern, angular melodic lines which draw strength from reiterated perfect fourths, provide the optimum setting for the opening text, "Zion is captive yet." A climactic moment early in the middle section is filled with expressive longing for the celestial country. The mode shifts to a bright, confident D major for the closing lines, "Zion rejoices."

Example 2

An uplifting modulation—literally up a minor second—introduces the majestic chorus of praise "Pars Mea, Rex Meus" with its impassioned question, "When shall we see thy face?", set to a staccato ascending line. A fully developed fugue unfolds after the opening homophonic phrases. Its majestic subject begets strong, assertive counterpoint and results in one of the many testimonies to the composer's masterful polyphonic craftsmanship. Near the end a brisk stretto leads into a final unison statement of the augmented subject, marked *maestoso* and triple-forte.

Flowing, expressive phrases in the tradition of 19th-century Italian opera characterize the soprano aria "O Bona Patria" (O Country Bright and Fair). As in the bass aria, simple ternary form and persistent two-bar phrase construction provide balance and coherence. Chorus number six "Thou Ocean Without Shore" opens with a bold reappearance of the main theme (Example 1) in the orchestral introduction. Solo quartet and chorus combine for this finale to Part One. Antiphonal exchanges in two-bar phrases, over a rippling orchestral background, picture the "fountain unknown." Brief four- and eight-bar imitative passages alternate between quartet and chorus alone. A brief orchestral interlude develops material from the introduction and the opening chorus and leads to a finale worthy of any Verdi opera.

Part Two begins with the tenor solo "Urbs Syon Aurea" (Golden Jerusalem). The thematic material is characteristic of the work, based on perfect fourths and perfect fifths in two-bar phrases. Unlike the other arias it is not in ternary form. Free vocal phrases climb higher and higher, seeming to seek the new life in the beauteous reaches of Heaven. The double chorus, "Stant Syon Atria," No. 8, notably contrasts with the others. Its text expresses the songs of consummate joy sung by the redeemed in an effervescent, scherzo-like movement. Quickly overlapping entrances of the two choirs and a spirited rhythmic vitality give this section buoyant urgency. Only once is the momentum interrupted by a change of meter and tempo, a majestic section in nine-four time for both choruses together, acting as a "trio." The "scherzo" returns ("The kingly throne is near them, joyful shouts we hear them"), moving with unbridled energy to a *maestoso* coda and final cadence over syncopated rhythms from the orchestral introduction. An alto aria, "Gens Duce Splendida" completes the sequence of alternating solos and choruses in Part Two. Intense, penetrating C-minor harmonies and short, pressing phrases over heavy triplet chords recall moods in Verdi's *Il Trovatore*. The text is "People victorious, In raiment glorious." This aria portrays a dark mood, relatively unrelated to the text, and provides an extraordinary contrast to the previous section.

Urbs Syon Unica," chorus ten, is written in 16th-century point-of-imitation motet style and is the only movement purely religious in tone. Waves of imitative polyphony ebb and flow into brief homophonic sections, always maintaining an ecclesiastical atmosphere. The choir sings "City of high renown, Home of the saints alone."

The finale, "Urbs Syon Inclyta," begins with a thematic recapitulation of the opening chorus material. An extended fugue subject of sweeping grandeur is introduced by the sopranos and leads to the most complex choral polyphony in the work (Example 3). Strands of the fugue subject together with new material weave a contrapuntal fabric that steadily increases in range and strength. The solo quartet leads the way to a climax in the highest tessitura. A brief, ten-measure orchestral bridge gathers fragments of thematic material with the verve of a Strauss symphonic poem. Then, as if all the company of heaven were assembled, the chorus recapitulates the fugue subject in a massive unison statement. Quartet and chorus seem to "strain the vaults of heaven" as their lines approach the final cadence of the work.

Example 3

The Legend of St. Christopher

Original Title: The Legend of St. Christopher, Op. 43
Original Language: English
Text: Verses by Isabella Parker.
Date of Writing: 1898
First Performance: April 15, 1898, in New York.
Form: The libretto is divided into three acts and nine scenes.
Cast: Seven character roles: three sopranos (The Queen, The Angel, The Child), two tenors (The King, The Hermit), high baritone (Satan) and bass (Offerus).
History of the Work: The Legend of Saint Christopher was premiered on April 15, 1898 by the New York Oratorio Society. A reviewer for *The New York Times* praised the oratorio but felt "it might easily have been written fifty years ago." This observation is certainly true regarding melodic and

harmonic styles, but Parker's use of "remembrance motives" is forward looking, even for this "post-Wagnerian" work. His understanding and structural handling of these motives is extensive and truly admirable, especially in the more subtle aspects of their relation to the drama.

In October 1902, *St. Christopher* was performed during a festival in Bristol, England. A comment by the reviewer for the *London Times* was accurate in a general historical appraisal of the work.

> The whole seems to be conceived operatically as if it were designed for Bayreuth, or some stage where religious subjects could be presented without offending pious susceptibilities. If the third act, with its abundance of church music and its likeness to *Parsifal*, be recognized as operatic in its higher sense, the first and second acts are even more distinctly operatic in character.

No doubt the *Brooklyn Eagle* gave the composer the most satisfaction in its review of the premiere. Citing the choral writing in particular, the commentator submitted that "the name of Parker will be classed among the musicians of renown." *St. Christopher* has never gained popularity equal to *Hora Novissima*, though the composer reportedly felt it was a better work. Modern performances have been given and a recording produced (1968) by the Washington Cathedral Choir.

Discussion of the Work: Parker's dramatic oratorio *The Legend of St. Christopher* was completed six years after *Hora Novissima*. There is no similarity in structure or content between the two works. The libretto for *St. Christopher* is narrative, with seven character roles and dramatic functions for the chorus. The music is through-composed. Throughout the score, explicit stage directions for costuming, action and scenery are indicated in detail. These directions are adequate to allow a fully staged "operatic" production, although certain long choruses do present static conditions which present challenges to effective staging. This dual nature of some oratorios and cantatas is not uncommon in the 19th century, as a number of works were written for optional concert or staged performance.

The legend focuses on a series of events through which the giant and servant, Offerus, the burden-bearer, becomes converted to Christianity. In his immediate desire to serve his new master, Offerus is called upon to carry the youthful Christ across a raging river and is thereafter called Christopher, the Christ-bearer.

In the first two scenes of Act One, Offerus gives himself in service to the King and Queen, following a festive scene at the King's victorious return from battle. The King accepts Offerus in a duet fit for the opera house. A flourish of hunting calls introduces scene three, the hunting scene, set in "an open glade in the forest." Offerus ignores the king's warning not to kill a deer which comes out of the forest, on the pretext that an evil force inhabits the woods. A strange, compelling power draws Offerus into the forest and the service of Satan. The King and chorus join in the closing number of Act One "Farewell, our hero, gallant Offerus".

Act Two opens on a desert plain, where Offerus meets Satan and his legions. In a bold, sinister aria, filled with furious, whiplashing motives, Satan proclaims himself to Offerus:

> Prince of all the world am I. Yield thee, body, mind and soul unto my supreme control.
> Storms and whirlwinds do not flee. Naught on earth can conquer me.

Offerus submits to Satan's power and joins with the male chorus in a long, diabolic march of Satan's host. The opening four-bar statement is reused in the manner of a refrain (Example 1). The movement of this march presses on, relentlessly. At the opening of scene two, a cross appears and a treble choir sings phrases of "Asperges Me" (Wash me and I shall be cleansed). Satan recoils. His followers are overcome, their movement gradually halted by the increasing power of the hymn. An arched, pentatonic "cross motive" appears in the chorus, leading to polyphonic imitations that symbolize the supreme power of the cross (Example 2). Offerus rejects Satan, espouses Christianity and goes to follow Christ. Satan attempts to restrain him in an impassioned "operatic" duet. The chorus "Farewell, our hero, gallant Offerus," closes the second scene.

Scene one of Act Three takes place in the cottage of a hermit, whom Offerus has sought out for guidance. As the hermit explains to Offerus the story of Christ's salvation he discloses his own past as a king who embraced a Christian life. Again, the vocal lines move with "operatic" gestures (Example 3).

A striking shift of scene to a cathedral takes place. The choir is singing "Asperges me, Domine" as at the appearance of the cross in Act Two. Offerus, deeply moved by the beauty of this music, asks "Tell me, good father, what can I do for the Christ, my Master?" With the hermit's response, "Come, and I will show you all the Church's beauty, in her worship lowly, learn thy constant duty," the orchestra introduces the magnificent chorus "Gloria in Excelsis Deo." This extensive, polyphonic masterpiece of some 200 measures exceeds any other portion of the oratorio in

Example 1

Example 2

Example 3

Example 4

Example 5

Example 6

craftsmanship and musical satisfaction. It was compared with other choral masterworks in the most flattering terms by all contemporary critics and may well be the composer's greatest single choral creation. The opening statement resounds through the vaults of the cathedral (Example 4). Passages in mixed chordal and contrapuntal style follow, continuing past mid-point in the liturgical text. As all voices come to an expressive pianissimo cadence on the words "miserere nobis" (have mercy upon on us), the orchestra sweeps into a restatement of the first motive and introduces the subject of a magnificent choral fugue (Example 5). Its buoyant energy propels the remainder of the text to a radiant "Amen," to which Offerus responds "In Gloria Dei Patris, Amen." In a beautiful and well-constructed trio with the Hermit and the Angel, Offerus learns that through giving himself to others and to God he will know immortal joy. The full chorus closes the scene in an a cappella setting of the Latin hymn "Iam sol recedit igneus" (As sets the blazing sun).

In the very brief third scene, Offerus asks again what he can do to serve Christ. The hermit instructs him to "build a hut" by a certain river and live there to carry burdened travellers through the deep and treacherous waters. The fourth scene opens at the hut. A violent storm rages through the night and Offerus hears the voice of a youth (soprano) calling to him "carry me over tonight." He responds and during a tempestuous orchestral interlude bears the youth across—"a quiet light upon the child's head" (Example 6). With a high, soaring melodic line over undulating arpeggios in the orchestra, Offerus sings "a power divine urges my spirit through the angry waves till I gain the great prize of my master's approval." As the chorus tells Offerus "Thou hast borne in thine arms the Holy One," the Hermit and the Angel join with the chorus and proclaim that Offerus will be named Christopher—the Christ-bearer. An extended choral finale with solo trio celebrates Christopher's mission as the helper and guardian of all travellers.

—Thurston Dox

Giovanni Pierluigi da Palestrina 1525?–1594

Giovanni Pierluigi, the renowned composer of sacred music, was named after the town of Palestrina, near Rome, where he was born. He has often been referred to as the "savior of sacred music" and as such was the hero of the opera bearing his name written by Hans Pfitzner in 1917. Today it seems certain that virtually nothing of the legend that had grown up around him, and provided the impetus for the opera, really took place. It is true that the Council of Trent devoted several spirited sessions to the matter of sacred music. Further, it is clear that church music in Palestrina's day was in a period of decadence replete with evidence of all kinds of abusive practices. But that the composer assured the continued place of polyphony in the liturgy with one of his masterly Masses, commissioned by the Cardinals, or that this Mass was dictated by an angel in a single night, is a beautiful story whose origin is unknown. Nevertheless, it is not unreasonable to regard Palestrina as the "savior of sacred music," by virtue of the strength and energy he imparted to it, thus silencing the noisy opposition voiced in clerical circles.

Palestrina entered his music career as a singer in the boys' choir of the Sistine Chapel in 1551;

he went on to direct that choir and to become choral director at the Cappella Giulia in St. Peter's Cathedral. After he served two Popes, Julius III and Marcello, Paul IV dismissed him under an ancient rule which forbade the employment of married musicians in the Vatican. He then worked in the churches of San Giovanni in Laterano and Santa Maria Maggiore, finally returning to St. Peter's in 1571, where he held a post until his death on February 2, 1594. He left some 950 works, of which 94 were Masses and ca. 300 motets. The best known of his works is the *Missa Papae Marcelli*, probably composed in 1562 and dedicated to his long-dead benefactor. It is still often heard today. It is said that this Pope once complained about composers of sacred music, claiming that because of all the ornamentation, coloratura passages, and complicated rhythms people could not understand a word of the text. The "Palestrina style" fulfilled the Pope's wishes for greater clarity of text, a sentiment that shortly thereafter led to the emergence of monody, or melodic homophony accompanied by chords.

Krzysztof Penderecki   1933–

Only a very few serious postwar composers have been successful in interesting more than a handful of experts or in having their works become part of the general repertory of public musical life. Few modern operas, orchestral compositions, vocal works, or teaching materials for the amateur musician have enjoyed any significant success. One of the exceptions is the Polish composer Krzysztof Penderecki. Despite his radical "modernism" his works are also attractive to the general public—indeed, Wolfram Schwinger coined a paradoxical bon mot, calling him "an avant-guardist of the establishment."

Penderecki was born on November 23, 1933, in Debica, near Krakow. His success came early and quickly, first in his native land, where he won anonymously all the first prizes in a composition competition (1959); later, in the West, one success followed another, notably at the Donaueschingen Festival. In 1966, he attracted enormous attention with his *St. Luke Passion*, commissioned by the West German Radio in Cologne. This "vocal-symphonic milestone" (Walter Labhart) has to be one of the most important musical works of our century. Its place is not simply due to the skillful use of the techniques of new music but also to their successful welding, to form an artistic unity in the service of the religious ideals to which he is committed. Though his later sacred works did not achieve the stunning effect of the *St. Luke Passion*, they should nevertheless be noted here. His music goes hand in hand with the development of his "new graphics," the only system of notation capable of recording the sounds introduced into music by him and like-minded contemporaries. This revolutionary means of indicating musical sounds is one with which young musicians must come to terms, just as young physicists, mathematicians, chemists, doctors and architects must come to terms with the revolutionary developments of our times. The old system of notation is clearly not adequate to represent such innovations as sounds inserted between adjacent chromatic notes, or nontraditional ways of playing instruments.

St. Luke Passion

Original Title: Passio et mors Domini nostri Jesu Christi secundum Lucam
Original Language: Latin
Text: From chapters 22 and 23 of the Gospel of *St. Luke*; also passages from the Gospel of *St. John*, and the *Lamentations of Jeremiah*, the *Psalms*, and the Roman Catholic Passion liturgy.
Date of Writing: Commissioned by the West German Radio in Cologne, 1963–1965.
First Performance: March 30, 1966, in Münster, Westfalia, for the 700th anniversary of the cathedral.
Scoring: Three solo voices (soprano, baritone, bass), a speaker, mixed chorus subdivided into many parts, two-part children's chorus; four flutes (with two piccolos), one bass clarinet, two saxophones, three bassoons, contrabassoon, six horns, four trumpets, four trombones, tuba, timpani, drums, cymbals, bongos, wood blocks, tam-tams, gongs, bells, vibraphone, harp, piano, harmonium, organ, and strings.
History of the Work: The West German Radio, where the European experiments with electronic music began in 1950, developed in the following decade into one of the leading centers of new music. Not surprisingly it commissioned this outstanding contemporary musician to compose a work to be performed at the great celebration for the Münster cathedral. At the time, Penderecki

was working on a *Stabat mater* (later worked into the *St. Luke Passion*), which called for three 16-part a cappella choruses. Penderecki had already used the new sounds and their attendant new notation in instrumental music, notably in his *Ode to the Victims of Hiroshima*. He now extended these concepts to vocal music. In spite of the unusual difficulty of performance and the unusual demands it made on the audience, the *St. Luke Passion* was a resounding success when it was performed March 30, 1966. Its popularity spread with surprising speed.

Discussion of the Work: The catchwords of modern music are inadequate to give the reader who is unacquainted with this work even a rough idea of it. Penderecki works with changing planes of tone color, thus expanding the expressive possibilities of both human and instrumental voices and introducing an incredible number of new effects. But such an explanation fails to provide the lay musician with much of an idea of the work.

Let us rather start with what it is that the music lover is accustomed to hearing and will not find here. He must forget the word "melody" in its traditional sense, because at the most there are only very short motives that may remain in the mind's ear. Nevertheless, the listener has the feeling that in long passages melodic events can be perceived. At first, however, it seems inconceivable to speak of harmony. Yet there is an idea of simultaneity—and that, after all, is what harmony really is, even if it no longer consists of triads or other easily recognized chords.

Nor can the listener expect the usual kinds of rhythm, yet the music is full of movement—and movement is rhythm, even when it is not grouped as the Classics did it 200 years ago. Sustained notes do not remain on a precise pitch but rise or fall. These fluctuations in pitch are not chromatic as in earlier music, the first flute phrase in Debussy's *L'apres-midi d'un faune* being an example, but rather move in smaller intervals, like a siren. Such small intervals usually are called "microtones." To notate microtones, new symbols had to be found.

In addition, Penderecki introduced other previously unused sound qualities: "Unspecified" pitches, expressed, for example, in symbols that mean "the highest possible" or "the lowest possible" tone without being more specific; arrhythmic playing or speaking or singing; aleatory music (free improvisation or an arbitrary succession of compositional elements); nontraditional ways of playing traditional instruments (such as bowing the strings of the violin between the bridge and the tailpiece); etc. In addition countless nuances of sound are called for in the choruses, from the faintest of breathy whispers to voice-cracking shouting. A glance at the score of the *St. Luke Passion* reveals a sound world that did not exist a generation ago, one that even today admits of multiple interpretations.

Nonetheless, Penderecki is not eager to break completely with all that has gone before, so we are suddenly surprised by "tonal" sonorities. Not only the previously composed *Stabat mater*, which the composer inserted into the work, but the entire composition ends on pure major chords. This "relapse" creates an unusually powerful effect; must Penderecki fall back upon the luminosity of these major harmonies, or upon the sad quality of a minor triad? Is it a conscious search for continuity? If so, this might also explain the appearance in the midst of this work of the motive B-A-C-H, which has been used by countless composers for almost 250 years in homage to the great cantor of St. Thomas. The listener is not aware of it, but the musicians are, and are moved by it. Penderecki, too, pays homage to Bach in this way—undoubtedly a testament to the living past. It is fascinating to observe the completely different musical means by which Bach and Penderecki convince their listeners of the overpowering force of the Passion story. We are indeed fortunate that in our era we can experience both.

Other Sacred Works

There is often a direct link between Penderecki's works and important contemporary events. Whether due to the search for the sensational, as his detractors maintain, or to a deeper participation in events is a question that will not be debated here. He has always been drawn to large works for voices and orchestra. One of the composition prizes he won in 1959 was for the *Psalmy Dawida* (David's Psalms). The Psalms are set in Polish and scored for mixed chorus with percussion. The first performance took place on October 9, 1959, in Krakow, with the chorus and orchestra of the Polish Radio, conducted by Jerzy Gert.

His *Dies Irae* was composed for the dedication of the memorial for the victims of the Nazi concentration camp Auschwitz-Birkenau on April 16, 1967. Similar to the *St. Luke Passion* in style, it is smaller in scope. The orchestra is unusual in that no violins or violas are used, only four flutes (with piccolo), three oboes, three saxophones, three bassoons, contrabassoon, six horns, four trumpets, four trombones, tuba, harmonium, piano, ten cellos, eight contrabasses, and again an unusual number of percussion instruments: six pairs of timpani, large and small drums, six cymbals, gongs, tam-tams, sirens, and so on. It is a powerful sound apparatus, one capable of creating images of the most strident urgency. The work is divided into three sections: Lamentatio, Apocalypse, and Apotheosis.

The next work in this series of sacred compositions is the two-part oratorio *Utrenja:* "Christ's Entombment" (first performed in the Altenberg cathedral near Cologne in April 1970) and "Christ's Resurrection" (1971, in the Münster cathedral). Two mixed choruses, subdivided into as many as 48 parts, five soloists, a large orchestra as well as a children's chorus in the *Resurrection* provide the means of tone painting in vast dimensions. The language is "Church Slavic," which corresponds to Old Bulgarian. Wolfram Schwinger said of it:

> All in all, a quiet, meditative work with an eminently Slavic aura . . . In the extremely concentrated, five-movement "Entombment" the interweaving of the two widely separated choruses is especially impressive, a surging volume of sound sinking again and again into an unearthly nothingness. He has composed the depths of the grave.

Penderecki composed a *Te Deum* to celebrate the election of the Polish Pope, John Paul II. He wrote the cantata *Kosmogonia* for the United Nations; its text is a compilation of passages in Greek, Latin, Italian, Russian, and English having to do with the universe. A song of praise in honor of space flight, expressing thoughts of the first astronauts, Gagarin and Glenn, is a work of historical importance if nothing else.

Ernst Pepping   1901–1981

Ernst Pepping was born in Duisburg on September 12, 1901, and died in West Berlin on February 4, 1981. For decades he was one of the leading practitioners of Protestant church music. From 1953–1968 he taught at the School for Church Music and later at the Academy of Music in West Berlin. He was one of those composers who could find musical expression for contemporary trends. He wrote in almost all genres, with the exception of opera: Symphonies, serenades, suites, variations, concertos, and instrumental music. More than any other, however, he wrote choral works, not a few of which have become classics of church music. His *Spandauer Chorbuch*, which appeared between 1934 and 1941 in 20 issues and was dedicated to the Protestant School for Church Music in Spandau, made him, together with Hugo Distler (1908–1942), one of the most important teachers in the field of theory and practice of church music. The *Deutsche Choralmesse* (1938), the *Missa dona nobis pacem* (1948), the *Weihnachtsgeschichte des Lukas* (1959), and the *139th Psalm* have long been part of the contemporary church repertory. He also wrote books on the nature and place of religious music, burning issues in our century.

His masterpiece was the *Passionsbericht des Matthäus*, completed in 1950. It calls for two double choruses subdivided into a total of 16 parts, a cappella, and is therefore accessible only to very capable ensembles, able to deal with its difficult polyphonic style, uncommon sonorities and complex rhythms. The work is in German, but the final song, entitled "Golgotha," includes a Latin "Crucifixus" in the second chorus. In the refrain, "Im Anfang war das Wort" (In the beginning was the word), which actually stands outside the work, the second chorus returns to German. The resolution of the last chord to D major, after the key of D minor has dominated the work from the beginning, is almost "Bach-like." There is undoubtedly a relationship here that spans the intervening years; a 20th-century Bach would probably have used a polyphony similar to Pepping's. His music is astringent and un-Romantic, looking back beyond the Baroque to the waning days of the Middle Ages. Harsh dissonances appear where expression requires them. The composer, like the masters of polyphony, pays little attention to declamation. The narrative, the "Passion report" (the term itself is matter-of-fact, in keeping with the demands of the 20th century), is in 12 sections: "Verrat des Judas" (Judas's betrayal), "Abendmahl" (the Last Supper), "Jesus und Petrus" (Jesus and Peter), "Gethsemane," "Gefangennahme" (the capture), "Jesus vor dem hohen Rat" (Jesus before the high council), "Petri Verleugnung" (Peter's denial), "Tod des Judas" (death of Judas), "Jesus vor Pilatus" (Jesus before Pilate), "Jesus vor dem Volk" (Jesus before the people), "Jesus und die Kriegsknechte" (Jesus and the soldiers), and "Golgotha," all based on the Gospel of *St. Matthew*. Pepping occasionally deviates from the Biblical text by interrupting the narrative flow with insertions of other material, as in the first words of the work from the prophet Isaiah: "Truly, he bore our sickness and took upon himself our pain." Only then does the report begin: "Höre die

Passion unseres Herrn Jesu Christi." (Hear now the Passion of our Lord, Jesus Christ). Further on he quotes from *Corinthians*; later yet, verses from *St. Luke*; and finally the Latin "Crucifixus etiam pro nobis." No solos are called for, as that which in similar works is related by the Evangelist is assigned to the chorus, sometimes monophonic, sometimes polyphonic. The demands made upon the choruses are extraordinary: objective narrative as well as dramatic description in passages of extreme complexity. At Christ's prophecy that he will "von diesem Gewächs des Weinstocks von nun an nicht mehr trinken" (henceforth not drink of this fruit of the vine) Pepping relies upon a little-used but very impressive effect: while the male voices of the first chorus sing a clearly metrical melody, the second chorus has a speaking role, which exactly imitates the rhythms of the first chorus but use the pitches of "natural speech," i.e., a different pitch for every voice. The division of the work into two parts corresponds to the content, with the break occurring after Jesus' capture. At this point an *Intermedium* is inserted: "Herr, bleibe bei uns, denn es will Abend werden und der Tag hat sich geneiget...." (Lord, stay with us, for night is falling and the day wanes); the beautiful words from *Luke* are joined spiritually and musically with two verses from *Matthew*. Thus there is a total of three pieces that in a certain sense stand apart from the "report": The introduction, the *Intermedium*, and the conclusion, which Pepping forms around a quotation from *St. John*: "In the beginning was the word and the word was with God."

Giovanni Battista Pergolesi   1710–1736

This South Italian master was born in Jesi, in the province of Ancona, on January 4, 1710, and died in Pozzuoli near Naples on March 16, 1736. He was one of the major figures not only of the Baroque era and the Neapolitan school, whose adherents were pathbreakers in opera and oratorio (although not always for the best), but also one of those geniuses who was called from the world at a pitifully young age—26. Like virtually all of his close contemporaries, he paid equal attention to sacred and secular music. We can ascribe four Masses to him with relative certainty, and the now world-famous *Stabat mater* assured him a place of honor in the realm of church music. His Intermezzo *La serva padrona* (The Maid as Mistress) established him as the probable inventor of comic opera. His sacred works call for double choruses and two orchestras, a usage characteristic of the time. The practice probably originated in St. Mark's church in Venice, where as early as 1490 a second organ was installed, making such antiphonal music possible. The use of two choruses and two orchestras soon followed.

Not much is known of Pergolesi's brief life, and it is unlikely much more will be discovered. When he was 20 he composed two oratorios: *La morte di San Giuseppe* and *La conversione di San Guglielmo d'Aquitania*, now forgotten like thousands of other works in this genre. It appears that after the terrible earthquake in Naples in 1732 he was commissioned to compose a Mass which he wrote for a 10-part chorus in F major and which made his fame in a single stroke. Two years later the C major Mass for five-part chorus followed, and at least two other similar works. In the course of his short life he also wrote several settings of the Miserere, Salve regina, Laudate pueri, and a Christmas oratorio (*La nascita del Redentore*). His crowning achievement is the *Stabat mater*, which he completed during the last year of his life, when severely ill with tuberculosis.

Stabat mater

Original Title: Stabat mater
Original Language: Latin
Text: The Stabat mater dolorosa sequence by the Franciscan monk Jacopone da Todi. (See Appendix)
Date of Writing: Probably at the end of 1735 or in the first two months of 1736, possibly at the Franciscan monastery at Pozzuoli. We do not know whether it was performed during his lifetime.
Form: The 20 strophes of the Marian sequence are divided into 12 musical numbers.
Scoring: Two solo voices (soprano and alto), strings, and organ. The common present practice of augmenting the solo voices with a chorus, especially in the "Fac, ut ardeat" and the final "Amen," is not authentic.
Discussion of the Work: The introduction is short and anticipates not only the anguished mood of the first number but also its typical dissonances. A canon at the second develops between the second

and first violins and is repeated later by the second and first voices, the alto and the soprano, while the basses in the orchestra beat a slow rhythm reminiscent of a funeral march. While all this is going on, harsh, clashing dissonances form in the canonic voices (F—G in the first measure, G—A-flat and A-flat—B-flat in the second, B-flat—C and C—D-flat in the third), evoking a feeling of deep sadness (Example 1).

It was to these places, which recur several times as the work progresses, that the prominent Late Classic musician Johann Adam Hiller was referring when he said (and he was thinking of a famous passage in Mozart's *Die Zauberflöte*) that he who is not moved by such sounds "does not deserve to be called human." This first number, "Stabat mater dolorosa" (The mother of Christ stands grieving) can be left to the two solo voices; but it has become the custom, for purely musical reasons as well as in the interests of maintaining a balance between the opening and last pieces, to have the chorus enter here, albeit in the most delicate way.

No. 2 is a soprano aria, "Cuius animam gementem" (Whose soul full of grief), in which a gentle, syncopated tempo with sudden forte beats at the end of the four-measure periods in no way alters the basically serious, melancholy mood. In the third piece, a duet (usually sung by the chorus), the G minor vocal melody expresses anguish, which is then intensified by the counter melody for the violins—how simple it is, and yet what an effect it achieves! (Example 2)

The lively tempo of the alto aria (No. 4) expresses the "agonizing distress of the heart," that "fearful anxiety" of which Clemens Brentano speaks in his version of the Stabat mater text (in the Latin original: "Quae moerebat et dolebat"). No. 5 begins with a duet. The alto responds to an expressive soprano solo with exactly the same phrase transposed a fourth down. The deeply intimate piece is in C minor, and when the lower voice enters, moves to G minor. (Not only Mozart attributed to this key a meaning of pain and grief.)

After the slow part of the duet, in whose last eight bars both voices move in thirds, comes a faster part in E-flat major, with a melody—and here everything depends upon interpretation—which makes it difficult to persist in the dark melancholy that is the underlying mood of the work: "Pro peccatis suae gentis" (For the sins of his people). Whether it is advisable to use the chorus here, as is usually done, is debatable.

No. 6 is a soprano aria ("Vidit suum dulcem natum"—She saw her sweet son). It is full of rhythmic variety and shaped melodically like a great rhapsody, its F minor key as bleak and gloomy as the mood it describes. The alto replies more simply, but her words, too, come from the depths of the soul: "Eia mater fons amoris" (O mother, fount of love). A word of warning—this passage should not be rendered too swiftly, as is often done.

In No. 8, Pergolesi introduces a more passionate tone. Here a choral setting is justified because of the emotion expressed: "Fac ut ardeat cor meum" (My heart burns with love). A duet for the two soloists follows; in it the previous G minor becomes a brighter E-flat major: "Sancta mater istud agas" (Holy Mother, do this thing). This movement is characterized by strong emotion in which lyrical expressivity often alternates with restless runs.

The alto aria No. 10 falls back once more into the deepest anguish: "Fac ut portem Christi mortem" (Let me feel Christ's death). Then, after the G minor of the aria, the mood lightens a bit. But it is incorrect to think of the melody, in gentle thirds, as carefree or even joyful (Example 3). The B-flat major and the loving words "Inflammatus et accensus" (Inflamed and enkindled) bring the work somewhat back down to earth. The voices are given coloratura passages and trills, and supple, melodic parallel sixths.

It may be that Pergolesi, like his Italian contemporaries, was too much an opera composer not to seek effective contrast wherever possible. Thus, after this perceptibly lightened duet, the last movement begins once more deep in grief. A noble melody in the violins to an accompaniment resembling a beating heart leads to a choral entry in dark F minor. The sopranos take up the violin melody while the altos imitate a little later. (Example 4).

The voices sing tranquilly to the sorrowful sobbing of the violins. Through their tears they see "paradisi gloria." Then there is a pause, and the chorus, suddenly lively, plunges into a fugue on the single word "Amen." Is it an accident that toward the end the dissonances of the opening return, that those suspensions that once meant pain and death can now no longer restrain the victory of light over darkness?

Uncertainty hangs over the last measures: Did Pergolesi seek to expand them with doubled note values, giving an almost opera-like effect, as an early copy in the Staatsbibliothek in Munich shows? Or did he imagine the version more effective where this "So be it!" led to the conclusion without any hesitation? Two hundred years later, even 100 years later, no tragedy of Mary would have included such a finale. But Pergolesi's *Stabat mater* is a work of the "old school," as we have seen in many other respects.

Hans Pfitzner 1869–1949

Pfitzner, the son of a German musician, was born on May 5, 1869, in Moscow, but lived in Germany from the age of three. He studied at the conservatory in Frankfurt/Main, and became Kapellmeister successively in Mainz, Berlin, and Munich. From 1908 to 1918 he was director of the opera and of the conservatory in Strasbourg, and from 1920 to 1929 conducted a master class in composition at the Berlin Academy of the Arts; from 1930 to 1934 he held a post at the Munich Academy of Music. He subsequently worked as a freelance composer, as his works had earned him a solid reputation. His first operatic works were very Wagnerian and soon forgotten, but *Palestrina* (1917) became part of the repertory of the major German opera houses. Pfitzner was one who was "born too late"; his ways of thinking and feeling were rooted in the Romantic era, and due to his contentious nature, clashes with representatives of contemporary composition could not be avoided. He wrote passionate diatribes against what he felt was a sickness in modern music, a harmful cancer, and he was discredited—unfairly for the most part—as being a querulous reactionary when he was really an idealistic dreamer. No one, however, dared to question his musical mastery. He, together with Richard Strauss, was thought of as one of the most important representatives of the old guard in German music in the first half of the century. After his Munich home was destroyed in a World War II air raid, he could no longer find peace. He lived for a time in Vienna and died in Salzburg on May 22, 1949.

His two great oratorios grew out of his deeply Romantic personality. They are timelessly beautiful works, which continue to be part of musical life and will always give pleasure. The Eichendorff cantata *Von deutscher Seele* Op. 28 (The German Soul) was composed in 1920 and 1921 and is one of Pfitzner's major compositions. He said of this work, "I chose the title *Von deutscher Seele* because I could find no better, more comprehensive expression for what these poems have to say about the German soul as to meditativeness, high spirits, earnestness, tenderness, strength, and heroism." The composition calls for four solo voices, mixed chorus, organ, and large orchestra. The first part is entitled "Mensch und Natur" (Man and Nature), the second, "Leben und Singen" (Life and Song), and the third, "Liederteil" (Songs). The work is a loose succession of a total of 20 poems by the great German Romantic poet Joseph von Eichendorff, in which Pfitzner connects the individual poem settings with imposing orchestral interludes. Many moods course through the work; the light and dark aspects of nature as well as of the human soul are treated with great love. Confidence in the good side of life is repeatedly emphasized, with mankind victorious over the demons and powers of darkness. The work requires no explanation for its music is easy to understand, full of tone-painting which is never obvious; it always touches the heart. Not only did Pfitzner believe in inspiration—again and again, he was blessed with it.

Das dunkle Reich (The Dark Kingdom), Op. 38, a choral fantasy with soprano and baritone soloists, organ, and orchestra, was written in 1930. It was conceived as a dirge upon the death of his wife. Far from offering religious or churchly consolation, it tries to come to terms with the dark kingdom of death and the hereafter. It is based on an unusual, very beautiful selection of poems by several authors: Michelangelo, Goethe, Conrad Ferdinand Meyer, and Richard Dehmel. This composition has deeply moving, even shocking moments; its basic mood is Romantic although the harmonies are completely typical of the 20th century. A mighty chorus of the dead (to Conrad Ferdinand Meyer's beautiful poem "Wir Toten, wir Toten sind grössere Heere als ihr auf der Erde, als ihr auf dem Meer" [We, the dead, are a mightier force than you on earth, than you in the sea]) is placed at the beginning and end of the work, giving it an undertone of darkness, but not despair.

Gabriel Pierné   1863–1937

Gabriel Pierné was an important figure in his lifetime and even for a time after his death, but his reputation has faded. His accomplishments in behalf of Parisian musical life are undisputed; he conducted the Colonne orchestra which premiered many modern masterpieces, including Stravinsky's *Firebird*. His compositions, however, have been forgotten including his operas (for example, *Ramuntcho*, after Pierre Loti), orchestral works, and chamber music. The musical legend *La Croisade des enfants* (The Children's Crusade) was his greatest success and for a time widely performed in Europe. Based on a text by Marcel Schwob, derived from the Latin accounts of Albert von Stade, Jacobus de Voragine, and Alberich de Trois-Fontaines it describes one of the most tragic and lunatic episodes of Medieval Christendom; ". . . children streamed out of the cities and towns of Europe, without leadership, and converged on the port cities. When asked where they were going, they replied 'To Jerusalem, to look for the Holy Land!'. No one knows what became of them. Those who returned could not say what roads they had taken." A few years before the account was written, hundreds, perhaps thousands of French and German children had fallen victim to a religious madness and had set out for the Near East to drive Islam from the holy places of Christianity. Their fate was terrible: Those who did not die or were murdered by strangers along the way were kidnapped by slave traders. The chronicle quoted here goes on to say that many women subsequently wandered the land in silence and despair, seeking their children who had embarked on that fateful journey. Pierné's oratorio turns on two of these children, the blind youth Alain and the maiden Allys. Additional roles include a mother, an old seaman, a narrator (a tenor), four undefined female solo voices, and a voice from on high, a baritone. In addition to the large chorus, which bears the main burden of the work, there is a children's chorus in from one to three parts. The city of Paris awarded *La Croisade des enfants* a prize in 1904. The premiere was on January 18, 1905, conducted by Edouard Colonne in the Théâtre Châtelet in Paris, where it met with great approval. The work is shaped effectively, but today its moralizing is no longer tenable. In the first part: "The Departure," the children follow a call purportedly from God. We accompany them on their journey (part 2: "On the High Road"; part 3: "The Sea") and experience their mystically transfigured demise (part 4: "The Savior in the Storm"). The work ends with a chorus of rejoicing.

Francis Poulenc 1899–1963

Poulenc was born on January 7, 1899 in Paris and died there on December 30, 1963. He is one of this century's foremost composers of opera and wrote a number of brilliant orchestral works as well. He is included in this book because a very substantial portion of his work was in the area of sacred music. His erotic opera *Les mamelles de Tirésias* seems a world apart from his *Stabat mater*, but he also wrote humorous choruses and the opera *Les dialogues des Carmélites*. He was able to do anything that was simply a question of technical mastery, something easily learned, but he was also sensitive to it and felt it. There is as little doubt about his wit as about his faith; his intelligence was as evident as his inclination toward simplicity. The music critic Claude Rostand said of him, he is a "mixture of monk and rascal." It is the former quality that is dwelt upon here. If, however, one knows only his *Stabat mater* or his *Gloria*, one should not think that one really knows Poulenc, one of the musical geniuses of our century.

Stabat mater

This work was composed during the summer of 1950 in Noizay. It calls for solo soprano, five-part mixed chorus (soprano, alto, tenor, baritone, and bass) and large orchestra with two flutes and a piccolo, two oboes and one English horn, two clarinets and one bass clarinet, three bassoons, four horns, three trumpets, three trombones, one tuba, timpani, two harps, and strings. The first performance took place on June 13, 1951, at the Strasbourg Music Festival, conducted by Fritz Münch; the choruses of St. Guillaume sang, the orchestra of the city of Strasbourg played, and the soloist was Geneviève Moizan.

Gloria

Commissioned by the Koussevitzky Foundation in the United States, the *Gloria* was composed between May and December 1959 and dedicated to the memories of Serge and Nathalie Koussevitzky. It was first performed on January 20, 1961 in Boston by the Boston Symphony Orchestra—of which the famous conductor and benefactor, Koussevitzky (1874–1951), had once been director—and the Pro Musica Chorus, directed by Charles Münch; Adele Addison sang the soprano solo. Shortly thereafter, on February 14, 1961, the first European performance was given in Paris, with the Orchestre National and the chorus of the R. T. F. (Radio-Télévision Française) conducted by Georges Prêtre; Rosanna Carteri was the soloist. This work, less than 30 minutes long, seems much more inspired than the *Stabat mater*; its harmonic structure is easier to understand even though here, too, Poulenc largely depends upon atonal and polytonal forms. Furthermore, the declamation of the Latin text presents fewer problems than in the other work. The chorus is in four parts, but the second female voice is called "mezzosoprano" instead of "contralto" as in the *Stabat mater*, without there being any perceptible difference.

Sergei Prokofiev 1891–1953

When Prokofiev died in Moscow on March 3, 1953, the musical world knew it had lost one of its greatest composers, one who had created new things with "enormous vitality, great boldness and optimism" (Benjamin Britten). Arthur Honegger called him "the most outstanding figure in contemporary music." The products of his genius included all musical genres save the sacred: operas, symphonies, ballet, concertos, chamber music, the children's classic *Peter and the Wolf*, music for films, and so on. In the 20s, while still living in his native land (he was born on April 23, 1891, in the little village of Sonzowka in the province of Jekaterinoslaw), Prokofiev wrote a work for solo tenor, chorus, and orchestra entitled *They are Seven*, to which the publisher added the subtitle, "cantata." The composer protested this designation, which he, as a young proponent of "new music" (as was his entire generation) thought old fashioned, and replaced it with *Chaldean Spells*. It is a barbaric work full of savagery and wild sound effects.

At the time, Prokofiev did not suspect that 15 years later he would call one of his most important works a cantata. The work was the magnificent music for *Alexander Nevsky*, the score originally written for the film made by the great director Sergei Eisenstein (*The Battleship Potemkin*). The film dealt with the historic victory of the Russians over the Germans in the 13th century. Eisenstein had been so enthusiastic about Prokofiev's music for the film *Lieutenant Kijé*, his first work after returning home from the West (Germany, France, the United States), that he asked him to compose the music for *Alexander Nevsky*. The film had its premiere on December 1, 1938. Shortly afterward, Prokofiev wrote a concert version of the music, as he had done with several others of his "utility" works; the cantata thus composed is in seven parts and bears the opus number 78. It is an extremely realistic, large-scale symphonic painting, whose structure follows the vivid images of the film: "Old Russia under the Mongol yoke" describes the oppressive atmosphere around the year 1240, when much of the country suffered under the invaders. Then Russia was exposed to a new danger: the independent northwestern part of the land was threatened by an invasion of an army of the Teutonic Knights of the Cross. The Russians called upon Prince Alexander Nevsky from Novgorod for help. (He was called Nevsky because of the battle he had won against Sweden on the banks of the Neva.) The second part, "Alexander Nevsky's Song," sings the hero's praises in a simple folklike melody. The third part reports the invasion by the Teutonic Knights of the Cross, announced with a Latin chorale; but behind their pious masks lies cruelty, even inhumanity ("The Knights in Pskow"). Alexander calls on all Russia to join in a battle for liberation; the words, "He who invades Russia will die" in retrospect sound like a prophecy. The next, extremely dramatic piece describes "The Battle on the Ice," the historic Russian victory on April 5, 1242, which resulted in the drowning of the entire army of knights; weighted down by heavy armor and weapons, they sank into Lake Peipus. Here, Prokofiev follows in the footsteps of his predecessor Tchaikovsky: The popular song from the second scene is set against the chorale of the invaders, just as in the *1812 Overture*, where Tchaikovsky opposed a Russian folk song to the *Marseillaise*. At this point, the music gathers force and rises to a mighty climax, making the following scene even more affecting. The voice of a young maiden mourns for those who have fallen on the "Field of Death." The seventh and final part depicts the triumphal "Entry of Alexander Nevsky into Pskow"; the simple hero's song becomes a magnificent hymn, a song of praise in honor of Russia's strength and invincibility. When the work was first performed at Moscow Philharmonic Hall on May 17, 1939, World War II was imminent; it seemed as if the audience's roar of exultation at the end of this brilliant, patriotic work would never end.

Another of Prokofiev's successful film scores, *Ivan the Terrible*, was transcribed for the concert hall into a full-length oratorio by Abram Stasewitch. It, however, fell far short of the enormous impact made by *Alexander Nevsky*. This transcription into 25 musical scenes and its first performance took place after the composer's death.

Henry Purcell   1659–1695

The 20th century was well along before it discovered the 17th-century master Henry Purcell, one of the great composers of all time. Long familiar only to specialists, he is now included among the truly important composers. Remarkably little is known about his life. His *Dido and Aeneas* is one of the most beautiful operas, on a par with those written by Monteverdi, one of the founders of the genre; he is known otherwise as the creator of much incidental music for plays. Efforts are being made today to revive many of his works. Not all were theater or chamber music, and since some relate to our subject, Purcell deserves a place here.

He was born in 1659, sometime between June and November; our information is no more precise than that. He was probably born in London; we know he died there on November 21, 1695, at the age of only 36. A year after his birth, the monarchy was restored; the 17-year-long republican interregnum, when the music-hating Puritans ruled, had come to an end. Once again the English, who had always been particularly partial to music, were allowed to indulge their fondness: Theaters reopened their doors, and audiences once more had their Shakespeare and other plays with more popular appeal. Especially beloved were the Masques—music theater, but not quite opera—employing spoken scenes, much dancing, and pantomime. For a time the public's taste for Masques even delayed the arrival of "true" opera in London.

Purcell served as a choir boy when he was about 10, as an organist at Westminster Abbey when he was 22 and in the same capacity at the Chapel Royal after 1682; he was involved with music throughout his life and was as familiar with secular music as with sacred. He left more than

100 sacred choral works, among them countless very beautiful anthems. The term "anthem" was used to designate all sacred choral music, usually based on Biblical texts, in England. It covered everything from simple songs to cantatas and reached its peak with Purcell and Handel. This "British Orpheus," as he was called even during his lifetime (he was obviously never one of the "unknowns"), also composed odes and secular cantatas, songs and hymns. Among the latter are six "Birthday Odes for Queen Mary," who died in 1695 of smallpox.

One of Purcell's sacred works seems to have become so popular during his lifetime that it was printed well before any of his other compositions. It was known under the title of *Te Deum* and *Jubilate* and consisted of two different elements that in practice (there is historic precedent for this) were usually combined; both are in D major. That the writer intended them to belong together is indicated by the word "and" in the title. Denis Arnold, in a foreword to a pocket score* of this double work, has this to say about its composition and first performance:

> St. Cecilia's Day was celebrated in England during Restoration times with a great festival of music.** When exactly this custom began is not known, but in 1683, the Gentlemen of the Musical Society of London organized a concert held before a large audience in Stationers Hall. The ode commissioned and composed for this occasion was Purcell's "Welcome to all the Pleasures." Usually, the music for the concert was composed to a specially written poem, and it was set for soloists, choir and orchestra. The soloists were among the best singers of the day, and their music was deliberately florid to show their virtuosity.
>
> It is in this tradition that Purcell wrote his festal *Te Deum and Jubilate* in D major. It was composed for St. Cecilia's Day, 1694, and shows the same ornate style as the odes composed in previous years. In spite of the fact that most settings of the English liturgy were designed for more modest resources, Purcell gives rein to his most pompous manner. The solo parts are full of ornamentation; the choral writing is elaborate, while the orchestra, with its prominent parts for trumpets, reminds us of the composer's dramatic music . . . It was this grand manner which assured the popularity of the work. After its initial performance, it was given annually on St. Cecilia's Day for many years. The festivals of the Sons of the Clergy given in St. Paul's Cathedral also provided an opportunity for its performance, and it was heard at these until Handel produced an equally splendid setting in 1743. . . .

It also seems that this work was especially well-suited for celebrating British military victories—an announcement on the title page of the second edition reads:

> *Te Deum et Jubilate* for voices and instruments perform'd before the Queen, Lords and Commons, at the Cathedral-Church of St. Paul on the Thanksgiving-Day for the glorious Successes of Her Majesty's Army the last campaign, compos'd by the late famous Mr. Henry Purcell.

We see that Purcell was called "famous" a few decades after his death; this also seems to have been the case during his lifetime. Around 1690, a leading English poet, John Dryden (author of the *Ode to St. Cecilia* and *Alexander's Feast*, set by Purcell, Handel, and others, as well as several stage works with music by Purcell) wrote, "We have at length found an Englishman, equal with the best abroad." The instrumentation described on the title page consists of two trumpets and the usual strings. According to the custom at the time, the low strings—cellos or gambas and contrabasses—were still played in unison, resulting in a doubling at the octave. It is entirely possible that a zealous search will turn up other examples of Purcell's enormous output, particularly odes, cantatas and the like, which he composed in large numbers.

Ariel Ramírez 1921–

Thanks to his extremely successful songs, dances, and choruses, Ariel Ramírez had long been one of Latin America's most popular composers. His horizons were suddenly expanded in an unexpected direction by the Second Vatican Council (convened by Pope John XXIII in Rome between 1962 and 1965). The new latitude to celebrate or sing the Mass in the vernacular evoked a

---

*Ernst Eulenburg, Ltd., London, Zurich, Mainz, New York: 1965

**Traditionally on November 22

spontaneous outpouring of sacred music in much of the world. The *Luba* Mass appeared in Africa. Native musicians in Mexico and Chile wrote sacred works in their own language based on native folklore.

By far the most successful of the latter was the *Misa criolla*, composed by Ariel Ramírez in 1963; since its first performance in Buenos Aires it has been performed throughout the world. To a degree found in hardly any other composition of its kind it combines musical inspiration, excellent craftsmanship, and a deeply religious feeling, based on a thorough familiarity with authentic South American folk music. The *Misa criolla* is both folk and art music to a degree almost unthinkable today in North America or Europe.

Criollo (creole) originally meant "of mixed blood." In the first centuries of the white settlement of the Americas, a creole was the son of a white father and a "native," or Indian mother. The meaning of the word gradually changed and today simply refers to anything "native to the land," whether it be a person, a custom, a dance, or whatever. The word is pronounced in the local Spanish dialect, ranging from *criojo* to *criosho* (with a very soft *sh*) or even to the often-used *crioljo*. Since the *Misa criolla* was written in Argentina, and more specifically, Buenos Aires, it should be pronounced *Missa criosha*, with the sounding similar to the *s* in "Asia. " (The word Misa—Mass—is written with only one *s* in Spanish.) Another title might be proposed—"Indoamerican Mass"— since the folklore Ramírez uses not only derives from various regions, but has Indian origins.

The movements of the *Misa criolla* are those of the Mass. The Kyrie uses the rhythm of the *Baguala-Vidala*, a melancholy song form from the northern, semiarid areas of Argentina. The Gloria is warmer, even cheerful; it uses a quick triple rhythm, called *Carnavalito* in Bolivia. The Credo is based on a *Chacarera* from central Argentina, which probably originated long ago in Indian music. The Sanctus comes once again from the especially rich and diverse folklore of Bolivia. The Agnus Dei is an *Estilo*, a simple song from the endless pampas of southern Argentina.

The instrumentation is especially interesting; it relies only on folk instruments: the *quena* (shepherd's flute) and the *zampona* (pan pipes) can be used ad libitum, while guitars form the backbone, as in much Latin American music. The *charango*, a very small stringed instrument made from an armadillo shell, plays a prominent role; it produces a sort of whirring sound, something like that of a zither, balalaika, or harp. Ramírez wrote this part for Jaime Torres, the greatest virtuoso on this instrument, who also plays in most recordings of the work. It is no surprise that more than a million of these recordings were sold in a short period of time. There is hardly a single country in which the *Misa criolla* has not dazzled and captivated a huge public. The Vatican newspaper, *Osservatore Romano*, wrote that ". . . the Pope was deeply moved, as we all were. The *Misa criolla* is unforgettable and lives on in every heart, no matter what one's particular faith."

Max Reger   1873–1916

Max Reger, whose star paled so quickly following his early death, was born on March 19, 1873, in Brand (near Marktredwitz, in Bavaria). In 1907 he became director of music at the university and teacher at the music conservatory in Leipzig; from 1911 to 1914 he was director of the tradition-rich, court orchestra at Meiningen and became its general music director in 1913. In 1914 he suffered a severe health problem and was forced to give up all public appearances, in particular his extensive concert tours as a pianist. Returning to Jena he then turned largely to composing, and in a surprisingly short time was widely heralded throughout Europe. At a time when efforts to overthrow the tonal system were brewing, and calls for a "new" music filled the air, Reger tried to expand the Classic-Romantic tonal system to the utmost from within. His accomplishments were astonishing; they made the rounds quickly and Reger seemed a "prophet." His works were not only eagerly played in concert halls and by chamber music societies but were analyzed and extolled by conservatory faculty as boldly progressive on one hand, and as bulwarks against complete dissolution on the other. But the revolution was too far advanced.

Reger died during World War I, in Leipzig, on May 11, 1916, at age 43. He would have been hard put to establish any kind of relationship with the atonality then descending upon the musical world. He was a liberal man, but one for whom rules were important, and the atonalists were intolerant of all who were not strictly loyal to their tenets. Few of Reger's compositions are now performed, save for his organ music. His name remains one of the greatest of the waning Romantic period, and he is considered a leader of the neo-Classical movement.

The 100th Psalm

After the *Gesang der Verklärten*, Op. 71 (1903, text by C. Busse) and a number of works for mixed, male and female choruses, Reger composed, in 1909, the *100th Psalm*, Op. 106, for mixed chorus, orchestra, and organ. It is considered his most important sacred choral work. The organization is similar to that of a four-movement sonata. The first movement begins so powerfully that the listener is instantly caught up in the work. First, a pedal point that builds from pianissimo to fortissimo; then, an exultant theme in the orchestra with the chorus calling out in unison an ever-mounting "Jauchzet!" (Rejoice!). This is more than bold, harmonic construction by an expert—it is true inspiration.

This storm of rapture, which leads through near and distant keys, sometimes with unusual modulations, ebbs only slowly. Then the lyrical "Dienet!" (Serve!) follows, like the second theme of a sonata. The two themes are in fact shaped and developed as in a symphonic movement, up to the point where an instrumental interlude leads back to the reprise.

The second movement is quite distinct from the first, just as the slow movement of a symphony differs from the preceding energetic one; it is lyrical, gentle, contemplative: "Erkennet!" (See, now!). The chorus comes to the fore with broad melodic passages; it is subdivided into as many as 10 parts, providing great beauty of sound as it describes the lovely scene of sheep in the pasture.

A sort of third movement follows: its allegretto con grazia in three-four time is reminiscent of the Scherzo of a sonata or symphony. The words are "Gehet zu seinen Toren ein mit Danken, zu seinen Vorhöfen mit Loben!" (Enter into His gates with thanksgiving, and into His courts with praise!). Excitement mounts again with "Lobet seinen Namen!" (Praise His name!).

And now, suddenly, in the midst of F-sharp, E, and B harmonies, sounds a triple fortissimo C major chord, luminous as the light of the sun's first rays on a summer morning. The device has often been used (since Haydn's *Schöpfung*) and here it is again, astonishingly beautiful as ever. The last, fourth part (or movement) appears. It builds through endless modulations from andante sostenuto to allegro maestoso. Reminiscences of the first movement appear. The conclusion is a single soaring passage: ". . . und seine Wahrheit für und für und für!" (And His truth is everlasting!). It is a magnificent piece, unfailingly powerful in its effect.

Other Choral Works

Two compositions entitled *Requiem* should be mentioned. One of them, a single movement based on the Latin text of the Mass for the dead, remained unfinished; it is for four soloists, mixed chorus, organ, and orchestra and bears the opus number 145a. The other is a one-movement German funeral dirge, Op. 144b, but it seems it may also be a fragment of a larger work that had been planned. It was written for solo alto or baritone, mixed chorus, and orchestra. The dedication reads, "In memory of the German heroes fallen in the Great War." The text, by Friedrich Hebbel (1813–1863), begins with the words, "Seele, vergiss sie nicht, Seele, vergiss nicht die Toten!" (My soul, forget not; my soul, forget not the dead!); for long passages it recalls a funeral ode. But as the work progresses an agitated, ghostly vision appears—a night scene of a storm pursuing the souls of the absent, forgotten ones, hunting them down through endless wilderness—for which Reger has composed powerful music.

Weihe der Nacht, Op. 119, could be called a lyrical choral ballad (the text is also by Hebbel, the *Weihegesang*, to words by Otto Liebmann), as could the *Einsiedler*, Op. 144a, written for solo baritone, five-part mixed chorus, and orchestra. The lovely text by Joseph von Eichendorff (1788–1857)—one of the Romantic poets most often used by composers—contains the words, so movingly set by Reger, "Die Jahre wie die Wolken gehn und lassen mich hier einsam stehn, die Welt hat mich vergessen." (The years pass like clouds and leave me to my solitude; the world has forgotten me.). Reger, who died soon after writing these last compositions, was not to suffer total neglect. He was loved by many, yet his music often reflects a profound loneliness and melancholy.

Aribert Reimann 1936–

Aribert Reimann, born on March 4, 1936 in Berlin, is one of the most important composers of our time. He is in the forefront of music theater; his ballets and operas have entered deeper into public awareness than any written by his contemporaries. In this book mention should be made of *Ein Totentanz* for baritone and orchestra (1960); *Verrà la morte*, after texts by Cesare Pavese, for soprano, tenor, chorus, and orchestra, first performed in 1967 by the Berlin Philharmonic, conducted by Wolfgang Fortner, who had been Reimann's teacher; *Inane*, a monodrama for soprano and orchestra (1968); *Lines*, for soprano and strings (1973); and *Wolkenloses Christfest*, for baritone, cello, and orchestra (1974). Special note must be made of his *Requiem*, which was commissioned to celebrate the 100th festival in Kiel. It is an odd birthday greeting for a festival of sports, celebrating life. But the artist sensitive to his times has the freedom, even the obligation to admonish; he is called upon to present a vision of eternity to a world out of joint, in what may be its last moment before it plunges into the abyss. Reimann's *Requiem* is not a work for the church; the liturgical text is supplemented by passages from the Old Testament Book of *Job*. The text is in many languages: German (the revised Luther translation), Hebrew, Classical Greek, Latin, English, French, and Hungarian. The orchestra is without the warm, high voices of violins and horns; dark sounds predominate, with alto and bass flutes, bass clarinet, and contrabassoon. The solo voices, soprano, mezzosoprano, and baritone, sing mainly the *Job* texts, while the mixed chorus follows the words of the Latin Requiem. After the Kiel premiere on January 9, 1973, the work was performed in the large broadcast studio of Radio Free Berlin, conducted by Gerd Albrecht, with soloists Julia Varady, Helga Dernesch, and Dietrich Fischer-Dieskau. Numerous subsequent radio performances and recordings have assured the work the place it deserves.

Joseph Rheinberger 1839–1901

Beside the great masters of the second half of the 19th century—Brahms being the foremost—were a number of "lesser masters" who lent much color and movement to the waning Romantic era. Many of them enjoyed unusual popularity and held a prominent place in the musical life of the time. That Late Romantic period has now largely been forgotten: Max Bruch lives on thanks to one of his beautiful violin concertos, but Carl Reinecke; Friedrich Hegar; the Zöllners, father and son; Franz Lachner; Joseph Rheinberger; and many others are names known only to the musically knowledgeable, for their works are seldom played today.

Rheinberger was born on March 17, 1839, in Vaduz, the capital of the principality of Liechtenstein. He achieved a position of stature in Munich, his works were performed brilliantly, and he died on November 25, 1901, after a full and productive life. Several of his numerous compositions deserve mention in this book: the Christmas cantata *Der Stern von Bethlehem*, Op. 164, for solos, chorus, and orchestra; 12 Masses (among them one for two choruses, Op. 109); and three Requiem and two Stabat mater settings.

Gioacchino Rossini 1792–1868

In many respects, Rossini, the "Swan of Pesaro" (he was born there on February 29, 1792) is unique in music history. He wrote more than 30 operas before he was 37, and the success he achieved with them was like nothing ever seen before. In 1829, when the premiere of *Guillaume Tell* gave every sign that the opera would be a sensational success (it was, in fact, repeated countless times), he explained that he no longer wanted to write for the stage, a decision to which he held for the rest of his long life. He died in Passy, near Paris, on November 13, 1868. Although he spent the "evening" of his life as a pensioner savoring life to the fullest, he occasionally interrupted this leisure to compose the odd sacred work. Few would have believed this ironic bon vivant capable of such undertakings. The most important of these were his *Stabat mater* and the *Petite Messe Solennelle*.

The history of the *Stabat mater* is an interesting story. In 1831, while travelling through Spain, Rossini met a cleric to whom he dedicated a manuscript entitled *Stabat mater* the following year.

This religious, named Francisco Verela, probably thought he had received a composition by Rossini for he presented it as such when it was performed on Good Friday of 1833, but his assumption was only partly true. Rossini had written only the first six parts, after which he requested an old friend, Giovanni Tadolini, to compose the rest. Rossini probably did so simply to please the Spaniard and thought no more about it. The cleric, however, died shortly thereafter, and after all kinds of misadventures, the manuscript ended up in the hands of a publisher, who announced plans to publish it. Rossini protested immediately, since he was well aware of the work's shortcomings. The publisher, Aulagnier, insisted on his right to the manuscript and would not be dissuaded from his plan by any threats from the alleged composer. Rossini then offered his own Parisian publisher, Troupenas, a *Stabat mater* he really had composed. It included the six parts already written plus supplementary material which Rossini supposedly composed in 1841. In the end, Rossini and Troupenas won the legal proceedings surrounding the publication rights; on January 7, 1842, the *Stabat mater*, composed entirely by Rossini, was performed for the first time in the Salon Ventadour in Paris. It was such a triumph that the work was performed in 29 other cities in that same year.

It was received with great enthusiasm everywhere, yet some critical opinions were also voiced. The most malicious came from Richard Wagner, published in the Leipzig journal *Neue Zeitschrift für Musik*. Wagner came to deeply regret these remarks, stimulated by nationalism and envy, and tried to repair the damage in a later essay. Some objections were also raised in orthodox religious circles, where it was thought that Rossini's musical language was too "secular," too "opera-like." Indeed many of the melodies recalled Rossini's writing for the stage, but it is difficult to make a case against his *Stabat mater* for that reason. A composer's style is his hallmark, and the more distinctive it is, the stronger is his musical personality. No composer would deny his own style when writing in a new genre; at most, he might modify some characteristics to better suit his style to the occasion. There were those who voiced similar misgivings about Mozart, even "proved" that the same melodies used in his Masses could be found almost note for note in *Figaro* and *Così fan tutte*. Did Beethoven change his style in any way when composing the *Missa solemnis*? Are Schubert's songs not also evident in his symphonies? Is there any fundamental difference between Bruckner's symphonic and sacred music?

Example 1

Example 2

Example 3

Heinrich Heine provided the most charming and perhaps most perceptive discussion of the premiere of Rossini's work. He referred to a religious procession of children he had once seen in the port town of Cette in southern France, saying it paralleled Rossini's music—deeply felt, yet naive; he thought the music equal to the "enormous martyrdom" it was intended to portray, yet called it childlike, and in the midst of all that horror perceived a "grace" like the heavenly blue sky that illuminated the procession that day in Cette. In its instrumentation, Rossini expands the forces used in opera buffa: two each of flutes, oboes, clarinets, bassoons, horns, and trumpets; three trombones, timpani, and strings. He calls for four solo voices (two sopranos, tenor, and bass) and a four-part mixed chorus (in which the lower female voices are not called alto, but soprano II, as was commonly done in Italy). The music is largely melodic and homophonic—a melodic line with harmonic accompaniment. But in a few places Rossini gives the sacred genre its due; the first vocal entry is in canon: bass, tenor, and soprano I (Example 1), and the finale even is a double fugue. The melodies, clear and beautiful, have a southern sensuousness about them, which makes the effect of the several noticeably chromatic passages, whether in the development of a melody (Example 2) or in the harmonic structure (Example 3), even more pronounced. It should come as no surprise that the solo parts, tender and heartfelt as they are, are full of dramatic verve and theatrical effect. In the "Inflammatus," the first soprano, supported fortissimo by the chorus and orchestra, twice rises to high C. Is this story not a drama? Why, then, not express it with all means available to the musical dramatist? Similar considerations will occupy us in dealing with Verdi's magnificent, spectacular *Requiem*.

There is less to say about the *Petite Messe Solennelle*. Rossini wrote it in 1863 for solos, chorus, two pianos, and harmonium, but in 1867 re-scored it for large orchestra. Unlike Bruckner with his symphony, Rossini did not dedicate his Mass to "the good Lord," but did accompany it with a letter that expressed similar thoughts: "Dear Lord, my little Mass is finished. Is it sacred music—or just the opposite? My real talent, as You well know, was for opera buffa. A little skill, a little heart is all I have to offer. Be merciful, then, and let me enter Paradise. G. Rossini. Passy, 1863."

Camille Saint-Saëns 1835–1921

Once counted among the great masters, Saint-Saëns is less popular today. His symphonies, chamber music, now and then one of his concertos for violin, cello, or piano, all are now only seldom played. His durable work is the opera *Samson et Dalila*, and of his symphonic poems, the ghostly *Danse Macabre* has retained some of its effect. His musical parody *Carneval des animaux*, which combines amusing pieces with a masterful melody—"Le cygne" (the swan) was once danced by the legendary Ana Pavlova as the "Dying Swan"—is played with some frequency.

Saint-Saëns, a leading figure in French music, was born in Paris on October 9, 1835, and died in Algiers, where he had gone to satisfy his interests by observing an eclipse of the sun, on December 16, 1921. His style was a combination of French Classical elegance and the tone set by Wagner and Liszt. He was a child prodigy, composing when he was 5, giving his first piano recital when he was 10. He obtained his first post as organist when just over 20 years old and in 1858 took the great step up to the Church of the Madeleine, where he became famous as an organist. His ties to the church moved him to compose works that had a religious air about them: the "Biblical opera" already mentioned, based on the Old Testament story of Samson and Delilah, as well as three oratorios: *Le déluge*, the *Oratorio de Noël*, and *The Promised Land* (in English).

The oratorio *Le déluge* (The Flood), Op. 45, subtitled "Poème Biblique," was written in 1874. It is divided into three parts entitled 1. Corruption de l'homme—Colère de Dieu—Alliance avec Noé

(Man's Corruption—God's Wrath—The Pact with Noah); 2. L'arche—Le déluge (The Ark—The Flood); 3. La colombe—Sortie de l'arche—Bénédiction de Dieu (The Dove—The Departure from the Ark—God's Blessing). As compared to the preceding, almost liturgical, *Oratorio de Noël*, *Le déluge* contains no passages of sacred music but, as its theme indicates, is deeply religious. There are four vocal soloists (soprano, alto, tenor, and bass-baritone), but they do not have sharply defined roles. The tenor, perhaps because of tradition, usually takes the role of narrator, while the bass-baritone sings God's proclamations, but there are exceptions. The mixed chorus is usually in four parts (soprano, alto, tenor, bass), but sometimes further subdivided, without, however, going beyond very simple, six-part singing. The orchestra has a very important, truly dominant role, one the composer handles brilliantly. The description of the flood, an almost symphonic piece of tone painting (in the second section of the work), is magnificent music. It rises from the softest tremolo to an unremitting, at times breathtaking feeling of oppression; the menacing elements gather force until the raging storm breaks, releasing its flood waters. The chorus enters, spiraling upwards in a continuous chromatic passage, then expands the intervals as if now all impediments have been swept away, and finally subsides only after all life on earth has been destroyed, leaving the ark to sail on through the night into the unknown. But weaker parts are evident, vulgar declamations and expressions of sentimentality. The concluding fugue, "Croissez donc et multipliez!" (Therefore be fruitful and multiply), is remarkably great music; after its elaboration in the chorus it draws in the solo voices, resulting in an extremely effective finale.

Alessandro Scarlatti   1660–1725

This master, effusively honored and highly esteemed in his time, founder of the Neapolitan opera "school," father of harpsichord master Domenico Scarlatti, not only wrote the almost unbelievable number of 115 operas (of which 87 remain, at least in part), but also 20 Masses, a *St. John Passion*, hundreds of Psalms, motets, and smaller liturgical compositions, as well as dozens of oratorios, all of which were probably performed in Naples and in Rome. Some of the titles are: *Il sagrificio d'Abramo*, *Il martirio di Santa Teodosia*, *L'assunzione della Beata Vergine Maria*, *San Felippo Neri*, *Passio secundum Johannem*, *Il trionfo della Gratia*, and *Il martirio di Santa Cecilia*. Alessandro Scarlatti was probably Sicilian, possibly born on May 2, 1660, in Palermo. His brilliant career evolved in Naples, then one of the leading musical centers of Italy; he died there on October 24, 1725.

Armin Schibler   1920–1986

Composers with a social conscience are a phenomenon not just of our own time. Few, however, have taken up the cause of saving mankind with such passionate ardor, few have conceived of a threat so all-encompassing, so dangerous, so outrageous, as did Schibler. Nearly every one of his works seeks to arouse awareness of those things threatening to annihilate mankind: the destruction of nature, weaponry of mass extermination, corrupting materialism, the anguish and enslavement of the spirit. His are not abstract works but rather hymns to life and love, seeking to revitalize what is most humane, before mankind takes the last step over the threshold to its doom. Even one of Schibler's earliest works, the *Grosse Psalm* (1945), addresses a specific example of destruction of nature, and he continued in the same vein, whether in vocal works, music drama, in "Hörwerke" (a new form of melodrama), or other forms. His work is experimental in every way without ever calling into question the primacy of music. Music in Schibler's view is as comprehensive as the widest definition of the term allows.

The composer was born on November 20, 1920, in Kreuzlingen, on the Swiss side of Lake Constance. Not only was he influenced by such varied mentors as Gustav Mahler, Carl Orff, and his teacher, Willy Burkhard; he searched through the many experiments of his century, including twelve-tone music and the "Darmstadt school" as well, but managed to stay free of their dangerous one-sidedness and absolutist claims. Rather, he sought to integrate those elements that seemed to him positive, primarily jazz and a partial return to tonality and the magic of sound.

Those of his works belonging in this book (not always easy to decide, since Schibler's thinking crosses boundaries that normally separate forms) are *Polyphem*, a dramatic cantata after Stefan

Zweig; the setting of the "Gilgamesh" epic *Der Tod Enkidus*; and *Epitaph auf einer Mächtigen, Später als du denkst, Greina,* and *The Point of Return* or *Concert pour le temps présent,* all based on his own texts, some with choreographic elements. Two of his works deserve to be examined in more detail.

Media in vita, Op. 48, is a full-length "symphonic oratorio" based on poems by Conrad Ferdinand Meyer and composed between 1956 and 1959. The work combines 18 poems by this great poet with two orchestral interludes to form a cycle of large proportions. By means of clever sequential arrangement of the most varied moods and by closely relating and connecting the music for the various parts, he welded all together to form an organic entity. The basic theme of the poems is the ancient *"media in vita"* (the entire expression is "media in vita morte sumus"—in the midst of life, we are surrounded by death). It is a memento mori (remember that you must die) without grief, without tragedy, without horror. Or, as Meyer wrote so affectingly in "Schnitterlied": "Von Garbe zu Garbe ist Raum für den Tod—Von Mund zu Mund ist Raum für den Tod" (Between one sheaf and the next, there is a space for death; between one mouth and another, there is a space for death).

The work is in three parts: Introitus (Chorus of the Dead); Fülle des Lebens (The Fullness of Life); Vision und Nähe des Todes (The Vision of and the Nearness of Death). At a later performance (the premiere took place in the Zürich Tonhalle in May 1962), Schibler noted,

> What inspired me then was the great economic boom that had just set the Western world on its feverish quest for progress. I joined texts by C. F. Meyer to form a symphonic-oratorio entity, a sequence of poems that would show mankind as a wary partner with animals and plants in the cycles of nature, as sower, as reaper, as one at the height of his physical powers, who ultimately himself feels the autumn of his life, his approaching end as a natural going home to the place from which he came. Were not people trying at every turn to put this "antiquated" view of humanity behind them, to do away with previous limits to existence?

It is a timeless, yet at every moment intensely topical work. Another very impressive performance on May 16, 1982 (at the same place, presented by Hans Erismann, to whom oratorio in Zürich owes much) provided convincing evidence of the validity of a genre that has achieved prominence in 20th-century Switzerland.

The *Messe für die gegenwärtige Zeit* (Mass for our time) is an entirely different kind of work. It was first performed in Zürich on November 22, 1980, to much acclaim. Its basic idea is not easily described in a few words; its scoring (mixed voices with two soloists, two pianos, and a jazz-rock group) gives it a modern sound, and the simultaneous concertante and danced scenic interpretation is a result of Schibler's efforts to combine all the arts to make an important intellectual point. The use of Latin in the text, written by the composer, points to his favorite concept for universal understanding (Stravinsky had paid tribute to the same idea in 1927 with his *Oedipus Rex*). To make the concept even more explicit, the basic idea of each section is anticipated by speakers in their various vernaculars. Karl Philipp carried out the rhythm of Schibler's Latin text to make the rock-style setting; thus the work's appeal is to the young, who are directly confronted with the problems of the time. It is a curious but urgent mixture of faith ("Ich glaube an Gott, von Anfang an war er gewesen, durch die Jahrhunderte war er, ist gegenwärtig heute und er wird sein in Ewigkeit"—I believe in God; He was there in the beginning, He was there through the centuries, He is present today, and will always be, for eternity) and accusation ("Verbrecher herrschen, Gottlose sind an der Macht, sinnlos und schändlich raffen sie alles an sich, den Erdkreis verwüsten sie, vor nichts schrecken sie zurück, sie foltern und morden, die wunderbare Welt verwirren und verunstalten sie, alles was göttlich ist, treten sie mit Füssen. "—Criminals rule, the godless are in power, infamously, without feeling, snatching everything for themselves; they lay waste to the earth, nothing is too horrible for them; they torture and murder, upset the wondrous world and disfigure it; they trample under foot all that is godly). This is a work that compels reflection, one that must interest even those for whom "Classical" music is foreign territory.

Karl Schiske   1916–

Although Karl Schiske was born on February 12, 1916, in Györ (formerly Raab) in Hungary, he is considered an Austrian composer, both because his father was Austrian and because he spent his life in Austria, mostly in Vienna and near the Grossglockner, in Styria, in self-imposed isolation. In addition to some notable symphonies, concertos, chamber and choral music, he early on (1946) composed an outstanding oratorio. It was given its premiere in Vienna under Karl Böhm and has since repeatedly proved its merit. It is certainly one of the more important products of the postwar period. *Vom Tode* is clearly part and parcel of the apocalyptic time in which it was created. Although the immediate inspiration for the work may have come from the death of a brother, to whom the score is dedicated, many people perceive in it the faltering beat of millions of hearts, victims of the time's unimaginable cruelty. With great sensitivity Schiske compiled the text for the almost two-hour piece from the works of great poets: Rilke's "O Herr, gib jedem seinen eignen Tod" (O Lord, give to each his own death) stands not only at the beginning but like a Leitmotif permeates all six parts: prologue, epilogue, and four movements named after the seasons. The work has a very distinctive style. It calls for four soloists (soprano, alto, tenor, and bass), a large mixed chorus, an organ, and a very large symphony orchestra (with piccolo, English horn, bass clarinet, contrabassoon, harp, piano, and numerous percussion instruments). Free use of tonality gives it a "contemporary" sound, but at every moment its connection with a great, bygone, musical era—the late Romanticism of the "Vienna School," Schreker and Franz Schmidt—is evident. The texts are by Liliencron, Weinheber, Eichendorff, Ina Seidel, Möricke, Hölderlin, Schiller, Hebbel, Klopstock, Thomas à Kempis, and, again and again, Rilke. The work is crowned by a choral fugue in which Goethe's lines (from *Faust II*) "Wer immer strebend sich bemüht" (Who, ever aspiring, strives) intertwine with the passage from Rilke's *Stundenbuch* noted earlier. Schiske's brilliant skill combined with deep inspiration permeates the work and provides its identity; it is a 20th-century masterpiece, one that raises its voice beyond time and space.

Franz Schmidt   1874–1939

"All music is rooted in the people," said the Rector of the Vienna Music Academy, Franz Schmidt, on the occasion of the ceremony marking the 100th anniversary of Schubert's death. Schmidt was mindful of tradition without being "conservative" in any limiting sense. His line of descent was from Brahms and Bruckner, but he opened natural paths to the tonality of the 20th century which was then bursting the bonds of tradition. Franz Schmidt was a music maker, in the best sense of the term, and an Austrian to boot. He was born on December 22, 1874, in a city that could be called a "suburb" of Vienna; typically for the Danube monarchy, it (like Brünn) had three names: Pressburg for the Germans, Bratislava for the Slavs, and Poszony for the Hungarians, for all three considered it their own. A Franciscan who was also a painter, named Father Felician, was his first teacher in harmony and organ, and made a decisive contribution to the youth's musical and idealistic world view. When 14, Schmidt went to Vienna; at the age of 18, he was a composer, and when 22 he played the cello so well that he was accepted into the Philharmonic Orchestra and the Court Opera. He served under the three-star hegemony of great composers: Richter, Jahn, and Mahler. In 1901 his First Symphony won the Beethoven prize offered by the Vienna Society of Friends of Music. In 30 years he so developed his mastery that his Fourth Symphony is now counted among the major works of the century. In 1904 he completed his opera *Notre Dame*, first performed in 1914. In the same year he joined the academy and became one of its leading teachers. His crowning work, the oratorio *Das Buch mit sieben Siegeln*, was the result of a narrow brush with death in 1935. He lived long enough to attend its premiere and died on February 11, 1939, in his villa in Perchtoldsdorf, just outside Vienna.

Das Buch mit sieben Siegeln (The Book of the Seven Seals)

Original Title: Das Buch mit sieben Siegeln
Original Language: German
Text: From the Book of *Revelation*, compiled by the composer.
Date of Writing: 1935–1937.
First Performance: June 15, 1938, in the large hall of the Vienna *Musikverein*.
Cast: John (tenor); the Voice of the Lord (bass); four solo voices (soprano, alto, tenor, bass), mixed chorus subdivided into as many as seven parts.
Orchestra: Three flutes (with piccolo), three oboes (with English horn), three clarinets (with bass and D clarinets), three bassoons (with contrabassoon), four horns, three trumpets, three trombones, tuba, four timpani, percussion (large and small drums, triangle, cymbals, xylophone,

three tam-tams of various sizes), organ, and strings.

History of the Work: The idea of setting such demanding material to music probably originated in conversations with his good friend Alexander Wunderer, president of the Vienna Philharmonic and a prominent Viennese musician. The intellectual planning must go back as far as the time of the Fourth Symphony, completed in 1933. Then, during the night of July 23, 1935, Schmidt suffered a severe heart attack which thanks to swift medical intervention did not prove fatal. The experience probably forced him to recognize his inner need to complete the oratorio.

The reclusive composer also shared the deepening and painful gloom of the times. He found with alarm signs of decline and dissolution—everything seemed to be rushing toward an upheaval that threatened to become an apocalypse. It seemed the time had come to use the mature artistic means of the foundering era to give expression to this nightmare. Many, particularly in Europe, tried to express this anguish—in literature, theater, painting, and film. Schmidt took up the difficult task in music. ("As far as I know, this is the first time anyone has tried to set the Apocalypse comprehensively to music.") As he finished it, Austria stood at the brink of collapse; Vienna's cultural landscape was about to be shaken by the worst earthquake in its history. By the time of its premiere, the work had acquired a dimension scarcely conceived of earlier. A far cry from the slogans of the moment, it was a final call to come to the senses before the unavoidable "End." The work, created to provoke introspection and reflection, struck a responsive chord in many of those who heard it, heightening their awareness that the first wave of the Apocalypse was at the gates.

Discussion of the Work: Schmidt, despite his belief that music should speak for itself, wrote an essay for the program of the premiere. It is matter-of-fact and deals only with the contents of the work—the text—but not with artistic questions.

When I approached this task it was clear to me that the first thing to be done was to shape the text in such a way that the essentials of the original would be retained while at the same time bringing the absolutely enormous dimensions of the work within the comprehension of the average human mind. In doing this, the outer lines of the structure and its inner cohesion were to remain intact. Except for combining John's letters to the seven congregations into a single welcoming address, I adhered faithfully to the original; the Lord's call to John, his appearance before the throne, the ceremony of homage, the book in the Lord's hand, the vision of the Lamb, the taking of the book by the Lamb—all this closely follows the original text. The following brief thanksgiving service rounds off the act—a "Prologue in Heaven." [Allusion is to Goethe's *Faust*—Ed.]

The next section of the work covers the breaking of the first six seals by the Lamb, in which the history of mankind is foretold. After a fruitful and hopeful spreading of the Christian teaching of redemption by the white horseman (Jesus Christ) and his heavenly hosts, mankind sinks into a night of chaos. The crimson horseman invades the world with his hellish forces and plunges mankind into war, every man against every other. The third (black) and the fourth (pale) apocalyptic horsemen deepen the consequences of that universal war by bringing famine and plague. Most of humanity has either perished or is in deep despair; only a few faithful remain. When the fifth seal is broken, the souls of the Martyrs and other victims of lawlessness appear. They call for justice and retribution. The Lord calls upon them to be patient and promises justice on Judgment Day. Because most of the survivors persist in sin and impenitence, the Lord annihilates them with earthquake, deluge, and fire, all revealed when the sixth seal is broken.

This brings the first section to a close. The pause here is the only opportunity to encompass musically the overflowing ocean of material in the original. From this point on, John wages his battle against the sinful city of Babylon (Imperial Rome was really the object) ever more fiercely with countless variations of parables and images, until it is finally destroyed, revealing the final, glorious victory of Christianity in the vision of the new Jerusalem. I ventured to eliminate the first two factors of the antithesis Babylon/Jerusalem, heathen/Christian, depravity/virtue and all material related to them. In my opinion, the fundamental antithesis has lost nothing in strength and meaning, and what is more, by unloading an enormous amount of material it was possible to construct a shapely second section, one completely in keeping with the original.

The second section begins with a great stillness in Heaven as the seventh seal is broken. During this stillness, John relates, almost parenthetically, the history of the true faith and its church, beginning with the Savior's birth, of its battles against the Devil's followers and their false teachings, and of its final victory.

After the great silence in Heaven, which it is assumed will last an eternity, until the end of earthly time, the seven angelic trumpets prepare to sound the terrifying call to the Day of Judgment. John reports this only briefly, as in the original, so as to give more urgency to his proclamation of the new world order—that from this time on a new earth will bear only those who have eternal life and that a new Heaven will arch over them. And the Lord speaks to the purified ones, telling them that He will abide with them, that they will be his children and He, their father. After the purified have thanked and praised the Lord with hallelujahs, John ends his Revelation with a brief explanatory farewell address.

There are too many high points in this work for each of them to be discussed individually. According to the dictates of the text and the images it contains, they are either melodic or harmonic, polyphonic or homophonic, for chorus or soloists in varied sequence, lyrical or dramatic, tranquil or powerful. These are portrayals whose luminosity and diversity of colors and figures are equal to those created by any painter and attain the poetic force of Dante, Milton, and Goethe.

The appearance of the four horsemen—on white, crimson, black, and pale horses—calls up visions whose musical strength has seldom been attained since the "Licht" (light) in Haydn's *Creation* and the "vor Gott" (before God) in Beethoven's Ninth Symphony. Perhaps the opening of the seventh seal somewhat outdoes what has gone before: the vision of the all-destroying earthquake, the stars falling from the sky, and the rising of the ocean is of breathtaking realism without ever losing itself in details of tone painting.

Several fugues, some enormous in scope but never too elaborate, reveal the composer as a man of consummate skill for whom technique is never an end in itself. He maintained complete mastery of all the resources provided by the enormous forces he chose to work with. The diversity of the work is almost impossible to comprehend, but again and again clear motives appear, whose beautiful melodic shapes are immediately effective. An example is the expression of eternity in few notes (Example 1), exactly what John must have seen in his vision. Another is the tenderness of the "Heilig, heilig" (Holy, holy) as, simply and movingly, it becomes a structural element in a fugue (Example 2).

But the transfiguration, the "silence in Heaven" after the breaking of the seventh seal, is beautiful beyond words. The high point of the work is the hallelujah; as a sublime hymn of thanks it is second to none, including that in Handel's *Messiah*. And there is more—the final moments before the conclusion are in no way a letdown. After this mighty outpouring, a passage of the utmost tranquility comes as a complete surprise. The male choral voices intone an antiphonal Gregorian chant, turning away from the world, ascetic, at one with God. Then John refers back to the beginning. Once more we hear his enormously simple, four-note motive; in spite of its structural simplicity, it imparts an undefinable feeling of endless time and space (Example 3).

Example 1

Example 2

Example 3

Is it significant that this motive appears seven times, both at the beginning and at the end? Is there something of numerology in the work (as is often claimed in the case of Bach)?

As a purely musical work, *Das Buch mit sieben Siegeln* is imposing. It is the near end of the vast arc of Romantic oratorio that began with Haydn and encompasses all the forms and possibilities created during the course of a long German, and no less Austrian or Viennese, tradition. Its scope, however, is due to its subject matter. John was an "initiate," as Paul was before him and Titurel, the founder of the Grail, after. The "Revelation" would not have been granted to any other sort; John received it at his rocky cave in the western slope of the highest mountain on the Greek island of Patmos, overlooking the endless blue of the Aegean Sea, far from the rest of humanity. A chapel stands there today built by St. Odilia, as a repository for the Grail, and dedicated to John, a visionary of Old Testament force, whom God permitted to see beyond time and to tell mankind of his vision. Whoever dares to deal with this theme and then masters it must have been inspired by otherworldly powers.

Deutsche Auferstehung (The German Resurrection)

It is too simple to place the blame for this "unholy" cantata (so called by Schmidt's biographer, Norbert Tschulik) on the deteriorating health of the composer; on his declining intellectual powers which sometimes, when he was very ill, led to loss of memory; too easy, too, to hold the people around him accountable for the choice of subject matter.

Schmidt was never a Nazi, would have nothing to do with anti-Semitism or any other kind of injustice. But a man as sensitive as he might easily have been caught up in the storm of enthusiasm that seized great numbers of people when Germany annexed Austria in March 1938. He truly believed that a time of happiness and prosperity was about to begin, and saw only the optimism that animated everyone he came into contact with. Furthermore, it seemed a fulfillment of his hopes for the ascendancy of art and culture.

Schmidt, basically a very religious man, failed to see the sharp division that should have separated him from the Third Reich. He allowed himself to be convinced by a former student to compose a hymn to Greater Germany, a cantata using the slogans and catchwords of the Hitler era. He was not able to complete the work; it was finished, based on his sketches, by Dr. Robert Wagner, and was first performed in the great hall of the *Musikverein* on April 24, 1940, 14 months after Schmidt's death. Less than two years had passed since the magnificent *Buch mit sieben Siegeln*. Schmidt's diminished musical and intellectual qualities are glaringly and sadly evident. But this aberration changes nothing in our total assessment of this great master.

Florent Schmitt   1870–1958

Inclusion of the French musician Florent Schmitt in this book is more than the settling of a debt of honor. Although he wrote glowing, passionate, even intoxicating music, some of it quite important, the musical world has ignored him badly. He was born on September 28, 1870, in Blamont, on the Moselle, studied in Paris with Massenet and Fauré, and won the Prix de Rome in 1900. He later became director of the Lyon conservatory. He wrote many choral compositions including two works that particularly deserve mention here: the *46th Psalm*, Op. 38, written in 1904 for soloists, chorus, and orchestra, and an even greater work, the magnificent *47th Psalm*, composed in 1934, which may be considered one of the most impressive works in the genre. It wittingly exploits a great panoply of sound to glorify God: "Rejoice, sing praises! God is king throughout the earth!" Vocal and instrumental voices build a towering song of praise so powerful it bursts all earthly bounds. The size of the forces he uses are akin to those of Berlioz and Mahler's Eighth Symphony, the *Symphony of a Thousand*, which makes it no easier to perform. Today, however, since radio networks in particular have access to such large forces, the work should be presented more often.

Arnold Schoenberg   1874–1951

Schoenberg once wrote that the second half of the century will wrongly overestimate his legacy, just as the first half had underestimated it. Looked at from today's standpoint, the correctness of this prophecy is confirmed. No other 20th-century musician, and only very few in the whole of music history, has so occupied the thought and practice of contemporaries and successors and so deeply divided the musical world as he. His twelve-tone theory, the "composition with twelve tones related only to each other," quickly attracted the world's attention. Yet though widely publicized in the media of the day by its fanatical devotees, it produced no more than a few works—including Schoenberg's own—that have found their way into "standard" musical life, that is to say, into the consciousness of music lovers. Schoenberg's disciples, in part on purpose and in part unconsciously, have succeeded in confusing theoretician and teacher with the composer.

In this book I do not have to deal with either aspect: save for the uncompleted oratorio *Die Jakobsleiter*, the only work of Schoenberg's of interest here is the *Gurrelieder*. The latter is one of the most important works of its time, but has nothing at all to do with Schoenberg's later theoretical experiments and perceptions. The *Gurrelieder*, Schoenberg's final work of this kind, is one last, magnificent monument to late Romanticism. He never again returned to its originality, to the richness of story and vision from which it sprang. In shaping this work, his critical, extremely keen intellect had yielded to overflowing inspiration.

Schoenberg was born on September 13, 1874, in Vienna. Thanks to his magnetic personality, he early on gathered people around him with whom he could seek new pathways in music. Among his first students were Alban Berg and Anton von Webern—musical historians would later call this group the core of the "second Vienna school," but as early as 1911 resistance from all sides forced Schoenberg to move to Berlin. The rise of Nazism once again forced him to emigrate, this time to California. He died in Los Angeles on July 13, 1951.

Gurrelieder

Original Title: Gurre-Lieder
Original Language: German
Text: A poem by the Danish poet Jens Peter Jacobsen, translated into German by Robert Franz Arnold.
First Performance: February 23, 1913, in Vienna, conducted by Franz Schreker.
Form: Oratorio, in three parts
Cast: Waldemar (tenor); Tove (soprano); the Wood Dove (mezzosoprano or alto); a Peasant (bass); Klaus the Fool (tenor); a Speaker; three four-part male choruses and an eight-part mixed chorus.
Orchestra: Four small and four large flutes; three oboes and two English horns; seven clarinets (including an E-flat and bass clarinets); three bassoons and two contrabassoons. 10 horns (four may be tubes); six trumpets and one bass trumpet; six trombones; one double-bass trombone; one tuba; six timpani; large drum, cymbals, triangle, glockenspiel, small drum, large side drum, xylophone, tam-tam, rattle, iron chains; four harps; celeste; first and second violin sections each divided into ten parts; violas, cellos, divided into eight, and contrabasses. (Schoenberg remarked that a minimum of 40 violins was essential and 60 desirable, which would mean that a minimum of 20 violas, 16 cellos, and a like number of contrabasses would be required.)
History of the Work: Schoenberg derived his earliest inspiration from contemporary poets such as the German Richard Dehmel (1863–1920), whose "Verklärte Nacht" was the basis for Schoenberg's string sextet of the same name, and the Danish Jens Peter Jacobsen (1847–1885), whose late Romantic verses portended the poetry of Impressionism.

Signs of disintegration, later called "decadence," the "fin de siècle" mood, marked this period; Impressionism, Jugendstil, and Expressionism converged, possibly accounting for the perceived dissolution of the dying Romantic era. Disquiet and ferment dominated the hearts and minds of young artists. Schoenberg in this same mood dreamed of a work of extraordinary dimension; his friend Alexander von Zemlinsky (a brilliant conductor and significant composer, only now gradually becoming recognized), with the best of intentions, advised him against it. But the idea was typical of its decade, just preceding the outbreak of World War I and the end of an era of European history.

The newly established Philharmonic Chorus in Vienna, whose director was Franz Schreker (on the way to becoming a very successful opera composer) and whose assistant director and piano accompanist was Richard Pahlen, was ready, with the necessary added forces, to take on the first performance of this mighty work; Schoenberg, then living in Berlin, was informed of their decision. There were problems at the rehearsals due to mistakes in the music, so the chorus and the publisher sent a telegram to Schoenberg: "Schreker wants you here immediately." The composer took offense and answered with a sharp letter, saying he would make the journey only to conduct his work, not to serve as "proofreader."

Feelings calmed down, and the premiere, on February 23, 1913, was enthusiastically acclaimed by an audience that until then had largely been unsympathetic to Schoenberg. The following year, 1914, the composer conducted *Gurrelieder* himself in Leipzig, achieving a new triumph. Fewer performances followed, due first to the war and to the years of crisis that followed, but more importantly to the turmoil in the musical world resulting from the advent of new styles.

Schoenberg became the leader of a "trend," of a "school," of a new system of composition, and in the ever increasing strife this work, composed before the innovations appeared, was almost forgotten. The rise of Nazism and the onset of World War II drove Schoenberg far from his old cultural environment. At his death, the conflict raging around the founder of the twelve-tone system continued with even greater intensity, but the man, by then a historic figure, was heaped with honors.

The *Gurrelieder* is unfortunately only seldom performed in the world's concert halls; Schoenberg's disciples regard it as a youthful work with no actual relationship to what they see as his life's mission: showing the way toward a "new" music. But the beauty of this very significant composition remains, and we can look for its resurgence in time.

Discussion of the Work: This is an epic tale of love and death, and of endless longing beyond the grave. A fine orchestral prelude, a symphonic poem, opens the work, depicting two people inexorably drawn together. King Waldemar, a 14th-century Danish prince, spurs his horse to Gurre castle, where the lovely young Tove awaits him. The love that binds them is indissoluble. Waldemar sings of it as he races along, as does Tove, until at last they fall into each other's arms to exchange tender words of love. Throughout we encounter reminders of other great love scenes, spoken and musical reminiscences from the second act of Wagner's *Tristan*. But despite natural similarities of mood, Schoenberg, here a full-blooded Romantic, sets his own particular tone, heart-rending, rapturous, wondrous ecstasy such as is granted only to lovers. Tove speaks tenderly, "Nun sag ich dir zum ersten Mal: 'König Volmer*, ich liebe dich!'" (Now I tell you for the first time, 'King Volmer, I love you') (Example 1), and like all lovers who believe every meeting is the first time, she

Example 1

too feels this is the first time, though she has told him of her love repeatedly before. Tove continues (Jacobsen's lines are high poetry): "Nun küss ich dich zum ersten Mal und schlinge den Arm um dich... Und sprichst du, ich hätt' es schon früher gesagt und je meinen Kuss dir geschenkt, so sprech'ich: 'Der König ist ein Narr, der nichtigen Tandes gedenkt.'" (Now, for the first time, I kiss you and throw my arms around you... And if you say I have said it before and earlier given you my kiss, I answer, 'The King is a fool and talks nonsense.'). Their love songs, music of utmost tranquility—only very great works take the time and repose needed to be understood in their full depth—carry intimations of death. But such thoughts hold no terrors for lovers:

---

*Probably a familiar form of Waldemar

"So kurz ist der Tod, wie ruhiger Schlummer von Dämm'rung zu Dämm'rung" (So brief is death, like a calm sleep from dusk to dawn), for they believe death will not separate them. Almost like a hymn Tove sings ". . . und wenn du erwachst, bei dir auf dem Lager in neuer Schönheit siehst du strahlen die junge Braut. So lass uns die goldene Schale leeren ihm, dem mächtig verschönenden Tod: Denn wir gehn zu Grab wie ein Lächeln, ersterbend im seligen Kuss!" (And when you awaken, you will see beside you your young bride, radiant with new-found beauty. So let us drain the golden cup to Death, who makes all beautiful beyond belief, for we enter the tomb smiling and expire in the bliss of our embrace). Death comes, but takes only the young Tove. In a long, intensely passionate orchestral interlude, all dreams of a love more profound than can ever be flow into the silence of the past. Who killed Tove? Was it the jealous queen, Waldemar's wife, who vengefully held high the single blazing torch, its flickering glow lighting the way as King Waldemar bore his dead love to the grave? The Wood Dove recounts the scene in a lengthy narrative that closes the first section. The second section is a single frenzied accusation by Waldemar against God. Insatiable longing for his lost love has driven the king to madness and death.

The third section is a ghostly dance: Every year, on the anniversary of Tove's death, Waldemar rides across the land with a wild army of the dead. A single obsession drives him: "Ich und Tove, wir sind eins!" (I and Tove—we are one). The male choruses sound otherworldly, the singing of hounded souls who, like Waldemar, can find no peace. "Des Sommerwindes wilde Jagd" (The Wild Chase of the Summer Wind) is the title of another lengthy orchestral interlude. A speaker makes the transition to a final reconciliation, and the precise pitch and rhythm of his words are indicated in the score—the first signs of a development which in a few years would lead Schoenberg to the revolutionary *Pierrot lunaire*, introducing a new form of melodrama into 20th-century art music.

An idyllic nature mood takes shape. Is it consolation? Apotheosis? Transfiguration? The sun rises in a radiant C major, as in Haydn's *Creation* and countless times since. All this is accomplished with the enormously enlarged musical forces of the dawning 20th century. Schoenberg's dawn is overpowering in its brilliance, yet it contains not the slightest hint that the dusk of an entire epoch has fallen over its world.

Die Jakobsleiter (Jacob's Ladder)

Schoenberg not only left his greatest work, the opera *Moses und Aron*, unfinished, but also, under very similar circumstances, discontinued work on an oratorio called *Die Jakobsleiter* when about halfway completed. Schoenberg had also written the text; the famous Viennese actor Wilhelm Klitsch read it at a matinee of Schoenberg's "Verein für musikalische Privataufführungen" (Society for Private Musical Performances) on May 22, 1921. The composer had worked on the composition since 1917, but despite repeated efforts later it remained unfinished. His student and friend Wilfried Zillig completed it later based on the composer's sketches. It is probably more than just accident that the composer either was unable or did not want to finish the problematic piece. Initially he thought the awkward, almost incomprehensible text required an enormous orchestra: 20 flutes (with 10 piccolos); 20 oboes (with 10 English horns); 24 clarinets; 20 bassoons (with 10 contrabassoons); 12 horns; 10 trumpets; eight trombones; six tubas; eight harps; 13 vocal soloists; and a chorus of 720. Zillig reduced this huge apparatus to the size of the typical Late Romantic orchestra. The Jacob's ladder of the title probably refers to the path of the soul to God; along the way the Archangel Gabriel acquaints it with the sufferings it will encounter. The cast includes an Authority, an Instigator, a Monk, a Chosen One (possibly a self-portrait of Schoenberg), a Dying One, a chorus of the Dissatisfied, the Despairing, and the Rejoicing. They declaim on and on in a language that even when read presents almost insurmountable obstacles, and is completely incomprehensible in music even if it were clearer and more inspired. It was presented for the first time in Vienna in 1961.

Franz Schubert 1797–1828

Schubert, gifted with wondrous creativity (probably only Haydn, Mozart, and Beethoven can compare), worked in all musical genres: opera, symphony, chamber music, choruses, sacred music, and songs. The oratorio was of little interest to him; he started only one and left it unfinished, just as with his most famous symphony, the Eighth, in B minor. And just as we know almost nothing of the reason why Schubert, after having sketched out the third movement, set the symphony aside never to take it up again, we have no idea what happened with his oratorio *Lazarus*. He seems to have lost interest after writing a few sketches of the last section, or perhaps it presented him with unsuspected difficulties. Difficulties? The word had no meaning for such a man who, like Mozart, composed with godlike ease. So why did *Lazarus oder: Die Feier der Auferstehung* (Lazarus, or the Celebration of the Resurrection) remain a fragment? Schubert left other works unfinished; for example, a string quartet in C minor; only one of its movements exists, probably the first one, to judge by its form. In this instance we do not even know whether he was really thinking of the beginning of a cycle, but we do know that he composed this string quartet movement in the same year as *Lazarus*. Two unfinished works at just about the same time? Is there some relationship, some depression, a general lassitude?

Schubert suffered several professional setbacks at that time, but when was that not true for him? In addition, Therese Grob, his young love, had rejected his suit, marrying a "respectable citizen." Did this hurt him so that he that he left the works unfinished? It is fairly certain that he broke off work on his single oratorio, *Lazarus*, in February 1820. Whether he had begun it in 1819 or not until 1820 is uncertain. It is also unclear how Schubert came to use the text, not really a good one. It seems to have been his fate to choose weak texts for his large works—operas and this one oratorio. The text for *Lazarus* was written by a Protestant theologian, a high councillor of the consistory in Halle, by the name of August Hermann Niemayer (1754–1828). The poem was published in 1778 under the title of "Lazarus oder Die Feier der Auferstehung," and had been set to music several times, but after 40 years surely had been forgotten, its style being "out of fashion." Schubert found it and sketched out a "religious drama in three acts," but it is highly unlikely he had a stage production in mind, because he also called the work an "Easter cantata." The first "act" describes the death of Lazarus. Strangely enough, the second contains a precise scenic instruction: "A greening field with many headstones, planted with palms and cedars," the site of Lazarus' grave. The third section was either never composed, (the most likely explanation) or has been lost. In its absence, the crux of the work is lacking: the Resurrection.

Nevertheless, the fragments are sometimes performed; they are well received by Schubert devotees since the completed portions are sufficiently inspired to hold and move an audience. The work was first performed at Easter, 1863, 35 years after Schubert's death, in the large hall of the Vienna *Musikverein*, conducted by Johann Herbeck (who also presented the premiere of the unfinished Symphony, No. 8, in B minor, among other Schubert works). Three years later, in 1866, the torso was first published following great efforts to gather it together. The first part was found in 1897 in the possession of Schubert's friend Josef von Spaun. It seems that Schubert's brother Ferdinand had the second part, but after his death it passed into the possession of Beethoven biographer A. W. Thayer, where Heinrich von Kreissle, the Schubert scholar, found it. Fritz Hug, who wrote one of the best biographies of the master, mentions Herbeck's claim that he discovered the last pages of the second section being used as "waste paper at a grocer's," for wrapping groceries. Hug added, "When we know the story of what became of the work, and when we think of the completely mature and consummate skill with which the first part and long passages of the second part are written, we hope against hope that the third part, the Resurrection, was also composed." The file on this only oratorio by Schubert must be closed, for the time being.

Toward the end of his life, Schubert wrote another work that could be called a cantata and is one of the most successful of his many choral works, *Mirjams Siegesgesang*. It was composed in March 1828 for solo soprano, mixed chorus, and piano. (Franz Lachner, a friend of Schubert's and Kapellmeister at the Kärntnertor Theater, later transcribed the piano part for orchestra.) This *Siegesgesang* describes the rejoicing of the Israelites upon their miraculous rescue from the Egyptian army led by the Pharaoh, all of whom drowned in the Red Sea. The text was written specifically for Schubert by Franz Grillparzer, a gesture of affection by of the famous Austrian dramatist which must have been one of the great satisfactions in Schubert's short life. The work, in which remarkably effective solos alternate with very forceful, sometimes fugal choral passages, is permeated with fiery inspiration and gives not the slightest hint of Schubert's imminent death. *Mirjams Siegesgesang* is one of many important works never heard by their creator. It was first performed on January 30, 1829, some 10 weeks after Schubert's death, at the hall of the Vienna *Musikverein*, at which for some unknown reason the solo part was sung by a tenor. It was next performed, in Lachner's orchestral transcription, on March 28, 1830, in the ballroom of the Hofburg—the solo sung by the prescribed soprano.

Schubert's Masses

Schubert composed six Latin Masses and the so-called *Deutsche Messe*. The first four Latin Masses are youthful works, composed in 1814, 1815, and 1816. Schubert's sacred works occupy a quite important place in his total output. In addition to the Masses, there is a Tantum ergo for a solo quartet, mixed chorus, and orchestra; an Offertory for solo tenor, mixed chorus, and orchestra; and many other works that I shall list chronologically. But first, a number of "semireligious" works should be noted, including: *Gott, der Weltschöpfer, Gott im Ungewitter*, the Schiller poem *Hymne an den Unendlichen*, and a *Chor der Engel* using a text by Goethe. There is the curious setting of the 92nd Psalm in Hebrew for a famous cantor of the time, Salomon Sulzer. And lastly this group is the best place to include a work played and sung a million times—the *Ave Maria*, by virtue of its deeply religious mood.

When only 15 (1812), Schubert wrote the Kyrie of a Mass in D minor, which he never completed, as well as a Salve Regina for solo soprano, orchestra, and organ. In 1813 he composed three Kyries (in B-flat major, D minor, and F major), which he seems to have conceived of as independent works, not as parts of a Mass. At the time he was living with his parents in Liechtenthal, a suburb of Vienna, not far from the church of the "Fourteen Intercessors" which his family not only attended but where they also occasionally participated as instrumentalists or vocalists. Here he presented his Mass No. 1 in F major, composed in 1814. A year later he wrote two Masses (in G major and in B-flat major) as well as Offertories, a Stabat mater, and a Gradual. In 1816, when barely 19, he composed for "his" church a fourth Latin Mass in C major, followed by a German Salve Regina, a second Stabat mater, a Latin Salve Regina, two Tantum ergos, and a Magnificat. In 1818 he composed the *Deutsche Requiem*.

In 1819 he began his largest Mass yet, No. 5 in A-flat major, which required three years to finish, totally out of keeping with his usual practice. He wrote a Salve Regina as well as an Offertory that can be viewed as either a sacred work or a song. The year 1820 saw the unfinished oratorio *Lazarus*, previously noted, as well as six Antiphons for Palm Sunday. The 23rd Psalm for four female voices and piano belongs here as well. In 1821 he produced "only" one Tantum ergo, and in 1822, two, as well as finishing the A-flat major Mass and starting an A minor Mass which remained a fragment. The composition of sacred works fell off somewhat in 1823 as a torrent of secular works flowed from his pen. From the year 1824, a Salve Regina and a *Gebet* for chorus and piano should be mentioned. In 1826 he composed the *Deutsche Messe*. The year of his death saw many sacred works: the sixth and last Mass, that in E-flat major, a second Benedictus for the much earlier D major Mass, a Tantum ergo, and an Offertory.

The Schubert authority Friedrich Spiro wrote that every important event in Schubert's life resulted in a sacred composition: his first love, his Alpine journey, his severe illness. In every case this devout composer felt even more intensely compelled to give expression to his feelings for God, Jesus, and Mary. No material consideration could have prompted him, for he had received neither money nor acclaim for any of his sacred pieces.

His piety is beyond doubt; about his relationship to the Church there are questions. We not only have accounts of comments by contemporaries but also the undeniable evidence of his Masses, in which he invariably omitted the article of faith in "unam sanctam catholicam et apostolicam Ecclesiam" (in one holy Catholic and apostolic church). In so doing, he was certainly aware that liturgical use of such "mutilated" Masses was out of the question; even performance in a church would probably be prohibited. Observers have long puzzled over this omission; he said nothing on the subject. Mass No. 1 in F Major was composed in 37 days and was intended for the centenary celebration of the Liechtental church. It was performed there for the first time on October 16, 1814, with his secret love, Therese Grob, singing the soprano solo part he had composed for her. The work made such an impression that only 10 days later it was repeated in the church of St. Augustine, a court church not in the suburbs but in the heart of the city.

Mass No. 2 in G major was written in 1815 in only five days. It went unnoticed during Schubert's lifetime and for a long time thereafter. A plagiarist seized this opportunity and presented it in Prague, in 1846, as his own: "Mass in G, Composed for the Inauguration of His Imperial Majesty . . . by Robert Führer, Kapellmeister at the cathedral of St. Veit in Prague."

Mass No. 3 in B-flat major was also composed in 1815, a few months after No. 2. We do not know when it was first sung. Ferdinand, faithful trustee for his brother Franz after his death, published it in 1838. In a letter to Franz in October 1824, from the town of Hainburg on the Danube, not far downriver from Vienna, Ferdinand advised that he had become acquainted with the director of the choir there, who invited him

to attend services the following Sunday; and when I asked him what Mass he was doing he replied, "a very beautiful one by a well-known, famous composer whose name I can't think of at the moment." And what Mass was it? If you had only been with me, I know you would have also been pleased, for it was the B-flat Mass—yours!

Mass No. 4 in C major seems to have been composed in July 1816. It was most certainly composed for the Liechtenthal church and its "Regens chori" (choral director), but why were nine years to pass before its first performance there on September 8, 1825? On September 3 of that year the Viennese publisher Anton Diabelli announced publication of the work; it bore a dedication to Schubert's friend Michael Holzer, also a choral director, whose importance in the composer's life cannot be underestimated. (Diabelli also played an important part in Beethoven's life—doubly so, as publisher and as composer of the theme upon which Beethoven composed his "Diabelli" piano variations.) Three weeks later, the *Berliner Allgemeine Zeitung* reported from Vienna that "the young composer tirelessly continues to compose songs; his firstborn, with the curious title *Der Erlenkönig* found an audience, but one that gradually seems to diminish. Diabelli has also published one of his Masses. His ballads are more successful." Schubert seems to have been less than completely satisfied with this Mass: a month before his death, in October 1828, he wrote a new Benedictus for it; his reason, "for lack of a good soprano singer" (in the first version, a large part of the movement and also the theme of the following Hosanna was written for this voice). Incidentally, the term "soprano singer" seems to indicate that Schubert's Masses were sung by boys rather than by women. Only the first of his Masses has a solo soprano role that seems to have been composed expressly for a young woman—for Therese Grob, who "was not meant for him."

Schubert's last two Masses are considered his best and most important. Mass No. 5 in A-flat major took three years to complete—an unheard of length of time for him. He was especially fond of it, worked on it devotedly, and revised the fugue "Cum sancto spiritu" again and again until it had the awe-inspiring magnificence he desired. He wrestled with the Osanna as well, composing more than one version. Little did he suspect that his idol, Beethoven, was working on a sacred work at the same time. In November 1819, Schubert sketched the first parts of the A-flat major Mass and on December 7, 1822 advised his friend Joseph von Spaun that it was finished. He said it would "very soon be performed," and that as an "old idea," he would dedicate it "to the Emperor or to the Empress" because he thought it had "turned out so well."

About this time Schubert applied for the position of second Hofkapellmeister but was no more successful than with any of the others for which he applied previously. He then visited Josef Eybler, first Hofkapellmeister, after which Schubert described the meeting to a friend:

> Eybler said he had heard of me but had not heard anything I had composed. I don't mean to flatter myself, but I certainly would have thought that the Hofkapellmeister of Vienna would have heard at least something of mine. When I returned a few weeks later and asked after the fate of my "child," [Schubert had taken one of his Masses on his first visit, probably the one in A-flat major] Eybler replied that the Mass was good but not in the style favored by the Emperor. I took my leave and thought to myself: Well, I am not so lucky as to be able to compose in the imperial style. . . .

When applying for another position in Vienna, Schubert mentioned that all his Masses had been performed "several times in Viennese churches." As they had not been published, they existed only in manuscript and could be used only in copies made with or without permission. So while Schubert's statement is probably true, it is far too late to establish when and where these performances took place.

Schubert called the A-flat major Mass a *Missa solemnis* (a great, solemn Mass), referring not only to the form but to the instrumentation, which consisted of two each of flutes, oboes, clarinets, bassoons, horns, and trumpets; three trombones; timpani; and a complete complement of strings. The scoring is richer than that of his earlier Masses, but the instruments are most economically used: they are at their most forceful only when solemnity or exultation require it.

Words cannot describe the beauty of this work. The fugue "Cum sancto spiritu" (Example 1) is the first so fully developed in any of Schubert's compositions. It surprises listeners who know him "only" as a master of homophony, or accompanied melody. It is then all the more surprising that shortly before his death, Schubert, who could compose such contrapuntal polyphony, sought out Simon Sechter, a teacher of theory, to learn more of this particular art.

This Mass contains many elements worthy of study in detail—the Credo, for example, is deeply moving, with its descent from Heaven ("Descendit de coelis") shrouded in mystery; or the way in which the Credo itself bursts forth. There can be no doubt as to the steadfastness of faith underlying it.

Example 1

Cum sancto spi—ri—tu in glo—ri—a De—i pa—tris, a— — —men,a— —men

The "Et incarnatus est" reveals a renewed sense of mysticism as Schubert divides the chorus into eight parts, begins in an almost whispered F minor and then carries the murmuring voices along through the boldest modulations—nothing less than a harmonic miracle.

When the dead are mentioned ("judicare vivos et mortuos") we feel the shiver so often evident when Schubert sings of death. It is not fear but a deeper belief in an eternity mortals can neither recognize nor understand. The movement is very long, leading us to recall Schumann's regard for Schubert's "Heavenly lengths," intended to stress the heavenly quality and not the length, which turns this so often misunderstood statement into highest praise.

Turning now to the last Mass, No. 6 in E-flat major: It was composed in June and July of the year he died, 1828, and as with so many of the great works of the final period of his brief life—Symphony No. 9 in C Major, *Mirjams Siegesgesang*, the 92nd Psalm, the F minor piano Fantasia for four hands, the three last piano sonatas in C minor, A major, and B-flat major, and the String Quintet in C major—he never heard it performed. It is hardly conceivable that any composer could produce so much within the space of 10 months. Fritz Hug sagely remarked on these last Masses:

> A deep, cheerful piety permeates all these works, as revealed in Schubert's letters to his father ... This piety had nothing to do with churches, nor was it limited by dogma or ritual. Everything about this composition is free yet tranquil, great and noble, convincing and full of life, sunny and mature. The harmony is typically Schubertian—rich, colorful, full of surprising modulations ... the instrumentation is graceful ... does not call for flutes ... a work of the most deeply felt piety, above all, a confession of faith in life but also in death, which has lost all its terror and is not far off.

It seems Schubert intended this Mass for the Holy Trinity parish church in Alser (a suburb at that time) for two important reasons: First, because a former fellow student, Michael Leitermeyer, was choral director there; and second, because Beethoven's body had been consecrated there a few months previously before being transported to the cemetery, a procession of enormous numbers in which Schubert was one of the torch bearers. When this Mass was finally performed, Schubert had been dead for almost a year; his brother Ferdinand directed the performance, probably on October 4, 1829, in that church.

The score calls for two each of oboes, clarinets, bassoons, horns, and trumpets, three trombones, and the usual strings. By way of exception, five soloists are used—soprano, alto, two tenors, and bass—but they are given less to do than in his earlier Masses.

In addition to the six Masses, of which the last two are the most outstanding, many of his other sacred works are still sung: For example the *Gesänge zur Feier des heiligen Opfers der Messe*, usually sung by male choruses, in an arrangement by Johann Herbeck, and commonly referred to as the *Deutsche Messe*. It was commissioned by the author of its text, J. Ph. Neumann, professor of physics at the Polytechnic Institute in Vienna, who sought to establish a musical tradition in the spirit of the Enlightenment and so help popularize church music. Schubert confirmed the commission:

> Honored Professor:
> I have received in good order the 100 florins W. W. [Viennese currency] that you sent me to compose the Mass, and only hope that the composition in question meets your expectations. With highest regards, your most devoted servant, Frz. Schubert. October 16, 1827.

The individual vocal sections are very simple and songlike; "they radiate a heartfelt, artless, folklike piety. Of them, the Sanctus, with its noble and very simple harmonies, is particularly affecting as it spans the restrained 'Heilig ist der Herr!,' the majestic 'Er, der nie begonnen,' and the delicate murmur of '. . . sein wird immerdar' in an arc completely organic in form" (Fritz Hug).

Church authorities in Vienna were offered all kinds of poetic works and compositions; rooted as they were in the era of Joseph II's "era of tolerance." They had to come to terms with Freemasonry even in the highest echelons of society, and they had no objection to the publication of this work. However, its use in religious services was forbidden.

In a high-handed way, church authorities added the missing articles of faith so that Schubert's

Latin Masses could be sung in church services. I firmly maintain that Schubert believed deeply in God but less so in his earthly representatives. And when pursuing such matters, the omission in his Mass No. 4 of the line "ex Maria virgine" from the "Et incarnatus est" must also be noted. A composer who had been brought up so firmly in the faith—at home and at the *Konvikt*, where he sang in the boys' choir—does not "forget" parts of the Mass, as is sometimes suggested to explain these omissions. Walter Pass has remarked, "there is a serious intent at work, which we are not yet able to explain. Without any doubt, however, these omissions are one of the most important keys to understanding Schubert's personality and way of thinking."

Schubert's church music is filled with the same faith that informs the entire body of his enormous oeuvre. Basically it is music for God rather than for the church.

Gunther Schuller 1925–

In 1970, Gunther Schuller received the Alice M. Ditson Conductor's Award, particularly in recognition of his warm professional support and concern for his fellow conductors and composers but, in general, for his noteworthy contributions to America's music. This award bestowed a special and lasting distinction upon the career of a leading American musician who became the esteemed Director of The New England Conservatory; taught on the faculties of Yale University and the Manhattan School of Music; played principal horn for the Cincinnati Symphony Orchestra and the orchestra of the Metropolitan Opera; directed musical activities at the Berkshire (Tanglewood) Music Center and the first International Jazz Festival (1962); guest conducted over 50 orchestras in Europe and North America; delivered a radio series on music for several years; received numerous awards, grants and academic honors; and composed over 150 major works, not including scores for films and television.

Schuller had studied privately at the Manhattan School of Music during his early years, but after finishing high school he was entirely self-taught in all academic and musical areas.

Prior to giving up his career as a professional horn player in 1962, freeing more time to compose, Schuller had written over 50 compositions. The first work to receive a major performance was his *Concerto for French Horn and Orchestra No. 1* (1945), premiered by the Cincinnati Symphony with the composer as soloist.

Schuller's personal style stems from the atonal idioms of Schoenberg and Stravinsky. He developed his own brand of "softer" serialism and combined this with his overriding devotion to American jazz, producing the mixed style for which he coined the phrase "third-stream jazz." His only major work for chorus and orchestra is *The Power Within Us: A Narrative Oratorio* (1972).

The Power Within Us

Original Title: The Power Within Us: A Narrative Oratorio for Baritone, Narrator, Chorus and Orchestra
Original Language: English
Text: The story is drawn from the published accounts of Alvar Núñez Cabeza de Vaca, the 16th-century Spanish explorer. His unique relationship with Indians (as a "miracle healer" during an ill-fated Spanish military expedition to the New World [1528–1536] under Pamfilo Narvarez) provides the dramatic focus.
Date of Writing: 1972
First Performance: March 11, 1972, at the Georgia Music Educators National Conference, with the composer conducting.
Form: One movement.
Cast: A narrator, baritone soloist and chorus share portions of the story as it unfolds in the first person. Neither soloist can be considered the voice of the explorer. The chorus never functions to comment and only in a few moments of dramatic intensity echoes the solo text. Hence the narration is unbroken; chorus and soloists providing effective contrast in its expression.
Scoring: Chorus and orchestra.
Discussion of the Work: The narrator begins, identifying de Vaca as a subject of the King of Spain (Emperor Charles V) and explaining the nature of de Vaca's report. De Vaca relates an earlier miraculous incident at the battle of Ravenna, when, as he was emotionally overcome by the carnage around him, a vision appeared: "I saw a far-off light; heard a far-off strain of music." An

ethereal polychord resounds through the orchestra under these last words. This incident assumes awesome significance for de Vaca: "What can describe a happening in the shadows of the soul?" An air of resignation characterizes the scene. Over ominous string tremolos the narrator recounts the disastrous expedition to America. Addressing the King, the baritone comments on the devastating reality—"five hundred eighty of us, to utter ruin." In staggered entrances, an a cappella choral phrase reaches a climax on the words "we would share the glory of Cortes," as the orchestra enters, forte, momentarily sustaining this fantasy for conquest. In polyphonic, half-whispered patterns the chorus paints a fleeting vision of past Spanish glories (Example 1). After a fruitless and demoralizing search for another Tenochtitlan (modern Mexico City) in the wastelands of Florida, the commander of the now depleted force elects to return to Cuba by sea. The baritone confesses, "This is what men can do when they must do something or die," and proceeds to describe the makeshift boats and the fateful attempt to navigate the open sea. In a telling passage revealing de Vaca's deep personal feeling for his fellow man, the chorus questions "Who knows what was lost in those boats?" The narrator depicts unbelievable scenes: "I saw men gnaw at corpses—these were Spanish gentlemen." Winds and brass appear to faint in short utterances. The strings dissolve into barely audible pianissimos on a long glissando. The vision at Ravenna appears again, surrounded by a glistening halo in the upper winds.

Although there is no formal division of any kind, it is at this point that the drama turns in a new direction. De Vaca and a few others finally reach land and are found by Indians, who treat them with unexpected concern and compassion: "They sat down beside us and cried too." The chorus utters a penetrating revelation in half-whispered rhythms (Example 2). Here de Vaca's unique relationship with the Indians is established. Initiated by the natives' desire for help, he and his band of forgotten conquerors discover that they possess miraculous powers of healing. The cause remains a mystery, but their power continues. De Vaca's companions die. He is left with the Indians until three other Spaniards are washed ashore—the final survivors of the original expedition. When approached by the Indians, these men likewise learn to perform acts of healing, exercising familiar rituals and prayers. Their fame spreads rapidly. Groups of diseased and ailing natives are brought to them. They are taken long distances, often under duress, to cure all manner of illness. De Vaca himself is actually summoned to bring one Indian back from the dead. In time these four are treated like gods of unlimited compassion, living unclothed and often near starvation. The chorus carries de Vaca's visionary words: "That European world of which we had been a

Example 1

Example 2

part grew fantastic and no longer plausible." He is consumed with the joy of his power, expressed in a momentous choral phrase. In a moment of final irony, de Vaca encounters a contingent of Spanish slave catchers. The baritone sings the words which seem to trap de Vaca's soul: "What, your Majesty, is so melancholy as to confront one's former unthinking and unfeeling self?"

Once more the scene shifts dramatically, with only a fermata to mark the change. De Vaca is rescued and returned to Spain. In the familiar semi-recitative style of the baritone lines, we hear the explorer's summary testimony:

> Baritone: At first I did not notice other ways in which our ancient civilization was affecting me. Yet soon I observed a certain reluctance to do good to others. While with them, I thought about doing the Indians good, but back among my fellow countrymen I had to be on guard not to do them positive harm. If one lives where all suffer and starve, one acts on one's own impulse to help, but where plenty abounds we surrender our generosity.

The chorus joins at the words "If one lives"—the only place in the work where different texts are heard simultaneously.

> Chorus: The power of maintaining life in others lives within each of us.

A response from the chorus completes de Vaca's witness to this remarkable experience (Example 3). In the few remaining measures, chorus and orchestra melt into pianissimo and the oratorio ends with the first violins alone.

Example 3

—*Thurston Dox*

Robert Schumann   1810–1856

Whereas Schumann made only one attempt at opera—his *Genoveva* received its premiere in Leipzig in 1850 but was never widely accepted—he returned again and again to the oratorio form, which he shaped in the most varied ways. His first work of this kind was composed in 1843: *Das Paradies und die Peri*, Op. 50. In 1851 came the oratorio *Der Rose Pilgerfahrt*, Op. 112. Whether the music for Lord Byron's poem "Manfred" should be considered an oratorio (Op. 115, composed in 1851) is questionable. Just as debatable is the classification of several choral ballads, among them *Beim Abschied zu singen* (1847); *Requiem für Mignon* (1849); *Nachtlied* (1849); *Der Königssohn* (1851); *Das Glück von Edenhall* (1853); *Des Sängers Fluch* (1852); and *Vom Pagen und der Königstochter* (1852), all of which are rarely encountered in modern performances. *Szenen aus Goethes "Faust,"* begun in 1849 and finished in 1850, is heard more often and is usually considered to be an oratorio. In 1852, Schumann composed a Mass (Op. 147) and a Requiem (Op. 148), his only liturgical works; his music was almost exclusively secular.

Tragedy surrounded not just his death, but his whole life, more so than that of almost any other composer. His insanity became publicly evident in 1854 when he threw himself into the icy Rhine near Düsseldorf. It had, however, been part of his makeup since his youth, causing from time to time attacks of anxiety so ferocious that those sound of mind cannot conceive of enduring them. As a consequence, his life was riddled with grave difficulties, somewhat strange and often fear-ridden. There were, of course, many happy, creative moments, particularly at the side of his beloved Clara, who even though she must have suspected what was in store remained devoted to him through joy and suffering. Mendelssohn, then Germany's most respected and influential musician, was Schumann's friend and guardian angel. Only after Mendelssohn's death did calamity really overtake Schumann, when he failed to live up to expectations as conductor at Düsseldorf and attempted suicide. One bright moment of those last years was his discovery of the young Johannes Brahms, who when 20 years old first came knocking on Schumann's door and received from him a veritable hymn of praise in the *Neue Zeitschrift für Musik*, almost unheard of for one so newly entered into the confraternity of composers.

Schumann's life spanned the period from June 8, 1810 to July 29, 1856, but his conscious one ended February 27, 1854. He was born in Zwickau, in Saxony, and died in an asylum at Endenich, near Bonn. His songs and piano works will live forever. His four symphonies are masterpieces of the Romantic era, and there is much beauty in his chamber music. The oratorios, discussed here, are equally lovely.

Das Paradies und die Peri (Paradise and the Peri)

Original Title: Das Paradies und die Peri
Original Language: German
Text: After the English epic "Lalla Rookh" by the Irish Romantic poet Thomas Moore (1779–1852); German version by Emil Flechsig.
Date of Writing: 1843
First Performance: December 4, 1843, in the Leipzig Gewandhaus.
Form: In three sections, with a total of 26 musical numbers.
Cast: The Peri, the Maiden (soprano); the Angel (alto); the Youth (tenor); the Man (baritone); Gazna (bass); four-part chorus.
History of the Work: The first years of Schumann's compositional life were devoted exclusively to works for piano. The year 1840—a thoroughly happy time, when the two lovers, Robert and Clara, were married—can be called his "Year of Song." The year 1841 became the "Year of the Symphony" and 1842, that of chamber music. In the same sense, and not to imply that the composer ever limited himself to a single genre, many have called 1843 Schumann's "Oratorio Year," since in that year he began and completed the setting of the Irish epic *Lalla Rookh* entitled *Das Paradies und die Peri,* his first effort in this genre. We can follow the story of the work's development from the diary that Robert and Clara jointly kept beginning with the day of their marriage. Under the date "April 1843" Clara entered, "At the end of last month, Robert finished the first section of his 'Peri' and will soon start the second. Unfortunately, that dreadful journal* has taken precedence over everything else for a week, which really annoys him. Why am I not a writer? It would be more useful to him than my piano playing ever was." At the end of that month she wrote, "Robert finished the second part of the 'Peri,' but has not said much about it to me. I look forward so very much to the premiere in the autumn, when I will once more luxuriate in my Robert's music, which is like no other I know." The following month, May 1843 (the entries in the diary, originally intended to be made at the end of each week, had long since been deferred to the end of each month), we read, once again in Clara's hand, "I wish you would finish the 'Peri' soon for the sake of our poor diary, because it completely loses interest when you do not write in it." The next entry ("June 28, 1843") was made by Robert; along with a report on the birth of their second child, he wrote, "On June 10, after many days of strenuous work, my 'Peri' was finally finished. This was a great joy for the Schumanns."

July and August 1843 are combined in the diary, the entry made by Clara: "At the end of July, I began to prepare the piano reduction for the 'Peri'—a task that gives me a great deal of pleasure."

On November 21, 1843, Robert entered,

> Clara is still in Dresden, where she gave a concert last evening; it is so deathly quiet in the house when she is not here. So I turn to you, dear diary . . . Otherwise, in the last few months everything we have done has had to do with the "Peri," and my Clara must have sometimes thought I was really egotistical because that is all I talked about. But other kinds of thoughts are related to this work, and if I wanted to tell you all about them, you should certainly not be cross with me. Clara did the piano reduction for the "Peri" with much love and at great sacrifice, and I've really not thanked her enough for it; but I do appreciate her efforts and love, and I often turned away deeply moved when I saw her at the piano so hard at work. Now the first performance will take place on

---

*The *Neue Zeitschrift für Musik,* founded and directed by Schumann

December 4, if all goes well. I've also tried my hand at conducting and see that I have some skill at it. My shortsightedness is the biggest problem, and I'll have to get glasses later.

Clara reported on the first performance in December 1843:

> On the 4th, Robert presented his "Peri" for the first time (for the benefit of the Music School) and also made his debut as a conductor. Even the morning of the rehearsal I was enchanted by the magnificent instrumentation, and you can just imagine how happy I was that evening—words can hardly express it. There was great applause—but at the second performance, on the 11th, it was enthusiastic. They sang with all their hearts and souls—I was with them! If ever I wanted to have a beautiful voice, it was then. What I wouldn't have given to have been able to sing Peri.

This was the last entry in their common diary. How would it have read as the decade ended and the next one began in ever increasing gloom?

Discussion of the Work: The oratorio begins with a tender, rapturous prelude. The writer of songs is clearly in evidence and shows Schumann more a lyricist than a dramatist. The alto then begins telling the story, first in a very melodic recitative and then an aria. The Peri—in Indian legend, a Peri is an angel who has fallen or been driven from Heaven—stands before the gates of Paradise and looks back sadly at her brothers and sisters, from whose midst she has been cast out. No matter how beautiful the human's earth below her appears, "ein Tropfen des Himmels ist schöner" (one drop of Heaven is more beautiful) than all else, sings the Peri in a soprano solo.

Then the tenor has a short solo; he fulfills the role of the narrator in classic oratorio, connecting the solos of the different characters. His role is the same as that of the testo in old Italian oratorios, and still in those of Bach and Handel, roughly a century before Schumann.

To a bright woodwind passage with softly beating chords an angel—once more the alto—proclaims the verdict inscribed in the book of fate: The expelled Peri may return to Paradise when she brings to its portals "des Himmels liebste Gabe" (the gift most favored by Heaven): "Geh', suche sie und werde rein: gern lass ich die Entsühnten ein!" (Go, seek it and be pure: I willingly admit the repentant ones!).

The Peri sets out to find this "most favored gift." She flies over India and sees its wondrous natural beauty. Solo voices extol it as a paradise, but the chorus paints a contrasting picture: rivers red with blood, death and suffering throughout the land, now under attack by a cruel enemy. In the midst of terrible strife—the "chorus of Indians" confronts the "chorus of conquerors"—the agitated orchestra depicts the battle, which ends in victory for the invaders.

The tenor reports, "Und einsam steht ein Jüngling noch, es fliesst sein Blut aus manchen Wunden, er beugt den Nacken nicht in's Joch." (A youth stands there all alone, blood flowing from his many wounds; he does not bend his neck to the yoke.). As the jubilant enemy surrounds Gazna, its leader, shouting triumphantly, the youth shoots his last arrow into their midst, but it misses the tyrant, who turns to him, saying (in a bass solo), "Komm, kühner Held, und huld'ge mir, willst du umsonst dein Blut verspritzen?" (Come, brave hero, pay homage to me. Do you want to shed your blood for nothing?) But the youth prefers to die at the side of his brothers and sisters. The Peri has observed this scene and, deeply moved, descends to the field of battle, "und nahm das letzte Tröpflein Blut, das aus dem Heldenherzen drang." (and took the last drop of blood pouring from the hero's heart.) The tenor reports, "denn heilig ist das Blut, für die Freiheit verspritzt vom Heldenmut!" (for holy is a hero's blood shed for freedom!). As the chorus accompanies the Peri back to Heaven, it repeats this line in a great chorale-like number, and the first section comes to an end.

In the second section, the narrator tells of the Peri's return to the gates of Heaven and how she is turned away: "Viel heil'ger muss die Gabe sein, die dich zum Tor des Lichts lässt ein!" (The gift that lets you through the gates of light must be much holier!). A chorus of angels confirms the refusal, in a passage vaguely reminiscent of Mozart's *Zauberflöte*, where an invisible chorus emphasizes the speaker's words. The Peri sets out again; she listens to a romantically vibrant "chorus of the Nile genies," and as they sing, the Peri joins in, creating a scene of pure enchantment.

The tenor describes the continuing journey: once again the Peri comes to an earthly paradise of indescribable beauty, but a pestilent miasma hangs over the land, and all that lives is expiring. The Peri begins to weep: a youth flees the poisoned atmosphere and awaits death by a lonely forest lake. As he lies dying, he thinks of the maiden he has loved truly through the years who is being held in her father's princely halls to protect her from contagion. But the maiden hurries to his side to join him in death. The soprano and the tenor sing a tender love duet in which the voices do not sound simultaneously—here, too, we see Schumann as the master of song he really was in all his compositions (Example 1).

Example 1

Example 2

Deeply moved, the Peri sings a lament for the dead with choral accompaniment (once again, completely songlike), and the second part comes to an end.

The third section begins with a lovely chorus of the Huri, those maidens or genies who dwell in Paradise, often mentioned in the Koran. Schumann gives them gently
lilting, almost dancelike music, emphasized by the "Turkish" instrumentation; he uses the same percussion that—at least since Mozart's *Entführung aus dem Serail*—has passed for "eastern," having become known in Central Europe through music made by Janissaries captured in the war with the Turks. (Beethoven used it, too, accompanying the tenor solo in the last movement of his Ninth Symphony.) The sound was characterized mostly by the use of large or small cymbals, small drums, and triangles (Example 2).

The Peri hears the music as she flies back to Heaven. This time she hopes to be admitted, for she takes with her "der reinsten Liebe Seufzer" (sighs of purest love). But once again, she is turned away with the same words as before: "Viel heil'ger muss die Gabe sein, die dich zum Tor des Lichts lässt ein! "Now in despair, she sets out a third time, but she will not rest until allowed back into Heaven. This time the baritone tells of the Peri's journey to Syria, to Lebanon, where once again radiant nature smiles upon her. Four other Peris meet her (two sopranos and two altos), singing "Peri, ist's wahr, dass du in den Himmel willst? Genügt dir nicht das Sonnenlicht und Sterne, Mond und Erde, so nimm uns eilig mit!" (Peri, is it true that you want to return to Heaven? If sunlight and stars, moon and earth are not enough for you, then quick—take us with you!).

The questing Peri's anguish grows; in the last light of evening, she descends to a temple of the sun. There, "über Balbeks Tal sich schwingend, erblickt im Spiele sie ein Kind" (hovering over Balbek's vale, she spies a child at play). The music is lovely but becomes menacing as a curious, mysterious man draws near; on his savage face all manner of vice and crime has left its mark. The child, tired from playing, has sat down and gazes at him fearlessly. From the minaret, the call to evening prayer fills the air; the boy kneels, looking like an angel who "sich hernieder verirrt hat und seine Heimat suchet wieder" (who is lost here below and is looking for his home).

Now, heavily, the words wrung from his heart with great effort, the man sings, "S' war eine Zeit, du selig Kind, da jung und rein wie Du mein Tun und Beten war." (Once upon a time, blessed child, my deeds and prayers were young and pure like you.). The baritone sings this in the simplest of melodies. The four-part chorus and four solo voices do not allow him to finish, for tears of bitterest remorse stream down his cheeks. The savage man kneels beside the child. The Peri's task is over; she takes to Heaven the most holy, the most beautiful gift—the tears of a repentant sinner. To joyful, finally hymnlike singing the Peri rejoins the company of the blessed.

Der Rose Pilgerfahrt (The Pilgrimage of the Rose)

Original Title: Der Rose Pilgerfahrt
Original Language: German
Text: Fairy tale by Moritz Horn
Date of Writing: In May and June 1851, Schumann composed a version of this oratorio with piano accompaniment which he orchestrated in the winter of 1851/52.
First Performance: The piano version in July 1851, at a concert in the Schumann home; the official premiere of the orchestrated work on February 5, 1852, in Düsseldorf.
Cast: Rose (soprano); Princess of the Elves (mezzosoprano); Marthe (alto); the Miller's Wife (alto); the Miller (baritone); the Gravedigger (bass); four solo voices (soprano, alto, tenor, bass); four-part mixed chorus (three-part female chorus in the scenes with elves and angels).
Orchestra: Two flutes, two oboes, two clarinets, two bassoons, four horns, two trumpets, three trombones, timpani, and strings (in the original score Schumann called for two each of hunting horns and valve horns as well as valve trumpets).
Form: The oratorio is in two sections and includes a total of 24 musical numbers, all connected.
History of the Work: On September 2, 1850, the Schumanns and their children arrived in Düsseldorf, where the master was to assume the duties of municipal music director. This is not the place to recount the tragedy of these three and a half years, which ended with the attempted suicide. There were unpleasant disagreements with the orchestra, with various local authorities, and with the press, all of which gradually induced a severe crisis in Schumann's physical and mental health. He suffered greatly, and Clara's unending love could only seldom dispel the melancholy thoughts and suspicions tormenting him. Despite these mounting difficulties his creative energy was not diminished, and the years 1850 to 1853 saw more than a few important works come into being. In the first of these years he composed the Symphony No. 3 in E-flat major, the *Rhenish*, and com-

pleted the *Faust* Scenes; he also composed the Cello Concerto in A minor, Op. 129. The year 1851 produced the beautiful *Märchenbilder,* Op. 113 (for viola or clarinet and piano), several chamber works, and two overtures, in addition to the oratorio under discussion here, *Der Rose Pilgerfahrt*. His output was reduced in 1852. Although the actual number of works produced in 1853, his last creative year, was surprisingly large, they were artistically inferior.

When he moved to Düsseldorf, his head was full of plans for oratorios. This genre, which offered almost limitless artistic freedom, had attracted him since the days of *Paradies und Peri*, but he could not seem to come up with a really brilliant work. He considered one dealing with Luther, whom he wanted to represent as a popular or folklike figure. The subject he finally chose, *Der Rose Pilgerfahrt*, was also to be treated simply, with freshness and vigor. The story upon which it is based can only be understood and presented in the light of its period—that of High Romanticism.

Discussion of the Work: The subject of this "pilgrimage" is pure Romanticism and was often treated in the literature and music of those decades. It may be that Friedrich de la Motte-Fouqué was the initiator of this theme, dealing with the relationship between the world of spirits and the world of men. He wrote a story called *Undine*, which served as model and prototype for many musical works, from the operas of E. T. A. Hoffmann (1816), Lortzing (1845), and Marschner's *Hans Heiling* (1833), to Dvorak's *Rusalka* (1901) and H. W. Henze's ballet *Undine*, to mention only a few of the most notable.

The inherent tragedy is found in the eternal separation between the human world and the invisible, supernatural kingdom of spirits, elves, water sprites, and other creatures whose existence has been depicted since earliest times in myths, fairy tales, and legends. The usual story is structured along these lines: A creature leaves its home in that "mysterious region" out of love for an earthly being, but because no lasting relationship between two such different natures is possible, the quest ends in tragedy. The spirit creature usually is the sufferer, for it cannot successfully survive in the atmosphere of the earthly world, nor among "cold-hearted" humans and their coarse, materialistic ways. Death is the penalty of the earthly journey, a fate which often befalls the mortal lover, more or less willingly, as well.

Schumann's oratorio describes such an earthly journey—librettist Horn and composer Schumann called it a pilgrimage—by a creature of the spirit world. The elf has heretofore played with her sisters in eternal joy, dancing the spring nights away, until her princess grants her secret wish: To become an earthly maiden and experience love.

Tradition has it that in fairyland all are born of roses, so the princess gives the elf a miraculous rose, which will protect her from all dangers. But if she gives the flower away or loses it she must die a mortal's death and return to her home in fairyland.

The "Pilgrimage of the Rose" on earth begins at the first door upon which she knocks. The scolding old woman refuses her quest for hospitality as she has no documentation to prove her identity. Following this first experience with sorrow, Rose meets a gravedigger preparing a grave for a young maiden who died of disappointment in love. In the gathering dusk, the funeral procession nears; deeply moved, Rose weeps for her unknown human sister.

Long after the other mourners have left, the gravedigger notices the maiden still kneeling at the graveside. The kindly old man invites her to his modest house, for night is falling. As Rose sleeps, an ethereal fairy chorus hovers above her bed. In the morning before setting out, she seeks the gravedigger's blessing. He is touched, and promises to take her to a couple who will adopt her as their own child. The couple, a miller and his wife, see in the elf a resemblance to their dead daughter and lovingly take her into their home.

Soon all the villagers take her to their hearts, after which love comes in the form of the forester's son. In time she agrees to marry him. Joyful, folklike songs ring out ("Ei, Mühle, liebe Mühle, wie schau'st so schmuck du heut!"—Ah, mill, dear mill, you look so handsome today!), announcing the wedding feast, a scene Schumann richly adorns with song and dance.

The scene shifts to the birth of Rose's child a year later. With the greatest tenderness, Schumann depicts Rose's happy motherhood, the music having a very close connection to the song cycle *Frauenliebe und -leben*, composed 11 years earlier. But this highest moment of Rose's mortal life carries within itself the end of her pilgrimage: She places the rose she has brought from fairyland on her child's heart, that it may always be protected as she herself has been. She knows it is her farewell: "Nimm hin mein Glück, du kleines Herz, ich geh beseligt heimatwärts, mein ward der Erde Seligkeit, nach dieser gibt es keine Freud!" (Take my happiness, tiny heart, I return home blessed; I have had mortal bliss—no joy is greater than this). Choruses of angels attend her as she ascends, returning to the spirit world or to Heaven—the fairy tale is over. Perhaps its time will come again.

Faust-Szenen (Scenes from Goethe's *Faust*)

Original Title: Szenen aus Goethes Faust
Original Language: German
Text: From *Faust*, Parts I and II, by Johann Wolfgang von Goethe.
Date of Writing: 1844–1853; Schumann began with the third section, originally conceived as a separate work entitled "Fausts Verklärung" (Faust's Transfiguration), finishing it in 1848. In 1849 and 1850 he composed the second and the first sections of the *Faust* scenes and in 1853 the Overture.
First Performance: The third section (Fausts Verklärung) in 1849 in Dresden, Leipzig, and Weimar (there conducted by Franz Liszt); the first complete performance of the *Faust* Scenes in January 1862, in Cologne.
Form: In three sections with a total of 13 musical numbers.
Cast: Faust (baritone); Pater Seraphicus (baritone); Doctor Marianus (baritone); Gretchen (soprano); Una Poenitentium (soprano); Evil Spirit (bass); Mephistopheles (bass); Pater Profundus (Bass); Ariel (tenor); Pater Ecstaticus (tenor); Care (soprano); Martha (soprano); Distress (soprano); Magna Peccatrix (soprano); Lack (alto); Mulier Samaritana (alto); Mater Gloriosa (alto); Guilt (alto); Maria Aegyptiaca (alto); eight-part double chorus with individual solos; four-part children's chorus with individual solos.
Orchestra: Two flutes (with one piccolo); two oboes; two clarinets, two bassoons; four horns; two trumpets; three trombones; one bass tuba; timpani; one harp; strings.
History of the Work: Since its appearance, Goethe's *Faust* (Part I, 1808; Part II, 1832) has stirred the imaginations of countless composers; settings of the first part, much easier to dramatize than the second, have clearly predominated. Early, long-since-forgotten incidental music was composed by Prince Anton Heinrich Radziwill and Peter Joseph von Lindpaintner, and an early Faust opera by Louis Spohr (1816) was very successful. At about the same time as Schumann was working on his composition, Hector Berlioz was composing *La damnation de Faust* in a very similar form, a large oratorio, after having previously set individual scenes. Liszt was quite taken with the subject matter, and Wagner wrote a *Faust* Overture. Charles Gounod attained worldwide attention in 1859 with his opera *Faust*. Operas by Arrigo Boito (*Mefistofele*) and Feruccio Busoni (*Doktor Faust*) were and remain greatly appreciated. Nor has interest abated in the 20th century (Reutter, Stravinsky, etc.). Gustav Mahler worked the final scene from *Faust II* into his Eighth Symphony ("Alles Vergängliche ist nur ein Gleichnis"—All that dies is only illusion).

Robert Schumann was excited by the subject matter and Goethe's play. In 1844, a few months after writing *Das Paradies und die Peri*, he not only thought of treating the material in oratorio form (as he wrote in a letter) but also began to compose the third section, at first conceived of as a separate work.

In 1845 he mentioned that he was "deeply moved by the sublime poetry." On September 24, 1845, in a letter to Mendelssohn, he wrote, "The scenes from Faust are lying in my desk drawer; I really shy away from looking at them again. . . . I do not know if I will ever publish them." The time we hear of them is in a letter to Carl Reinecke dated June 30, 1848: "Last Sunday, for the first time, we presented the final scene from Faust, with orchestra, but only for a small group of people. I thought I would never finish it, particularly the final chorus—now I'm really quite pleased with it."

A few days later, in letters to his student (and later Beethoven scholar) Martin Gustav Nottebohm and to Franz Brendel, whom he had made editor of his musical journal in 1844, he said that this presentation had more greatly affected him than *Peri*, probably largely attributable to the magnificence of the poetry.

In 1849, the scenes composed up to that point were performed in Dresden, Leipzig, and Weimar under the title of "Fausts Verklärung" at several festivals in memory of Goethe's 100th birthday. "How odd—the thing lay in my desk for five years, known to no one, almost forgotten by me—and now it comes to light just in time for this rare occasion!" wrote Schumann to his publisher, Dr. Härtel (Breitkopf & Härtel).

The performance for which we have the best account, that in Leipzig, did not make much of an impression. Schumann blamed the "incorrect" sequence of pieces on the concert program—his work should not have been placed first. But these performances strengthened his resolve to proceed with setting more of the poem. And so, in a certain sense, the work grew backwards, from the conclusion to the beginning. Most of the music was composed in 1849 and 1850. Then the work was put aside, this time for three long years. Not until 1853 did the overture appear. Thus the end—the third section, "Fausts Verklärung"—came from Schumann's most inspired, creative period, his stay in Dresden. On the other hand, the beginning was from the time in Düsseldorf and gives evidence of the last, tragic phase of his life.

Schumann never heard it, one of his favorites, in its totality. In 1862, in Cologne, Ferdinand Hiller, a noted musician and highly esteemed composer in his own time and closely tied to the Mendelssohn-Schumann circle, took up the cause of the composition, which has remained a highly praised but seldom performed contribution to German secular oratorio.

Discussion of the Work: The oratorio opens with a long overture which begins "langsam, feierlich" (slowly and solemnly) and becomes more lively as Faust's brooding, contradictions, and struggles are revealed. One has the feeling that one is hearing an opera rather than an oratorio. The Garden Scene not only depicts the meeting of Faust and Gretchen in a completely operatic duet, but even includes stage directions ("She picks a daisy and pulls a petal off... she plucks the petals and murmurs... plucking the last petal" and so on).

It continues in this operatic vein, so it is surprising efforts to stage this oratorio have so seldom been made, unlike frequent stagings of Berlioz's *Damnation de Faust.* Gretchen kneels before the statue of the Virgin: "Ach neige, du Schmerzensreiche..." (Ah, give me a sign, Thou who art full of sorrows), but Schumann's setting is not equal to the famous text. The same is not true of the following scene in the cathedral, in which Evil Spirit speaks to Gretchen as she prays and is driven to despair. Here, Schumann is truly dramatic, as he hardly was in his only opera, *Genoveva.*

The chorus intones the "Dies irae," in unison at first, causing Gretchen's terror to mount. Without attaining significant intrinsic value musically, this is nevertheless a remarkably theatrical scene, strengthened primarily by the chorus singing the Requiem while the rich orchestration sometimes produces organlike effects.

Out of respect for the illustrious text, Schumann even set the passage, omitted by most composers, "Nachbarin, euer Fläschchen" (Neighbor, your vial), which immediately precedes Gretchen's loss of consciousness. In this passage he has her unwittingly repeat the sequence of tones just used by the chorus at the end of its passage: a fine psychological touch indicating that Gretchen is no longer in her right mind.

The second section begins at sunrise in an imaginary landscape where Faust has gone after the tragic ending of the affair with Gretchen. He begins to feel a renewal of life, to music which has thrown off all melancholy. Ariel, ruler of the spirits of the air, and a charming group of spirits call upon Faust, still caught up in the recent drama, to cheer him up and urge him to undertake new deeds, to make new discoveries, to return to joy. Choruses and groups of soloists join Ariel's tenor in charming, lively melodies.

Faust, who until then lay "auf blumigen Rasen gebettet, ermüdet, unruhig" (in a flowery meadow, exhausted, restless), trying to sleep, awakens to the beguiling voices hovering about him. He greets the new day as its first light touches the mountain peaks; the sun begins to shine and a feeling of closeness with nature pervades his entire being (Example 1). The mood of the next scene, composed in 1850, is just the opposite. "Vier graue Weiber" (Four gray, old women) appear—Lack, Guilt, Care, and Distress; their ghostly conversation develops mysteriously, full of deeper meaning, even philosophical (and therefore very difficult to express in music); such is the dialogue between Care and Faust, who falls back blinded.

Example 1

The second part concludes with "Fausts Tod" (Faust's Death). A chorus of lemurs (in Antiquity, restless spirits of the dead) bend to Mephistopheles' command to dig graves. But Faust hears only the clatter of the spades and, taking it for the music of life, imagines dams being built to hold back the sea, creating new land for men.

At this point, Schumann turns to very realistic tone painting. In his imagination, Faust experiences the highest moment of his life: "Solch ein Gewimmel möcht'ich seh'n, auf freiem Grund mit freiem Volke steh'n. Zum Augenblicke dürft' ich sagen: verweile doch, du bist so schön! Es kann die Spur von meinen Erdentagen nicht in Äonen untergeh'n. . . ." (Such a throng I would like to see, a free people on free land. That's the moment I would say, now stay, oh stay—you are so beautiful! The passing eons will not obliterate the traces of my days on earth.) In this moment of elation, he dies; the lemurs sing him into his grave with "Es ist vollbracht" (It is finished).

The third and final section turns on Faust's "transfiguration." Once again, the scene is hardly intelligible if presented only as an oratorio, without explanation. Goethe's stage directions read, "Bergschluchten, Wald, Fels, Einöde. Heilige Anachoreten, gebirgauf verteilt, gelagert zwischen Klüften" (Mountain gorges, forest, rocky cliffs, wilderness. Holy anchorites [hermits] lodged in crevices high up the mountain sides). The souls of Gretchen and Faust, more closely bound to one another than their brief earthly encounter would lead one to expect, meet in the regions between Heaven and earth. Supernatural voices are heard: Pater Ecstaticus and Pater Profundus, Pater Seraphicus and a chorus of blessed children. A choir of angels brings "Faustens Unsterbliches" (Faust's immortality).

Here, where mysticism sets the tone and Goethe's play moves farther and farther from mortal understanding, Schumann seems to have been most at home. The closing chorus, the "Chorus mysticus," is truly a great composition; in eight parts, pianissimo, completely transfigured, the voices enter with "Alles Vergängliche ist nur ein Gleichnis, das Unzulängliche, hier wird's Ereignis, das Unbeschreibliche, hier ist es getan, das Ewig-Weibliche zieht uns hinan" (All that must die is only illusion; here, inadequacy is made whole; the indescribable becomes fact; the eternally feminine leads us on). The solo voices join the double chorus. Schumann's creativity, springing from Romantic delicacy of feeling, from the deepest, most secret emotion, here experiences one of its finest hours.

Manfred

In 1848, shortly after he had completed his only opera, *Genoveva*, and was beginning the long, two-year wait for its less-than-successful premiere, he became enthralled by one of the most Romantic poems of his time: Lord Byron's dramatic poem *Manfred* (1817). At the time of Byron's death (1824), Goethe called him "the greatest talent of the century." With Manfred, the English poet had created the quintessential Romantic figure which repeatedly attracted musicians. The closest in spirit was perhaps Tchaikovsky's "Manfred" Symphony.

Schumann altered the original poem (translated into German for Schumann by F. W. Suckow); rather significantly and—contrary to Byron's intention—he provided it with a religious ending: As Manfred dies, a Requiem is heard. The story is set "high in the Alps, partly in the mountains and partly in Manfred's castle"; the characters are Manfred (speaking voice), Ariman, Nemesis, the Chamois Hunter, an Abbot, Manfred's Servants, Goddesses of Fate, and the Alpine Fairy. At the beginning of the work, Schumann inscribed as a motto the famous passage from Shakespeare's *Hamlet:* "There are more things in heaven and earth, Horatio, than are dreamt of in your philosophy."

Schumann once remarked that he "really wrote this work with distaste for the stage and with the intention of making even the thought of staging it impractical." Is it then an oratorio? Not according to the rules for the genre observed at the time, because a large part of the work, if not most of it, is melodrama—recitation or declamation with orchestral background.

Franz Liszt was probably the first to circumvent Schumann's wish to limit this composition to the concert hall by presenting an operatic performance in Weimar. Thereafter it was given a number of stage performances, among them those in Munich, Berlin, Hamburg, and Vienna, but without lasting success. Yet the outcome was little better when performed in concert. Manfred does contain some of Schumann's most beautiful work, especially in the magnificent overture—one long, raging, storm of passion.

There are other orchestral sections equally deserving of attention. The entr'acte, and the close of the second section display short but impressive symphonic passages. An Alpine herder's dance, (*ranz des vaches*) mentioned here as a curiosity, occurs in the middle of the work.

The Romantic era was preoccupied with what we call "folklore" (the term was coined later). Both composer and listener were fascinated by distant lands (though with very little reference to the music actually played in such places), but also—and this was especially popular—to the unsophisticated, remote world of the high mountains. Examples of this interest in Alpine settings occur in Berlioz's *Symphonie fantastique* and in Rossini's opera *Guillaume Tell*. Schumann gave this scene from *Manfred* to the English horn, but was probably thinking of a shepherds' pipe or even of a real Alphorn (Example 1).

Example 1

Manfred is seldom performed today, which is a pity, because it contains much beauty. But its requirements are considerable: Very good speakers, several vocal soloists, a four-part chorus and a large symphony orchestra with two each of flutes, oboes, clarinets, and bassoons, four horns, three trumpets, three trombones, timpani, and strings, as well as an organ at the end to provide the churchly atmosphere.

Sacred Works

Finally, it should be mentioned that Schumann's oeuvre includes few sacred works, but they are not among his most important. He decided to compose the Mass, Op. 147, and the Requiem, Op. 148, in 1852, a time of all kinds of crises in Schumann's life. Nevertheless, the Mass contains enough beauty and "passages of mighty grandeur and strength" (H. Kretzschmar) to justify occasional performances.

Less can be said in behalf of the (posthumous) Requiem. At the time of its composition, Schumann was no longer capable of sustained concentration, so passages of great nobility are placed next to banalities. The most terrible thing was that Schumann was unaware of it.

Heinrich Schütz   1585–1672

Heinrich Schütz (who sometimes Latinized his name to Henricus Sagittarius, as was the custom for educated public figures) was one of the great masters of 17th-century music. To label him a "predecessor of J. S. Bach," as earlier writers have done, is unfortunate and does not do him justice. Certainly, every creative genius is someone's successor and someone's predecessor, but to label him as such is only justified when his importance lies only in that particular relationship. Schütz, however, born exactly 100 years before Bach and Handel, was a great artist in his own right. To see him in a larger context, his transitional role between the monodic style that had recently appeared in Italy and the German music tradition must be understood. His four-year stay in Italy, between 1609 and 1613, influenced him greatly. There he studied with Giovanni Gabrieli in Venice, came into contact with the early, revolutionary works of Claudio Monteverdi, and became familiar with the art of the madrigal, to which he dedicated his Opus I, *Il primo libro de Madrigali* (1611).

He was born on October 8, 1585, in Köstritz near Gera, in Thuringia, was educated on a scholarship provided by Landgrave Moritz of Hesse and was sent to Italy. Upon his return he became an organist in Kassel, from where he went "temporarily," "on loan," as it were, to Dresden, where he finally settled in 1617.

He held the post of court Kapellmeister for 55 years in that royal Saxon city where he lived through the worst of times: The Thirty Years War laid waste to more than half of Germany, including the decimation and dissolution of court chapels such as the one in Dresden. Slowly and with great effort, Schütz had to build it up again from nothing, for which he must be given a great deal of credit, as he turned down a very good position in Copenhagen, where he had made several very successful guest appearances, to do so. In addition, he had to deal with the intrigues and difficulties in Dresden's musical life. Schütz composed until he was quite old, at the end primarily in Weissenfels, and died in Dresden on November 6, 1672. Music history usually names him in the same breath with the two other "great Sch's," Johann Hermann Schein (1586–1630) and Samuel Scheidt (1587–1654). Of the former's work we should at least mention a 14-part Te Deum and from the latter, the *Geistliche Gesänge*, both of which belong in this book only marginally.

Die sieben Worte (Jesu Christi) (Seven Words from the Cross)

Schütz composed primarily sacred music: In 1619 *Psalmen Davids*, in 1625 *Cantiones sacrae* (Religious songs). Later he published three volumes of his very important *Symphoniae sacrae* (1629, 1647, 1650), polyphonic choruses with instrumental accompaniment, some in Latin and some in German. The polyphonic work discussed here, *Die sieben Worte*, probably was composed in 1645. Schütz compiled the text from the Gospels, but the errors in several passages lead us to believe he wrote them from memory.

On the other hand, some of the passages that his relatively early biographer Philipp Spitta (1841–1894) attributed to error on Schütz's part are today considered probably correct. For example, the Roman soldier who offered a sponge to the crucified Jesus when he was thirsty could well have soaked it in "Essig und Ysopen" (vinegar and hyssop), for the hyssop taken exception to is an herb from the Orient, which possibly intensified the tormenting effects of the vinegar.

The title page of the first edition bore the following inscription: "Die sieben Wortte unseres lieben Erlösers und Seeligmachers Jesu Christi so er am Stamm des Heiligen Creutzes gesprochen, gantz beweglich gesetzt von Herrn Heinrich Schützen, Chur Sächsischen Capellmeistern." (The seven words of our dear Redeemer and Savior Jesus Christ as he spoke them on the Holy Cross, in a very moving setting by Herr Heinrich Schütz, Kapellmeister for the Elector of Saxony.). The music for the Evangelist's role is divided into as many as four parts, Jesus is assigned to a tenor, and the words of the two thieves are sung by an alto and a bass. The instrumental accompaniment is spare: The entire work is accompanied by continuo—a harpsichord, to which was usually added a string instrument of the lower range. Unlike the ensembles and solos, which are accompanied only by the continuo, Jesus' words are supported by five instruments, which following common practice were not positively indicated, but which were probably a string quintet. If old instruments are available, it is advisable to use various viols and gambas.

Two purely instrumental movements (Symphonie) are included. The end of the work is a vocal ensemble called a *Conclusio*, supported by the continuo. It would be interesting to know whether at this point the other instruments fell silent or whether their participation at such a time went without saying, in order to intensify the effect of the conclusion. In those days, was it really a question of "effect," in the sense the word later acquired? In the instance of opera, also a very young form at the time, the answer might be yes, but in the case of a sacred work, one that was both contemplative and soulful, we really do not know. One detail should be mentioned: When Jesus calls out to his Father, he does so first in Hebrew ("Eli, Eli, Eli lama asabthani"), whereupon the Evangelist (in four-part singing) comments in German: "Das ist verdolmetschet" (this means:). And then Jesus calls out in German, "Mein Gott, mein Gott, mein Gott, warum hast du mich verlassen?" (My God, why hast Thou forsaken me?), singing the same melodic line, with little embellishments, as he did the first time. In its naiveté, the effect of this small work—it is only about 20 minutes long—is striking, like that of old paintings or engravings whose supposed primitiveness is really highly artistic.

Die Weihnachts-Historie (The Christmas Story)

This work, too, had a much longer title in the original: "Historia, Der Freuden-und Gnadenreichen Geburth Gottes und Marien Sohnes, Jesu Christi, Unseres Einigen Mitlers, Erlösers und Seeligmachers. Wie dieselbige Auff gnädigste Anordnung Churfl. Durchl. zu Sachsen. ec. H. Johann Georgen des Andern, Vocaliter und Instrumentaliter in die Musik versetzet worden ist von Henrico Schützen, Churfl. Durchl. zu Sachsen ec. ältisten Capel-Meistern" (Story of the joyous, grace-giving birth of the Son of God and Mary, Jesus Christ, our only Intercessor, Redeemer, and Savior. How the same, upon the most gracious orders of His Grace, the Elector of Saxony etc., H. Johann Georg the Younger, was set to music for voices and instruments by Henrico Schütz, Senior Kapellmeister for His Grace the Elector of Saxony).

This *Christmas Oratorio* calls for larger vocal and instrumental forces than the last Passions, which were composed at about the same time. The oratorio employs in solo roles: Evangelist (tenor), an Angel (soprano), three Shepherds (altos), three Kings (tenors), four High Priests (basses), Herod (bass), and a Group of Angels composed of six soloists. In addition, there is a four-part mixed chorus.

There is not much we can say about the specific instrumentation—that is, about the make-up of an orchestra that Schütz might have used or hoped to use—that could be considered authentic. Studies done in connection with recent editions, including the finding of parts (at the University of

Uppsala, Sweden), although very worthwhile, have not been able to clarify this question.

But because the Baroque orchestra is no longer as hazy a concept as it was a century ago or even half-century ago, it is easier to assemble a Schütz ensemble than formerly. Cornetts, gambas, early trombones, viols, lyres, lutes, theorbos, recorders and transverse flutes, clarinos (instead of modern trumpets)—all might be used. The use of an organ in this work seems to have been understood.

It is striking that the vocal parts are mostly written unusually low, sometimes in registers that today's singers, especially altos and basses, find difficult. In spite of the importance of specific key characteristics, transposition of all vocal parts up a second or even a minor third must be considered for modern performances.

Much of this *Christmas Oratorio* may have been new at the time. The musicologist Arnold Schering said, at the beginning of the 20th century, that this work was the first German oratorio, "which went beyond the simple dialogue form—that is to say, which presented not just a single scene, but combined various situations, making use of all the means available to art music at that time."

The Passions

The three Passions ascribed to Schütz with certainty, based on *St. Luke, St. John,* and *St. Matthew,* were most likely composed in the years between 1653 and 1666. No original manuscript has been found for any of the three; we have them in a beautifully written copy that was probably not made before 1692 (by one Johann Zacharias Grundig) and which is now in Leipzig. There is a fourth work in this copy, a *St. Mark Passion,* which was long thought to be Schütz's, but today, is generally regarded as by a different hand. Only the first work in the volume—the *St. Matthew Passion*—bears the name Schütz. Nevertheless, there is no longer any doubt as to the authenticity of the *St. Luke* and the *St. John* Passions. The three have in common the fact that they are a cappella—purely vocal, with no instrumental support at all. Today's music lovers hardly need to be reminded of the vocal skill required to perform such a work, roughly 50–60 minutes long.

The *St. Luke Passion,* composed in 1653 and, therefore, the oldest of the three, seems to have been inspired by a similar work by the Cantor Christoph Schultze (1606–1683), from Delitzsch, near Leipzig. This assumption is based primarily on the text. Schütz assigned the role of Jesus to a bass, as he did in several other works, and that of the Evangelist to a tenor. Peter is also a tenor; Pilate is a bass; two soldiers are a tenor and a bass; two robbers (Latri) are tenors; a maid, soprano; a Roman Centurion, bass.

The work begins with a chorus: "Das Leiden unseres Herren Jesu Christi, wie uns das beschreibet der heilige Evangeliste Lucas" (The suffering of our Lord Jesus Christ, as described by the Evangelist St. Luke)—a polyphonic, four-part announcement. The same manner of announcing the program is found in Medieval plays, a necessary device in a day when printed programs could not be produced. Not only does the announcement carry us back to ancient times, the music itself does so as well. At first we think we are hearing the "modern" key of F major, but in the eighth bar there is a B instead of the B-flat called for today. This gives the music a different, almost medieval character. Schütz stood at the frontier of modern harmony—of the tonal system that was then beginning to take shape in the Western world.

This mixture of the old church modes and modern tonality is very attractive to the ear and is natural for Schütz and typical of his music. The long unaccompanied recitatives, which Schütz wanted "to flow freely and naturally," sound odd to today's listener. At such places the debt to Gregorian chant is quite evident.

The choruses of the people—the *turbae,* a special kind of chorus found from the time of earliest oratorios until long after Bach—are very dramatic with their staggered, imitative entrances, but simple compared with those of later times (Bach's, for example), just as a Giotto painting might seem when compared to a Titian, or a woodcut compared to a modern color print. Much in Schütz's music depends upon emotion, and the listener who finds it particularly well suited to express the simple words of the Gospels will understand its meaning and value.

The *St. John Passion* was probably written in 1665, for this is the date given in a much later copy. In it the choruses display remarkable dramatic force, achieving a characterization that is almost modern and contains elements of tone painting (entirely vocal; no instruments are used) to depict mockery, anger, indignation, and deception. Such descriptions, however, are limited to the ensembles, whereas the recitatives show an almost ceremonial austerity—a curious contrast that leads the listener to reflect upon the era in which this master lived and how it influenced its music.

The *St. Matthew Passion*, one of his last works, was probably composed in 1666, when the composer was over 80 years old. Its original title was also different from that used today: "Historia des Leidens und Sterbens unseres Herrn und Heilandes Jesu Christi nach dem Evangelisten S. Matheus in die Musik übersetzet von Heinrich Schützen, Churfürstlichen Sächsischen dero Zeit ältesten Capell-Meistern" (Story of the suffering and death of our Lord and Savior Jesus Christ, as told in the Gospel of *St. Matthew*, set to music by Heinrich Schütz, Senior Kapellmeister of the Elector of Saxony).

Once again, the Evangelist is a tenor and Jesus, a bass—exactly as was done a century later when Bach was writing. Peter is a tenor, as is Pilate; Caiphas is a bass, whereas Judas is an alto. The two False Witnesses are sung by tenors, two Maids by a soprano and an alto, and Pilate's wife by an alto. This "Historia," too, begins with the announcement: "Das Leiden unseres Herren Jesu Christi, wie es beschreibet der heilige Evangeliste Matthaeus" (The suffering of our Lord Jesus Christ as described by the Evangelist St. Matthew).

In general, the choral passages are extremely short, and for long stretches of the work none is longer than a minute. The recitatives, often in dialogue form, are much longer. Therefore, no larger forms, in particular fugues, can be contained within these brief choral movements.

No extended form occurs until the chorus that follows upon Jesus' death, in which the High Priests and the Pharisees demand that Pilate provide watchmen for Christ's grave, to prevent his friends from stealing the body and then proclaiming him risen from the dead. Here imitative entries and pronounced modulations are used.

The conclusion of the work is once more a contemplative, prayerful, peaceful chorale: "Ehre sei dir, Christe . . . hilf uns armen Sündern zu der Seligkeit, Kyrie eleison, Christe eleison" (Glory to Christ . . . help us poor sinners to blessedness; Kyrie eleison, Christe eleison).

It is not easy to weigh Schütz's three Passions one against another; each has its admirers and devotees, and each justifies the position its composer enjoys in music history. In many respects, he deserves some of the honor of being called the "Father of Music," a distinction that all masters of subsequent centuries, in a rare show of unanimity, have awarded to Bach.

Dimitri Shostakovich 1906–1975

Shostakovich was born on September 25, 1906, in Petersburg (Leningrad) and died on August 9, 1975, in Moscow. One of Russia's most notable composers, probably second only to Prokofiev, he was not recognized in the West until late and only gradually gained the acceptance he deserved. His 15 symphonies are played increasingly frequently as are his 15 string quartets and numerous piano works. The position of his vocal works is more problematic due to the difficulty of satisfactorily translating the Russian into other languages. He wrote numerous songs and operas, among them, *The Nose* and *Katerina Ismailowa*. For the same reasons his choral works are far less well known and less often performed in the West than in his own country.

We must mention here the oratorio *The Song of the Forests*, written in 1949, for two solo voices, children's chorus, mixed chorus, and orchestra which was awarded the highly remunerative Stalin Prize. Its agricultural social theme is quite unusual: The reforestation of bare, uncultivated land to create new ecological foundations for the expansion of Soviet agriculture. In 1951 Shostakovich wrote the *Ten Whitman Poems* for children's chorus, mixed chorus, and large orchestra; followed in 1965 by the fine cantata, *The Execution of Stepan Razin*, for bass, mixed chorus, and orchestra, Op. 119, based on a text by the leading Russian poet Yevgeny Yevtushenko.

Louis Spohr 1784–1859

Louis Spohr was in his own time a leading name in the world of music. He was a virtuoso violinist, a composer, a conductor, and a quite influential teacher. Ludwig (called Louis) Spohr was born on April 5, 1784. When only 15 years old, he was employed as a string player in Braunschweig and in 1805 went to Gotha. He held several positions as Kapellmeister: from 1812 to 1815 in Vienna; in 1817 in Frankfurt/Main; and from 1822 on in Kassel, where he died on October 22, 1859. As a violinist, he rivaled for a time the "wizard" Paganini. His operas (among them, *Jessonda*, often performed in his day, and his very interesting *Faust*), nine symphonies, and even his violin concertos have faded considerably. A few worthwhile pieces of his chamber music have continued in the repertory, including the Octet, Op. 32, in E Minor, and the Nonet, Op. 31, in F Major. Among his oratorios (*Das jüngste Gericht, Das befreite Deutschland, Der Fall Babylons*) only *Die letzten Dinge*, composed in 1826, in Kassel, and *Des Heilands letzte Stunden* (Kassel, 1835) are still programmed now and then. In addition, the Mass, Op. 54, in C Minor should be mentioned as it is also sometimes sung.

Alessandro Stradella 1645–1682

Neither the place, nor the day, nor even the year of Alessandro Stradella's birth is known with certainty. Nor do we know whether this brilliant singer, outstanding violinist, and composer with a great gift of melody came from northern or southern Italy. Genoa, Venice, Naples, and the area around Modena (probably the most likely) all have presented documents, or at least hypotheses, to support their claim as the birthplace of this curious musician. His life story has come down to us so encrusted with legend that no one can any longer sort out fact and fiction. He seems to have composed a considerable body of work, even when pieces which appeared under his name but which are most likely not his (a number of well-known songs and arias) have been eliminated from the total. But we must add back those pieces, turning up slowly but steadily in the archives of half of Europe, which can be attributed to him with a fair degree of certainty. There are operas not really worth reviving and a number of oratorios: *Santa Editta, Ester, San Giovanni Crisostomo, Santa Pelagia, Susanna*, as well as a *San Giovanni Battista* (St. John the Baptist), which has recently been rediscovered and successfully performed in two Swiss concerts. It is said that when he went to Venice to complete and perform one of his operas, he ran off with a senator's mistress—an affair that became the subject of Friedrich von Flotow's once successful opera, *Alessandro Stradella* (1844). After a life filled with hair-raising incidents—exciting incidents including hired assassins, who, carried away by his magnificent singing, failed to kill him—Stradella met his end as the victim of a dagger, drawn to avenge the abduction previously mentioned or perhaps another. He died in Genoa on February 25 or 28, 1682.

San Giovanni Battista is a Baroque oratorio based on the story of John the Baptist, who was beheaded at the court of the Tetrarch Herod. The latter, surnamed Antipas, ruled Judea at the time of Jesus' death, and was the son of the "great" Herod who built the great temple at Jerusalem, but who also had decreed the slaughter of the innocents in Bethlehem. John the Baptist was a beloved itinerant preacher, whom Herod the son, traditionally believed to have been a luxury-loving oriental despot, had arrested for being a "troublemaker." From the state's point of view, John was likely a problem, but once in detention Herod could not decide what to do with him. Many hailed John as a great prophet, comparable to those who appeared from time to time in the Old Testament, while others saw in him the messenger sent by God to proclaim the coming of the Messiah. But a curious turn of events removed the decision from Herod's hands. Legend has it that Herod's step-daughter attempted to win John to her charms, in vain. In revenge, she demanded his head. This legend has provided the stuff of innumerable stories, poems and plays.

A graphic and dramatic comparison of the profound differences in thought, feeling, and spirit between the Baroque of about 1680 and the Expressionist era of about 1900, marked by altered psychological perceptions, can be had by performing, sequentially, two staged versions of this historical drama: The first by Girardo Ansaldi, *San Giovanni Battista*, with music by Alessandro Stradella, and the other of *Salome* by Oscar Wilde, with music by Richard Strauss. What in Wilde is expressionistic, passionate, highly dramatic, even breath-taking, in the Baroque authors is distanced, objective, allegorical, contemplative, moralizing. Ansaldi, who adapted texts by Filippo Acciaioli, divided his work into the main story—the death of the Baptist—and subsidiary actions in the prologue and intermezzi, to illuminate the "incident" from all possible perspectives. To do so he allowed mythical and archetypical figures (Pluto, Proserpina, the Furies, Lust, Prodigality, Modesty, Deception, as well as popular figures from the Commedia dell'arte) to offer observations on the decadence of the time and human weakness in general. In the Baroque manner, other allegorical figures appear who do not immediately have anything to do with the action, but rather symbolize the spiritual condition of the people in the drama. In a manner of speaking, they shed light on the main action. Baroque theater, which is receiving renewed interest in our era, differs in fundamental ways from that to which we have become accustomed since the Classical era. And fundamentally different, too, is the music. The will to form and the feeling for form of that distant era so thoroughly dominate Baroque practice that the emotional factor—as surely present in music as in other forms of theater—cannot be easily felt. The Baroque oratorios included in this book are—and this is an important observation—works of music theater. They may be performed either in concert or on the stage. Indeed they often gain interest when performed partially staged, as was doubtless a frequent practice 300 years ago, especially in the churches.

Returning to Stradella; his *San Giovanni Battista* was successfully performed several times in 1979/1980, after lying in oblivion for nearly three centuries.

Igor Stravinsky   1882–1971

In the course of his career, which spanned more than 65 years, this great 20th-century master served as mirror, focal point, and synthesis of the musical developments of his time. It was an extremely turbulent and revolutionary period, yet Stravinsky was able to come to terms with all its various forms. He wrote operas, but few of them had anything in common with the genre that until shortly before had still been clearly defined. He wrote symphonies, most of which did not correspond to the Romantic canons. The work of this highly intelligent Russian did not, however, reflect confusion, but rather clarity. To achieve this quality in a time of Late Romantic haze and fin-de-siècle weariness required bold, often painful experimentation. And Stravinsky—very like his great friend, the painter Pablo Picasso—was the eternal experimentalist, but because he was also a genius, the results were often masterpieces.

He was born in Oranienbaum, near St. Petersburg, on June 5, 1882. He met Rimsky-Korsakov in 1902 and decided to make music his career. After early works, influenced by this teacher as well as Glazunov, Stravinsky went to Paris and began his momentous collaboration with Sergei Diaghilev, the prophet of modern ballet. After two very substantial examples of his talent (*The Firebird* and *Petrushka*) came, on the eve of the World War I, *Le sacre du printemps*, which produced an enormous scandal in the theater and marks the dawn of a new age. The tumult of war led Stravinsky to move to Switzerland, then back to France, and finally, due to the growing terror in Europe, further west to the United States.

Stravinsky was wildly acclaimed during his early years, after which he was for decades the highly respected spokesman for "New Music." His late works, although difficult to comprehend, earned him respect as a "great musician" and as the symbol of the music of the century, for he was frequently in the vanguard of the enduring trends of the modern era. He died on April 6, 1971.

During his long life he produced an extremely rich variety of music, touching again and again on the subject matter of this book. Indeed, *Oedipus Rex* is a mixed genre, as is the *Symphony of Psalms. L'histoire du soldat* is difficult to classify, and even more so the later *Persephone*. The closest we can come is to call them a new form of music theater (in reality, probably a very old one); therefore we shall not consider them in this book. This decision leaves four works suitable for this volume: the Mass of 1948, the Cantata of 1951/52, the *Canticum sacrum* of 1955, and *Threni*, from 1958—all late works, marked by the maturity of age but exhibiting nonetheless the composer's continuing satisfaction in experimentation found in his earlier works.

Stravinsky explored other choral forms of greatly varying types which should be at least noted here: *King of the Stars*, a Russian cantata for six-part male chorus with orchestra, whose text by K. Balmont treats an apocalyptic vision of Christ (1911); a short cantata entitled *Babel*, based on *Genesis*, for male chorus, orchestra, and narrator, in which the voice of God is represented by a two-part chorus (1944); a Bach transcription, *Vom Himmel hoch*, for mixed chorus and orchestra (1956); *Monumentum pro Gesualdo da Venosa*, an homage to that brilliant Renaissance prince and composer of madrigals, so far ahead of his time, for mixed chorus and orchestra (1960); *A Sermon, a Narrative, and a Prayer*, a cantata based on Biblical and English religious texts for speaker, soloists, chorus, and orchestra; *Anthem*, for four-part mixed chorus, based on poems by T. S. Eliot (1962); and an *Introitus in memoriam T. S. Eliot*, for this leading American-English poet and Nobel Prize winner, whose death greatly affected Stravinsky, for male chorus and chamber orchestra (1965).

As early as 1932 and the *Symphony of Psalms*, the influence of Catholicism was evident; Latin particularly fascinated Stravinsky in those years. But 16 years passed before the composer ventured to undertake a composition for the church: in 1948 he composed the *Mass* for mixed chorus and double wind quartet (two oboes, one English horn, two bassoons, two trumpets, and three trombones). The singularly homogeneous tone of this accompanying ensemble was exceptionally well suited to the severe, primeval, almost ascetic character of this Mass. Stravinsky sought here the very roots of traditional sacred music, and the spirit of Gregorian Chant and Catholic liturgical music by old French and Flemish masters clearly pervades the work. The composer conceived of it as purely sacred, to be performed in the church sanctuary and without applause.

Among Stravinsky's other important works is the *Cantata* composed in 1951/52 for soprano and tenor soloists, women's chorus, and small orchestra. The work very much fits into the realm of traditional church music, but there are secular, even clearly erotic elements intermixed. The composer chose for the text anonymous English verse from the 15th and 16th centuries, which—as he demonstrated—contributed decisively to the musical form. The ancient form of the dirge (wake) is the basis of the work, which is in four main parts (Verses I–IV), between which he inserted two ricercares and a duet for the two solo voices. The *Cantata* was composed during the period when Stravinsky, thanks to his association with his much younger colleague, Robert Craft, began to work with serial music. Traces of this method of composition are clearly evident in this interesting work.

Canticum sacrum

This "sacred song" sings of the three cardinal virtues of Christianity; Faith, Hope, and Love, using Latin passages from both the Old and the New Testament. The work is dedicated "to the city of Venice, in honor of its holy patron saint, the Apostle Mark"; these words not only stand at the head of the score, but also supply the text of the *Dedicatio* preceding the first part, sung by both soloists, tenor and baritone, and accompanied by three trombones. Its effect is archaic, the linear construction austere as it was in the *Mass*, the counterpoint much informed by the severity of medieval music before the advent of harmony.

The small orchestra includes one flute, two oboes, one English horn, two bassoons, contrabassoon, three trumpets, one bass trumpet, three trombones, one bass trombone, one harp, organ, violas, and contrabasses. The orchestration is as notable for the instruments it does *not* use as for those it does: only one flute (as opposed to three each of oboes and bassoons), no clarinets, no violins, no cellos to entice us with sensuous cantilenas. Brighter tone colors are not part of his concept of sacred music. Is this a recollection of the old Russian Orthodox liturgy he had probably seldom heard since his childhood?

The chorus, employed with the greatest economy of sound, is mixed and in four parts. Musicians will find the score very interesting to read for in it will be discovered extremely subtle relationships, artful technique, and imposing skill. But all of this is completely imperceptible and impossible to reconstruct, even for a finely attuned music amateur. Is there a parallel here to Beethoven's last quartets?

About this time Stravinsky became interested in Schoenberg's twelve-tone theory, which he had heretofore scorned. He found it "interesting," as he said in conversations with his colleague, Robert Craft, and an aid to composition. Until that time, he had maintained the free creative spirit, unfettered by strict rules, could continuously produce new, gripping, "beautiful" (a concept that changes with the times) music. Then, in his 70s, after the creator of the twelve-tone system had died and the system was open to freer interpretation, he moved toward dodecaphony.

Stravinsky did not follow Schoenberg's precepts to the point that they conflicted with his own lifelong convictions. But he started using tone rows, sometimes only four or five notes long, that were consistent with the dodecaphonic principle only in the way they were used, allowing as it did development only by inversion, mirror, or retrograde motion.

Stravinsky also used these techniques in cases where tone rows were not used at all. A technical analysis of the *Canticum* reveals, for example, that the final chorus ("Domino cooperante") is the exact, note-for-note inversion of the opening chorus ("In mundum universum"). But no one could detect this inversion simply by listening. The *Canticum sacrum* also contains one authentic twelve-tone row. It is in the organ part, in a mighty unison spanning four octaves, at the beginning of the third part, in which the three virtues are set forth: Caritas (love), Spes (hope) and Fides (faith), each time in a different transposition.

Canticum sacrum is a product of both great skill and the wisdom of age. If listened to repeatedly, provocative, perhaps beautiful elements can be discovered that are far removed from Romanticism. It was composed in 1955 and performed for the first time that year in St. Mark's church in Venice.

Threni

The complete title of this work is *Threni id est Lamentationes Jeremiae Prophetae*. The text for this approximately 35-minute-long work comes from the *Lamentations* of Jeremiah. It is scored for six soloists: soprano, alto, two tenors, bass, low bass, and a four-part mixed chorus. Before each verse Stravinsky composed a letter of the Hebrew alphabet. After the two female soloists announce "Incipit lamentatio Jeremiae Prophetae" (The lamentations of the Prophet Jeremiah begin), the chorus enters with the first letter: "Aleph."

Close analysis of the score reveals that the entire work is based on a dodecaphonic tone row, which, however—to a much greater extent than in *Canticum*—is imperceptible to the ear, since its notes often sound simultaneously in different voices.

The very beautiful Latin text is in three sections and contains contemplation, lament, hope, consolation, and prayer. Especially striking is a very piercing minor second interval that is heard throughout the work: the notes F, F-sharp, F not only appear in immediate sequence, but are also often played simultaneously.

The composer had always objected strongly to "imagining"—that music represented an external reality, that music could or should represent or express something concrete. But this almost leitmotivic use of the harsh dissonance so brings to mind anguish, unhappiness, and despair that from the very beginning the listener is brought to a mood in keeping with Jeremiah's laments. Stravinsky dedicated this work, extremely difficult to perform and even more so to listen to, to the North German Radio, which, in 1957, commissioned the 75-year-old composer to write it, and in 1958 gave it its premiere.

Karol Szymanowski   1882–1937

This Polish composer, far too little known outside his own country, was born on September 21, 1883, in Tymoszowka (Polish Ukraine). He composed a deeply felt, beautiful, masterfully written *Stabat mater* in addition to other choral works, such as *Litania*. The former is one of the immortal creations of our fast-paced era, when mundane glitter blinds all too easily. Szymanowski was a restless man: In 1900 he joined a group of young Polish composers who, in the face of opposition in their own land, laid the groundwork for Poland's unusual thrust toward 20th-century music. In 1908 he went to Italy, then lived for a few years in Vienna, and finally returned to his own country where, in 1920, he began to delve into folklore. He developed a new style in which Western (Debussy's and, even more, Ravel's Impressionism), Eastern (Scriabin), and medieval influences came together in an enchanting mixture bearing his own, unmistakable stamp. To protect his fragile health, which early on had prevented him from taking an active part in international musical life, Szymanowski moved to Switzerland in 1930. On March 29, 1937, he died in a sanatorium in Lausanne.

The idea for a Stabat mater came to him in 1924, when he was asked to compose a Requiem; he thought first he would compose a short composition of this type, one that could be performed at peasant ceremonies, using traditional texts. In 1925 he worked out the plan for a Stabat mater, constructing a succinct, six-part choral work. For the text he used a Polish liturgy that had been translated from the Latin by Czeslaw Jankowski. (The music is such that it can also be sung with the original Latin text.) From the first note, the listener is transported back into a distant past, although the sounds are thoroughly contemporary; the times of Machault and Dufay seem to have returned, but there is nothing forced or artificial in these archaic sounds. We can only marvel at how closely they are fused with the sometimes effusive Romantic melody, with "modern" harmonies, to form a great unity, devout and beautiful. Directors of larger concert choirs are urged to try this work, completed in 1926. It calls for soprano, alto, and baritone soloists of outstanding ability, a large mixed chorus, and a symphonic orchestra. The work is timeless, not easy, but a pleasure, even a joy, for performers and listeners alike.

Georg Philipp Telemann 1681–1767

Telemann belongs to the generation of Bach and Handel, of Rameau and Vivaldi. Though we may judge his importance somewhat differently today, in his time he was one of the most admired of musicians, one of the most successful masters of the 18th century, and probably the most prolific composer in Europe. He was born on March 14, 1681, in Magdeburg, and after his father's early death he had to assume responsibility for his own musical education. An assiduous student, primarily self-taught, he rose to become one of the most respected organists of his time, active in Leipzig and Sorau (1704) and then in Eisenach (1708), where he became friends with the Bach family (he was godfather to Bach's second eldest son, Carl Philipp Emanuel). In 1712 he became organist and Kapellmeister in Frankfurt am Main, from where he was called to Hamburg as the music director for the five main churches, a position he held until his death on June 25, 1767.

Telemann composed an incredible number of works. When only 12 years old, he surprised the music world with his first opera, *Sigismundus*; in the next decades 44 others followed (among them *Pimpinone*, 1725, and *Der geduldige Sokrates*, 1721). In addition to operas there were countless concertos, orchestral suites, and overtures; furthermore, he wrote an almost unbelievable number of chamber works—for every instrument, for every scoring, for every conceivable musical occasion. His great collections *Essercizii musici*, 12 each of solo and trio sonatas for various instruments; *Der Getreue Musikmeister*, which includes a total of 70 chamber works; and the three volumes of the popular *Tafelmusik* became well known and remain much beloved by chamber musicians today.

Telemann's output of vocal works is particularly striking: 23 years' worth of sacred cantatas, more than 70 secular cantatas, 15 Masses, 46 Passions, 35 oratorios (among them *Der Messias*, based on the epic by Friedrich Gottlieb Klopstock; *Der Tod Jesu*; *Das befreiete Israel*; and *Die Tageszeiten*). Interest in several of the Passions has been renewed; 23 of the total 46 settings remain. The forces Telemann could enlist when performing his works were relatively modest, as he did not have the musicians of the outstanding Hamburg opera orchestra at his disposal, so for the most part he relied only on amateurs. Compared to Johann Sebastian Bach's two Passions, the scores are relatively simple; the chorales, for example, are those in the hymn books used in the Hamburg churches, in both text and melody. They were intended to be sung by the congregation, so their harmonies are quite simple. Nevertheless, the dramatic force of the *turbae* choruses is striking; and some tone painting is used to illustrate the Passion text in a plain, direct way. Here, too, Telemann shows himself a master of the concise form: Choruses and arias seldom last more than three minutes—again unlike what we find in Bach—maintaining the dramatic tension of the events of the Passion story at each moment. With all its thrifty scoring, this work, too, shows Telemann's unmistakable mastery and his ability to incorporate the profusion of German, French, Italian, and last but not least, Polish influences into a new, personal, forward-looking style.

Randall Thompson 1899–1984

The durable qualities and appeal of Thompson's choral works have earned them a secure place in the American repertoire. His name is a byword in the choral field and his music is acclaimed as purely American. Yet prior to completing the a cappella cantata *The Peaceable Kingdom* (1936), Thompson's success as a composer rested with his large instrumental works: The Second Symphony (1931) received several hundred performances. Two string quartets, three symphonies, an opera and several works for keyboard and small ensembles are testimony to his prowess in other media.

After receiving two degrees from Harvard, Thompson studied composition with Ernest Bloch. In the course of his career, he held positions on the faculties of Harvard, Princeton, Wellesley College and the University of Virginia, and was Director of the Curtis Institute. In 1965, after a tenure of 16 years, he retired from the faculty of Harvard as Professor Emeritus.

Thompson's large works for chorus and orchestra, excepting *The Testament of Freedom* (1943), have received less attention than many of the shorter works—his classic *Alleluia* and the *Frostiana* suite. A striking work which requires unusual forces and a novel performing space is *The Nativity According to Saint Luke* (1961). On the score it is designated "A Musical Drama in Seven Scenes," a staged theater piece using an entire sanctuary as its setting. Ten character roles are required, plus choruses representing the Faithful, the Angels and the Shepherds. Using movement, dramatic action, costumes, lighting and a chamber orchestra, the Christmas story is dramatized from the scene of Zacharias and the Angel, through the Annunciation, The Visitation, The Naming of John, The Apparition, The Adoration and The Song of Simeon. The didactic overtones at the close and its overall dramatic character relate it to the historical oratorio, but it is clearly a theater piece—an opera-oratorio.

The most enduring tribute to Randall Thompson's genius as a choral composer is *The Passion According to Saint Luke* (1963), a companion piece to *The Nativity*.

The Passion According to Saint Luke

Original Language: English
Text: From the Gospel of Luke.
Date of Writing: 1963
First Performance: March 28, 1965, in Boston.
Form: Two major parts (each requiring 45 minutes to perform) subdivided into 10 sections, beginning with the "Entry into Jerusalem" and concluding with "The Entombment."
Cast: Ideally, 11 soloists are needed, though the tenor may also cover the roles of Peter, Pilate and the Second Malefactor. Seven come from the chorus, taking minor roles; one (The Maid) is the only female soloist. The major roles are Jesus (baritone) and Peter (tenor). Long reflective arias for soprano and alto soloists have no place in this Passion setting.
Scoring: Full orchestra and chorus.
History of the Work: The Passion According to Saint Luke was commissioned by the Handel and Haydn Society of Boston and premiered by the Society on March 28, 1965, on the occasion of its 150th Anniversary Celebration.
Discussion of the Work: Traditional settings of the Passion story in oratorio form call for a soloist (Evangelist) to function as narrator, but Thompson uses the chorus in this role. This additional presence of the chorus and the omission of meditative hymns give this setting a unique feeling of musical unity and narrative flow, when compared with familiar masterworks. There are no individual numbers.

Choral narration sets the first scene at the Mount of Olives. In rapid exchanges involving Jesus, the disciples, the owner of the colt and the narrating chorus, the entry into Jerusalem is prepared. The chorus becomes a cheering crowd. Jesus enters during this chorus with a brief arioso—his lament for Jerusalem. This section concludes with the chorus "Blessed be the King" (Example 1). [Musical examples Copyright 1965 by E. C. Schirmer Music Company, Boston. Used by permission.] Without pause, two sharp chords by percussion and strings introduce a brief section for chorus alone, "The Passover." In recitative style, often in unison, the chorus exposes the plot of Judas to betray Jesus. Choral recitative in parallel chords continues into the third section, "The Institution of the Lord's Supper." As Jesus prepares to take the last supper with his disciples, his words follow a poignant motive expressing his compassion and love for the Twelve (Example 2). Jesus conducts the Passover ritual in chant-like lines which become active only for moments of dramatic import (Example 3). In response, the disciples ask "Which of us shall do this thing?" In four straightforward measures of contrapuntal parallel lines, those words are repeated exactly 11 times. Here the composer does acknowledge a traditional practice in setting this moment in the Passion narrative: the voice of Judas is not heard. The orchestra reflects feelings of strife and frustration which beset the disciples. Jesus interrupts, crying out to Simon Peter (Example 4): Peter professes unyielding faithfulness, but Jesus foresees his weakness and subsequent denial, as the motive of compassion appears again in the orchestra.

The scene moves to Gethsemane. In long, suppliant tones, Jesus prays (Example 5). This highly emotional description of Christ's agony at Gethsemane evokes harmonic and melodic chromaticism which exceeds the normal perimeter of Thompson's style. The text, "And his sweat was as it were great drops of blood," is set to intense dissonance; such anguished harmonies do not occur in his other choral works. Also, the narrating chorus brings an emotional quality to this passage not possible for the traditional solo narrator.

To the sound of the "compassion" motive, Jesus wakens the disciples as Judas and the multitude approach. Angered, the disciples rush to defend Jesus. Luke simply reports, "One of them smote the servant of the High Priest and cut off his right ear." In the phrase that follows, one can feel the gentle touch of Jesus' healing hand (Example 6). Jesus calls out to those who condemned him: "When I was daily with you, you stretched forth no hand against me." Part One ends here.

Division of the work in two parts is for convenience in performance only. Choral recitative

Example 1

Example 2

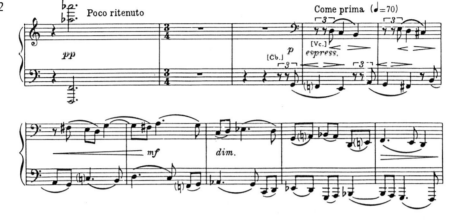

Example 3

Example 4

begins Part Two without a break in action. Jesus is led "into the High Priest's house," followed by Peter, who is immediately recognized. In dramatic recitative Peter denies association with Christ, and after the third denial a clarinet sends out the prophesied "crowing of the cock" (Example 7). In a brief orchestral interlude, the "compassion" motive is transformed into the dolorous sobbing of the despondent Peter, melting into pianissimo as this section ends.

Section six, "The Mocking of Jesus," begins with an abrupt fortissimo and a hammering rhythm pattern of three repeated chords. The chorus begins a narration: "And the men that held Jesus mock'd him and smote him". Incessant rhythms press with mounting anger under shouts of "mocked him—prophesy!—blasphemously"—from the chorus.

An instrumental interlude represents the dawn of the next day, recalling a theme used during the Passover scene. Jesus is brought to trial. The hammering rhythms of the earlier chorus return, while the voices lash out against the innocent Jesus in harsh, percussive chords. A long orchestral interlude, based on a transformed "compassion" motive, creates a mood of dark foreboding at the

316 Randall Thompson

Example 5

Example 8

Example 9

Example 10 JESUS

outset of scene seven, "The Trial." The multitude brings to Pilate its charges against Jesus (Example 8). Accusations are thrown in vehement phrases of choral and solo recitative. Accompanied by transformed thematic material from the prelude, the scene shifts to Herod's court and back again to Pilate. Declaring Jesus guiltless, Pilate calls for his release, but the mob demands Barabbas. As Pilate offers to release Jesus, the crowd shouts "crucify him" in violent repeated notes over hammer blows from the orchestra (Example 9). Jesus is lead to Calvary. Simon bears his cross, and the lines of choral recitative bend to their deepest range. Slowly, the processional music moves on, gradually climbing in range and increasing in dynamic. In a dramatic arioso, Jesus attempts to calm his followers, "weep not for me, but for yourselves and your children." The chorus adds textless wails to the mounting fervor. An impassioned climax is reached after Jesus' words of comfort, "Blessed are the barren." The steady, unhesitating steps of Jesus are marked in the lower registers of the orchestra, picturing the passion procession as it moves away.

A drum-roll crescendo confirms the arrival on Calvary. Exchanges of derisive recitative among the soldiers and officials are directed at Jesus—"He saved others, let him save himself." The inscription "This is the King of the Jews" is emblazoned on the cross, sung by the chorus in slow, widely-spaced chords, and Jesus speaks to the malefactors about the paradise to come. Then, in the stark undulations of parallel recitative, the chorus pictures the ultimate moment: "And the sun was darkened, and the veil of the temple was rent in the midst." Jesus utters His final words, singing "quasi senza voce" (Example 10).

The closing section of the oratorio, "The Entombment," involves only chorus, singing slow, quiet chords to complete the story.

> And behold, there was a man named Joseph. This man went unto Pilate and begged the body of Jesus, and laid it in a sepulchre that was hewn in stone, wherein never man before was laid. And the Sabbath drew on.

The "compassion" motive rises from the orchestra in single fortissimo utterances, and then is absorbed into the final chords.

—*Thurston Dox*

Michael Tippett 1905–

At the turn of the century, with the generation of Elgar, Delius, Holst, and Vaughan Williams, England re-entered the circle of great, musically creative nations which it had abandoned upon the deaths of Purcell and Handel. The succeeding generation, represented principally by Benjamin Britten, William Walton, and Michael Tippett, proved that this reawakening was not a fleeting moment. Although the oratorio was not their primary medium, all three must be given a place in this book: Britten, with his very important *War Requiem* and his church operas; Walton, with the cantata *Belshazzar's Feast*; and Tippett, with the oratorio *A Child of Our Time*.

This latter should be thought of as a documentary and, more than that, as an effort to give artistic expression to horrifying events in a form that will withstand the test of time. After the Nazi regime established its concentration camps, a Jewish youth escaped persecution and found his way to Paris, where he vainly sought assistance in rescuing his imprisoned mother. In a final act of desperation, the 14-year-old shot one of the diplomats in the German embassy, hoping to incite action against such injustice and abuse of power. Unhappily he helped precipitate the ugly pogrom aimed at the complete elimination of the centuries-old Jewish presence.

This incident, which immediately preceded World War II, was set by Tippett to verse and music. A narrator reports the events, and we hear the voices of the mother, of relatives, of the youth himself. Just as in the old Passion settings, the chorus has several roles: It describes events, embodies the persecutors as well as the persecuted, and reflects on the action. In addition, in five places it stands outside the work, as a devout congregation singing Negro spirituals, among them "Steal Away," "Go Down, Moses," and "Deep River."

The work is in three parts: The first and the third are general observations on human despair, on the darkness closing in on the entire era, on the existential fear that attacks man again and again when he becomes aware how far his image has strayed from that of God. The second part treats the deed and the cruel terror surrounding it. Tippett wrote it in the first years of the war and it was first performed in London in 1944, one year before the war's end and before it became known to the public at large that under Hitler's rule, death factories and extermination camps existed. Only then was the oratorio's indictment fully realized. It will probably live on in music history as a prophetic work.

Alfred Uhl 1909–

Alfred Uhl was born on June 5, 1909, in Vienna. When only 13 he undertook his first compositional efforts and later became a student of Franz Schmidt at the Vienna Academy of Music. He traveled extensively and composed, among other things, some fine film music before World War II broke out. He was drafted into the army and severely wounded in 1941, after which, in 1943, he became a professor at the Vienna Academy for Music and Performing Arts—the former Academy of Music. He wrote a number of notable works, which won him the Austrian Government Prize in 1959, the Prize of the City of Vienna in 1961, the Vienna Gold Medal of Honor in 1969, and the Austrian Medal of Honor for Art and Science in 1980. From 1970 to 1975, Uhl was president of the Austrian Society of Composers.

Uhl's principal contributions to the genre of oratorio are *Gilgamesch* and *Wer einsam ist, der hat es gut*. In our era, the Gilgamesh epic has inspired a surprisingly large number of composers, witness the works on this theme by Martinu and Schibler already included in this book. Seldom, however, have so many of its mythical events been included as in Uhl's version based on a text by Franzis Jordan, adapted by Andreas Liess and Uhl himself for this full-length "oratoriolike music drama." It includes in solo roles: Gilgamesh (baritone); Enkidu (tenor); Ishtar, the Goddess of Love (soprano); the "wise" and "remote" Utnapishtim (bass); as well as smaller parts for a Temple Maiden and Siduri (soprano); a Hunter, a Scorpion Man, a Ferryman (tenor); and the Ghost of Enkidus (speaking role). The Narrator is a speaking role. In addition, a mixed, eight-part chorus and a monophonic boys' chorus are called for. The orchestra includes two flutes (with piccolo), two oboes (with English horn), two clarinets (with bass clarinet), two bassoons (with contrabassoon), four horns, four trumpets, three trombones, tuba, timpani, percussion, harp, organ, and strings.

Uhl uses a simple but expressive tonal language to depict many of the important episodes (see Martinu entry for story): The tyranny of the godlike Gilgamesh as he built the city of Uruk; his encounter with his equal, Enkidu, and their close friendship; their common deeds and trials; Enkidu's death and Gilgamesh's despair as his doubts about immortality grow stronger; and finally, his own death. Uhl rejected the twelve-tone system, serialism, aleatory music and the jazz idiom adopted by many of his contemporaries. Rather, he followed the practice of his teacher, Franz Schmidt (see Schmidt entry), which derives from traditional tonality, treated freely to suit the contemporary mood but never fully abandoned. The *Gilgamesh* oratorio received its premiere on

December 3, 1957, in Vienna; a revised version was heard for the first time on June 13, 1969, also in Vienna.

I would like to call special attention to the "cheerful cantata" *Wer einsam ist, der hat es gut* (If You're Lonely, You've Got it Good). Here, 26 poems by three of the greatest humorists in the German language—Wilhelm Busch, Christian Morgenstern, and Joachim Ringelnatz—are brought together. Uhl's music is no less humorous, creating one of the very few truly funny, really hilarious musical works of this century and, for that matter, in the entire musical literature. The original version of this cantata for three soloists (soprano, tenor, baritone), mixed chorus, and large symphony orchestra was first heard on June 24, 1961, in Vienna; the revised version, on January 27, 1964, in Linz.

Ralph Vaughan Williams 1872–1958

The English composer Ralph Vaughan Williams shares the fate of Gustav Holst, his contemporary, and Edward Elgar, a few years his elder: In his native England he is among the highly respected figures of the musical world, but is very seldom performed elsewhere, even though he left an extensive and very important body of work: A total of nine great symphonies, important chamber music, songs, and opera.

He composed choral works as well, some of them small, such as the deeply felt *Benedicite* for solo soprano, chorus, and orchestra (1930), or the *Five Mystical Songs* for baritone solo, chorus, and orchestra (composed in 1906, revised 1910/11). A more important work, however, is the *Mass in G minor*, composed 1920/21 and intended by the composer expressly for liturgical use. The scoring of the work, for eight-part, a cappella double chorus and four solo voices (to be sung by boy soprano and alto voices, in the choral portions as well) is in keeping with this usage. Recollections of the English Tudor period, masterfully interwoven with the composer's tonal language, give this Mass its special attraction. Sounds from a long vanished past mingle with Vaughan Williams's completely 20th-century principles of composition in a very natural, straightforward way.

Williams's *Magnificat*, composed in 1932, has probably attracted less attention. The reasons for this have largely to do with performance: This passionate, deeply religious work calls for enormous forces (an alto voice, large chorus, and orchestra), but lasts barely a quarter of an hour. In spite of its brevity, it is a powerful choral piece with many musical high points. The treatment of the flute is especially impressive, which, the composer indicates, describes Mary's spiritual state at the time of the Annunciation.

Vaughan Williams also wrote an oratorio: *Sancta Civitas* for tenor and baritone solos, chorus, half-chorus, off-stage chorus, and large orchestra. This work, composed between 1923 and 1925 (first performed on May 7, 1926, in the Sheldonian Theater in Oxford) is considered the composer's most personal work. It has certain characteristics in common with the *Mass in G Minor* in that it combines traditional stylistic ideas with an individual, contemporary musical language. The composer selected the text from the *Revelations* of St. John; in addition, there are passages from the English "Taverner's Bible" and—in Greek—a quotation from Plato's *Phaidon*. Once again, Vaughan Williams calls for an immense performance apparatus. The director has to coordinate music on three different levels: in addition to the large chorus and the orchestra there are a half-chorus (with about 20 singers) and a "distant chorus" (an off-stage chorus, preferably children).

Vaughan Williams's most famous choral work is the cantata *Dona nobis pacem*, composed in 1935 and 1936 and performed for the first time in Huddersfield on October 2, 1936. This passionate, very expressive work, written for soprano and baritone solos, chorus, and orchestra, was intended by the composer as a warning—a warning to his contemporaries that a disastrous war was at hand. The words "Dona nobis pacem" are heard at both the beginning and the end of the cantata and are taken up again and again in the individual sections. The six-part work is based mainly on poems by Walt Whitman (Hindemith, too, based his *Lilacs* Requiem on verses by this magnificent lyricist); in addition, there are passages from the Bible and, in the fifth part, words by John Bright. In *Dona nobis pacem*, Vaughan Williams uses harsh, chilly sounds to depict the horror of war with stunning force. But he also employs affecting musical means for the recurring pleas, each expressive in a different way, of inner peace and peace on earth.

Just as important and similarly relentless in its musical demands is Vaughan Williams's last large choral work, the Christmas cantata *Hodie*, composed in 1953–54. It is divided into 16 musical numbers, and its structure, with its chorales, choruses, narrative by an Evangelist, and contemplative episodes, reminds us of the great Passions of Johann Sebastian Bach. Once again the composer had recourse to passages from the Bible, especially to the Gospels of *St. Matthew* and *St. Luke*. Between these he set verses by Milton (from the "Hymn on the Morning of Christ's Nativity") and passages from contemporary poems. The work, almost an hour long, received its premiere on September 8, 1954, in the Worcester Cathedral and was conducted by the elderly composer. It achieves its effect with a somewhat detached, yet always cheerful, relaxed mood. Of all the late works of Vaughan Williams, none can compare with this in confidence, serenity, and otherworldly peace.

Giuseppe Verdi   1813–1901

Twenty-four operas (not all successful) had already assured Verdi a place at the highest levels of international music theater when he attracted worldwide attention with his Mass for the Dead. Audiences could not imagine him as anything other than an opera composer, and so the doubters and carpers never tired of referring to his *Requiem* as an opera transplanted to the church or the concert hall. They did not even suspect how right they were—in a much higher sense than they intended—and how little their comments detracted from the work. Is there more profound drama than that found in the Mass and the Requiem? Are not the ultimate questions treated there? Are not the sharpest conflicts between principle and worldly conduct involved? Where is it written that this confrontation can only be dealt with in an unworldly, transcendental way? It is about human beings, and human beings, as long as they live and breathe, are not unworldly and transcendental, but participate passionately in all that lies between birth and death and go on to extend this burning concern to what awaits their bodies and souls after death. Verdi, born dramatist that he was, could not address the human drama, death, the confrontation with the incomprehensibility of eternity, other than dramatically. And so, the *Requiem* differed in no fundamental way from his previous subjects; it was the musical representation of a drama, albeit a very special one, that called for a very special spiritual and intellectual perspective so as to evoke a similar one in the listener.

Giuseppe Verdi, this greatest of musicians among peasants, but certainly also the greatest peasant among musicians, was born on October 10, 1813, in the tiny village of Roncole, near Busseto, close to Parma. In his middle years, Verdi found the lovely retreat that served him to the end of his life—the estate at Sant'Agata, located on the plains of Lombardy, near the place where he was born. He lived as a "peasant" (as he liked to call himself), building walls, raising livestock, and planting crops, all in the grand manner. At his side was Giuseppina Strepponi, a great singer and, surely, an even greater woman, whom he married in 1859. They were together for more than half a century, following the tragic death of his young wife and their two children. They grew old together, died at almost the same time, and were buried together near the home for old and ailing musicians that Verdi had endowed. His death, on January 27, 1901, was the occasion for one of the most enormous funeral services ever staged for a musician.

Requiem

Original Title: Missa da Requiem
Original Language: Latin
Text: Mass for the Dead from the Catholic liturgy (Missa pro defunctis).
Date of Writing: The last movement, the "Libera me," was composed in 1869; the rest, between June 1873 and the first months of 1874. After the first performance, the "Liber scriptus" in the Dies irae movement was reworked as a solo for mezzosoprano.
First Performance: On May 22, 1874, on the first anniversary of the death of Alessandro Manzoni, conducted by Verdi in the church of St. Mark, in Milan. The version used today (with the "Liber scriptus" as mezzosoprano solo) was heard for the first time on May 12, 1875, in London's Royal Albert Hall.
Form: In seven movements: 1. Requiem and Kyrie; 2. Dies irae (with nine connected musical numbers); 3. Offertorium; 4. Sanctus and Benedictus; 5. Agnus Dei; 6. Lux aeterna; 7. Libera me.
Scoring: Four solo voices (soprano, mezzosoprano, tenor, bass); four-part mixed chorus (further subdivided in the Dies irae, expanded to an eight-part double chorus in the Sanctus); three flutes (with piccolo), two oboes, two clarinets, four bassoons, four horns, four trumpets, three trombones,

one bass tuba, three timpani, one large drum, and strings; off-stage, four trumpets.

History of the Work: "There are so many Masses for the dead! It doesn't make sense to add another one," Verdi once said when a patron approached him about composing one. But within a few years death carried off several from his family and circle of friends who were dear to him, and he began to think of composing a Requiem as a way of dealing with the pain. Then, in 1868, the famous, even legendary Italian composer, Gioacchino Rossini, died. Verdi responded with an idea: 13 of the leading composers in the land should each compose a section of a Requiem to be performed on the first anniversary of Rossini's death, under the baton of the prominent conductor and friend of the dead composer, Angelo Mariani.

The composers Verdi had in mind, and to whose generosity he appealed, for they were to pay the costs of printing and performance, were: Saverio Mercadante, Errico Petrella, Federico Ricci, Alessandro Nini, and others. Who remembers them today? Verdi was to compose the last number himself. This Requiem was indeed finished in time, but disagreements among the musicians prevented its performance, a turn of events which embittered Verdi and led to the end of his friendship with Mariani. Thus, in 1869, the "Libera me" was put away in the master's desk at Sant'Agata and lay there unused.

Then, on May 22, 1873, Italy's greatest poet, hero, and beloved champion of liberty, Alessandro Manzoni, died; Verdi greatly admired him calling him a "saint." He was now so consumed by thoughts of a Requiem that he decided to compose one himself. The "Libera me" contained the seeds of further movements, and it was not difficult for Verdi to expand upon it. After *Aida*, now two years behind him and an enormous success all over the world, he had thought that his opera career was over. But when he set to work on the Requiem, he realized how many unsung melodies he still had in him and even believed he was at one of his inspirational peaks. He wrote the work in about eight months, partly in Sant'Agata, partly in Paris, where he had business in the summer and fall of 1873.

The city of Milan organized the memorial service. Exactly one year after Manzoni's death, on May 22, 1874, Verdi conducted the first performance of his Requiem in the church of St. Mark. This was probably the first time he had ever conducted a church performance, for while a believer he was not on the best footing with the officials of the Church.

The Requiem made a tremendous impression in Milan. When Verdi conducted the work again a few days later at the Teatro alla Scala, the audience exploded in an ovation that seemed to never end. A year later the maestro performed his work (which he firmly believed to be his last) in Vienna and three years later at the Lower Rhine Music Festival at Cologne. It should be noted that he had never personally conducted any of his operas as often as he did the Requiem.

Discussion of the Work: The opening brings a quiet melody in the cellos, which descends an octave, in two phases. This is repeated, now softly harmonized in the strings, as the chorus sings its first words, almost in a whisper: "Requiem, requiem aeternam." Then the first of the countless emotional melodies to appear in this work unfolds: Like a prayer, a plea, the choral sopranos truly implore: "Dona, dona eis, Domine." A crescendo passage in the orchestra peaks in an ethereal pianissimo, as if from another world (Example 1).

It is the "Et lux perpetua," eternal light, that Verdi depicts here in such tender tones. Then the music becomes more earthly: "Te decet hymnus" sing the choral basses in an almost marchlike rhythm. A small fugato arises from it before the quiet, deeply felt opening passages return. The soloists now are heard, radiantly praising God in a sweeping melody, taken up in turn by the tenor, bass, soprano, and mezzosoprano (Example 2).

Out of it Verdi develops an eight-part ensemble (soloists and chorus). Does it remind us of one of his masterful choral ensembles? The stage never gave him the time and leisure to develop such an extended, polyphonic tissue, to let the voices sing unhurriedly, for the "plot" was always urging the composer to get on with it. What follows cannot be described in words: the greatest section of the work, the Dies irae (itself subdivided into nine sections: Dies irae, Tuba mirum, Liber scriptus, Quid sum miser, Rex tremendae, Recordare, Ingemisco, Confutatis, and Lacrymosa) bursts forth with an elemental power such as even Berlioz, with the combined forces of his several orchestras, could not surpass. Four mighty blows, rushing passage work in the strings, terrified cries for help in the frenzied chorus, descending and ascending, reintensified, driven on. The thundering bass drum reverberates after the four hammer blows announcing the end of the world: A vision at once eerie and magnificent, which only slowly subsides (Example 3).

It is as if humans, scattered by the world's impending doom, were gathering once more, arduously, faltering, seeking each other in the dark. Trumpets are heard in the distance—they call out, are answered, and then coalesce into a mighty chorus of wind instruments: "Tuba mirum spargens sonum." All must appear before the eternal judge.

Example 1

Example 2

Example 3

Example 4

Example 5

Sal-va me, fons pi-e - ta - tis,

Example 6

Re - cor-da - re Je - su pi - e, quod sum cau - sa

Example 7

Qui Ma - ri - am ab-sol-vi - sti,

Example 8

La-cry-mo-sa di-es il-la, qua re-sur-get ex fa-vil-la,

Example 9

The image of death arises as from a mist: to the lower strings, barely touched, the drum beats a mysterious rhythm; the voices of the basses rise in fear, plunge, and then whisper ominously: "Mors . . . mors . . . mors . . ." The connecting mezzosoprano solo is just as unrelenting; God holds the book in which all sins and evil deeds are written—"Liber scriptus proferetur."

Yet there is melody everywhere; Verdi cannot compose without it. We are astounded when we realize how many kinds of melody there are and how each is able to express human feelings and experiences. The picture painted by the mezzosoprano is gloomy, and finally she, too, can only stammer the terrible word, "nil . . . nil . . . nil": nothing, no sin will remain unexpiated. The choruses burst forth again: "Dies irae, dies illa." Full of remorse, man feels his hour approaching: "Quid sum miser" (Who am I, poor wretch, and what will I say?). Three soloists await the fearful hour, the orchestra waits in silence, and one after the other, the voices hopelessly run their courses. With stunning force, the "Rex tremendae majestatis," the terrible majesty of the Lord, draws near; the basses ponderously announce His appearance, and the tenors, as if trembling in fear, repeat it in the softest pianissimo (Example 4). The soloists plead with a melody that pierces the heart (Example 5).

This is probably one of the most beautiful melodies Verdi ever wrote; modulating gently, it courses through all the voices and forms a counterpoint to the menacing "Rex tremendae" of the basses—and once again, a great ensemble forms, as if of its own accord. Scarcely has it faded away when the soprano and mezzosoprano soloists begin a new, deeply felt duet (Example 6). The pleading melody of the solo tenor (Example 7) is no less affecting.

Verdi never talked of his creative process: It was a private matter, of concern only to him; only the results were for the world. But in this work we are surely not wrong if we imagine that the uninterrupted stream of melodies came first, each melody then being adapted to the passage most suited to it. Finally, Verdi rounds off this extremely lyrical movement with a renewed eruption of the destruction of the world—the four thunderclaps, the raging strings, the pleading chorus. But all does not end in destruction. The mezzosoprano sings the wondrous, sorrowful song of the day of weeping, "Lacrymosa dies illa." (Example 8).

The bass seconds her, and, once again, Verdi forms a great ensemble of all the voices around this melody, which leads into a calm prayer: "Dona eis requiem," (Give them eternal rest . . . Amen). For the following Offertorium, Verdi composed a melody of heavenly consolation (Example 9), sung first by the solo bass and then, like a salutation from infinite heights, by a delicate solo violin.

In the old Requiem tradition, Verdi composed the "Quam olim Abrahae promisisti" (As Abraham once promised) as a recurring choral fugato. As the dramatic tension of the ensemble mounts, the solo tenor separates from it, and once more, a magnificent melody (Example 10) becomes the backbone of an ensemble that grows more intense with the renewed drama of the "Quam olim Abrahae."

The conclusion of the movement, however, belongs to a pleading melody sung softly in unison by all the soloists; it dies away slowly. The Sanctus is a great double chorus introduced by resounding trumpets. The beginning of the Agnus Dei, sung in unison by the soprano and the mezzosoprano without any accompaniment, seems to come from another world; it is a song for angels (Example 11).

The Lux aeterna is also brief, but very sonorous. The conclusion is formed by the part that Verdi had composed first: "Libera me. . . ." (Free me from eternal death). It begins with the voice of the solo soprano, psalmodizing, almost reciting; it is taken up by the whole chorus. Then, again—for the third time!—the tumultuous storm of the end of the world bursts forth (No. 3); it was probably one of the earliest themes he composed for the work. (We mention only in passing that he used very similar melodic lines and tone-painting in the storm scene of Otello.)

A soprano melody floats above an a cappella choral movement in which the theme in example No. 1 is repeated, transposed from an instrumental to a vocal passage. At the conclusion, another weighty choral fugue: "Libera me, Domine." Alto, soprano, bass, and tenor announce its seven-bar theme, and in the development there is a series of contrapuntal details (inversion, stretto, and so on) we would not have expected from Verdi, the composer of Romantic opera. The movement, at times very dramatic, gradually calms; it fades away with a whispered "Libera me."

A work of imposing grandeur and overwhelming emotion comes to an end, as beautiful as any work man ever dedicated to God. We recall Tchaikovsky's words, "God needs no prayers; it is we who need them." God needs no music, either; His Heaven is so perfect and so beautiful that man can never create anything to equal it. But we need music like this—it is our bulwark, our consolation, our light in a dark, chaotic world.

Example 10

dolcissimo

Ho - sti - as et pre - ces ti - bi, Do - mi - ne,

ppp   *pp*

Example 11

Andante

Sopran

dolcissimo

A - gnus De - i, — a - gnus De - i, qui — tol-lis pec-ca-ta mun-di,

Mezzosopran

dolcissimo

A - gnus De - i, — a - gnus De - i, qui — tol-lis pec-ca-ta mun-di,

Quatro Pezzi Sacri (Four Sacred Pieces)

In the final years of his long life, coinciding with the final years of the century, Verdi wrote several sacred compositions. He was almost 80 years old when his triumphant masterpiece *Falstaff* received its premiere at La Scala in Milan; he would write no more operas. Everything a composer could hope for, he had attained: Great fame, wealth, innumerable performances of his works. However, the "grand old man of Sant'Agata," as his fellow countrymen called him, refused to spend his remaining days in idleness, and so he turned his hand to writing four sacred pieces. They were not initially planned to relate to each other, but perhaps upon the advice of his friend Arrigo Boito or his publisher, Giulio Ricordi, he joined them loosely in the form they have come down to us.

The *Quattro pezzi sacri*, the "Four Sacred Pieces" are:
1. Ave Maria for four-part, unaccompanied mixed chorus (1889)
2. Stabat Mater for four-part female chorus with orchestra (1896/97)
3. Laudi alla Vergine Maria for four-part, unaccompanied female chorus (1887)
4. Te Deum for double chorus, each in four mixed voices (1896)

The premiere, without the Ave Maria, was given during Holy Week, on April 7, 1898, at the Paris Opera. Shortly thereafter, the complete *Pezzi sacri* were performed for the first time in Turin, on May 26, 1898, under the baton of Arturo Toscanini. In the following winter there were performances in Milan, London, Vienna, Berlin, Munich, and Hamburg—in a concert hall or church, as was customary north of the Alps—and in Milan, at La Scala.

The writing of the Ave Maria was prompted by a curious event. In 1889, the *Gazetta musicale*, a respected Italian musical magazine, posed its readers, mostly skilled professionals, a "brain teaser": It published a *Scala enigmatica*, an "enigmatic scale," and challenged them to use it as the basis of a composition (Example 1). To all outward intents and purposes, it was no more than a diversion, a sort of crossword puzzle for musicians, but its underlying significance was more serious. A new century was not far off, and various composers had been calling for new directions by expanding the harmonic system, which had been deeply shaken by Wagner's *Tristan*.

Example 1

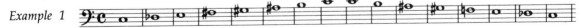

The "enigmatic scale" was an invented one and contained both major and minor elements (without assuming the identity of either mode); an augmented fifth, which completely obscured any notion of key; three half-tone steps; and an augmented second. In those days, it was extremely difficult to use this scale as the foundation for a logical, harmonic structure; probably no one expected that the oldest of all the participants would work out the most skillful and durable solution to the "assignment."

Verdi went beyond what had been asked for: He used the scala enigmatica not only in the ascending form in which it had been presented, but led it back to its point of departure (implicit in every scale) by arranging it somewhat differently each time, in half, whole, or one-and-a-half-step intervals. He used this scale the way cantus firmus was used in old music; as the "skeleton" of a composition whose other voices wind in and out of it contrapuntally. In the first section, the cantus firmus of the enigmatic scale is in the bass; in the second, in the alto; in the third, in the tenor; and in the fourth, in the soprano. In the two latter voices, it is transposed upwards a fourth, thereby extending from F to f. The result is a sonorous, polyphonic movement, "modern" in a way unusual for Verdi (this "modernity" predetermined, of course, by the scala enigmatica), with exciting harmonies. Each of the four sections is 16 bars long; the length of the scale, eight bars ascending, eight bars descending. A brief coda, with two "Amen's" leads back to the opening key of C major.

The Stabat Mater is a beautiful composition, one of the most affecting settings of this ancient text. Verdi's tonal language often sounds ancient, probably unintentionally. The text moves along without a single word repetition, a very unusual practice. A unified narrative thus is formed, one not divided into different sections, as was customary in earlier major settings (Pergolesi, Emmanuele d'Astorga, Rossini, and others). Much here is reminiscent of the Requiem, composed 20 years earlier, an example being the expressive melody for the basses (Example 2).

Example 2

Nevertheless, the work's structure is complex, with lyrical passages and dramatic high points, forceful orchestral background and completely unaccompanied vocal passages. This Stabat Mater, finished in 1897, was Verdi's last complete composition.

The *Laudi alla Vergine Maria* (Hymns in honor of the Virgin Mary) differ from the other three *Pezzi*, primarily in their use of an Italian rather than a Latin text. Verdi used the last verse of the "Paradise" from Dante's *La Divina Commedia*, a work to which he was completely devoted. Like the Ave Maria, this piece is written for a cappella chorus, but female rather than mixed. The sound is consequently ethereal, truly "paradisical." Musicologists sense here a relation to Palestrina, whom Verdi revered. Is there a link between Verdi and that last great High Renaissance master of polyphony, dead exactly 300 years before? Verdi once said, "In order to go forward, let us return to the past." Some musicians have erroneously construed this now famous saying, taking it to mean that Verdi's attitude was basically conservative. The truth is that at no point in his life could this have been said of him. What he meant was that the future, likely to depart from many of the Romantic principles, had much to learn from the masters of the past. There are moments in the *Laudi* that remind us of the greatest old polyphonic works, without seeming "old" or, more to the point, "old-fashioned"—a confirmation of Verdi's meaning.

The cycle closes with a Te Deum, composed in 1896; it and the Stabat Mater are the only liturgical pieces in the set. The Te Deum is the most beautiful, the largest in scope and, perhaps, the most significant of the four pieces. The basses of the first chorus sing the Gregorian chant "Te Deum laudamus," and the tenors of the second reply in the age-old way "Te Deum confitemur" (Example 3).

Example 3

The work continues prayerlike as the chorus, still a cappella, sings antiphonally, softly and with little melodic change. Then the mighty, eight-part Sanctus bursts forth, and the orchestra enters fortissimo. The movement continues in a sort of ecstasy, the high sopranos of both choruses, each in three parts, singing the Sanctus as if from very far away; the high strings' reply is just as soft and exalted. Next we hear the majestic ten-part a cappella choral passage "Patrem immensae majestatis," followed by the thrilling build-up in chorus and orchestra to a point where suddenly a soprano voice floats alone on high, with a new melody full of sweetness and tenderness ("Sanctus quoque paraclitum Spiritum"). Mysticism alternates with strength, fear with hope. Verdi all the while achieves exciting, ever-changing effects from the alternation of major and minor modes. Wondrous is the unaccompanied Miserere, with its echo effects, which appear toward the end. Finally, a solo soprano, timid at first, bursts forth with, "In te, Domine, speravi" (Lord, my hope rests in Thee). The thundering ten-part chorus takes up the avowal, after which the overpowering work ebbs slowly and fades away to its conclusion. A work of old age, remarkable down to the smallest detail—a deeply moving legacy.

Tomás Luís de Victoria 1547?–1611

If one lists the greatest masters of the waning 16th century, the Spaniard Tomás Luís de Victoria must be included with Palestrina and Orlando di Lasso. He dedicated himself exclusively to sacred music, and his magnificent, mystical Masses are among the most beautiful of all time. He came from Avila, a very old city in Castile, but we are not certain of the year of his birth. As a youth, he was sent to Rome to be educated in sacred music. In 1571 he became director of a boys' chorus in the Jesuit "German School" and in 1575 director of the school itself. His early works appeared under his Italianized name, Tommaso Luigi da Vittoria, a name still used occasionally today. We are not certain whether he was a student of Palestrina, but the two men were friends in later years. Victoria lived sometimes in Rome, sometimes in Madrid, and died in the latter city on July 27, 1611. Felipe Pedrell, Spain's leading musicologist, believes the *Officium Hebdomadae Sanctae* and the *Officium Defunctorum*, two monumental compositions in polyphonic, a cappella style, to be Victoria's greatest. The first relates the Passion of Christ, while the second is dedicated to the souls of the dead. In addition, Pedrell lists 20 Masses, 44 motets, 34 hymns, and various Magnificats. Among his Masses, the *Missa quarti toni* and the *Missa Ave maris stella* stand out. Three other Masses—*Salve Regina*, *Alma Redemptoris*, and *Ave Regina*—are written for double chorus. An abundance of splendid music still waits to be discovered in the works of this great Spaniard.

Antonio Vivaldi 1678–1741

Vivaldi was considered one of the greatest violin virtuosos of his day; triumphant concert tours led him across Europe as far as Vienna and Hamburg. Very little is known of his origins; until recently we did not even know the exact date and place of his birth. Scholars have now located Vivaldi's baptismal certificate, dated May 6, 1678, issued by the church of San Giorgio in Venice. Nor do we know much about Vivaldi's life. His father was a violinist in the San Marco orchestra who surely gave Antonio his first musical instruction. In order to continue with music, Vivaldi chose a career in the church and was educated for the priesthood. As a consecrated priest he was permitted to accept the position of choral director at the Ospedale della Pietà, where each Saturday and Sunday evening public concerts were presented. Word of Vivaldi's capabilities both as a composer and a virtuoso violinist soon spread from Venice throughout Western Europe. Leading musicians such as Johann Joachim Quantz traveled to Venice to meet the *prete rosso* ("red priest"), as he was often called because of his red hair. In 1718 he took leave of his duties at the Ospedale to spend five years concertizing through Europe. Following this triumphal tour he resumed his post in 1723, and remained there until 1740. He undertook another concert tour on which he died in 1741, in Vienna. We do not know the exact date, but he was buried in Vienna on July 28 of that year.

Vivaldi's entire output, much of which has not been published, is impressive in its almost limitless scope. There are more than 400 concertos, for from one to four solo instruments, orchestra, and continuo; *Le quattro Stagioni* (The Four Seasons), four short, three-movement violin concertos, each representing one of the seasons of the year, have become famous throughout the world. Then there are more than 50 chamber works, mostly sonatas. Vivaldi also composed for the stage: A total of 49 operas, of which 19 remain in their entirety. In addition, he wrote numerous choral works, mostly for his concerts at the Ospedale della Pietà: among them are the large oratorio *Juditha triumphans* (1716) and a *Sacrum* (Mass) in C major for four solo voices, chorus, and orchestra. Some musicologists question the authenticity of this Mass, for it is written in a style more German and Austrian than typically Italian. He also wrote numerous smaller choral works: A *Magnificat in G minor*, which has come down to us in two versions (with different scorings and in highly divergent forms) and various settings of the *Dixit Dominus* (*Psalm* 109) and the *Beatus vir* (*Psalm* 111); these, too, are for several solo voices, chorus, and orchestra. A *Te Deum* and various separate Mass movements have also come down to us, among them a particularly imposing *Kyrie a 8* for two four-part choruses, two orchestras, and double continuo. The *Gloria in D Major* for two solo voices (soprano and alto), chorus, and orchestra has become well known and quite popular; it is justifiably one of Vivaldi's most famous works, for the orchestration, with the added radiant sound of a trumpet, is especially sumptuous.

Richard Wagner 1813–1883

Richard Wagner's role as a music dramatist is so imposing that all other works he created in the course of his life pale in comparison with his stage works. Even his devotees might be surprised to learn that he wrote a large concert work for male chorus with orchestra. This "Biblical scene," entitled *Das Liebesmahl der Apostel* (The Love Feast of the Apostles), is more interesting for biographical reasons and when seen in relation to Wagner's total output than as a composition in its own right. It is one of hundreds or even thousands of similar compositions written in Germany in the 19th century for the male choruses then so popular, but which are now a thing of the past and likely to remain so.

Wagner probably wrote the work on commission: When he assumed the position of Hofkapellmeister in Dresden—in a certain sense a reward for the triumph of *Rienzi* on October 20, 1842, and the moderate success of *Der fliegende Holländer* on January 2, 1843—he also took on the direction of the Dresden *Liedertafel* (male choir). This organization, which played a considerable social and artistic role in the city, was preparing a "Second Song Festival for Male Choruses in Dresden" for the summer of 1843, for which Wagner was requested to compose something. He chose the scene in which Christ's Disciples, Apostles, and other followers gather after his death to remember him and to renew their promises to spread the Gospel. During this period Wagner had toyed with the idea of composing a music drama based on Jesus; Christ would be described as a social revolutionary, as savior of the poor and vanquisher of the rich and powerful. The work never progressed beyond sketches and a prose draft, but some of its ideas doubtless spilled over to influence the basic concept of *Siegfrieds Tod* (the later *Gotterdämmerung*) as well as of the *Ring des Nibelungen*.

It is even more noteworthy that the design and contents of the *Liebesmahl der Apostel* are prophetic: In a work composed in 1843 we find clear signs of the "staged consecrational play," *Parsifal*, the last of Wagner's dramas to appear on the stage at Bayreuth, in 1882. The "Biblical scene" is conceived of as purely concert music, but the parading of the choruses, who represent a religious society, as well as the announcement of salvation by invisible "voices from on high" prefigure the Grail scenes in *Parsifal*. Basically, the *Liebesmahl* scene deals with the exaltation of the miracle of Pentecost, the outpouring of the Holy Ghost: in *Parsifal*, the analogous scene has a different meaning, but religious ecstasy and the suggestion of supernatural powers are present in both.

Wagner divided the "scene" into two parts: the first traces the fear and anxiety of the Disciples and disclosure of new threats, given over exclusively to long a cappella choruses. Then, as if from a great distance, far removed from all that is earthly, the solace of the Holy Spirit descends; voices "from on high" proclaim "Be of good cheer, for I am with you." Here is the moment present even in the weakest of Wagner's works, which reveals his genius: The orchestra, heretofore silent, enters very softly, ascending from the depths, and the chorus, as if sensing the supernatural, asks the Disciples, "Welch Brausen erfüllt die Luft, welch Tönen, welch Klingen! Bewegt sich nicht die Stätte, wo wir stehen?" (What a rushing fills the air, what sounds, what music! Does it not move— the ground upon which we stand?) The balance of the "scene" is given over to an increasingly imperious call to the ceaseless battle for the faith, resulting in the kind of *Liedertafel* singing so loved in the 19th century.

The work was first performed on July 6, 1843, as part of the choral festival. Wagner, ever a man of the theater, incorporated the architecture of the Frauenkirche, where the event took place, into the performance: Members of the male chorus, probably quite a large one, were posted at different places so as to appear to be the groups of Disciples gathering for their meeting. The orchestra sat behind one of these groups and was, consequently, almost invisible, thus maintaining the illusion. Wagner had the "voices from on high" singing from the dome, just as did the angels' voices in *Parsifal*, 40 years later.

William Walton   1902–1983

Walton was born on March 29, 1902, in Oldham, Lancashire. At an early age he became one of the leading English composers of his generation, together with Britten, Tippett, and others. They were the successors to Elgar, Vaughan Williams, Delius, and Holst, the generation that reestablished the international musical standing of the British Isles. Walton wrote the score for the film versions of Shakespeare's *Henry V*, *Hamlet* and *Richard III*; he composed the official ceremonial marches for the coronations of George VI (1937) and Elizabeth II (1953), as well as several operas, orchestral music, concertos, and chamber works. One of his most brilliant creations, second only to the *Coronation Te Deum*, falls within the scope of this book: the oratorio *Belshazzar's Feast*, first performed in 1931.

Belshazzar's Feast, scored for large chorus, is practically unknown outside of England, and seldom performed there, largely due to its monumental scale. When Walton was commissioned to compose a large choral work for the Leeds Festival of 1931, he happened to learn from the famous English conductor Sir Thomas Beecham that among other works to be performed at the Festival was the grandiose *Requiem* by Hector Berlioz. In light of the enormous choral and orchestral forces which were to be mustered for the Berlioz *Requiem*. Walton decided to use the same forces for his composition as well. With this in mind, he called for a large double chorus, solo baritone, and a vast orchestra. Biblical passages describing the sad fate of the Jews in captivity in Babylonia, compiled by Osbert Sitwell, constitute the text for this three-part work. Its structure is quite symphonic. The high points of the first part are the recurring lines from *Psalm* No. 137: "By the waters of Babylon, there we sat down, yea, we wept." In the second part, the baritone soloist and the choruses report the dramatic event: The mysterious appearance of handwriting on the wall during a feast given by the Babylonian King: "Mene, mene tekel upharsin." The last part is a magnificently constructed hymn of praise to God the Father, in whom all must trust even when under the Babylonian yoke. The monumental work comes to an incomparable conclusion with the crowning "Hallelujah."

David Ward-Steinman   1936–

In his own words, David Ward-Steinman viewed all the music he had composed prior to completing *The Song of Moses* (1964) as preparation for writing this 70-minute oratorio. His career to that point included study with Burrill Phillips, Gordon Binkerd, Milton Babbitt, Darius Milhaud and Nadia Boulanger, and his professorship at San Diego State University had just begun. A personal style evolved through his commitment to integrating avant garde techniques with music that communicates more easily to the general listener. Species of serialism mix with neo-classical structures; third-stream jazz mixes with ancient modes; all converge on a pinpoint of post-romantic tonality. Explorations in electronic sound production, aleatory techniques, mixed-media, and his own "fortified" piano are the continuation of that evolution.

The Song of Moses

Original Language: English
Text: Compiled by the composer from scripture and original writings.
Date of Writing: 1964

First Performance: May 31, 1964, by the San Diego State Symphony Orchestra and Chorus and the Aztec Choir.

Form: The libretto divides into a prologue and four parts: "The Call," "Battle and Triumph," "The Heresy," and "The Death of Moses." Subdivision of the parts results in 22 titled numbers. The passages of narration are spoken and generally placed at the beginnings or ends of numbers or parts. In its adherence to a traditional formal plan, this oratorio is similar to many familiar 18th-century and 19th-century works, but it differs because of one unique feature. The Prologue and Part Four ("The Death of Moses") are enactments of the same scene—Moses viewing the Promised Land at the point of his death—which positions the middle three parts as dramatic flashback.

Cast: Narrator, Moses (baritone), Pharaoh (tenor) and Aaron (tenor). God's voice speaks through the chorus.

Scoring: Narrator, soprano, two tenors, baritone, double mixed chorus, and a large Romantic orchestra, including an alto saxophone and a battery of 26 percussion instruments.

Discussion of the Work: At the opening, attention quickly focuses on the double chorus "And There Arose not a Prophet in Israel" (whom the Lord knew face to face). Warm sonorities, gentle rhythms and antiphonal exchanges between the choirs characterize the aged deliverer of Israel according to the composer's personal view: "The Moses of my imagination is the Moses of Michelangelo."

The opening of Part One, "The Call," places Moses before the burning bush. Crackling flames suddenly appear in the orchestra, and in a brief but powerfully expressive chorus God summons Moses to deliver Israel (Example 1). [Musical examples copyright 1968 San Diego State College Press. Used by permission of the composer.] Moses complains and shrinks from the call: "Who am I, that I should go unto Pharaoh." God convinces Moses to have faith that He will supply the power to speak and act. In a chorus filled with joyous excitement, the Israelites praise the power of God (Example 2). The earthy language in Pharaoh's rejoinders to Moses ("Who is the Lord," No. 6), delivered in cutting recitative-like phrases, is characteristic and appropriate in this modern setting.

> Who is the Lord, that I should obey his voice and let
> Israel go. Ye are lazy, ye are idle;
> Be off now to your work!

Part Two opens with the narrator who confirms God's resolve to force the hand of Pharaoh. Pounding orchestral chords introduce the narrative chorus "And the Lord spoke Unto Moses," bringing the plagues of blood and frogs down on Pharaoh (Example 3). In a leaping, staccato recitative, Pharaoh relents and promises deliverance.

> Take the frogs away from me and my people,
> Take the blood away from the lakes and wells,
> for I really can't stand the smells.

The agitated choral narrations about this plague and those to follow use modifications of the same thematic material (Example 4). A driving triplet figure in broken octaves provides a rhythmic dynamic for these sections. With a unity of style maintained for the entire section dealing with the plagues, there is little need for the descriptive word painting so common in other settings of this story. When the final plague is sent, "Thus saith the Lord, all the first born shall die," textless choral melismas release the anguish of the beleaguered Egyptians (Example 5). In a recitative that becomes slower and slower, the wearied Pharaoh summons Moses to receive the words of release, "Rise up and get ye forth from my people, and be gone."

A short march (No. 8), with descriptive narration above the music, pictures the movement of the Israelites to the Red Sea. But Pharaoh turns against Israel once again and orders his army to destroy them (Example 6). Fear besets the Israelites, and they confront Moses: "Why hast thou led us away to die in the wilderness?" Moses rebukes them, and invokes "the Salvation of the Lord." Accelerating orchestral phrases, undulating broken chords and swelling chromatic lines support the narrator's description of the parting Red Sea waters. Moses commands the sea to engulf the Egyptians, and the chorus converges on a unison to represent total destruction (Example 7). This epochal scene closes with the text "And the Lord saved Israel that day." These words pass through the chorus in a sequence of melodic arches, symbolizing the rainbow which appeared as a sign of God's covenant after the flood. The chorus of Israelites concludes Part Two in a whirling jubilation: Miriam's song of triumph.

Three months elapse before Part Three begins. The male voices carry God's admonishment to Israel in a concise chorus, "You Have Seen What I Did to the Egyptians" (No. 12). Streams of imitating lines by muted strings represent the enveloping smoke that veils God's descent to Mount

Example 1

Example 2

Sinai. Above a flurry of muted brass and strings the narrator describes the meeting of God and Moses, "face to face." The Israelites protest to Aaron and demand a new god to lead them: "As for this Moses, we know not what has become of him." Aaron forgets his covenant vow and presents them a golden calf, igniting a frenzied chorus which erupts into the satanic "Dance to the Golden Calf" (No. 16), for orchestra alone. All the brilliance and power of this orchestra, with its battery of percussion, is unleashed in this easily choreographed interlude. Strains of third-stream jazz are heard, culminating at mid-point in a celebrated solo for alto saxophone. When the voice of God thunders over the orchestra, warning Moses of this corruption, the motion of this orgiastic dance is quickly subdued. Moses berates Aaron for his sinful laxity and Aaron "sheepishly" replies, using the same melodic material with which the Israelites had taunted him. Moses demands "Who is on the Lord's side?", and one by one, over an ominous tremolo in the orchestra, members of the chorus speak: "I, Lord." The entire chorus responds together in extreme vocal ranges: "I Lord; I Lord; I!" Then the basses begin a section in rhythmic speech "Would to God We Had Died" (No. 17), which becomes the subject of a whispered fughetta. Later in the chorus a similar line is the main thematic material for short dramatic episodes, as the Israelites again become distrustful and restless over the lack of food. Moses reminds them that God promised food. The soprano soloist, who has not been heard until this point, sings at length about the manna from heaven. A soft, fluffy triplet figure appears in the orchestra, but the chorus of Israelites continues its complaint, calling for meat. Driven to despair by their protests, Moses chides the people with the same melodic phrases they had sung to ridicule his lengthy sojourn on Mount Sinai. Moses continues: "O ye who

Example 3

Example 4

Example 5

Example 6

Example 7

Example 8

weep in the ears of the Lord! The Lord will give you meat to eat." The soprano describes the miracle of the quail providing meat, but the people are dissatisfied and blame Moses for the lack of water. Angered, Moses proposes to "get water for you from this rock." Two sharp clusters in the orchestra underscore his resolve to "strike twice with my staff," without God's help. Trickles of water spring from the orchestra, turning into a flowing stream. Now God threatens to destroy Israel. Moses pleads for mercy in a long and impassioned arioso: "Pity, Lord, Pity" (No. 18), and God proclaims to Moses that neither he nor any Israelites who "have put me to the test" will inhabit the Promised Land. In the closing chorus of Part Three, "Out of the Depths" (No. 19), the Israelites repent and plead for mercy. In one moment of piercing irony, the identical, textless sounds of wailing Egyptians heard during the last plague reappear. The only gesture in the direction of fugal imitation in the entire work occurs in this chorus (Example 8).

Part Four, "The Death of Moses," contains four brief numbers. The scene returns to the opening prologue. In the aria "Be Strong and of Good Courage" (No. 20) Moses commissions Joshua to be Israel's new leader. A soprano aria, "The Lord Bringeth Thee" follows, and Moses praises God in a final profession of faith ("Give Ear, O Heavens").

> He is the rock
> His work is perfect,
> For just and right is He.

A narration of Moses' death begins the final section. The text and music of the choral prologue return, this time with reverently augmented rhythms (Example 9). This chorus continues to the final words, "Whom the Lord knew face to face."

Example 9

—*Thurston Dox*

Elinor Remick Warren 1900–

Although she published her first work while still in high school, this composer began her career as a concert pianist. Tours with famous operatic singers were part of an active concert life, but her interest shifted towards composition. Study with Paolo Gallico, Clarence Dickinson and Nadia Boulanger set her course firmly in that direction. The Neo-romantic style holds strong appeal for her and choral composition is her primary interest. Certain works in larger forms, *The Harp Weaver* (1933), *Abram in Egypt* (1960), *Requiem* (1966) and *The Legend of King Arthur* (1974) are outstanding and widely performed.

The Legend of King Arthur

Original Title: The Passing of Arthur *(1939)*
Original Language: English
Text: Based upon the poem "The Passing of King Arthur" by Alfred Lord Tennyson.
Date of Writing: 1974
First Performance: 1940, in Los Angeles, under the original title.
Form: Two major divisions written in a continuous operatic style: dramatic recitative, interspersed with arioso and choral passages. Performance requires one hour.
Scoring: Baritone (King Arthur), tenor (Sir Bedivere), full orchestra and chorus.
History of the Work: The Legend of King Arthur *was premiered in Los Angeles in 1940 under the original title* The Passing of Arthur. *The reviewer of a performance by the Roger Wagner Chorale in*

1954 called it "the most impressive and well-organized of Miss Warren's larger works."
Discussion of the Work: The Legend of King Arthur is a modified version of an earlier work, *The Passing of Arthur* (1939). Warren designates the work as a Choral Symphonic Poem, a formal concept which proves appropriate and satisfying for this scenic drama. In another sense, considered as choral music alone, the composition resembles a gigantic madrigal: a continuous, non-repetitive procedure, depending for musical logic on the balance of its text-related musical impressions. The text is taken literally from portions of Tennyson's "The Passing of Arthur," found among the *Idylls of the King*.

The story begins at midpoint in Tennyson's poem. An impassioned introduction, filled with ominous phrases and punctuated by "regal" rhythms, leads directly into the opening chorus. Warren's Post-romantic manner eloquently depicts King Arthur's last battle (Example 1). [Musical examples copyright 1939 (renewed 1964) J. Fisher & Bros. Assigned to Belwin-Mills Publishing Corp. c/o CPP/Belwin, Inc., Hileah, FL 33014. International Copyright secured. Made in U.S.A. All rights reserved. Used by permission.] The first words of the chorus "All day long the noise of battle rolled among the mountains" are severed by sword-like lines in the orchestra. Arthur's knights have been killed and the king mortally wounded. At the words "Their Lord, King Arthur," a fanfare motive sounds in the orchestra, which will be associated with the king at later moments. Sir Bedivere carries Arthur to a chapel which has a "broken chancel, broken cross." The rhythms of the lower voices separate abruptly. Arthur summons Bedivere to take his sword, Excalibur. A long ascending line accompanies his description of the Lady of the Lake, when she offered Excalibur to him with "outstretched arm" (Example 2). The king orders Bedivere to return the sword to the lake—to "fling him far." At these words the notes leap up an octave. Bedivere's journey to the lake through ancient burial grounds is narrated by the chorus. Orchestral sounds evoke the text in fleeting frames of singing thirds, piercing octaves, icy parallel fifths and staccato flakes of foam. Male voices and orchestra release dazzling, radiant chords on the word "Excalibur," as Bedivere draws the sword. He gazes at the jeweled hilt. Staccato chords and circling lines in the upper winds and strings reflect the light of the winter moon. Reluctant to relinquish the sword, Bedivere conceals it and returns to Arthur. "I heard the ripple washing in the reeds," he reports, over impressionistic undulations in the orchestra. Angered, Arthur sends him out a second time. The chorus narrates how Sir Bedivere, stiffened by conceit, reasons the sword must not be lost to the ages and concludes, "The King is sick, he knows not what he does." With a liquid melody over placid, shimmering tremolo in the strings, Bedivere sings a doleful arioso depicting the Lady of the Lake fashioning the sword. Bedivere returns to Arthur. The full chorus alludes to his new bearing as pompous, swaggering chords resound in the orchestra: "And so strode back slow to the wounded King" (Example 3).

Example 1

Example 2

Example 3

Example 4

Sir Bedivere reports as before, to similar musical phrases, and with renewed anger Arthur reproves him, threatening his life should he fail a third time. Bouncing jagged lines in contrary motion accompany Bedivere in his haste to retrieve the sword. As he flings it into the lake, darting scales and leaping thirds flash through the chorus like lightning. In a rare a cappella passage the chorus vividly pictures the arm of the Lady of the Lake. An eerie whir of rapidly descending tritones accompanies the words "and drew him [Excalibur] under the mere." Arthur receives the penitent Bedivere with compassion and requests to be taken to the lake: "Quickly, quick! I fear it is too late and I shall die." The chorus narrates in phrases of relentless energy as Bedivere braves all obstacles to do the King's bidding (Example 4).

Example 5

Part Two begins with a lengthy intermezzo for orchestra alone, which serves as a transition of mood to enhance the view of a barge waiting to carry Arthur. The chorus sings of the "black stoled, black hooded forms" and the "three queens with crowns of gold" (sung by an obbligato trio). Now, alone at the time of death, Arthur calls "Place me here in the barge." The orchestra is silent. While the chorus sings "for all his face was white and colorless" the orchestral lines are in "white notes" for the last words, giving a visual as well as musical picture. At this moment, Sir Bedivere sings an aria of great emotional fervor and deep reflection on the changes that are ahead in his own life. In despair, he pleads to Arthur for guidance. With the celebrated verses from this poem, "The old order changeth, yielding place to new," Arthur's words unfold their transcendent meaning in the work's most uplifting solo passage. Broad, soaring phrases rise above flowing arpeggios in the orchestra, reaching an overpowering climax on the final line, "wherefore, let thy voice rise like a fountain for me night and day." By giving the succeeding lines to the a cappella chorus ("more things are wrought by prayer than this world dreams of") these reverent words stand out in relief. No other musical setting could allow them to speak more effectively. This chorus glows with moments of sublime beauty.

Over gentle, floating chords and Puccini-like counter-melodies, Arthur bids a final farewell. Mysterious, measured harmonies dip into the deep orchestral ranges as the chorus intones "The barge with oar and sail, moved from the brink." The sound of an English horn emerges, symbolizing the arm of the Lady of the Lake, to offer a brief "arioso" of lament. Bedivere is left alone on the shore. In wailing chromaticism the chorus bemoans Arthur's passing as Bedivere cries out: "The King is gone." Immediately, celestial string tremolos and the female chorus suggest the sounds of a new dawn. The upper three voices of the chorus describe Bedivere's view from the shore—"The speck that bare the King down that long water opening on the deep, pass on from less to less and vanish into light." On the word "light," divisi sopranos, alone, fade into pianissimo in the extremes of range. Harp arpeggios rise through the orchestra and a brilliant crescendo announces the "new sons" and the "new year" as the full chorus enters.

Nowhere in the work does imitative counterpoint play a role until the entire ensemble moves into these closing moments. A powerful fugato carries the poem to a majestic and glorious conclusion.

> For so the whole round earth is every way bound by golden chains about the feet of God. (Example 5)

—Thurston Dox

Carl Maria von Weber   1786–1826

For decades, *Der Freischütz* drove all Weber's other compositions out of general public awareness. His later operas did indeed sometimes attain the musical level of this early Romantic masterwork but never touched it dramatically. Nevertheless, among his many other works—orchestral pieces, symphonies, concertos, overtures—there are many fine things, some of which fall within the scope of this book.

When only 13 Weber, always very devout, tried his hand at a Mass; the result understandably lacked the necessary depth of feeling. In 1815, the other basic aspect of his nature came to light: A burning love for his country. He celebrated the victory of the Alliance over Napoleon, "Germany's Archenemy," with the patriotic cantata *Kampf und Sieg* (Struggle and Victory), which in places indulges in very superficial tone painting—not much different from Beethoven's *Wellington's Victory or the Battle of Vittoria*, composed at almost the same time, and many other "battle pieces" then in fashion. Nevertheless, it does demonstrate some ideas, and Weber's pure, noble enthusiasm is often in evidence.

Not until 1818 and 1819 did he compose mature, contemplative, sacred works. He had become Hofkapellmeister in Dresden, for which he wished to offer thanks to God. But there were practical reasons as well. An entry in his diary dated January 4, 1818 states: "Mass begun, Kyrie." Two days later, the work had been sketched out in its entirety, and on February 23, the *Missa sancta in E-flat Major* (also called *Missa Solemnis*) was finished. It was intended to honor King August I of Saxony and was performed at his nameday celebration; the royal couple, however, did not attend. Nevertheless, a few months later, Weber wrote the cantata *Natur und Liebe*, Op. 58, for the 50th anniversary of that king's reign, and in that same year began a new *Mass in G Major* (sometimes called the *Jubelmesse*), which was completed in 1819. With the exception of the short, insignificant cantata *Wo nehm' ich Blumen her* (Where shall I find the flowers), Weber never again composed vocal concert or sacred music.

Egon Wellesz 1885–1974

Wellesz, an Austrian composer, was born on October 21, 1885, in Vienna, and died on November 9, 1974, in Oxford; he had emigrated to England in 1938 and never returned. His role in music is not to be underestimated. In 1916 he succeeded in deciphering the Byzantine system of notation, thereby opening for musicologists a fascinating new aspect of early Christian music. Wellesz was a professor at the University of Vienna and later, at Oxford.

Among his important compositions are nine symphonies, a number of operas, chamber works and other kinds of instrumental music. Early on he also composed works that belong in this book; a *Cantata*, Op. 45; the *Mass in F Minor*, Op. 51; the "Little" Masses in C, Op. 58 and in G, Op. 80; and the *Missa brevis*, Op. 89. In 1963 he set Rainer Maria Rilke's *Duino Elegies*, Op. 90, for solo soprano, mixed chorus and medium-sized orchestra, which, like the following oratorios, were given their premiere by the ORF/Austrian Radio. From 1967 came *Mirabile Mysterium*, Op. 101, for soprano and baritone solos and voices echoing them, speaker, mixed chorus, and orchestra. The texts were taken from 7th-century Byzantine hymns compiled by the composer; 1) The Prophecy; 2) Hymn to Bethlehem (Et tu Bethlehem); 3) Joseph's Lament; 4) Hymn; 5) The Adoration of the Angels; 6) The Miracle; 7) Hymn of the Faithful. There is a glowing luminosity about some of these that never seems archaic. On October 25, 1969, when the composer was 84, the first performance of the *Canticum sapientiae*, Op. 104, for solo baritone, mixed chorus, and orchestra was given in Graz. It is not only a product of the wisdom of age, but also an exciting world view; "From recognition of the transitoriness of all that is worldly, to the comprehension of eternal wisdom," as one critic remarked.

APPENDIXES

A. Liturgical Texts

The Ordinary of the Mass

Kyrie

Kyrie eleison, Christe eleison. Kyrie eleison.

Lord, have mercy upon us. Christ, have mercy upon us. Lord, have mercy upon us.

Gloria

Gloria in excelsis Deo. Et in terra pax hominibus bonae voluntatis. Laudamus te. Benedicimus te. Adoramus te. Glorificamus te. Gratias agimus tibi propter magnam gloriam tuam. Domine Deus, Rex coelestis, Deus Pater omnipotens. Domine Fili unigenite, Jesu Christe. Domine Deus, Agnus Dei, Filius Patris, Qui tollis peccata mundi, miserere nobis. Qui tollis peccata mundi, suscipe deprecationem nostram. Qui sedes ad dexteram Patris, miserere nobis. Quoniam tu solus sanctus. Tu solus Dominus. Tu solus Altissimus, Jesu Christe. Cum Sancto Spiritu, in gloria Dei Patris. Amen.

Glory be to God in the highest. And on earth peace to men of good will. We praise Thee. We bless Thee. We adore Thee. We glorify Thee. We give Thee thanks for Thy great glory. O Lord God, heavenly King, God the Father almighty. O Lord Jesus Christ, the only-begotten Son. Lord God, Lamb of God, Son of the Father. Who taketh away the sins of the world, have mercy upon us. Who taketh away the sins of the world, receive our prayer. Who sitteth at the right hand of the Father, have mercy upon us. For Thou alone art holy. Thou alone art Lord. Thou alone, O Jesus Christ, art most high. Together with the Holy Ghost, in the glory of God the Father. Amen.

Credo

Credo in unum Deum, Patrem omnipotentem, factorem coeli et terrae, visibilium omnium, et invisibilium. Et in unum Dominum Jesum Christum, Filium Dei unigenitum. Et ex Patre natum ante omnia saecula. Deum de Deo, lumen de lumine, Deum verum de Deo vero. Genitum, non factum, consubstantialem Patri: per quem omnia facta sunt. Qui propter nos homines, et propter nostram salutem descendit de coelis. Et incarnatus est de Spiritu Sancto ex Maria Virgine; et homo factus est. Crucifixus etiam pro nobis; sub Pontio Pilato passus, et sepultus est. Et resurrexit tertia die, secundum Scripturas. Et ascendit in coelum: sedet ad dexteram Patris. Et iterum venturus est cum gloria, judicare vivos et mortuos: cujus regni non erit finis. Et in Spiritum Sanctum, Dominum et vivificantem: qui ex Patre Filioque procedit. Qui cum Patre et Filio simul adoratur, et conglorificatur; qui locutus est per prophetas. Et unam sanctam catholi-

I believe in one God, the Father almighty, maker of heaven and earth, and of all things visible and invisible. And in one Lord Jesus Christ, the only-begotten Son of God. Born of the Father before all ages. God of God, light of light, true God of true God. Begotten, not made; of one substance with the Father: by whom all things were made. Who for us men, and for our salvation, came down from heaven. And was made flesh by the Holy Ghost of the Virgin Mary: and was made man. He was also crucified for us, suffered under Pontius Pilate, and was buried. And on the third day He rose again, according to the Scriptures. And ascended into heaven: He sitteth at the right hand of the Father. And He shall come again with glory to judge the living and the dead; and of His Kingdom there shall be no end. And in the Holy Ghost, the Lord and Giver of life, who proceedeth from the Father and the Son. Who together with the

cam et apostolicam Ecclesiam. Confiteor unum baptisma in remissionem peccatorum. Et expecto resurrectionem mortuorum. Et vitam venturi saeculi. Amen.

Father and the Son is adored and glorified: who spoke by the prophets. And in one holy, catholic and apostolic Church. I confess one baptism for the remission of sins. And I expect the resurrection of the dead. And the life of the world to come. Amen.

Sanctus

Sanctus, Sanctus, Sanctus Dominus Deus Sabaoth. Pleni sunt coeli et terra gloria tua. Osanna in excelsis.

Holy, Holy, Holy Lord God of hosts. Heaven and earth are filled with Thy glory. Hosanna in the highest.

Benedictus

Benedictus qui venit in nomine Domini. Osanna in excelsis.

Blessed is He that cometh in the name of the Lord. Hosanna in the highest.

Agnus Dei

Agnus Dei, qui tollis peccata mundi, miserere nobis. Agnus Dei, qui tollis peccata mundi, miserere nobis. Agnus Dei, qui tollis peccata mundi, dona nobis pacem.

Lamb of God, who taketh away the sins of the world, have mercy upon us. Lamb of God, who taketh away the sins of the world, have mercy upon us. Lamb of God, who taketh away the sins of the world, grant us peace.

Missa pro defunctis (Requiem Mass)

Introit

Requiem aeternam dona eis, Domine: et lux perpetua luceat eis. Te decet hymnus Deus in Sion, et tibi reddetur votum in Jerusalem: exaudi orationem meam: ad te omnis caro veniet. Requiem.

Eternal rest give unto them, O Lord: and let perpetual light shine upon them. A hymn, O God, becometh Thee in Sion; and a vow shall be paid to Thee in Jerusalem. O hear my prayer: all flesh shall come to Thee. Eternal rest.

Kyrie eleison

Kyrie eleison. Christe eleison. Kyrie eleison.

Lord, have mercy upon us. Christ, have mercy upon us. Lord, have mercy upon us.

Gradual

Requiem aeternam dona eis, Domine: et lux perpetua luceat eis. In memoria aeterna erit justus: ab auditione mala non timebit.

Eternal rest give to them, O Lord: and let perpetual light shine upon them. The just shall be in everlasting remembrance: he shall not fear the evil hearing.

Sequence

1. Dies irae, dies illa,
   Solvet saeclum in favilla:
   Teste David cum Sibylla.

   Day of wrath, O day of mourning,
   See fulfilled the prophets' warning;
   Heav'n and earth in ashes burning.

2. Quantus tremor est futurus,
   Quando judex est venturus,
   Cuncta stricte discussurus!

   Oh, what fear man's bosom rendeth
   When from heaven the Judge descendeth,
   On whose sentence all dependeth!

3. Tuba mirum spargens sonum
   Per sepulcra regionum,
   Coget omnes ante thronum.

   Wondrous sound the trumpet flingeth,
   Through earth's sepulchers it ringeth,
   All before the throne it bringeth.

4. Mors stupebit et natura,
   Cum resurget creatura,
   Judicanti responsura.

   Death is struck, and nature quaking,
   All creation is awaking,
   To its Judge an answer making.

5. Liber scriptus proferetur,
   In quo totum continetur,
   Unde mundus judicetur.

Lo! the book exactly worded,
Wherein all hath been recorded:
Thence shall judgment be awarded.

6. Judex ergo cum sedebit,
   Quidquid latet apparebit:
   Nil inultum remanebit.

When the Judge His seat attaineth,
And each hidden deed arraigneth,
Nothing unavenged remaineth.

7. Quid sum miser tunc dicturus?
   Quem patronum rogaturus,
   Cum vix justus sit securus?

What shall I, frail man, be pleading?
Who for me be interceding,
When the just are mercy needing?

8. Rex tremendae majestatis,
   Qui salvandos salvas gratis,
   Salva me, fons pietatis.

King of majesty tremendous,
Who dost free salvation send us,
Fount of pity, then befriend us!

9. Recordare, Jesu pie,
   Quod sum causa tua viae:
   Ne me perdas illa die.

Think, good Jesu, my salvation
Caused Thy wondrous Incarnation,
Leave me not to reprobation.

10. Quarens me, sedisti lassus:
    Redemisti crucem passus:
    Tantus labor non sit cassus.

Faint and weary Thou has sought me,
On the cross of suffering bought me;
Shall such grace be vainly brought me?

11. Juste judex ultionis,
    Donum fac remissionis,
    Ante diem rationis.

Righteous Judge! for sin's pollution
Grant Thy gift of absolution,
Ere that day of retribution.

12. Ingemisco, tamquam reus:
    Culpa rubet vultus meus:
    Supplicanti parce, Deus.

Guilty, now I pour my moaning,
All my shame with anguish owning;
Spare, O God, Thy supplicant groaning.

13. Qui Mariam absolvisti,
    Et latronem exaudisti,
    Mihi quoque spem dedisti.

Thou the sinful woman savedst;
Thou the dying thief forgavest;
And to me a hope vouchsafest.

14. Preces meae non sunt dignae:
    Sed tu bonus fac begnigne,
    Ne perenni cremer igne.

Worthless are my prayers and sighing;
Yet, good Lord, in grace complying,
Rescue me from fires undying.

15. Inter oves locum praesta,
    Et ab haedis me sequestra,
    Statuens in parte dextra.

With Thy favored sheep O place me,
Nor among the goats abase me,
But to Thy right hand upraise me.

16. Confutatis maledictis,
    Flammis acribus addictis,
    Voca me cum benedictis.

While the wicked are confounded,
Doomed to flames of woe unbounded,
Call me with Thy saints surrounded.

17. Oro supplex et acclinis,
    Cor contritum quasi cinis:
    Gere curam mei finis.

Low I kneel, with heart-submission,
See, like ashes, my contrition;
Help me in my last condition.

18. Lacrimosa dies illa,
    Qua resurget ex favilla

Ah, that day of tears and mourning!
From the dust of earth returning

19. Judicandus homo reus:
    Huic ergo parce Deus.

**Man for judgment must prepare him.
Spare, O God, in mercy spare him!**

20. Pie Jesu Domine, dona eis
    requiem. Amen.

Lord, all pitying, Jesu blest, grant them
Thine eternal rest. Amen.

Offertory

Domine Jesu Christe, Rex gloriae, libera animas omnium fidelium defunctorum de poenis inferni, et de profundo lacu: libera eas de ore leonis, ne absorbeat eas tartarus, ne cadant in obscurum: sed signifer sanctus Michael repraesentet eas in lucem sanctam: Quam olim Abrahae promisisti, et semini ejus.

Hostias et preces tibi, Domine, laudis offerimus: tu suscipe pro animabus illis, quarum hodie memoriam facimus: fac eas, Domine, de morte transire ad vitam: Quam olim Abrahae promisisti, et semini ejus.

O Lord, Jesus Christ, King of Glory, deliver the souls of all the faithful departed from the pains of hell and from the deep pit: deliver them from the lion's mouth, that hell may not swallow them up, and may they not fall into darkness; but may Thy holy standard-bearer, Michael, lead them into the holy light; which Thou didst promise to Abraham and to his seed.

We offer to Thee, O Lord, sacrifices and prayers: do Thou receive them in behalf of those souls whom we commemorate this day. Grant them, O Lord, to pass from death unto life; which Thou didst promise to Abraham and to his seed.

Sanctus

Sanctus, Sanctus, Sanctus Dominus Deus Sabaoth. Pleni sunt coeli et terra gloria tua. Osanna in excelsis.

Holy, Holy, Holy Lord God of Sabaoth. Heaven and earth are filled with Thy glory. Hosanna in the highest.

Benedictus

Benedictus qui venit in nomine Domini. Osanna in excelsis.

Blessed is He who cometh in the name of the Lord. Hosanna in the highest.

Agnus Dei

Agnus Dei, qui tollis peccata mundi, dona eis requiem. Agnus Dei, qui tollis peccata mundi, dona eis requiem. Agnus Dei, qui tollis peccata mundi, dona eis requiem aeternam.

Lamb of God, who takest away the sins of the world, grant them rest. Lamb of God, who takest away the sins of the world, grant them rest. Lamb of God, who takest away the sins of the world, grant them eternal rest.

Communion

Lux aeterna luceat eis, Domine: cum sanctis tuis in aeternum, quia pius es. Requiem aeternam dona eis, Domine, et lux perpetua luceat eis. Cum sanctis tuis in aeternum, quia pius es.

May light eternal shine on them, O Lord: with Thy saints forever, for Thou art merciful. Eternal rest give to them, O Lord: and let perpetual light shine upon them: with Thy saints forever, for Thou art merciful.

Responsory After Absolution

Libera me, Domine, de morte aeterna, in die illa tremenda: quando coeli movendi sunt et terra: Dum veneris judicare saeculum per ignem. Tremens factus sum ego, et timeo, dum discussio venerit, atque ventura ira. Quando coeli movendi sunt et terra.

Dies illa, dies irae, calamitatis et miseriae, dies magna et amara valde. Dum veneris judicare saeculum per ignem. Requiem aeternam dona eis Domine: et lux perpetua luceat eis. (The Responsory is then repeated up to "Tremens.")

Deliver me, O Lord, from eternal death in that awful day: when the heavens and the earth shall be moved: when Thou shalt come to judge the world by fire. Dread and trembling have laid hold on me, and I fear exceedingly because of the judgment and the wrath to come. When the heavens and the earth shall be shaken.

O that day, that day of wrath, of sore distress and of all wretchedness, that great and exceeding bitter day. When Thou shalt come to judge the world by fire. Eternal rest grant to them, O Lord, and let perpetual light shine upon them. (The Responsory is then repeated up to "Dread.")

Te Deum

1. Te Deum laudamus: te Dominum confitemur.
2. Te aeternum Patrem omnis terra veneratur.
3. Tibi omnes Angeli, tibi Coeli et universae Potestates:
4. Tibi Cherubim et Seraphim incessabili voce proclamant:
5. Sanctus, Sanctus, Sanctus, Dominus Deus Sabaoth.
6. Pleni sunt coeli et terra majestatis gloriae tuae.
7. Te gloriosus Apostolorum chorus:
8. Te Prophetarum laudabilis numerus:
9. Te Martyrum candidatus laudat exercitus.
10. Te per orbem terrarum sancta confitetur Ecclesia.
11. Patrem immensae majestatis:
12. Venerandum tuum verum, et unicum Filium:
13. Sanctum quoque Paraclitum Spiritum.
14. Tu Rex gloriae, Christe.
15. Tu Patris sempiternus es Filius.
16. Tu ad liberandum suscepturus hominem, non horruisti Virginis uterum.

17. Tu devicto mortis aculeo, aperuisti credentibus regna coelorum.

18. Tu ad dexteram Dei sedes, in gloria Patris.

19. Judex crederis esse venturus.

20. Te ergo quaesumus, tuis famulis subveni, quos pretioso sanguine redemisti.

21. Aeterna fac cum Sanctis tuis in gloria numerari.
22. Salvum fac populum tuum Domine, et benedic haereditati tuae.
23. Et rege eos, et extolle illos usque in aeternum.
24. Per singulos dies, benedicimus te.
25. Et laudamus nomen tuum in saeculum, et in saeculum saeculi.
26. Dignare Domine die isto sine peccato nos custodire.
27. Miserere nostri Domine, misere nostri.

28. Fiat misericordia tua Domine super nos, quemadmodum speravimus in te.
29. In te Domine speravi: non confundar in aeternum.

We praise Thee, O God: we acknowledge Thee to be the Lord.
All the earth doth worship Thee, the Father everlasting.
To Thee all Angels cry aloud, the Heavens, and all the Powers therein:
To Thee Cherubim and Seraphim continually do cry:
Holy, holy, holy, Lord God of Sabaoth.

Heaven and earth are full of the majesty of Thy glory.
The glorious company of the Apostles praise Thee:
The goodly fellowship of the Prophets praise Thee:
The noble army of Martyrs praise Thee:
The holy Church throughout all the world doth acknowledge Thee:
The Father, of an infinite majesty:
Thine honorable, true, and only Son:

Also the Holy Ghost, the Comforter.
Thou art the King of Glory, O Christ.
Thou art the everlasting Son of the Father.
When Thou tookest upon Thee to deliver man, Thou didst not abhor the womb of a Virgin.
When Thou hadst overcome the sharpness of death, Thou didst open the kingdom of Heaven to all believers.
Thou sittest at the right hand of God, in the glory of the Father.
We believe that Thou shalt come to be our Judge.
We therefore pray Thee, help Thy servants, whom Thou has redeemed with Thy precious blood.
Make them to be numbered with Thy Saints in glory everlasting.
O Lord, save Thy people, and bless Thine heritage.
Govern them, and lift them up forever.

Day by day, we magnify Thee.
And we worship Thy name ever, world without end.
Vouchsafe, O Lord, to keep us this day without sin.
O Lord, have mercy upon us, have mercy upon us.
Let Thy mercy be upon us, as our trust is in Thee.
In Thee, O Lord, have I trusted: let me never be confounded.

Sequence: *Stabat Mater*

1. Stabat Mater dolorosa
Juxta crucem lacrimosa
Dum pendebat Filius.

2. Cujus animam gementem
Contristatam et dolentem
Pertransivit gladius.

3. O quam tristis et afflicta
Fuit illa benedicta
Mater Unigeniti.

4. Quae maerebat et dolebat,
Pia Mater, dum videbat
Nati poenas incliti.

5. Quis est homo qui non fleret,
Matrem Christi si videret
In tanto supplicio?

6. Quis non posset contristari,
Christi Matrem contemplari
Dolentem cum Filio?

7. Pro preccatis suae gentis
Vidit Jesum in tormentis,
Et flagellis subditum.

8. Vidit suum dulcem natum
Moriendo desolatum,
Dum emisit spiritum.

9. Eia Mater, fons amoris,
Me sentire vim doloris
Fac, ut tecum lugeam.

10. Fac ut ardeat cor meum,
In amando Christum Deum,
Ut sibi complaceam.

11. Sancta Mater, istud agas,
Crucifixi fige plagas
Cordi meo valide.

12. Tui nati vulnerati,
Tam dignati pro me pati,
Poenas mecum divide.

13. Fac me tecum pie flere,
Crucifixo condolere,
Donec ego vixero.

14. Juxta crucem tecum stare,
Et me tibi sociare
In planctu desidero.

15. Virgo virginum praeclara,
Mihi jam non sis amara:
Fac me tecum plangere.

16. Fac ut portem Christi mortem,
Passionis fac consortem,
Et plagas recolere.

17. Fac me plagis vulnerari,
Fac me cruce inebriari,
Et cruore Filii.

18. Flammis ne urar succensus,
Per te Virgo, sim defensus
In die judicii.

At the cross her station keeping
Stood the mournful Mother weeping
Close to Jesus at the last.

Through her heart, His sorrow sharing,
All His bitter anguish bearing,
Now at length the sword has passed.

Oh, how sad and sore distressed
Was that Mother, highly blest,
Of the sole-begotten One.

Christ above in torment hangs;
She beneath beholds the pangs
Of her dying glorious Son.

Is there one who would not weep,
Whelmed in miseries so deep,
Christ's dear Mother to behold?

Can the human heart refrain
From partaking in her pain,
In that Mother's pain untold?

Bruis'd, derided, curs'd, defil'd,
She beheld her tender Child:
All with bloody scourges rent.

For the sins of His own nation,
Saw Him hang in desolation
Till His spirit forth He sent.

O thou Mother, fount of love!
Touch my spirit from above;
Make my heart with thine accord.

Make me feel as thou hast felt,
Make my soul to glow and melt
With the love of Christ our Lord.

Holy Mother, pierce me through,
In my heart each wound renew
Of my Savior crucified.

Let me share with thee His pain,
Who for all my sins was slain,
Who for me in torments died.

Let me mingle tears with thee,
Mourning Him who mourned for me,
All the days that I may live.

By the cross with thee to stay,
There with thee to weep and pray,
Is all I ask of thee to give.

Virgin of all virgins best,
Listen to my fond request:
Let me share thy grief divine.

Let me, to my latest breath,
In my body bear the death
Of that dying Son of thine.

Wounded with His every wound,
Steep my soul till it hath swoon'd
In His very blood away.

Be to me, O Virgin, nigh,
Lest in flames I burn and die
In His awful Judgment day.

19. Christe, cum sit hinc exire,
    De per Matrem me venire
    Ad palmam victoriae.

20. Quando corpus morietur,
    Fac ut animae donetur
    Paradisi gloria.
    Amen. Alleluia.

Christ, when Thou shalt call me hence,
Be Thy Mother my defense,
Be Thy cross my victory.
While my body here decays
May my soul Thy goodness praise, Safe in
Paradise with Thee.
Amen. Alleluia.

B. Glossary

In this list, an effort is made to define the technical terms used in the book in the simplest way possible, to make them intelligible to the layman.

I hope that professional musicians will kindly overlook the fact that occasionally the definitions lack technical detail. [*The New Harvard Dictionary of Music* (Cambridge MA, 1986) is a good source for further information—Ed.]

A cappella: Vocal (usually choral) music without any instrumental accompaniment.

Ad libitum: Latin: "at the (performer's) pleasure." Used several ways in music. Thus, to denote freedom in performance at certain places in a work; for example, the cadenza in a concerto may be played in a "free" tempo or even improvised; the same is true for a vocal cadenza toward the end of an *aria*. *Ad libitum* (abbreviation, ad lib.) can also refer to the participation of instruments in a work; for example, in this book, the phrase "organ ad lib." often appears, meaning that the work can be performed with or without the organ.

Agnus Dei: Latin: "Lamb of God." The last section of the Ordinarium Missae.

Antiphonal: Describes alternate singing, usually by two choruses or two groups within the same chorus, or even by the leading soloist and the chorus (which might also be called "responsorial"). Surely one of the oldest forms of collective musical practice, in evidence in Byzantium as early as A. D. 300; it appeared soon thereafter in Milan, where it seems to have been introduced by Bishop Ambrosius, one of the most important figures in early Christian music.

Aria: A self-contained musical number for a single voice with orchestral accompaniment, part of a larger work (oratorio, opera, cantata). Usually melodic and songlike. Developed from song, but more artistic, longer, and usually more complex, and usually also more difficult to perform. Related to it are the following: *air*, used by Bach and others: an expressive, slow instrumental movement, as part of a suite, for example; *arietta*, a short aria, perhaps also limited in range of expression and difficulty.

Arioso: "Arialike," that is to say, melodically expressive; the term is usually used for a piece stylistically between *recitative* and *aria*.

Arpeggio: From the Italian word for harp: *arpa*. The striking of the several notes of a chord not all at once, but one after the other in quick succession. The arpeggio can proceed from the lowest tone upward (most common) but also from the highest tone downward—in both directions, the notes follow in sequence. In German, it is usually called *Brechung*. In scores, it is indicated by *arp., arpegg., arpeggiando*, or by a perpendicular wavy line placed in front of the chord. It is quite common in playing harpsichord music.

Atonality: Twentieth-century music that no longer abides by the rules of tonality, but rather combines the notes in a completely free way.

Basset horn: A type of alto clarinet (in the key of F) invented around 1770; it fell out of use toward the middle of the 19th century. Mozart used it in his Requiem and even gave it solos in his opera *La clemenza di Tito*.

Basso continuo: See *continuo*.

Benedictus: The fifth section of the Ordinarium Missae (or the second half of the fourth section, if the Sanctus and the Benedictus are counted together). To be sung after the transubstantiation (the transformation of the bread into the flesh, and of the wine into the blood of Christ).

Bourrée: Old French dance, a lively, lighthearted round dance in duple meter.

Cadence: There are closing formulas for musical works just as there are for letters. They serve to reinforce—to impart to the listener—at the conclusion of the work, the strong feeling of the principal key or, one might say, of the point of departure and of the goal. This is accomplished by the use of the chords best suited to leading the ear in the right direction. They can be combined and tied to each other in various ways, but just as the signature stands at the end of a letter, so the chord of the principal key stands at the end of a cadence. This was true in the Baroque, the Classic, and the Romantic eras; not until the 20th century did these rules, too, become relaxed or suspended. Atonal music (see *tonality*) knows no principal key and therefore, no cadence. It is related to the meaning of *Cadenza* (see above, *Ad Libitum*).

Canon: In one way, the simplest form of polyphony. All the members of a vocal or instrumental group present the same melody, not at the same time but at intervals, as in a "round." One voice begins with the melody or theme, and before it ends, a second voice joins in with exactly the same melody while the first proceeds steadfastly with its line. The number of voices, or entries, is really limited only by the length of the work. Canons or canonlike forms were present in the early days of polyphony; the English "Sumer is icumen in" dates from the 13th century. Canon is the simplest of all polyphonic forms, but also the strictest; because all participants perform exactly the same material, variations and deviations from the theme are excluded. Artistic development of the form led to a loosening of its rules, and through freer *imitations* and forms, the *fugue* came about. For the layman unfamiliar with polyphony, the singing of canons is the simplest and best way to begin to understand several melodic lines sounded at once.

Canonic forms: Successive entrances similar to those in a canon, but which do not strictly follow the rules for a canon.

Cantata: A musical work for vocalists with instrumental accompaniment, with either sacred or secular text. The oldest cantatas—probably from the 17th century—were simple in form, often in one movement, with only one or two soloists. The form continued to expand and came to include several movements: arias, recitatives, choruses, and so on; many cantatas (Bach, Handel, and A. Scarlatti composed hundreds of them) came to resemble oratorios.

Cantus firmus: (Latin: fixed, stable, preexisting melody.) Precursor of the concept *theme*. In medieval *polyphony*, there usually was a main melody, called *cantus firmus*. It was not found in the highest voice, as was usually true later, but mostly in a voice called the tenor. The other voices were arranged around or above it; in a sense, it represented the backbone of the composition, and the counter-voices were called *counterpoint*. Often folk songs or well-known tunes were used as *cantus firmus*.

Cavatina: A short aria; in opera, often the same as a song.

Chaconne: A slow, solemn musical form, originally a dance, in which a short bass melody is repeated over and over (see also *Ostinato*).

Chorus: A large group of vocalists who sing either without instrumental accompaniment (*a cappella*) or accompanied by an orchestra, or by a single instrument such as a piano or organ. There are male choruses (usually in four parts: tenors I and II, basses I and II; in modern works, sometimes in three parts: tenor, baritone, bass); female choruses (soprano, mezzosoprano or soprano II, alto); children's choruses (one- to three-part or possibly even four-part, according to their ability); and mixed choruses. The word *mixed* refers less to the gender of the performers than to the range of the voices. The church, which for centuries forbade the participation of women in musical performance, formed *mixed choruses* from the high voices of boys and the low ones of men—boy sopranos and altos, adult tenors and basses. Today, *mixed chorus* usually means a chorus composed of both men and women: soprano, alto, tenor, bass. Normally it is in four parts, but each section can be further subdivided.

Chorale: The word has various meanings. The oldest probably refers to the early Christian music called *Gregorian chant*. Luther gave the word a new meaning. The *Protestant chorale* is a church hymn with a single melody, which can be sung as is, homophonically, either with or without organ accompaniment, or in four parts by a mixed chorus.

Bach worked chorales into his oratorios in many places, to provide a contemplative element in the midst of drama. The musical form of the chorale is fairly well fixed: it usually includes several four-bar phrases with a brief pause at the end of each. An overall AAB form is common.

Chromaticism: Melodic progression in the smallest "neighboring" intervals or pitches, for example, C, C-sharp, D, D-sharp, E, and so on. If this progression extends to an octave, a chromatic scale is formed, which includes 12 tones, all those existing within one octave. The word comes from the Greek *chroma*, which means color. The word *chromatic* is also used outside of music for colors and refers to the almost imperceptible transition from one color to its "neighbor." The musical term *chromatic* or *chromaticism* is not only used to describe melody but also harmony—the sequence of chords.

Church modes: In medieval Western music, Church modes were scales that for centuries were transitional forms between the old Greek modes, used in the ancient Mediterranean world, and "modern" keys. There are eight different church modes, or "tones", each of which resembles a modern scale, differing from it usually in only one note, or at the most, two. The most important difference between the old Greek and medieval scales—the *church modes*—and the "modern" system of keys or tonalities lies in the fact that not until the latter came into existence was the principle of a leading tone introduced. This means that the seventh, penultimate tone of each scale is a half step below the eighth, or octave and is heard to "lead" to it. Because this principle is lacking in the church modes, they sound ancient, archaic to our ear. They do not yet include the major and minor modes and, in contrast to our scales, are built individually, so that each of the eight *church modes* has its own distinctive structure and sound.

Col legno: The striking or bowing of the strings with the wooden part of the bow.

Comes: The first appearance of the theme of a fugue is called **dux** (from the Latin word for leader); its second appearance is called *comes* (Latin: the one that accompanies) and is slightly different from the dux; it usually enters on the fifth degree, whereas the dux usually does on the first. As it runs its course, it must modulate back to that position, for the third entry is once again a dux (on the first degree), the fourth, a comes (and so on, if there are more than four voices).

Consonance: The "satisfying," "good" combination of two or several notes in a chord or interval. (See also *dissonance*.) Classical theory (based on physics and mathematics) holds that the "best" consonances are the octave, the fifth, and naturally, the unison (which the ear does not hear as an interval). For folk and popular music throughout much of Europe, it is usually the third and the sixth that are the "best" intervals.

Continuo: (Abbreviation for *basso continuo*, thorough bass or figured bass.) When polyphony yielded its prominence to homophony (or monody), at the end of the 16th century and the beginning of the 17th, it was the custom when composing music to set down on paper only the melody and the bass. To establish the harmonies, the composer provided the bass part with numbers, which everyone who knew harmony could immediately transform into chords. In this new style, the one who played the thorough

bass had the job of filling in, between the melody and the bass, the harmonies called for by the numbers; there was always some leeway in the way the chords could be combined, allowing performers to use their imagination. At the end of the Baroque era, the practice of continuo playing declined; Haydn and Mozart, and still Beethoven, were capable continuo players, but in their own works they indicated the harmonies they wanted so exhaustively that not much was left to interpretation. Here is an example, to clarify the practice for the layman: In the bass, beneath the note C are the figures 5/3; according to the principles of thorough bass, this means that above the C, harmonies at the third (3) and the fifth (5) are to be formed, resulting in the C Major triad C, E, G. In a way this system is a kind of musical shorthand. The continuo was usually played on the harpsichord or organ, but there often were additional continuo instruments (a cello or a contrabass, possibly a bassoon) which simply played the bass line. This small group of instruments was also called the *continuo*. In Baroque instrumental music, the scoring almost always calls for a few melody instruments "and continuo," meaning the small group of instruments that played with the harpsichord or organ.

Counterpoint: When a guitarist accompanies a song, the chords supply harmony; the notes are arranged vertically on the page, as are all notes that are to be sounded simultaneously. Harmony, then, is a vertical principle; as a field of study it deals with chords and their relationships. There is also a horizontal system for combining sounds: when one part (vocal or instrumental) has a melody, and a second part has a counter melody—one that does not simply parallel the first but is quite independent—the latter then forms a *counterpoint* to the first; it could be called simply a counter voice, or counterpart. Such counterpoint does not lead to music that is essentially harmonic, or homophonic, composed of a single melodic line with accompaniment, but to *polyphony* (which see). The simplest example of counterpoint is seen in the *canon*; there, in a certain sense, the melodic line forms a counterpoint to itself, although the second voice presents it somewhat later. The *fugue*, consequently, is also a contrapuntal form. The voices, developing simultaneously, may result in harmonies, or chords, but this does not change the fact that they develop horizontally, and can be comprehended only in time. Photographically, harmony can be compared to a snapshot, and counterpoint only to a (moving) film.

The strong tendency in the late Baroque era to compose polyphonically, or contrapuntally, yielded in the Classic and Romantic eras to a preference for essentially homophonic, harmonic style. In the 20th century we encounter both styles. Contrapuntal composing has produced several terms such as *retrograde* and *inversion*, which will be defined separately.

Credo: The creed or confession of faith; third part of the Ordinarium Missae. It includes statements of belief in God the Father, in Christ, in the Holy Ghost, and in the Church.

Crescendo: Italian, "growing." An expression mark indicating gradual increase in loudness.

Decrescendo: Italian, "becoming softer." Expression mark.

Diminuendo: Same as *decrescendo*.

Dissonance: Traditional harmony divides simultaneous combinations of sound into "good" and "bad," a distinction based not only on how they sound, but also on physics: the "simpler" the ratio of rates of vibration (1 : 2, 2 : 3, 3 : 4, and so on), the more harmonious the interval sounds. The "good" combinations are called *consonances* and the "bad," *dissonances*. Theory requires that the latter must be "resolved"—led back to the consonances from which they sprang. In the Classic era, a work could not end on a dissonance. In the Romantic era this rule slowly began to weaken.

Double fugue: A *fugue* with two themes, which appear simultaneously at each entry. There are also double fugues in which the two themes enter one after the other and are developed alternately.

Dux: The first appearance of a *fugue* theme is called *dux*, "the leader" (Latin). The second entry is called *comes*, "the follower"; the third voice follows, again in the form of the *dux*.

Figured bass: See *thorough bass.*

Fugal, fugal entrances: Different voices using the same theme enter one after the other. The word comes from *fugue*, for the idea of staggered entrances of the same theme reaches its highest artistic expression in the fugue.

Fugato: A musical concept similar to *fugue* in that a theme makes several entrances, but strict fugal form is not adhered to. These appearances are called "fugal entries." The form of their development is free and thus different from that in a fugue. Whereas strict fugal form was used primarily in the Baroque era, appearing less frequently afterward, the fugato technique persists and occurs frequently.

Fugue: One of the most important musical forms or principles, preferred especially in the Baroque era. In this form, a single theme is presented by different voices (vocal or instrumental), one after the other. The first entrance, called *dux*, is in the main key; the second, the *comes*, follows at the fifth (the dominant). In a three-voice fugue there is a third entry (again as *dux*), and in a four-voice fugue, there is a fourth (again, the *comes*), whereupon the first section of the fugue, the exposition, comes to a close. The next section is called the development; in it, the theme undergoes all kinds of changes and developments. The third section is called the reprise and is similar to the first section, and the conclusion usually consists of a coda, long or short, which introduces no new material, but reinforces the feeling of conclusiveness. There are also *double fugues* and *triple fugues*.

Gloria: The second section of the Ordinarium Missae.

Gradual: (from Latin *gradus*, or steps to the altar.) Sometimes refers to the book in which the parts of the Mass not included in the *Ordinarium Missae* are found. It is also the term used for the sung section heard between the Epistle and the Gospel in the Catholic Mass.

Half tone: The smallest interval, or distance between two tones of our musical system. This system, which matured slowly during the Middle Ages, divides the octaves—the basis of all systems—into twelve equidistant tones: C, C-sharp, D, D-sharp, and so on. This tempering, or equalizing, of intervals was established in 1693 by Andreas Werckmeister, among others; Bach was the first to put it to practical use, in his *Das wohltemperierte Klavier* (The Well-Tempered Clavier). The smallest of these steps is called a half tone. (Not until our own time were smaller intervals introduced, such as quarter tones; they can be produced on string instruments and sometimes, with difficulty, on wind instruments, but not at all on keyboard instruments.) These "mini-intervals" require a new system of notation, for the old system can record only half-tone intervals. (See *chromaticism* and *notation*.)

Historia: Many early Baroque composers preferred this term to designate oratorios with Biblical content, particularly the Passions.

Homophony: (From Greek, sameness of sound). Used in the sense of a single melody, as opposed to *polyphony*. We say that accompanied music is homophonic if there is clearly only a single melody and everything else is accompaniment.

Imitation: When one voice repeats exactly or

with only slight variation a phrase that has just been sung or played by another, we call it imitation. *Imitative style* is a way of composing in which this principle becomes the basis of the work. *Canon* and *fugue* belong to this style.

Imperfect cadence: Traditional, simple melodic structure ordinarily consists of two phrases, called the antecedent and the consequent, giving an effect like question and answer. Only the second phrase ends with a complete stop (see also *cadence*); the first phrase often ends with a kind of intermediate stop, an imperfect or half cadence, which provides only a temporary break and demands continuation. Consequently, this imperfect cadence takes place not on the first degree of the melody's main key, but on a different degree of the scale, often at the fifth, or dominant.

Interval: The distance between two tones, whether in a melodic line or a chord. (See also *consonance* and *dissonance*.) The intervals are named according to their size: second (2 notes); third (3); fourth (4); fifth (5); sixth (6); seventh (7); octave (8, and, therefore, the beginning of the next octave).

Inversion: A way of treating a theme contrapuntally. There are various ways to present a theme: the "usual" way, retrograde, inversion, and retrograde inversion. By inversion is meant the transformation of the intervals in the theme to their opposites. If the theme begins with the melody ascending a fourth (C to F), then the inversion begins with exactly the same interval, only descending (C down to G). It is as if the theme were held up to a mirror. There is also the inversion of the reversed or retrograde theme. Not all of these techniques are easily perceptible to the ear.

Lamento: A song of lament or mourning, a favorite component of early opera and oratorio.

Libretto: Literally, Italian for "small book." It is the text of a large vocal composition (opera, oratorio, Passion, cantata).

Litany: In the Middle Ages, a popular song of prayer; later incorporated into the Catholic liturgy. The uniform, even monotonous delivery (with often-repeated refrains) has also given the word the meaning of a very monotonous kind of music or recitation, without high points, lacking in verve.

Mass: The central religious service of the Catholic Church; the ritual of the Eucharist—the commemoration of Christ's sacrificial death. The Mass can be quiet or silent (Missa lecta: the text is read by the priest), recited, or presented musically, and ranges from the relatively simple Missa brevis (short) to the Missa solemnis. It may include vocal solos, choruses, and orchestra. Almost without exception, the musical Mass consists of the five or six parts of the Ordinarium Missae: Kyrie, Gloria, Credo, Sanctus (with Benedictus), Agnus Dei. (See Appendix.)

Melisma: In Greek, usually "rustic singing." Today, it refers to musical embellishments such as trills or coloratura—in other words, those in which several notes of the melody are sung to one syllable. The liturgy of the Greek and Russian Orthodox Church is especially melismatic; this is also true, but to varying extent, of Gregorian chant.

Monody: Greek, meaning "single voice"; originally, it meant without accompaniment. In the Middle Ages, this term was applied to vocal solos with simple instrumental accompaniment, such as those sung by troubadours and minnesingers. The term also describes the music of early operas and oratorios, which began to appear around 1600, in which a single, dominant melody began to replace the older polyphonic style.

Motet: Originally a polyphonic vocal composition without accompaniment and usually religious in nature. Developed and cultivated during the Middle Ages (Machaut, later by Josquin des Prez, Palestrina and Bach). Later, it often was a larger work with several movements, resembling the *cantata*.

Notation: The use of conventional symbols to write down music. Our system of notation has developed over the centuries to accommodate the demands of Western music as it grew and changed and became more complex. In the 20th century, music has developed in such ways as to exceed the limitations of traditional notation. Consequently, since about 1950, efforts have been made to develop new systems of notation or graphic layout.

Oboe d'amore, oboe da caccia: Two members of the oboe family; beautiful sounding instruments that appeared in the first half of the 18th century. Bach was especially fond of them. The *oboe d'amore* (love oboe), so called, perhaps, because of its sweet, soft, longing sound, was pitched a third lower than the usual oboe. It has been copied in modern times; Maurice Ravel used it in his *Bolero*. The oboe da caccia (hunting oboe) is an alto oboe, pitched a fifth lower than the usual instrument. In the early 19th century it was modified to become the English horn, for whose beautiful, melancholy sound many important composers have written solos.

Ordinarium Missae: The order of the principal Catholic liturgy; composed of the five constant parts of the Mass: Kyrie, Gloria, Credo, Sanctus and Benedictus, and Agnus Dei. Almost without exception, these five sections are the textual basis for Mass compositions.

Ornamentation: This term refers to the embellishment of a melody, accomplished by the addition of variations, such as runs, trills, appoggiaturas etc.

Ostinato: A recurring phrase mostly in the bass (vocal or instrumental), above which the other voices develop their own material. (See also *passacaglia* and *chaconne*.)

Passacaglia: A dance from southern Europe which probably spread throughout Europe at the end of the Middle Ages. Its name comes from the Spanish *pasacalle* and means "strolling through the streets." A Baroque musical form developed from the dance: a short melody, continuously repeated, mostly in the lower instruments, was its hallmark. Above this bass melody variations develop in the higher voices, which always relate to the *ostinato* (or *basso ostinato*, persistently repeated bass).

Passion: The story of Jesus' suffering, from the Last Supper to his death on the cross. It began to be presented theatrically in the early Middle Ages and musically, not long after. It is usually based on one of the four Gospels: Sts Matthew, Mark, Luke, or John. These texts have been set again and again, and continue to be used in the present.

Polyphony: From the Greek, meaning "many voices." The term does not mean that there are many performers in a given musical work, but rather that there are several or many melodies developing and unfolding at the same time. A thousand people singing one melody do not produce polyphony; but two children singing a *canon* do. The rules governing the writing of polyphony are collectively called *counterpoint*.

Polytonality: The simultaneous appearance of two or more keys in a piece of music. Because in this technique the foundations of tonality are loosened, *polytonality* is one of the phenomena indicative of the dissolution of Classic/Romantic harmony which also led to atonality.

Proprium Missae: (From the Latin *proprium*, "special"). The Proper—the changing parts of the Mass. Introit, Gradual, Sequence, Offertory, Communion, and Alleluia are of special musical importance.

Responsory: First, a richly embellished vocal solo in the liturgy; second, the choir's response (hence the name, from the Latin *respondere*, to answer) to the parts of the Mass intoned by the priest (called *responsoria*).

Recitative: A way of singing that resembles speech, used in large, dramatic musical works such as opera and oratorio. In the Baroque and Classic eras, two types of recitative were distinguished: the *secco recitative* (literally, dry recitative) in which the material presented was accompanied only by the *continuo*—by a harpsichord and a low string instrument; and the *accompagnato* (accompanied) recitative, in which the voice part is more melodic and is accompanied by the orchestra. The secco recitative is especially suited to carry the action forward, for in the set pieces (arias, duets, etc.), the action is necessarily suspended. In recitative, the voice is quite free as to tempo and expression. This is the form usually used for the narrator or Evangelist in an oratorio. The *secco recitative* has also been called "musical declamation"; it is something between speech and song, must be presented very clearly, and can be quite dramatic. *Accompagnato recitative* is somewhat similar to an *arioso* and usually is followed by an *aria*.

Retrograde: Just as we can turn a word around, that is, read it from back to front, so a melodic line can also be "read backward;" this procedure is called *retrograde*. A retrograde melody is just as difficult to discern at first glance or upon first hearing as a word that has been reversed. This is a technical device of composition that was used in polyphonic musical works such as *fugues* to enrich the structure. The ear does not perceive it as variation of the theme, but as a new theme, but an experienced musician will see in the score that the theme has been reversed, that is to say, is retrograde.

Ripieno: A term from Baroque music that means about the same thing as *tutti*. It is Italian and means "full:" it is used by the composer or director to call in the full orchestra when previously only a few musicians (as soloists or concertino) have been performing. A violinist who played only during the "tutti" passages, could be called a *ripienist*.

Sanctus: The fourth part of the Ordinarium Missae: it immediately precedes the transubstantiation.

Sequence: In music, the word has two completely different meanings. First, it refers to the repetition of the same musical phrase at different pitches. Second, it is a song form of early Christian liturgy (Stabat mater, Dies irae, and others), which probably developed around the year 850 from Hallelujah chants.

Stabat mater: The first words of the sacred sequence "Stabat mater dolorosa," attributed to the Franciscan monk Jacopone da Todi, who died shortly after 1300. It has often been set to music. It depicts the suffering and pain of the mother of Jesus at His death. (The complete text is in the Appendix.)

Stretto: Technical compositional term meaning that the different themes or entrances of a fugue do not follow each other at the normal distance but are more closely compressed. Stretto, or *stretta*, can also refer to the particularly lively or dramatic conclusion of a piece of music, especially in opera.

Suspension: When one or more notes of a dissonant chord do not lead to the resolution chord with the other notes, but delay the resolution, the result is a suspension. Two individual voices can also form a suspension, which calls for resolution in one of the voices.

Te Deum: The hymn that begins with the Latin words *Te Deum Laudamus* (Lord, we praise Thee), the so-called Ambrosian song of praise. St. Ambrose either composed it or inserted it into the Catholic liturgy around A. D. 380. It is often composed, even today. See Appendix.

Thorough bass: See *continuo*.

Toccata: Old instrumental musical form, which begins with a number of imposing chords, which then lead into rapid, elaborate passages. The toccata essentially is a free, improvisatory piece, especially in the hands of Baroque organists.

Tonality: The term tonality simply refers to the tonal or harmonic system—the traditional Classic and Romantic major-minor system with its scales and chords. It manifests itself in the main key in which a work is composed: sonata in C Major, symphony in B Minor, and so on. Even though a work may also modulate—move from one key to another—it eventually returns to its main key, just as a ship, after a long cruise, returns to its home port. The feeling of tonality has long been considered satisfying to the ear, and not until our own century has it been called into question. Thus, tonality is a term not really coined until the 20th century, when the opposing system, atonality, came into use.

Triple fugue: A fugue with three subjects instead of only one; they are closely related and always appear simultaneously.

Tritone: Traditional harmony (which developed gradually during the 16th and 17th centuries and was codified by Jean-Philippe Rameau among others) distinguishes between consonances and dissonances, "good" and "bad" combinations of sounds. Without going into more detail here, let it be said that the "worst" combination is the

tritone. This term refers to three notes, three whole-tone steps—for example, the interval between C and F-sharp (first whole-tone step: C to D; second, D to E; third, E to F-sharp). This interval can be considered to be both an augmented fourth or a diminished fifth. In the Middle Ages, musical theory strictly forbade the use of this interval and gave it the unflattering name *diabolus in musica*, "the devil in music." Its use was not only frowned upon in the formation of harmonies (vertically) but also in the formation of melodies (horizontally). None of this, however, hindered less orthodox composers from using it anyway and often in interesting ways; indeed, it was sometimes used specifically for its shock value (which lessened over time), to achieve either surprise or tone painting. The tritone is the progression of three successive whole tones, no matter on which note it begins: C-sharp to G; d to G-sharp; F to B, and so on. It measures exactly one-half of the octave.

Tutti: Italian, literally means "all." In Baroque music fewer dynamic nuances were notated than later. Contrasts in volume were not achieved by *crescendi* and *diminuendi*, but often resulted from increasing or decreasing the number of performers at a particular entry. At points where the music was to be loud and forceful, all the members of the ensemble played—*tutti*—and where it was to be soft, only a few—*soli*.

Twelve-tone system: A system of musical composition developed independently by the Austrians Josef Matthias Hauer and Arnold Schoenberg, and further developed by the latter "with 12 notes of equal value, related only to each other." Its impact revolutionized 20th-century composing. It negated the traditional harmonic system while trying to put a stop to the chaos of atonality, which had spread during the early part of this century and has never really disappeared. The twelve-tone system, also called dodecaphony (Greek, "12-tone"), regulated with mathematical precision the entire course of a piece of music, in both its harmonic and melodic aspects. Consequently, this way of composing is largely dependent upon calculation, and in spite of the fact that it attracted many famous composers, it never found favor with a broad public.

Unisono: Latin, "one sound": all the voices sing (or play) the same melody. Octaves can be doubled, and men and women can sing together, although their natural registers differ by about an octave, yet the effect is still considered unison.

Virginal: Old keyboard instrument, related to

the harpsichord and spinet. English composers and virtuosos of the Elizabethean era—Byrd, Bull, Gibbons, Morley, and so on—were called virginalists; it was the favorite instrument of the age.

C. Sources of Illustrations

Archiv Kurt Pahlen, Männedorf
A. de Baenst, Ghent
Carinthischer Sommer, Villach/Ossiach
Decca Record Company Limited, Publicity Department, London
Alfred Linares, Vienna
Österreichische Nationalbibliothek, Vienna
Pressebüro der Salzburger Festspiele/Steimetz
R. Rinnethaler, Salzburg
Salzburger Landestheater, Salzburg
Susanne Schimert-Ramme, Zürich
Schweizerische Verkehrszentrale, Zürich
H. G. Trenkwalder, Klagenfurt